Berlin-Brandenburgische Akademie der Wissenschaften

Die Griechischen Christlichen Schriftsteller
der ersten Jahrhunderte

(GCS)

Neue Folge · Band 15

Iulius Africanus
Chronographiae

The Extant Fragments

Edited by
Martin Wallraff

with Umberto Roberto
and, for the Oriental Sources, Karl Pinggéra

Translated by William Adler

Walter de Gruyter · Berlin · New York

Herausgegeben im Auftrag der
Berlin-Brandenburgischen Akademie der Wissenschaften
von Christoph Markschies
Gutachter dieses Bandes:
Jürgen Hammerstaedt und Christoph Riedweg

⊗ Gedruckt auf säurefreiem Papier,
das die US-ANSI-Norm über Haltbarkeit erfüllt.

ISSN 0232-2900
ISBN 978-3-11-019493-7

Library of Congress Cataloging-in-Publication Data
A CIP catalogue record for this book is available from the Library of Congress.

Bibliografische Information der Deutschen Nationalbibliothek
Die Deutsche Nationalbibliothek verzeichnet diese Publikation in der Deutschen Nationalbibliografie;
detaillierte bibliografische Daten sind im Internet über http://dnb.d-nb.de abrufbar.

© Copyright 2007 by Walter de Gruyter GmbH & Co. KG, 10785 Berlin

Dieses Werk einschließlich aller seiner Teile ist urheberrechtlich geschützt. Jede Verwertung außerhalb der engen Grenzen des Urheberrechtsgesetzes ist ohne Zustimmung des Verlages unzulässig und strafbar. Das gilt insbesondere für Vervielfältigungen, Übersetzungen, Mikroverfilmungen und die Einspeicherung und Verarbeitung in elektronischen Systemen.

Printed in Germany
Einbandgestaltung: Christopher Schneider, Berlin
Druck und buchbinderische Verarbeitung: Hubert & Co. GmbH & Co. KG, Göttingen

PREFACE

Modern research on Christian chronography was inaugurated 400 years ago by Joseph Justus Scaliger with his magisterial *Thesaurus temporum* (1606). The work drew scholars' attention to the author of the first Christian chronicle, Iulius Africanus (3rd cent.), a writer who effectively transformed the heritage of Hellenistic universal historiography by adapting it to a Christian framework. Although Africanus' work is lost in its entirety, the preserved fragments—including those of the *Cesti*, his second main work—reveal a multifaceted and broad-based intellectual, writing in an era rich in culture and change.

Given the importance of Africanus, it was obvious that his works be inserted into the editorial program of the GCS series which was initially planned as "Die Griechischen Christlichen Schriftsteller *der ersten drei Jahrhunderte*." Although the idea of limiting the series to the first three centuries was later abandoned, Africanus was still retained. The editions were entrusted to Karl Konrad Müller for the *Cesti* and to Heinrich Gelzer for the *Chronographiae*. Unfortunately, for a variety of reasons, neither project was ever completed, although Gelzer's work was already at an advanced stage when he died 100 years ago (†1906).

After more than a century, the chronicle is about the only significant work of the original project[1] for which still no modern edition exists. Thus, it is with particular gratitude that the main editor of this volume has taken the opportunity of publishing the present edition in the distinguished GCS series. This invitation was first extended by Prof. Albrecht Dihle, in 1999, on behalf of the commission working under the aegis of the Berlin-Brandenburg academy, an invitation that was later repeated by Prof. Christoph Markschies. However, this publication is more than just a sign of intellectual continuity during a century, marked otherwise by turmoil and ruptures. It also heralds an important innovation. This is in fact the first edition in the series in which the original text is accompanied by a translation into a modern language and in which the introduction and translation are in English.

Such an undertaking was made possible thanks to a felicitous transatlantic collaboration between William Adler (North Carolina State University) and a European *équipe*. The former, referred to on the front cover as the translator of the fragments, was also able to offer a great deal of invaluable advice concerning many other aspects of the edition. The texts were discussed between him and the European *équipe* in numerous details during three intensive meetings in three successive phases of the project in Bonn, Jena and Basel. On the European side, the project was generously funded by the *Deutsche Forschungsgemeinschaft* as part of the *Gerhard-Hess-Programm*. In addition to the editors already

---

1 See Stefan Rebenich, Theodor Mommsen und Adolf Harnack. Wissenschaft und Politik im Berlin des ausgehenden 19. Jahrhunderts, Berlin 1997, 175f.

mentioned on the front cover, the team consisted of Gregor Staab, Sebastian Kaas and Christof Kraus, all of whom gave important assistance in different phases of the project. Indeed, many of the problems in the text could only be resolved collectively and only after many hours of discussion. As a consequence, the single contributions are no longer distinguishable. The introduction has been written by the main editor together with Umberto Roberto (except for 4.4., written by William Adler, and 4.6., written by Karl Pinggéra). In the notes to the English translation, the contributions of all four scholars are conflated.

Some of the results of the project were discussed at a conference in Eisenach in May 2005. The conference proceedings were published in the series "Texte und Untersuchungen", parts of which can be consulted as a useful supplement to the introduction of this edition.[2]

Over the years many colleagues from all over the world have helped in the production of this work with innumerable suggestions and advice. Only some of them can be mentioned here. During his work on the edition of the Symeon Logothete chronicle, Prof. Staffan Wahlgren (University of Lund, Sweden) shared some of his results with us. In particular, he put a microfilm of cod. Vat. gr. 163 at our disposal. Unfortunately, his edition appeared[3] when our edition was already near completion. Therefore, it was only possible to refer to his chapter numbers in the *index locorum* (p. 325). With the help of this list, however, it should be easy for readers to locate our texts in Wahlgren's edition and vice versa. Apart from a few very minor details, the new text neither alters the quantity of relevant material, nor changes the shape of the texts themselves.

Special thanks are also due to the manuscript department of the University library in Jena and its director Dr. Joachim Ott, who, for more than five years allowed us to use the manuscript of Heinrich Gelzer for his planned edition in our office. Close collaboration with the library also led to the creation of a common project and a small publication on Christian world chronicles.[4]

The preparation of a bilingual edition of this sort is a complex undertaking, not only philologically, but also for the many technical difficulties encountered along the way. It would not, for example, have been possible to provide a camera-ready copy for publication without the use of a specific kind of software. This edition has been executed using "Classical Text Editor", whose author, Dr. Stefan Hagel (Austrian Academy of Sciences, Vienna), was on hand to give practical advice and in some cases even modify the program for our own specific purposes.

Dr. Philip Ditchfield (Rome) assumed the tedious task of correcting and improving the English text. Over the years, many student assistants spent many hours with various technical tasks. They can be referred to only collectively here.

---

2 Julius Africanus und die christliche Weltchronistik, ed. Martin Wallraff (TU 157), Berlin 2006.
3 Symeonis Magistri et Logothetae Chronicon, ed. Staffan Wahlgren (CSHB 44,1), Berlin 2006.
4 Welt-Zeit. Christliche Weltchronistik aus zwei Jahrtausenden in Beständen der Thüringer Universitäts- und Landesbibliothek Jena, ed. Martin Wallraff, Berlin 2005.

Last but not least, the two referees for the GCS series ought to be mentioned with gratitude: Prof. Christoph Riedweg (Rome) and Prof. Jürgen Hammerstaedt (Cologne). The former saved us from a few fatal errors in the final phase, the latter also gave precious advice in intensive discussions on the text at the University of Jena in the summer of 2003.

Iulius Africanus could never have foreseen, nor could the editors themselves ever have anticipated, that after nearly 1800 years, exactly 100 fragments of the *Chronographiae* have survived. Surely the chronicler, who was fascinated almost to the point of obsession by the symbolism of numbers, would have liked the thought.

Basel, December 2006   Martin Wallraff

CONTENTS

Preface	V
Introduction	XIII
1. Iulius Africanus: The Man and his Work	XIII
2. The *Chronographiae*: Date and Place of Writing, Literary Character	XVII
3. The Chronological System	XXIII
4. The Text and its Transmission	XXIX
4.1. Eusebius	XXXI
4.2. Chronicles from the Alexandrian Tradition	XXXIV
4.2.1. Panodorus and Annianus	XXXV
4.2.2. The *Excerpta Barbari*	XXXVI
4.3. Chronicles from the Antiochene Tradition	XXXVIII
4.3.1. John Malalas	XXXVIII
4.3.2. John of Antioch	XXXIX
4.3.3. Anonymous Material in the *Excerpta Salmasiana* (Ps. John of Antioch)	XL
4.4. Georgius Syncellus	XLII
4.5. The Logothete Chronicle and Related Texts	XLIV
4.5.1. Symeon Logothete	XLIV
4.5.2. Ps. Symeon and Cedrenus	XLVI
4.6. Oriental Authors	XLVII
4.7. Minor Authors and Texts	XLIX
4.7.1. Ps. Eustathius of Antioch	XLIX
4.7.2. The *Chronicon Paschale*	XLIX
4.7.3. The *Anonymus Matritensis*	L
5. Earlier Editions	L
6. Principles of the Edition	LV
7. Bibliography	LIX
Conspectus Siglorum	LXIX
Abbreviationes	LXXIX
1. Opera in apparatu adhibita	LXXIX
2. Editores et Emendatores	LXXXVII
3. Cetera	LXXXVIII
Iulius Africanus, *Chronographiae*	1
Testimonia on the Life of Iulius Africanus	2
T1 Africanus under Pertinax and Septimius Severus (AD 193)	2
T2 Africanus' Mission on behalf of Nicopolis	4
T3 Africanus under Gordian III (AD 238-244)	8

T4	Africanus under Decius (AD 249–251)	10
T5	Africanus as a Contemporary of Origen	10

Testimonia on General Aspects of the *Chronographiae* 12

T6	Chronological Overview	12
T7	Jerome	14
T8	Church Historians in Constantinople	16
T9	Isidore of Seville	16
T10	John Malalas	18
T11	Photius	18
T12	Suda	20
T13	Michael Syrus	20

Material from Books 1/2: From Adam to Moses 22

F14	The Creation	22
F15	The Fabricated Chronology of the Egyptians and the Chaldeans	24
F16	The Generations from Adam to Abraham	26
T17	Adam's Tomb	42
F18	Seth, the Inventor of the Hebrew Alphabet	42
F19	Enosh, called by the name of God	44
F20	God's Immanence	44
F21	Quotation from the Book of Enoch	44
F22	The Years of Methuselah and the Names of the Sons of Cain	46
F23	The Circumstances of the Flood	48
F24	The Pagan Gods	52
F25	From the Division of the Earth to Abraham's Migration	58
F26	Abraham in Egypt, Lot's Land and the Dead Sea	58
T27	The Toponym Gerar	60
T28	The Chronology of Jacob's Life	62
F29	Jacob's Tent	64
F30	The Terebinth Tree in Shechem	66
F31	Job, the Descendant of Esau	68
T32	The Chronology of Joseph's Life	68
F33	The Date of Joseph's Death	70

Material from Book 3: From Moses to the First Olympiad 72

F34	Synchronism of the Exodus and Ogygus	72
F35	The Chronology from Adam to Samuel	82
T36	Synchronism of Ehud and the Flood of Deucalion	84
T37	The Family of Abimelech	84
T38	Abdon the Judge	84
T39	The Chronology after Joshua	86
T40	The Chronology of the Judges and the One-year Rule of Shamgar	88
T41	The Chronology from the Exodus to the Building of the Temple	90

T42	The Date of the Building of the Temple	92
F43	The Pre-History of Egypt	94
F44	Mestrem, the Eponymous Father of the Egyptians	96
T45	The Date of the Flood and the Date of Abraham	98
F46	Dynasties of Egypt	100
T47	King Amosis and Moses	124
T48	Moses and Inachus	128
T49	Chronology of the Assyrian Kingdom	130
F50	The Kings of the Argives	132
F51	The Rulers of the Sicyonians	138
T52	From Aeneas to the Foundation of Rome	146
F53	The Kings of Rome	146
F54	The Rulers of the Athenians	148
T55	The Chronology of the Floods among the Greeks	164
F56	Atlas and Prometheus	168
T57	The Years from Inachus to Cecrops	170
F58	The Kings of the Lacedaemonians	170
F59	The Kings of the Corinthians	174
F60	The First Festival of Olympian Zeus	178
T61	The Kings of Thebes	178
F62	The Kings of the Medes	180
F63	The Kings of the Lydians	182
F64	The Date of the First Olympiad	186

Material from Books 4/5: From the First Olympiad to the End of the
Chronographiae 192

F65	Victors in the Olympic Games	192
F66	The Prophet Jonah	218
T67	Pekahiah, King of Israel	218
T68	Pekah, King of Israel	220
T69	The End of the Northern Kingdom	220
F70	Manasseh's Supplication and Liberation	220
T71	The High Priest Hilkiah	222
F72	King Jehoahaz and the First Tribute	222
F73	The Kings of the Persians	224
F74	Cyrus and the Samians	228
T75	The Identification of Cambyses and Nebuchadnezzar II	230
F76	The Chronology from Adam to the Babylonian Captivity	232
T77	Daniel and the Captivity	232
F78	The Seventy Weeks of Daniel	236
F79	Ezra the Priest	238
T80	Africanus as a Source for post-biblical Jewish History	240
F81	The Beginning of the Peloponnesian War	242

F82 The Kings of the Macedonians 244
T83 From Adam to Seleucus I 250
F84 The Jews under Greek Domination 252
F85 Jonathan, Simon's son, the High Priest 252
F86 The Ptolemies 254
F87 The Father of Herod 258
T88 Africanus and the Archive of Edessa 260
F89 Herod and Cleopatra 262
F90 Omissions in Jesus' Genealogy 270
T91 The Arrival of the Magi 274
T92 The Date of the Incarnation 274
F93 The Passion and Resurrection of the Savior 276
F94 The Millennialist Framework of History 290
F95 John the Apostle in Ephesus 290
F96 Abgar VIII, King of Edessa 290
F97 Clement of Alexandria 292
F98 Africanus' Journey to Alexandria 292
T99 The End of the *Chronographiae* 292
F100 Final Doxology 294

Indices 297
   1. Index textuum adhibitorum et locorum citatorum 297
      1.1. Biblia sacra 297
      1.2. Textus antiquitatis et medii aevi 299
   2. Index nominum propriorum 328
   3. Comparatio numerorum 348
      3.1. Routh ^{2}1846 348
      3.2. Gallandi 1766 (= PG 10,63–94) 350
Appendix: The Chronological System 351

INTRODUCTION

1. Iulius Africanus: The Man and his Work

Even by the standards of the versatile social elite of the 3rd century, Iulius Africanus was not only a very intelligent man, he was also a remarkably well-connected figure. A Christian with good knowledge of Jewish culture, he was fluent (at least) in both Greek and Latin, had interests in virtually all fields of human knowledge and possessed good contacts with various political leaders all over the world. From the viewpoint of the extant sources, Iulius Africanus is so multifaceted that modern historiography has even gone as far as to hypothesize that there were actually two authors named Africanus, one pagan, the other Christian.[1] Although this hypothesis has now been abandoned for over a century, the man still remains an enigma.

In the transmission of his works, he is usually referred to quite simply by his *cognomen* Ἀφρικανός. That being said, the *nomen gentilicium* Ἰούλιος is also attested in the tradition of his two main works, *viz.* the *Chronographiae*[2] and the *Cesti*[3], a fact which would certainly be hard to explain if we really were dealing with two different authors. Less convincing is the evidence for the conventional *praenomen Sextus*. At one point, the Suda refers to him as Ἀφρικανός, ὁ Σέκτος χρηματίσας (T12). Since the word Σέκτος is not the normal transliteration of *Sextus*, scholars have emended it into Σέξτος.[4] The full name "Sextus Iulius Africanus" was once widely adopted (by the influential Gelzer, amongst others, in the title of his book), and indeed it is sometimes still used, although recent scholarship does tend to avoid it—and rightly so. The basis of just one reference in a late and notoriously imprecise source (and even here the reading is problematic) is perilously weak.[5] Due to the character of his work, other honorary

---

1 See the opinions quoted by Gelzer 1,2f. On Africanus' biography and profile, see Sickenberger 1918; Bardenhewer 1913–32, 2,263–271; Vieillefond 1970; Crehan 1977; Rampoldi 1981 and 1997; Winkelmann 2002; Adler 2004.
2 T2 (Eusebius); T75b (Suda).
3 In the *explicit* of two books: *cestus* 7 and 18 (cest. 1,20,66; 5,55); the second case is particularly interesting, because it is preserved on a papyrus dated to around 265 (cest. 5 = Pap. Oxy. 412), thus only one generation after the date of the writing of the *Cesti*.
4 E.g. Gelzer 1,1. This is apparently also the way in which the lexicographer himself understood the epithet (which he probably found in his source), see the variant Σέξτος in Suda Σ 856 (given in the third app. to T12). Cf. also Adler 2004,523, n. 18, who gives a few examples of papyri where Σέκτος actually stands for *Sextus*.
5 An alternative interpretation would be the transliteration of Latin *sectus*; Crehan 1977,635 translates "Africanus der Eunuch". Some scholars also suggest an emendation into Κεστός, an analogy to Clement of Alexandria, author of the *Stromata*, who is sometimes called Στρωματεύς, see Vieillefond 1970,15.

epithets crop up in the sources to describe him, especially ἱστοριογράφος[6] and χρονογράφος[7]. It is interesting to note that the attribution σοφός/σοφώτατος is a near constant in John Malalas' Chronicle,[8] but it also occurs in other writers.[9]

The Church historian Socrates of Constantinople cites Clement of Alexandria, Africanus and Origen in this order (T8a) as important "ancient" Christian writers (i.e. pre-Constantinian). This listing not only expresses the high esteem for Africanus, but one might presume also, the correct chronological sequence. In fact, Clement was born in c. 140–150, Origen was born around 185, and Africanus must have come somewhere in between, perhaps around 170. Unfortunately, this is all that can be said with any degree of certainty. The literary activity of Africanus is attested from the early 220's up to the 240's (see below), which implies that he was younger than Clement; however, since he calls Origen in a letter κύριέ μου καὶ υἱέ,[10] he must have been older than the famous Alexandrian theologian. This letter is presumably his last work, but unfortunately it can only be loosely dated to the 240's[11] and it represents the only *terminus post quem* we have for Africanus' death. It may be that he was still alive under Decius (249–251), although a note of Symeon Logothete to this effect (T4) is of dubious credibility.

The life story of Africanus was certainly both interesting and eventful, although we are only able to glean snippets of it from his own writings. We first find him in Edessa, at the court of king Abgar VIII of Osrhoene, for whom he apparently had much admiration (F96) and whose son he helped to educate. It was here that he came into contact with the fascinating intellectual Bardesanes (cest. 1,20), in whom he may have found a congenial thinker and source of inspiration. All this must have occurred some time before 216.[12] It was here also that he might have seen what was alleged to have been the tent of Jacob, venerated in Edessa and later destroyed (F29). On his travels he saw mount Ararat in Armenia (referred to as Parthia, F23) and also visited Apameia in Southern Phrygia, formerly Celaenae (F23). He was acquainted with the Dead Sea (F26) and was also familiar with the library of Nysa in Caria (cest. 5,52).[13] Later, he made a trip to Alexandria, where he met Heraclas (F98).[14] Possibly on

---

6 F100 (Basil of Caesarea).
7 T10; F54f; T61; F95 (Malalas); F97 (app., Cedr.).
8 F51b; F54f; F58b; T61; F74; F95.
9 T1b (app.); F24 (app.); F53; F97; all belong to the Logothete tradition.
10 ep. Orig. (78,2 Reichardt).
11 See below note 22.
12 Vieillefond 1970,18.
13 The edifice has been recently excavated by Prof. Dr. Volker Michael Strocka (University of Freiburg, Germany).
14 This is normally dated to a phase in which Heraclas replaced Origen as the head of the famous catechetical school (i.e. after 215); see Winkelmann 2002,510. However, it may also have been

the same occasion, he was able to acquire a copy of the ancient book written by the pharaoh Suphis in Egypt—"a colossal possession" (F46,54). It would appear that the re-foundation of Emmaus in Palestine as a *polis* with the name "Nicopolis" was achieved thanks to an initiative at the court of the Roman emperor in the early 220's presided over by Africanus himself (T2). This may or may not mean that Africanus was a resident of Nicopolis (or Palestine in general) at that time. Nevertheless, his links to the town were certainly profound and went well beyond that of any normal sightseer. A little later, we find him in Rome at the court of Alexander Severus, where he was entrusted with the task of instituting (ἀρχιτεκτονεῖν) the library of the Pantheon.[15] Whatever that might mean, it must have been quite a prestigious post in the society of the capital.

Given such a high profile position, it is highly plausible that Africanus was well-acquainted with Latin. Most likely, his mother tongue was Greek, the language in which his works are written. Moreover, he certainly knew some Hebrew, and probably quite well, since he mentions the measure κάβος (from the Hebrew קב) as an equivalent of the Greek κόγγιον, adding that it was used by "us."[16] This could be taken to imply that Hebrew was his first language. More likely, however, is that he spoke a form of Greek which was current in Palestine and which was open to Semitic influences. He also used his knowledge of Hebrew's linguistic structures for his exegetical argumentation in the letter to Origen.[17] Given his role at the court of Edessa, it is not impossible that he knew some Syriac as well, although this cannot be proved.[18]

Africanus was certainly both a polyglot and a polymath and the man may well have been as equally multifaceted in his daily life; even his religious beliefs are difficult to pin down. There are good reasons for believing that he was a Roman citizen and that he had some sort of Palestinian background. Of the places already mentioned, Palestine is clearly prominent. In addition, the Dead Sea and Nicopolis (Emmaus) crop up and he may also have seen the terebinth tree at Shechem (F30). More interestingly, on one occasion he speaks of Aelia Capitolina, the Roman name of Jerusalem, as "the old home (ἡ ἀρχαῖα πατρίς)" (cest. 5,51). This certainly expresses a particular emotional link to Palestine and Jerusalem, although it is difficult to establish exactly what the author meant by this phrase. It might mean a general identification with Jerusalem as a "spiritual home" for all Jews (and perhaps even Christians).[19] It seems more likely, however, that Africanus was actually referring to his own home town, which

---

much earlier, even before Heraclas' conversion to Christianity, since Eusebius in his text does not give any specific Christian motivation for the trip.
15 cest. 5,53f; see Harnack 1921.
16 cest. 4,55 (if the text is considered genuine).
17 ep. Orig. (79,13–15 Reichardt); see also the Hebrew etymology in F16d.
18 A text in the *Cesti* points in that direction: the Syriac name of a serpent is given as βαθανηραθά (cest. 1,2,119).
19 Vieillefond 1970,41f argued that Africanus must have been a Jew.

strongly suggests that he could not have been a Jew, since, from the time of Hadrian, the Jews had been banned from Aelia Capitolina.[20]

Whatever the case may be, it is interesting to note that Africanus actually refers to Hebrew words as "our" way of speaking (κάβος, see above). Indeed, when quoting Herodotus by heart he automatically replaces Ἀράβιοι (here understood in a broad sense of "Easterners") with "those near us (οἱ παρ' ἡμῖν)" (cest. 7,5) and he speaks of Jerusalem as the "old home". On the other hand, his Roman affiliations are impossible to ignore: he uses the Latin name of the city, he publishes under a Latin name and in certain circumstances he identifies himself with the Romans, using "us" to distinguish himself from the Persians (cest. 1,1,4f). What might seem at first sight to be a contradiction ought perhaps to be seen as an expression of a multiple cultural and religious identity which was possible and even desirable in the upper echelons of society in the Severan age.

As regards his alleged Christianity, it has always puzzled scholars how his *Cesti* shows no pro-Christian leanings whatsoever. However, since only 10% or less of a lengthy work of 24 books has come down to us, it is clear that all arguments on this issue are extremely difficult to substantiate. Even on the basis of the few surviving segments, it is clear that the work, which was dedicated to Alexander Severus (T2d), did not have any aim in supporting one religious tradition or another, or indeed of attacking one faith to ingratiate the other. Even if it is true that the surviving fragments of the *Cesti* do not reveal any hints of Jewish or Christian faith, it is also true that they attest no anti-Jewish or anti-Christian sentiments. Of course, a reader steeped in any profound orthodox creed might find otherwise.

The *Cesti* is usually dated to between 227 and 231, that is to say after the construction of the baths of Alexander Severus in Rome and before the latter's victory over the Persians in 231;[21] along with the *Chronographiae* it forms the main work of Africanus. In addition, two letters have been preserved, both of which are very learned and both of which contain exegetical material. One is addressed to a certain Aristides and discusses the genealogies of Christ; it cannot be dated (CPG 1693). The other is a letter to Origen, dealing with the story of Susanna, preserved in the book of Daniel (CPG 1692). Origen's answer has also come down to us, although the correspondence can only vaguely be dated to the 240's.[22] There may also have been a work called Περὶ ἑβδομάδων (F93,102f) dealing with the interpretation of the seventy weeks in the book of Daniel and thus perhaps some sort of precursor to certain elements of the

---

20 This is the *communis opinio* of most recent authors, see Crehan 1977,635; Rampoldi 1981,74; Winkelmann 2002,509; Adler 2004,521f.
21 Vieillefond 1970,60–64.
22 It used to be dated to 240 (Reichardt 1909,65), but de Lange 1983,498–501 rightly pointed out that there is not much evidence to support this dating. He suggests 248, but his arguments are also weak.

chronicle. Occasionally texts have been falsely attributed to Africanus. These include a Syriac fragment dealing with the appearance of Moses and Elijah (CPG 1695), parts of the account of an "inter-religious dialogue" at the Persian court,[23] a text referred to as the *Passio Symphorosae* in certain manuscripts[24] and a large number of quotations from a collection of Byzantine agricultural texts—the *Geoponica*—the analysis of which is still ongoing.[25]

2. The *Chronographiae*: Date and Place of Writing, Literary Character

Iulius Africanus wrote his chronicle in the early 220's, most probably in the summer or early autumn of the year 221. This date, which represents the end of his historical account, is confirmed by various independent texts and by various forms of dating. Photius for example says that the entire chronology covered a period of 5723 years (T11,7), which would correspond to AD 221/22.[26] In addition, the complex synchronism found within F54d provides us with the following dates:

- Ol. 250, which was held in the summer of 221
- the names of the consuls for the year 221
- the third year of Elagabalus, which runs either from May 220 to May 221, or, counting in complete Roman years, the whole of 221.

The last piece of evidence comes from the text which deals with the dating of Christ (F93). According to Africanus, his *parousia* occured in AM 5531, effectively 192 years before the 250th Olympiad (F93,109). This would again lead to the year given by Photius: AM 5723 = AD 221/22. All transmitted dates, therefore, coincide with the year 221 and probably sometime during the second half of it.

Technically speaking, the end of the historical account would only be a *terminus post quem* for the time of writing. However, there are several reasons why it seems unlikely that much time elapsed between that date and the end of

---

23 *De gestis in Perside,* CPG 6968; see Bratke 1899,51.
24 BHL 7971; see Ruinart 1859,70.
25 It is clear that the work contains both genuine and spurious material. The brief remarks of Vieillefond 1970,69f are not all that can be said on the issue. However, whatever is genuine most likely comes from the *Cesti*.
26 Calculated with the standard equation, according to which Africanus' years "from Adam" begin in 5502/01 BC (established since Pétau 1627, shared by many others, *inter alia* Finegan 1998, 154–160, see Mosshammer 2006,84). This consensus is challenged by Mosshammer 2006, who suggests a beginning in 5501/00 BC and thus comes to the equation AM 5723 = AD 222/23. His reconstruction, which is based on a new interpretation of the intricate text F93, creates more problems than it solves, especially in conjunction with the evidence of F54d (see above in the main text). The information given by Photius, that AM 5723 was in the reign of Macrinus (217–218), is in any case faulty.

its redaction and publication. In F93,84f Africanus says that after the Passion and Resurrection of Christ "nearly 200 years have elapsed up to our time". These years would seem to coincide more or less with the above-mentioned 192 years, and in any case they leave very few years for the redaction of the work after AD 221. More evidence comes from the Olympic victor list. The list ends with the winner of Ol. 249, that is to say with the games held in the summer of 217 (F65,399). If the work had been finished much after 221, Africanus would probably have added the name of the winner of Ol. 250, held in the summer of that year. It may be that he finished his work during the summer/autumn of 221, before he was able to learn the name of its winner.

Finally, if 221 was not in fact the time of writing, it would be very difficult to explain why the historical account stops in that year. There is not the slightest hint that Africanus considered this particular year in any way important for the general course of history. It is not an epochal year and "nothing out of the ordinary" happened in it (nor, for that matter, in the whole of the period following the death of Christ, F93,85). The most logical hypothesis, therefore, is that Africanus finished and published his work in 221.[27]

While the time of writing can be determined with a relatively high degree of certainty, nothing is known about the place of writing. As has been said in the previous section, Africanus was a cosmopolite, who was able to visit and reside in numerous places. We know that he "instituted" the library near the Pantheon in Rome (cest. 5,53f), although this will have been after 221. The *Chronographiae* must have been written in a place where the author had access to a good library; this could have been Rome, but there is no way of knowing for certain.

It has been hypothesized that the *Chronographiae* was published in two "editions".[28] The theory is based on a passage in which Syncellus speaks of a δευτέρα ἔκδοσις Ἀφρικανοῦ (F46,33). However, to surmise the existence of two editions on this basis alone would be imprudent to say the least. There are in fact more logical ways of understanding this phrase (see note ad loc.). That being said, it is also true that the preserved material contains traces of earlier strata than that of the final version of 221. The heading of the Olympic victor list sets out a catalogue of names extending as far as Ol. 247 (= AD 209–13, i.e. the reign of Caracalla, whose name is also given, F65,42f.397). But the actual list goes further, up to Ol. 249 in fact. This should not be interpreted as a trace of a first (published) version, but rather the result of a long process of collecting and

---

27 This dating is shared and accepted by most scholars; see *inter alia* Gelzer 1,50f; Winkelmann 2002,511; Burgess 2006,40.
28 See discussion in Gelzer 1,29f.

2. The Chronographiae: Date and Place of Writing, Literary Character XIX

elaborating the material. The end of T6 could also be taken as a sign of an earlier redaction, although the evidence remains weak.²⁹

The oldest sources call the work χρονογραφίαι,³⁰ that is to say a "description of time", as Syriac and Armenian authors rightly translate.³¹ The expression could thus be considered the most likely form of the original title, although occasionally other titles are also attested, such as ἱστορικόν (Photius: T11), τὰ ἱστορικά (Syncellus: T64e), ἱστορία (anonymous: F14a), τὸ χρονογραφεῖον (Annianus: T39b) or τὰ χρονικά (Eusebius: T2a; John Chrysostom: F90a). The fact that Basil of Caesarea speaks of the ἐπιτομὴ τῶν χρόνων (F100) suggests that the *Chronographiae* also existed in an epitomized form. This theory appears to be endorsed by Syncellus, who at one point actually quotes Africanus ἐν ἐπιτόμῳ (F89,2) and furnishes a heavily-abridged text which is barely understandable. Nevertheless, the evidence for the existence of an epitomized version of the whole work is insufficient. It might be more prudent to assume that certain passages were detached for circulation and were quoted in abridged versions. As used by Syncellus, the word ἐπιτομή might also simply refer to a style of historiography whose broad chronological scope precluded in-depth analysis.

The sources generally agree on the fact that the whole chronicle consisted of five books,³² which leads us to believe that the work in its entirety was of quite a considerable size. Judging by the book lengths of later Church histories (Eusebius and his successors), it can be surmised that the surviving parts of the chronicle represent only a small part of the whole work. Although this is difficult to estimate, it is reasonable to suppose that no more than 10–20% of the entire text has been preserved. In all likelihood, the overall structure of the work was chronological, i.e. the five books corresponded to five consecutive periods of history. The subdivision was not according to sections in different literary characters (section of prose, section of tables, or the like), although there may have been some sort of appendix with one or more tables.³³ That being said, it seems unlikely that the material was organized in such a way that the narrative remained distinct from the numbers and the tables, or that there was a division into a historical account and a synoptic "canon-table" as found in Eusebius.

---

29 The text speaks of 184 years after the Resurrection (T6,21). This would lead to the year AM 5716 = AD 214/15 (AM 5532 + 184 = AM 5716), under Caracalla. However, the names given immediately before are totally confused and in any case do not coincide with the reign of Caracalla. *Moricaviti* probably comes from Marcus Avitus, which would be Elagabalus. *Alexandri* could be Alexander Severus.
30 Eusebius: T3,5; T41,6; introductory formulations (fourth app.) to F34,1; F93,22; John of Scythopolis: F20; T93a. See also Gelzer 1,26f.
31 Syriac: T13b; Armenian: T80c; similarly Jerome in Latin: T7b,6 (*Africanus temporum scriptor*).
32 Eusebius: T3a; Jerome: T2b; Paschale Campanum: T92; Photius: T11, see also the references to books 1–5 below.
33 T6 might reflect such an appendix; see below, pp. XXVI f. T39a,7f could imply that at the end of the fifth book controversial issues were discussed.

As for its literary character, the preserved material reveals a variety of styles, including straightforward lists (e.g. the lists of kings, see below pp. XXXVI f), annotated lists (e.g. F89, see ll. 18.38.58.66) and discourse or narrative prose (e.g. F34, F93). It is reasonable to suppose that the material that has been lost was also presented in the same way. The perusal of such interminable tables and texts must have been tedious in the extreme. Nevertheless, they offered reliable information which would have been otherwise difficult to find in one place—maybe this is another reason why the work was so widely used and why it has not survived as a whole.

If the five books correspond to five consecutive periods of history, the question arises as to where the demarcation points actually were. Unfortunately, the structure cannot be entirely reconstructed and therefore the attribution of individual fragments to particular books remains in many cases uncertain.[34] For book 3, our knowledge is relatively good, both for the quantity of material and for the chronological limits. The long discussion of the synchronism between the Exodus and Ogygus of Athens (F34) must have been placed at the beginning of this book.[35] The synchronism between the first Olympiad and the first year of Ahaz is also mentioned in this book, although it is taken up again in book 4 (T64e). It seems plausible to assume, therefore, that book 3 extended from the Exodus to the first Olympiad. Book 4 would then open with the period in which Greek chronology becomes firmly established on the basis of Olympiads. Book 5 must have started at the latest with the Incarnation: the genealogy of Jesus (F90a,1f), his Passion and Resurrection (F93, app. to l. 22; T93a), and a final doxology (F100) are all attested for this book. Unfortunately, the limits between book 4 and 5 cannot be defined any more precisely than this. The same applies for the history dealing with the period from Adam to Moses, i.e. books 1 and 2. Book 1 might have finished with the division of the earth in AM 2661 or with the death of Peleg in AM 3000, but this is no more than a supposition.

The literary character of Africanus' chronology is equally difficult to determine, particularly since the author did not adhere to any established genre. Indeed, his work is highly innovative in a number of ways, possessing varied and far-flung roots. The chronicle might be considered a rendition and re-adaptation of Hellenistic universal historiography, founded in a Christian theological framework, with a particular bias for Jewish history. As early as the second century, historical debates were becoming increasingly important within learned Christian circles. Such arguments not only concerned the history of Christianity itself (which was disappointingly new anyway) but also its older Jewish roots. In

---

34 The discussion that follows takes account of whatever is known about Africanus' subdivision of the *Chronographiae* into five books and the original placement of individual excerpts in them (for T39a see previous note); see also Gelzer 1,27–29.

35 Attested by Syncellus, text in the fourth app. to F34,71; see also the more general formulations in the app. to ll. 1.38.104.

apologetic contexts, the truth of the Christian message depended above all on the age of its doctrine.[36] As a consequence, the chronological relationship that existed between Moses and Plato, or of that between Moses and Homer, already attracted a certain level of interest. Theophilus of Antioch and Clement of Alexandria pushed the argument even further, affirming the existence of a historical continuum that went from creation right up to the present day.[37] In such a way, Christian roots were traced back to the remotest possible point, beyond which no history could be conceived.

The apologetic tradition in general, and Theophilus and Clement in particular, represent the most important Christian antecedents to the *Chronographiae* of Africanus. That being said, his work is much more than just a simple continuation of this tradition. To write five tomes of historical miscellanea would have been far too much of an undertaking, if it was meant just to make a point that in principle had already been made by previous authors with a great deal less effort. In fact, almost no trace of any controversial theological thinking can be found in any of the preserved fragments,[38] and it is clear that a work of such dimensions could only have been written by someone with a genuine scholarly interest in historiography. In this sense, the approach of Africanus might best be termed as scientific, the implication being that his interest in precise historical knowledge was mainly for the sake of knowledge.

The Christian character of his work is clear, especially given the importance attributed to the date of the Incarnation in AM 5500 and the detailed discussion concerning the date of the Crucifixion and Resurrection of Christ (F93). Nevertheless, it would be a mistake to try and reduce the *Chronographiae* to a purely apologetic work. In the same way, there is no trace of any interest in chiliastic or anti-chiliastic thought, although Africanus must have been aware of these currents and of the possible impact his system had for this sort of debate (see also below p. XXVIII).

Heinrich Gelzer was indubitably right in calling Africanus the "father of Christian chronography".[39] The *Chronographiae* was a benchmark and as such it went on to become a model for the new genre of Christian chronicles. Henceforth, all later chroniclers implicitly or explicitly had to take account of this work.[40] This is especially true of Eusebius whose work is based upon Africanus to a much higher degree than one might initially suppose.

---

36   See Droge 1989 and Pilhofer 1990 on early Christian construction of the beginnings of history and its theological value.
37   Theoph. Ant., Autol. 3,16–28; Clem. Alex., str. 1,21,101–147. On the origins of Christian universal history, see Croke 1983 and Wallraff 2004 and 2005. For Africanus' Christian predecessors, see Gelzer 1,19–24.
38   An exception would be the polemic against the Marcionites in F93,104–106.
39   Gelzer 1,1.
40   See Croke 1990,32f., Wallraff 2004,161–166.

Nevertheless, the Hellenistic roots of Africanus' historiography should always be borne in mind.[41] At the beginning of F34, which was probably the preface to book 3, he gives a fascinating insight into his role as an intermediary of the Jewish and Hellenistic traditions. For Africanus, just as it was for his Hellenistic predecessors, the description of primordial history was a thorny issue. When it came to the origins of mankind, the Greek tradition renounced the use of the term "history" resorting instead to the word "myth". Up until that point, all historians had agreed on considering Ol. 1,1 as the beginning of historical time.[42] Here, Africanus overcomes the incertitude of Greek historians concerning their archaic past—that is to say for the period of time from the beginning of the world to Ol. 1,1—by distinguishing between Jewish *history* and Greek *mythical history*.

For such a long time period (4727 years according to Africanus) only the Jewish chronology was able to provide a secure basis upon which to reconstruct a viable sequence of historical events. That does not mean to say that Africanus entirely rejected the Greek tradition. By means of synchronization, he attempted to link the comparatively fragile mythical Greek history to the much firmer Jewish one. Thanks to Africanus, synchronism thus became a means of mediating between two different chronological and historical systems.[43]

Despite the predominance of Jewish history as a general base, Africanus still managed to retain some traditional topics of Hellenistic universal history. A good example is his interest in the history of human knowledge and progress. In the preserved fragments, he mentions many of the most important discoveries of mankind, in accordance with the Greek tradition of the *heuremata*.[44] Another good example is his adoption of the *translatio imperii*, a concept which was part and parcel of Hellenistic historiography. The *translatio imperii* crops up in many passages in the list of kings and elsewhere (see in particular F89,53–57, F93,50–53, also T6,14–21). The series of kingdoms culminates in the Roman empire, which is presented as the historic scene for the advent of Christ.[45]

The methodology of Africanus was also influenced by a number of other traditional Hellenistic models. For example, his approach to Greek mythology is

---

41 The article of Burgess 2006 gives an excellent overview of the antecedents of Iulius Africanus—primarily, but not only, in the Hellenistic sphere. For the Hellenistic roots of Africanus, see also Schwartz 1895,23; for his methodology, see Roberto 2006.
42 This view is also referred to by Africanus, F34,1–5. On the problem of primordial history in the Greek tradition, see Momigliano 1966,14–22 and Adler 1989, in particular 15–18.
43 See F34,4–11 and F15,9–14 for a comparison between Jewish chronology and other Oriental systems. On the synchronism in the *Chronographiae*, see Sirinelli 1961,509–515 and Roberto 2006,8–15. For the synchronisation between Jewish and Greek history in preceding universal historiography see Wacholder 1968 (esp. 463–477).
44 F18; F24,34–37; F54a,17f; F56,7–9. The interest in *heuremata* is connected to a general interest for cultural history, as shown for example by F81b.
45 F15,9–14, see also T6,17.

based on a sort of criticism of myth, recalling both the euhemeristic tradition and the interpretation of Palaephatus.[46] According to the traditional criterion of autopsy, Africanus occasionally refers in his narrative to his own personal experiences (e.g. F23,18–20; F29). From these texts it can be inferred that at least some parts of the *Chronographiae* were composed not only as a strict chronological account, but also as a history which was designed to include descriptions of natural phenomena and exotic places. The *Chronographiae* was much more than just a monotonous book of tables and lists, in some parts the author actually tried to entertain his readers.[47]

Africanus' use and quotation of various sources also hark back to the Greek tradition. Even though he may only have known some of them second hand, his quotations still show a good knowledge of such authors.[48] The most important example is the insertion of an epitomized Jewish version of the list of the Egyptian kings of Manetho (F46). In the 9th century, Syncellus considered this the best preserved version of the list (T46a).

3. The Chronological System

Africanus' presiding idea was to insert the whole of the history of mankind into one great chronological system. Not only was such a system intended to be arithmetically coherent, it was conceived in such a way as to encompass all branches of history, including the Semitic and Hellenistic traditions. Everything was subordinated to this idea, sometimes to an almost obsessive extent and occasionally even at the cost of factual truth. Large parts of the work served little other than to support the impressive numerical framework that he re-calculated in order to fit various historical perspectives. Underpinning the entire system was the old Christian (and Jewish) conviction that the duration of history as a whole amounted to 6000 years, in accordance with the six days of creation, whereby each day equaled 1000 years.[49] In this framework, the most decisive dates are the death of Peleg (in whose time the earth was divided), which would be the "mid-point" of history occurring in the year 3000, and the Incarnation of Jesus Christ in 5500.[50] Everything else, and in particular the traditional elements of Hellenistic historiography, is woven into this framework.

---

46 F24. On this question, see Sirinelli 1961,180–189; Roberto 2006,11–13.
47 See, e.g., F26,13–23; F30.
48 See, e.g., F34,26–36.75–87.96–102; F56,4f; F65,30–37; F81a,3–5; F93,14–17.
49 Ps 89[90],4 ("For a thousand years in your sight are like yesterday when it is past, or like a watch in the night"); II Petr 3,8 ("with the Lord one day is like a thousand years, and a thousand years are like one day"); see also Barn 15,4; Iren., haer. 5,28,3; 5,23,2; Hipp., Dan. 4,23,5 f.
50 Here and in the following pages, references to the Africanus material can be found in the "reference" section of the fold-out table in the appendix.

Obviously, it is no longer possible to reconstruct the whole system in its original form as Africanus would have presented it. Not only are large parts of the work lost, but the numerals themselves are particularly prone to error in transmission, both intentional and unintentional. Indeed, given all the problems and pitfalls, it is actually quite surprising how coherent all the extant material is. Even the *Excerpta Barbari*, which textually speaking, represents an extremely distorted branch of the transmission, preserves numerals which, in many cases, dovetail perfectly with the system as we know it from other sources.

The present edition is based on the hypothesis that Africanus' chronological system was internally coherent, although this does not exclude the presence of discrepancies and inconsistencies in a few minor places. Hence, in many problematic passages it is better to assume an error in transmission rather than an oversight in the original. Of course, this could lead to an attitude of over-confident conjecture and of papering over all the chronological cracks in the text. Therefore, the present edition adopts a rather cautious method. The chronological discrepancies that remain are too many and too grave to be resolved convincingly by means of simple emendations. Several inconsistencies and contradictions can be found in the text, and as a rule the notes to the English translation draw the reader's attention to these points. However, wherever the text would appear to be corrupt and where an obvious solution was at hand, the text has been emended (with the original reading in the critical apparatus). That being said, it has to be admitted that in many cases, the borderline between the obvious and the hypothetical is not always completely clear-cut.[51]

The debate over the correct reconstruction of Africanus' chronological system has been ongoing for some 400 years (since Scaliger 1606) and some *quaestiones vexatae* have emerged, for which we admit to having no ready answers. As a result, the present edition aims neither to prolong this debate nor resolve any of the questions definitively. The aim of this edition is simply to place at the disposal of scholars a better working basis from which to analyze all of the available material. As a consequence, the table illustrating the chronological system in the appendix is intended primarily as an aid to help guide the reader through the material, not a new and innovative hypothetical reconstruction. In large parts, it reflects a broad scholarly consensus, although parts have been challenged in recent publications.[52]

The table can be folded out and opened in order to permit a better synoptic use in conjunction with the texts. Not all the dates have the same degree of

---

51 In F89,57, for example, we did correct 11 to 14, but not Ol. 187,4 to 187,2; the notes to the English translation explain the differing degrees of certainty.

52 The most important contributions are Routh 507–509, Trieber 1880, Schwartz 1895, Gelzer 1,26–52, Finegan 1998,154–160, Burgess 2006, Mosshammer 2006 (where more bibliography can be found). Our reconstruction of the system owes a great deal to Schwartz, who in many cases (but not in all) still seems to be the most convincing.

3. The Chronological System

relevance nor indeed the same level of certainty. Particularly important events, whose dates are both well-attested and fundamental to the entire chronological system, are printed in bold-face. In the second and third columns (from Adam and the Olympiads) the corresponding figures are printed in bold only when they are actually attested explicitly in the sources. Although some dates are not attested directly, they can still be deduced with a high degree of certainty (e.g. the Exodus in AM 3707 and the first Olympiad in AM 4727). Braces { } have been used to indicate cases where well-attested dates fail to concur with the overall chronological system and where we have been unable to offer a logical emendation. A recurring problem is the numbering of the first year of each king/emperor. For example, "1 Saul" should actually be read as "0 Saul", i.e. the beginning of his reign. Therefore the period of time from "1 Saul = AM 4382" to "20 Saul = AM 4402" is 20 years, not 19.

It should be noted that, although Africanus' chronicle included the Mosaic cosmogony (F14, see also Photius in T11), he typically numbers years from the creation of Adam (ἀπὸ Ἀδάμ).[53] As a consequence, the use of the conventional abbreviation AM (*annus mundi*) is, strictly speaking, not appropriate. However, for the sake of clarity and brevity, it has been adopted in the translation and in the notes to the edition.

In most cases, the textual basis for the material found within the fold-out table is sufficiently documented in the "reference" section accompanying it. The discussion that follows refers only to fundamental questions and a few particularly complex details.

First and foremost, it is important to distinguish between Africanus' own method of dating and that of modern historiography (i.e. BC/AD). Since the latter is of secondary importance for the reconstruction of Africanus' chronological system, it appears in the table merely as an additional aid.[54] Africanus basically uses two systems of dating and part of his great historiographical achievement consists in the coordination of the two. By combining the years from Adam with the Greek system of dating according to Olympiads, he was able to graft the Hellenistic tradition onto a Jewish historical framework (see above pp. XXII f).

Unfortunately, only three texts have been preserved containing a direct equation between the years from Adam and the Olympiads: F54d, F89 and F93. In the case of the second text (F89,57), the interpretation is problematic; all scholars agree on the fact that the text is corrupt in its transmitted form.[55] It probably ought to be emended to give the equation AM 5472 = Ol. 187,2. In the long fragment F93, dealing with the Passion and Resurrection of Christ, the Olympiad date 202,2 (l. 58) is not immediately equated with a year from Adam.

---

53 On the theological distinction between 'Adam-years' and 'world-years', see Gelzer 1,35f.
54 According to the standard equation AM 1 = 5502/01 BC; see above n. 26.
55 See notes 5 and 6 to the translation of the fragment.

It might be 5531, which is quoted by Syncellus further down, but from a slightly different context in Africanus (l. 109), or it could be 5532, as found in Michael the Syrian (T93d). Most scholars prefer the second option,[56] since the equation Ol. 202,2 = AM 5532 is coherent with the third and best piece of evidence. In F54d, the year Ol. 250,1 is equated with AM 5723, which is presumably the date of the end of the *Chronographiae*.

All these indications lead us to the fundamental date of AM 4727, which represents the year of the first Olympiad, a hypothesis confirmed by various calculations within the *Chronographiae*.[57] In sum, Africanus' entire chronological system is founded upon the following three coherent equations:

AM 4727 = Ol. 1,1
AM 5532 = Ol. 202,2
AM 5723 = Ol. 250,1

Given the complexity of the system as a whole, it is quite possible that Africanus composed a short summary in tabular form at the beginning or at the end of his work. This would certainly not have had the form of a "second book" as in the canons of Eusebius, but rather a brief one or two page overview (see above p. XVIII). It is tempting to think that the enigmatic text (T6)—attested only in Latin from the 9th century onwards—might ultimately derive from Africanus' own summary, although this cannot be proven.[58] The table includes a striking number of dates which are all well-attested in other authentic fragments of Africanus. Even if the text is the work of a learned reader of later times, this reader must have been very well acquainted with the *Chronographiae*.[59] Since references to known fragments are given in the apparatus of the edition, only a few points need further explanation here. The whole chronological scheme is based on the Hellenistic idea of the *translatio imperii*: i.e. a history of the Jews followed by a history of the Persians, Macedonians and Romans.[60] The only

---

56 Gelzer 1,48f; Schwartz 1895,27f; Burgess 2006,40–42; Mosshammer 2006,107.
57 The most prominent confirmation comes from F34,41, according to which the period from the Exodus to Ol. 1,1 is 1020 years, i.e. AM 3707 + 1020 = AM 4727. The information on the Sicyonian kingdom (F51a) also points in the same direction: the kingdom begins 114 years after the migration of Abraham (AM 3277, F16d,6), from there to the first Olympiad, 1336 years have elapsed: AM 3277 + 114 + 1336 = AM 4727. Similarly with the Lacedaemonians (F58a): their kingdom began in the 20th year of Saul, which is 325 years before Ol. 1,1. According to F35, Saul began his reign in AM 4382, and AM 4382 + 20 + 325 = AM 4727.
58 The text was first published in 1688 by Henry Dodwell (1641–1711), on whom see Quantin 2006.
59 This becomes immediately plausible from the high number of cross references to other fragments in the apparatus.
60 It should be remarked that Africanus seems to adopt an Egyptian perspective. The Persian kingdom ends with the conquest of Egypt by Alexander. In the same year (AM 5172) the Macedonian (Ptolemaic) hegemony begins, which lasts until the conquest of Egypt by Augustus.

slight imprecision lies in the time-span attributed to the Roman empire (74 years). Instead of giving the period beginning with the death of Cleopatra (end of the Ptolemaic dynasty) running up to the Crucifixion and the Resurrection (60 years, F93,53), the text calculates the period starting from the death of Caesar and Augustus' own accession to the throne. This is not wrong in itself, but it does not concur with the precept of the *translatio imperii*, since it could lead to the period of 14 years between 1 Augustus and the death of Cleopatra being counted twice. This is effectively what happens at the end of the text when the calculation of the total number of years from Adam to the Resurrection is given. This number has been calculated independently on the basis of the numbers mentioned before. Two errors occurred in the process. One is a simple error of calculation (or, more likely, a scribal error); the text reads 5726, whereas the correct sum should be 5526. The other is the double counting of the first 14 years of Augustus; the total should therefore amount to 5512. Moreover, one has to consider that the only number that actually managed to creep in from the Eusebian tradition, which is definitely not from Africanus, is the date of the Flood (2242 in the text, opposed to 2262 which is quite definitely that of Africanus). Therefore, the correct sum for Africanus' system can be rectified to 5532, which supports once again the dating of the Crucifixion and Resurrection given above.

Syncellus already considered the date of the Flood in AM 2262 a characteristic feature of Africanus' (and only Africanus') system (T16g with note 2; T22a; T45). This is not only 20 years later than the date given by Eusebius, it is also 20 years later than the date that could have been calculated on the basis of the Bible as it was known to Syncellus, i.e. the Septuagint (in its Byzantine *textus receptus*). Behind all this lies an old problem of biblical chronology: if one takes the numbers given in the Greek Bible seriously, Methuselah should have survived the Flood. According to the figures, Methuselah lived 969 years, 167 up to the birth of his son Lamech, 188 up to the birth of Noah (Gen 5,25–32); from there 600 years elapsed up to the Flood (Gen 7,6), thus placing his death 14 years after the Flood. In the Hebrew Bible, this problem is avoided by the assumption that Lamech was born 20 years later (and Noah 6 years earlier), therefore putting Methuselah's death exactly in the year of the Flood itself.[61] Africanus followed this tradition, although he normally used the Septuagint and it is quite possible that he studied a little textual criticism for the purpose. Indeed, formulations of the *Chronicon Paschale* ("the accurate copies of the book of Genesis", T16g) and Syncellus ("on the basis of a few copies", T16h) both suggest this.

A similar case is the problem of the "second" Kenan, that is to say the son of Arpachshad after the Flood ("second" because there is another person of that name before the Flood). Although Kenan is mentioned both in the Septuagint

---

61 On the chronology of the various versions of the Hebrew Bible, see Rösel 1994,129–144.

and the Gospel of Luke (Gen 10,24; 11,13; Lc 3,36), he does not appear in the Hebrew Bible. Africanus follows the Hebrew text and omits the 130 years up to the generation of Kenan's son Shelah (F16c with note 1; T16i–o). Therefore, in comparison with the Byzantine tradition (including Syncellus), the chronology of Africanus is lacking 110 years (Kenan's 130 years – Methuselah's 20 years = 110 years, T16q).

The death of Peleg in AM 3000 is another important feature of Africanus' system. As stated in F94 (see also F16c,7–12, 3rd app.), this date falls precisely midway through the 6000 year period, a span of time which Africanus equates with the entire period from the creation to the end of the world.[62] Whether and how Africanus actually dealt with eschatological issues is a moot point. Although no preserved text addresses questions of this sort,[63] it is obviously in the logic of his chronological system to attempt calculations concerning the end of the world. Indeed, since he wrote in AM 5723, there would be 277 years left until the end of the sixth millennium and the beginning of the "great Sabbath", the seventh millennium belonging to God. 277 years were almost certainly enough to quiet the eschatological fervor of his own generation and several succeeding ones. Africanus probably did not reflect on the possibility that his system would stir up agitation in AD 500, although this is precisely what happened.[64] Since nothing is known about Africanus' view of the future, the "Chronological System" in the appendix ends in AM 5723 and not in AM 6000.

In "historical" times, i.e. after Ol. 1,1, the chronology becomes increasingly complex. At the beginning of book 3, Africanus inserts a fundamental discussion of the synchronization of the Jewish chronological system with the Greek one (F34). According to this text, the two principal dates are the Exodus of Moses (AM 3707) and the first Olympiad, which, in Hellenistic historiography, represents the beginning of a continuous chronological narrative. The time-span from the Exodus to Ol. 1,1 is 1020 years, the first Olympiad (AM 4727) occurring in the first year of the reign of king Ahaz in Israel.[65]

From this point onwards, the two dating systems run parallel. However, it can be demonstrated that Africanus actually continues calculating on the basis of years "from Adam". This corresponds with his chronological method formulated in F34, according to which the principal historical thread is the Jewish one. It also explains two important inconsistencies in the system which probably go

---

62 The birth of Peleg in AM 2661 corresponds to the division of the earth after the Flood (F25). Gelzer 1,29 suggests that this date was the point of division between books 1 and 2.
63 F94,3 gives a calculation of the time remaining from the *parousia* of Jesus Christ until the end of the world. However, there is no real reason to think that this still derives from Africanus (hence printed in small letters).
64 Brandes 1997. On the history of millenarianism, see Landes 1988.
65 For the fall of Troy, which was the earliest possible historical event in the Hellenistic tradition, Africanus follows the widely accepted chronology of Eratosthenes and assumes that this took place 407 years before Ol. 1,1, i.e. AM 4727 – 407 = AM 4320 (F50,28), 1183/82 BC.

back to the original version of the *Chronographiae*. These are the beginning of the Persian kingdom in Ol. 55,1 and the rebuilding of Jerusalem in Ol. 83,4. Both dates are well-attested and both dates fail to correspond with Africanus' system. Although in both cases no AM date is given, there is sufficient evidence to calculate with a high degree of certainty what must have been Africanus' dates: AM 4942 and AM 5057 (corresponding to Ol. 54,4 and Ol. 83,3). However, in two important and well-attested fragments, Africanus' calculations are clearly based on the AM dates and not on those of the Olympiads. Curiously, however, he omits the AM dates, even while citing those of the Olympiads (F34, see note 6, and F93, see note 6).

4. The Text and its Transmission

The *Chronographiae* of Africanus is lost. No complete copy of it survives. Unlike the *Cesti*, where an interesting fragment on papyrus was discovered in Oxyrynchus,[66] no fragments of its direct transmission have ever been found. As a consequence, all attempts at reconstructing the work depend totally on later authors using or quoting Africanus. With the exception of a few excerpts (T6, F14), the nature of the source material consists almost entirely of quotations (where the term is understood as an insertion of text in an independent context with its own literary aspirations). Put succinctly, almost everything we possess from Africanus has come down to us in the context of independent works, mostly chronicles, with their own inclinations, agendas and interests. Those who quoted Africanus usually did so because they either wanted to confirm their own view of world history or falsify somebody else's—as a result some criticize him, others praise him. Even when Africanus is used purely as a historical source, those citing him have a particular interest in quoting a precise piece of data. Any textual criticism has to take all of these elements into account. The

---

[66] cest. 5 = Pap. Oxy. 412. In the case of the chronicle also, there might be an interesting case of fragmentary direct transmission. Berendts 1904,75–79 (hence Bardenhewer 1913–32, 2,266) analyzes the scarce information on a Meteora manuscript given by the Russian bishop Porfirij Uspenski (†1885). He saw the manuscript in 1859 and his notes were published posthumously in 1896 (Richard 1995, nr. 1676). All he says on the "ms. 34" of the monastery of the transfiguration (Metamorphosis) is the following: "Ἱστορικὸν ἀπὸ τῆς ὀπτασίας τοῦ Δανιὴλ ἕως τῆς βασιλείας τοῦ Ἀντωνίνου Καρακάλλα... Anfang und Ende fehlen. Μοναρχία Τιβερίου Καίσαρος. ... (sic) μὲν οὖν Αὔγουστος ἀπεβίω, ὡς εἴρηται· τὴν δὲ μοναρχίαν ὁ Τιβέριος διεδέξατο· ὃς εὐπατρίδης μὲν ἦν καὶ πεπαίδευτος, τὴν δὲ γνώμην ἦν ποικιλώτατος..." (Berendts 1904,75). Berendts rightly infers that there is a certain likelihood that the text is linked to Africanus. Unfortunately, it was not possible to find the manuscript, nor does the detailed catalogue by Bees 1967 show any trace of it. The manuscript may be irretrievably lost. The only remaining possibility is that Uspenskij actually took the manuscript with him, in which case it might ultimately have ended up in an ecclesiastical library in Russia. Cf. also Richard 1995, nr. 1676 on Uspenskij: "De nombreux mss des bibliothèques signalées ont depuis disparu."

following paragraphs, therefore, are intended to assist the reader in assessing the principal authors who are thought to constitute the Africanus tradition.

Explaining why the *Chronographiae* has not survived is a difficult task. Whatever the reasons, Africanus is not alone in this literary category. Of Hippolytus' work we have nothing but a few woeful fragments. As for Eusebius, large parts of his work are known only in ancient translations (Latin and Armenian), while of a certain chronicler named Judas (3rd cent.) we know not much more than that he actually existed.[67] The loss of such works is perhaps due to the fact that chronicles, despite the high esteem in which the authors were often held, were largely considered *Gebrauchsliteratur*. That is to say, as soon as a more up-to-date and (allegedly) more correct chronicle existed, the older ones were no longer used and copied. Occasionally quoted and consulted, the more ancient works were all eventually superseded by newer versions.

As a genre, chronicles were very popular in the Greek literature of the Later Roman and Byzantine Empire, answering to a broad spectrum of interests and needs. It would be a mistake however to group such works under the title of *Trivialliteratur* or *Mönchschroniken*.[68] While it is true that some chronicles were minor works written by monks, it is also true that other works were composed by authors forming part of an intellectual elite, possessing high literary and scholarly ambitions. It was men belonging to such lofty groups, men such as Eusebius, Syncellus and Michel the Syrian that invariably had recourse to Africanus' chronology. Although in a few cases the (direct or indirect) use of his chronology also "sank down" into the lower strata of the genre, we are mostly dealing with scholarly products, written for an intellectual elite audience.

Given the popularity of the genre and the interdependence of the works among themselves, it is virtually impossible to establish any kind of stemma explaining who copied what and from whom. The task becomes even harder because of the highly fragmented state of preservation of the works and, in many cases, the lack of critical editions. Although a viable "stemmatization" will always remain an illusion, the number of available editions has increased somewhat in the last decades. A hundred years ago, when Gelzer first attempted to edit the fragments, the situation was dire. Although some good editions have appeared in the meantime,[69] the situation is still far from satisfactory. Some of the works in question have never been edited, while others are still only available

---

67 According to Eus., h.e. 6,7 his chronicle was inspired by the seventy weeks of Daniel; the author thought the coming of the Antichrist was near.
68 On Byzantine chronicles in general, see Gelzer 2,129–410; Hunger 1978, 1,257–278 (fundamental, despite his classification under *Trivialliteratur*); Adler 1989; Rochow 1990; Croke 1990. Already in 1965 Hans-Georg Beck has shown that the so-called *Mönchschroniken* were not necessarily written or primarily read by monks (Beck 1965).
69 Since Gelzer, good critical editions have appeared for Eus., can.^{Hier}; Eus., h.e.; Io. Mal.; (ps.) Io. Ant.; Sync.; Sym. Log. and others.

in editions going back to Renaissance or Baroque times.[70] Even with better texts, a great deal of scholarly debate is still needed to clarify many aspects of this literature. Hence, what follows is only a snapshot of the present state of research, a brief synopsis of the sources underpinning this edition.

The first author assumed to have used and criticized Africanus is Hippolytus. However, too little of his work has been preserved to take any material from it and collate it with our collection of fragments.[71] Therefore, our first relevant author is Eusebius of Caesarea, who also happens to be one of the most important.

4.1. Eusebius

Eusebius almost certainly knew Africanus right at the beginning of his scholarly career. If the man hadn't inspired and fascinated him to some extent, it would be hard to explain why, in the wake of Africanus' *Chronographiae*, he began his activity with a similar monumental historical work. Already in the first few lines, Eusebius associates himself with the Christian chroniclers, mentioning by name Clement of Alexandria, Africanus, and Tatian,[72] of whom the second is doubtlessly the most important. The literary genre chosen by Eusebius is that of Africanus. Eusebius also copied his basic chronological structure, attempting to bind together the various historiographical traditions of the Hellenistic and Semitic world and place them in a Christian perspective. In many points, however, Eusebius succeeds in maintaining a certain critical distance from his predecessor. This applies both to some historical details[73] and to the more general issue of his whole historiographical conception: his most important innovation is the presentation of the material in the form of a series of chronological tables (*Canones*).

Given the literary impact of the *Chronographiae* as a genre and all the criticism it received, it is hard to conceive that Eusebius knew the work of Africanus

---

[70] This applies, for instance, to ps. Sym. Log. (unpublished); Cedr.; ps. Eust., in hex.; Ioh. Scyth., scholia in epp. Dion. Areop.

[71] On Hippolytus' use of Africanus, see Bauer 1905,150–152 and Bauer 1955, XXVII.

[72] T48a = Eus., can.^{Hier} 7,10–17. On Eusebius' chronicle, see Schwartz 1907,1376–1384; Sirinelli 1961; Mosshammer 1979; Winkelmann 1991,88–104; Burgess 1999; Jeanjean/Lançon 2004.

[73] Eusebius considers, for example, his dating of Moses to the period of Cecrops as an important chronological achievement. This is completely different from Africanus' system (Moses under Ogygus, therefore c. 200 years earlier). Opinion also diverges concerning the duration of the period from the exodus to the building of the temple (T41) and the interpretation of the passage in the book of Daniel (9,24–27), also known as the "apocalypse of 70 weeks" (F78, T78a). On both problems, cf. Adler 1992,471f and Adler 2006,148–150. In general, Africanus seems much more confident about the possibility of establishing a coherent chronology on the basis of the Bible. He tries to make everything fit into his system. This is why Adler 1992,479 speaks of "Africanus' dogmatism" as opposed to "Eusebius' reserve".

in excerpts or fragments only. Indeed, in a later work he actually refers to a complete copy of the chronicle which had come into his possession,[74] and it is highly likely that he had it at his disposal already when he was writing the chronicle. It is for this reason that his testimony is so precious for the reconstruction of Africanus' work, but for various reasons this treasure is not easy to rescue. The most serious impediment is the unfortunate transmission of Eusebius' text itself and the lack of a satisfactory modern edition. This complex situation requires some explanation. The original work (*Chronica*) essentially consisted of two parts—two volumes as it were—which for the sake of simplicity are here referred to as *Chronographia* and *Canones*.[75] The literary character of the former was probably quite similar to that of Africanus' own work. A prose text with many inserted tables, it contained various historical themes which were collated and placed into direct relationship with one another by means of theoretical discussions and synchronisms. This part of Eusebius' work is only preserved in its entirety in an early Armenian translation and in a number of Greek fragments.[76] The latter part/volume constitutes Eusebius' main innovation: a juxtaposition of the whole history of mankind from Abraham to the present day in a large table, containing several columns for the various historical themes. Understandably, such a work fascinated later authors, in particular Jerome, and, therefore, apart from the Armenian translation and some fragments of the Greek original, this part is also preserved in Jerome's Latin version.[77] It became one of the standard history books of the Latin middle ages. For the purposes of the present edition, it has been necessary, on occasion, to anticipate the work of a future editor of Eusebius, i.e. reconstituting a text on the basis of the Greek, Latin and Armenian witnesses.

---

74 T3a = h.e. 6,31,2.
75 This terminology follows Fotheringham 1923,III–V, who has collected all relevant material and comes to the conclusion that this is closest to the sources, without claiming that Eusebius actually used these titles. Schwartz 1907,1376 did not see the two parts as "two volumes", rather he considered the first part only an introduction to the main work which would be the χρονικοὶ κανόνες. This was due to an exaggerated tendency to exalt Eusebius' originality.
76 The Armenian text is easily accessible in a German translation in the GCS edition by Karst 1911; this does not, however, replace the useful edition of Aucher 1818, which is a sound work of scholarship, where the Armenian text is provided along with a literal Latin translation and with the corresponding Greek fragments. On the Armenian text, see also Drost-Abgarjan 2006. The Greek material still awaits a comprehensive modern analysis and edition. At present, the best version can be found in Schoene 1875–76, 1,1–286 (especially the texts preserved in the ms. Paris. gr. 2600, the so called *Excerpta Eusebiana*, collated by Paul de Lagarde, see p. XII). The value of this edition is often underestimated; it is by no means superseded by Helm 1956 and Karst 1911. Although it is less reliable, the older Cramer edition also remains useful for the *Excerpta Eusebiana*, because it gives the whole relevant section of the ms. Paris. gr. 2600 (ff. 193^r–219^r) in its context. On the codex see Christesen/Martirosova-Torlone 2006,41–43.
77 Helm's GCS edition of Jerome's chronicle can be considered a masterpiece. Apart from the edition itself, the appendix should also be used, where Helm gives references in condensed form to many useful parallels (including the preserved Greek fragments).

A second obstacle in evaluating the material in Eusebius' chronicle is the heterogeneous way in which he exploits his predecessor. In some cases, he quotes him directly, mostly in order to criticize him.[78] In a few cases, the critique is not explicit in that he quotes in an affirmative way, but then goes on to add implicit corrections, which has a habit of rendering his quotes rather misleading to say the least.[79] But by far the biggest and most difficult group of citations are those in which Eusebius simply cites the historical material of his predecessor without questioning him or even mentioning his name. Such cases are difficult to identify. Parallels drawn between the material of Syncellus, which are attributable to Africanus and passages in Eusebius' chronicle are in some cases conclusive.[80] The series of texts in the *Excerpta Salmasiana* (ps. Ioh. Ant., fr. 2*–21*), which contain rationalizing explications of myths, are all probably taken from Africanus and sometimes reveal striking parallels with Eusebius.[81] As for the various kings' lists,[82] these all basically go back to Castor, but often it is impossible to say whether Eusebius copied them from him directly, or whether he took them straight from Africanus. This is why the Eusebian numerals have been noted in the apparatus for each of the relevant fragments.[83] It is unlikely that all of Africanus' material has been identified in Eusebius' chronicle so far.

In only one spectacular case has it been possible to firmly attribute material of this category to Africanus. The latter concerns the long list of Olympic victors stretching from the beginning of the games to Ol. 249, which effectively constitutes the only surviving antique list of its kind (F65). The attribution to Africanus was initially surmised by Scaliger and although some doubts were recently cast over it, a detailed analysis demonstrates that the hypothesis still carries a high degree of plausibility.[84]

---

78   T48a; T78a; mention without critique: T80a.b.c; F85. For Eusebius' critique of Africanus in general, see Adler 2006.
79   This is the case in F64d, where a verbatim quotation from Africanus is given (ll. 11f = F64c). The quotation is given with the intention of confirming, with his predecessor's authority, Eusebius' main point, namely the dating of the first Olympiad. Closer analysis, however, reveals that the quoted text has nothing to do with this problem and that Eusebius actually disagrees with Africanus' dating (as Syncellus rightly pointed out, T64e).
80   F56; F81.
81   See Roberto 2005b and below, pp. XL ff.
82   Africanus' material is partly preserved in the *Excerpta Barbari*; see below, pp. XXXVI f.
83   An additional problem is presented by the lists transmitted both in Armenian and in Latin in the context of the chronicle, although apparently neither of them belong to it ("regum series", not in Helm's edition, but in Schoene 1875–76, 1,19–40 [Appendix 1B] and Karst 1911,144–155). They might derive from Eusebius' preparatory work in the form of a collection of material.
84   Scaliger's hypothesis won general acceptance until Mosshammer 1979,138–146 argued that if Eusebius had really had the list from him, he would have mentioned Africanus in the record of sources that follows shortly after (Eus., chron. 125,8–25). However, this *argumentum ex silentio* remains weak. An analysis of the historical notices contained within the list and a study of the transmission of the text suggest otherwise, see Wallraff 2006,50–53. The most recent study of

In a similar fashion, it has also been hypothesized that Eusebius used a list of bishops, relating to the most important sees, which was itself originally compiled by Africanus.[85] However, the argumentation here is much more complex and although the hypothesis cannot be totally ruled out, the evidence is much too scanty to justify its inclusion in the present edition.[86]

Even in Eusebius' later works, Africanus always remained an important intellectual model. However, although he continued to use and quote him, the tone becomes somewhat more irenic. It would have been pointless for Eusebius to stress differences in chronological detail in literary works that no longer pertain to the genre of a chronicle. Although Eusebius still tends not to agree with everything Africanus says, he now seems prepared to admit at least that Africanus belonged to the "men of learning, second to none in the cultivated class" (p. e. 10,9,26), and that he was "no ordinary historian" (h. e. 1,6,2). Moreover, in some instances he cites Africanus in longer passages without interruption or correction. In his theological works, the *Eclogae propheticae*, the *Praeparatio* and the *Demonstratio evangelica*, we have a small number of lengthy quotations belonging to the most important and well-attested surviving texts. These are F34, which presumably formed part of Africanus' *prooemium* to book 3, and F93, the intricate discussion of the date of the Passion and the Resurrection of Christ. The quality of the text in these cases is very high as can be inferred from parallels in Syncellus.[87]

4.2. Chronicles from the Alexandrian Tradition

The chronicle of Eusebius soon became a standard work, and to a large extent it superseded that of his predecessor Africanus. However, interest in the father of Christian chronography still lingered. In the fifth century, this interest is attested

---

the list (Christesen/Martirosova-Torlone 2006, appeared after our edition was finished) does not discuss the question of authorship (see only p. 38f, quoting Mosshammer). However, it gives useful information on the transmission of the text. Further studies of the list are by Moretti 1957 and Wacker 1998.

85   The argument was developed with acumen and in detail by Harnack 1897,70–230 and Schwartz 1903–09, 3,CCXXVIII–CCXLIII. Harnack 1897,124–127 even gave a hypothetical reconstruction of Africanus' list.

86   For a detailed analysis, see Wallraff 2006,53–56.

87   In the case of F93, there is also a double transmission within Eusebius' oeuvre. He quotes the same passage both in his *Eclogae propheticae*, dating to around 305 and his *Demonstratio evangelica* ca. ten years later (for the dating, see Winkelmann 1991,188–191). However, this doublet is no check on the quality of the transmission, because it is quite possible that in the second case Eusebius took the quotation from his older work (rather than looking it up again in the original). Another fragment is transmitted in the *Church history* (F87, The Father of Herod, again with a doublet in the *Eclogae*), a rather short text, where the positive judgment on the quality of the transmission has to be attenuated: considerable differences between Eusebius and Syncellus appear and it is impossible to know which author modified the original wording.

in the Alexandrian intellectual milieu by a reference to him in the chronicle of Annianus (T39b). Around the same time, a Greek chronicle, composed in Alexandria during the reign of Zeno or Anastasius and preserved in a Latin epitome, referred to as the *Excerpta Barbari* (8th century), contains yet more of his quotations.

4.2.1. Panodorus and Annianus

The monks Panodorus and Annianus were both writing at the beginning of the fifth century. Although their works do not survive, some general features and excerpts are known, many of them coming through the quotations of Syncellus. Apparently both authors attempted a new chronological system, continuing and commenting on the work of their predecessors, Africanus and Eusebius.

Syncellus tells us that Panodorus composed a universal chronicle far surpassing Annianus in both length and astronomical learning.[88] Establishing his own reckoning system, known as the Alexandrian era, Panodorus calculated 5493 years from Adam to the Incarnation.[89] Another important feature of his work was the reconciling of pagan sources and scholarship with biblical chronology. Syncellus criticizes him for some chronological errors (e.g. calculating the birth and the death of Jesus) and he questions his orthodoxy.[90] In his attempt to form a new Christian chronological system, it is highly probable that Panodorus took an interest in Africanus' *Chronographiae* and that he knew his work. Unfortunately, this cannot be proved on the basis of the preserved material.[91]

Although Annianus may have been less innovative than Panodorus, Syncellus viewed his chronicle far more favorably. While containing much of the same material as Panodorus, it was less prolix, structured, according to Syncellus, in the form of tables of 532-year Easter cycles. Unlike Panodorus, Annianus also adhered to the traditional dating of the Incarnation in AM 5500. As a consequence, his work exerted more influence than that of Panodorus, especially among Syriac chronographers.[92]

In one preserved fragment (T39b), Africanus is directly mentioned. Here, Annianus criticizes Eusebius for forgetting to mention the 40 years of anarchy

---

88 Sync. 35,20–36,5.
89 See Serruys 1907,251–260.
90 Sync. 378,5–10, see also 17,26f and 42,20–24.
91 On Panodorus, see Unger 1867,40f, Gelzer 2,189–204 (in particular 190f on the originality of his work), Seel 1949, and, more recently, Adler 1983, Adler 1989,97–101. Expanding an hypothesis of Unger, Gelzer asserts that the main sources of Panodorus were Africanus, Eusebius and Dexippus. Furthermore, he presumes that the excerpts of these authors came to Annianus and to Syncellus mainly through Panodorus, see, e.g., his hypothesis on the transmission of Africanus' list of Egyptian kings to Syncellus via Panodorus, 196–198. This view is basically shared by Mosshammer 1979,77f.81.147; cf., however, Seel 1949,633f and Adler 1989,101–105, who are much more cautious (see also below, pp. XLII ff).
92 See Adler 1989,102f. For Annianus' chronological system, see Serruys 1907,260–262.

after the death of Samson the judge. On the other hand, he affirms that Africanus was right in inserting these years in the total sum of his chronography. This information is interesting for two reasons. Firstly, it shows that Annianus, who was writing in Alexandria at the time of bishop Theophilus (388–416), knew and used the *Chronographiae* for his own chronological calculations. Secondly, it is methodologically remarkable that Annianus used Africanus to prove the inconsistency of Eusebius' chronological system. The same approach is also frequent in Syncellus' criticism of Eusebius.

Regrettably, due to their poor state of preservation, both Panodorus and Annianus are of little use for the concrete reconstruction of Africanus' chronicle.

4.2.2. *The* Excerpta Barbari

The *Excerpta Latina Barbari* constitutes an 8th century Latin translation of an earlier Greek chronicle, which was composed in Alexandria during the reign of Zeno (474–491) or Anastasius (491–518). It begins with Adam and breaks off abruptly in AD 387. The translation was made in Merovingian France by an anonymous author, who shows scarce knowledge of both Greek and Latin. Scaliger refers to him as a *homo barbarus ineptus Hellenismi et Latinitatis imperitissimus*, hence the conventional name *Excerpta barbari*, or *Barbarus Scaligeri*. The text was first published by Scaliger in 1606, in his *Thesaurus Temporum*,[93] using a copy (now Hamburg Ms. hist. 269) of the original manuscript (now Paris. Lat. 4884). Two centuries later, the *Excerpta* was edited once again, first by A. Schoene in 1875 and then by C. Frick in 1892.[94]

Despite the ignorance of the translator, Scaliger was quick to point out that the *Excerpta Barbari* was an important text for the understanding of the Christian chronographic tradition after Africanus and Eusebius. Indeed, there is now general agreement on the fact that the anonymous Alexandrian chronicler had good knowledge of the Africanus material, whether it be direct or indirect.[95] This applies chiefly, though not exclusively, to the second part, which contains various lists of kings, whose attribution to Africanus seems highly probable.[96] Although the section does not derive from Africanus in its entirety, much more

---

93 Scaliger 1606, 2nd pagination, p. 44–70 (= ²1658,58–85); the quoted epithets are to be found in the title.

94 On the central value of the *Excerpta Barbari* in Scaliger's study of Christian chronology, see Grafton 1983–93, 2,560–569. For a general view of the text and its problems, see the preface in Frick 1892, furthermore Gelzer 2,316–329, Jacoby 1909, Bardenhewer 1913–32, 4,91–93.

95 Scaliger 1606, 4th pagination, p. 239 (reprinted and translated in Grafton 1983–93, 2,560f; the text is missing in the second edition of 1658); Frick 1880,7f; Gelzer 1,137; Jacoby 1909,1570.

96 280,14–330,3 Frick. This section has the form of an excursus; it is inserted between the historical account from Adam to Cleopatra (first part) and from Caesar to AD 387 (third part); see Jacoby 1909,1568f. The relevant fragments are: F50 (Argives); F51a (Sicyonians); F54a (Athenians); F58 (Lacedaemonians); F59a (Corinthians); F62 (Medes); F63a (Lydians); F73 (Persians); F82 (Macedonians).

goes back to him than what is directly attributed by means of explicit quotation. As a result, each list has been discussed separately, the specific reasons for each attribution being provided in the notes to the translation to the text. In what follows some general criteria are given:

1) The list of the Sicyonians (F51a) is explicitly attributed to Africanus. This list with its specific features can serve as a model for similar material in the *Chronographiae*. It contains the names and dates of kings who are recorded in synchronism with major events in Jewish history. Both at the beginning and at the end of the list there is an accurate calculation of the years of the kingdom until the beginning of Ol. 1,1. Where similar features occur in other lists within the *Excerpta Barbari*, there is a strong likelihood that the information derives from Africanus.

2) Parallel texts in other witnesses which explicitly mention Africanus aid in the attribution of some of the lists in the *Excerpta* to him. It is interesting to note that such parallel texts often come from the chronicle of John Malalas. Gelzer had already surmised that there was a common Alexandrian source for both authors, proposing the lost chronicle of Annianus as the intermediary.[97] The lists in the *Excerpta Barbari* which show a striking affinity with the those of Malalas (where they actually carry the name Africanus) are those dedicated to the Athenians (F54) and the Lacedaemonians (F58). In other cases, Syncellus can be particularly useful when it comes to attributing list material of the *Excerpta Barbari* to Africanus. Even if highly abridged, the list of Egyptian dynasties in the *Excerpta* clearly belongs to a version of Manetho's list. The total number of years attributed to the duration of each dynasty in the *Excerpta Barbari* agrees with that given in the list which Syncellus explicitly identifies as Africanus' version of the list originally composed by Manetho. As a result, it is not unreasonable to suppose that the Egyptian list in the *Excerpta Barbari* actually comes from the tradition of the *Chronographiae* (F46, see app. 3).

3) Some other lists can be attributed to Africanus on the basis of a close parallel with his chronological system. One decisive criterion is the equation Ol. 1,1 = 1 Ahaz. Further reasons are explained in the notes to the translation of each list.

It is also worth reminding the reader that not all lists of the *Excerpta* belong to the tradition of Africanus. The Latin kings, the list of Seleucids and the list of the Ptolemies,[98] for example, are all inconsistent with the chronological system of Africanus. This observation suggests that the *Grundschrift* of the *Excerpta Barbari* was using Africanus indirectly, drawing from an intermediary work which mixed Africanus with other sources.

The relevant material is not limited, however, to just barren lists of kings. The *Excerpta Barbari* also plays an important role in the reconstruction of Afri-

---

97 Gelzer 2,329.
98 300,13–302,29, 316,19–320,2 and 320,3–21 Frick respectively.

canus' understanding of Greek history before and after Ol. 1,1. Occasionally, historical notes are inserted into the lists of kings. Another fragment, which explicitly quotes Africanus as a source, gives a list of famous Greek writers, philosophers and artists who allegedly lived under the Persian king Artaxerxes (F81b).[99]

Even if the author of the *Excerpta* only knew Africanus indirectly and even if the underlying chronicle is preserved only in a poor Latin translation, the quality of the transmission is surprisingly high. This can be shown in F78 which deals with the 70 weeks of Daniel and where the wording of the *Excerpta* seems to be closer to a parallel in the *Chronicon Paschale* than to the one in Eusebius (see n. 1 to the text). This is a sign of the high quality of the former two sources which were otherwise compiled independently of each other.

4.3. Chronicles from the Antiochene Tradition

4.3.1. John Malalas

John Malalas wrote a chronicle in Antioch during the first half of the 6th century. A second edition (or version) of his work was composed in Constantinople after the death of Justinian in 565. The chronicle is eighteen books long and deals with the period reaching from Adam down to AD 565. As explained in the preface of his work, the *Chronographia* of Malalas was divided into two parts. The first part deals with universal history from the creation of Adam down to the emperor Zeno (AD 474). In the second part, Malalas records the events from Zeno down to his own day (books 15–18). The main sources for the first part were indicated in the preface. Among these authors, Malalas included Iulius Africanus the chronographer (T10). In various passages in books 2–8, Malalas actually cites him as a source.[100]

Most of the references to Africanus concern the lists of kings, in particular those of archaic Greece.[101] The list of the Ptolemaic dynasty found in Malalas ought also to be considered as another Africanus fragment (F86). Some other texts attributed to Africanus provide us with different kinds of information, but they are always used in a context which is linked to the king lists. Examples are F74 which records the Samian thalassocracy, together with the conquests of Cyrus, the first king of Persia, or F60 which deals with the first festival of the

---

99   For the *Excerpta Barbari* as evidence for Greek history in Africanus, see Gelzer 1,118–137.
100 On the relationship between Africanus and Malalas, see Jeffreys 1990,172f. For the importance of Malalas' framework of the ancient past (from the creation to the Trojan war) and Byzantine chronography in general, see Jeffreys 1979. An excellent general introduction with recent bibliography on Malalas is Jeffreys 2003.
101 Sicyonians (F51b), Athenians (F54c), Lacedaemonians (F58b), Corinthians (F59b) and Thebans (T61). The same applies to the list of Lydian kings (F63b).

Olympian Zeus, recorded after a brief reference to the Lacedaemonian and Corinthian kings.

As in other sources, the fact that Malalas quotes Africanus does not necessarily mean that he had direct knowledge of his work. By comparing different traditions, such as Malalas and the *Excerpta Barbari*, it becomes clear that Malalas usually reduces the text of the *Chronographiae* to scant and inaccurate information. In some of his more developed discourses, it is not always clear what data Malalas is actually attributing to Africanus as a source. The record of the flood under Ogygus in Malalas 3,11 (= T54c) reveals, for example, a confusing contamination of at least two sources. Even if the words resemble those of Africanus (see F54b for Syncellus' version), the quotation of Africanus ought to be strictly confined to the reckoning of the number of years from the flood to 1 Cecrops. The statement that Ogygus perished in the flood does not come from Africanus himself (see F34,38f). Either it comes from another source or it is the result of confusion in Malalas' reasoning.[102]

The general opinion is that Malalas only knew Africanus second-hand, through an intermediary. He does not adhere to the chronological framework of the *Chronographiae*. A familiarity that was only indirect might also explain why Malalas seems to use information which only deals with the lists of kings, failing to quote Africanus on other matters. Gelzer presumed that the lost work of the Alexandrian Annianus was an important source for the first part of Malalas' chronicle.[103] This theory could explain the high level of concordance between Malalas and the *Excerpta Barbari*, in particular for the lists of kings; however, this is only a hypothesis.

4.3.2. John of Antioch

John of Antioch wrote his *Historia chronica* in Constantinople at the beginning of the reign of Heraclius (610–641). His knowledge of Africanus is clearly second-hand; it depends wholly on John Malalas to whom he was closely related. It has also been observed that in his first two books, John of Antioch supplements Malalas' scant information on biblical history with another unknown Christian chronicle (e.g. the histories of king David and king Solomon). However, there is no evidence that this second source pertains to Africanus or to that

---

102 Another significant example could be mentioned. Malalas relates that Africanus wrote on the kingdom of Thebes (see T61). However, this information follows a long excursus on the mythical history of Boetia and Thebes, which cannot automatically be attributed to Africanus (see Io. Mal. 2,14–17). We know from other passages in the work (e.g. F34,90f) that Africanus included some of these themes in his description of Greek history after Moses; but we have very little evidence of them in the surviving fragments (F50,17f; F54a,17f). It seems, therefore, safer to include only the section of this long excursus, where Africanus is quoted by Malalas. For a different perspective, see Gelzer 1,140.

103 Gelzer 2,137f.

of a closely related chronicle. Indeed, this source does not follow the chronological system of Africanus.[104] Nevertheless, the text of John of Antioch is still useful, since it occasionally offers a better version of Malalas' text than the codex Baroccianus 182, which is the only manuscript to have come down to us belonging to the direct transmission in Greek. A good example is the calculation of the years from the Exodus of Moses up to the first year of Cecrops in Athens. While the codex Baroccianus 182 attributes 270 years to this time-span, John of Antioch, using his copy of Malalas, gives it only 206 years. This number corresponds exactly with the chronology of Africanus (T54c) and allows us to correct the reference to 208 years in the *Excerpta Barbari* (F54a,4).

4.3.3. Anonymous Material in the Excerpta Salmasiana *(Ps. John of Antioch)*

The *Excerpta Salmasiana* constitutes a collection of texts copied by Claudius Salmasius at the beginning of the 17th century from a codex in Heidelberg (now Vat. Pal. 93, 12th cent.). It consists of two groups of excerpts, the first of which was published by Karl Müller, in 1851 in his *Fragmenta Historicorum Graecorum*, vol. 4, as fr. 1, under the name of John of Antioch. In a note on the same page, however, he explains that these fragments do not belong to John of Antioch, contrary to the second part, which does. Furthermore, he indicates that they demonstrate a clear connection with the chronographic tradition of Africanus, Eusebius and Syncellus.[105] Gelzer considered them as original excerpts from books 3 and 4 of the *Chronographiae*. Unfortunately, he neglected to consult the footnote in Müller's edition and assumed—falsely—that these excerpts came from John of Antioch. After Gelzer, the *Excerpta Salmasiana* was generally considered to derive from John of Antioch, whose *Historia chronica* was therefore incorrectly seen as a key work in the transmission of Africanus. The new edition of John of Antioch (Roberto 2005a) put them—*faute de mieux*—under the name of an anonymous ps. John of Antioch.[106] We do not know who the

---

104 On the problem, see Roberto 2005a,CXXX. For a different interpretation, cf. Sotiroudis 1989,145f.
105 *Quae hucusque de priscis Graecorum barbarorumque temporibus legimus optime conveniunt cum melioris notae chronicis Africani, Eusebii, Syncelli. Exspectaveris excerptorum istorum seriem iisdem ducibus iam ad certiorem historiam nos deducturam esse. At non ita se res habet. Nam quae deinceps in Salmasii codice leguntur, denuo redeunt ad antiquissimam Assyriorum, Aegyptiorum, Graecorum memoriam, eamque eodem plane modo explicant, quem ex deterioris farinae chronologis, ex Malala, Cedreno, similibus, bene novimus. Ad posteriorem hanc antiquae historiae expositionem pertinent, quae ex Ioanne excerpta praebent Tituli Constant. Περὶ ἀρετῆς et Περὶ ἐπιβουλῶν, nec non codex Paris. 1630. Quae quum ita sint, haud temere contenderem mihi videor Excerpta ista Salmasiana ex duobus chronicis fluxisse eorumque partem priorem, quam modo apposui, ab Ioanne nostro alienam esse.* Müller 1851,538, referring to his fr. 1.
106 First ed. in Müller 1851, 538–540 as fr. 1, new edition: Roberto 2005a,556–575, which is followed here. See also Sotiroudis 1989,139–141, Roberto 2005a,LXXIV–LXXVII, Roberto 2005b.

author of the collection was, nor do we know how these excerpts were transmitted, or why they were connected to the second part of the *Excerpta Salmasiana*, deriving from John of Antioch.[107]

Such problems do not diminish in any way the importance of these texts in the transmission of the *Chronographiae*. As Müller pointed out, the excerpts are identical to some well-attributed fragments of Africanus, quoted by Eusebius or Syncellus. However, the transmission of these texts is not directly related to either Eusebius or Syncellus, since part of the material has parallels only in one of the authors and not the other.[108]

The material can be divided into the following groups:
- fr. 1*: this excerpt includes three different texts, each of which deals with the chronological relationship between the Exodus of Moses from Egypt and the first year of Cyrus in Ol. 55,1. Comparison with the version of Syncellus (F34) clearly shows that the texts are taken from the *Chronographiae* of Africanus.
- fr. 2*–22*: these texts deal with Greek mythology and ancient history up to the first Olympiad. At first sight, there does not seem to be any evidence of some sort of textual connection with any of the surviving fragments of Africanus. However, several elements reveal a certain affinity with the *Chronographiae*. These elements include the structure, some lexical features, the topics, such as the rationalizing interpretation of myths (e.g. the interpretation according to Palaephatus), and the attempt to create synchronisms between Greek and Jewish history.
- fr. 23*–30*: these texts come from the list of Egyptian kings of Manetho in the version of Africanus (F46). A striking confirmation of this attribution comes from an insertion within the Egyptian excerpts of a text about Semiramis, queen of Assyria. This information is attested in the *Chronographiae* (in a different section: F34,51–53).
- fr. 31*: this small fragment, dealing with the late Seleucid dynasty, shows no evidence of any relationship with Africanus; in addition, Africanus' list of Seleucid kings is lost.
- fr. 32*: this excerpt, concerning Aegialeus, king of Sicyon, is completely in keeping with Africanus' interest in the archaic kings of Greece (F51).
- fr. 33*–36*: this group of short texts derives from Africanus' list of victors in the Olympic games (F65).
- fr. 37*: this excerpt, dealing with Holophernes and identifying Cambyses as Nebuchadnezzar II, also comes from Africanus (T75).

---

107 For a general discussion of the *Excerpta Salmasiana*, see Roberto 2005b. The whole collection has a 12th century *terminus ante quem*, when the manuscript Vat. gr. 96—the first codex containing both groups of excerpts—was written.
108 A detailed analysis can be found in Roberto 2005b,271–288.

As regards the edition of Africanus, the following conclusions are pertinent: most of the first part of the *Excerpta Salmasiana* are directly connected to the tradition of the *Chronographiae*. Hence, they are usually quoted in apparatus 3 of the edition. Two excerpts, which come from the first part of Manetho's list in the *Chronographiae* and which are absent in Syncellus, are presented as an original text from Africanus (F43b and F44). Apart from fr. 31*, which does not belong to Africanus, the group of excerpts dealing with the mythical history of Greece (fr. 2*–22*) still remains dubious. Gelzer notes that many excerpts concur with the arguments expounded by Africanus in book 3 as part of his discourse on Greek mythical history after Moses (see F34,89–92). Furthermore, some of the excerpts reveal various synchronisms between Greek and Jewish history. As a result, Gelzer was inclined to consider all these texts as fragments of Africanus.[109] But since this cannot be proven beyond all reasonable doubt, the texts have not been included here. Nevertheless, it seems plausible, even likely, that they do indeed stem from Africanus. One hopes that more evidence will be forthcoming in the future, allowing a more secure attribution.

4.4. Georgius Syncellus

The *Ecloga Chronographica*, composed by Georgius Syncellus in Constantinople between the years 808–810, is a chronicle of world history, beginning with the creation.[110] When Syncellus' death prevented him from completing the work, it was left to a fellow monk Theophanes to continue the chronicle from the reign of Diocletian down to his own day.[111] Because much of what is known of Africanus' chronicle survives only in Syncellus, the reconstruction of the *Chronographiae*'s contents, structure and chronological foundation depends to a large extent on this source.

The assorted material taken from Africanus reveals varying degrees of editorial intervention, ranging from excerpts to epitomes, paraphrases and *testimonia*. The headings of several of his excerpts include descriptive summaries of the passage contents (F15, F23, F79, F93). In two places, Syncellus ascribes Africanus' analysis of comparative Greco-Jewish chronology to the third book of the *Chronographiae* (see app. to F34,38.104). Direct quotations from Africanus are commonly distinguished with formulaic phrases, indicating literal citation (e.g.,

---

109 Gelzer[ms] and Gelzer 1,118–137.
110 Critical edition by Mosshammer 1984. For an English translation, see Adler/Tuffin 2002. The older CSHB edition of Dindorf 1829 is still useful. For discussion of Syncellus' use of and dependence on earlier authorities, including Africanus, see most recently Adler/Tuffin 2002,lx–lxix. For the more important previous studies, see Mosshammer 1984,xxvi–xxx; Huxley 1981; Laqueur 1932; Gelzer 2,176–189; G. G. Bredow, Dissertatio de Georgii Syncelli Chronographia, in Dindorf 1829, 2,3–49; J. Goar, Praefatio, in Dindorf 1829, 2,53–73.
111 Ed. de Boor 1883–85. For an English translation of Theophanes, see Mango/Scott 1997.

ἐπὶ λέξεως) and textual lacunae (e.g., καὶ μετ᾽ ὀλίγα, καὶ μεθ᾽ ἕτερα). An originally continuous narrative of the Flood (F23) survives in Syncellus' chronicle as two separate excerpts. The fact that Syncellus describes a lengthy passage of Africanus' chronicle (F89) as an "epitome" implies that it was either a précis of a longer passage, or a collection of material culled from various places in his chronicle. Tables and lists originating in Africanus' chronicle may also have been condensed. Africanus' list of the biblical patriarchs from Adam to Abraham probably contained expository narrative that Syncellus chose to exclude (see F16a, n. 1). Although Africanus' version of Manetho's list of Egyptian kings probably included the dynastic successions of the divine and semi-divine rulers before the Flood (cf. F43, n. 1), Syncellus only transcribes the 30 dynasties of the human kings of Egypt (F46).

Ambiguities in Syncellus' method of quoting sometimes make it difficult to ascertain the extent and literalness of the source material taken from Africanus' chronicle. Use of phrases such as κατὰ δὲ Ἀφρικανόν or ὥς φησιν ὁ Ἀφρικανός do not necessarily mean that Syncellus is quoting directly. Comparison with other sources shows, for example, that Syncellus' references to Africanus' account of the miraculous terebinth tree (F30a) and the ancestry of Herod the Great (F87b) were paraphrases. An unattributed passage dealing with the rulers of Athens (F54d) conflates Africanus' chronology of the annual Athenian archons with chronological information from other sources. Even in attributed excerpts, the scope of the citation can be ambiguous (cf. F19, F84).

Corruptions of Africanus within the work of Syncellus are most common in the transcription of numerical data. The original numbers of Africanus' intricate exposition of the calendar underlying Daniel's apocalypse of 70 weeks (Daniel 9,24–27) are now almost irrecoverable from Syncellus' faulty transcription of them (F93,70–77). Emendations by a later editor are particularly noticeable in Syncellus' summary of Africanus' account of the dissolution of the Ptolemaic kingdom (F89). In this passage, a correction of Africanus' 300-year chronology of the Persian empire to "300 less two" (l. 54) harmonizes his reckoning with Syncellus' own system (see n. 4 ad loc.). A reference to the "24th year according to the Antiochenes" in the same passage may be a later addition by an editor of Syrian provenance (see ll. 66f and n. 7 ad loc.). In his paraphrase of Africanus' account of the miraculous terebinth tree, a term for prayers used in the Byzantine liturgy (τὰς ἐκτενάς) has replaced a reference to burnt offerings (τὰς ἑκατόμβας), which, according to Africanus, were positioned on the altar before the tree (F30a,10, cf. F30b,10). Confusion about Africanus' use of the word *parousia* probably accounts for the later and ungrammatical insertion of the words καὶ τῆς ἀναστάσεως into a sentence dealing with the beginning of the ministry of Jesus in AM 5531 (F93,109f and n. 18 ad loc.).

As he does with his other sources, Syncellus frequently volunteers his own judgments on Africanus' abilities as a chronographer and a historian. Africanus' date of Abraham's migration to Canaan (T16p), the age that he assigns to Jacob when he arrives in Mesopotamia (T28a), his chronology of the Argive kingdom (T49) and his identification of Cambyses as Nebuchadnezzar (T75a), all elicit from Syncellus the same one-word reaction: ἀδύνατον. Interestingly, a few of Syncellus' comments are embedded in the actual excerpt.[112] The word ἄπιστον ("not credible") is added at the end of Africanus' discussion of how terms such as the "sons of God" and the "daughters of men" in Genesis (6,2–4) might best be interpreted (F23,11). In addition, a refutation of Africanus' dating of the Exodus during the reign of the Egyptian king Amosis appears twice and in identical wording in Africanus' list of Egyptian kings (F46,134f and n. 6 ad loc.).

The rough and unfinished character of the editing of some of these excerpts supports R. Laqueur's conjecture that Syncellus' death prevented him from completing the revisions to what was really only a first draft.[113] Nor should we assume that Syncellus or the later manuscript tradition was solely responsible for the glosses, corrections, corruptions and reworkings of the text of Africanus. Although an entry in Photius implies that a complete copy of the *Chronographiae* existed in Constantinople (T11), it is entirely possible that Syncellus' knowledge of Africanus depended on a previously edited corpus of citations, transmitted to him by intermediaries.

4.5. The Logothete Chronicle and Related Texts

This title covers a number of Byzantine chronicles in which it is sometimes unclear whether we are dealing with a single manuscript, an independent redaction of an existing work, or an autonomous chronicle. Research on these texts is still at a preliminary stage and therefore only provisional statements are possible here. A further problem lies in the fact that current research still tends to focus on the latter part of these chronicles, at the expense of the less original earlier sections. But because the earlier parts are largely derivative, they are highly relevant for the reconstruction of older works, including Africanus'.

4.5.1. Symeon Logothete

The chronicle bearing the name Symeon Logothete runs from the creation of the world up to the year 948 and was written presumably shortly after its end date in the second half of the 10th century. Previous versions can be hypothetically reconstructed back to the time of Justinian II (†711) and the year 842.[114] The text has come down to us in over thirty different Greek manuscripts and a

---

112 For further discussion, see Laqueur 1932,1389.
113 Laqueur 1932,1407.
114 See Kazhdan 1991; Wahlgren 2006.

new critical edition by Staffan Wahlgren is awaited.[115] Older editions of certain manuscripts are available, the two most important being "Leo Grammaticus"[116] and "Theodosius Melitenus"[117], although the names are more or less arbitrary and carry no historical weight. In a few cases, the manuscript Vat. gr. 163 has also been consulted.[118]

According to some earlier studies on the question, a text published under the name of "Iulius Pollux" or "ps. Polydeuces"[119] was also considered part of the Symeon Logothete tradition. However, Staffan Wahlgren has shown that this text is an independent parallel source, which, in the early parts—up to Julius Caesar—coincides with Symeon. It seems plausible, therefore, that the text goes back to a common source, chronicling the period from creation up to the first century BC; this *Grundschrift* can be hypothetically dated to the 6th century.[120] For the purpose of our edition, only this text is relevant (with the one exception of F97). As an independent testimony for the chronicle of Symeon Logothete, therefore, the text of "Iulius Pollux" deserves particular attention. Purely for the sake of simplicity, the latter has been included in the *siglum* "Sym. Log". In dealing with these two sources, it must always be remembered that the consensus of Symeon properly speaking and Iul. Pol. goes further back than the 10th century.

Gelzer has long since underlined the importance of the Logothete chronicle for the reconstruction of the *Chronographiae*.[121] Although the author draws heavily upon Africanus, very little of the material concerns explicitly attributed quotations (only F24, F53, F97). In the majority of cases, the origin can be ascertained only on the basis of parallel texts preserved elsewhere (mostly Syncellus). In such cases, the text of Symeon Logothete is placed in the third apparatus of the main (attributed) text. Obviously, with such extensive, but unattributed use of Africanus, one cannot help but conjecture that much more material exists than has actually been identified through parallels with external sources. This is probably true and more fragments might be forthcoming in the future, especially for the early parts, dealing with the period from Adam to Abraham.[122] Nevertheless, for methodological reasons the present edition

---

115 Wahlgren's edition appeared after completion of the work on our edition, see above p. VI.
116 Paris. gr. 1711, 11th cent., ed. Bekker 1842.
117 Monac. gr. 218, 11th cent., ed. Tafel 1859; for the name, see Kresten 1976,208–212.
118 Staffan Wahlgren kindly put a microfilm of this manuscript at our disposal.
119 Ironically, for this text there is a reliable edition on the basis of a late manuscript (Monac. gr. 181, 16th cent., used by Hardt 1792) and a flawed edition on the basis of the best manuscript (Ambr. D34 sup., 11th cent., used by Bianconi 1795). Because of the important Milan manuscript, this text has also been called *Chronicum Ambrosianum*—certainly a better name than the ones used in the two editions. On names, transmission and editions, see Kresten 1969.
120 Wahlgren 2003. These findings were partially anticipated by Gelzer (unpublished), who at the beginning of his manuscript gave the reconstruction of an "Epitome der jüdischen Geschichte" (Gelzer^{ms}, file 1, section A).
121 Gelzer 1,57–72.
122 See Wallraff 2006,56–58.

remains cautious. Where there is neither an explicit attribution, nor a direct parallel in Syncellus or elsewhere, cases in which we have actually been able to ascribe material to Africanus with a sufficient degree of certainty remain very few (F25, F35, F76).

It is virtually impossible to establish where Symeon Logothete (or rather his *Grundschrift* for the early parts) took the Africanus material from. It would perhaps be prudent to assume that he had some sort of indirect knowledge, working with other chronicles or handbooks. Whatever the channel of transmission, it seems to have been independent of our two other main sources —Eusebius and Syncellus—making it all the more precious for the edition of Africanus.

4.5.2. Ps. Symeon and Cedrenus

Among the Byzantine chroniclers, the so-called ps. Symeon and Georgius Cedrenus also seem to have had a good knowledge of Africanus' *Chronographiae*, albeit indirectly. Since Cedrenus would appear to have taken nearly all his material from ps. Symeon, the two authors can be treated together. In only one case does Cedrenus actually quote a text from Africanus that is not preserved in ps. Symeon (F93, app. to ll. 3–19). Unfortunately, due to the lack of a complete edition of ps. Symeon, establishing the exact relationship between the two chroniclers is hazardous.

The name ps. Symeon refers to a Byzantine chronicle, which is preserved in the manuscript Paris. gr. 1712, ff. 18^v–272^r and deals with the period running from Adam down to the year 963. The text was probably written in the last third of the tenth century and represents a reworked and enriched version of the chronicle of Symeon Logothete.[123] In only one case does ps. Symeon provide a quotation from Africanus which is not taken up by Cedrenus (F66, dealing with the interpretation of the toponym Tarshish).

Georgius Cedrenus composed a world chronicle from Adam to the year 1057, a *quisquiliarum stabulum*[124] in which he uses almost everything useful (or useless) that was available to him in the preceding Byzantine tradition. Like ps. Symeon, Cedrenus seems to be acquainted with Africanus through two different channels. In most cases, he clearly relies on Syncellus. In transcribing Syncellus, he usually changes his wording, abridging the text and often omitting to mention that Africanus is the original source (see, e.g., F23, F26, T36 etc.). Another group of quotations is taken from the chronicle of Symeon Logothete or rather from Symeon Logothete's source. An interesting case is preserved in

---

123 On ps. Symeon, see Gelzer 2,357–384, Markopoulos 1978, and Kazhdan 1991c. Markopoulos has announced an edition of the chronicle, which is still awaited.

124 Scaliger ^{2}1658, 3rd pagination, p. 402. On Cedrenus see Schweinburg 1929/30; Maisano 1983; Kazhdan 1991a.

F24, where ps. Symeon and Cedrenus both provide us with a more elaborate version, in comparison to that found in Leo Grammaticus and Theodosius Melitenus.[125]

In ps. Symeon-Cedrenus, the interest in Africanus is particularly focused on his account of Jewish history down until the Babylonian captivity. Hebrew etymologies also seem to attract both authors (F16d and, only in ps. Symeon, F66).

4.6. Oriental Authors

Agapius (*Maḥbūb ibn Qusṭanṭīn*), Bishop of Mabbug, is the author of a universal history, which is known under the name *Kitāb al-'Unvān* ("book of the title").[126] The book chronicles the beginning of the history of mankind and extends as far as the author's own times (10th cent.). While the preserved manuscripts break off in 776/77, a remark of the author shows that he must have at least gone as far as 941/42. Like Eusebius, Agapius associates the *floruit* of Africanus (T3b) with the emperor Gordian III (238–244), although his information seems independent. The fragments dealing with the invention of the Hebrew alphabet by Seth (F18) and the arrival of the Magi (T91) are unattested elsewhere. However, the evidence is too scanty to allow us to decide whether or not Agapius was acquainted with the entire work of Africanus (in Greek?).[127] Agapius also attributes—probably erroneously—a list of the Chaldean kings to Africanus.[128]

---

125 Along with F86 (the list of Ptolemies) this text could lead to the assumption that one possible channel of transmission of the Africanus material in ps. Symeon was somehow related to John Malalas.

126 See Graf 1947,39f; Breydy 1989; Pančenko 2000. The title derives from a scribal error in a late manuscript. The oldest preserved witness (ms. Sinai arab. 580, late 10th cent.) shows that the original title was *Kitāb al-Tarīkh* ("book of history"). There are two editions of the work: CSCO 65 arab. 10 (Cheikho) and PO 5,4–11,1 (Vasiliev, see below *Conspectus*, p. LXIX). For the first part (up to the birth of Christ) the manuscripts of both editions derive from Sinai arab. 580, for the second part both editions use the same manuscript. In the present edition Vasiliev was preferred, since he directly uses the Sinai manuscript (as opposed to Cheikho) and since he gives a critical apparatus. The quoted texts can be found in Cheikho in the following places: T3b at p. 269,15f, F18 at p. 13,16f, T 91 at p. 138,8–13.

127 A comprehensive analysis of Agapius' sources is lacking. The existing case studies show that Agapius often used Syriac sources or Syriac translations of Greek authors (e.g. Eusebius); see Baumstark 1912 and Lindner 1916.

128 PO 7,553,9 – 554,9 (Vasiliev); CSCO 284,12 – 285,3 (Cheikho). A similar list is also transmitted in Eusebius (chron. 5,24–33) as a quotation from Alexander Polyhistor (FGrHist 680 F4), and anonymously in Syncellus (18,11–20). In Agapius, the list is inserted into a biblical framework, beginning with Adam and ending with the Flood. The beginning is in contrast with Africanus' dismissal of the Chaldean tradition (F15,9f; see note ad loc.), while the end is compatible with Eusebius' system, not with Africanus' (2242 years from the creation to the Flood). Therefore, it seems likely that Agapius took the text from a chronicle in the Eusebian tradition and erroneously attributed it to Africanus; see also the arguments in Wallraff 2006,48f, n. 17.

Michael the Syrian, Patriarch of the West Syrian Church from 1166 to 1199, was the author of a universal history extending to 1194/95.[129] In the preface, he mentions Africanus as one of his sources (T13a). He considers the *Chronographiae* not a "Church history", but a "description of time", i.e. a universal history.[130] Among Greek world chronicles, he makes extensive use of Eusebius, but in a few places he also refers to the chronological calculations of Africanus (T16f, T77b, T83). In T71, he gives a vague and otherwise unattested reference to Africanus' account of the high priest Hilkiah. It is uncertain whether Michael had direct knowledge of the work of Africanus. His knowledge may have been mediated by lost Syriac sources.

All references to Africanus in the world chronicle of Gregor Barhebraeus, maphrian of the West Syrian Church (1264–1286), can be traced back to Michael the Syrian. In his biblical commentary *Horreum Mysteriorum*, probably written around 1271/72,[131] there are two fragments on the genealogy of Christ (F90b.c) which may derive from the *Chronographiae* of Africanus.[132] Since Barhebraeus probably knew little Greek, it is likely that he read the texts in a Syriac translation.[133]

In his *History of Armenia*, Moses of Chorene[134] claims to use Africanus as a source for a potentially long text, but the value of this attribution is dubious. In his second book, Moses refers to the fifth book of the *Chronographiae* as the main source for the history of the Armenian kings. Africanus is supposed to have based his knowledge of Armenian history on the archives of Edessa, but critical research now mostly rejects this.[135] Attempts at ascribing at least part of the material to Africanus via the use of Greek parallel texts remain unconvincing.[136] This does not exclude the possibility that Moses might have had some

---

129 See Weltecke 2003.
130 The preface does not survive in the Syriac original; it is known only in two Armenian translations, one written shortly after the other (between 1246 and 1248). The translations are based on the Syriac autograph, but in both cases there are alterations, presumably intended to stress the identity of the Armenian Church. The translation of the monk Vardan in many cases expands and elaborates the text (*versio longior*). The shorter version could be a correction and revision on the basis of the original text, see Schmidt 1996 and 1998. Therefore, in T13 the *versio brevior* is given along with the additions of the other version in the apparatus.
131 See Takahashi 2005,92f.
132 See below F90a, n. 1.
133 Takahashi 2005,31–35.
134 The discussion on the date of the author and his work is still open. The work purports to be written at the beginning of the reign of Sahak Bagratuni (482). Scholarly debate has proposed dates which vary from the late 5th to the 9th century; possibly, a dating in the 7th/8th cent. would be the most plausible, see Mahé 1993, 88–91.
135 See e.g. Thomson 1978,12f; Traina 1991,61–63. The information in Moses that is allegedly taken from Africanus can mostly be traced back to other sources, Mahé 1993,66–68.
136 Topchyan 2001 has argued that large parts of Moses' book 2 are taken from Africanus. This has been rightly criticized by Terian 2001/02, esp. 113, n. 40. Topchyan has reacted to the criticism in his recent monograph (Topchyan 2006), where he presents the thesis in a moderate form.

contact with the transmission of the *Chronographiae,* but at present this remains totally uncertain and no concrete fragment can be ascribed (beyond the *testimonium* in T88).[137]

4.7. Minor authors and texts

4.7.1. Ps. Eustathius of Antioch

The work commonly referred to as the "commentary on the hexaëmeron", and transmitted under the name of Eustathius of Antioch, is actually part exegesis and part chronicle. The unknown author was writing sometime between 370 and the end of the 5th century. The fact that he was familiar with the homilies on the hexaëmeron of Basilius of Caesarea gives us a *terminus post quem*, while a *terminus ante quem* is given implicitly in the text in F94. The work probably comes from an Antiochene milieu.[138]

The author would appear to have known and consulted Africanus' *Chronographiae,* either directly or through a tradition closely related to him.[139] Two quotations are important. In the first instance (F30b), his text can be juxtaposed with that of Syncellus, allowing us to check his account of the terebinth tree in Shechem—taken from Africanus—but slightly emended in both cases. Another text (F94), which gives precise information on the chronological framework of Africanus, is only preserved by ps. Eustathius. The words καὶ ἀνάστασιν are probably a later gloss and show that ps. Eustathius may have shared a similar source with Syncellus (F93,109).

4.7.2. *The* Chronicon Paschale

The anonymous author of the *Chronicon Paschale* (of ca. 630) uses some quotations from Africanus and exploits his chronological system for the period before the Flood (see e.g., app. to F16b, F33). The material from the *Chronographiae* would appear to come down to him via at least three different channels.[140]

His main source is the chronicle of Eusebius. In some cases, the *Chronicon Paschale* transcribes Eusebius almost verbatim (see, e.g., F64c and T64d), allowing us to restore the original wording. Another channel of transmission is John Malalas. While ultimately derived from Africanus, the information about the pagan gods preserved in the *Chronicon Paschale* was mediated to the author through Malalas (see app. to F24).[141]

---

137 See Wallraff 2006,49f, n. 20.
138 See Zoepfl 1927.
139 See Zoepfl 1927,22.
140 On the *Chronicon Paschale* and the *Chronographiae* of Iulius Africanus, see Gelzer 2,138–176.
141 On the relationship between the *Chronicon Paschale* and Malalas, see Scott 1990,38f.

Finally, there is a third unknown source of the *Chronicon Paschale* which also preserves passages from the *Chronographiae*. Striking evidence of this can be found in F78. In this case, the interpretation of the seventy weeks of Africanus is mentioned twice. In the first instance, the source reproduces Eusebius (T78a). In the second instance (F78), the text preserved by the *Chronicon Paschale* is independent of Eusebius, using wording which would appear to be very close to that of Africanus, as a comparison with the *Excerpta Barbari* shows. This source is probably a lost chronicle. Gelzer assumed that it was of Egyptian provenance and suggested Annianus or Panodorus.[142]

4.7.3. The Anonymus Matritensis

Under this name an anonymous chronicle is known, which is transmitted in a Madrid codex of the 10th century (Matritensis gr. 4701). The codex has become famous for the precious material from Hippolytus' chronicle preserved in its second part (from f. 51 onwards). The independent value of the first part[143] passed unnoticed for a long time, since this small chronological text greatly resembles the *Chronicon breve* of patriarch Nicephorus (806–15). Hence, Adolf Bauer in his first study of the codex considered it to be a copy of that work.[144] When he noticed his error shortly afterwards, he decided to prepare a small independent edition of the text, in which he typographically distinguished the parts taken from Nicephorus (italics) and those taken from other sources (upright). Only the latter are of interest here.

The author of the text might have been a monk or a cleric in Constantinople. He was writing probably one or two generations after Nicephorus (between 848 and 886),[145] whose chronicle he used as a basis and which he supplemented with the fruits of his own studies. While Nicephorus apparently did not know and use Africanus, his follower must have had some contact with him—be it directly or indirectly. Unfortunately he does not normally name his sources,[146] which makes it difficult to identify the material taken from Africanus.

5. Earlier Editions

Joseph Justus Scaliger (1540–1609) was the first modern historian to have fully understood and appreciated the importance of Iulius Africanus, both for his contribution to the literary genre of Christian chronicles as a whole and for his

---

142 Gelzer 2,154–156.
143 f. 1ʳ–29ᵛ; see Bauer 1909,69f for an analysis of the smaller texts between the two main blocks.
144 Bauer 1905,16.
145 See Bauer 1909,XIIf and Sartori 1988,415.
146 The only exception is the small discussion in 3,6–4,4 Bauer (= T16m).

legacy in the domain of ancient historical chronology. The research conducted by him for his monumental *Thesaurus temporum*[147] was a milestone not only for having brought Africanus to light, but also for bringing to the fore Eusebius and various other minor texts of the Greek chronographic tradition. Many of his findings remain valid and fundamental up to this day.[148] Scaliger also discovered the *Excerpta Barbari*, whose conventional name (still in use today) reflects his pejorative view of it. He first published the Olympic victor list of cod. Paris. gr. 2600, in a section known as the *Excerpta Eusebiana*. Scaliger continues to be cited by modern scholars, although the latter have a regrettable habit of quoting him secondhand and thus not always correctly.

Scaliger's significance for our understanding of Africanus can hardly be overestimated. In his monumental work, he effectively lays down the basis for the reconstruction of the *Chronographiae*. Nevertheless, Scaliger never made any attempt at collecting and editing the extant fragments of the lost work. On the contrary, his editions of manuscript material, hypothetical reconstructions and scholarly considerations are often so mingled, they have provoked misunderstandings and confusion in later scholars.[149] A generation later, the work of Dionysius Petavius (Pétau, 1583–1652) was a major achievement for research on chronology (*Opus de doctrina temporum*, 1627). However, scholars would have to wait over a century before they could consult the first collection of fragments of the *Chronographiae*.

The Venetian Oratorian Andrea Gallandi (1709–1779)[150] has the merit of being the first scholar to publish such a collection. However, this is about the only positive remark that can be made of it. His *Bibliotheca veterum patrum* (14 vols., Venice 1765–1781) is one of a series of comprehensive collections of patristic texts, produced during the 18th century. Its *differentia specifica* to other monumental enterprises resides in the fact that he devoted particular attention to minor authors, especially those that had not been published previously,[151] among them Iulius Africanus. In his second volume, dating to 1766, he published the correspondence with Origen, the letter to Aristides and nineteen fragments of the *Chronographiae*, most of which were drawn from Syncellus, although some came from Eusebius and other sources.[152] The work was of course far from complete, even by the standards of the texts known at that time, a fact the editor himself soon became aware of when he had to write the preface

---

147 Scaliger 1606, a 2nd edition appeared posthumously in 1658, enlarged by notes left by the author.
148 On Scaliger and the study of chronography, see Mosshammer 1979,38–41 and the brilliant book of Grafton 1983–93, especially 2,581–591 on Africanus.
149 Nevertheless Grafton 1983–93, 2,591 is right in saying: "Scaliger's failures—if failures they were —can still teach lessons."
150 See Godet 1920.
151 On the 18th century collections and on Gallandi in particular, see Bardenhewer 1913–32, 1,50–52.
152 Gallandi 1766,339–341 (letter to Origen); 341–357 (letter to Africanus); 358–362 (letter to Aristides, from Eus., h.e. 1,7); 363–376 (*Chronographiae*). He knew nothing of the *Cesti*.

to the huge volume.¹⁵³ As a result, his introduction to Africanus comes almost in the form of a supplement to the edition. It is in fact here that we find the central texts of Eusebius in the *Eclogae propheticae* (F93), the Latin fragment first published by Henry Dodwell in 1688 (T6), the excerpt of Photius (T11) and various others.

It is particularly unfortunate that the Abbé Jacques-Paul Migne decided to reprint this edition (rather than the later edition of Routh) in his *Patrologia graeca* (vol. 10, coll. 63–94). The sad consequence is that in certain cases this deficient edition continues to be used and quoted up to this day. If the Migne text must be consulted, the introductory remarks of Gallandi are indispensable and really ought to be read (reprinted on coll. 45–50).

A new era of studies focusing on Africanus is marked by the famous Oxford scholar Martin Joseph Routh (1755–1854).¹⁵⁴ Renowned for his meticulous precision, his collection of pre-Nicene Christian authors, entitled *Reliquiae sacrae* (4 vols. 1814–18, ²1846–48), was certainly a major achievement and not just for the text of Africanus. Routh's edition of the *Chronographiae* remained the standard edition for nearly two centuries, whereas in almost all the other cases his work has been superseded by better and more recent editions. The Greek texts are accompanied by a Latin translation which is still occasionally useful, while the notes to the text contain many significant comments on many problems of textual criticism and chronology. In difficult cases, these notes are still worth consulting. The material basis of the edition is good and the methodology is not far removed from what would be expected today and indeed applied—we hope—here. The main critique would be that he fails to distinguish between fragments and *testimonia* and in the case of multiple attestations (e.g. Sync. and Eus.), his presentation of the text is not always very clear. Obviously, Routh had to rely on the best available editions of his time and in many cases a better textual basis is now available.

Routh took into consideration 56 fragments, most of which were in Greek with only a very few in Latin. The present edition contains almost double that number. This was made possible thanks to a complete analysis of all the available sources, most notably the *Excerpta Barbari* and the Oriental material, together with several texts that were only published after Routh. Our corpus also contains the Olympic victor list (F65), a long and important text which was inexplicably missing in Routh.¹⁵⁵

At least in passing it ought to be mentioned that at the beginning of the 19ᵗʰ century, Iulius Africanus also attracted the interested of a gifted young scholar

---

153 Gallandi 1766,XXXVII–XLI.
154 On his biography, see Hunt 1897.
155 The reason could be that he did not trust the Greek text given by Scaliger. Only after the publication of the Armenian version was he convinced that the transmission was good and that the text actually ought to be attributed to Africanus (Routh 504f).

who was to become one of the greatest poets of Italian literature. In 1815, the 17 year old student, Giacomo Leopardi (1798–1837) collected all the available material by and on Africanus. His work is preserved in a manuscript which is now conserved in the National Library of Florence.[156] The manuscript was critically edited in 1997 by Claudio Moreschini. Leopardi was, of course, unaware of Routh's edition, which had appeared the year before. But it is amazing how comprehensive his knowledge of the sources was and how well he understood the texts. The material is rarely provided with the full Greek text, but carries references to the edition used; in many cases, Latin translation and notes are provided. Although his translation and notes are still worthy of consultation, the work was basically superseded by Routh and Gelzer. The same could not be said however of the *Cesti*. Here, Leopardi has the merit of having been the first scholar to systematically engage in an analysis of this enigmatic work, which was totally missing from Routh's collection.[157]

The last important contribution to the research on the *Chronographiae* was conducted by Heinrich Gelzer (1847–1906). Descendant of an old Basel family of scholars, he was a student of Jacob Burckhardt in Basel and later went on to become professor of Greek at the University of Jena.[158] For a nineteenth century scholar of classical philology, his interests were surprisingly wide, focusing on relatively late literature. Indeed, he is now regarded as one of the fathers of Byzantine studies. His passion for Christian chronography and for Iulius Africanus in particular grew in the 1870's and remained with him throughout his entire scholarly career, right up to his death. The *érudit* made his debut in 1880 with the first volume of the magisterial monograph entitled "Sextus Julius Africanus und die byzantinische Chronographie." The original idea was remarkably ambitious: an initial first volume on Africanus, a second volume providing a general overview of Byzantine chronography and a third crowning volume containing an edition of the extant fragments of the "father of Christian chronography". Although the work proceeded well up to vol. 2 (1885), the edition of the extant fragments soon got bogged down. Finally, in 1894 Adolf Harnack, who was in search for manuscripts for his newly founded series "Die Griechischen Christlichen Schriftsteller", persuaded Gelzer to abandon his original plan of publishing the edition as a final part of the monograph (with Teubner in Leipzig) and instead, put it at the disposal of the new series (with the publisher Hinrich, also in Leipzig).[159]

---

156 Banco Rari 342 n. 20; see esp. Moreschini 1997,20–31 and 65–116 for the *Chronographiae*.
157 See Vieillefond 1970,88–99.
158 The most comprehensive biographical account is Reichardt 1907, in particular 17–19 which deals with Africanus. See also the obituaries by Gerland 1907 and Kornemann 1907.
159 Rebenich 1997,176. The monograph was concluded with a third volume (vol. 2,2, to be precise, published at Hinrich's, Leipzig 1898 and much smaller than the two preceding parts) on the Oriental authors.

Gelzer complied, but this did not accelerate the work's completion. On several occasions, he was invited by the *Kirchenväterkommission* of the Berlin academy, which was responsible for the series, to submit his manuscript and on each occasion he informed the commission that the work was near completion.[160] In the meantime, Gelzer became rector of his university, which obviously further retarded the work on Africanus. Finally, in 1906, he died without having completed the edition. At the time, nobody had a clear idea of how far the work had really proceeded and how much still needed to be done. The commission of the academy was of the conviction that the task was too difficult and since critical editions of important authors such as Eusebius and Syncellus were missing, it abandoned the project.[161]

In the year 2000, during the preparatory work for the present edition, Gelzer's manuscript finally resurfaced. It had been kept in the library of Jena University and because it had been given a misleading label, it was thought to be the manuscript of the published monograph and therefore of little interest. It was Gregor Staab who discovered that it was actually the long-awaited edition. Not only that, but what Gelzer had written to Harnack turned out to be largely true—that the edition was very near completion. The material is kept in ten files,[162] the first two of which contained preparatory work for the edition; five files then follow, corresponding to the five books of the *Chronographiae*, succeeded finally by three files of miscellaneous notes. Within the main block (files 3-8) the quality of the manuscript deteriorates towards the end. The first four books are in reasonable condition. The writing is not always legible, but as a rule the text is clear and comprehensible. The final book comes in the form of disorganized and incomplete notes. In keeping with his reputation, Gelzer had done an excellent work on the text. Since there was no reliable edition of Syncellus at his time, he collated the two most important manuscripts (A and B in Mosshammer). In many textually problematic cases, his edition is worthy of consultation. This has been done for the present edition and wherever Gelzer's readings seem to have some weight, they are registered in the apparatus (Gelzer^{ms}).

The main problem of his work, and probably the ultimate reason why he never completed the edition, lies in his methodology. Over the years, Gelzer had cocooned himself in a fragile web of theories, where one hypothetical attribution was the basis for another, with the effect that many texts were attributed to Africanus, when this was no more than just a vague possibility. Some theories were not impossible, some are even likely, but many were not sound enough to be presented to the scholarly world as a certainty. Gelzer was clearly aware of the

---

[160] Rebenich 2000, 116 and 121; see also Rebenich 1997, 186, n. 240.
[161] Rebenich 2000, 140 and 150.
[162] See the more detailed description and reproduction of two sample pages in Krönung 2005. Particular thanks are due to Thomas Krönung, who compiled a full index of Gelzer's manuscript to facilitate access to the material in the project.

problem and it was this that made him reluctant to consign the material to the printer. A similar problem also characterizes the published monograph. The latter still remains the best and most exhaustive work on Africanus' chronicle and therefore continues to be quoted—also in the notes of our edition—but it is fraught with highly speculative suppositions, in many cases presented in an apodictic tone of certainty. Both the unpublished manuscript and the published monograph ought to be considered as extremely precious documents, which attest to an unparalleled, almost intuitive familiarity with the material, but also to a lack of methodological clarity and systematic reflection.

6. Principles of the Edition

Fragments and Testimonies. The preceding discussion (see above, section 4) illustrates the complexity of the transmission of extant material from the *Chronographiae*. In some cases, we possess the original wording of Africanus with a high degree of certainty; in others the extent to which the material corresponds to the original is unclear. There are still other cases in which we know for certain that the text has been altered, abridged or garbled. However, it would be futile to subdivide the material into too many different categories: each case needs to be analyzed separately. Therefore, the present edition has limited itself to the two main categories of "fragment" (F) and "*testimonium*" (T). Those texts that include original wording of Africanus are classified as "F". All others—*viz.* sources which talk *about* Africanus rather than quoting him—are considered as "T". Since the "F" category encompasses various degrees of proximity to the original text, readers are advised to pay careful attention to the notes accompanying the English translation. In a strict sense, only a portion of the excerpts designated "F" transmit Africanus' original wording with certainty. The highest degree of confidence can be given to texts independently attested in two branches of the transmission (F34 and F93). Stylistic analysis of the *Chronographiae* would thus have to consider primarily these cases.

Columns and subdivisions within a fragment. Fragments are numbered according to "clusters" of contents; texts listed under the same number presumably go back to the same passage in the original text. In a few cases, it is possible to reconstruct the wording of Africanus on the basis of two or more independent witnesses (e.g. F34). In other cases, two or more texts cannot be united into a single hypothetical original. Where the degree of similarity is sufficient, pertinent texts are printed in parallel columns (e.g. F30) and the extent to which the original can be recognized is expressed by means of italicization (see below). In other instances the relationship between texts dealing with the same topic cannot be determined (e.g. F14). In these cases, the texts are presented seriatim under the same number with additional lower case letters. The same applies to all those texts where the sequence is clear, but which may have been divided by other lost entries. Here also lower case letters are assigned to indicate that they belong together (e.g. F16). Only where there is reason to think that very little or nothing is missing between adjoining blocks of text, are the texts lined up under the same number, separated only by "[…]" (e.g. F46). Lower case letters are also used when we have one fragment followed by *testimonia*, usually in the form of discussion or commentary by various later authors (e.g. F93).

Apparatuses. The four apparatuses are as follows, beginning from the bottom:

1. The critical apparatus is normally based on the consulted edition, but has been standardized according to our syntax and in some cases is slightly abridged. When our reading differs from the one found in the edition, the decision of the original editor is documented in the apparatus. This can occur, for example, when additional parallels make it possible to constitute a text that is presumably closer to the original than the text of the quoted author. Where needed, a list of all relevant witnesses (manuscripts) is provided at the beginning of the apparatus in square brackets (unless a fourth apparatus is needed, see below). The *sigla* can be found in the *Conspectus siglorum* (pp. LXIX ff). When a text is divided into two columns, two apparatuses might be required.

2. The apparatus *locorum similium* documents quotations in the text (both biblical and non-biblical). References to sources, parallels and users of Africanus are also cited, usually preceded by "cf." Abbreviations for the quoted works can be found below (pp. LXXIX ff). Texts that use Africanus are included only when they have little or no value for the constitution of the text; otherwise they appear in the third apparatus with the full text.

3. The apparatus of secondary textual witnesses gives those texts which are secondary to the main text, but which are of some interest to the reconstruction of the original wording (or in some cases the chronological system) of Iulius Africanus. Typically, the main text would be explicitly attributed to Africanus, whereas the origin of the secondary material is less certain. Verbatim parallels with the main text often suggest that they originate from the same source. Because the main text might in some cases be an epitome, these secondary testimonies also sometimes contain fuller texts, possibly of independent value. Material in these sources which overlaps with the main text is identified in upright print; the remainder is in italics (see below). In the case of *testimonia*, the secondary witnesses are those texts which draw upon the main text, although it cannot be excluded that they also had independent sources of information. In a few cases, this apparatus also supplements *testimonia* with "likely candidates" for the original text of Africanus, to which the *testimonium* refers (e.g. T36).

While some particularly important witnesses appear in the notes to the translation, material cited in this apparatus is not normally rendered into

English. Texts preserved in languages other than Greek or Latin are therefore provided in the best available translation in a Western language.

In many cases, secondary evidence also comes from other independent fragments. These texts are referred to with an arrow (→). As a result, the third apparatus provides the reader with a network of inter-textual references within the *Chronographiae*.

4. The apparatus of attestation (beginning with "test.:") is employed when more than one source attests to the same original text (e.g. F34). In such cases, the relevant source material is listed in the heading of the fragment along with the pertinent *sigla* used in the apparatus (e.g. "Eus.", "Sync.²"). The fourth apparatus specifies where a single source begins ("inc.") or ends ("des."); when they are of interest, the words immediately before or after the quotation are provided here (rather than in small letters in the main text, as would be the case with fragments that are attested by one source only). Information about all available witnesses is repeated at the beginning of the apparatus on each page. After the first mention of any given source, a list of all manuscripts is given in square brackets (rather than at the beginning of the critical apparatus). Note that in these cases the critical apparatus indicates the readings of single manuscripts within the transmission of one of the quoted authors in the form of "Siglum:ms." (e.g. "Sync.:A").

Use of small letters. Small letters in the main text of a fragment serve two functions. They can identify material which, although not from Africanus, gives helpful information on the context (such as quoting formulations or further discussion of an issue by the quoting author). More rarely, they can identify parts of the text whose attribution to Africanus is ambiguous. The latter case might occur when it is difficult to determine the precise ending of a quotation that begins with a clear attribution. In the case of *testimonia*, small letters are used for those parts of the text bearing no direct connection to Africanus or his chronicle, but of possible value to the context.

Use of normal print and italics. The existence of two or more independent sources attesting the same text increases the probability that it reflects Africanus' own original wording. To indicate such agreements, overlapping words and phrases in texts appearing in facing columns are printed in normal type; material not common to both texts is italicized. Where there are verbal correspondences between the main text and a secondary testimony (in the third apparatus, see above), the system of italics and upright print is used only for the secondary source. Italics are also used in the first apparatus for variants in Latin or other languages to differentiate from the Latin language of the apparatus itself.

Oriental languages. Where they appear in the main text, all texts preserved in Oriental languages (Syriac, Arabic, Armenian) are reproduced in the original language. As with the Greek and Latin texts, they are translated into English on the facing page. However, where additional material in the apparatus is preserved in one of the Oriental languages, only a translation in a Western language is given (usually the most recent available).

Translation and notes. The English translation aims to facilitate access to texts that are sometimes difficult to understand. It also seeks to clarify how the editors have understood the text and why they have preferred certain solutions over others. In this sense, the translation is part of the critical edition itself. Occasionally, the English version may more closely approximate to Africanus than the "original text". Some sections of the *Excerpta barbari*, for example, are barely understandable and at best imprecise representations of Africanus' intentions. On the basis of other Greek sources and some speculative combinations, it is possible to provide an English text that is more than just a translation of the problematic Latin "original".

In the rendering of proper names, the English translation does not adhere to strict rules of transliteration, preferring instead more readily recognizable Latinized forms. The spelling of proper names from the Hebrew Bible conforms to the practice of the New Revised Standard Version (NRSV). For the sake of consistency with usage elsewhere in the edition, the translation and introduction spell Africanus' *nomen* as "Iulius", even though he is better known to English readers by the name "Julius Africanus". Where the spelling of proper names is obviously corrupt, as is often the case in the *Excerpta barbari,* the translation has supplied the more conventional spelling of these names found in other witnesses (e.g., Syncellus or Eusebius).

For easier orientation, short English titles have been added to the fragments. These titles have no critical value and do not purport to be fully descriptive of the fragments' contents.

An important part of the work conducted by the editors is documented in the notes. These are not commentaries, i.e. many important problems connected with the texts are not discussed or even mentioned. Likewise they do not pretend to give a complete record of recent (or not so recent) bibliography on relevant issues. Their role is limited to giving further arguments for:

a) questions of textual criticism (especially where they are too long or too complicated to be dealt with in the apparatus)

b) questions of attribution (especially for the relatively few cases in which texts are not explicitly attributed to Africanus)

c) complex calculations of dates etc.

Only in a few cases do they also serve to give translations of material contained in the apparatus which would not normally be translated.

7. Bibliography

Bibliographical abbreviations are according to Schwertner 1992.

Adler, William, Berossus, Manetho, and 1 Enoch in the World Chronicle of Panodorus, HThR 76, 1983, 419–442.
Adler, William, Time Immemorial. Archaic History and its Sources in Christian Chronography from Julius Africanus to George Syncellus (DOS 26), Washington D.C. 1989.
Adler, William, The Origins of the Proto-Heresies. Fragments from a Chronicle in the First Book of Epiphanius' Panarion, JThS 41, 1990, 472–501.
Adler, William, Eusebius' Chronicle and Its Legacy, in: Eusebius, Christianity, and Judaism, ed. H. W. Attridge/G. Hata, Leiden 1992, 467–491.
Adler, William, Sextus Julius Africanus and the Roman Near East in the Third Century, JThS 55, 2004, 520–550.
Adler, William, Eusebius' Critique of Africanus, in: Julius Africanus und die christliche Weltchronistik, ed. M. Wallraff (TU 157), Berlin 2006, 147–157.
Adler/Tuffin 2002: see *Editores et emendatores*
Alexakis, Alexander, Codex Parisinus Graecus 1115 and Its Archetype (DOS 34), Washington 1996.
Aucher 1818: see *Conspectus* s.v. Eusebius, Chronica
Bardenhewer, Otto, Geschichte der altkirchlichen Literatur, 5 vols., Freiburg ²1913–1932.
Bauer, Adolf, Die Chronik des Hippolytos im Matritensis Graecus 121 (TU 14,1), Leipzig 1905.
Bauer 1909: see *Abbreviationes* s.v. Anon. matr.
Bauer 1955: see *Abbreviationes* s.v. Hipp., chron.
Baumstark, Anton, Die Lehre des römischen Presbyters Florinus, ZNW 13, 1912, 306–319.
Beck, Hans-Georg, Zur byzantinischen „Mönchschronik", in: Speculum historiale. Geschichte im Spiegel von Geschichtsschreibung und Geschichtsdeutung, ed. C. Bauer/L. Boehm/M. Müller, Freiburg 1965, 188–197 (= id., Ideen und Realitäten in Byzanz. Gesammelte Aufsätze, London 1972, Nr. XVI).
Bees, Nikos A., Τὰ χειρόγραφα τῶν Μετεώρων. Κατάλογος περιγραφικὸς τῶν χειρογράφων κωδίκων τῶν ἀποκειμένων εἰς τὰς μονὰς τῶν Μετεώρων. 1. Τὰ χειρόγραφα τῆς μονῆς Μεταμορφώσεως, Athens 1967.
Berendts, Alexander, Die handschriftliche Überlieferung der Zacharias- und Johannes-Apokryphen. Über die Bibliotheken der Meteorischen und Ossa-Olympischen Klöster (TU 9,3), Leipzig 1904.
Boeckh, August, Manetho und die Hundsternsperiode. Ein Beitrag zur Geschichte der Pharaonen, Berlin 1845.
de Boor, Carl (ed.), Theophanis Chronographia, 2 vols., Leipzig 1883–85.

de Boor, Carl, Neue Fragmente des Papias, Hegesippus und Pierius in bisher unbekannten Exzerpten aus der Kirchengeschichte des Philippus Sidetes (TU 5/2), Berlin 1888, 165–184.

Brandes, Wolfram, Anastasios ὁ δίκορος. Endzeiterwartung und Kaiserkritik in Byzanz um 500 n.Chr., ByZ 90, 1997, 24–63.

Bratke, Eduard, Das sogenannte Religionsgespräch am Hof der Sasaniden (TU 19/4), Leipzig 1899.

Breydy, Michael, Agapius von Manbiğ und sein historisches Werk, OrChr 73, 1989, 90–96.

Brooke, Alan E./Norman McLean, The Old Testament in Greek, vol. 1.4, Cambridge 1917.

Burgess, Richard W. (with the assistance of Witold Witakowski), Studies in Eusebian and Post-Eusebian Chronography (Historia. Einzelschriften 135), Stuttgart 1999.

Burgess, Richard W., Apologetic and Chronography. The Antecedents of Julius Africanus, in: Julius Africanus und die christliche Weltchronistik, ed. M. Wallraff (TU 157), Berlin 2006, 17–42.

Carr 1925: see *Conspectus* s.v. Gregorius Barhebraeus, Commentarium in Evangelia

Christesen, Paul/Zara Martirosova-Torlone, The Olympic Victor List of Eusebius. Background, Text and Translation, Traditio 61, 2006, 31–93.

Crehan, Joseph, Africanus, Julius, in: TRE 1, Berlin 1977, 635–640.

Croke, Brian, The Origins of the Christian World Chronicle, in: History and Historians in Late Antiquity, ed. B. Croke/A. M. Emmett, Sydney 1983, 116–131 (= id., Christian Chronicles and Byzantine History, 5th–6th Centuries, Aldershot 1992, III).

Croke, Brian, Byzantine Chronicle Writing, in: Studies in John Malalas, ed. E. Jeffreys/B. Croke/R. Scott, Sydney 1990, 27–54.

D'Alfonso, Francesca, Euripide in Giovanni Malala, Torino 2006.

De Sanctis, Gaetano, ΑΤΘΙΣ. Storia della repubblica ateniese dalle origini alla età di Pericle. Torino ²1912.

Dindorf, Wilhelm (ed.), Georgius Syncellus et Nicephorus Constantinopolitanus, 2 vols. (CSHB), Bonn 1829.

Dittenberger, Wilhelm/Karl Purgold, Die Inschriften von Olympia (Olympia. Die Ergebnisse der von dem deutschen Reich veranstalteten Ausgrabung 5), Berlin 1896.

Droge, Arthur J., Homer or Moses? Early Christian Interpretations of the History of Culture (HUTh 26), Tübingen 1989.

Drost-Abgarjan, Armenuhi, Ein neuer Fund zur armenischen Version der Eusebios-Chronik, in: Julius Africanus und die christliche Weltchronistik, ed. M. Wallraff (TU 157), Berlin 2006, 255–262.

Finegan, Jack, Handbook of Biblical Chronology. Principles of Time Reckoning in the Ancient World and Problems of Chronology in the Bible, Revised edition, Peabody 1998.
Fotheringham, John Knight, The Bodleian Manuscript of Jerome's Version of the Chronicle of Eusebius, reproduced in collotype, Oxford 1905.
Fotheringham, John Knight (ed.), Eusebii Pamphili Chronici canones latine vertit, adauxit, ad sua tempora produxit S. Eusebius Hieronymus, London 1923.
Frick 1892: see *Conspectus* s.v. Excerpta latina Barbari
Frick, Carl, Beiträge zur Griechischen Chronologie und Literaturgeschichte, Jahres-Bericht über das König Wilhelms-Gymnasium zu Höxter an der Weser 13, 1880, 3–14.
Gallandi, Andrea (ed.), Bibliotheca veterum patrum antiquorumque scriptorum ecclesiasticorum, vol. 2, Venezia 1766.
Gelzer: see *Editores et emendatores*
Gelzer[ms]: see *Editores et emendatores*
Gerland, Ernst, Heinrich Gelzer, ByZ 16, 1907, 417–430.
Goar[(m)]: see *Editores et emendatores*
Godet, P., Galland, André, in: DThC 6,1, Paris 1920, 1095.
Graf, Georg, Geschichte der christlichen arabischen Literatur, vol. 2. Die Schriftsteller bis zur Mitte des 15. Jahrhunderts (StT 133), Roma 1947.
Grafton, Anthony, Joseph Scaliger. A Study in the History of Classical Scholarship, 2 vols. (Oxford-Warburg Studies), Oxford 1983–93.
Harnack, Adolf, Geschichte der altchristlichen Litteratur bis Eusebius, 2. Teil. Die Chronologie, vol. 1, Leipzig 1897 (reprint Berlin 1958).
von Harnack, Adolf, Julius Afrikanus, der Bibliothekar des Kaisers Alexander Severus, in: Aufsätze, Fritz Milkau gewidmet, Leipzig 1921, 142–146.
Helm 1956: see *Conspectus* s.v. Eusebius, Canones
Heyden, Katharina, Die *Christliche Geschichte* des Philippos von Side. Mit einem kommentierten Katalog der Fragmente, in: Julius Africanus und die christliche Weltchronistik, ed. M. Wallraff (TU 157), Berlin 2006, 209–243.
Hunger, Herbert, Die hochsprachliche profane Literatur der Byzantiner, 2 vols. (HAW 12,5), München 1978.
Hunt, William, Joseph Martin Routh, in: DNB 17, Oxford 1897, 324–326.
Huxley, George L., On the Erudition of George the Synkellos, Proceedings of the Royal Irish Academy 81c/6, 1981, 207–217.
Huxley, George L., A Theban Kinglist in Malalas, Philologus 131, 1987, 159–161.
Inglebert, Hervé, Aphraate, le «sage persan». La première historiographie syriaque, Syria 78, 2001, 179–208.
Jacoby, Friedrich, Excerpta Barbari, in: PRE 6,2, Stuttgart 1909, 1566–1576.
Jeanjean, Benoît/Bertrand Lançon (ed.), Jérôme, Chronique. Continuation de la Chronique d'Eusèbe, années 326–378, suivie de quatre études sur les chro-

niques et chronographies dans l'Antiquité tardive (IVe–VIe siècles), Rennes 2004.

Jeffreys, Elizabeth, The Attitudes of Byzantine Chroniclers towards Ancient History, Byzantion 49, 1979, 199–238.

Jeffreys, Elizabeth, Malalas' Sources, in: Studies in John Malalas, ed. E. Jeffreys/B. Croke/R. Scott, Sydney 1990, 167–216.

Jeffreys, Elizabeth, The Transmission of Malalas' Chronicle, in: Studies in John Malalas, ed. E. Jeffreys/B. Croke/R. Scott, Sydney 1990, 245–268.

Jeffreys, Elizabeth, The Beginning of Byzantine Chronography. John Malalas, in: Greek and Roman Historiography in Late Antiquity. Fourth to Sixth Century A.D., ed. G. Marasco, Leiden 2003, 497–527.

Jeffreys, Elizabeth/Brian Croke/Roger Scott (trans. and eds.), The Chronicle of John Malalas. A Translation (Byzantina Australiensia 4), Melbourne 1986.

Jeremias, Joachim, Golgotha, ed. V. H. Kanus-Credé, Allendorf an der Eder ^{2}2002.

Karst 1911: see *Conspectus* s.v. Eusebius, Chronica

Kazhdan, Alexander P., Kedrenos, George, in: Oxford Dictionary of Byzantium 2, New York 1991, 1118 (= Kazhdan 1991a).

Kazhdan, Alexander P., Symeon Logothete, in: Oxford Dictionary of Byzantium 3, New York 1991, 1982f (= Kazhdan 1991b).

Kazhdan, Alexander P., Symeon Magistros, Pseudo-, in: Oxford Dictionary of Byzantium 3, New York 1991, 1983 (= Kazhdan 1991c).

Kienast, Dietmar, Römische Kaisertabelle. Grundzüge einer römischen Kaiserchronologie, Darmstadt 1990.

Klijn, Albertus Frederic Johannes, Seth in Jewish, Christian and Gnostic Literature (NT.S 46), Leiden 1977.

Kornemann, Ernst, Heinrich Gelzer, Klio 7, 1907, 302.

Kresten, Otto, Andreas Darmarios und die handschriftliche Überlieferung des Pseudo-Julios Polydeukes, JÖB 18, 1969, 137–165.

Kresten, Otto, Phantomgestalten in der byzantinischen Literaturgeschichte. Zu vier Titelfälschungen des 16. Jahrhunderts, JÖB 25, 1976, 207–222.

Krönung, Thomas, Die Wiederentdeckung des Manuskripts von Heinrich Gelzer zur kritischen Edition der *Chronographien des Iulius Africanus,* in: Welt-Zeit. Christliche Weltchronistik aus zwei Jahrtausenden in Beständen der Thüringer Universitäts- und Landesbibliothek Jena, ed. M. Wallraff, Berlin 2005, 20–31.

Landes, Richard, Lest the Millennium Be Fulfilled, in: The Use and Abuse of Eschatology in the Middle Ages, ed. W. Verbeke, Leuven 1988, 137–211.

de Lange, Nicholas, Origène, La lettre à Africanus sur l'histoire de Suzanne, in: Origène..., ed. M. Harl/N. de Lange (SC 302), Paris 1983, 469–578.

Laqueur, Richard, Synkellos (1), in: PRE 4 A2, Stuttgart 1932, 1388–1410.

Leopardi: see Moreschini 1997

Lepsius, Carl Richard, Königsbuch der alten Aegypter, Berlin 1858.
Lindner, Josef, Papias und die Perikope von der Ehebrecherin (Joh 7,53–8,11) bei Agapius von Mambiğ, ZKTh 40, 1916, 191–199.
Mahé, Annie et Jean-Pierre, Histoire de l'Arménie par Moïse de Khorène. Nouvelle traduction de l'arménien classique, Paris 1993.
Maisano, Riccardo, Note su Giorgio Cedreno e la tradizione storiografica bizantina, Rivista di studi bizantini e slavi 3, 1983, 227–248.
Mango, Cyril/Roger Scott, The Chronicle of Theophanes Confessor. Byzantine and Near Eastern History AD 284–813, Oxford 1997.
Markopoulos, Athanasios, Ἡ Χρονογραφία τοῦ Ψευδοσυμεὼν καὶ οἱ πηγές της, Ioannina 1978.
Momigliano, Arnaldo, Time in Ancient Historiography, in: History and the Concept of Time (History and Theory. Beiheft 6), Middletown 1966, 1–23.
Moreschini, Claudio (ed.), Giacomo Leopardi. Giulio Africano. Introduzione, edizione critica e note (Istituto Italiano per gli Studi Storici. Testi Storici, Filosofici e Letterari 7), Napoli 1997.
Moretti, Luigi, Iscrizioni agonistiche greche, Roma 1953
Moretti, Luigi, Olympionikai. I vincitori negli antichi agoni olimpici, Roma 1957.
Mosshammer, Alden A., The Chronicle of Eusebius and the Greek Chronographic Tradition, Lewisburg 1979.
Mosshammer 1984: see *Conspectus* s.v. Georgius Syncellus
Mosshammer, Alden A., The Christian Era of Julius Africanus. With an Excursus on Olympiad Chronology, in: Julius Africanus und die christliche Weltchronistik, ed. M. Wallraff (TU 157), Berlin 2006, 83–112.
Müller, Carl (ed.), Fragmenta Historicorum Graecorum, vol. 4, Paris 1851.
Palmer, Andrew/Sebastian Brock/Robert Hoyland, The Seventh Century in the West-Syrian Chronicles. Introduced, translated and annotated by Andrew Palmer. Including two seventh-century Syriac apocalyptic texts introduced, translated and annotated by Sebastian Brock with added annotation and an historical introduction by Robert Hoyland (Translated Texts for Historians 15), Liverpool 1993.
Pančenko, K. A., Агапий Манбиджский, in: Православная Энциклопедия 1, Moskva 2000, 221.
Pétau, Denis, Opus de doctrina temporum, 2 vols., Paris 1627 (many reprints).
Pilhofer, Peter, Presbyteron Kreitton. Der Altersbeweis der jüdischen und christlichen Apologeten und seine Vorgeschichte (WUNT 2,39), Tübingen 1990.
Quantin, Jean-Louis, Anglican Scholarship Gone Mad? Henry Dodwell (1641–1711) and Christian Antiquity, in: History of Scholarship, ed. Ch. Ligota/J.-L. Quantin, Oxford 2006, 305–356.
Rampoldi, Tiziana, Giulio Africano e Alessandro Severo, RIL 115, 1981, 73–84.

Rampoldi, Tiziana, I Kestoi di Giulio Africano e l'imperatore Alessandro Severo, in: ANRW II 34,3, Berlin 1997, 2451–2470.

Rebenich, Stefan, Theodor Mommsen und Adolf Harnack. Wissenschaft und Politik im Berlin des ausgehenden 19. Jahrhunderts. Mit einem Anhang: Edition und Kommentierung des Briefwechsels, Berlin 1997.

Rebenich, Stefan (ed.), Adolf von Harnack. Protokollbuch der Kirchenväter-Kommission der Preußischen Akademie der Wissenschaften 1897–1928, Berlin 2000.

Reichardt, Walther, Heinrich Gelzer. Geb. am 1. Juli 1847, gest. am 11. Juli 1906, in: Biographisches Jahrbuch für die Altertumswissenschaft, founded by Conrad Bursian, ed. W. Kroll, 30, 1907, 1–48.

Reichardt 1909: see *Abbreviationes* s.v. Iul. Afr., ep. Arist.

Reuss, Joseph, Matthäus-, Markus- und Johannes-Katenen nach den handschriftlichen Quellen untersucht (Neutestamentliche Abhandlungen 18,4–5), Münster 1941.

Richard, Marcel, Florilèges Damascéniens, in: DSp 5, Paris 1964, col. 476–486.

Richard, Marcel, Répertoire des bibliothèques et des catalogues de manuscrits grecs, Troisième édition entièrement refondue par Jean-Marie Olivier, Brepols 1995.

Riedweg, Christoph, Ps.-Justin (Markell von Ankyra?), Ad Graecos de vera religione (bisher „Cohortatio ad Graecos"). Einleitung und Kommentar (SBA 25), Basel 1994.

Routh: see *Editores et emendatores*

Roberto 2005a: see *Conspectus* s.v. Ioannes Antiochenus

Roberto, Umberto, Gli Excerpta Salmasiana di storia greca e orientale dello Ps. Giovanni Antiocheno e le Chronographiae di Giulio Africano, Selecta colligere II, Beiträge zur Technik des Sammelns und Kompilierens griechischer Texte von der Antike bis zum Humanismus, ed. R. M. Piccione/M. Perkams (Hellenica 18), Alessandria 2005, 253–293 (= Roberto 2005b).

Roberto, Umberto, Julius Africanus und die Tradition der hellenistischen Universalgeschichte, in: Julius Africanus und die christliche Weltchronistik, ed. M. Wallraff (TU 157), Berlin 2006, 3–16.

Rochow, Ilse, Chronographie, in: Quellen zur Geschichte des frühen Byzanz (4.–9. Jahrhundert), ed. F. Winkelmann/W. Brandes, Berlin 1990, 190–201 and 364f.

Rösel, Martin, Übersetzung als Vollendung der Auslegung. Studien zur Genesis-Septuaginta (BZAW 223), Berlin 1994.

Ruinart, Theodoricus (ed.), Acta martyrum, Regensburg 1859.

Rutgers, Iosephus, Sexti Julii Africani Olympiadōn anagraphē, adiectis ceteris quae ex Olympionicarum Fastis supersunt, Leiden 1862.

Sartori, Franco, Mario e i Cimbri nell'Anonymus Matritensis, in: Alte Geschichte und Wissenschaftsgeschichte. Festschrift für Karl Christ zum 65. Geburtstag, ed. P. Kneissl/V. Losemann, Darmstadt 1988, 411–430.

Scaliger, Joseph Justus, Thesaurus temporum, Eusebii Pamphili Caesareae Palaestinae episcopi, Chronicorum canonum omnimodae historiae libri duo, interprete Hieronymo, ex fide vetustissimorum codicum castigati…, Leiden 1606 (reprint Osnabrück 1968, 2nd edition Leiden 1658, quoted hereafter).

Schamp, Jacques, Photios historien des lettres. La *Bibliothèque* et ses notices biographiques, Paris 1987.

Schmidt, Andrea Barbara, Die zweifache armenische Rezension der syrischen Chronik Michaels des Großen, Le Muséon 109, 1996, 299–319.

Schmidt, Andrea Barbara, Syrische Tradition in armenischer Adaption. Die armenische Rezeption des Geschichtswerkes von Michael Syrus und der antichalcedonensische Judenbrief an Kaiser Markianos, in: Symposium Syriacum VII, ed. René Lavenant (OCA 256), Roma 1998, 359–371.

Schoene, Alfred, Eusebi chronicorum libri duo, 2 vols., Berlin 1875–76.

Schwartz, Eduard, Die Königslisten des Eratosthenes und Kastor. Mit Excursen über die Interpolationen bei Africanus und Eusebios (AGWG.PH 40), Göttingen 1895.

Schwartz 1903–09: see *Conspectus* s.v. Eus., h. e.

Schwartz, Eduard, Eusebios, in: PRE 6,1, Stuttgart 1907, 1370–1439 (= id., Griechische Geschichtsschreiber, Leipzig 1957, 495–598).

Schweinburg, Kurt, Die ursprüngliche Form der Kedrenchronik, ByZ 30, 1929/30, 68–77.

Schwertner, Siegfried, Internationales Abkürzungsverzeichnis für Theologie und Grenzgebiete (IATG²), Berlin ²1992 (reprint in: Theologische Realenzyklopädie. Abkürzungsverzeichnis, Berlin ²1994, 1–488).

Scott, Roger, The Byzantine Chronicle after Malalas, in: Studies in John Malalas, ed. E. Jeffreys/B. Croke/R. Scott, Sydney 1990, 38–54.

Seel, Otto, Panodoros, in: PRE 18 A2, Stuttgart 1949, 632–635.

Serruys, D., Les transformations de l'aera alexandrina minor, Revue de Philologie 31, 1907, 251–264.

Sickenberger, Joseph, S. Iulius Africanus, in: PRE 10, Stuttgart 1918, 116–125.

Sirinelli, Jean, Les vues historiques d'Eusèbe de Césarée durant la période prénicéenne, Dakar 1961.

Sotiroudis, Panagiotis, Untersuchungen zum Geschichtswerk des Ioannes von Antiocheia, Thessaloniki 1989.

Staab, Gregor, Chronographie als Philosophie. Die Urwahrheit der mosaischen Überlieferung nach dem Begründungsmodell des Mittelplatonismus bei Julius Africanus (Edition und Kommentierung von Africanus *Chron.* fr. 1), in: Julius Africanus und die christliche Weltchronistik, ed. M. Wallraff (TU 157), Berlin 2006, 61–81.

Takahashi, Hidemi, Barhebraeus. A Bio-Bibliography, Piscataway 2005.
Terian, Abraham, Xorenacʻi and Eastern Historiography of the Hellenistic Period, REArm 28, 2001/02, 101–141.
Thomson, Robert W., Moses Khorenatsʻi. History of the Armenians. Translation and Commentary on the Literary Sources, London 1978.
Topchyan, Aram, Julius Africanus' Chronicle and Movsēs Xorenacʻi, Le Muséon 114, 2001, 153–185.
Topchyan, Aram, The Problem of the Greek Sources of Movsēs Chorenacʻi's History of Armenia (Hebrew University Armenian Studies 7), Leuven 2006.
Traina, Giusto, Il complesso di Trimalcione. Movsēs Xorenacʻi e le origini del pensiero storico armeno (Eurasiatica. Quaderni del Dipartimento di Studi Eurasiatici dell'Università degli Studi di Venezia 27), Venezia 1991.
Trapp, Erich et al. (eds.), Lexikon zur byzantinischen Gräzität besonders des 9.–12. Jahrhunderts, vol. 1, Wien 2001.
Trieber, Conrad, Die Chronologie des Julius Africanus, Nachrichten von der königlichen Gesellschaft der Wissenschaft, Göttingen 1880, 49–75.
Trieber, Conrad, Die Idee der vier Weltreiche, Hermes 27, 1892, 321–344.
Unger, Georg Friedrich, Chronologie des Manetho, Berlin 1867.
Vieillefond 1970: see *Abbreviationes* s.v. Iul. Afr., cest.
Wacholder, Ben Zion, Biblical Chronology in the Hellenistic World Chronicles, HThR 61, 1968, 451–481.
Wacker, Christian, The Record of the Olympic Victory List, Nikephoros 11, 1998, 39–50.
Waddell, William G., Manetho (LCL 350), London 1940 (various reprints).
Wahlgren, Staffan, Original und Archetypus. Zu Zustandekommen und Transformation einer byzantinischen Weltchronik (Pseudo-Polydeukes/Symeon Logothetes), ByZ 96, 2003, 269–277.
Wahlgren, Staffan, Die Logotheten-Chronik. Form – Inhalt – Ideologie, in: Julius Africanus und die christliche Weltchronistik, ed. M. Wallraff (TU 157), Berlin 2006, 245–251.
Wallraff, Martin, Protologie und Eschatologie als Horizonte der Kirchengeschichte? Das Erbe christlicher Universalgeschichte, in: Historiographie und Theologie. Kirchen- und Theologiegeschichte im Spannungsfeld von geschichtswissenschaftlicher Methode und theologischem Anspruch, ed. W. Kinzig/V. Leppin/G. Wartenberg (Arbeiten zur Kirchen- und Theologiegeschichte 15), Leipzig 2004, 153–167.
Wallraff, Martin, Von der antiken Historie zur mittelalterlichen Chronik. Die Entstehung christlicher Universalgeschichtsschreibung, in: Welt-Zeit. Christliche Weltchronistik aus zwei Jahrtausenden in Beständen der Thüringer Universitäts- und Landesbibliothek Jena, ed. M. Wallraff, Berlin 2005, 1–19.
Wallraff, Martin, Die neue Fragmentensammlung der Chronographie des Julius Africanus. Bemerkungen zur Methodik anhand einiger Dubia vel Spuria, in:

Julius Africanus und die christliche Weltchronistik, ed. M. Wallraff (TU 157), Berlin 2006, 45–59.

Weltecke, Dorothea, Die „Beschreibung der Zeiten" von Mōr Michael dem Großen (1126–1199). Eine Studie zu ihrem historischen und historiographischen Kontext (CSCO 594, Sub. 110), Louvain 2003.

Wevers, John William (ed.), Genesis (Septuaginta. Vetus Testamentum Graecum 1), Göttingen 1974.

Winiarczyk, Marek, Euhemeros von Messene. Leben, Werk und Nachwirkung (Beiträge zur Altertumskunde 157), München 2002.

Winkelmann, Friedhelm, Euseb von Kaisareia. Der Vater der Kirchengeschichte, Berlin 1991.

Winkelmann, Friedhelm, Iulius Africanus, in: RAC 19, Stuttgart 2002, 508–518.

Xeres, Saverio, L'oscuramento del sole durante la Passione di Cristo nelle fonti cristiane e pagane dei primi due secoli, in: Fenomeni naturali e avvenimenti storici nell'antichità, ed. Marta Sordi (Contributi dell'Istituto storico 15), Milano 1989, 219–226.

Zoepfl, Friedrich, Der Kommentar des Pseudo-Eustathios zum Hexaëmeron, Münster 1927.

CONSPECTVS SIGLORVM

continens omnes textus e quibus fragmenta vel testimonia hausta sunt
(* = codices qui in praeparanda editione consultati sunt)

Agapius Mabbugensis, Historia universalis, ed. A. Vasiliev, 4 vol. (PO 5,4 [= pars I,1], 11,1 [= I,2], 7,4 [= II,1], 8,3 [= II,2]), Paris 1909–15.

Anonymus Matritensis, ed. A. Bauer, Leipzig 1909.
                Matritensis gr. 4701 (olim 121), saec. X

ps. Athanasius, Fragmenta varia, PG 28,1252–1257.

Barhebraeus → Gregorius Barhebraeus

Basilius Caesariensis, De spiritu sancto, ed. B. Pruche (SC 17bis), Paris ^{2}1968.
    A   Parisinus gr. 506, saec. X
    C   Parisinus gr. 966, saec. XI
    F   Parisinus gr. 969, saec. XIV
    G   Oxoniensis Bodleianus XXXVII, saec. XI
    K   Mosquensis Sancti Synodi 23, saec. XI
    M   Vindobonensis theologicus gr. 18, saec. XIV

Catena in Ioannem, excerptum in: Collectio Nova Patrum et Scriptorum Graecorum, ed. B. Montfaucon, vol. 2, Paris 1707, p. 105 (= PG 26,1321B).
                * Parisinus gr. 209, saec. XI/XII

Catena in Matthaeum, ed. J. A. Cramer, in: Catenae graecorum patrum in Novum Testamentum, vol. 1, In evangelia S. Matthaei et S. Marci, Oxford 1840 (ed. anast. Hildesheim 1967), 1–257, 449–496.
    C   Coislinianus gr. 23, saec. XI
    B   Oxoniensis Bodleianus gr. auct. T I 4, saec. X/XI

Cedrenus → Georgius Cedrenus

Chronicon Epitomon, ed. A. Pusch, Jena 1908.
    T   Vindobonensis theologicus gr. 40, saec. XIII
    H   Vindobonensis historicus gr. 99, saec. XIV

Chronicon Paschale, ed. L. Dindorf, vol. 1 (CSHB), Bonn 1832.
    V   Vaticanus gr. 1941, saec. X

Didymus Caecus (Alexandrinus), Commentarius in Genesim, ed. P. Nautin, 2 vol. (SC 233, 244), Paris 1976-1978.

Dionysius bar Salibi, Commentarii in Evangelia I,1, trans. I. Sedláček (CSCO 16, Syr. 16), Louvain 1906.

Ecloga Historiarum, in: Anecdota graeca e codicibus manuscriptis Bibliothecae Regiae Parisiensis, ed. J. A. Cramer, Oxford 1839, 2, 165 – 230.
 P   Parisinus gr. 854, f. 71–146, saec. X

Elenchus anonymus historiographorum
    Parisinus syr. 9, p. 165, saec. XIII, ed. F. Nau, in: ROC 20 (1915–1917) 101–104

Eusebius Caesariensis, Chronica (Chronographia et Canones)
 Versio armeniaca
 E   Erewan, Matenadaran 1904, saec. XIII/XIV
 Aucher ed. J. B. Aucher, 2 vol., Venezia 1818
 Karst trans. J. Karst (GCS 20, Eusebius Werke 5), Leipzig 1911

Excerpta Eusebiana (e textu graeco), ed. J. Cramer, Anecdota graeca e codd. manuscriptis bibliotheceae regiae Parisiensis, vol. 2, Oxford 1839, 118–163 (ed. anast. Hildesheim 1967) (= ed. A. Schoene, Eusebi chronicorum libri duo, vol. 1, Berlin 1875, 1–286).
 P   * Parisinus gr. 2600, f. 193^r–219^r, saec. XV

Canones, Versio latina Hieronymi, ed. R. Helm (GCS 47, Eusebius Werke 7), Berlin ²1956 (ed. anast. cum praefatione U. Treu 1984), codices ad textum T6 pertinentes vide apud "Excerptorem anonymum in calce chronici".
 O   Oxoniensis Bodleianus lat. auct. T II 26, saec. V
 S   Fragmenta Floriacensia, in diversis bibliothecis, saec. V (ed. photographica, L. Traube, Leiden 1902)

Eusebius Caesariensis, Demonstratio evangelica, ed. I. Heikel (GCS 23, Eusebius Werke 6), Leipzig 1913.
 P   Parisinus gr. 469, saec. XII
 O   Bononiensis gr. 3644, saec. XIII
 S   Oxoniensis Collegii S. Ioannis Baptistae 41, saec. XV
 V   Vaticanus gr. 1153/1154, saec. XII

Eusebius Caesariensis, Eclogae propheticae, ed. Th. Gaisford, Oxford 1842 (= PG 22,1021–1262).

   * Vindobonensis gr. 55, saec. XII

Eusebius Caesariensis, Historia ecclesiastica, ed. E. Schwartz (accedit versio latina Rufini, ed. Th. Mommsen), 3 vol. (GCS 9, Eusebius Werke 2), Leipzig 1903–1909 (ed. anast. Berlin 1999).

B	Parisinus gr. 1431, saec. XI/XII
b	Marcianus gr. 339, saec. XIV
β	Parisinus gr. 1432, saec. XIII/XIV
D	Parisinus gr. 1433, saec. XI/XII
M	Marcianus gr. 338, saec. XII
A	Parisinus gr. 1430, saec. XI
a	Vaticanus gr. 399, saec. XI
T	Laurentianus 70,7, saec. X/XI
E	Laurentianus 70,20, saec. X
R	Mosquensis Sancti Synodi 50, saec. XII
Σ	versio syriaca
$Σ^a$	versio syriaca, anno 462
$Σ^b$	versio syriaca, saec. VI
$Σ^{arm}$	versio armenica, translata e versione syriaca
Λ	versio latina Rufini
Π	textus manuscriptorum graecorum
^{1}	prima manus
^{c}	correctio antiqua alterius manus
^{r}	correctio recentior

Eusebius Caesariensis, Praeparatio evangelica, ed. K. Mras/E. Des Places (GCS 43, Eusebius Werke 8), 2 vol., Berlin ²1982–1983.

A	Parisinus gr. 451, anno 914
B	Parisinus gr. 465, saec. XIII
D	Parisinus gr. 467, saec. XVI
G	Laurentianus pluteus 6,9, anno 1344
H	Marcianus gr. 343, saec. XI
I	Marcianus gr. 341, saec. XV
N	Neapolitanus II AA 16, saec. XV
O	Bononiensis 3643, saec. XIII
V	Vatopedinus 180, saec. XIV

ps. Eustathius Antiochenus, Commentarius in hexaemeron, ed. L. Allatius, Leiden 1629, 1–94 (= PG 18,708–793).

Excerpta Eusebiana → Eusebius Caesariensis, Chronica

Excerpta latina Barbari, in: Chronica Minora, ed. C. Frick, vol. 1, Leipzig 1892, 183–371.
      Parisinus lat. 4884, saec. VII/VIII

Excerptor anonymus in calce chronici Hieronymiani
  T   * Oxoniensis MertonCollege 315, saec. IX
  U   * Vaticanus Ottobonianus lat. 743, saec. XV
  V   * Vaticanus lat. 244, anno 1467

Florilegium anonymum
  P   * Parisinus gr. 1115, saec. XIII (cf. Alexakis 1996, inprimis p. 86 et p. 307).

Georgius Cedrenus, Compendium historiarum, ed. I. Bekker, vol. 1 (CSHB), Bonn 1838.
  R   Parisinus gr. 1713/1713A, saec. XII
  C   Coislinianus gr. 135, saec. XIII/XIV

Georgius Monachus, Chronicon, ed. C. de Boor/P. Wirth, 2 vol., Stuttgart ²1978.

Georgius Monachus [continuatus], Chronicon ab orbe condito ad annum p. Chr. n. 842 et a diversis scriptoribus ad a. 1143 continuatum, ed. E. de Muralt, Sanktpeterburg 1859 (= PG 110,41–1286).

Georgius Syncellus, Ecloga chronographica, ed. A. Mosshammer (BiTeu), Leipzig 1984.
  A   Parisinus gr. 1711, saec. XI
  A^c lectio codicis A post correctionem
  A^m scriptura marginis cod. A
       (eadem ratione Moss. in ceteris usus est)
  B   Parisinus gr. 1764, saec. XI
  E   Excerpta codicis Vatopedini 645, saec. XV
  C   Coislinianus gr. 133, saec. XII
  O   Oxoniensis Christ Church Wake 5, saec. IX
  T   Vaticanus gr. 154, saec. XII
  V   Vaticanus gr. 155, saec. IX/X
  x   consensus codicum C, O, T, V

M	Monacensis gr. 391, saec. XVI
P	Palatinus gr. 395, saec. XVI
Q	Vaticanus gr. 979, anno 1571
R	Vallicellianus 92, saec. XVI
S	Basiliensis 82, saec. XVI
Par. 1336	Parisinus gr. 1336 f. 143–160 excerpta chronographica variorum auctoribus (Syncelli et aliorum), saec. XI
z	archetypus familiae codicum M, P, Q, R, et S sed animaduertendum est R ex M et M, Q, S ex P descriptos esse
t	archetypus familiae z et antiquiorum codicum quos siglo x Moss. comprehendit

Gregorius Barhebraeus, Chronographia, trans. E. A. Wallis Budge, vol. 1, London 1932 (ed. anast. Amsterdam 1976).

Gregorius Barhebraeus, Commentarium in Evangelia ex Horreo Mysteriorum, ed. et trans. W. E. W. Carr, London 1925.

Gregorius Barhebraeus, Historiae dynastarum (arabice), ed. et trans. E. Pococke, Oxford 1663.

Hieronymus, Chronicon → Eusebius Caesariensis, Chronica

Hieronymus, Commentarii in Danielem, ed. F. Glorie (CChr.SL 75A), Turnhout 1964.

Hieronymus, Commentarii in Matthaeum, ed. D. Hurst (CChr.SL 77), Turnhout 1969.

R	Karlsruhe, Augiensis Pergamentum CCLIII, saec. VIII
G	Sangallensis 126, saec. VIII
O	Salispurgenis Sancti Petri a. VII. 2, saec. VIII
C	Karlsruhe, Augiensis Pergamentum CCLXI, saec. VIII/IX
K	Karlsruhe, Augiensis Pergamentum CXCIV, saec. IX
E	Parisinus lat. 9529, saec. IX
B	Bononiensis 42, saec. VIII/IX
P	Palatinus lat. 177, saec. VIII/IX

Hieronymus, De uiris illustribus, ed. A. Ceresa-Gastaldo, Firenze 1988.

α	Bambergensis B. IV. 21, saec. VI
β	Londinensis Cottonianus Calig. A.XV, saec. VIII
γ	Leidensis Vossianus lat. O. 69, saec. IX
δ	Herfordiensis Bibliothecae Cathedralis O. 3. 2, saec. X

Hieronymus, Epistula 70, in: Epistularum pars prima, ed. I. Hilberg (CSEL 54), Wien ²1996, 700–708.

K	Spinaliensis 68, saec. VIII
L	Coloniensis 35, saec. IX
M	Coloniensis 60, saec. IX/X
Φ	Guelferbytanus 4156, saec. IX/X
l	Vaticanus lat. 341, saec. X/XI
m	Vaticanus lat. 354, saec. XI
B	Berolinensis lat. 18, saec. XII

Ioannes Antiochenus, Fragmenta ex Historia chronica, ed. U. Roberto (TU 154), Berlin 2005.

ps. Ioannes Antiochenus, Anonymi excerpta chronographica, in: Ioannes Antiochenus, Fragmenta ex Historia chronica, ed. U. Roberto (TU 154), Berlin 2005, 556–575.

V	* Vaticanus gr. 96, saec. XII
D	* Parisinus gr. 1763, anno 1606

Ioannes Chrysostomus → Catena in Matthaeum

Ioannes Damascenus, Sacra parallela, in: Opera Omnia, ed. M. Lequien, vol. 2, Paris 1712, 274–730 (= PG 95,1033–1588; 96,9–442).

* Vaticanus gr. 1236, saec. XV
* Vaticanus Ottobonianus gr. 79, saec. XV

Ioannes Lydus, De magistratibus populi Romani (American Philosophical Society, Memoirs 149), ed. et trans. A. C. Bandy, Philadelphia 1983.

Ioannes Malalas, Chronographia, ed. J. Thurn (CFHB 35), Berlin 2000.

P	Parisinus suppl. 682, saec. X
V	Vatopedinus 290 (membrum discissum codicis praecedentis saec. X)
B	Parisinus gr. 1630, saec. XIV
Tusc.	Cryptoferratensis Z.a.XXII, saec. VI
O	Oxoniensis Baroccianus 182, saec. XII
A	Parisinus gr. 1336, saec. XI
EI	Constantinus VII Porphyrogenetus, Excerpta de insidiis, ed. C. de Boor, Berlin 1905
EV	Constantinus VII Porphyrogenetus, Excerpta de virtutibus et vitiis, ed. Th. Büttner-Wobst, 2 vol., Berlin 1906

Sl editiones Istrini translationis slavicae
Soph. Gos. Pulicn. Biblioteka, Sofijsk sobr. Nr. 1454

Ioannes Niciensis, The chronicle of John, bishop of Nikiu, translated from Zotenberg's Ethiopic text by R. H. Charles, Oxford 1916.

Ioannes Scythopolitanus (ps. Maximus Confessor), Scholia in Dionysii Areopagitae epistulas, in: Dionysius Areopagita, Opera, ed. B. Cordier, vol. 2, Antwerpen 1634, 61–184 (= PG 4,527–576).

Iordanes, De summa temporum vel origine actibusque gentis Romanorum, ed. Th. Mommsen (MGH AA 5,1), Berlin 1882.

Isidorus Hispalensis, Chronica maiora, in: Chronica minora saec. IV.V.VI.VII., vol. 2, ed. Th. Mommsen (MGH AA 11,2), Berlin 1894, 391–488.

Išodad Mervensis, Commentarius in vetus testamentum, ed. C. van den Eynde (CSCO 229/230, Syr. 96/97), 2 vol., Louvain 1962–1963.

Iulius Pollux (= ps. Polydeuces), Historia physica seu Chronicon, ed. I. Hardt, München 1792.

                  * Monacenis gr.181, saec. XVI (quem secutus est Hardt)
Bianconi   ed. J. B. Bianconi, Bologna 1795
                  Ambrosianus D 34 sup. (227), saec. XI (quem secutus est Bianconi)

ps. Iustinus, Cohortatio ad Graecos, ed. M. Marcovich (PTS 32), Berlin 1990.

Leo Grammaticus → Symeon Logothetes

Michael Psellus, Historia Syntomos, ed. W. J. Aerts (CFHB 30), Berlin 1990.

Michael Syrus, Descriptio temporum
        Syriace, ed. et trans. I. B. Chabot, Chronique de Michel le Syrien, 4 vol., Paris 1899–1910.
        Prooemium armeniace, recensio brevior, ed. [T. Sawalaneanc'], Jerusalem 1871; recensio longior, ed. [T. Sawalaneanc'], Jerusalem 1870 (vide Schmidt 1996, inprimis p. 299, n. 8 necnon p. 301, n. 13).

Moses Chorenensis, Historia Armeniorum, ed. M. Abełean/S. Yarout'iwnean, Tiflis 1913 (ed. anast. cum praefatione R. W. Thomson, Delmar NY 1981).

Nicephorus Callistus Xanthopulus, Excerpta ex historia ecclesiastica (vide de Boor 1888).
     * Oxoniensis Baroccianus 142, saec. XIV

Paschale Campanum anno 464–599. Epitoma temporum et indiculum pascae, in: Chronica minora saec. IV.V.VI.VII., vol. 1, ed. Th. Mommsen (MGH.AA 1), Berlin 1892, 744–750.
  V   * Vaticanus Reginae Suedicorum 2077, saec. VI
  W   Guelferbytanus Helmstadiensis 597, anno 820

Petrus Alexandrinus, Ekthesis chronon, ed. S. G. Samodurova, Vizantijskij Vremennik 18, 1961, 150–197.

Photius Patriarcha, Bibliotheca, ed. R. Henry, vol. 1–8 (CBy), Paris 1959–1977.
  A   Marcianus gr. 450, saec. X/XV
  M   Marcianus gr. 451, saec. XII/XV

Socrates Constantinopolitanus, Historia ecclesiastica, ed. G. Ch. Hansen (GCS N.F. 1), Berlin 1995.
  M   Laurentianus 70,7, saec. X
  F   Laurentianus 69,5, saec. XI
  A   Xeropotamu 226 (Athous 2559), saec. XIV
  T   Theodorus Lector in Marciano gr. 344, saec. XIII
  Cassiod. Cassiodorus, Historia tripartita

Sozomenus, Historia ecclesiastica, ed. J. Bidez/G. Ch. Hansen (GCS N.F. 4), Berlin ²1995.
  B   Oxoniensis Baroccianus 142, saec. XIV
  B^2 folia nova in B, saec. XV
  C   Alexandrinus 60, saec. XIII
  T   Theodorus Lector in Marciano gr. 344, saec. XIII
  Cassiod. Cassiodorus, Historia tripartita

Suidae lexicon, ed. A. Adler (Lexicographi Graeci 1), 5 vol., Leipzig 1928–1938.
  A^2 Parisinus gr. 2625 pars recentior, saec. XIV
  G   Parisinus gr. 2623, saec. XV
  I   Angelicanus 75, saec. XV
  F   Laurentianus 55,1, anno 1422
  V   Lugdunensis Vossianus 2 fol., saec. XII
  M   Marcianus 448, saec. XIII

Sulpicius Severus, Chronica, ed. G. de Senneville-Grave (SC 441), Paris 1999.

Symeon Logothetes, Chronicon
        V   * Vat. gr. 163, saec. XII
        Leo Grammaticus, Chronographia, ed. I. Bekker (CSHB), Bonn 1842.
        P   Parisinus gr. 1711, anno 1013
        Theodosius Melitenus, Chronographia, ed. Th. L. F. Tafel (Monumenta Saecularia Academiae Scientiarum Monacensis 3,1), München 1859.
                * Monacensis gr. 218, saec. XI
        vide etiam: Cedrenus et Iulius Pollux

ps. Symeon, Chronicon anonymum ineditum
                * Parisinus gr. 1712, f. 18–271, saec. XIII

Theodosius Melitenus → Symeon Logothetes

ABBREVIATIONES

1. Opera in apparatu adhibita

Aldhelmus Malmesbiriensis
    de metris   De metris et enigmatibus ac pedum regulis, ed. R. Ehwald, Aldhelmi opera (MGH.AA 15), Berlin 1919, 59–204.

Aelian.   Claudius Aelianus
    nat. animal.   De natura animalium, ed. A. F. Scholfield, 3 vol., London 1958–59.
    varia hist.   Varia Historia, ed. M. R. Dilts, Leipzig 1974.

Alex. Polyh.   Alexander Polyhistor, FGrHist 273

Anon. Matr.   Anonymus Matritensis, ed. A. Bauer, Leipzig 1909.

Anth. Graec.   Anthologia Graeca, ed. H. Beckby, 4 vol., München ²1965–68.

App.   Appianus
    bell. civ.   Bellum civile, ed. L. Mendelssohn/P. Viereck, Leipzig 1905.

Ar.   Aristophanes
    Ach.   Acharnenses, ed. V. Coulon, vol. 1, Paris 1952, 12–66.

Arist.   Aristoteles
    Pol.   Politica, ed. J. Aubonnet, 5 vol., Paris 1986–1991.

ps. Ath.   ps. Athanasius Alexandrinus
    fr.   Fragmenta varia, PG 28,1252–1257.
    pass.   Homilia in passionem et crucem domini, PG 28,185–250.

Aug.   Aurelius Augustinus
    retract.   Retractationes, ed. A. Mutzenbecher (CChr.SL 57), Turnhout 1984.

Aur. Vict.   Sextus Aurelius Victor
    Caes.   Liber de Caesaribus, ed. F. Pichlmayr, Leipzig 1911 (ed. anast. Stuttgart 1993).

Barhebr.   Gregorius Barhebraeus
    Chronographia, ed. et trans. E. A. Wallis Budge, vol. 1, London 1932.
    hist. dyn.   Historiae dynastarum (arabice), ed. et trans. E. Pococke, Oxford 1663.
    hor. myst.   Commentarium in Evangelia ex Horreo Mysteriorum, ed. et trans. W. E. W. Carr, London 1925.

Bas.   Basilius Caesariensis
    hex.   Homiliae in hexaemeron, ed. E. Amand de Mendieta/St. Y. Rudberg (GCS N.F. 2), Berlin 1997.

ps. Bas. ps. Basilius Caesariensis
    Enarratio in proph. Isaiam
        Enarratio in prophetam Isaiam, ed. P. Trevisan, 2 vol. (CPS.G 4–5), Torino 1939.

Callimachus
    fr. Fragmenta, ed. R. Pfeiffer, Oxford 1949.

Cassiod. Cassiodorus, Historica ecclesiastica tripartita, ed. R. Hanslik (CSEL 71), Wien 1952.

Cass. Dio Cassius Dio, Historiarum Romanorum quae supersunt, ed. U. Ph. Boissevain, 5 vol., Berlin 1895–1931.

Cat. Gen. Catena in Genesim, ed. F. Petit, 4 vol. (Traditio exegetica graeca 1–4), Louvain 1991–1996.

Cat. Mt. Catena in Matthaeum, ed. J. A. Cramer, in: Catenae graecorum patrum in Novum Testamentum, vol. 1, In evangelia S. Matthaei et S. Marci, Oxford 1844, 1–257, 449–496.

Cedr. Georgius Cedrenus, Compendium historiarum, ed. I. Bekker, vol. 1 (CSHB), Bonn 1838.

Chron. Epit. Chronicon Epitomon, ed. A. Pusch, Jena 1908.

Chron. Pasch. Chronicon Paschale, ed. L. Dindorf, vol. 1 (CSHB), Bonn 1832.

Chron. Synt. Chronographeion Syntomon, ed. A. Schoene, Eusebii chronicum libri duo, vol. 1, Berlin 1875, Appendix 4, 59–102.

Cic. Marcus Tullius Cicero
    div. De divinatione, ed. R. Giomini (BiTeu), Leipzig 1975, 1–148.

Clem. Alex. Clemens Alexandrinus
    paed. Paedagogus, ed. M. Marcovich/J. C. van Winden (SVigChr 61), Leiden 2002.
    strom. Stromata I–VI, ed. O. Stählin/L. Früchtel/U. Treu (GCS 52, Clemens Alexandrinus 2), Bonn ⁴1985.
        Stromata VII–VIII, ed. O. Stählin/L. Früchtel (GCS 17, Clemens Alexandrinus 3), Berlin ²1970.

Constantinus Manasses
    chron. Chronicon, ed. I. Bekker (CSHB 15), Bonn 1837.

Cyr. Cyrillus Alexandrinus
    c. Iul. Contra Iulianum imperatorem, PG 76,504–1064.
    Os.-Mal. Commentarius in XII prophetas minores, ed. P. E. Pusey, 2 vol., Oxford 1868 (ed. anast. Bruxelles 1965).
    fr. Mt. Commentarii in Matthaeum, fragmenta, ed. J. Reuss, Matthäus-Kommentare aus der griechischen Kirche (TU 61), Berlin 1957, 153–269.

Didym.	Didymus Caecus (Alexandrinus)
in Gen.	Commentarius in Genesim, ed. P. Nautin, 2 vol. (SC 233, 244), Paris 1976–1978.
Diod. Sic.	Diodorus Siculus, Bibliotheca historica, ed. F. Vogel et al., 6 vol., Leipzig 1888–1906.
Diog. Laert.	Diogenes Laertius, Vitae philosophorum, ed. H. S. Long, 2 vol., Oxford 1964–66.
Dionys. Sal.	Dionysius bar Salibi
comm. Ev.	Commentarii in Evangelia I,1, trans. J. Sedláček (CSCO 16, Syr. 16), Roma 1906.
Dion. Hal.	Dionysius Halicarnassensis, Antiquitates Romanae, ed. V. Fromentin (Collection des Universités de France, Série grecque 386), Paris 1998.
Ecl. Chron.	Ecloga Chronicarum, ed. J. A. Cramer, Anecdota graeca e codicibus manuscriptis Bibliothecae Regiae Parisiensis, vol. 2, Oxford 1839 (ed. anast. Hildesheim 1967), 231–242.
Ecl. Hist.	Ecloga Historiarum, ed. J. A. Cramer, Anecdota graeca e codicibus manuscriptis Bibliothecae Regiae Parisiensis, vol. 2, Oxford 1839 (ed. anast. Hildesheim 1967), 165–230.
Elias Nisib.	Elias Nisibenus, Opus chronologicum I, trans. E. W. Brooks (CSCO 63*, Syr. 23), Roma 1910.
Epiph.	Epiphanius Constantiensis
anc.	Ancoratus, ed. K. Holl (GCS 25, Epiphanius 1), Leipzig 1915, 1–149.
haer.	Panarion seu adversus lxxx haereses, 1–33, ed. K. Holl (GCS 25, Epiphanius 1), Leipzig 1915.
	Panarion seu adversus lxxx haereses, 34–64, ed. K. Holl/J. Dummer (GCS 31, Epiphanius 2), Berlin ²1980.
	Panarion seu adversus lxxx haereses, 65–80, ed. K. Holl/J. Dummer (GCS 37, Epiphanius 3), Berlin ²1985.
Eus.	Eusebius Caesariensis
chron.	Chronographia (prima pars chronicorum), versio armeniaca, trans. J. Karst (GCS 20, Eusebius Werke 5), Leipzig 1911, 1–143.
Exc. Eus.	Excerpta Eusebiana, ed. J. Cramer, Anecdota graeca e codicibus manuscriptis Bibliotheceae Regiae Parisiensis, vol. 2, Oxford 1839 (ed. anast. Hildesheim 1967), 115–163 (= ed. A. Schoene, Eusebi chronicorum libri duo, vol. 1, Berlin 1875, 1–286).
can.	Canones (secunda pars chronicorum) = can.[Hier] et can.[armen]
can.[Hier]	Canones, versio latina Hieronymi, ed. R. Helm (GCS 47, Eusebius Werke 7), Berlin ²1956 (= ³1984).

can.^{armen}	Canones, versio armeniaca, trans. J. Karst (GCS 20, Eusebius Werke 5), Leipzig 1911, 156–227.
reg. ser.^{armen}	Regum series secundum versionem armeniacam, trans. J. Karst (GCS 20, Eusebius Werke 5), Leipzig 1911, 145–155.
reg. ser.^{Hier}	Regum series secundum versionem latinam Hieronymi, ed. A. Schoene, Eusebi chronicorum libri duo, vol. 1, Berlin 1875, Appendix 1B, 25–40.
dem. ev.	Demonstratio evangelica, ed. I. Heikel (GCS 23, Eusebius Werke 6), Leipzig 1913.
ecl. proph.	Eclogae propheticae, ed. Th. Gaisford, Oxford 1842 (= PG 22,1021–1262).
fr. Lc.	Fragmenta in Lucam, PG 24,529–606.
h. e.	Historia ecclesiastica, ed. E. Schwartz (accedit versio latina Rufini, ed. Th. Mommsen), 3 vol. (GCS 9, Eusebius Werke 2), Leipzig 1903–1909 (= ²1999).
onomasticon	Onomasticon, ed. E. Klostermann (GCS 11,1, Eusebius Werke 3,1), Leipzig 1904, vide etiam textum syriacum, ed. S. Timm (TU 152), Berlin 2005.
praep. ev.	Praeparatio evangelica, ed. K. Mras/E. desPlaces, 2 vol. (GCS 43, Eusebius Werke 8), Berlin ²1982–1983.
reg. ser.	vide supra sub can.
v. C.	Vita Constantini, ed. F. Winkelmann (GCS Eusebius Werke 1,1), Berlin ²1991.
ps. Eust.	ps. Eustathius
in hex.	Commentarius in hexaemeron, ed. L. Allatius, Leiden 1629 (= PG 18,708–793).
Exc. Barb.	Excerpta latina Barbari, in: Chronica Minora, ed. C. Frick, vol. 1, Leipzig 1892, 183–371.
Exc. Eus.	vide Eus.
Exp. off.	Anonymi auctoris Expositio officiorum ecclesiae, Georgio Arbelensi vulgo adscripta, vol. 1, trans. R. H. Connolly (CSCO 71, Syr. 28), Paris 1913.
FGrHist	Fragmente der griechischen Historiker, ed. F. Jacoby, Berlin/Leipzig 1923ss.
FHG	Fragmenta historicorum Graecorum, ed. C. Mueller, 5 vol., Paris 1841–1873.
Georg. Mon.	Georgius Monachus, Chronicon, ed. C. de Boor/P. Wirth, 2 vol., Stuttgart ²1978.
cont.	Georgius Monachus continuatus, ed. E. de Muralt, Sanktpeterburg 1859 (= PG 110,41–1286).

Gregorius Barhebraeus, vide Barhebr.

ps. Gr. Nyss.		ps. Gregorius Nyssenus
	hom. 1 cr.	Homilia 1 de creatione hominis, ed. H. Hörner (Gregorii Nysseni opera. Supplementum), Leiden 1972, 2–40 (= PG 30,9–37; 44,257–277).
	imag.	Quid sit, ad imaginem dei, PG 44,1327–1346.
Hdt.		Herodotus, ed. H. B. Rosén, 2 vol., Leipzig 1987–1997.
Hier.		Hieronymus
	ep.	Epistulae, 4 vol., ed. I. Hilberg (CSEL 54–56), Wien ²1996.
	in Dan.	Commentarii in Danielem, ed. F. Glorie (CChr.SL 75A), Turnhout 1964.
	vir. ill.	De viris illustribus, ed. A. Ceresa-Gastaldo, Firenze 1988.
Hilarian.		Hilarianus
	curs. temp.	De cursu temporum, ed. C. Frick, Chronica Minora, vol. 1, Leipzig 1892, 155–174.
Hipp.		Hippolytus
	chron.	Chronicon, ed. A. Bauer/R. Helm (GCS 46, Hippolytus Werke 4), Berlin ²1955.
	Dan.	Commentarii in Danielem, ed. G. N. Bonwetsch/M. Richard (GCS N.F. 7), Berlin ²2000.
	haer.	Refutatio omnium haeresium, ed. M. Marcovich (PTS 25), Berlin 1986.
Hist. Dynast.		vide Barhebr.
Hom.		Homerus
	Il.	Ilias, ed. T. W. Allen, Oxford 1931.
	Od.	Odyssea, ed. P. von der Mühll (Editiones helveticae. Series graeca 4), Basel ³1962.
Iambl.		Iamblichus
	vit. Pythag.	De vita Pythagorica, ed. L. Deubner/U. Klein, Stuttgart ²1975.
Io. Anag.		Ioannes Anagnostes, Chronographia inedita in codice Atheniensi Bibl. Nat. 2492, f. 108ᵛ–116ʳ (secundum Mosshammer in editione Syncelli).
Io. Ant.		Ioannes Antiochenus, Fragmenta ex Historia chronica, ed. U. Roberto (TU 154), Berlin 2005.
ps. Io. Ant.		Anonymi excerpta chronographica, ed. U. Roberto, in: Ioannes Antiochenus (vide supra), 556–575.
Io. Chrys.		Ioannes Chrysostomus
	hom. in Gen.	Homiliae in Genesim, PG 53,21 – 54,580.
	hom. in Mt.	Homiliae in Matthaeum, PG 57,13 – 58,794.
	hom. in Io.	Homiliae in Ioannem, PG 59,23–482.
Io. Lyd.		Ioannes Lydus
	mens.	De mensibus, ed. R. Wünsch, Leipzig 1898.

Io. Mal.	Ioannes Malalas, Chronographia, ed. J. Thurn (CFHB 35), Berlin 2000.
Io. Nic.	Ioannes Niciensis, The chronicle of John, bishop of Nikiu, translated from Zotenberg's Ethiopic text by R. H. Charles, Oxford 1916.
Iordanes	Iordanes Gothus
Rom.	De summa temporum vel origine actibusque gentis Romanorum, ed. Th. Mommsen (MGH AA 5,1), Berlin 1882.
Ios.	Flavius Iosephus
ant. Iud.	Antiquitates Iudaicae, ed. B. Niese, 4 vol., Berlin 1885–1896.
bell. Iud.	Bellum Iudaicum, ed. O. Michel/O. Bauernfeind, 3 vol., Darmstadt 1959–1969.
c. Ap.	Contra Apionem, ed. Th. Reinach, Paris ²1972.
Iren.	Irenaeus Lugdunensis
haer.	Adversus haereses, ed. A. Rousseau/L. Doutreleau, 2 vol. (SC 211), Paris ²2002.
Išodad Merv.	Išodad Mervensis, Commentarius in vetus testamentum, ed. C. van den Eynde (CSCO 229, 230 = SS 96, 97), 2 vol., Louvain 1962–1963.

Itinerarium Burdigalense, ed. P. Geyer/O. Cuntz, in: Itineraria et alia geographica (CChr.SL 175), Turnhout 1965, 1–26.

Iub.	Liber Iubilaeorum
Iul. Afr.	Iulius Africanus
cest.	Cesti, ed. J.-R. Vieillefond (PIFF.H 20), Firenze 1970.
ep. Arist.	Epistula ad Aristidem, ed. W. Reichardt, Die Briefe des Sextus Julius Africanus an Aristides und Origenes (TU 34,3), Leipzig 1909, 53–62.
ep. Orig.	Epistula ad Originem, ed. W. Reichardt, Die Briefe des Sextus Julius Africanus an Aristides und Origenes (TU 34,3), Leipzig 1909, 78–80.
Iul. Pol.	Iulius Pollux (= ps. Polydeukes), Historia physica, ed. J. Hardt, München 1792.
Iust.	Iustinus Martyr
dial.	Dialogus cum Tryphone Iudaeo, ed. M. Marcovich (PTS 47), Berlin 1997.
ps. Iust.	ps. Iustinus
coh. Gr.	Cohortatio ad Graecos, ed. M. Marcovich (PTS 32), Berlin 1990.
Iustin.	M. Iuniani Iustini Epitoma historiarum Philippicarum Pompei Trogi, ed. O. Seel, Leipzig 1935 (ed. anast. 1985).
Leo Gr.	vide Sym. Log.

Liber Genealogus	Liber Genealogus anni CCCXVII, in: Chronica minora saec. IV.V.VI.VII., vol. 1, ed. Th. Mommsen (MGH.AA 9), Berlin 1892, 160–196.
Lucian.	Lucianus
verae hist.	Verae historiae, ed. M. D. Macleod, in: Luciani opera, vol. 1, Oxford 1972, 82–125.
Mich. Syr.	Michael Syrus, Chronicon, ed. et trans. J. B. Chabot, 4 vol., Paris 1899–1910.
Mich. Psellus	Michael Psellus
hist. synt.	Michaeli Pselli Historia Syntomos, ed. W. J. Aerts (CFHB 30), Berlin 1990.
Mos. Choren.	Moses Chorenensis, Historia Armeniorum, ed. M. Abełean/S. Yaroutʻiwnean, Tiflis 1913 (ed. anast. cum praefatione R. W. Thomson, New York 1981).
Niceph.	Nicephorus patriarcha Constantinopolitanus
chron. syn.	Chronicon breve, ed. C. de Boor, Nicephori archiepiscopi Constantinopolitani opuscula historica, Leipzig 1880, 79–135.
OrMan	Oratio Manassis
Or.	Origenes
Cels.	Contra Celsum, ed. H. Borret, 5 vol. (SC 132.136.147.150. 227), Paris 1967–76.
comm. in Gen.	Commentarii in Genesim (fragmenta), PG 12,45–145.
comm. in Mt.	Commentarii in Matthaeum, 2 vol., ed. E. Klostermann/E. Benz (GCS 38.40, Origenes Werke 10), Leipzig 1935–37.
sel. in ps.	Selecta in Psalmos (fragmenta), PG 12,1053–1686.
Oros.	Paulus Orosius
hist.	Historiae adversus paganos, ed. M.-P. Arnaud-Lindet, 3 vol., Paris 1990–1991.
Paus.	Pausanias, Graeciae descriptio, ed. M. Casevitz, vol. 1–4, Paris 1998–2002 (libri 1,2,7,8); ed. M. H. Rocha-Pereira, vol. 1–3, Leipzig 1989–1990.
Petr. Alex.	Petrus Alexandrinus, Ekthesis chronon, ed. S. G. Samodurova, Vizantijskij Vremennik 18, 1961, 150–197.
Phil. Sid.	Philippus Sidensis, Christiana historia, cf. Heyden 2006.
Philo	Philo Alexandrinus
migr. Abr.	De migratione Abrahami, ed. P. Wendland, in: Philonis Alexandrini opera, vol. 2, Berlin 1897, 268–314.
op.	De opificio mundi, ed. L. Cohn, in: Philonis Alexandrini opera, vol. 1, Berlin 1896, 1–60.
post.	De posteritate Caini, ed. P. Wendland, in: Philonis Alexandrini opera, vol. 2, Berlin 1897, 1–41.

Philostr.	L. Flavius Philostratus
gym.	De gymnastica, ed. J. Jüthner, Leipzig/Berlin 1909.
VA	Vita Apollonii, ed. J. Keyser, Flavii Philostrati opera, Leipzig 1870, 1–344.
Phleg. Trall.	Phlegon Trallianus, FGrHist 257
Photius	Photius Patriarcha, Bibliotheca, 8 vol., ed. R. Henry (CBy), Paris 1959–1977.
Pind.	Pindarus
olymp.	Carmina Olympiaca, ed. A. Puech (CUFr), Paris ^{4}1958.
Pl.	Plato
Ti.	Timaeus, ed. J. Burnet, in: Platonis Opera, vol. 4, Oxford 1902, p. III, 17a–92c St.
Plinius	C. Plinius Secundus
nat. hist.	Naturalis historia, ed. L. Ian/K. Mayhoff, 5 vol., Leipzig 1892–1909.
Plut.	Plutarchus
de Daed. Plat.	De Daedalis Plataeensibus, in: Moralia, vol. 7, ed. F. H. Sandbach (BiTeu), Leipzig 1967, 94–99.
Plat. quaest.	Platonicae quaestiones, ed. C. Hubert, in: Plutarchi Moralia, VI/I, Leipzig 1954, 113–142.
Numa	Vita Numae, ed. R. Flacelière et al., in: Plutarque, Vies, vol. 1 (CUFr), Paris ^{3}1993, 256–318.
Proc. G.	Procopius Gazaeus
in Gen.	Commentarius in Genesim usque ad cap. XVIII, ed. A. Mai (CAVC 6), Rom 1834 (= PG 87/1,21–512).
Prosp.	Prosper Tiro (Aquensis)
chron.	Epitoma chronicorum, in: Chronica minora saec. IV.V.VI. VII., vol. 1, ed. Th. Mommsen (MGH.AA 9), Berlin 1892, 385–485.
Quintil.	Marcus Fabius Quintilianus
instit. orat.	7 vol., ed. J. Cousin (CUFr), Paris 1975–80.
SIG^3	Sylloge Inscriptionum Graecarum, 4 vol., ed. G. Dittenberger, Leipzig ^{3}1915–1924.
Socr.	Socrates, Historia ecclesiastica, ed. G. Ch. Hansen (GCS N.F. 1), Berlin 1995.
Sol.	Gaius Iulius Solinus, Collectanea rerum memorabilium, ed. Th. Mommsen, Berlin ^{2}1895.
Soz.	Sozomenus, Historia ecclesiastica, ed. J. Bidez/G. Ch. Hansen (GCS N.F. 4), Berlin ^{2}1995.
Strabo	Strabo, Geographica, 5 vol., ed. S. Radt, Göttingen 2003–06.
Suda	Suidae lexicon, 5 vol., ed. A. Adler (Lexicographi Graeci 1), Leipzig 1928–1938.

Suet.		Caius Suetonius Tranquillus
	Nero	De vita Caesarum, lib. VI. Nero, ed. M. Ihm, Leipzig 1908, 222–259.
Sulp. Sev.		Sulpicius Severus
	chron.	Chronica, ed. G. de Senneville-Grave (SC 441), Paris 1999.
ps. Sym.		ps. Symeon, Anonymi opus ineditum in codice Parisino gr. 1712, f. 18–271; vide et Gelzer 2, 276–297; 357–384.
Sym. Log.		Symeon Logothetes
	Leo Gr.	Leo Grammaticus, Chronographia, ed. I. Bekker, Bonn 1842.
	Th. Mel.	Theodosius Melitenus, Chronographia, ed. Th. L. F. Tafel (Monumenta Saecularia Academiae Scientiarum Monacensis 3,1), München 1859.
	vide etiam Cedr., Iul. Pol.	
Sync.		Georgius Syncellus, Ecloga chronographica, ed. A. A. Mosshammer (BiTeu), Leipzig 1984.
Tac.		Cornelius Tacitus
	dial.	Dialogus de Oratoribus, ed. R. Mayer, Cambridge 2001.
Tat.		Tatianus
	orat.	Oratio ad Graecos, ed. M. Whittaker, Oxford 1982.
TGFr		Tragicorum graecorum fragmenta, ed. A. Nauck, Leipzig ²1889.
Th. Mel.		vide Sym. Log.
Theodorus Lector		
	epitome	Historia ecclesiastica, ed. G. C. Hansen (GCS N.F. 3), Berlin ²1995.
Theoph. Ant.		Theophilus Antiochenus
	Autol.	Ad Autolycum, ed. et trans. R. M. Grant, Oxford 1970.
Thuc.		Thucydides, Historiae, ed. H. S. Jones/J. E. Powell, 2 vol. (SCBO), Oxford 1942.
Vard.		Vardan Arawelc'i, Opus historicum, trans. R. W. Thomson, DOP 43, 1989, 125–226.
Zon.		Ioannes Zonaras, Epitome historiarum, lib. 1–12, 3 vol., ed. L. Dindorf, Leipzig 1868–1875.

2. Editores et emendatores

Adler/Tuffin	The Chronography of George Synkellos. A Byzantine Chronicle of Universal History from the Creation, translated with introduction and notes by W. Adler/P. Tuffin, Oxford 2002.
Chilm.	E. Chilmead, Johannis Malalae Historia chronica, Oxford 1691.

Cr.	J. A. Cramer
Di.	L. Dindorf
Gelzer	H. Gelzer, Sextus Iulius Africanus und die byzantinische Chronographie, 2 vol. et add., Leipzig 1880–1898 (ed. anast. 1 vol. New York 1967).
Gelzer^{ms}	Sextus Iulius Africanus, Chronographia, editio manuscripta, ed. H. Gelzer, apud Bibliothecam Universitatis Jenensis (Nachlass Heinrich Gelzer).
Goar	Georgii monachi quondam Syncelli chronographia et Nicephori patriarchae breviarium chronographicum, ed. I. Goar (Corpus byzantinae historiae 15), Roma 1652.
Goar^m	in margine editionis, Roma 1652.
Gutschmid	A. von Gutschmid, in: Eusebi chronicorum libri duo, ed. A. Schoene, vol. 1, Berlin 1875.
Kamb.	A. Kambylis, in: Ioannes Malalas, Chronographia, ed. J. Thurn (CFHB 35), Berlin 2000.
Moss.	Georgius Syncellus, Ecloga chronographica, ed. A. A. Mosshammer (BiTeu), Leipzig 1984.
Routh	Julius Africanus, Libri quinque de temporibus seu chronicon, ed. M. J. Routh, in: Reliquiae Sacrae, vol. 2, Oxford ²1846, 238–309, 357–509 (ed. anast. Hildesheim/New York 1974).
Rutgers	I. Rutgers, Sexti Julii Africani Olympiadōn anagraphē, Leiden 1862.
Scal.	J. J. Scaliger, Thesaurus Temporum, Leiden 1606 (²1658).
Vig.	F. Vigerius

3. Cetera

Abbreviationes bibliographicae secundum Schwertner 1992.

[ ]	litterae in codicibus deperditae coniectura suppletae
< >	litterae additae
{ }	litterae deletae
<	omisit/omiserunt
[...]	lacuna
+	addidit/addiderunt
~	transposuit/transposuerunt
≈	similiter etiam
→	vide etiam (in hac editione)
ad loc.	ad locum
AM	annus mundi
app.	apparatus/apparatu/apparatum

3. Cetera

cf.	confer
cod.	codex
codd.	codices
corr.	correxit/correxerunt
del.	delevit/deleverunt
des.	desinit/desinunt
ed.	edidit/editio
f.	folium/folia
fort.	fortasse
fr.	fragmentum
ibd.	ibidem
inc.	incipit/incipiunt
in ms.	in manuscripto
l.	linea/lineae
marg.	in margine
man. prim.	manus prima
Ol.	Olympias
p.	pagina/paginae
prop.	proposuit/proposuerunt
r	recto
sc.	scilicet
scrips.	scripsit/scripserunt
suppl.	supplevit/suppleverunt
v	verso

IULIUS AFRICANUS
CHRONOGRAPHIAE

T1

T1a Georgius Syncellus (434,11–21 Mosshammer)

Σευῆρος δὲ βασιλεύσας εὐθὺς τοὺς Περτίνακος φονευτὰς ἀνεῖλε.
Κλήμης ὁ Στρωματεὺς πρεσβύτερος Ἀλεξανδρείας ἄριστος διδάσκαλος ἐν τῇ κατὰ Χριστὸν φιλοσοφίᾳ συντάττων διέλαμπε.
Πάνταινος φιλόσοφος ἀπὸ στωικῶν ἐν τῷ θείῳ λόγῳ διέπρεπεν.
5 Ἀφρικανὸς ἱστορικὸς Χριστιανὸς ἤκμαζε.
Λεωνίδης Ὠριγένους πατὴρ ἐμαρτύρησε διωγμοῦ γεγονότος ἐν Ἀλεξανδρείᾳ.
Μουσιανὸς ἐκκλησιαστικὸς συγγραφεὺς ἐγνωρίζετο.
Ὠριγένης ὁ ματαιόφρων ἐν Ἀλεξανδρείᾳ κενοδοξῶν Ἑλληνικοῖς δόγμασιν ἐνεωτέριζε. τοῦτον Εὐσέβιος ὁ Παμφίλου ὡς ὁμόφρων ἐκθειάζων σὺν αὐτῷ λογισθείη.

1 cf. Cass. Dio 74,1,1s; Aur. Vict., Caes. 20,1   2–4 cf. Eus., can.[Hier] 211[a]   6 cf. Eus., can.[Hier] 212[c]
7 cf. Eus., can.[Hier] 212[g]   8 cf. Eus., can.[Hier] 212[l]

[At = x (= COTV) + z (= MPQRS)] 1 σευῆρος AxPMRS σεβῆρος QS[c]   4 πάνταινος P[c] πένταινος A πάντενος t | διέπρεπεν t διέπραττεν A   9 ὁμόφρων At ὁμόφρονα C[c]

T1b Georgius Cedrenus (441,17–21 Bekker), cf. etiam Symeon Logothetes (Leo Grammaticus [71,16–18 Bekker] = Theodosius Melitenus [54,18–20 Tafel])

Ἐπὶ τούτου (sc. Pertinax), ὥς φησιν Εὐσέβιος, ἦν ὁ Σύμμαχος, εἷς τῶν ἑρμηνευτῶν τῆς τῶν Ἑβραίων γραφῆς, Ἐβιωναῖος τὴν αἵρεσιν· ἀλλὰ καὶ Πορφύριος ὁ φιλόσοφος ὁ κατὰ Χριστιανῶν γράψας, καὶ
Ἀφρικανὸς ὁ χρονογράφος.
Ἐπὶ τούτου Λεωνίδης ὁ τοῦ κακόφρονος Ὠριγένους πατὴρ ἐμαρτύρησεν.

1–4 cf. Iul. Pol. 228,23 – 230,3; ps. Sym. f. 80[r]; Mich. Psellus, hist. synt. 34   1 cf. Eus., h.e. 6,16,4–17

1 Ἐπὶ Περτίνακος Sym. Log. | ὡς…Σύμμαχος < Sym. Log.   1s τῆς…γραφῆς < Sym. Log.   2 τὴν αἵρεσιν + ἦν Sym. Log. | ὁ < Sym. Log.   3 Ἀφρικανὸς + ὁ σοφώτατος Sym. Log. | ὁ χρονογράφος marg. Leo Gr. < Th. Mel.   4 Ἐπὶ…ἐμαρτύρησεν < Sym. Log.

Testimonia on the Life of Iulius Africanus

T1 *Africanus under Pertinax and Septimius Severus (AD 193)*[1]

T1a

After becoming emperor, Severus immediately executed the murderers of Pertinax.
Clement, the author of the *Stromata*, a presbyter of the Alexandrian church and a most outstanding teacher, was showing brilliance in his writing in Christian philosophy.
Pantaenus, a Stoic philosopher, was becoming eminent in divine doctrine.
The Christian historian Africanus was flourishing.
Leonides, the father of Origen, was martyred when persecution broke out in Alexandria.
Musianus, an ecclesiastical author, was becoming known.
Through the use of Greek doctrines, the feeble-minded Origen formulated in Alexandria meaningless and radical ideas. As one who had the same beliefs and treated Origen like a god, Eusebius, [pupil] of Pamphilus, should be classed with him.

T1b

Symmachus lived during his [sc. Pertinax'] reign, as Eusebius states. He was one of the translators of the Scripture of the Hebrews, a member of the Ebionite heresy. There was also Porphyry the philosopher, who wrote against Christians, and **Africanus the chronographer.**
During his reign, Leonides, the father of the evil-minded Origen, was martyred.

---

1 Although the two notices that follow have overlapping material (see the sentence immediately following the note about Africanus), they disagree about the *floruit* of Africanus and the death of Origen's father Leonides. The first one dates them to the reign of Septimius Severus, the second to his predecessor Pertinax.

T2

T2a Eusebius, Canones (Chronicon Paschale [499,5–7 Dindorf] ≈ armeniace [224 Karst] ≈ Hieronymus [214ʰ Helm])

Παλαιστίνης Νικόπολις, ἡ πρότερον Ἐμμαοῦς, ἐκτίσθη πόλις, πρεσβεύοντος ὑπὲρ αὐτῆς καὶ προϊσταμένου Ἰουλίου Ἀφρικανοῦ τοῦ τὰ χρονικὰ συγγραψαμένου.

1–3 Iordanes, Rom. 279 (36 Mommsen) Emmaus in Iudaea constructa et Nicopolim nominata. tunc et Africanus egregius temporum scriptor pro ipsa legationem suscepit ad principem. Mich. Syr. 6,7 (187,29s Chabot, unde etiam Barhebr. [59 Wallis-Budge]) De son temps (sc. Helagabalus) fut bâtie Nicopolis de Palestine, qui est Emmaus; le chroniquer Iulius Africanus présidait à sa construction.

1–3 cf. Soz., h. e. 5,21,5

T2b Hieronymus, De uiris illustribus 63 (166–168 Ceresa-Gastaldo)

Iulius Africanus, cuius quinque de temporibus extant uolumina, sub Imperatore Marco Aurelio Antonino, qui Macrino successerat, legationem pro instauratione urbis Emmaus suscepit, quae postea Nicopolis appellata est.
⁵Huius est epistula ad Origenem super quaestione Susannae: eo quod dicat in Hebraico hanc fabulam non haberi nec conuenire cum Hebraica etymologia ἀπὸ τοῦ πρίνου πρίσαι καὶ ἀπὸ τοῦ σχίνου σχίσαι, contra quem doctam epistulam scripsit Origenes. Extat eius ad Aristidem altera epistula, in qua super διαφωνίᾳ, quae uidetur esse in genealogia Saluatoris apud Matthaeum et Lucam plenissime disputat.

4–9 → T3; T11,8–11 **6s** → T12,3s

8 Mt 1,1–17; Lc 3,23–38

[αβγδ] **2** legationem] *legatione* γ *relegationem* δ **2s** instauratione] *instaurationem* αβ **3** Nicopolis] *Nocopolis* β **4** Huius < Gebhardt *cuius* γ | est] *extant epistulae* γ | quaestione] *questionem* βγ **6** doctam] *dogma* γ **7** eius < δ | altera epistula] *alteram epistulam* β **9** disputat] *disputauit* γ

T2 *Africanus' Mission on behalf of Nicopolis*

T2a

Nicopolis of Palestine, formerly Emmaus, was founded as a *polis*, when Iulius Africanus, the author of the *Chronica*, acted as ambassador on its behalf and presided over the undertaking.[1]

T2b

During the reign of the emperor Marcus Aurelius Antoninus, who was the successor to Macrinus, Iulius Africanus, whose five books on chronology are still in circulation, undertook an embassy on behalf of the restoration of the town of Emmaus, which was subsequently named Nicopolis.

There is a letter by him to Origen concerning the question of Susanna: namely, he asserts that this story is not found in the Hebrew, nor is the word-play in 'ἀπὸ τοῦ πρίνου πρίσαι καὶ ἀπὸ τοῦ σχίνου σχίσαι' consistent with Hebrew etymology. Against him, Origen wrote an erudite letter. There is in circulation another letter by him to Aristides, in which he discusses at very great length the disagreement that appears to exist in the genealogy of the Savior in Matthew and Luke.

---

[1] Although the three witnesses to Eusebius' report of Africanus' mission to Rome on behalf of Emmaus textually agree, they date the event differently. According to the Latin and the Armenian version of the chronicle, the embassy occurred during the reign of Elagabalus, in AD 221. The *Chronicon Paschale* dates the embassy two years later, during the reign of his successor Alexander Severus.

T2c Nicephorus Callistus Xanthopulus, Excerpta ex historia ecclesiastica (Eusebius Caesariensis et Philippus Sidensis?) in codice Barocciano 142, f. 212ʳ, l. 18–20 (169 de Boor)

Ἄριστα ὁ Ἀφρικανὸς δι᾽ ἐπιστολῆς πρὸς Ἀριστείδην γεγράφηκε περὶ τῆς δοκούσης διαφωνίας ἐν τῇ γενεαλογίᾳ ἕνεκεν τῶν γενεῶν παρὰ τοῖς εὐαγγελισταῖς Ματθαίῳ τε καὶ Λουκᾷ.
  Ἦν δὲ ὁ Ἀφρικανὸς ἀπὸ Ἐμμαοῦς τῆς κώμης τῆς ἐν Παλαιστίνῃ, ἐν ᾗ οἱ περὶ
5 Κλεόπαν ἐπορεύοντο, ἥ τε ὕστερον δίκαια πόλεως λαβοῦσα κατὰ πρεσβείαν Ἀφρικανοῦ Νικόπολις μετωνομάσθη.

1–3 Eus., h.e. 1,7,1   4–6 Phil. Sid., frg. 4.1 Heyden

T2d Georgius Syncellus (439,15–20 Mosshammer)

Ἐμμαοῦς ἡ ἐν Παλαιστίνῃ κώμη, περὶ ἧς φέρεται ἐν τοῖς ἱεροῖς εὐαγγελίοις, Νικόπολις ἐτιμήθη καλεῖσθαι ὑπὸ Ἀλεξάνδρου τοῦ αὐτοκράτορος, Ἀφρικανοῦ πρεσβευσαμένου τὰς ἱστορίας ἐν πενταβίβλῳ συγγραψαμένου.
  Ἀφρικανὸς τὴν ἐννεάβιβλον τῶν Κεστῶν ἐπιγεγραμμένην πραγματείαν ἰα-
5 τρικῶν καὶ φυσικῶν καὶ γεωργικῶν καὶ χυμευτικῶν περιέχουσαν δυνάμεις Ἀλεξάνδρῳ τούτῳ προσφωνεῖ.

4–6 → T3,1s; T11,1s; T12,2–4

1 cf. Lc 24,13

[At = x (= COTV) + z (= MPQRS)]   **1** τοῖς < t   **4** ἐννεάβιβλον Goar ἐννάβιβλον At | κεστῶν A καιστῶν t

T2c[2]

In a letter to Aristides, Africanus has written most admirably about the apparent disagreement in the genealogy of the generations recorded by the evangelists Matthew and Luke.

Africanus was from Emmaus, the village in Palestine to which those with Cleopas were traveling.[3] Through Africanus' embassy, it later received the legal standing of a city and was renamed Nicopolis.

T2d

Emmaus, the village in Palestine mentioned in the holy gospels, was honored with the name Nicopolis by the emperor Alexander, when Africanus, the author of a history in five books, acted as its ambassador.[4]

Africanus addressed to this Alexander a treatise in nine books entitled the *Cesti*, which deals with the properties of medical, natural, agricultural and alchemical agents.

---

2   The collection of excerpts from various historians found in codex Baroccianus 142 was probably compiled by the 14th cent. historian Nicephorus Callistus Xanthopulus; for discussion of this codex, see most recently Pouderon 1994. The first paragraph of the text originates in Eusebius' *Ecclesiastical History*. For Philip of Side as the possible source of the second part of the notice, see Heyden 2006,223–225.
3   On the problematic identification of Emmaus, see Gelzer 1,6f; Adler/Tuffin 2002,517, n. 7.
4   Cf. above T2a, which dates the mission of Africanus during either the reign of Elagabalus or of Alexander Severus. Syncellus' report that Alexander Severus was the emperor who conferred the name Nicopolis on the city does not state under which emperor the actual mission occurred.

T3

T3a Eusebius, Historia ecclesiastica 6,31,1–3 (584,21 – 586,13 Schwartz)

Ἐν τούτῳ (sc. sub Gordiano Augusto) καὶ Ἀφρικανὸς ὁ τῶν ἐπιγεγραμμένων Κεστῶν συγγραφεὺς ἐγνωρίζετο. ἐπιστολὴ τούτου Ὠριγένει γραφεῖσα φέρεται, ἀποροῦντος ὡς νόθου καὶ πεπλασμένης οὔσης τῆς ἐν τῷ Δανιὴλ κατὰ Σουσάνναν ἱστορίας· πρὸς ἣν Ὠριγένης ἀντιγράφει πληρέστατα.

5   Τοῦ δ' αὐτοῦ Ἀφρικανοῦ καὶ ἄλλα τὸν ἀριθμὸν πέντε Χρονογραφιῶν ἦλθεν εἰς ἡμᾶς ἐπ' ἀκριβὲς πεπονημένα σπουδάσματα· ἐν οἷς φησιν ἑαυτὸν πορείαν στείλασθαι ἐπὶ τὴν Ἀλεξάνδρειαν διὰ πολλὴν τοῦ Ἡρακλᾶ φήμην, ὃν ἐπὶ λόγοις φιλοσόφοις καὶ τοῖς ἄλλοις Ἑλλήνων μαθήμασιν εὖ μάλα διαπρέψαντα, τὴν ἐπισκοπὴν τῆς αὐτόθι ἐκκλησίας ἐγχειρισθῆναι ἐδηλώσαμεν.

10   Καὶ ἑτέρα δὲ τοῦ αὐτοῦ Ἀφρικανοῦ φέρεται ἐπιστολὴ πρὸς Ἀριστείδην, περὶ τῆς νομιζομένης διαφωνίας τῶν παρὰ Ματθαίῳ τε καὶ Λουκᾷ τοῦ Χριστοῦ γενεαλογιῶν· ἐν ᾗ σαφέστατα τὴν συμφωνίαν τῶν εὐαγγελιστῶν παρίστησιν ἐξ ἱστορίας εἰς αὐτὸν κατελθούσης, ἣν κατὰ καιρὸν ἐν τῷ πρώτῳ τῆς μετὰ χεῖρας ὑποθέσεως προλαβὼν ἐξεθέμην.

1   Sym. Log. (Leo Gr. [75,17s Bekker] = Th. Mel. [56,14 Tafel] = Iul. Pol. [236,3s Hardt] ≈ Georg. Mon. cont. [PG 110,545B] ≈ Zon. [12,17 Dindorf]) Ἐπὶ Μαξίμου καὶ Γορδιανοῦ (κατὰ τούτους τοὺς χρόνους Iul. Pol. τότε δὲ καὶ Zon.) Ἀφρικανὸς ὁ συγγραφεὺς ἐγνωρίζετο.   **1s**   → T2c,4–6; T11,1s; T12,1–3   **2–4** → T2b,3–6; T11,6–9; T12,3–5   **6s** = F98   **10–13** → T11,12–14; T2b,6s

1s Iul. Afr., cest.   **2–4** Iul. Afr., ep. Orig.; cf. Mich. Syr. 6,7   **8s** cf. Eus., h.e. 6,26; 6,29,4; 6,35; Eus., can.[Hier] 215[h] (sub anno 231 p. Chr. n.)   **10–12** Iul. Afr., ep. Arist.

[ATERBDMΣ[arm]Λ]   **1** καὶ] δὲ καὶ M   **1s** ὁ…ἐγνωρίζετο ATERBDM *war ein bekannter Schriftsteller* Σ[arm] *erat … vir inter scriptores ecclesiasticos nobilis* Λ   **3** ὡς TERBDM ὥς ἂν Α   **6** πεποιημένα M   **8** ἑλλήνων ATERM τῶν ἑλλήνων TER *Graecorum* Λ < Σ[arm]   **11** τοῦ E rasura BD τῶν ATE[1]RM   **12** σαφέστατα τὴν] σαφεστάτην M | συμφωνίαν τῶν εὐαγγελιστῶν BDM τῶν εὐαγγελιστῶν συμφωνίαν ATER

T3b Agapius Mabbugensis, Historia universalis (PO 7/4, 526,1s Vasiliev)

وفى هذا الوقت عرف ابرقيانوس صاحب التاريخان ووضع كتبًا كثيرة فى الازمنة وسير الملوك وغير ذلك

1 التواريخ] التاريخان marg. codd. (recte)

T3 *Africanus under Gordian III (AD 238–244)*

T3a

At this time [i.e. during the reign of Gordian Augustus], Africanus, the author of the work entitled the *Cesti*, was becoming known. A letter by him, written to Origen, is in circulation; there he raises the question as to whether the story of Susanna in the book of Daniel was a spurious fabrication. In his response to this letter, Origen writes at very great length.

From the same Africanus, there has also come to us the *Chronographiae*, five books in number, a project that was pursued with painstaking accuracy. In this work, he states that he himself set out on a journey to Alexandria because of the great fame of Heraclas. As we stated, Heraclas, very well-known for his discourses in philosophy and other branches of Greek learning, was entrusted with the oversight of the church there.

Another letter, from the same Africanus, is in circulation, written to Aristides. It concerns the supposed contradiction between the genealogies of Christ in Matthew and Luke. In this letter, he establishes most clearly the agreement between the evangelists on the basis of information that came down to him, which I have already set out at the appropriate place in the first book of the present work.

T3b

At this time [i.e. during the reign of Gordian Augustus], there was known Africanus, the author of chronicles, who composed many books on the times and the biographies of the kings and others.[1]

---

1   Note that the information in Agapius, which appears to be independent of that in Eusebius, confirms his dating of Africanus' *floruit*.

T4

T4a Symeon Logothetes (Leo Grammaticus [76,14 – 77,1 Bekker] = Theodosius Melitenus [56,25 – 57,2 Tafel]) ≈ Georgius Monachus continuatus (360,4–6 Muralt = PG 110, 552C)

Δέκιος ἐβασίλευσεν ἔτη δύο, […] ἐπὶ τούτου ἦν Κλήμης ὁ στρωματεὺς καὶ Ἀφρικανὸς καὶ Γρηγόριος ὁ θαυματουργός.

T4b Michael Psellus, Historia syntomos 44 (28,94s Aerts)

Ἐπὶ τούτου (sc. Decius) Κλήμης ὁ στρωματεὺς ἐγνωρίζετο Ἀφρικανός τε ὁ φιλόσοφος καὶ Ναυᾶτος πρεσβύτερος.

T5 Georgius Syncellus (445,27 – 446,7 Mosshammer)

Ὅς (sc. Eusebius) μείζω πάντων ἁγίων καὶ διδασκάλων αὐτὸν (sc. Origenem) ἀποδεῖξαι σπουδάζων ἐν ἕκτῳ τῆς ἐκκλησιαστικῆς αὐτοῦ ἱστορίας λόγῳ ὁμοφρονῶν αὐτῷ πολλοῖς ἐγκωμίοις αὐτὸν ἐνυβρίζει, μὴ εἰδὼς ἃ λέγει ἢ περὶ ὧν διαβεβαιοῦται. πάνυ γὰρ ὀλίγον περὶ τῶν κατὰ τούσδε τοὺς χρόνους ἱερῶν καὶ μακαρίων πατέρων ἐπιμνησθείς, Κλήμεντος λέγω τοῦ
5 στρωματέως, Ἱππολύτου τοῦ ἱερομάρτυρος, Ἀφρικανοῦ τοῦ ἱστορικοῦ, Διονυσίου τοῦ μεγάλου Ἀλεξανδρείας καὶ ἄλλων, μόνου τοῦ ματαιόφρονος Ὠριγένους τὴν ἐκ παιδὸς ἀναγωγὴν ἐκθειάζει μέχρι τῆς ἐν τῷ μαρτυρίῳ λειποτακτήσεως.

[At] 3 ὀλίγον A ὀλίγων t   4 λέγω τοῦ t λεγομένου A

T6 Excerptor anonymus in calce chronici Hieronymiani

Item secundum Africanum, qui de temporibus et historiis Hebraeorum et Graecorum et Persarum et Macedonum cum Alexandrinorum, itemque Romanorum V libris omnia complexus est.

Ab Adam usque ad cataclysmum Noe   anni $\overline{II}CCXLII$.
5 Item a cataclysmo usque ad Abraham et transmigrationem in terram Chanaan
                                                                 anni MXV.
Habitatio omnis generis Israhel in terra Chanaan et in terra Aegypti
                                                              anni CCCCXXX.
Moyses in heremo   anni XL.
10 Hiesus Naue et qui post ipsum presbyteri   anni LV.
Iudicum et sine principibus et pacis tempore   anni CCCCXC.
Sacerdotum et Iudicum   anni XC.
Regum Hebraeorum   anni CCCCXC.
Captiuitatis et destructionis Hierusalem   anni LXX.
15 Persarum regnum   anni CCXXX.
Macedonum principatus cum Alexandrinis et Ptolemaeis   anni CCC.
Et imperium Romanorum usque ad Saluatorem et resurrectionem eius
                                                                 anni LXXIIII.
In se omnes anni in tempus supra scriptum   anni $\overline{V}DCCXXVI$.
20 Exinde ad imperium Alexandri, hoc est Moricauiti, qui Antoninus cognominatus est,   anni CLXXXIIII.

6 → F16d,4s   7s → F34,68s (exod. – Ol. 1,1: 1020 anni); F51,4–6.10s (Abr. – Ol. 1,1: 1336 + 114 = 1450 anni)   9–14 → F34,61–67   14 → T76; T77a,5s   15 → F73,7.22s; F93,51   16 → F86,22; F89,53s; F93,52   17s → F89,56; F93,52s

[TUV] **1** Africanum] *Aphricanum* UV   **2** cum T *ac* U *et* V   **4** IICCXLII] *IICCLXII* Iul. Afr. (F16b,2 etc.)   **5** Item < UV | cataclysmo + *Noe* UV   **7** in¹ < V   **10** Hiesus T *Ihesus* UV   **15** regnum T *regum* UV   **16** CCC < UV   **17** Et < UV   **19** VDCCXXVI] *VDXXVI* Routh   **20** Moricauiti] *Marci Auiti* Routh | qui + *et* UV | Antoninus T *Antonius* UV

Testimonia on General Aspects of the *Chronographiae*

T6 *Chronological Overview*[1]

Also according to Africanus, who has in five books included everything pertaining to the chronology and history of the Hebrews, Greeks, Persians and Macedonians, together with the Alexandrians, as well as the Romans.

From Adam to the Flood of Noah:	2242 years.[2]
And from the Flood up to Abraham and the migration to the land of Canaan:	1015 years.
The sojourn of all the offspring of Israel in the land of Canaan and the land of Egypt:	430 years.
Moses in the wilderness:	40 years.
Joshua son of Nun and the elders succeeding him:	55 years.
For the judges and period without rulers and the time of peace:	490 years.
For the priests and judges:	90 years.
For the kings of the Hebrews:	490 years.
For the captivity and destruction of Jerusalem:	70 years.
The kingdom of the Persians:	230 years.
The dominion of the Macedonians, together with the Alexandrians and Ptolemies:	300 years.
And the Roman empire up to the time of the Savior and his resurrection:	74 years.[3]
In sum all the years for the period of time recorded above:	5726 years.[4]
From that point to the principate of Alexander, that is Marcus Avitus, surnamed Antoninus [sc. Elagabalus]:	184 years.

1   Although this summary of Africanus' chronology appears in some manuscripts as an appendix to Jerome's version of Eusebius' *Canons,* it does not belong to the original work. Absent from the earliest witnesses to Jerome's version (O and S in Helm, 5th cent.), it is first attested in Codex Merton 315, Oxford (T, 9th cent.). Two of the several later witnesses to the text (U and V) have also been collated for the present edition. While it is conceivable that the passage, which is mostly an accurate representation of Africanus' chronology, originated in his chronicle (cf. Theoph. Ant., Autol. 3,28 and Jerome, both of whom added chronological summaries to their own works), it is safer to classify it as a later *testimonium* from a learned reader (in or before the 9th cent.). A better dating and understanding would require further analysis of the manuscript tradition of Jerome's chronicle (the best analysis so far is Fotheringham 1923,1–7). Much of the information in the text can be confirmed by other fragments (see the parallels in the app. and introduction, pp. XXVI f; "incorrect" numbers are printed in italics in the text).
2   Africanus reckoned 2262 years from Adam to the Flood (F16b,2). 2242 is Eusebius' chronology.
3   The number 74 represents the total years from 1 Augustus. Africanus counted 60 years from the end of the Ptolemaic dynasty (= 14 Augustus) to the Resurrection (F93,53f).
4   The total years add up to 5526. The addition of 20 years to the date of the Flood (l. 4) and the subtraction of the overlapping 14 years of Macedonian and Roman rule (ll. 17f) would produce the required 5532 years, see introduction, p. XXVII (and p. XIX, n. 29 for the confused data in ll. 20f).

T7

T7a Hieronymus, Epistula 70,4 (706,6 – 707,3 Hilberg)

Extant et Iulii Africani libri, qui temporum scripsit historias, et Theodori, qui postea Gregorius appellatus est, uiri apostolicorum signorum atque uirtutum […]: qui omnes in tantum philosophorum doctrinis atque sententiis suos referserunt libros, ut nescias, quid in illis primum admirari debeas, eruditionem saeculi an scien-
5 tiam scripturarum.

[KLMΦlmB] **1** Iulii] *Iuli* KB | Africani] *affricani* ΦB *affricā* L | temporum…qui < L | historias] *hystorias* m *historiam* K *ystoriam* B *storiam* Φ | Theodori] *teodori* ex *eodori* K *theodorii* Φ **3** referserunt] *referunt* Llm *refferunt* M ante correctionem manus secundae *resarciunt* ς **4** nescias quid] *nescis quod* Φ

T7b Hieronymus, Commentaria in Matheum (9,46–56 Hurst)

«Iacob autem genuit Ioseph.» hunc locum obicit nobis Iulianus Augustus dissonantiae euangelistarum, cur euangelista Matheus Ioseph filium dixerit Iacob, et Lucas filium eum appellauerit Heli, non intellegens consuetudinem scripturarum quod alter secundum naturam, alter secundum legem ei pater sit. scimus enim hoc per Moysen Deo iubente praeceptum ut, si frater aut propinquus
5 absque liberis mortuus fuerit, alius eius accipiat uxorem ad suscitandum semen fratris vel propinqui sui. super hoc et Africanus temporum scriptor et Eusebius Caesariensis in libris diaphonias euangeliorum plenius disputarunt.

6 → F90

1 Mt 1,16   **1–6** cf. Iul. Afr., ep. Arist. ≈ Eus., h.e. 1,7; Aug., retract. 2,7,2

[BPGOCKMELR] **1** obicit] *obiecitur* RG^(corr.) | Iulianus] *lucianus* C | Augustus] *agustus* OC | dissonantiae] *dissonantia* R *dissonantium* BP   **2** filium eum < C   **3** consuetudinem] *consuetudine* K secundum legem < C (lacuna)   **4** propinquus] *propinquos* OB^(corr.)   **7** diaphonias] διαφωνιας E *diafonias* OBP < K | disputarunt] *disputabunt* K

T7 *Jerome*

T7a

There are also in circulation the books of Iulius Africanus, who wrote historical works on chronology, and of Theodore, who was subsequently called Gregory, men endowed with the miracles and virtues of the apostles. … All of them interweave the teachings and sayings of the philosophers to such an extent in their books that you might be at a loss as to which to admire in them first, their secular learning or their knowledge of the Scriptures.

T7b

'Now Jacob begot Joseph.' With this passage Iulianus Augustus presents us with a disagreement of the evangelists: why did the evangelist Matthew state that Joseph was the son of Jacob, whereas Luke called him the son of Heli? He does not understand the scriptural usage, according to which one is his father according to nature, the other according to law. For we know that this has been ordained through Moses by the command of God: if a brother or relative dies childless, another is to take his wife in order to raise up offspring for his brother or relative. Concerning this, both Africanus the chronographer[1] and Eusebius of Caesarea have examined more fully the disagreements of the gospels in their books.

---

1   Although Africanus does treat the genealogies of Jesus in his chronicle (F90), Jerome's description of Africanus as *temporum scriptor* does not necessarily mean that he is referring here to his chronicle. The explanation of the gospel genealogies that he provides summarizes the portion of Africanus' *Epistle to Aristides* cited in the *Ecclesiastical History* of Eusebius.

T8

T8a Socrates, Historia ecclesiastica 2,34,10s (151,3–10 Hansen)

Οὕτω δὲ ἦν ὀλιγομαθὴς ὁ Ἀέτιος καὶ τῶν ἱερῶν γραμμάτων ἀμύητος, τὸ ἐριστικὸν δὲ κατωρθώκει μόνον, ὅπερ ἂν καὶ ἄγροικός τις ποιήσειεν, ὡς μηδὲ τοὺς ἀρχαίους τοὺς τὰ Χριστιανικὰ λόγια ἑρμηνεύσαντας ἀσκηθῆναι. πολλὰ γὰρ χαίρειν φράσας τοῖς περὶ Κλήμεντα καὶ Ἀφρικανὸν καὶ Ὠριγένην, ἀνδράσι πάσης φιλοσοφίας ἐπιστήμοσι, ἐπιστολάς συνεκάττυεν
5 πρός τε τὸν βασιλέα Κωνστάντιον καὶ πρὸς ἑτέρους τινάς, ἐρεσχελίας συμπλέκων καὶ σοφίσματα μελετῶν.

[MFATCassiod] **1** δὲ¹] δὴ Mʳ **2** ὡς μηδὲ] μήτε M¹FA | τὰ < T **3** γὰρ < MFA Cassiod. **3s** Ἀφρικανὸν] ἀφρικιανὸν A **4** ἀνδράσι...ἐπιστήμοσι] ἄνδρας ... ἐπιστήμονας MFA | φιλοσοφίας] σοφίας MFA *sapientiae* Cassiod. **5** τε < MFA | τινάς < M

T8b Sozomenus, Historia ecclesiastica 1,1,12 (8,23–31 Bidez/Hansen)

Ὡρμήθην δὲ τὰ μὲν πρῶτα ἀπ' ἀρχῆς ταύτην συγγράψαι τὴν πραγματείαν. λογισάμενος δὲ ὡς καὶ ἄλλοι ταύτης ἐπειράθησαν μέχρι τῶν κατ' αὐτοὺς χρόνων, Κλήμης τε καὶ Ἡγήσιππος, ἄνδρες σοφώτατοι, τῇ τῶν ἀποστόλων διαδοχῇ παρακολουθήσαντες, καὶ Ἀφρικανὸς ὁ συγγραφεὺς καὶ Εὐσέβιος ὁ ἐπίκλην Παμφίλου, ἀνὴρ τῶν θείων γραφῶν καὶ τῶν παρ' Ἕλλησι
5 ποιητῶν καὶ συγγραφέων πολυμαθέστατος ἵστωρ, ὅσα μὲν τῶν εἰς ἡμᾶς ἐλθόντων ταῖς ἐκκλησίαις συνέβη μετὰ τὴν εἰς οὐρανοὺς ἄνοδον τοῦ Χριστοῦ μέχρι τῆς Λικινίου καθαιρέσεως, ἐπιτεμόμενος ἐπραγματευσάμην ἐν βιβλίοις δύο.

5–7 cf. Theodorus Lector, epitome 1

[B² CTCassiod] **1** ὡς < T **3** διαδοχῇ T Cassiod. διδαχῇ B²C **4** ὁ] ὢν T **5** μὲν + οὖν B²C **6** οὐρανοὺς B² *caelos* Cassiod. οὐρανὸν CT

T9 Isidorus Hispalensis, Chronica maiora 1 (424,1–4 Mommsen)

Brevem temporum per generationes et regna primus ex nostris Iulius Africanus sub imperatore Marco Aurelio Antonino simplici historiae stilo elicuit. deinde Eusebius Caesariensis atque sanctae memoriae Hieronymus chronicorum canonum multiplicem ediderunt historiam regnis simul ac temporibus ordinatam, post hos alii atque alii.

T8 Church Historians in Constantinople

T8a

Aetius was a man of so little knowledge, so unfamiliar with the sacred Scriptures, and successful only in disputation—something that any boor could do—that he had not been carefully trained in those ancient writers who interpreted the Christian oracles. **For while he completely renounced Clement, Africanus and Origen, men knowledgeable in every branch of philosophy,** he would cobble together letters both to the emperor Constantius, and to some other persons, entwining them with idle argumentation and making displays of sophistry.

T8b

I was initially inclined to compose this treatise from the very beginning. **But after I considered that others had already undertaken this task up to their own times**—both Clement and Hegesippus, extremely wise men and closely following in the succession of the apostles, **and Africanus the historian,** and Eusebius surnamed [pupil] of Pamphilus, a learned man highly knowledgeable in the sacred Scriptures and the writings of the Greek poets and authors—I drew up an epitome in two books of all that we have received about events in the churches, after the ascension of Christ up to the overthrow of Licinius.

T9 Isidore of Seville

During the reign of the emperor Marcus Aurelius Antoninus,[1] Iulius Africanus was the first among us to establish a brief [chronology] arranged according to generations and kingdoms and using a simple historical style. Thereafter, Eusebius of Caesarea and Jerome of hallowed memory published the multifaceted history of the *Chronici Canones,* arranged both by kingdoms and in chronological order. After them were various others.

1   On the composition of the *Chronographiae* during the reign of Marcus Aurelius Antoninus (Elagabalus), see introduction, p. XVII.

T10 Ioannes Malalas, prooemium (3,4–11 Thurn)

Δίκαιον ἡγησάμην μετὰ τὸ ἀκρωτηριάσαι τινὰ ἐκ τῶν Ἑβραϊκῶν κεφαλαίων ὑπὸ Μωυσέως <καὶ τῶν> χρονογράφων Ἀφρικανοῦ καὶ Εὐσεβίου τοῦ Παμφίλου καὶ Παυσανίου καὶ Διδύμου καὶ Θεοφίλου καὶ Κλήμεντος καὶ Διοδώρου καὶ Δομνίνου καὶ Εὐσταθίου καὶ ἄλλων πολλῶν φιλοπόνων χρονογράφων καὶ ποιητῶν καὶ σοφῶν ἐκθέσαι σοι μετὰ πάσης ἀληθείας τὰ συμβάντα ἐν μέ-
5 ρει ἐν τοῖς χρόνοις τῶν βασιλέων ἕως τῶν συμβεβηκότων ἐν τοῖς ἐμοῖς χρόνοις ἐλθό<ν>των εἰς τὰς ἐμὰς ἀκοάς, λέγω δὴ ἀπὸ Ἀδὰμ ἕως τῆς βασιλείας Ζήνωνος καὶ τῶν ἑξῆς βασιλευσάντων.

1-4 Inscriptio cod. Parisini gr. 1630, f. 234ʳ (= B in app. infra) ex Historia chronica Ioannis Antiocheni (app. ad fr. 1 Ro.) *Ἀπὸ τῆς ἐκθέσεως Ἰωάννου Ἀντιοχέως τῆς περὶ χρόνων καὶ κτίσεως κόσμου πονηθείσης, ὥς φησιν, ἀπὸ βίβλων Μωσέως, Ἀφρικανοῦ, Εὐσεβίου, Παππίου καὶ Διδύμου καὶ ἑτέρων.*

[PB(abbrev.) S|EI] **1s** καὶ τῶν Kamb. < P   **2** Διδύμου BSl Σισινίου P   **3** Εὐσταθίου Sl Καὰθ P < B
4 καὶ σοφῶν post ἐκθέσεσι P transposuit Kamb. ἐκθέσαι σοι Kamb. ἐκθέσεσι P fort. ἐκθέσθαι Sl < B
5 ἐλθόντων Sl ἐλθότων P < B   **6** Ἀδὰμ ἕως P < BSl

T11 Photius, Bibliotheca 34,7a7-24 (1,19s Henry)

Ἀνεγνώσθη Ἀφρικανοῦ ἱστορικόν.
 Οὗτός ἐστιν ὁ καὶ τοὺς λεγομένους κεστοὺς ἐν λόγοις συντάξας ιδ΄.
 Ἔστι δὲ σύντομος μέν, ἀλλὰ μηδὲν τῶν ἀναγκαίων ἱστορηθῆναι παραλιμπάνων. ἄρχεται δὲ ἀπὸ τῆς Μωυσαϊκῆς κοσμογενείας καὶ κάτεισιν ἕως τῆς Χρι-
5 στοῦ παρουσίας. ἐπιτροχάδην δὲ διαλαμβάνει καὶ τὰ ἀπὸ Χριστοῦ μέχρι τῆς Μακρίνου τοῦ Ῥωμαίων βασιλέως βασιλείας, ὅτε αὐτῷ, ὥς φησι, καὶ ἥδε ἡ συγγραφὴ συνετελεῖτο, ἐτῶν οὖσα ‚εψκγ΄. τεύχη δὲ τὸ βιβλίον πέντε.
 Οὗτος καὶ πρὸς Ὠριγένην γράφει περὶ τοῦ κατὰ Σωσάνναν διηγήματος ὡς οὐκ εἴη αὐτῷ ἐν τοῖς Ἑβραϊκοῖς ἀνεγνωσμένον, καὶ ὡς οὐδ' ἀκόλουθον τῇ
10 ἑβραϊκῇ ἐτυμολογίᾳ οὔτε τὸ ἀπὸ τοῦ πρίνου πρῖσαι οὔτε τὸ ἀπὸ τοῦ σχίνου σχίσαι· ἃ καὶ ἐπιλαβόμενος Ὠριγένης ἀντέγραψε.
 Γράφει δὲ Ἀφρικανὸς καὶ πρὸς Ἀριστείδην, ἐν οἷς ἱκανῶς τὴν νομιζομένην διαφωνίαν παρὰ Ματθαίῳ καὶ Λουκᾷ περὶ τῆς τοῦ σωτῆρος ἡμῶν γενεαλογίας σύμφωνον ἔδειξεν.

2 → T2d,4–6; T3a,1s   **4s** → T6; T13a,3s; F14; T92,3s; F93,108–110   **5s** → T80a.b.d; F93,84s; T99
6s → F54d,9–11   **8–11** → T2b,4–7; T3a,2–4; T12,3s   **12–14** → T2b,7–9; T3a,10–14; F90

2 Iul. Afr., cest.   **8–11** Iul. Afr., ep. Orig.   **12–14** Iul. Afr., ep. Arist.

[AM] **2** ὁ καὶ M ὃ A   **6** φησι A φασι M   **7** τὸ βιβλίον A τοῦ βιβλίου M   **10** τοῦ σχίνου A σχίνου M
11 ἐπιλαβόμενος A ἐπιλυόμενος A²M

T10 *John Malalas*[1]

After abridging some material from the chapters of the Hebrew books composed by Moses <and the> chronographers Africanus, Eusebius, [pupil] of Pamphilus, Pausanias, Didymus, Theophilus, Clement, Diodorus, Domninus, Eustathius, and many other industrious chronographers, poets and sages, I have deemed it proper to set forth with all truthfulness a summary of events in the times of the emperors up to the events in my own time that have come to my attention, by which I mean from Adam up to the emperor Zeno and those who ruled in succession after him.

T11 *Photius*[2]

The history of Africanus was read.

He is the one who also composed in 14 volumes the work called the *Cesti*.

Although he is concise, he overlooks nothing in need of historical record. He begins with the Mosaic cosmogony and continues down to the *parousia* of Christ. He also gives a cursory account of events from Christ up to the reign of the Roman emperor Macrinus, at which date, as he tells us, the work concludes, consisting of 5723 years.[3] The book is comprised of five volumes.

He also wrote a letter to Origen concerning the story of Susanna, stating that it was not in the Hebrew books known to him, and that neither the word-play 'ἀπὸ τοῦ πρίνου πρῖσαι' nor 'ἀπὸ τοῦ σχίνου σχίσαι' is consistent with Hebrew etymology. Origen answered and refuted these objections.

Africanus also wrote a letter to Aristides, in which he ably demonstrated no supposed discrepancy in the genealogy of our Savior in Matthew and Luke.

---

1 On the problems of the transmission of this text, see Jeffreys 1990,251f; Roberto 2005a,XXIV, n. 25.
2 On the fragment, see Schamp 1987,301–306.
3 Cf. F54d,9f, which puts the year 5723 in the third year of the emperor Elagabalus. See introduction, pp. XVII and XXV f.

T12 Suda Ἀφρικανός A 4647,1-5 (1,433,30 – 434,3 Adler)

Ἀφρικανός, ὁ Σέκτος χρηματίσας, φιλόσοφος, Λίβυς, ὁ τοὺς Κεστοὺς γεγραφὼς ἐν βιβλίοις κδ΄. εἰσὶ δὲ οἱονεὶ φυσικά, ἔχοντα ἐκ λόγων τε καὶ ἐπαοιδῶν καὶ γραπτῶν τινων χαρακτήρων ἰάσεις τε καὶ ἀλλοίων ἐνεργειῶν. κατὰ τούτου ἔγραψεν Ὠριγένης ἔνστασιν ποιησάμενος περὶ τοῦ τῆς Σωσάννης βιβλίου, τοῦ
5 εἰς τὸν Δανιήλ.

1–3 → T2c,4–6 (sed libri 9); T3a,1s; T11,2 (sed libri 14)   3–5 → T2b,5s; T11,8–11; Suda Σωσάννα Σ 856 (4,408,8s Adler; id ipse lexicographus desumpsit ex Suda A 4647,3s) Σωσάννα· ὅτι κατὰ τοῦ Ἀφρικανοῦ Σέξτου ἔγραψεν Ὠριγένης, ἔνστασιν ποιησάμενος περὶ τοῦ τῆς Σωσάννης βιβλίου, τοῦ εἰς τὸν Δανιήλ.

1s cf. Suda Κεστός K 1428   1–3 Iul. Afr., cest.   3–5 cf. Iul. Afr., ep. Orig.

T13

T13a Michael Syrus, prooemium (2,4–15 Sawalaneancʿ 1871, cf. etiam 1870)

Բայց պարտ է նախ զնէզ զանուանս պատմագրացն ուսանի Հանդերձեալ եմք
ժողովել զնիւթ շինուածոյս մերոյ:
Աֆրիկանոս և Յեւս և Հերիպոս և Յովսեպոս Հրեայքն գրեցին մինչև ՚ի
գալուստն Քրիստոսի:
5 Եւսանոս կրճատոր Աղէքսանդրացի, գրեաց ՚ի Մզամեայ մինչև ՚ի
Կոստանդիանոս Թագաւորն:
Եւսեբի Պամփիլեայ, յորոց գրոց ժողովեաց զիւն և անուանեաց
Եկեղեցականս:

3s → T6; T11,4s; T92,3s; F93,108–110; Elenchus anonymus historiographorum (103 Nau) Combien d'écrivains écrivirent l'histoire ecclésiastique depuis Adam jusqu'au Christ: Africanos, Hégésippos, Josephos et Jude (Yhouda) qui écrivit sur les semaines de Daniel.

3   գրեցին + արդ. ՚ի յարմառոց անոնի մարդկութեանոս 1870   7   յորոց] ՚ի ասցանէ և յայլոց պատմագրաց 1870

T13b Michael Syrus 10,20 (4, 378,23–26 Chabot)

T12 *Suda*

Africanus, the one called Sectus,[1] a philosopher and Libyan, and the author of the *Cesti* in 24 books. It is a kind of Physica, containing cures from words, charms, written figures of some kind, and operations of various sorts. Origen wrote against him, taking an opposing position on the subject of the book of Susanna, which belongs to the book of Daniel.

T13 *Michael Syrus*

T13a[2]

But first it is necessary to give the names of those historians from whom we shall collect the material for our edifice.
Africanus and 'Yesov' and Hegesippus and Josephus, the Jews, wrote until the advent of Christ.[3]
Annianus, the Alexandrian monk, wrote from Adam to the emperor Constantine.
Eusebius [pupil] of Pamphilus composed a book from these, and he called it the *Ecclesiastical [History]*.

T13b

Even so [their] chronicles are not called *Ecclesiastical [Histories]*, but rather *Chronographies*, that is a description of times, like those that Josephus, Andronicus, Africanus, Annianus, Georg[ius] *rgty*',[4] John of Antioch, and finally Eusebius [pupil] of Pamphilus have produced.

---

1   Σέκτος in the main text, Σέξστος in the résumé Σ 856 (text in the third app.). Scholars mostly interpreted this as an equivalent of the Latin 'Sextus', hence the name 'Sextus Iulius Africanus', see introduction, p. XIII. However, the information given here is generally not very reliable. The following epithet 'Libyan' is probably just a faulty inference, based on the name 'Africanus'. For the 'philosopher', see above T4, n. 1.
2   The text of Michael's preface is preserved only in two Armenian translations (ed. by T. Sawalaneanc' 1870 and 1871, see Schmidt 1996, 299, n. 8 and 301, n. 13). The shorter version (1871, whose text is given here) is considered closer to the Syriac original. This section is part of the preface of the lost history of Dionysius of Tel-Maḥrē (Syrian Orthodox Patriarch AD 818–845).
3   It is not clear to which of the named authors the epithet 'Jews' applies. On Hegesippus' Jewish origins, see Eus., h.e. 4,22,8. The identity of Yesov is uncertain. Cf. the parallel list of ecclesiastical historians in the *Elenchus anonymus historiographorum* (in app.): "Africanus, Hegesippus, Josephus and Judas, who wrote on the weeks of Daniel." For the identity of Judas, see Eus., h.e. 6,7.
4   George of Raggath (?); this could be George Syncellus, see Palmer 1993,95, n. 230: he was from Palestine and we know of the existence of a place called Raggath/Rakkat.

F14

F14a Florilegium anonymum in codice Parisino gr. 1115, f. 224ᵛ–225ʳ

Ἀφρικανοῦ ἱστορίας·
Ἐν ἀρχῇ ἐποίησεν ὁ θεὸς τὸν οὐρανὸν καὶ τὴν γῆν, τουτέστι τὸ πᾶν κατ' ἰδέαν ἢ ἀπὸ μέρους τῶν ἄκρων, εἴ τι ἕτερον διὰ τούτων σημαίνεται.
α' πρώτη μὲν ἡμέρᾳ τὸ φῶς, ὃ ἐκάλεσεν ἡμέραν.
5 β' δευτέρᾳ δὲ στερέωμα πρὸς διάκρισιν ὕδατος, οὐρανὸν ἐπονομάσας.
γ' τρίτῃ δὲ ἦν γῆς φανέρωσις καὶ θαλάσσης σύνοδοι.
δ' τετάρτῃ φωστῆρες.
ε' πέμπτῃ ἐξ ὑδάτων ψυχαὶ νηκτῶν τε καὶ ἀερίων.
ϛ' ἕκτῃ τε ἐκ τῆς γῆς ζῷα. ἄνθρωπος κατ' εἰκόνα θεοῦ τὸ χοϊκὸν ἀπὸ γῆς
10 πλασθείς, καθ' ὁμοίωσιν δὲ ἐμψυχωμένος, ἢ ὅτι τὸ μὲν κατ' εἰκόνα προσφυές, τὸ δὲ καθ' ὁμοίωσιν προσδοκᾶται.

2-11 → T11,4s; T92,3s

2-8 cf. Gen 1,1–23   3 cf. Plato, Ti. 35C2–36A6   9-11 cf. Gen 1,26s; 2,7; I Cor 15,47; Clem. Alex., strom. 2,22,131,6; Clem. Alex., paed. 1,12,98,2s; Didym., in Gen. 1,26–28 (59,2–5 Nautin); ps. Gr. Nyss., imag. 1328BC; ps. Gr. Nyss., hom. 1 de creatione hominis 28,13–31,5

2 εἰδέαν cod.   3 εἴ] fort. ἢ vel ἢ εἰ   8 νηκτῶν Alexakis ψυκτῶν cod.   9 τε] τὲ cod., fort. τὰ (cf. Gen 1,25)   10 ἐμψυχώμενος cod.   10s προσφυές Staab προσδεὺς cod. προσδοὺς Alexakis

F14b Georgius Syncellus (3,1–18 Mosshammer)

Τὴν πρώτην ἡμέραν ὁ Ἀφρικανὸς νοητὴν λέγει διὰ τὸ ἀδιοργάνιστον εἶναι τέως τὸ πρωτόκτιστον φῶς καὶ κεχυμένον. ἐν τῷ πρωτοκτίστῳ νυχθημέρῳ, τῇ πρώτῃ τοῦ παρ' Ἑβραίοις πρώτου μηνὸς Νισάν, ὡς προδέδεικται, παρὰ δὲ Ῥωμαίοις κε' τοῦ Μαρτίου μηνός, καὶ παρ' Αἰγυπτίοις κθ' τοῦ Φαμενώθ, ἐν ἡμέρᾳ κυριακῇ, ἤτοι μιᾷ τῶν σαββάτων, ἐποίησεν ὁ θεὸς τὸν οὐρα-
5 νὸν καὶ τὴν γῆν, τὸ σκότος καὶ τὰ ὕδατα, πνεῦμα καὶ φῶς καὶ νυχθήμερον, ὁμοῦ ἔργα ἑπτά. ἐν τῷ

1-5 ps. Sym. f. 19ʳ = Cedr. (7,2–21 Bekker) …Ἡ πρώτη ἐστὶ τοῦ παρ' Ἑβραίοις λεγομένου Νισὰν τοῦ πρώτου μηνός, εἰκοστὴ δὲ πεμπτὴ τοῦ παρὰ Ῥωμαίοις Μαρτίου μηνός, παρὰ δὲ Αἰγυπτίοις ζ' Φαμενὼ τοῦ κθ' καλουμένου (< ps. Sym.) παρ' αὐτοῖς μηνός. … ὅτι ἐν αὐτῇ τῇ πρώτῃ ἡμέρᾳ, ἥτις ἦν κυριακή, ἤγουν τῇ μιᾷ τῶν σαββάτων, ἐποίησεν ὁ θεὸς τὸν οὐρανὸν καὶ τὴν γῆν, τὸ σκότος καὶ τὰ ὕδατα (τ.σ.κ.τ.υ. < Cedr.), πνεῦμα καὶ φῶς καὶ νυχθήμερον (+ καὶ ἐκ τοῦ συμβεβηκότος τὸ σκότος Cedr.), ὁμοῦ ἔργα ἑπτά. ὁ δὲ Ἀφρικανὸς τὴν πρώτην ἡμέραν νοητὴν λέγει διὰ τὸ ἀδιοργάνιστον (ἀδιάγνωστον Cedr.) εἶναι τέως τὸ πρωτόκτιστον φῶς καὶ (< ps. Sym.) κεχυμένον. **1-13 →** T11,4s

1s cf. Philo, op. 29–33; Bas., hex. 1,5   5-13 cf. Iub 2,2–23; Io. Anag. f. 109ʳ

[A] 1 ἀδιοργάνιστον A ps. Sym. ἀδιάγνωστον Cedr.   2 καὶ < ps. Sym. | κεχυμένον ps. Sym. κεχυμμένον A   3 Νισάν Di. νισσᾶν A   4 μιᾷ τῶν σαββάτων ps. Sym. μιᾶς σαββάτου A μιᾷ Σα Io. Anag.

Material from Book 1/2: From Adam to Moses

F14 *The Creation*[1]

F14a

From the history of Africanus:

In the beginning, God created the heaven and the earth, that is everything according to its form, or from a part of the extremes,[2] if something different is signified by this.
1. On the first day, [God created] the light, which he called 'Day.'
2. On the second, [God created] the firmament for the separation of the water, giving it the name 'Heaven.'
3. On the third, the appearance of land and the gathering together of the sea.
4. On the fourth, the luminaries.
5. On the fifth, from the waters, living creatures of things that swim and things of the air.
6. And on the sixth, animals from the earth. Man was created 'according to the image' of God, a thing of dust from the earth, but endowed with a soul 'according to his likeness'; or else that which 'according to his image' belongs to him by nature, whereas that which is 'according to his likeness' is awaited.[3]

F14b

The first day Africanus calls 'intelligible', because the first-created light was yet unformed and diffuse.[4] On the first-created full day, the first day of the first Hebrew month of Nisan, as has been shown above, the 25th of the Roman month of March, and the 29th of the Egyptian month of Phamenoth, on the Lord's day, that is on the first of the week, God created the heaven

---

1 F14a was originally published by Alexakis 1996,86, along with photographs of the relevant manuscript pages. For a new edition and analysis of the Platonic background of the fragment, see Staab 2006. Staab suggests that F14a is an epitome of what was in Africanus' chronicle a list and commentary on the works of creation. In his opinion, F14b, which made up part of this commentary, originally followed the word ἡμέραν in l. 4 of the preceding fragment.
2 For discussion of the meaning of the phrase ἀπὸ μέρους τῶν ἄκρων and its relationship to Plato, Ti. 35C2–36A6, see Staab 2006,75 (and 74f on τὸ πᾶν κατ' ἰδέαν).
3 Although Gen 1,26 states that God intended to create man "according to our image and likeness," the following verse from Genesis states only that he created man according to "the image of God." Africanus offers here two explanations as to why God did not actually create man "according his likeness".
4 Because the first-formed light was diffused throughout the atmosphere before the sun was created as a receptacle for it, Africanus calls the first day 'intelligible'. On the 'intelligible light (φῶς νοητόν)' of the first day of creation, cf. also Philo and Basil (see app.).

δευτέρῳ νυχθημέρῳ ἐγένετο τὸ στερέωμα, ἔργον αʹ. ἐν τῷ τρίτῳ νυχθημέρῳ ἐγένετο ἔργα δʹ, φανέρωσις γῆς καὶ ἀναξήρανσις, παράδεισος, δένδρα παντοῖα, βοτάναι καὶ σπέρματα. τῇ δʹ ἡμέρᾳ ἐποίησεν ὁ θεὸς τὸν ἥλιον καὶ τὴν σελήνην καὶ τοὺς ἀστέρας. τῇ εʹ ἡμέρᾳ ἐποίησεν ὁ θεὸς τὰ ἑρπετὰ καὶ τὰ νηκτὰ πάντα, κήτη καὶ ἰχθύας καὶ ὅσα ἐν τοῖς ὕδασι, ἔτι τε πετεινά, ὁμοῦ ἔργα γʹ. τῇ ςʹ ἡμέρᾳ
10 ἐποίησεν ὁ θεὸς τὰ τετράποδα καὶ τὰ ἑρπετὰ τῆς γῆς, τὰ θηρία καὶ τὸν ἄνθρωπον, ἔργα δʹ. ὁμοῦ τὰ πάντα ἔργα κβʹ ἰσάριθμα τοῖς κβʹ Ἑβραϊκοῖς γράμμασι καὶ ταῖς κβʹ Ἑβραϊκαῖς βίβλοις καὶ τοῖς ἀπὸ Ἀδὰμ ἕως Ἰακὼβ εἴκοσι δύο γενεαρχίαις, ὡς ἐν λεπτῇ φέρεται Γενέσει, ἣν καὶ Μωϋσέως εἶναί φασί τινες ἀποκάλυψιν. αὕτη τὰς οὐρανίους δυνάμεις τῇ πρώτῃ ἡμέρᾳ λέγει ἐκτίσθαι.

6-10 similiter etiam in ps. Sym. et Cedreno, nonnullis additis

7 παράδεισος Di. παράδεισσος A Io. Anag. παράδησος ps. Sym.

F15 Georgius Syncellus (17,28 – 18,10 Mosshammer)

Ἀφρικανοῦ περὶ τῆς τῶν Αἰγυπτίων καὶ Χαλδαίων μυθώδους χρονολογίας·

Αἰγύπτιοι μὲν οὖν ἐπὶ τὸ κομπωδέστερον χρόνων περιττὰς περιόδους καὶ μυριάδας ἐτῶν κατὰ θέσιν τινὰ τῶν παρ' αὐτοῖς ἀστρολογουμένων ἐξέθεντο, ἅς τινες τῶν ταῦτα ἀκριβοῦν δοξάντων συστέλλοντες σεληνιαίους εἶπον ἐνιαυ-
5 τούς, οὐδὲν <δὲ> ἔλαττον ἐπὶ τὸ μυθῶδες ἀπονενευκότες συμπίπτουσι ταῖς ὀκτὼ καὶ ἐννέα χιλιάσιν ἐτῶν, ἃς Αἰγυπτίων οἱ παρὰ Πλάτωνι ἱερεῖς εἰς Σόλωνα καταριθμοῦντες οὐκ ἀληθεύουσιν.

Καὶ μετ' ὀλίγα·

Τὰ γὰρ Φοινίκων τρισμύρια ἔτη ἢ τὸν τῶν Χαλδαίων λῆρον, τὸ τῶν μηʹ μυ-
10 ριάδων, τί δεῖ καὶ λέγειν; ἐκ τούτων γὰρ Ἰουδαῖοι τὸ ἀνέκαθεν γεγονότες ἀπὸ Ἀβραὰμ ἀρξάμενοι ἀτυφότερόν τε καὶ ἀνθρωπίνως μετὰ τοῦ ἀληθοῦς διὰ τοῦ Μωυσέως πνεύματος διδαχθέντες, ἔκ τε τῶν λοιπῶν Ἑβραϊκῶν ἱστοριῶν, ἀριθμὸν ἐτῶν πεντακισχιλίων πεντακοσίων εἰς τὴν ἐπιφάνειαν τοῦ σωτηρίου λόγου τὴν ἐπὶ τῆς μοναρχίας τῶν Καισάρων κηρυσσομένην παραδεδώκασιν.

2s → F43a,1-4; F43b,7-9 **12-14** → T92,3s; T93c,8s; Sym. Log. (Leo Gr. [57,8-12 Bekker] = Th. Mel. [46,31-34 Tafel]) ≈ Iul. Pol. [164,6-21 Hardt]) Τῷ δὲ ‚εφʹ ἔτει ἀπὸ κτίσεως κόσμου καὶ τεσσαρακοστῷ δευτέρῳ ἔτει Αὐγούστου ἐξῆλθε δόγμα παρ' αὐτοῦ ἀπογράφεσθαι πᾶσαν τὴν οἰκουμένην, ἐν ᾧ ἔτει καὶ ὁ κύριος ἡμῶν ἐγεννήθη, Ἡρώδου βασιλεύοντος τῆς Ἰουδαίας, ὃν ὁ Καῖσαρ Αὔγουστος προεχειρίσατο.

2-5 cf. Diod. Sic. 1,26,1-5; Io. Lyd., mens. 3,5; Io. Mal. 1,15; 2,1; Io. Ant. fr. 7.1-2 **5-7** cf. Plato, Ti. 23E **9s** cf. Cic., div. 1,19; Eus., chron. 4,8 – 6,12; Sync. 18,11-20; 40,26-31 **12-14** cf. Hipp., Dan. 4,23,3; Hipp., chron. 698

[A] **2** τὸ Scal. τῶν A | περιττὰς Scal. περὶ τὰς A **3** κατὰ θέσιν Scal. κατάθεσιν A **5** δὲ Gelzer[ms]

and the earth, the darkness and the waters, wind and light and a full day: altogether seven works.[5] On the second full day, the firmament came into being: one work. On the third full day, there were four works: the manifestation and drying of the land, Paradise, all kinds of trees, and plants and seeds. On the fourth day, God created the sun and the moon and the stars. On the fifth day, God created all reptiles and swimming things (sea monsters and fish and whatever is in the waters), as well as birds: altogether three works. On the sixth day, God created four-footed animals, land reptiles, wild beasts, and man: four works. Altogether there are 22 works, equal in number with the 22 letters of the Hebrew alphabet, and the 22 books of the Hebrew Bible, and the 22 generations of patriarchs from Adam up to Jacob, as it is reported in the *Little Genesis*, which some say is also a revelation of Moses.[6] This work says that the heavenly powers were created on the first day.

F15 *The Fabricated Chronology of the Egyptians and the Chaldeans*[7]

From Africanus, concerning the mythical chronology of the Egyptians and the Chaldaeans:

The Egyptians, then, in order to make something of an impression, have set forth outlandish chronological cycles and myriads of years according to some sort of system based on astronomical calculations made by them; which some of them, reputed for their accuracy in these matters, compress, saying that they are lunar years. But inclining no less than the others to the mythical, they manage to reconcile these years with the eight and nine thousand years that the Egyptians priests in Plato falsely enumerate to Solon.

And after some other words:

Of the 30,000 years of the Phoenicians or of the absurdity of the Chaldaeans, with their 480,000 years, why should one even speak?[8] For although it is from the Chaldaeans that the Jews as descendants of Abraham derive their origins, they have received through the spirit of Moses more modest and moderate teaching, together with the truth. And from their remaining Hebrew histories, they have handed down a period of 5500 years up to the advent of the Word of salvation that was announced during the sovereignty of the Caesars.

5 The description of the 22 works of creation that follows the excerpt from Africanus forms a single block of material and is thus cited in full. Syncellus' enumeration is based on Iub 2,2–23.
6 'Little Genesis' is a commonly used Greek title for the *Book of Jubilees.* In conformity with the text of the Hebrew Bible, Iub 2,23 counts 22 patriarchs from Adam to Jacob. This is also Africanus' numbering. Syncellus' own list of the patriarchs from Adam up to Jacob, which includes the second Kenan found in the Septuagint version of Genesis, comes to a total of 23.
7 Resemblances to the prooemium to the third book (F34,1–11) suggest that Africanus' discussion of the chronology of the Egyptians, Chaldaeans, Phoenicians and Hebrews may have served as a programmatic introduction either to book one of his chronicle or to the entire work.
8 This is the only reference to Chaldaean chronology in the surviving fragments of the *Chronographiae*. Africanus, who seems to have known the Babylonian historian Berossus (3rd cent. BC) in some form (F34,14), may have based the 480,000 years of Chaldean history on Berossus' *Babyloniaca;* but cf. Alexander Polyhistor's version of Berossus, which assigns 215,000 years to Babylonian history (in Eus., chron. 6,19f). The list of Chaldaean kings that follows this excerpt in Syncellus (18,11–20) does not originate in Africanus' chronicle, see Gelzer 1,208f and Wallraff 2006,48, n. 17.

F16

F16a Georgius Syncellus (91,23 – 92,4 Mosshammer)

Ἀφρικανοῦ·
Ἀδὰμ γενόμενος ἐτῶν σλ' γεννᾷ τὸν Σήθ· καὶ τούτοις ἐπιζήσας ἔτη ψ' ἀπέθανεν, ἤτοι δεύτερον θάνατον.
Σὴθ γενόμενος ἐτῶν σε' ἐγέννησε τὸν Ἐνώς· ἀπὸ Ἀδὰμ τοίνυν μέχρι γενέσεως
5 Ἐνὼς ἔτη τὰ σύμπαντα υλε'.
Ἐνὼς ὑπάρχων ἐτῶν ρϙ' γεννᾷ τὸν Καϊνᾶν.
Καϊνᾶν δὲ ἐτῶν ρο' γεννᾷ τὸν Μαλελεήλ.
Μαλελεὴλ δὲ ἐτῶν ρξε' γεννᾷ τὸν Ἰάρεδ.
Ἰάρεδ δὲ ἐτῶν ρξβ' γεννᾷ τὸν Ἐνώχ.
10 Ἐνὼχ δὲ ὑπάρχων ἐτῶν ρξε' γεννᾷ τὸν Μαθουσάλα· καὶ εὐαρεστήσας τῷ θεῷ ἐπιζήσας ἔτη σ' οὐχ εὑρίσκετο.
Μαθουσάλα γενόμενος ἐτῶν ρπζ' ἐγέννησε τὸν Λάμεχ.
Λάμεχ ὑπάρχων ἐτῶν ρπη' γεννᾷ τὸν Νῶε.

2–13   Sym. Log. (Leo Gr. [8,22 – 10,20 Bekker] = Th. Mel. [14,2 – 15,7 Tafel] = Iul. Pol. [58,2 – 60,18 Hardt])

Ὁ δὲ Ἀδὰμ γενόμενος ἐτῶν σλ' *ἐγέννησε* τὸν Σήθ· καὶ τούτοις ψ' (*ἑπτὰ* Th. Mel.) *ἐπιζήσας ἔτη θνήσκει* ...

Σὴθ *Ἀζουρὰν ἀγόμενος τὴν ἀδελφὴν* (*Ἀζουρὰν ... ἀδελφὴν* < Iul. Pol.), σε' *ὑπάρχων* (*γενόμενος* σε' Iul. Pol.) *ἐτῶν, ἐγέννησε τὸν Ἐνώς.* ...

Ἐνὼς *ἐγήματο Ἐμμὰν τὴν ἀδελφὴν αὐτοῦ* (< Th. Mel. | *ἐγήματο ... αὐτοῦ* < Iul. Pol.)· ρϙ' (sic codd.) *γενόμενος ἐτῶν* (+ *καὶ* Leo Gr. Th. Mel.) *γεννᾷ τὸν Καϊνᾶν.*

Καϊνᾶν ρο' *ἐτῶν ὑπάρχων ἐγέννησε τὸν Μαλελεήλ.*

Μαλελεὴλ *ἐτῶν* ρξε' (ξε' Th. Mel.) *γενόμενος ἐγέννησε τὸν Ἰάρεδ.*

Ἰάρεδ *γενόμενος* ρξβ' (σξβ' Leo Gr.) *ἐτῶν* (Ἰάρεδ ρξβ' *ἐτῶν γενόμενος* Iul. Pol.) *ἐγέννησε τὸν Ἐνώχ.*
...
Ἐνὼχ *γενόμενος* ρξε' *ἐτῶν ἐγέννησε τὸν Μαθουσάλαν* (Μαθουσάλα Th. Mel.), *καὶ* σ' *πρὸς τούτοις ἐπιβιώσας ἔτη,* ...

Μαθουσάλα ρπζ' (ρξε' Iul. Pol. *ἑκατὸν ὀγδοήκοντα* Leo Gr.) *ἐτῶν γενόμενος ἐγέννησε τὸν Λάμεχ.*

Λάμεχ *ἐτῶν* ρπη' *ὑπάρχων ἐγέννησε τὸν Νῶε.*

Νῶε *ἐτῶν* φ' *γενόμενος ἐγέννησε τὸν Σὴμ καὶ μετ' αὐτὸν* (+ *ἐγέννησε* Leo Gr.) *τὸν Χὰμ καὶ μετ' αὐτὸν τὸν Ἰάφεθ.*

6 → T16f   **12** → T16o; T16q,2–4; F22

2–13   cf. Gen 5,3–29; Hipp., chron. 23–32; Eus., chron. 38,7 – 39,21; 40,21 – 41,4 = Sync. 92,8–26; 92,30 – 93,14; 93,17–34; Chron. Pasch. 34,17–35,10; 36,10–16; Niceph., chron. syn. 81,7 – 83,2

[AB]   **4** σε' B σνε' A   **6** ρϙ' Sym. Log. Mich. Syr. (T16f) Goar^m Gelzer 1,52 (cf. Gen 5,9) ρϙε' AB
7s μαλελεὴλ B μαλελεὴλ A   **12** ρπζ' B ρπη' A

F16 *The Generations from Adam to Abraham*[1]

F16a

From Africanus:

Adam, when he was 230, begot Seth. And after living another 700 years, he died (that is a second death).

Seth, when he was 205, begot Enosh: from Adam, then, up to the birth of Enosh, there is a total of 435 years.

Enosh, being 190,[2] begot Kenan.

Kenan, at age 170, begot Mahalalel.

Mahalalel, at age 165, begot Jared.

Jared, at age 162, begot Enoch.

Enoch, being 165, begot Methuselah. As one pleasing to God, he lived another 200 years and was not found.

Methuselah, when he was 187,[3] begot Lamech.

Lamech, being 188, begot Noah.

---

1   The material that appears in the following cluster of texts consists mainly of lists of the names and dates of biblical patriarchs from Adam to Abraham, along with chronological information about significant events (e.g., the Flood and Abraham's entrance into Canaan). Because Africanus used a biblical text whose chronology sometimes departed from the version of the Greek Bible known to later chroniclers, much of the criticism found in later *testimonia* faults him for deviating from the chronology of the Septuagint (see T16e–q). It is possible that Syncellus' own version of Africanus' list of the biblical patriarchs represents only a chronological summary of an originally more developed exposition. Some of the more ample notices about the patriarchs found in the Logothete group may also have originated in the chronicle of Africanus. Only a few of these notices are attributed to him, however (e.g. F16d, F22); for discussion, see Wallraff 2006,56–58.

2   In the apparatus, Enoch's age according to the text of Sym. Log. (190, as in the Septuagint) is based on Leo Gr. and the Munich mss. of Th. Mel. and Iul. Pol. The printed editions of these two authors give his age as ρζ′ and ρη′ respectively.

3   Cf. the *textus receptus* of the Septuagint, which gives 167 years as Methuselah's age when he begot Methuselah. 187 is the number found in the Masoretic text and some Septuagint mss. (Wevers 1974 ad loc.). See further T16g, n. 2 and introduction, p. XXVII.

F16b Georgius Syncellus (94,15–17 Mosshammer)

Ἀφρικανοῦ·
Νῶε ἦν ἐτῶν χ', ὅτε ὁ κατακλυσμὸς ἐγένετο.
Γίνεται τοίνυν ἀπὸ Ἀδὰμ μέχρι Νῶε καὶ τοῦ κατακλυσμοῦ ἔτη ˏβσξβ'.

2s Sym. Log. (Leo Gr. [12,3–5 Bekker] = Th. Mel. [16,11s Tafel] = Iul. Pol. [64,18 – 66,1 Hardt])
Ἐγένετο (+ οὖν Iul. Pol.) ὁ κατακλυσμὸς τῷ χ' ἔτει τοῦ Νῶε. γίνονται (+ οὖν Iul. Pol.) ἀπὸ Ἀδὰμ μέχρι Νῶε καὶ (Νῶε καὶ < Iul. Pol.) τοῦ κατακλυσμοῦ ἔτη ˏβσμβ' (ˏβσμη' Th. Mel. + γενεαὶ ι' Iul. Pol.). **3** → F16d,4–6; T16g,1s; T16h,2–4; T16q,3; T22a; T45,9–12

2 cf. Gen 7,6   **2s** cf. Hipp., chron. 34s   **3** cf. Chron. Pasch. 403,13; 526,7; Epiph., haer. 1,173,16s (omnes 2262 anni); Eus., can.[Hier] 15,4s; 70[a]; 174,5; 250,23s; Eus., chron. 38,31–34 = Sync. 94,20–23; ps. Sym. f. 26[r] = Cedr. 27,21–23; Ecl. Hist. 170,17s; Anon. Matr. 2,12s; Cat. Gen. 699; 865 (2242 anni); Io. Mal. 1,4; Io. Ant. fr. 2,18s (2552 anni)

[AB]   **3** ἔτη ˏβσξβ' B ~ A

F16c Georgius Syncellus (97,4–15 Mosshammer)

Ἀφρικανοῦ·
Μετὰ δὲ τὸν κατακλυσμὸν Σὴμ ἐγέννησε τὸν Ἀρφαξάδ.
Ἀρφαξὰδ δὲ γενόμενος ἐτῶν ρλε' γεννᾷ τὸν Σαλά, ˏβτϛζ'.
Σαλὰ γενόμενος ἐτῶν ρλ' γεννᾷ τὸν Ἕβερ, ˏβφκζ'.
5 Ἕβερ γενόμενος ἐτῶν ρλδ' γεννᾷ τὸν Φαλέκ, ˏβχξα', οὕτως ἐπικληθέντα διὰ τὸ ἐν ἡμέραις αὐτοῦ μερισθῆναι τὴν γῆν.

2–6   Sym. Log. (Leo Gr. [12,6 – 14,12 Bekker] = Th. Mel. [16,13 – 17,31 Tafel] = Iul. Pol. [66,1 – 80,6 Hardt])
Ἐν δὲ τῷ δευτέρῳ ἔτει μετὰ τὸν κατακλυσμὸν Σὴμ γενόμενος ρ' (ρβ' Iul. Pol.) ἐτῶν ἐγέννησε τὸν Ἀρφαξάδ (Καϊνᾶν Leo Gr., + ἀφ' οὗ πρώτη βασιλεία Χαλδαίων Iul. Pol.).
Ἀρφαξὰδ (Καϊνᾶν Leo Gr.) δὲ (< Leo Gr.) γενόμενος ρλε' (ρλ' Leo Gr. ρλζ' Iul. Pol.) ἐτῶν ἐγέννησε τὸν Σάλα (Σάλαμ Leo Gr. Iul. Pol.). …
Σάλα (Σάλαμ Leo Gr. Iul. Pol.) γενόμενος ρλ' ἐτῶν ἐγέννησε τὸν Ἕβερ. …
Ἕβερ γενόμενος ρλδ' ἐτῶν ἐγέννησε τὸν Φαλέκ. ἐν ἀρχῇ τῶν ἡμερῶν Φαλὲκ (ἐν … Φαλὲκ < Iul. Pol.) οἱ τοῦ Νῶε υἱοὶ διχονοήσαντες τῆς γῆς εἰς ἑαυτοὺς ποιοῦνται τὴν διανέμησιν.
3s de secundo Cainan deficiente → T16i; T16k; T16l; T16m; T16n; T16o; T16q,1s; T45,13–15

2–6 cf. Hipp., chron. 36–41   **2–12** cf. Gen 11,10–26; Eus., chron. 41,33 – 42,28; 43,4–22; 43,29 – 44,13 = Sync. 97,20 – 98,13; 98,20 – 99,6; 99,12–30; Chron. Pasch. 43,3–13; 86,18 – 87,5; Niceph., chron. syn. 83,21–84,15   **5s** cf. Gen 10,25; Niceph., chron. syn. 84,5–7; Chron. Epit. 11,1–4; Exc. Barb. 191,13–15

F16b

From Africanus:

Noah was 600 years when the Flood occurred.
From Adam to Noah and the Flood, there are, therefore, 2262 years.

F16c

From Africanus:

After the Flood, Shem begot Arpachshad.
Arpachshad, when he was 135, begot Shelah,[1] in 2397.
Shelah, when he was 130, begot Eber, in 2527.
Eber, when he was 134, begot Peleg, in 2661; he received this name[2] because of the division of the earth during his life.

---

[1] At Gen 10,24; 11,13 (hence Lc 3,36), most manuscripts of the Septuagint mention a second, post-diluvian Kenan between Arpachshad and Shelah, see Wevers 1974 ad loc. Lacking in the Masoretic text and, according to Sync. (T16i), in some Septuagint manuscripts, this second Kenan is also missing in Africanus' and Eusebius' lists of the biblical patriarchs. For Syncellus' critique of their omission of the second Kenan, see T16i-o and Gelzer 1,89.

[2] According to Gen 10,25 ("To Eber were born two sons: the name of the one was Peleg, for in his days the earth was divided and his brother's name was Joktan"), the name Peleg derives from the verb פלג ("divide"), see also the following note.

T4 *Africanus under Decius (AD 249–251)*

T4a

Decius reigned for two years; … living during his rule were Clement, author of the *Stromata,* and Africanus and Gregory Thaumaturgus.

T4b

During his [Decius'] reign, Clement, author of the *Stromata*, was becoming known as well as Africanus the philosopher[1] and Navatus a presbyter.

T5 *Africanus as a Contemporary of Origen*

In the sixth book of his *Ecclesiastical History,* he [Eusebius] strives to prove that he [Origen] was greater than all the other saints and teachers. As one holding the same views that Origen did, he actually insults him with his lavish words of praise, since he knows neither whereof he speaks nor what he affirms. **For he makes only the briefest remarks about the holy and blessed fathers of the time, I mean Clement, author of the *Stromata*, and the holy martyr Hippolytus, and Africanus the historian, and Dionysius the Great of Alexandria, and others.** The conduct of only the feeble-minded Origen from his childhood up to his desertion in the face of martyrdom does he exalt to the status of divinity.

---

1 Psellus' description of Africanus as a 'philosopher' may have been inspired by his wide-ranging learning, especially apparent in the *Cesti*. Cf. T12, where the Suda's reference to Africanus the 'philosopher' precedes a summary of the contents of the *Cesti*.

Φαλὲκ ἐτῶν ρλ' ἐγέννησε τὸν Ῥαγαῦ, καὶ ἐπιζήσας ἔτη σθ' ἐτελεύτησεν.
Ἀπὸ Ἀδὰμ ἐπὶ τελευτὴν Φαλὲκ ἔτη ,γ, κατὰ δὲ Εὐσέβιον ,β϶π'
Ῥαγαῦ ἐτῶν ρλβ' γενόμενος ἐγέννησε τὸν Σερούχ.
10 Σεροὺχ ρλ' τὸν Ναχώρ.
Ναχὼρ οθ' τὸν Θάρα.
Θάρα ο' ἐτῶν ὢν τὸν Ἀβραὰμ καὶ Ναχὼρ καὶ Ἀρράν. ... (→ F16d,4)

7s Io. Mal. 2,10 (25,21-23 Thurn) *Ἐν τοῖς χρόνοις τούτοις ἐγένετο Φάλεκ, υἱὸς Ἔβερ, ἀνὴρ θεοσεβὴς καὶ σοφός, ζήσας ἔτη τλθ' (= ρλ' + σθ'!), περὶ οὗ Μωσῆς ὁ προφήτης συνεγράψατο. ἔστιν οὖν ἀπὸ Ἀδὰμ ἕως τοῦ Φάλεκ ἔτη ,γ κατὰ τὴν προφητείαν.*
7-12 Sym. Log. (Leo Gr. [14,4 – 19,10 Bekker] = Th. Mel. [20,13 – 21,7 Tafel] = Iul. Pol. [80,11 – 82,20 Hardt])
Φαλὲκ γενόμενος ρλ' ἐτῶν ἐγέννησε (γεννᾷ Iul. Pol.) τὸν Ῥαγαῦ, καὶ ἐπιβιώσας ἔτη σθ' ἐτελεύτησε.
Συνάγεται τὰ πάντα ἔτη ἀπὸ Ἀδὰμ ἐπὶ τὴν τοῦ Φαλὲκ τελευτὴν ἔτη ,γ. ὥστε εἰκότως ταύτης ἔτυχε τῆς ὀνομασίας ὁ Φαλέκ, μερὶς γὰρ ἑρμηνεύεται, ἑκατέρας προαναφωνῶν τὰς διαιρέσεις. τῆς τε γὰρ γῆς τὴν διακλήρωσιν οἱ τοῦ Νῶε παῖδες ἐπὶ τούτου ποιοῦνται, καὶ τοῦ ὑπονοουμένου τῶν ἑξακισχιλίων ἐτῶν χρόνου ἡ διαίρεσις ἐπὶ τῆς τελευτῆς τῶν ἡμέρων γίνεται τούτου, ἡ (ὁ Th. Mel.) μὲν ἐν ἀρχῇ, ἡ (ὁ Th. Mel.) δὲ ἐπὶ τῷ τέλει τῆς ζωῆς αὐτοῦ (καὶ ἐπιβιώσας ... αὐτοῦ < Iul. Pol.). ...
Ῥαγαῦ γενόμενος ρλβ' (ρλ' Th. Mel.) ἐτῶν ἐγέννησε τὸν Σερούχ. ...
Σεροὺχ γενόμενος ρλ' ἐτῶν ἐγέννησε τὸν Ναχώρ ...
Καὶ Ναχὼρ γενόμενος οθ' (ρλ' Leo Gr.) ἐτῶν ἐγέννησε τὸν Θάρα (Θάρρα Th. Mel. Leo Gr.). ...
Θάρα (Θάρρα Th. Mel. Leo Gr.) γενόμενος ἐτῶν ο' ἐγέννησεν ἐκ γυναικὸς Ἔδνας, θυγατρὸς Ἀβραὰμ πατραδέλφου αὐτοῦ (ἐκ ... αὐτοῦ < Iul. Pol.), τὸν Ἀβραάμ ... ἐγέννησε δὲ ἔτι ὁ Θάρα (Θάρρα Th. Mel. Leo Gr.) τὸν Ἀρρὰν (αραν Iul. Pol.) καὶ τὸν Ναχώρ.
8 → F94,1; ps. Sym. f. 26ʳ ≈ Cedr. (28,4–6 Bekker) *Ὅτι καὶ (< Cedr.) ὁ Φάλεκ πρὸ τοῦ πατρὸς αὐτοῦ Ἔβερ τελευτᾷ, συνάγεται δὲ τὰ πάντα ἔτη ἀπὸ τοῦ (< ps. Sym.) Ἀδὰμ ἐπὶ τὴν τοῦ Φάλεκ τελευτὴν ἔτη ,γ. ὥστε εἰκότως ταύτης ἔτυχε τῆς ὀνομασίας ὁ Φαλέκ, μερισμὸς γὰρ ἑρμενεύεται (ὥστε ... ἑρμενεύεται < Cedr.).*

7-12 cf. Hipp., chron. 616–619 **8** cf. Cat. Gen. 860,1; Proc. G., in Gen. 11 (PG 87/1,315C); Cedr. 22,4

7-9 [AB] **7** et **9** ῥαγαῦ B ῥαγὰμ A **10** σεροὺχ A σεροὺγ B **11** et **12** θάρα A θάρρα B

Peleg, at age 130, begot Reu, and after living another 209 years, he died.

From Adam up to the death of Peleg, there are 3000 years,[3] according to Eusebius 2980 years.

Reu, when he was 132, begot Serug.

Serug, at age 130, begot Nahor.

Nahor, at age 79, begot Terah.

Terah, being 70, begot Abraham, Nahor and Haran.

---

3 For Africanus, the name Peleg refers both to the division of the earth during his lifetime and the completion of the first half of universal history at the time of his death. Cf. Sym. Log. (in the app.): "The years from Adam to the death of Peleg come to a total of 3000. Fittingly, then, Peleg received this name, for it means 'division', anticipating each of the two divisions. The sons of Noah made the allotment of the earth during his time, and the division of the supposed period of 6000 years occurred at the end of his life; the one division was at the beginning, the other at the end of his life." Some of the material in the ample geographical excursus that follows may originate from Africanus.

F16d

Sync.[1]: Georgius Syncellus (112,16–21 Mosshammer)
Sync.[2]: ibd. (97,16–18 Mosshammer)

Ἀφρικανοῦ περὶ Ἀβραάμ·
Ἔνθεν ἄρχεται τῶν Ἑβραίων ἡ προσωνυμία. Ἑβραῖοι γὰρ οἱ περάται ἑρμηνεύονται, διαπεράσαντος Εὐφράτην Ἀβραάμ, καὶ οὐχ, ὥς οἴονταί τινες, ἀπὸ Ἕβερ τοῦ προειρημένου. συνάγεται τοίνυν εἰς τὴν ἐπίβασιν τῆς κατηγγελμένης
5 γῆς Ἀβραὰμ ἀπὸ μὲν τοῦ κατακλυσμοῦ καὶ Νῶε γενεῶν ι´ ἔτη ͵αιε´, ἀπὸ δὲ Ἀδὰμ γενεῶν κ´ ἔτη ͵γσοζ´.

test.: **1–6** Sync.[1] [AB] **4** inc. Sync.[2] [AB] (→ F16c) … καὶ Ἀρράν. συνάγεται τοίνυν …

2–4 ps. Sym. f. 30ᵛ = Cedr. (49,11–13 Bekker) *Διαπεράσας δὲ τὸν Εὐφράτην τὴν προσωνυμίαν ἔλαβεν· Ἑβραῖοι γὰρ περάται λέγονται. οἱ δὲ ἀπὸ Ἕβερ λέγουσιν αὐτοὺς καλεῖσθαι Ἑβραίους.* **4–6** Sym. Log. (Leo Gr. [20,18–20 Bekker] = Th. Mel. [22,1–3 Tafel]) … *ἀπὸ δὲ τοῦ διαμερισμοῦ τῆς γῆς ἔτη ͵χις´ (͵ας´ Leo Gr.), ἀπὸ δὲ τοῦ κατακλυσμοῦ ἔτη ͵αιε´, ἀπὸ δὲ Ἀδὰμ ἔτη ͵γσοζ´* **4–6** → F16b; T16g,2–4; T16o; T16p; T16q,2–4; T45,9–10.15–18 **5s** → T6,6; F51a,10s

2s cf. Philo, migr. Abr. 20; Or., comm. in Gen. PG 12,113,9s; Io. Anag. f. 115ᵛ **3s** cf. Gen 10,21; 14,13; Ios., ant. Iud. 1,146; Io. Mal. 1,5 (8,19 Thurn in apparatu); Exc. Barb. 205,24; Sym. Log. (Leo Gr. 13,4–7 = Th. Mel. 17,5–7 = Iul. Pol. 68,7–11) **4–6** cf. Eus., chron. 45,20–28 = Sync. 100,32 – 101,3 **5s** cf. Hipp., chron. 621; Io. Mal. 3,3; Io. Ant. fr. 18,8s; Iul. Pol. 86,9–11

5 δὲ < Sync.[2] **6** ͵γσοζ´ Sync.[2] Leo Gr. ͵γσζ´ Sync.[1]

T16e Georgius Syncellus (91,1–11 Mosshammer)

Οὕτως ἀποδεδειγμένου τοῦ χρόνου, καθ᾽ ὃν ὁ Ἕβερ τὸν Φαλὲκ ἐγέννησε ις´ ὄντα ἀπὸ Ἀδάμ, ἄξιον οἶμαι ἐκ παραλλήλου τῶν ἡμῖν ἐπιλογισθέντων ἐν δευτέρῳ κανονίῳ παραθέσθαι καὶ τὰ παρὰ τῷ Ἀφρικανῷ ἔτη ἕως τοῦδε χρόνου, καὶ ἀπὸ τοῦδε μέχρι Ἀβραάμ (καὶ γὰρ προγενέστερος ὁ ἀνὴρ ὑπάρχει τοῦ Εὐσεβίου ἔτε-
5 σί που), εἶθ᾽ οὕτω καὶ τὰ παρὰ Εὐσεβίου τριχῶς ἐκτεθέντα, ὡς ἐκεῖνός φησι, κατά τε τοὺς ο´ σοφοὺς ἑρμηνέας καὶ κατὰ τὸ παρ᾽ Ἑβραίοις καὶ ἔτι κατὰ τὸ παρὰ Σαμαρείταις ἀντίγραφον.

Οὕτω γὰρ ἐν πέντε κανονίοις κειμένων τῶν ἀπὸ Ἀδὰμ ἕως τοῦ Φαλὲκ καὶ ἀπὸ τοῦ Φαλὲκ ἕως Ἀβραὰμ ἐτῶν, εὐμαρῶς δειχθήσεται ἡ σύμφωνος τῇ τε Μω-
10 υσαϊκῇ καὶ εὐαγγελικῇ γραφῇ γενεαρχία τε καὶ χρονολογία.

[AB] **1** ις´ scripsimus δέκατον AB ιε´ Goar Gelzerᵐˢ **5** που + ρ´ Gelzerᵐˢ

F16d

From Africanus, concerning Abraham:

From this originates the appellation of the Hebrews. For 'Hebrews' interpreted means 'crossers',[1] from Abraham's crossing of the Euphrates, and not, as some believe, from the previously mentioned Eber. Therefore,[2] from the Flood and Noah up to Abraham's entrance into the promised land, there is a total of 1015 years in 10 generations, but from Adam there are 3277 years in 20 generations.

T16e[3]

Now that I have thus demonstrated the date at which Eber begot Peleg, the 16th descendant[4] from Adam, I think it fitting to juxtapose our calculations with Africanus' numbering of years up to this point, and from there up to Abraham. Africanus' version is in a second table (because after all he predates Eusebius by some years). And then in the same way I shall furnish as well Eusebius' numbering of years, set out in three tables and based, so he says, on the sages who translated the Septuagint, the textual version used by the Hebrews, in addition to the one used by the Samaritans.

Once the years have been arranged accordingly in five tables from Adam up to Peleg and from Peleg up to Abraham, the genealogy of the patriarchs and the chronology that coincides with the writing of Moses and the gospels will be readily evident.

---

1   The Septuagint translates "Abraham, the Hebrew (העברי)" (Gen 14,13) as Ἀβράμ τῷ περάτῃ ("Abraham the crosser," deriving from the verb עבר). For ancient discussion of the two opposing etymologies of the word "Hebrew," see Adler/Tuffin 2002,140, n. 4.
2   Syncellus quotes the following sentence twice with identical wording, although in both cases the preceding text is different. In F16c he probably gave an abridged list. In this particular case we can be sure that the original of Africanus had more information than the list (see n. 1 to F16a); it certainly contained the etymology of "Hebrews," although it is hard to reconstruct the precise structure of the text.
3   This passage precedes Syncellus' chronological tables of the biblical patriarchs up to Abraham, as calculated by Africanus, Eusebius and Syncellus himself.
4   The number '10' found in the manuscripts is corrupt. Syncellus counted 16 patriarchs from Adam to Peleg (cf. Sync. 90,22; 101,16 and T16i,4). Goar and Gelzer emend it to '15', which represents Africanus' numbering of the patriarchs.

T16f Michael Syrus 1,3 (4, 2a,17–20 Chabot)

ܐܘܠܐ ܐܢܐ ܡܢ ܐܝܟ ܐܦܪܝܩܢܘܣ ܐܘܣܒܝܘܣ ܕܚܫܒܘ ܕܡܢ ܩܝ ܥܣܪܝܢ ܐܠܦ̈
ܘܐܝܟ ܣܒܪܝܐ ܕܡܢ ܩ ܥܣܪܝܢ ܕ̄

→ F16a,10s

cf. Gen 5,9; Elias Nisib. 7,35 (Annianus?)

T16g Chronicon Paschale (36,17–21 Dindorf)

Ἐν τῷ ἑκατοστῷ ἔτει τοῦ Σήμ, ἑξακοσιοστῷ δὲ τοῦ Νῶε καὶ ‚βσξβ′ ἔτει γενέσεως κόσμου ἐγένετο ὁ κατακλυσμὸς ἐπὶ τῆς γῆς· τοσαῦτα δὲ μέχρι τὸν ἐνταῦθα
καὶ ὁ Ἀφρικανὸς συνήγαγεν, ἐπειδὴ καὶ τὰ ἀκριβῆ τῆς Γενέσεως βιβλία ρπζ′
φαίνει τοῦ Μαθουσάλα ἔτη, καὶ οὕτως αὐτὸν γεννῆσαι τὸν Λάμεχ.

1–4 → T16q; T45,6–18   1s → T22a; F16b,3s; T16h   2–4 → F16a,12; F16d,4–6; T16o; F22,2s; T22b

1s cf. Chron. Pasch. 403,13; 526,7

3 ἐπήγαγεν du Cange

T16h Georgius Syncellus (94,4–14 Mosshammer)

Ἀπὸ Ἀδὰμ ἕως τοῦ κατακλυσμοῦ ἔτη ‚βσμβ′. οὕτω δὲ καὶ Εὐσέβιος καὶ ὁ ἀληθὴς λόγος καὶ τὰ πλεῖστα τῶν Μωυσαϊκῶν ἀντιγράφων περιέχουσι κατὰ τὴν τῶν ο′ ἔκδοσιν. Ὁ μέντοι Ἀφρικανὸς
‚βσξβ′ ἐπελογίσατο ἔκ τινων σπανίων ἀντιγράφων οὕτω περιεχόντων, οἷς οὐ
χρὴ πείθεσθαι. Μέχρι τοίνυν τοῦ κατακλυσμοῦ καθὼς πρόκειται διαφωνοῦσι τὰ Ἑβραϊκὰ ἀντί-
5 γραφα πρὸς τὸ Σαμαρειτῶν ἀρχαιότατον καὶ τοῖς χαρακτῆρσι διαλλάττον, ὃ καὶ ἀληθὲς εἶναι καὶ
πρῶτον Ἑβραῖοι καθομολογοῦσιν, ἔτεσι τμθ′, πρὸς δὲ τὴν τῶν ο′ ἔκδοσιν τὸ μὲν Ἑβραϊκὸν ἔτεσιν
φπϛ′, τὸ δὲ Σαμαρειτῶν ꜙλε′. Ἀφρικανὸς δὲ πρὸς Εὐσέβιον ἀπὸ Ἀδὰμ ἕως τοῦ κατακλυσμοῦ διαφωνεῖ ἔτη κ′.

1–8 → T16g; T16p; T22a; T45,13–15   2–4 → F16b,3s; T16g,1s   7s → T16o; T16q,2–4; T22b

1s   cf. Hipp., chron. 35; Eus., chron. 45,20–28 = Sync. 100,32 – 101,3; ps. Sym. f. 26ʳ = Cedr. 27,21;
Eus., can.^Hier 15,4s; 70,15s; 174,5; 250,23   4–7 cf. Eus., chron. 39,28; 41,10

[AB]   7 ꜙλε′ A ꜙλ′ B 935 Eus., chron. 36,3

T16f

But Enosh according to the chroniclers Annianus and Africanus fathered a child at the age of 190, according to the Syrians 90 years.[1]

T16g[2]

In the 100th year of Shem, the 60th year of Noah, and the 2262nd year from the creation of the universe, the Flood came upon the earth. This is the sum of years that Africanus also calculated up to this time, for the accurate copies of the book of Genesis make it clear that Methuselah was 187 years old when he begot Lamech.

T16h

From Adam to the Flood, there are 2242 years. This is what Eusebius and the true tradition and the large majority of the manuscripts of Mosaic writings report, in accordance with the Septuagint version. Notwithstanding, Africanus reckoned 2262 years, on the basis of a few copies that report this tradition. But no credence should be put in these copies. Up to the Flood, therefore, as the preceding has shown, the copies of Hebrew Scriptures disagree by 349 years with the most ancient Samaritan text, which is composed in a different Hebrew script, and which the Hebrews acknowledge is both true and original. Compared with the Septuagint version, the Hebrew version differs by 586 years; the Samaritan version differs from it by 935 years. From Adam to the Flood, Africanus differs from Eusebius by 20 years.

---

1   The divergence reflects the variations in the biblical versions. Unlike Annianus and Africanus, both of whom followed the chronology of the Septuagint, the Syriac text reflects a variant chronology also found in the Masoretic text and the Samaritan Pentateuch.
2   In the following two texts, Syncellus criticizes Africanus' treatment of two related issues: the age of Methuselah when he begot Lamech and the date of the Flood. Because chronographers established biblical chronology by adding up the ages of the patriarchs when each of them fathered a successor, Africanus' addition of 20 years to the age of Methuselah (187 instead of 167, see above F16a,12) put the date of the Flood in AM 2262 instead of 2242. 187 is the age of Methuselah found in the Hebrew text, and, as Syncellus notes, in some manuscripts of the Septuagint (see Wevers 1974 ad loc.; Adler/Tuffin 2002,27, n. 3). Although this reading is already reflected in the biblical chronology of Demetrius the Jewish chronographer (2nd cent. BC), it is probably a correction of 167, designed to avoid a discrepancy created by the latter number. If Methuselah was only 167 years when he begot Lamech, then his death in 2256 would have been 14 years after the Flood in AM 2242, see below T22a.

T16i   Georgius Syncellus (132,15–22 Mosshammer)

Τινὰ δὲ τῶν ἀντιγράφων, ὡς καὶ Εὐσεβίου, υγ′ ἔχουσι τοῦ Ἀρφαξὰδ μετὰ τὸ γεννῆσαι αὐτὸν τὸν Σάλα, οἷς οὐδ᾽ ὅλως ἑπόμεθα, πάντη τῆς ἀληθείας τῶν χρόνων καὶ τῶν γενεῶν διημαρτηκόσιν. ἀντὶ γὰρ τοῦ Καϊνᾶν τὸν Σάλα φασὶ γεννηθῆναι τῷ Ἀρφαξὰδ Ἀφρικανός τε καὶ Εὐσέβιος, καὶ τὴν ιδ′ γενεὰν τοῦ Σάλα ιγ′ τάττουσι, μνήμην τοῦ δευτέρου
5   Καϊνᾶν οὐδ᾽ ὅλως ποιησάμενοι, ὃν αἱ πανταχοῦ τῆς Γενέσεως ἱεραὶ βίβλοι καὶ τὸ κατὰ Λουκᾶν Εὐαγγέλιον τοῦ Ἀρφαξὰδ υἱὸν ἐκδεδώκασι καὶ ιγ′ ἀπὸ Ἀδάμ, πατέρα δὲ τοῦ Σάλα ιδ′ ἀπὸ Ἀδὰμ ὄντος.

3–7 → F16c,3s; T16k; T16l; T16m; T16n; T16o; T16q; T45,12–17

1 cf. Eus., chron. 42,1s = Sync. 97,22s   2 cf. Hipp., chron. 38s   3–5 cf. Eus., chron. 42,1; 43,6; 43,31 = Sync. 97,22; 98,22; 99,14; Elias Nisib. 8,7–16 (Annianus?); Niceph., chron. syn. 83,25–28   5s cf. Lc 3,36

[AB]   1 αὐτὸν τὸν Moss. αὐτὸν A τὸν B   2 διημαρτηκόσιν B διημαρτηκέναι A   3 τῷ B τὸν A

T16k Georgius Syncellus (89,28 – 90,7 Mosshammer)

Τῷ ͵βφ′ ἔτει Καϊνᾶν ἔλαβε γυναῖκα καὶ τῷ ͵βφε′ ἐγέννησε τὸν Σαλά. τοῦτον δὲ τὸν Καϊνᾶν ὁ Εὐσέβιος οὐκ ἐστοιχείωσε, τῷ Ἑβραϊκῷ ἀντιγράφῳ κακῶς ἀκολουθήσας, διὸ καὶ ἐσφάλη ἔτη ρλ′. ὁμοίως δὲ καὶ ὁ Ἀφρικανὸς διήμαρτε μὴ στοιχειώσας τοῦτον τὸν δεύτερον Καϊνᾶν, ὅθεν καὶ ἐν τοῖς ἀπὸ Ἰησοῦ τοῦ Ναυῆ καὶ τῶν πρεσβυτέρων ἕως Ἠλὶ καὶ
5   Σαμουὴλ ἠναγκάσθη ἔτεσι προσθεῖναι χρόνους ἐγγὺς ρμ′. περὶ ὧν ὁ Καισαρεὺς Εὐσέβιος οὗτος σφόδρα αὐτὸν καταμέμφεται πλειοτέρως σφαλεὶς ἐν ταὐτῷ καὶ ἐν τοῖς λοιποῖς, ὡς προδεδήλωται, ἕως ἐτῶν σϛ′. ὁ μέντοι θεῖος εὐαγγελιστὴς Λουκᾶς ιγ′ αὐτὸν ἀπὸ τοῦ Ἀδὰμ ἐγενεαλόγησε.

3–5 → F16c,3s; T16i; T16l; T16m; T16n; T16o; T16q,1s; T45,12–15   5–7 → T41

1–3 cf. Eus., chron. 42,1; 43,6; 43,31 = Sync. 97,22; 98,22; 99,14   5–7 cf. Eus., chron. 47,22 – 48,8 6s cf. Sync. 36,29s   7s cf. Lc 3,36

[AB]   1 ͵βφ′ B ͵αφ′ A | ͵βφε′ B ͵αφε′ A ͵βφζ′ Sync. 88,10   5 προσθεῖναι A προσθῆναι B 6 πλειοτέρως A πλειωτέρως B | ταὐτῷ A ταὐτὸ B   7 ἐτῶν B τῶν A

T16i[1]

According to some of the manuscripts, as well as Eusebius, Arpachshad lived another 403 years after begetting Shelah. But these manuscripts we utterly disregard, since they have gone quite astray from a truthful account of the chronology and the generations. **Both Africanus and Eusebius say that Shelah was born to Arpachshad instead of Kenan, and they put Shelah in the 13th, not the 14th generation. And they entirely neglect to mention the second Kenan, whom the sacred books at every point in Genesis, as well as the Gospel according to Luke, have declared to have been Arpachshad's son, the 13th descendant from Adam, and the father of Shelah, the 14th from Adam.**

T16k

In the 2500th year, Kenan took a wife and begot Shelah in the year 2505. This Kenan is omitted in the computation of Eusebius, who, by erroneously following the Hebrew version, was consequently 130 years off in his reckoning. **Likewise, Africanus was also in error by failing to include this second Kenan in his computation. For this reason, in the period of years from Joshua son of Nun and the elders up to Eli and Samuel, he was forced to add on almost 140 years.** For these additional years, this man Eusebius of Caesarea severely criticizes him, although, as we have previously demonstrated, on this very point and on the other matters, the magnitude of his error was even greater, extending to 290 years. The divine evangelist Luke, on the other hand, in his genealogy of Christ counted Kenan 13th from Adam.

---

1   T16i–o deal chiefly with Africanus' omission of the post-diluvian Kenan, on which see above, F16c,3, n. 1.

T16l Georgius Syncellus (96,13–18 Mosshammer)

Κατὰ τὸ παρὸν χρονογραφεῖον· ἔτους β' μετὰ τὸν κατακλυσμὸν Σὴμ ἐγέννησε τὸν Ἀρφαξάδ. Ἀρφαξὰδ γενόμενος ἐτῶν ρλε' ἐγέννησε τὸν Καϊνᾶν ,βτοζ'. Καϊνᾶν γενόμενος ἐτῶν ρλ' ἐγέννησε τὸν Σαλὰ ,βϡζ'. τοῦτον τὸν Καϊνᾶν Εὐσέβιος καὶ Ἀφρικανὸς οὐκ ἐστοιχείωσαν· διὸ καὶ τὰ ρλ' ἔτη αὐτοῦ σφάλλονται.

3s → F16c,3s; T16i; T16k; T16l; T16m; T16o; T16p; T16q,1s; T45,13–15

1–4 cf. Gen 11,10–13   3s cf. Eus., chron. 42,1; 43,6; 43,31 = Sync. 97,22; 98,22; 99,14

[AB]   1 χρονογραφεῖον B   χρονογραφίον A   2 ἐτῶν[1] B < A   3 ἐστοιχείωσαν B   ἐστοιχείωσεν A

T16m Anonymus Matritensis (3,6 – 4,4 Bauer)

Καϊνᾶν γενόμενος ἐτῶν ρλ' ἐγέννησε τὸν Σάλα καὶ ἐπέζησεν ἔτη τλ'· ἐγένοντο δὲ πᾶσαι αἱ ἡμέραι Καϊνὰν ἔτη υξ'· ἰστέον ὅτι τὸν Καϊνᾶν παραλελοίπασιν Ἀφρικανός τε καὶ Εὐσέβιος ἐν τοῖς χρόνοις· οὐ γὰρ εὑρήκασιν αὐτὸν ἐν πολλοῖς τῶν ἀντιγράφων. ὁ δὲ ἅγιος Λουκᾶς γενεαλογῶν τὸν σωτῆρα μέμνηται αὐτοῦ.

2s → F16c,3s; T16i; T16k; T16l; T16n; T16o; T16q,1s

2s cf. Eus., chron. 42,1; 43,6; 43,31 = Sync. 97,22; 98,22; 99,14   3 cf. Niceph., chron. syn. 83,25–28
3s cf. Lc 3,36

T16n Chronicon Epitomon (10,16–26 Pusch)

Ἀρφαξὰδ γενόμενος ἐτῶν ρλε' ἐγέννησε τὸν Καϊνᾶν· οὗτος δὲ ὁ Καϊνᾶν ἐν τῷ Ἑβραϊκῷ οὐδ' ὅλως εὑρίσκεται ἐμφερόμενος, ἀλλ' ἀπὸ τοῦ Ἀρφαξὰδ τὸν Σαλὰ γεννηθῆναι οἱ ο' ἡρμήνευσαν καὶ καθεξῆς τοὺς λοιπούς. ἔοικε δὲ ἀρχῆθεν ἁμαρτῆσθαι τὰ ἀντίγραφα καὶ διὰ τοῦτο ἔνιοι τῶν χρονογράφων οὔτε αὐτὸν οὔτε τοὺς χρόνους αὐτοῦ ἀριθμοῦσιν. ὁ μέντοι
5 ἀπόστολος καὶ εὐαγγελιστὴς Λουκᾶς σαφῶς καὶ τοῦ Καϊνᾶν τούτου ὡς υἱοῦ μὲν τοῦ Ἀρφαξάδ, πατρὸς δὲ τοῦ Σαλὰ μνημονεύει ἐν τῇ παρ' αὐτοῦ ἐκτεθείσῃ ἀναποδιστικῇ γενεαλογίᾳ, τῇ κατὰ τὸ εὐαγγέλιον, ᾧτινι καὶ ἡμεῖς ἑπόμενοι ὡς ἀξιολογωτέρῳ· καὶ τὸν Καϊνᾶν τοῦτον καὶ τοὺς χρόνους αὐτοῦ δεχόμεθα.

3s → F16c,3s; T16i; T16k; T16l; T16m; T16n; T16q,1s

1 cf. Gen 11,12   4–7 cf. Lc 3,35s

[TH]   2 ἐμφερόμενος T ἐκφερόμενος H | γεννηθῆναι T γεγεννῆθαι H   3 δὲ < H   4 αὐτοῦ + δέχονται καὶ H | μέντοι + θεῖος H   5 Λουκᾶς < H   6 μνημονεύει T μνημονεύων H | κατὰ T ἐν H

T16l

According to the present chronography: In the second year after the Flood, Shem begot Arpachshad. Arpachshad, when he was 135, begot Kenan, in 2377. Kenan, when he was 130, begot Shelah, in 2507. **Eusebius and Africanus did not count this Kenan. Therefore, they are in error by omitting his 130 years.**

T16m

When Kenan was 130 years of age, he begot Shelah and lived an additional 330 years. All the days of Kenan totaled 460 years. **It should be recognized that both Africanus and Eusebius omitted him in their chronology. For they did not find him in many of the manuscripts.** However, Saint Luke mentions him in his genealogy of the Savior.

T16n

When Arpachshad was 135 years of age, he begot Kenan. There is no reference at all to this Kenan found in the Hebrew version; moreover, according to the Septuagint translation, Shelah was begotten from Arpachshad, and then the others were begotten in succession. **It seems likely that, at the very outset, there was an error in the manuscripts, as a result of which some of the chronographers[1] number neither him nor his years.** However, the apostle and evangelist Luke clearly also mentions this Kenan as both son of Arpachshad and father of Shelah in the reverse genealogy set out by him, which is in his gospel. We also follow it, since it is more deserving of consideration. And we accept both this Kenan and his years.

---

1   The reference to "some chronographers" would include Africanus and Eusebius, both of whom omitted the second Kenan.

T16o Georgius Syncellus (104,16–23 Mosshammer)

Εὐσέβιος τῷ ˏγρπδ' ἔτει τοῦ κόσμου φησὶ τὸν Ἀβραὰμ γεννηθῆναι. σφάλλεται ὁ Εὐσέβιος ἐν τοῖς ἀπὸ Ἀδὰμ ἕως Ἀβραὰμ χρόνοις τὰ ρλ' ἔτη τοῦ δευτέρου Καϊνᾶν μὴ στοιχειώσας υἱοῦ Ἀρφαξάδ, ὃν οἱ ο' ἀριθμοῦσι καὶ τὸ κατὰ Λουκᾶν εὐαγγέλιον ιγ' ἀπὸ Ἀδάμ.

Ἀφρικανὸς ἀπὸ Ἀδὰμ ἐπὶ τὸ πρῶτον ἔτος Ἀβραὰμ ἔτη ˏγσβ' ἐπελογίσατο.
5 σφάλλεται δὲ καὶ οὗτος τὰ αὐτὰ ρλ' ἔτη τοῦ δευτέρου Καϊνᾶν υἱοῦ Ἀρφαξάδ, ὑφαιρουμένων τῶν κ' ἐτῶν τοῦ Μαθουσάλα, ἅτινα προσομοίως τῷ Εὐσεβίῳ καὶ οὗτος τῷ ˏγρπδ' ἔτει τοῦ κόσμου.

4s → F16c,3s; T16d,4–6; T16i; T16l; T16m; T16n; T16q; T45,13–17   **6** → F16a,12; T16g,2–4; T16h,7s; T16k; F22; T45,9–11

1 cf. Eus., chron. 45,20–22 = Sync. 100,32–34   **2s** cf. Lc 3,36   **6s** cf. Eus., chron. 42,33 = Sync. 98,17

[AB]   **2** υἱοῦ B οἱ υἱοῦ A   **6** προσομοίως Di. πρὸς ὁμοίως AB   **7** οὗτος B οὕτως A | τῷ...κόσμου delere maluerunt Goar et Di.

T16p Georgius Syncellus (105,3–5 Mosshammer)

Κατὰ Ἀφρικανὸν τῷ ˏγσοζ' ἔτει τοῦ κόσμου ἐπέβη Ἀβραὰμ τῆς ἐπηγγελμένης Χανανίτιδος γῆς, ὅπερ ἀδύνατον πέφυκε.

→ T6,5–8; F16d,4–6; T16h; T16l; T16o; T45,6–18

T16q Georgius Syncellus (112,22 – 113,2 Mosshammer)

Λείπεται πρὸς τὴν προκειμένην ἀκριβῆ χρονολογίαν ἡ παρὰ τῷ Ἀφρικανῷ χρόνοις ρι' ἐκ τῶν ρλ' ἐτῶν τοῦ δευτέρου Καϊνᾶν. τὰ γὰρ ἄλλα κ' ἐκ τῶν αὐτῶν ρλ' ἡ ἀπὸ Ἀδὰμ ἐπὶ τὸν κατακλυσμὸν τῶν ˏβσξβ' ἐτῶν παραύξησις προαφήρπασε, προστεθέντων αὐτῶν τοῖς τοῦ Μαθουσάλα χρόνοις.

1–4 → F16b; T16g; T16o; T22b   **1s** → F16c,3s; T16i; T16k; T16l; T16m; T16n   **2–4** → F16a,12; T16d,4–6; T16h,7s; F22; T45,9–11;

[AB]   **2** ρλ' B ρλε' A   **3** παραύξησις B παράξησις A

T16o

Eusebius states that Abraham was born in AM 3184. But Eusebius errs in his dating from Adam to Abraham, since he did not count the 130 years of the second Kenan, the son of Arpachshad, whom the Septuagint and the Gospel according to Luke number as the 13th from Adam.

Africanus reckoned 3202 years from Adam up to the first year of Abraham. But he too is mistaken by omitting the same 130 years of the second Kenan son of Arpachshad. For if one subtracts the 20 additional years that he assigns to Methuselah, he also dates it, much like Eusebius, in AM 3184.[1]

T16p

According to Africanus, in AM 3277, Abraham went up to the promised land of Canaan. This dating cannot possibly be correct.

T16q

Compared with the accurate chronology presented here, Africanus' chronology is lacking 110 of the 130 years of the second Kenan. The remaining 20 of these 130 years were previously offset by the lengthened period of time represented by the 2262 years from Adam up to the Flood; these 20 years were added on to the years of Methuselah.

---

[1] Since 3202 − 20 = 3182, Goar and Dindorf favor the deletion of the number. However, Syncellus states only that Africanus' date was "nearly the same (προσομοίως)" as Eusebius' (= 3184).

T17 Catena in Ioannem in codice Parisino gr. 209, f. 298ᵛ (2,105 Montfaucon = PG 26,1321B)

Οὗτοι δέ εἰσιν οἱ περὶ τῆς ταφῆς τοῦ Ἀδὰμ εἰρηκότες, Ἀφρικανὸς καὶ ὁ ἅγιος Ἀθανάσιος.

1   Sym. Log. (Leo Gr. [9,4–7 Bekker] = Th. Mel. [14,5–7 Tafel] = Iul. Pol. [58,6–9 Hardt]; cf. Cedr. [18,11–13 Bekker]) = Georg. Mon. (43,16s de Boor/Wirth) Τοῦτον (ὃς Georg. Mon.; sc. Adam → F IA32,2s) λέγεται πρῶτον (πρῶτος Georg. Mon.) εἰς τὴν γῆν, ἐξ ἧς ἐλήφθη, ταφῆναι, καὶ (+ τὸ Leo Gr.) μνῆμα αὐτῷ (αὐτοῦ Leo Gr.) κατὰ τὴν (+ τῶν Leo Gr., Iul. Pol.) Ἱεροσολύμων γεγονέναι γῆν, Ἑβραϊκή τις ἱστορεῖ παράδοσις (+ ὥς φησιν Ἰώσηπος Georg. Mon.).

1   cf. Or., comm. in Mt. 265; Epiph., haer. 2,208,15 – 209,10; Io. Chrys., hom. 85 in Io (PG 59,459); ps. Bas., enarratio in proph. Isaiam 5,141,13   **2** cf. ps. Ath., pass. 208,5–8

F18 Agapius Mabbugensis, Historia universalis (PO 5/4, 587,8s Vasiliev)

وزعم افريقون الحكيم ان شيث ابن ادم هو اوّل من اظهر الحروف ودل على الكتاب واللسان العبراني

→ F16a,2–4; Sym. Log. (Leo Gr. [9,22 – 10,1 Bekker] = Th. Mel. [14,20s Tafel]) Οὗτος ὁ Σὴθ πρῶτος τὰ Ἑβραϊκὰ γράμματα ἐξευρὼν συνεγράψατο. Io. Mal. 1,1 (4,18 Thurn) Καὶ γράμματα Ἑβραϊκὰ ἐφεῦρεν πρῶτος καὶ αὐτὸς ἀνεγράψατο.

1 cf. Gen 4,25; 5,3   **1s** cf. Io. Ant. fr. 1,13s; Georg. Mon. 10,5; ps. Sym. f. 21ᵛ,36 = Cedr. 16,16; Mich. Syr. 1,4

T17 *Adam's Tomb*[1]

These are the authors who write about Adam's tomb: Africanus and Saint Athanasius.

F18 *Seth, the Inventor of the Hebrew Alphabet*[2]

Africanus the sage claims that Seth, the son of Adam, was the first to bring to light letters and taught writing and the Hebrew language.

---

1. On this type of *catena* on John, see Reuss 1941,210–215 ("Typus F"), in particular pp. 210f on the Paris ms. Although this short notice is late and unspecific, the information found in Sym. Log. may provide a fuller understanding of Africanus' version of the tradition (on which, see Gelzer 1,60f): "It is said that Adam was the first to be buried in the ground (cf. Iub 4,29), from which he was taken. And his tomb was in the ground of Jerusalem, according to what is reported in a Hebrew tradition." See also Georg. Mon. cont., who attributes the tradition to "Josephus." Christian writers from the time of Origen situated the burial site of Adam on Mount Golgotha, cf. the *loci similes* and Jeremias 2002,35–43.
2. About Seth and the discovery of the letters see Klijn 1977,48–51. Other passages in the *Chronographiae* attest Africanus' strong interest in the history of culture. For his account of the discovery of arts and crafts and of cultural heroes (πρῶτοι εὑρεταί) see F24,35–37; F54a,17f; F56,7–9 and Roberto 2006,13f. His specific interest in the Hebrew language also appears in the various etymologies and aetiologies found elsewhere (T2b,4–7; T11,8–11; F16d,1–4; F19,3f; F44,2, see also Wallraff 2006,57f). Furthermore, there is a tradition, found in Sym. Log. (Leo Gr. 10,6f and parallels), according to which Enoch first learned and taught letters, see also Iub 4,17.

F19 Georgius Syncellus (10,7–11 Mosshammer)

Ἀπὸ Ἀδὰμ ἕως γεννήσεως Ἐνὼς ἔτη τετρακόσια τριάκοντα πέντε, δηλούσης τῆς γραφῆς· Ἐνὼς «ἤλπισεν ἐπικαλεῖσθαι τὸ ὄνομα κυρίου τοῦ θεοῦ» πρῶτος, τοῦτ' ἔστι προσαγορεύεσθαι ὀνόματι θεοῦ. ἑρμηνεύεται γὰρ ὁ Ἐνὼς ὡσανεὶ ἄνθρωπος κατὰ τὸν Ἑβραϊκὸν νοῦν. οὕτω δὲ καὶ ὁ σωτὴρ υἱὸς τοῦ ὄντος ἀνθρώπου, κατὰ τὸν φυσικὸν λόγον. Ἀφρικανοῦ.

1–4   Didym., in Gen. 4,26 (144,27 – 145,8 Nautin) *Ὁ Σὴθ οὖν ἀντὶ τοῦ δικαίου τεχθεὶς γεννᾷ τὸν Ἐνὼς δίκαιος δίκαιον, ὃς ἀντὶ τοῦ κυρίου ὀνόματος ἄνθρωπος καλεῖται, τῆς τοιαύτης προσηγορίας, τῆς ψυχῆς αὐτοῦ τὴν ἀρετὴν δηλούσης, σῳζούσης τὸ «κατ' εἰκόνα» καὶ τὴν τοῦ ὄντως ὄντος ἀνθρώπου κατάστασιν· Ἐνὼς γὰρ παρ' Ἑβραίοις ἄνθρωπός ἐστιν. ἀμέλει γοῦν καὶ τὸ ἴδιον τοῦ ἀνθρώπου προσάπτει αὐτῷ· «οὗτός» φησιν «ἤλπισεν ἐπικαλεῖσθαι τὸ ὄνομα κυρίου»· προσήκουσα δὲ αὕτη ἀνθρώπῳ ἐναρέτῳ πρᾶξις· ἐλπὶς δὲ ἡ τῷ ὄντι αὕτη ἐστὶν τὸ ὁμοιωθῆναι τῷ θεῷ κατὰ τὸ δυνατόν· ἐλπίζειν δὲ ἐπικαλεῖσθαι τὸ ὄνομα κυρίου τοῦ θεοῦ ἅμα καὶ ὑπὸ ἐξουσίαν καὶ ὑπὸ τὴν διδασκαλίαν τὴν θείαν ἐστὶν ἑαυτὸν ὑποτάττοντος.*

1s Gen 4,26   1–4 cf. Cat. Gen. 574 (= Eusebius Emesenus); ps. Sym. f. 22ʳ = Cedr. 17,9–12; Sym. Log. (Leo Gr. 9,13–15 = Th. Mel. 14,11–14); Iul. Pol. 58,13–15

[AE]   4   τοῦ ὄντος AE   ὄντως ps. Sym. | κατὰ τὸν φυσικὸν λόγον Africano attribuerunt Routh, Gelzer[ms] κ. τ. φ. λ. Ἀφρικανοῦ Moss.

F20 Ioannes Scythopolitanus (ps. Maximus Confessor), Scholion in Dionysii Areopagitae ep. 4 (76 Cordier = PG 4,532B)

Τοῦτό φησι καὶ Ἀφρικανὸς ἐν ταῖς Χρονογραφίαις·

Λέγεται γὰρ ὁμωνύμως ὁ θεὸς πᾶσι τοῖς ἐξ αὐτοῦ, ἐπειδὴ ἐν πᾶσίν ἐστιν. ἐν δὲ τῇ οἰκονομίᾳ, ὡς κατὰ τὴν οὐσίαν ὅλην οὐσιωθεὶς ἄνθρωπος λέγεται, κατὰ τὸ εἰρημένον· «ἐν ᾧ κατοικεῖ πᾶν τῆς θεότητος τὸ πλήρωμα σωματικῶς».

4 Col 2,9

F21 Nota in margine codicis Parisini gr. 1711, p. 13 (ad textum Georgii Syncelli [20,29s Mosshammer])

Ἀφρικανοῦ· | ἐπὶ †...† | φησὶ φερ[...] | φατ Ἐνὼχ | ἐν βίβλῳ | τῶν ἀποκρ<ύφων>.

†...†] Νξα Gelzer[ms] | φατ] φάτις ? | ἀποκρύφων Gelzer[ms]

F19 *Enosh, called by the name of God*

From Adam until the birth of Enosh were 435 years, Scripture revealing that Enosh was the first 'to hope to make use of the name of the lord God', that is to be called by the name of God.[1] For Enosh is interpreted as 'man' according to the Hebrew sense. Thus also the Savior is the son of the 'one who is man', according to the natural sense. From Africanus.[2]

F20 *God's Immanence*

Africanus also says this in the *Chronographiae*:

For God is called by the same name as all that is from him, since he is in everything. But in the divine economy, he is called 'human', since in his whole being he is invested with existence, in accordance with what has been said, 'For in him the whole fullness of deity dwells bodily'.

F21 *Quotation from the Book of Enoch*

From Africanus: About … he states … an oracle (?) (of ?) Enoch is reported in a book of the apocrypha.[3]

---

1. To preserve the ambiguity of the word ἐπικαλεῖσθαι found in the Septuagint text of Gen 4,26, the translation renders the word as 'make use of the name of'. ἐπικαλεῖσθαι can mean either 'to call upon' (in the middle voice) or 'to be called by the name of' (in the passive voice). Later Christian interpreters often preferred the latter, in part because it explained how the descendants of Seth and Enosh could be identified as 'the sons of God' of Gen 6,2 (see, e.g., Io. Chrys., hom. 22 in Gen. 189,4–35). By this interpretation, Enosh could also be seen as a foreshadowing of Christ. While the name Enosh means 'man' in Hebrew, he was also called by the name 'God.'
2. Mosshammer's punctuation, which removes the full stop before Ἀφρικανοῦ, would attribute only the last sentence of this passage to Africanus (beginning with the words "thus also"). Because the meaning of the phrase 'the natural sense (λόγος) of Africanus' is doubtful, the punctuation presented here follows Routh's text; cf. also Gelzer 1,61f.
3. Found in the margin of ms. A (= Parisinus gr. 1711), this notice originates in a note to one of Syncellus' lists of the early biblical patriarchs (20,26–29). Because the text is mostly illegible, Mosshammer did not include it in his edition. Gelzer did provide it in his planned edition of Africanus (Gelzer[ms]). While fragmentary, the text suggests Africanus' familiarity with the *Book of Enoch*.

F22 Georgius Syncellus (21,1–8 Mosshammer)

Ὁ γὰρ Μαθουσάλα ἐν τῷ κατακλυσμῷ τέθνηκε, περὶ οὗ Ἀφρικανός·
Οὗτος ἁπάντων πλείονα χρόνον βιοῖ, τῶν τε πρὸ αὐτοῦ καὶ τῶν ἑξῆς εἰς ἡμᾶς, εἰς ἔτη τὰ σύμπαντα ͵Ϡξθʹ. τάχα τι σημαίνει τὸ πολυχρόνιον αὐτοῦ διὰ τὴν ὑπερκόσμιον ὀγδοάδα κυριακὴν ἡμέραν. ὄγδοος γὰρ ἀπὸ τοῦ αʹ τυγχάνει. ὃ δ᾽
5 ὑστερεῖ, τοῦτο πρὸς ἀναπλήρωσιν τῆς χιλιάδος, πρῶτον ὑπάρχον πλήρωμα, ἀνεπλήρωσεν ὁ σωτήρ.
Εἶτά φησιν· εἰσὶ τρεῖς ὁμωνυμίαι πως ἀπὸ Κάιν τοῖς ἀπὸ Σήθ, ὡς Ἐνὼχ καὶ Μαθουσάλα καὶ Λάμεχ.

2s → F16a,12; T16o; T16q,2–4

2s cf. Gen 5,27; Eus., chron. 38,22–26; 39,18s; 41,1s = Sync. 92,22s; 93,13s; 93,31s 3–6 cf. Or., sel. in ps. 118,164; Bas., hex. 2,8 (36,14–16) 7s cf. Gen 4,17–19; Philo, de posteritate Caini 40s

[A] **1** Μαθουσάλα Di. μαθουσάλας A

T22a Georgius Syncellus (20,5–13 Mosshammer)

Τῷ ͵ασοζʹ ἔτει ἐγέννησεν Ἐνὼχ τὸν Μαθουσάλα. Μαθουσάλα γενόμενος ρξζʹ ἐτῶν ἐγέννησε τὸν Λάμεχ. Τῷ ͵αυνδʹ ἔτει τοῦ κόσμου, τινὰ δὲ τῶν ἀντιγράφων τῷ ρπζʹ ἔτει αὐτοῦ Μαθουσάλα φέρουσι τὴν γέννησιν Λάμεχ· οἷς καὶ ὁ Ἀφρικανὸς ἀκολουθήσας τῷ ͵βσξβʹ ἔτει τοῦ κόσμου τὸν ἐπὶ Νῶε κατακλυσμὸν ἐστοιχείωσεν, ὅπερ οὐ δοκεῖ ἡμῖν ὑγιῶς ἔχειν. δοκεῖ δέ μοι ὁ Ἀφρικανὸς
5 τῷ ͵βσξβʹ ἔτει τοῦ κόσμου τὸν κατακλυσμὸν στοιχειῶσαι διὰ τὸ τοὺς ͵Ϡξθʹ χρόνους τῆς ζωῆς Μαθουσάλα ἀρχομένους ἀπὸ τοῦ ͵ασπζʹ ἔτους τοῦ κόσμου λήγειν εἰς τὸ ͵βσνςʹ ἔτος τοῦ κόσμου ἐντὸς τῶν ͵βσξβʹ ἐτῶν.

3–7 → F16b,2s; T16g,1s; T16o; T16q; T45,15–17

1 cf. Gen 5,21 1s cf. Gen 5,25 LXX 2s cf. Io. Chrys., hom. 21 in Gen. 5 (PG 53,181,23–25)

[A] **6** ͵ασπζʹ Goar^m ͵ασπξʹ A **7** ἔτος Goar^m ἔτους A

F22 *The Years of Methuselah and the Names of the Sons of Cain*

For Methuselah died in the Flood, concerning whom Africanus wrote:

This man lived longer than anyone else, both those who preceded him and those who succeeded him up to our time, 969 years in all. Perhaps his longevity has some meaning, because of the supramundane eighth day, the Lord's day. For he happens to be numbered eight from the first.[1] And what he is lacking, this the Savior has completed in order to fulfil the millennium, the primary and the complete period of time.[2]

Then he says: There are three descendants of Cain, whose names are in a certain way identical with those of the descendants of Seth, namely Enoch, Methuselah and Lamech.

T22a

In the 1277th year, Enoch begot Methuselah. When Methuselah was 167 years of age, he begot Lamech. This was in AM 1454, but some of the manuscripts report the birth of Lamech in the 187th year of this Methuselah.[3] With them is Africanus also in agreement, who reckoned the date of the Flood at the time of Noah in AM 2262. But this does not seem to us to be sound. For in my opinion Africanus reckoned the date of the Flood in AM 2262 because the 969-year duration of Methuselah's life began in AM 1287 and continued up to AM 2256, within the period of 2262 years.[4]

---

1   Methuselah, the eighth patriarch from Adam, prefigures not only the Resurrection of Christ on the first day after the Jewish Sabbath, but also the end of the 7000-year millennial week.
2   969 (the age of Methuselah at the time of his death) added to 31 (the age of Jesus at the time of the Crucifixion) equals the perfect millennial number of 1000. For Africanus' dating of the Crucifixion of Jesus at age 31, see T93b.
3   For Septuagint mss. reading 187 years, see Wevers 1974 ad loc.
4   See above, T16g, n. 2.

T22b Georgius Syncellus (131,7–16 Mosshammer)

Ἔσται δὲ καὶ Ἰάρεδ μακροβιώτερος αὐτοῦ ἔτη ιγ′, ϡξβ′ ζήσας ἔτη, ὅπερ οὐδενὶ συμπεφώνηται. διόπερ οὐ χρὴ διὰ τὸ φάναι συναπολέσθαι αὐτὸν τοῖς ἐν τῷ κατακλυσμῷ, διὰ τοῦτο ϡμθ′ μόνα ἔτη βεβιωκέναι. Ἀλλὰ οὐδὲ τῷ Ἀφρικανῷ πειθόμεθα προστιθέντι τὰ αὐτὰ κ′ ἔτη καὶ ϡπθ′ λέγοντι τοῦ Μαθουσάλα ἀντὶ ϡξθ′. λοιπὸν οὖν κρεῖσσον εἶναι δοκεῖ ταῖς καθ᾽ ὅλην
5 τὴν οἰκουμένην ἑπομένους ἱεραῖς βίβλοις ϡξθ′ λέγειν τῆς ζωῆς Μαθουσάλα, εἰ καὶ τὸν κατακλυσμὸν ὑπερβέβηκεν ἔτεσι ιε′, τοῦ θεοῦ κἀκεῖνον ἴσως, ὡς τὸν Ἐνώχ, περισώσαντος παραδόξως καθ᾽ οὓς οἶδε τρόπους καὶ τόπους.

3s → F16a,12; T16f,3–5; T16g,7s; T16l; T16n,2–4

[AB] **1** ιγ′ Goar^m κγ′ AB **2** συναπολέσθαι B συναπολλέσθαι A **5** ἑπομέναις A ἐπωμέναις B

F23

Sync.¹: Georgius Syncellus (19,24 – 20,4 Mosshammer)
Sync.²: Georgius Syncellus (21,27 – 22,10 Mosshammer)

Πλήθους ἀνθρώπων γενομένου ἐπὶ τῆς γῆς ἄγγελοι τοῦ οὐρανοῦ θυγατράσιν ἀνθρώπων συνῆλθον. ἐν ἐνίοις ἀντιγράφοις εὗρον· οἱ υἱοὶ τοῦ θεοῦ. μυθεύεται δέ, ὡς οἶμαι· <οἱ μὲν> ἀπὸ τοῦ Σὴθ ὑπὸ τοῦ πνεύματος οἱ υἱοὶ θεοῦ προσαγορεύονται διὰ τοὺς ἀπ᾽ αὐτοῦ γενεαλογουμένους δικαίους τε καὶ πατριάρχας ἄχ-
5 ρι τοῦ σωτῆρος. τοὺς δ᾽ ἀπὸ Κάϊν ἀνθρώπων ἀποκαλεῖ σποράν, ὡς οὐδέ τι θεῖον ἐσχηκότας διὰ πονηρίαν γένους καὶ διὰ τὸ τῆς φύσεως ἀνόμοιον. ἐπιμιχθέντων αὐτῶν τὴν ἀγανάκτησιν ποιήσασθαι τὸν θεόν.

test.: **1** inc. Sync.¹ [A]: Ἀφρικανοῦ περὶ τῶν ἐγρηγόρων

1–10   Sym. Log. (Leo Gr. [10,21 – 11,3 Bekker] = Th. Mel. [15,8–13 Tafel] = Iul. Pol. [60,18 – 62,4 Hardt]) *Οἱ ἐγρήγοροι πρὸς τὰς θυγατέρας τῶν ἀνθρώπων ἐπιμιξίαν* ποιησάμενοι *γεννῶσι τοὺς γίγαντας, μαντείας τε αὖ* (οὖν Iul. Pol.) *καὶ* γοητείας *ἀνθρώποις εἰσηγηταὶ γενόμενοι, ἔτι δὲ* (καὶ Iul. Pol.) *ἀστρονομίας τε καὶ ἀστρολογίας καὶ πάσης ὑψηλῆς καὶ μετεώρου κινήσεως, καὶ ταῖς γυναιξὶ τούτων ἁπάντων παραδεδωκότες τὴν γνῶσιν, εἰς ἄκρον ἐλθεῖν πονηρίας τοὺς ἀνθρώπους* παρεσκεύασαν.

1–23 cf. Sym. Log. (Leo Gr. 10,21 – 12,5 = Th. Mel. 15,8 – 16,12 = Iul. Pol. 60,18 – 64,20)   **1–7** cf. Iul. Pol. 62,7–22   **1s** cf. Gen 6,1s (in traditione manuscripta modo ἄγγελοι modo υἱοί)   **2–7** cf. Ios., ant. Iud. 1,73s; Or., Cels. 5,55,1–9; Proc. G., in Gen. 6 (86,5 – 87,10 Mai = PG 87/1,265C – 268C)

1 Πλήθους Goar^m   πλῆθος A   **3** οἱ μὲν Scal.   **5** ἀποκαλεῖ Goar^m   ἀποκαλεῖν A

T22b

And Jared, who lived to age 962, will have outlived him by 13 years—an opinion with which no one agrees. Therefore, to say that he was swept away with the others in the Flood does not necessarily mean that as a result he lived only 949 years. But neither are we convinced by Africanus, who adds on these 20 years, and assigns 989 instead of 969 years to Methuselah.[1] In my opinion, then, it is better for us to follow the sacred books used throughout the whole world and assign 969 years to his life, even if it means that he survived the Flood by 15 years; for perhaps God kept him alive miraculously, as he did Enoch, through means and locations that only he knows.

F23 *The Circumstances of the Flood*

When humankind became numerous upon the earth, angels of heaven had intercourse with daughters of men. In some manuscripts, I found: 'the sons of God'. In my opinion, this is to be understood figuratively:[2] <the descendants> of Seth are called 'the sons of God' by the Spirit, since the genealogies of the righteous and the patriarchs up until the Savior are traced from him. But the descendants of Cain it designates as human seed, as having had nothing divine because of the wickedness of their line and the dissimilarity of their nature, so that when they were mingled together, God grew angry.

---

1   Syncellus' statement that Africanus lengthened the life of Methuselah from 969 to 989 years is a misunderstanding of Africanus' chronological system. The additional 20 years refer to the date when Methuselah begot Lamech (187 instead of 167), not the number of his years.
2   Lit.: 'this is related mythically'.

Εἰ δὲ ἐπ' ἀγγέλων νοοῖτο ἔχειν τούτους, τῶν περὶ μαγείας καὶ γοητείας, ἔτι δὲ ἀριθμῶν κινήσεως τῶν μετεώρων ταῖς γυναιξὶ τὴν γνῶσιν παραδεδωκέναι,
10 ἀφ' ὧν ἐποιήσαντο παῖδας τοὺς γίγαντας, δι' οὓς τῆς κακίας ἐπιγενομένης ἔγνω πᾶν ἀφανίσαι ζῴων γένος ὁ θεὸς ἐν κατακλυσμῷ, ἀπειλήσας ρκ' ἔτη οὐχ ὑπερβήσεσθαι τοὺς ἀνθρώπους. μηδὲ νομιζέσθω ζήτημα διὰ τὸ πλείονα χρόνον τινὰς ὕστερον βιῶναι· τὸ γὰρ διάστημα τοῦ χρόνου γέγονεν ἑκατὸν ἔτη μέχρι τοῦ κατακλυσμοῦ κατὰ τῶν ἁμαρτωλῶν τῶν τότε· ἦσαν γὰρ εἰκοσαετεῖς.
15 Τῷ Νῶε διὰ δικαιοσύνην εὐαρεστήσαντι κιβωτὸν ὑπέθετο κατασκευάσαι θεός· καὶ γενομένης εἰσῆλθον εἰς αὐτὴν αὐτός τε Νῶε καὶ οἱ υἱοί, ἡ γυνὴ καὶ αἱ νύμφαι, καὶ ἀπὸ παντὸς ζῴου ἀπαρχὴ εἰς διαμονὴν τοῦ γένους. ἦν δὲ ἐτῶν ἑξακοσίων ὁ Νῶε, ὅτε ὁ κατακλυσμὸς ἐγένετο. ὡς δὲ ἔληξε τὸ ὕδωρ, ἡ κιβωτὸς ἱδρύθη ἐπὶ τὰ ὄρη Ἀραράτ, ἅτινα ἴσμεν ἐν Παρθίᾳ, τινὲς δὲ ἐν Κελαιναῖς τῆς
20 Φρυγίας εἶναί φασιν· εἶδον δὲ τὸν τόπον ἑκάτερον. ἐπεκράτησε δὲ ὁ κατακλυσμὸς ἐνιαυτόν· καὶ τότε ἐξηράνθη ἡ γῆ. οἱ δὲ ἐξῆλθον τῆς κιβωτοῦ κατὰ συζυγίας, ὥς ἐστιν εὑρεῖν, καὶ οὐχ ὃν εἰσῆλθον τρόπον κατὰ γένη, εὐλογοῦνταί τε πρὸς τοῦ θεοῦ.

test.: Sync.[1]   **10** ἔγνω inc. Sync.[2] [A]: Ἀφρικανοῦ (marg.)   **11** κατακλυσμῷ des. Sync.[1]: ἄπιστον **23** des. Sync.[2]: τούτων μὲν οὖν ἕκαστον τῶν διαφερόντων τι σημαίνει.

18-20 Io. Mal. 1,4 (7,86–92 Thurn) Μετὰ τὸ παῦσαι τὸν κατακλυσμὸν καὶ τὰ ὕδατα λωφῆσαι εὑρέθη αὕτη ἡ κιβωτὸς καθίσασα ἐν τοῖς ὄρεσιν Ἀραρὰτ τῆς Πισιδίας ἐπαρχίας, ἥστινός ἐστιν μητρόπολις Ἀπάμεια (quae olim etiam Κελαιναί vocabatur) καὶ ἔστιν τὰ ξύλα αὐτῆς ἐκεῖ ἕως τῆς νῦν, ὡς συνεγράψατο Πέργαμος ὁ Παμφύλιος. Ἰώσηπος δὲ καὶ Εὐσέβιος ὁ Παμφίλου καὶ ἄλλοι χρονογράφοι ἐξέθεντο, ὅτι τὰ ὄρη Ἀραρὰτ ἐστιν ἐπὶ τὴν Ἀρμενίαν καὶ μεταξὺ Πάρθων καὶ Ἀρμενίων καὶ Ἀδιαβηνῶν. κἀκεῖ ἐκάθισεν ἡ κιβωτός. ps. Sym. f. 20ᵛ = Cedr. (20,18s Bekker) Ὅτι τὰ ὄρη Ἀραρὰτ ἴσμεν ἐν Παρθίᾳ τῆς Ἀρμενίας εἶναι· τινὲς δέ φασιν, ἐν Κελαιναῖς τῆς Φρυγίας.   **19** Proc. G., in Gen. 8 (88,3–6 Mai = PG 87/1,285A, cf. Georg. Mon. 47,15–18) Περὶ δὲ τῆς κιβωτοῦ φησιν Ἰώσηπος ὁ Ἑβραῖος ἐν τοῖς περὶ Ἀρχαιότητος οὕτως· ἧς κιβωτοῦ τὰ λείψανα μέχρι νῦν πρὸς ἀπόδειξιν τῶν γεγονότων δείκνυται ἐν ὄρει λεγομένων Ἀραρὰτ, ἃ τυγχάνει ἀνὰ μέσον τῆς Ἀρμενίας καὶ Παρθικῆς χώρας κατὰ τὴν τῶν Ἀδιαβηνῶν γῆν.

11-14 cf. Gen 6,3   **15-18** cf. Gen 7,6–16   **18s** cf. Gen 8,4   **18-20** cf. Io. Ant. fr. 2,17–23; Ecl. Chron. 233,9–11; Mich. Syr. 2,1   **19** cf. Ios., ant. Iud. 1,93–95 = Eus., praep. ev. 9,11 (= Berossus Babylonius FGrHist 680 F4c; Hieronymus Aegyptius FGrHist 787 F2; Nicolaus Damascenus FGrHist 90 F72); Theoph. Ant., Autol. 3,19,21s; Epiph., haer. 1,175,18; Eus., onomasticon 1,1; Eus., chron. 11,35 – 12,2; Sync. 31,28 – 32,1   **20-23** cf. Gen 8,13–19

8 μαγείας] μαντείας Sym. Log.   **11** ἀφανίσαι ζῴων γένος ὁ θεὸς Sync.[1] ~ (ὁ θ. ἀ. ζ. γ.) Sync.[2] **19** ἱδρύθη Di. ἱδρύνθη A

But let us suppose they refer to 'angels'. Then it was they who transmitted knowledge about magic and sorcery, as well as the numbers of the motion of astronomical phenomena, to their wives, from whom they produced the giants as their children;[3] and when depravity came into being because of them, God resolved to destroy every class of living things in a flood,[4] after threatening that humankind would not live beyond 120 years. Let it not be considered a problem because some later lived more years than that. For the interval of time invoked against the sinners of that age was 100 years up to the Flood (for they were 20 years old).

To Noah, who was well-pleasing to him because of his righteousness, God gave orders to prepare an ark. And when it was completed, there entered into it Noah himself and his sons, his wife and their young wives, the firstlings from every living thing, in order to ensure the survival of their species. And Noah was 600 years of age when the Flood occurred. But when the water receded, the ark came to rest on the mountains of Ararat, which we know to be in Parthia, but some say they are in Celaenae of Phrygia. I have seen both places. The Flood persisted for a year. And then the earth became dry. And they came out of the ark in pairs, as can be discovered, and not in the same manner in which they entered, according to species; and they were blessed before God.

---

3   Africanus' account of the revelation of forbidden knowledge by the angels is first attested in I Hen 6–8, where the angels are also identified as 'Watchers'. This is also the way they are described in the parallel text from Symeon Logothete: 'The Watchers had intercourse with the daughters of men and begot the giants, after having introduced to humankind both divination and sorcery, as well as the motion of everything exalted and heavenly; in having transmitted knowledge of all these things to women, they caused humankind to reach the height of depravity.'

4   Sync.¹ appends the word ἄπιστον ('not credible'). Since it is lacking in the repetition of the same text in Sync.², it is most likely a gloss either by Syncellus himself or an earlier editor, meant to express disapproval of the notion that heavenly angels actually had intercourse with women, see also introduction p. XLIV.

F24

F24a Symeon Logothetes (Leo Grammaticus [15,5 – 16,3 Bekker] = Theodosius Melitenus [18,15 – 19,2 Tafel])

F24b ps. Symeon (cod. Par. gr. 1712, f. 26ᵛ – 27ʳ = [inc. a l. 10] Georgius Cedrenus 28,20 – 29,12)

Ἀφρικανοῦ·

Ἐκ δὲ τῆς φυλῆς τοῦ Σὴμ ἀνεφάνη ἄνθρωπος γιγαντογενής, ὀνομασθεὶς ὑπὸ τοῦ πατρὸς Κρόνος εἰς ἐπώνυμον τοῦ
5 πλανήτου ἀστέρος, ὃς πρῶτος κατέδειξεν ἄρχειν καὶ βασιλεύειν Ἀσσυρίων. ἔσχε δὲ γυναῖκα Σεμίραμιν τὴν καὶ Ῥέαν καλουμένην, ἐξ ἧς ἔσχεν υἱόν, ὃς ἐπεκλήθη Ζεὺς ὁ καὶ Πῖκος, γήμας τὴν
10 ἰδίαν ἀδελφὴν Ἥραν. ἔσχε δὲ Κρόνος καὶ ἕτερον υἱὸν ὀνόματι Ἄφρον, ᾧ ἀπεκλήρωσε τὴν πρὸς Λιβύην γῆν· ὃς ἔγη-

Ἐκ τῆς φυλῆς τοῦ Σὴμ ἀνεφάνη ἄνθρωπος γιγαντογενής, ὠνομάσθη δὲ ὑπὸ τοῦ πατρὸς Κρόνος εἰς μὲν ἐπώνυμον τοῦ πλανήτου ἀστέρος, ὃς 5
πρῶτος ἦρξεν Ἀσσυρίων. ἔσχε δὲ γυναῖκα Σεμίραμιν τὴν καὶ Ῥέαν καλουμένην, ἐξ ἧς ἔσχεν υἱόν, ὃς ἐπεκλήθη Ζεὺς ὁ καὶ Πῆκος, γήμας τὴν ἰδίαν ἀδελφὴν Ἥραν. ἔσχε δὲ Κρόνος καὶ 10
ἑτέρους δύο υἱούς· Ἄφρον ἐξ οὗ καὶ Ἄφροι, καὶ Νῖνον. ὁ Ἄφρον γήμας

---

test. F24a: **2** Σὴμ + ὥς φησιν Ἀφρικανὸς ὁ σοφώτατος Vat. gr. 163, f. 5ᵛ   **5** Leo. Gr. marg. ὥς φησιν Ἀφρικανὸς ὁ σοφώτατος   test. F24b: **10s** inc. Cedr.: ὡς δὲ Ἀφρικανός φησι, καὶ ἕτερον υἱὸν ἔσχε ὁ Κρόνος τὸν Ἄφρον κτλ.

2–10 Io. Mal. 1,8 (9,47 – 10,62 Thurn) *Ἐκ δὲ τῆς αὐτῆς φυλῆς τοῦ Σὴμ τῆς κρατησάσης τὴν Συρίαν καὶ τὴν Περσίδα καὶ τὰ λοιπὰ μέρη τῆς ἀνατολῆς τοῦ αʹ υἱοῦ Νῶε ἐγεννήθη καὶ ἀνεφάνη ἄνθρωπος γιγαντογενὴς ὀνόματι Κρόνος, ἐπικληθεὶς ὑπὸ Δαμνῶ τοῦ ἰδίου αὐτοῦ πατρὸς εἰς τὴν ἐπωνυμίαν τοῦ πλανήτου ἀστέρος. ἐγένετο δὲ δυνατὸς οὗτος, ὅστις πρῶτος κατέδειξεν τὸ βασιλεύειν ἤτοι ἄρχειν καὶ κρατεῖν τῶν ἄλλων ἀνθρώπων. ... οὗτος εἶχεν γυναῖκα τὴν Σεμίραμιν τὴν καὶ Ῥέαν καλουμένην παρὰ Ἀσσυρίοις διὰ τὸ αὐτὴν εἶναι ὑπερήφανον καὶ ἀλαζόνα. ἦν δὲ καὶ αὕτη ἐκ τῆς αὐτῆς φυλῆς τοῦ Σήμ, υἱοῦ Νῶε. ἔσχεν δὲ ὁ Κρόνος υἱὸν ὀνόματι Πῖκον ὅστις ἀπὸ τῶν γονέων ἐκλήθη Ζεὺς εἰς ὄνομα καὶ αὐτὸς τοῦ πλανήτου ἀστέρος. ἔσχεν δὲ καὶ ἄλλον υἱὸν ὁ αὐτὸς Κρόνος ὀνόματι Νίνον καὶ θυγατέρα δὲ ἔσχεν ὀνόματι Ἥραν. ἔλαβεν δὲ γυναῖκα Πῖκος ὁ καὶ Ζεὺς τὴν ἰδίαν αὐτοῦ ἀδελφὴν τὴν Ἥραν ὀνόματι.*   **10–14** Io. Mal. 1,9 (10,71–76 Thurn) *Καὶ ἔμεινεν* (sc. Κρόνος) *κρατῶν καὶ βασιλεύων τῆς δύσεως πάσης ἔτη πολλὰ καὶ ἔσχεν ἐκεῖ γυναῖκα ὀνόματι Φιλύραν, ἐξ ἧς ἔσχεν υἱὸν ὀνόματι Ἄφρον, ᾧτινι ἔδωκε τὴν πρὸς Λιβύην γῆν· καὶ ἐκράτει τῶν ἐκεῖ βασιλέων ὁ Ἄφρος, ὅστις ἐγάμησε τὴν Ἀστυνόμην ἐκ τῆς Λακερίας νήσου καὶ ἐγέννησε θυγατέρα, ἣν ἐκάλεσεν Ἀφροδίτην εἰς ὄνομα καὶ αὐτὴν τοῦ πλανήτου ἀστέρος τῆς οὐρανίας Ἀφροδίτης...* (→ vide infra ad l. 38–43).

2s cf. Gen 10,21s; Io. Mal. 1,7   **2–10** cf. Io. Ant. fr. 4,1–19; Chron. Pasch. 64,19 – 65,16; Io. Nic. 6,1–3; Georg. Mon. 11,17 – 12,8   **10–14** cf. Io. Ant. fr. 4,22–26; Chron. Pasch. 66,5–11 (omnes ex Io. Mal.)

5a πλάνητος Th. Mel. | πρῶτος + nota marginalis Leo. Gr. vide supra   **7a** Σεμιράμην Th. Mel.   **11** Ἄφρον] Ἄφρων Sym. Log. corr. Bekker Tafel τὸν Ἄφρον Cedr.   **12b** καὶ Νῖνον < Cedr. | ὁ Ἄφρον ps. Sym. ὃς Cedr.

F24 *The Pagan Gods*[1]

F24a

F24b

From Africanus:

From the tribe of Shem arose a man of the race of giants.[2] He was given the name Cronus by his father, after the planet of that name.[3] He first revealed how to rule and exercise kingship over the Assyrians.[4] He had a wife Semiramis, also called Rhea, from whom he had a son who was surnamed Zeus, also known as Picus,[5] who married his own sister Hera. Cronus also had another son named Afer,[6] to whom he allotted the land in the direction of Libya. He married Astynomê,[7] and begot	From the tribe of Shem arose a man of the race of giants. He was given the name Cronus by his father, after the planet of that name. He was the first to rule the Assyrians. He had a wife Semiramis, also called Rhea, from whom he had a son who was surnamed Zeus, also known as Picus, who married his own sister Hera. Cronus also had two other sons: Afer, after whom the Afri are named, and Ninus. After marrying

---

1. In ps. Symeon, the heading of the entire passage is Ἀφρικανοῦ. In Cedrenus, the attribution to Africanus ὡς δὲ Ἀφρικανός φησι ('as Africanus says') appears before the account of the birth of Afer. Among the Logothete group, the words ὥς φησιν Ἀφρικανὸς ὁ σοφώτατος ('as the most learned Africanus says') appear in a marginal note to l. 5 in Leo Grammaticus, at the beginning of the text in the codex Vat. gr. 163. John Malalas, who has a version of the story, quotes Diodorus Siculus as his source in the context of the death of Zeus-Picus (Io. Mal. 1,13 [14,49–52 Thurn] = Diod. Sic. 6, fr. 5).
2. Because the eastern part of the inhabited world, including Assyria and Babylonia, was allocated to Shem (see, for example, Leo Gr. 14,22 – 15,1), Cronus and his descendants belong to the tribe of Shem. The description of Cronus as a 'giant' may be connected with the biblical Nimrod, the legendary giant and founder of Babylon (Gen 10,8f), who is also sometimes identified as a descendant of Shem (against Gen 10,6), see Io. Mal. 1,7.
3. Cf. Io. Mal. 1,8, which identifies Cronus' father as 'Damno'; in the Chron. Pasch. 65,3, he is named 'Damnos.'
4. Cf. Eus., chron. 30–35; Sync. 109,16, which list 'Belus' as the first king of Babylon and the father of Ninus. For the identification of Belus as Cronus, see Eus., praep. ev. 9,17,9 (quoting Alexander Polyhistor).
5. On the identification of the Roman god Picus with Zeus, see also, for example, Sync. 200,14–16.
6. 'Afer' is thus the eponymous father of the Afri ('Africans'). Cf. Cleodemus Malchus (in Ios., ant. Iud. 1,239,4–8), who identifies him with Afer, son of Midian and grandson of Abraham and Keturah (Gen 25,1–4).
7. Cf. Gelzer 1,70, who suggests a possible connection between the mentioned Astynomê and the Phoenician mother goddess Astronoê.

με τὴν Ἀστυνόμην, γεννήσας ἐξ αὐτῆς θυγατέρα, ἣν ἐκάλεσεν Ἀφροδίτην.

Ὁ δὲ Κρόνος ἐξωσθεὶς τῆς βασιλείας ὑπὸ τοῦ ἰδίου υἱοῦ Διὸς κατέλιπε Δία καὶ Νῖνον, υἱοὺς αὐτοῦ, μετὰ τῆς μητρὸς αὐτῶν Ῥέας βασιλεύειν Ἀσσυρίων· αὐτὸς δὲ κατιὼν ἐν τῇ δύσει κρατεῖ καὶ βασιλεύει πάσης Ἰταλίας.

Ζεὺς οὖν ὑποχωρήσας τῶν Ἀσσυρίων παρεγένετο πρὸς τὸν πατέρα· ὁ δὲ παραχωρεῖ αὐτῷ βασιλεύειν *πάσης* Ἰταλίας, *καὶ* κρατήσας πολλοῖς ἔτεσι *καὶ* τελευτήσας κατατίθεται ἐν Κρήτῃ.

Ἀστυνόμην, ἐποίησε θυγατέρα τὴν Ἀφροδίτην.

Ὁ δὲ Κρόνος ἐξωθεὶς τῆς βασιλείας ὑπὸ τοῦ ἰδίου υἱοῦ Διὸς κατιὼν ἐν τῇ δύσει κρατεῖ τῆς Ἰταλίας.

Εἶτα ὁ Ζεὺς οὖν ὑποχωρήσας τῶν Ἀσσυρίων *παραγίνεται* πρὸς τὸν πατέρα· ὁ δὲ παραχωρεῖ αὐτῷ βασιλεύειν τῆς Ἰταλίας, καὶ πολλοῖς ἔτεσι *βασιλεύσας εἶτα* τελευτήσας κατατίθεται ἐν Κρήτῃ.

15-20 → F34,49–53; Io. Mal. 1,9 (10,66–71 Thurn) Ὁ δὲ προπάτωρ Κρόνος ἐάσας τὸν ἑαυτοῦ υἱὸν Πῖκον ἐν τῇ Ἀσσυρίᾳ καὶ τὴν ἑαυτοῦ γυναῖκα Ῥέαν τὴν Σεμίραμιν μετὰ Πίκου τοῦ καὶ Διὸς υἱοῦ αὐτοῦ καὶ λαβὼν πολλὴν βοήθειαν ὄχλου ἀνθρώπων γενναίων ἀπῆλθεν ἐπὶ τὴν δύσιν ἀβασίλευτον οὖσαν, μὴ κρατουμένην ὑπό τινος κελεύοντος, καὶ ἐκράτησε τῶν δυτικῶν μερῶν ἀφανὴς ἐκ τῆς Ἀσσυρίας γενόμενος.   21-25 Io. Mal. 1,10 (11,89–97 Thurn) Μετὰ δὲ τὸ βασιλεῦσαι τὸν Πῖκον τὸν καὶ Δία τῆς Ἀσσυρίας ἔτη λ' ἐάσας καὶ αὐτὸς τὴν ἑαυτοῦ μητέρα καὶ τὴν Ἥραν τὴν ἑαυτοῦ ἀδελφὴν καὶ γυναῖκα καὶ ποιήσας τὸν ἑαυτοῦ υἱὸν Βῆλον βασιλέα τῆς Ἀσσυρίας ἀπῆλθεν ἐπὶ τὴν δύσιν πρὸς τὸν ἑαυτοῦ πατέρα τὸν Κρόνον ... ὁ δὲ Κρόνος ἑωρακὼς τὸν ἴδιον αὐτοῦ υἱὸν Πῖκον τὸν Δία ἐλθόντα πρὸς αὐτὸν ἐν τῇ δύσει παρεχώρησεν αὐτῷ τὴν βασιλείαν τῆς δύσεως ... καὶ ἐβασίλευσε τῆς δύσεως ἤτοι τῆς Ἰταλίας ὁ Πῖκος ὁ καὶ Ζεὺς ἄλλα ἔτη ξβ'.   25s Io. Mal. 1,13 (13,45 – 14,52 Thurn) Μέλλων δὲ τελευτᾶν ὁ αὐτὸς Πῖκος ὁ καὶ Ζεὺς ἐκέλευσε τὸ λείψανον αὐτοῦ ταφῆναι ἐν τῇ Κρήτῃ νήσῳ. καὶ κτίσαντες αὐτῷ ναὸν οἱ αὐτοῦ παῖδες ἔθηκαν αὐτὸν ἐν τῇ Κρήτῃ νήσῳ ἐν μνήματι, ὅπερ μνῆμα ἦν ἐν τῇ αὐτῇ Κρήτῃ, κεῖται δ' ἕως τοῦ παρόντος, ἐν ᾧ ἐπιγέγραπτο· ἐνθάδε κεῖται θανὼν Πῖκος ὁ καὶ Ζεύς, ὃν καὶ Δίαν καλοῦσιν. περὶ οὗ συνεγράψατο Διόδωρος ὁ σοφώτατος χρονογράφος, ὃς καὶ ἐν τῇ ἐκθέσει τοῦ συγγράμματος αὐτοῦ τοῦ περὶ θεῶν εἶπεν, ὅτι Ζεύς, ὁ τοῦ Κρόνου υἱός, ἐν τῇ Κρήτῃ κεῖται.

15-20   cf. Io. Ant. fr. 4,20–22; Chron. Pasch. 65,19 – 66,3 (omnes ex Io. Mal.); Exc. Barb. 234,25 – 236,3   21-26   cf. Io. Ant. fr. 4,29–32; Chron. Pasch. 66,15 – 67,3 (omnes ex Io. Mal.); Exc. Barb. 236,4–22   24-26   cf. Theoph. Ant., Autol. 1,10,12s; Tat., orat. 27,1; Io. Ant. fr. 6.2,4–13; Chron. Pasch. 80,1–10 (ambo ex Io. Mal.)

15b ἐξωθεὶς ps. Sym. ἐξωσθεὶς Cedr.   16b κατιὼν ps. Sym. κατελθὼν Cedr.   21b οὖν < Cedr.   26b ἐν + τῇ Cedr.

from her a daughter whom he called Aphrodite.[8]	Astynomê, Afer had a daughter Aphrodite.
When Cronus was forced out of his kingdom by his own son Zeus, he left behind his sons Zeus and Ninus to reign over the Assyrians with their mother Rhea.[9] Cronus himself moved away to the West, took control, and became king of all Italy.	When Cronus was forced out of his kingdom by his own son Zeus, he moved away to the West and took control of Italy.
Zeus, then, withdrew from the Assyrians and came to his father. And he allowed him to be king of all Italy. And after controlling it for several years, he died and was buried in Crete.[10]	Zeus, then, withdrew from the Assyrians and came to his father. And he allowed him to be king of Italy. And after reigning for several years, he then died and was buried in Crete.

---

8   The passage interprets the meaning of the name Aphrodite as 'born to Afer (= Ἄφρος)'.
9   For Africanus' discussion of the Assyrian kingdom after Ninus, see F34,49–53, T49a.b, and ll. 27–31 below.
10 The tradition according to which Zeus was buried in Crete was wide-spread in antiquity; it may originate in Euhemerus, see Winiarczyk 2002,35–43.

Μετὰ δὲ Νῖνον ἐβασίλευσεν Ἀσσυρίων Θούρας, ὃν μετωνόμασαν Ἄρεα ὡς πολεμικώτατον καὶ γενναῖον ὄντα· ὃν οἱ Ἀσσύριοι Βάαλ θεὸν μετωνόμασαν καὶ ἀναστηλώσαντες σέβονται.

Μετὰ δὲ τὴν τοῦ Διὸς τελευτὴν Φαῦνος υἱὸς αὐτοῦ ἐβασίλευσεν, ὃς μετωνομάσθη Ἑρμῆς· ἦν γὰρ λογιώτατος πάνυ καὶ μαθηματικός· ὅστις καὶ τὴν τοῦ χρυσοῦ ποίησιν ἐφεῦρεν ἐκ μετάλλων ἀνθρώποις.

Μετὰ δὲ Νῖνον ἐβασίλευσεν Ἀσσυρίων Θούρας, ὁ καὶ Ἄρης κληθεὶς ὡς πολεμικότατος. τοῦτον οἱ Ἀσσύριοι Βάαλ θεὸν ἢ Βὴλ μετωνομάσαντες καὶ ἀναστηλώσαντες σέβονται.

Μετὰ δὲ τὴν Διὸς τελευτὴν Φαῦνος ὁ υἱὸς αὐτοῦ ἐβασίλευσεν, ὃς μετωνομάσθη Ἑρμῆς· ἦν γὰρ λογιώτατος πάνυ καὶ μαθηματικός· ὃς καὶ τὴν τοῦ χρυσοῦ ποίησιν ἐφεῦρεν ἐκ μετάλλων ἀνθρώποις.

Ἡ μέντοι Ἀφροδίτη λογικὴ καὶ ποικίλη λεγομένη ἐγαμήθη τῷ Ἀδώνιδι τῷ υἱῷ τοῦ Κινύρου, φιλοσόφῳ ὄντι καὶ αὐτῷ· οὓς καὶ ἄχρι θανάτου φιλοσοφοῦντας σὺν ἀλλήλοις βιῶσαι ἱστοροῦσι.

27-37 Io. Mal. 1,12-14 (12,19 - 14,56 Thurn) Μετὰ δὲ Νῖνον ἐβασίλευσεν Ἀσσυρίων Θούρας ὀνόματι, ὅντινα μετεκάλεσεν ὁ τούτου πατὴρ Ζάμης, ὁ τῆς Ῥέας ἀδελφός, εἰς ὄνομα τοῦ πλανήτου ἀστέρος Ἄρεα. οὗτος ἐγένετο πικρὸς πολεμιστής, ὅστις ἐπολέμησεν ἐπὶ τὰ ἀρκτῷα μέρη. ... ᾧτινι Ἄρεϊ ἀνέστησαν πρώτην στήλην οἱ Ἀσσύριοι καὶ ὡς θεὸν προσεκύνουν αὐτόν, ὃν καὶ ἕως νῦν καλοῦσι περσιστὶ τὸν Βάαλ θεόν, ὅ ἐστιν ἑρμηνευόμενον Ἄρης πολέμων θεός. ... ἔσχεν δὲ ὁ αὐτὸς Πῖκος ὁ καὶ Ζεὺς υἱὸν ὀνόματι Φαῦνον, ὃν καὶ Ἑρμῆν ἐκάλεσεν εἰς ὄνομα τοῦ πλανήτου ἀστέρος. ... μετὰ δὲ τὴν τελευτὴν Πίκου τοῦ καὶ Διὸς ἐβασίλευσεν ὁ αὐτοῦ υἱὸς Φαῦνος ὁ καὶ Ἑρμῆς τῆς Ἰταλίας ἔτη λε', ὃς ἦν ἀνὴρ πανοῦργος καὶ μαθηματικός· ὅστις ἐφηῦρεν τὸ μέταλλον τοῦ χρυσοῦ ἐν τῇ δύσει πρῶτος καὶ τὸ χωνεύειν. **38-43** Io. Mal. 1,9 (10,75-78; 11,86 Thurn) ... (→ vide supra ad l. 10-14) Ἀφροδίτην ... φιλόσοφον γενομένην, ἥτις ἐγαμήθη Ἀδωνίδη τῷ υἱῷ τοῦ Κινύρου Ἀθηναίῳ, καὶ αὐτῷ φιλοσόφῳ, ἐκ τῆς οἰκείας αὐτοῦ θυγατρός. ... λέγονται δὲ ὁμοῦ περιφιλοσοφηκέναι μέχρις θανάτου.

27-31 cf. Io. Ant. fr. 6.1; Chron. Pasch. 68,1-11; Georg. Mon. 13,4-10 (omnes ex Io. Mal.) **32-37** cf. Io. Ant. fr. 6.2,14-24; Chron. Pasch. 80,11-16 (omnes ex Io. Mal.); Exc. Barb. 238,3-5 **38-43** cf. Io. Ant. fr. 4,26-28; Chron. Pasch. 66,11-13 (omnes ex Io. Mal.).

28 Θούρας ps. Sym. Cedr. Routh Θούρρας Sym. Log. | μετωνόμασαν Leo Gr. μετονομάσαντες Th. Mel. **30b** ἢ ps. Sym. ἤτοι Cedr. **32b** τοῦ Διὸς Cedr. **34s** λογιώτατος] λογικώτατος Cedr. **35s** τὴν ... ἐφεῦρεν] τοῦ χρυσοῦ τὴν φύσιν ἐξεῦρεν Cedr. **38** Ἀφροδίτης ps. Sym.

After Ninus, the king of the Assyrians was Thuras,[11] whom they renamed Ares, since he was extremely warlike and brave. The Assyrians renamed him as a god with the name Baal, and after erecting a monument to him, worshipped him.[12]

After the death of Zeus, Faunus his son became king, who was renamed Hermes. He was exceedingly eloquent and fond of learning; he also discovered for mankind the art of making gold from metals.

After Ninus, the king of the Assyrians was Thuras, also known as Ares, since he was extremely warlike. The Assyrians renamed him as a god with the name Baal, or Bel, and after erecting a monument to him, worshipped him.

After the death of Zeus, Faunus his son became king, who was renamed Hermes. He was exceedingly eloquent and fond of learning; he also discovered for mankind the art of making gold from metals.

However, Aphrodite, said to be intellectual and sophisticated, was married to Adonis the son of Cinyras; he too was a philosopher. It is reported that the two of them lived together up to the time of their deaths practicing philosophy.[12]

---

11 The name 'Thuras' is probably derived from the Greek word θοῦρος ('furious'), one of the Homeric epithets for Ares (see Il. 5,507; 24,498).
12 'Ares' is probably an *interpretatio Graeca* of the early Assyrian king 'Areios'. For the dates and reign of Areios, see Eus., chron. 30,36 (from Castor of Rhodes), Sync. 117,20, and especially Chron. Pasch. 68,2–4. For further discussion, see Routh 409f, n. ad loc.
13 While unattested in the Symeon Logothete tradition, the narrative concerning Aphrodite and Adonis appears both in the ps. Symeon tradition and in John Malalas' description of the gods of paganism (itself based on Africanus). Routh 264f attributes the notice also to Africanus.

F25 Symeon Logothetes (Leo Grammaticus [20,16–20 Bekker] = Theodosius Melitenus [22,1–3 Tafel])

Ὁμοῦ τοίνυν γίνεται ἔτη μέχρι τῆς παροικεσίας Ἀβραὰμ τοσαῦτα. ὁ διαμερισμὸς τῆς γῆς γέγονε τῇ ἀρχῇ τῶν ἡμερῶν Φαλέκ. ἀπὸ δὲ τοῦ διαμερισμοῦ τῆς γῆς ἔτη ,χις′, ἀπὸ δὲ τοῦ κατακλυσμοῦ ἔτη χίλια δεκαπέντε, ἀπὸ δὲ Ἀδὰμ ἔτη τρισχίλια διακόσια ἑβδομήκοντα ἑπτά.

1s → F16c,5 (ann. 2661)   2s → F16b,2 (ann. 2262)   3 → T6,6; F16d,5s; T16m

1 ἔτη...τῇ < Th. Mel.   2 ἀρχῇ Leo Gr. ἀρχὴ Th. Mel. | ,χις′ Th. Mel. ,ας′ Leo Gr.

F26 Georgius Syncellus (114,1–24 Mosshammer)

Ἀφρικανοῦ·

Λιμοῦ κατασχόντος τὴν γῆν τὴν Χανανίτιδα κατῆλθεν εἰς Αἴγυπτον Ἀβραάμ, δεδιὼς δὲ μὴ διὰ τὸ κάλλος τῆς γυναικὸς ἀναιρεθῇ, ἀδελφὸς εἶναι σκέπτεται. ἐπαινεθεῖσαν δὲ ἠγάγετο Φαραώ (οὕτω γὰρ Αἰγύπτιοι τοὺς βασιλεῖς ἑρμη-
5 νεύουσι), καὶ ὁ μὲν δίκας ἔτισε τῷ θεῷ, ὁ δ' ἅμα τοῖς ἰδίοις Ἀβραὰμ ἤδη πλουτῶν ἀπηλλάσσετο.

Ἐν Χαναὰν διεπληκτίσαντο ποιμένες τοῦ τε Ἀβραὰμ καὶ τοῦ Λώτ, καὶ δόξαντος αὐτοῖς ἐχωρίσθησαν, ἑλομένου Λὼτ ἐν Σοδόμοις οἰκεῖν δι' ἀρετὴν καὶ κάλλος τῆς γῆς ἐχούσης πέντε πόλεις, Σόδομα, Γόμορρα, Ἄδαμα, Σεβωείμ, Ση-
10 γώρ, καὶ τοσούτους βασιλεῖς. τούτοις οἱ πλησιόχωροι τέσσαρες βασιλεῖς Σύρων ἐπολέμησαν, ὧν ἡγεῖτο Χοδολλαγομὸρ βασιλεὺς Αἰλάμ. συνέβαλλον δὲ παρὰ τὴν θάλασσαν τὴν ἁλικήν, ἣ καλεῖται νῦν θάλαττα νεκρά.

7–12   ps. Sym. f. 31ʳ = Cedr. (51,5–14 Bekker) Ἀφρικανοῦ· (< Cedr.) Ὅτι ὁ Λὼτ χωρισθεὶς τοῦ Ἀβραὰμ κατῴκησεν εἰς Σόδομα δι' ἀρετὴν καὶ κάλλος τῆς γῆς, ἐχούσης πέντε πόλεις, Σόδομα Γόμορρα Ἄδαμα Σεβοήν (Σεβόϊν Cedr.) καὶ Σηγώρ, καὶ τοσούτους βασιλεῖς. τούτοις οἱ πλησιόχωροι τέσσαρες βασιλεῖς Σύρων ἐπολέμησαν, ὧν ἡγεῖτο Χοδολλογομὸρ βασιλεὺς ὁ Αἰλάμ (Ἰλάμ Cedr.). συνέβαλον δὲ παρὰ τὴν θάλασσαν τὴν ἁλικήν, ἣ (καὶ Cedr.) καλεῖται νῦν θάλασσα νεκρά, πλεῖστα θαυμάσια ἔχουσα, ἅ ἐγὼ ἐθεασάμην. ζῷόν τε γὰρ οὐδὲ ἐκεῖνο φέρει τὸ ὕδωρ, καὶ νεκρὰ μὲν σώματα ὑποβρύχια γίνεται (γίνονται ps. Sym.), ζῶν δέ τις οὐδ' ἂν ῥᾳδίως βαπτίσαιτο. (καὶ Cedr.) λύχνοι δὲ (μὲν Cedr.) καιόμενοι μὲν (< Cedr.) ἐπιφέρονται, σβεννύμενοι δὲ καταδύουσιν.

2s cf. Gen 12,10; Iub 13,10   3–5 cf. Gen 12,11–17; Iub 13,13; Ios., ant. Iud. 1,162–164   5–10 cf. Gen 13,1–11; Iub 13,14–17; Ios., ant. Iud. 1,170   7–22 cf. ps. Eust., in hex. 761B–D   10–13 cf. Gen 14,1–10; Iub 13,22; Ios., ant. Iud. 1,171–175

[AB]   3 δὲ < A   5 ἔτισε A αἴτισε B   7 διεπληκτίσαντο A διεπληκτήσαντο B   9 σεβωείμ AB σεβοήν ps. Sym.   11 συνέβαλλον AB συνέβαλον ps. Sym.

F25 *From the Division of the Earth to Abraham's Migration*[1]

Altogether, then, the years up to the migration of Abraham are the following: The division of the earth occurred at the beginning of the days of Peleg. From the division of the earth, there are 616 years. From the Flood there are 1015 years, from Adam 3277 years.

F26 *Abraham in Egypt, Lot's Land and the Dead Sea*

From Africanus:[2]

When a famine gripped the land of Canaan, Abraham went down to Egypt. Fearing that he might be killed on account of the beauty of his wife, he made a plan to pretend to be her brother. And Pharaoh (for this is the name that Egyptians use to mean 'kings') took her for himself when she was commended to him. And whereas he was punished by God, Abraham, now enriched, departed with his household.

In Canaan, the shepherds of Abraham and Lot were in dispute, and by mutual consent they separated. Lot chose to live in Sodom because of the fertility and beauty of the land; it had five cities, Sodom, Gomorrah, Admah, Zeboiim, and Segor, and as many kings. The four neighboring kings of the Syrians made war with them, led by Chedolaomer king of Elam. They met by the Salt Sea, which is now called the Dead Sea.

---

1 The dates provided in large print accurately represent the chronology of Africanus. For his dating of Abraham's migration in AM 3777 and the Flood in AM 2262 (3277 – 1015), see F16d, 3–6. For the division of the earth in the first year of Peleg's life, AM 2661 (3277 – 616), see F16c,5f.
2 Although the endpoint of this excerpt, consisting of several parts, is not clearly demarcated in the text of Syncellus, its contents can be verified from parallel material preserved in the secondary witnesses to the tradition (Cedrenus, ps. Eustathius and ps. Symeon). The recollection of a personal visit to the vicinity of the Dead Sea is also consistent with Africanus' own documented interest in autopsy and travel, see F23,19–24; F46,52–55.

Ἐν ταύτῃ πλεῖστα τῶν θαυμασίων τεθέαμαι. ζῴων τε γὰρ οὐδὲν ἐκεῖνο φέρει τὸ ὕδωρ, καὶ νεκροὶ μὲν ὑποβρύχιοι φέρονται, ζῶντες δὲ οὐδ' ἂν ῥᾳδίως βαπτί-
15 σαιντο. λύχνοι δὲ καιόμενοι μὲν ἐπιφέρονται, σβεννύμενοι δὲ καταδύουσιν.

Ἐνταῦθά εἰσιν αἱ τῆς ἀσφάλτου πηγαί· φέρει δὲ στυπτηρίαν καὶ ἅλας, ὀλίγον τι τῶν ἄλλων διαφέροντα· πικρά τε γάρ ἐστι καὶ διαυγῆ. ἔνθα δ' ἂν καρπὸς εὑρεθῇ κάπνου πλέον εὑρίσκεται θολερωτάτου. τὸ δὲ ὕδωρ ἰᾶται τοὺς χρωμένους αὐτῷ, λήγει τε παντὶ ὕδατι πάσχον τὰ ἐναντία. εἰ δὲ μὴ Ἰορδάνην εἶχε τὸν
20 ποταμὸν τροφὴν ὡς πορφύραν διατρέχοντα καὶ ἐπὶ πολὺ ἀντέχοντα, ἔληξεν ἂν θᾶττον ἢ φαίνεται. ἔστι δὲ παρ' αὐτῇ πάμπολυ τοῦ βαλσάμου φυτόν. ὑπονοεῖται δὲ ἀνατετράφθαι ὑπὸ τοῦ θεοῦ διὰ τὴν τῶν περιοικούντων ἀσέβειαν.

13-15 ps. Eust., in hex. (59,26–30 Allatius = PG 18,761C) *Ῥιφέντες γὰρ ἐπ' αὐτῇ ζῶντες ἄνθρωποι ἀναβλυστάνουσι· νεκροὶ δὲ καταδύνουσι· καὶ λύχνοι δὲ καιόμενοι ἐπιφέρονται, σβεσθέντες δὲ καταποντοῦνται.* **16-22** ps. Sym. f. 31ʳ–31ᵛ = Cedr. (51,14–23 Bekker) Ἐνταῦθά εἰσιν αἱ τῆς ἀσφάλτου πηγαί. φέρει δὲ στυπτηρίαν καὶ ἅλας ὀλίγον τι τῶν ἄλλων διαφέροντα· πικρά τε γάρ *εἰσι* καὶ διαυγῆ. ἔνθα δ' ἂν καρπὸς εὑρεθῇ, καπνοῦ πλέον εὑρίσκεται θολερωτάτου (*οὐδέν* Cedr.). τὸ δὲ ὕδωρ ἰᾶται τοὺς χρωμένους αὐτῷ (*αὐτό* ps. Sym.), λήγει τε παντὶ ὕδατι πάσχον τὰ ἐναντία. εἰ δὲ μὴ Ἰορδάνην εἶχεν *ὁ τόπος* τροφὴν ὡς πορφύραν διατρέχοντα καὶ ἐπὶ πολὺ ἀντέχοντα, ἔληξεν ἂν θᾶττον ἢ φαίνεται. ἔστι δὲ παρ' αὐτῇ πάμπολυ *τὸ* βαλσάμου φυτόν. ὑπονοεῖται δὲ ἀνατετράφθαι ὑπὸ τοῦ θεοῦ διὰ τὴν τῶν περιοικούντων ἀσέβειαν.

[AB] **13** ζῴων AB ζῷον ps. Sym. **13s** φέρει τὸ ὕδωρ B ps. Sym. ~ A **14** νεκροὶ...φέρονται AB νεκρὰ μὲν σώματα ὑποβρύχια γίνονται ps. Sym. | ζῶντες δὲ AB ζῶν δέ τις ps. Sym. **14s** βαπτήσαιντο A βαπτήσαιντο B **15** λύχνοι δὲ καιόμενοι μὲν B ps. Sym. λύχνοι μὲν καιόμενοι δὲ A **16** ἐνταῦθα + δὲ A **16s** ὀλίγον A ps. Sym. ὀλίγων B **19** αὐτῷ A Cedr. αὐτό B ps. Sym. **19s** τὸν ποταμὸν AB ὁ τόπος ps. Sym. **20** διατρέχοντα AᶜB διατρέφοντα ante corr. A **21** αὐτῇ A ps. Sym. αὐτὴν B | τοῦ AB τὸ ps. Sym.

T27 Georgius Syncellus (113,25s Mosshammer)

Ἀβραὰμ παρῴκησεν ἐν Γεράροις, ἥν τινες Ἀσκαλῶνά φασιν εἶναι, ὡς καὶ Ἀφρικανός.

cf. Gen 20,1; ps. Sym. f. 31ʳ = Cedr. 51,1s

In this sea, I have witnessed a great many marvellous things. For that body of water sustains no living thing. Corpses are carried beneath its depths, but the living would not easily even dip under it. Lighted torches are borne upon it, but when they are extinguished they sink.

In that place are the springs of bitumen; and it produces alum and salt, somewhat different from other kinds in that they are bitter and translucent. And wherever you can find fruit, it turns out rather to consist of the most foul smoke. But the water is medicinal for those who use it. And it drains in a way different from all other water. For if it did not have the Jordan River as nourishment flowing through it like purple dye and holding out for a long time, it would have drained more quickly than it fills. And there is by it a very large crop of balsam. It is believed that the sea was made sterile by God because of the impiety of the neighboring peoples.

T27 *The Toponym Gerar*[1]

Abraham settled in Gerar, which some, including Africanus, say is Ashkelon.

---

[1] Portions of the historical narrative in which this small notice about Abraham's settlement of Gerar is inserted (Sync. 112,16 – 113,28) may also have come from Africanus' chronicle. Routh's edition (415f) provides additional text from Cedrenus (see app.), on the basis of a marginal note mentioning Africanus in a manuscript used by Xylander for his 1566 Cedrenus edition.

T28

T28a Georgius Syncellus (120,18–21 Mosshammer)

Ὁ Ἀφρικανὸς οζ' ἐτῶν λέγει τὸν Ἰακὼβ ἐλθεῖν εἰς Μεσοποταμίαν, ὡς ἐκ τῆς γραφῆς. ἡ δὲ γραφὴ οὐδαμοῦ τοῦτο φαίνεται λέγουσα, ἄλλως τε, εἰ τοῦτο δῶμεν, ἔσται ὁ Ἰωσὴφ κατὰ τὸ ϙϛ' τοῦ Ἰακὼβ γεννηθείς, ὅπερ ἀδύνατον.

1s → F51,10s

1 cf. Eus., can.[Hier] 30[e] (anno 78); Eus., praep. ev. 9,21,1s (= Demetrius FGrHist 722 F1,1; Alex. Polyh. FGrHist 273 F19a); Georg. Mon. 112,11s; Sym. Log. (Leo Gr. 21,16–18 = Th. Mel. 22,20–22) (omnes anno 75); ps. Sym. f. 32[r] ≈ Iub 29,13; Cedr. 59,17–19; Sync. 120,22 (omnes anno 73); Chron. Pasch. 106,21 – 107,3 (anno 63)   **2s** cf. Sync. 133,23 – 134,28 (→ T28c)

[AB]   1 λέγει B λέγεται A | τὸν Ἰακὼβ ἐλθεῖν B ~ A

T28b Georgius Syncellus (121,8–13 Mosshammer)

Οὔτε κατὰ τὸν Ἀφρικανόν μοι δοκεῖ δυνατὸν εἶναι τὸν Λευὶ γεννηθῆναι τῷ πζ' ἔτει τοῦ Ἰακὼβ οὔτε κατὰ τὸν Εὐσέβιον τῷ αὐτῷ πζ'. εἰ γὰρ ὁ Ἰωσὴφ μ' ἐτῶν ἦν τῷ ρλ' ἔτει τοῦ Ἰακώβ, ἡνίκα κατῆλθε πρὸς αὐτὸν εἰς Αἴγυπτον, ἀνάγκη πᾶσα τὸν Ἰακὼβ ϙα' αὐτοῦ ἔτει γεννῆσαι τὸν Ἰωσὴφ ἐκ τῆς Ῥαχήλ.

1s cf. Chron. Pasch. 107,14s; Exc. Barb. 222,17–19 (omnes anno 83); Eus., praep. ev. 9,21,1–3 (= Demetrius FGrHist 722 F1,1–3; Alex. Polyh. FGrHist 273 F19a) (anno 85); Hipp., haer. 285,11; Sym. Log. (Leo Gr. 23,3s = Th. Mel. 23,20 = Iul. Pol. 92,2s); Niceph., chron. syn. 85,10; Suda Μωυσῆς Μ 1348,15s; Georg. Mon. 115,17 (omnes anno 87); Anon. Matr. 9,4 (anno 86); Epiph., anc. 110,5 (anno 89)   **2** cf. Eus., chron. 46,29 (anno 86); can.[Hier] 31[a] (anno 87)   **2s** cf. Gen 41,46; 45,6; 47,8s

[AB]   2 πζ' AB πϛ' Sync. infra (T28c,3) 3 ἔτει < A

T28 *The Chronology of Jacob's Life*

T28a

Africanus says that at age 77 Jacob came to Mesopotamia, as if he was quoting from Scripture.[1] But it is clear that Scripture nowhere says this; besides, if we grant this, Joseph will have been born in the 96th year of Jacob, which is impossible.

T28b

In my opinion, Africanus cannot possibly be right that Levi was born in the 87th year of Jacob;[2] nor can Eusebius be right, who dates it in the same year 87.[3] For if Joseph was age 40 in the 130th year of Jacob, at which time he came down to him in Egypt, it is absolutely necessary that when Jacob was 91 he begot Joseph from Rachel.

---

1   The Bible does not give a precise chronology of Jacob's life. Africanus may have arrived at the number '77' by the following reasoning: According to Gen 41,46, Joseph was 30 years of age when he entered the service of the Pharaoh. Another nine years elapsed before his brothers' arrival in Egypt (Gen 45,6). If Jacob and his family spent 17 years in Egypt before Jacob died at the age of 147 (Gen 47,28), then Joseph was 56 years of age at the time of his father's death. Jacob was thus 91 years old at the time of Joseph's birth. Since the sequence of events described in Gen 30–31 implied that Joseph was born at the end of Jacob's 14-year service to Laban, Africanus concluded that Jacob was 77 years old when he arrived in Haran (see Adler/Tuffin 2002,149, n. 5). Africanus' chronology is similar to the dating proposed by the Jewish chronographer Demetrius, see Gelzer 1,88. For Syncellus' own opposing calculation of Jacob's age, see Sync. 133,23 – 134,30.
2   If Jacob married Leah after seven years of service to Laban, then it follows from Africanus' chronology that Jacob was 84 years of age at the time (77 + 7, see T28a). Africanus then determined that the birth of Levi, Jacob's third son (Gen 29,31-35), occurred three years later, in Jacob's 87th year; see Adler/Tuffin, 2002,151, n. 1.
3   Cf. below, T28c,3, where Syncellus states that Eusebius dated Levi's birth in the 86th year of Jacob. The witnesses to Eusebius' chronicle also disagree about the date (see the *loci similes*).

T28c Georgius Syncellus (134,2–13 Mosshammer)

Ζ' γὰρ ἔτη δουλεύσας ὑπὲρ τῆς Ῥαχὴλ πρῶτα καὶ παρὰ γνώμην τῇ Λείᾳ μιχθεὶς τρίτον ἔσχε παῖδα τὸν Λευὶ παρ' αὐτῆς ἐν τρισὶν ἔτεσι δηλονότι. ὥστε οὔτε τῷ Ἀφρικανῷ πιστευτέον πζ' ἔτει τοῦ Ἰακὼβ λέγοντι γεννηθῆναι τὸν Λευὶ οὔτε τῷ Εὐσεβίῳ λέγοντι τῷ πς' ἔτει. κατ' ἄμφω γὰρ ἢ τῷ ϛς' ἢ τῷ ϙε' τῆς ζωῆς Ἰακὼβ εὑρεθήσεται γεννηθεὶς ὁ Ἰωσήφ· ὅπερ ἀσύμφωνον τῇ
5 θείᾳ γραφῇ παριστώσῃ τοῦτον ἐτῶν λ' ἄρξαντα τῆς Αἰγύπτου καὶ μετὰ τὰ δέκα ἔτη, ἑπτὰ λέγω τῆς εὐθηνίας καὶ τρία τῆς λιμοῦ, ἀπολαβόντα τὸν πατέρα Ἰσραὴλ πανοικὶ ρλ' ἐτῶν, τεσσαρακοντούτην ὄντα δηλονότι. ὥστε ἐκ τούτων ἀκριβῶς παρίσταται ἡ ἑκατέρου γένεσις, καὶ οὕτως ἡμῖν στοιχειωθήσεται ἔχουσι καὶ ἑτέρους μεταγενεστέρους ἐκκλησιαστικοὺς ἱστορικοὺς συνᾴδοντας, μὴ μέντοι μετὰ τῆς προκειμένης αἰτιολογίας καὶ ἀκριβοῦς ἀποδείξεως.

2s → T28b,1s

1 cf. Gen 29,30   **3s** cf. Eus., praep. ev. 9,21,1–5 (= Demetrius FGrHist 722 F1,1–5; Alex. Polyh. FGrHist 273 F19a) (anno 89); Eus., can.[Hier] 31[d]; ps. Sym. f. 32[r]; Cedr. 59,15 – 60,3; Sync. 134,14–28 (omnes anno 91); Chron. Pasch. 107,14s; 109,17s; Ecl. Hist. 174,22s (omnes anno 92)   **4–7** cf. Gen 41,46–49; 45,6; 47,8s

[AB] **1** ὑπὲρ Β περὶ Α **3** ἔτει[1] Β ἔτη Α **5** θείᾳ < Β **6** τῆς Β τοῦ Α | τεσσαρακοντούτην Goar, Di. σερακοντούτην ΑΒ

F29 Georgius Syncellus (123,8–12 Mosshammer)

Τῷ ρκ' ἔτει τοῦ Ἰακὼβ ἐτελεύτησεν ὁ Ἰσαὰκ ὁ πατὴρ αὐτοῦ ζήσας ἔτη ρπ'. ἐτάφη δὲ ὑπὸ Ἰακὼβ καὶ Ἠσαῦ τῶν παίδων αὐτοῦ. ἡ ποιμενικὴ σκηνὴ τοῦ Ἰακὼβ ἐν Ἐδέσῃ σῳζομένη κατὰ τοὺς χρόνους Ἀντωνίνου Ῥωμαίων βασιλέως διεφθάρη κεραυνῷ, ὥς φησιν ὁ Ἀφρικανός, ἕως τῶν χρόνων αὐτοῦ Ἀντωνίνου ἱστορήσας.

2–4 = T99 **4** → T11,5–7; T6,20s

1 cf. Gen 35,28   **1s** cf. Gen 35,29; ps. Sym. f. 32[v] = Cedr. 62,8–10

[AB] **3** Ῥωμαίων βασιλέως Β ~ Α

T28c

For on account of Rachel he served for the first seven years; and having had unintended relations with Leah, he had a third son Levi by her, obviously after the period of three years. **Therefore, one should trust neither Africanus' assertion that Levi was born in Jacob's 87th year**, nor Eusebius' that he was born in his 86th. For if we follow one or the other of them, we shall find that Joseph was born when Jacob was either 96 or 95 years of age. And this contradicts what is set forth in divine Scripture: namely (1) that Joseph was 30 years of age when he began to rule Egypt, and (2) that after 10 years elapsed (I am referring to the seven years of plenty and the three years of famine), he was reunited with Israel and his whole household, Israel being 130 years of age and Joseph obviously 40. From this, we have thus precisely established the date of birth of each of these two patriarchs. And in doing the calculations in this way, we shall also have the agreement of other church historians who succeeded them, but who do not provide the explanation and careful argumentation given above.

F29 *Jacob's Tent*

In the 120th year of Jacob, his father Isaac died, having lived 180 years. He was buried by his sons Jacob and Esau. **The shepherd's tent of Jacob preserved in Edessa was destroyed by a thunderbolt around the time of Antoninus the emperor of the Romans,** as Africanus states, who has written his history up to the time of this Antoninus.[1]

---

1 For Syncellus' concluding notice about the endpoint of the *Chronographiae* and the identity of Antoninus, see T99 and notes.

F30

F30a Georgius Syncellus (123,13–21 Mosshammer)

F30b ps. Eustathius, Commentarius in hexaemeron (77,21 – 78,6 Allatius = PG 18,777D–780A)

Ἰακὼβ ἀπαρεσθεὶς τοῖς ὑπὸ Συμεὼν καὶ Λευὶ πραχθεῖσιν ἐν Σικίμοις διὰ τὴν τῆς ἀδελφῆς φθορὰν εἰς τοὺς ἐπιχωρίους, *θάψας ἐν Σικίμοις οὓς ἐφέρετο θεοὺς παρὰ τὴν πέτραν ὑπὸ τὴν θαυμασίαν τερέβινθον, ἥτις μέχρι νῦν εἰς τιμὴν τῶν πατριαρχῶν ὑπὸ τῶν πλησιοχώρων τιμᾶται, μετῆρεν εἰς Βαιθήλ·* ταύτης παρὰ τὸ πρέμνον βωμὸς ἦν, ὥς φησιν ὁ Ἀφρικανός, τῆς τερεβίνθου, ἐφ' ὃν τὰς ἐκτενὰς ἀνέφερον ἐν ταῖς πανηγύρεσι τῆς χώρας ἔνοικοι, ἡ δ' οὐ κατεκαίετο δοκοῦσα πιπρᾶσθαι. παρὰ ταύτην ὁ τάφος Ἀβραὰμ καὶ Ἰσαάκ.

Φασὶ δέ τινες ῥάβδον εἶναί τινος τῶν ἐπιξενωθέντων ἀγγέλων τῷ Ἀβραὰμ *φυτευθεῖσαν αὐτόθι.*

Ἐπὶ τέλει δὲ καὶ τὸν Ἰωσήφ, τῆς Αἰγύπτου ἀποχωρήσαντες, κηδεύουσιν *ἔνθα ὁ προπάτωρ αὐτῶν Ἀβραὰμ προκεκήδευτο· ἐν ᾧ τόπῳ ὑπῆρχε καὶ ἡ τερέβινθος, ὑφ' ᾗ ἔκρυψεν Ἰακὼβ τῆς Λάβαν τὰ εἴδωλα, ἥτις ἔτι καὶ νῦν εἰς τιμὴν τῶν προγόνων ὑπὸ τῶν πλησιοχώρων θρησκεύεται· ἔστι γὰρ ἄχρι τοῦ δεῦρο παρὰ τὸν πρέμνον αὐτῆς βωμός, ἐφ' ὃν τά τε ὁλοκαυτώματα καὶ τὰς ἑκατόμβας ἀνέφερον.*

Εἶναί τε φασὶ ῥάβδον αὐτὴν ἑνὸς τῶν ἐπιξενωθέντων ἀγγέλων τῷ Ἀβραάμ, *ἥνπερ τῷ τόπῳ τότε παρὼν ἐνεφύτευσε, καὶ ἐξ αὐτῆς ἡ ἀξιάγαστος ἐνεφύη τερέβινθος.* ὑπαφθεῖσα γὰρ ὅλη πῦρ γίνεται, καὶ νομίζεται τοῖς πᾶσιν εἰς κόνιν ἐκ τῆς φλογὸς ἀναλύεσθαι, καίτοι σβεσθεῖσα μέντοι ἀσινὴς ὅλη καὶ ἀκέραιος δείκνυται.

5–7 Eus., dem. ev. 5,9,7 (232,5–8 Heikel) ὅθεν (sc. Mamre!) εἰσέτι καὶ νῦν παρὰ τοῖς πλησιοχώροις ὡς ἂν θεῖος ὁ τόπος εἰς τιμὴν τῶν αὐτόθι τῷ Ἀβραὰμ ἐπιφανέντων θρησκεύεται, καὶ θεωρεῖταί γε εἰς δεῦρο διαμένουσα ἡ τερέβινθος.

1–6 cf. Gen 34,30 – 35,5   **b:1s** cf. Gen 50,25; Exod 13,19; Ios 24,32   **b:2s et a:13s** cf. Act 7,16; Liber Genealogus 352s; Sync. 176,4–6   **3–14** cf. Ios., bell. Iud. 4,533; Eus., v. C. 3,53; Eus., onomasticon 237; Soz., h. e. 2,4; Itinerarium Burdigalense 587,5 – 588,6   **8s** cf. Gen 12,6s; 33,18–20   **15–23** cf. Gen 18,1–15

[AB] **8** βαιθήλ B βεθήλ A   **8s** παρὰ τὸ πρέμνον A παρὰ πραίμνον B   **13** πιπρᾶσθαι A πηπράσθαι B πίπρασθαι Di. πιμπράσθαι Goar^m   **17** φυτευθεῖσαν A φυτεύθησαν B

8 ἔστι] ἔσται Allatius   **22** καίτοι σβεσθεῖσα] κατασβεσθεῖσα Routh | μέντοι < Gelzer^ms

F30 The Terebinth Tree in Shechem

F30a

Jacob was displeased by what Simeon and Levi had done in Shechem against the inhabitants there in retaliation for their sister's defilement. And he buried in Shechem[1] the gods that he brought with him by the rock underneath the wonderful terebinth tree, which is even to this day venerated by the neighboring peoples in honor of the patriarchs. He removed thence to Bethel. By the trunk of this terebinth tree there was an altar, as Africanus says, to which the residents of that region would offer prayers in their festal assemblies. Even though it appeared to be in flames, it was not consumed. Near it is the tomb of Abraham and Isaac.

Some say that (it) is a staff of one of the angels received as guests by Abraham and planted on that spot.

F30b

And finally, after departing from Egypt, they buried Joseph in the location where their forefather Abraham had been previously interred. At that site the terebinth tree was also standing, under which Jacob had hidden the idols of Laban. Even to this very day, it is an object of religious observance by the neighboring peoples in honor of their ancestors.[2] For up to the present time, there is an altar at its trunk, on which they would offer both burnt offerings and hecatombs.[3]

It is said that it is a staff of one of the angels received as guests by Abraham, which he planted at the site when he was present there at that time. And from it sprouted the remarkable terebinth. For when set aflame, it turns entirely into fire and is supposed by everyone to be reduced to dust by the flame; and yet once the fire is extinguished, it proves to be entirely unscathed and intact.

---

1. According to the book of Genesis, Mamre, not Shechem, was the place where Abraham entertained the angels (Gen 18,1–10), and the burial site of Abraham and Isaac (Gen 23,1–20; 25,9f; 50,13f; cf. Act 7,16). Cf. also Eus., dem. ev. 5,9,7, which describes in very similar language a ritual performed at the terebinth at Mamre. Either Africanus was describing another festival of Samaritan origin (see Gelzer 1,10), or the terebinth at Shechem (where Jacob buried the idols) somehow became confused with the terebinth at Mamre.
2. The pagan character of the sacrifices performed at the terebinth suggests that 'ancestors' is closer to the original text than 'patriarchs'.
3. Here again the text of ps. Eust. more closely reflects the original wording of Africanus. The ἐκτεναί mentioned in Syncellus' text are public prayers in the Byzantine liturgy, see Trapp 2001, s. v. ἐκτενή.

F31 Georgius Cedrenus (76,23 – 77,3 Bekker)

Ὡς δὲ λέγει ὁ Ἀφρικανός, ὅτι ἐκ τοῦ Ἡσαῦ ἄλλοι τε πολλοὶ καὶ Ῥαγουὴλ γεννᾶται, ἀφ᾽ οὗ Ζαρέθ, ἐξ οὗ Ἰώβ, ὃς κατὰ συγχώρησιν θεοῦ ὑπὸ διαβόλου ἐπειράσθη καὶ ἐνίκησε τὸν πειράζοντα.

2   cf. Eus., praep. ev. 9,25,1 (= Alexander Polyhistor FGrHist 273 F19a, Aristeas FGrHist 725 F1); Eus., fr. Lc. 540D; Epiph., haer. 1,180,19 – 181,2; Cedr. 126,8–11

T32   Georgius Syncellus (126,10–17 Mosshammer)

Τῷ α΄ ἔτει τῆς ζωῆς Καάθ, ὅπερ ἦν τοῦ μὲν Ἰακὼβ ρλ΄, τοῦ δὲ Λευὶ μη΄, κατῆλθεν Ἰακὼβ εἰς Αἴγυπτον πρὸς Ἰωσήφ, ὥς φησιν ἡ θεία γραφή, ὅτι «εἶπε δὲ Ἰακὼβ τῷ Φαραώ· αἱ ἡμέραι τῶν ἐτῶν τῆς ζωῆς μου ἃς παροικῶ ρλ΄ ἔτη.» Ἰωσὴφ δὲ ἦν ἐτῶν μ΄ τῷ αὐτῷ ρλ΄ ἔτει τοῦ Ἰακώβ, διότι, ὥς φασιν οἱ περὶ τὸν Ἀφρικανόν, ο΄ ἔζησεν ὁ Ἰωσὴφ ἔτη μετὰ τὸ παροικῆσαι τὸν
5 Ἰακὼβ ἐν Αἰγύπτῳ.
    Τὸ ζ΄ καὶ τελευταῖον ἔτος τῆς λιμοῦ, τὸ ε΄ ἔτος Καάθ, τοῦ δὲ κόσμου ἦν ἔτος ͵γχς΄.

4s → T28c,3s

1–3 cf. Eus., can.[Hier] 33[a]; 33[d]; Sym. Log. (Leo Gr. 24,22 – 25,4 = Th. Mel. 24,23 – 25,1); ps. Sym. f. 32[v] = Cedr. 62,12–14; Ecl. Hist. 174,27.30–32   2 cf. Gen 41,46s; 45,6; 50,26   2s Gen 47,9   4s cf. Eus., can.[Hier] 36[c]; Sym. Log. (Leo Gr. 25,4s = Th. Mel. 25,1s); ps. Sym. f. 32[v] = Cedr. 62,16

[AB]   4 ὁ < B   6 τῆς B τοῦ A

F31 *Job, the Descendant of Esau*

Africanus states that Esau begot many children, among them Reuel, from whom was begotten Zerah, from whom was begotten Job. With the consent of God, he was put to the test by the devil and prevailed over the one testing him.

T32 *The Chronology of Joseph's Life*

In the first year of the life of Kohath, which was the 130th year of Jacob and the 48th year of Levi, Jacob went down to Joseph in Egypt, as Scripture says, 'The days of my life in which I sojourn are 130 years'. Now Joseph was 40 years old in the same 130th year of Jacob, since, as the school of Africanus says, Joseph lived another 70 years after Jacob had come to dwell in Egypt.[1]

The seventh and final year of the famine, the fifth year of Kohath, AM 3606.

---

1 According to Africanus, Joseph's family came to Egypt when he was 39 years of age (T28a, n. 1). If Joseph died aged 110, then he would have lived another 71 (not 70) years after Jacob's arrival. The difference might be explained by the fact that Syncellus apparently did not quote directly from Africanus, but from a member of his 'school' (οἱ περὶ τὸν Ἀφρικανόν).

F33

Sync.¹: Georgius Syncellus (128,1–3 Mosshammer)
Sync.²: Georgius Syncellus (122,1–3 Mosshammer)

Ἀφρικανοῦ·
   Ἀπὸ Ἀδὰμ τοίνυν ἐπὶ τὴν τελευτὴν Ἰωσὴφ καὶ τῆσδε τῆς βίβλου γενεαὶ μὲν κγ′, ἔτη δὲ ͵γφξγ′.

test.: Sync.¹ [AB] (→ T33a) ... οὕτω γράφει· Ἀφρικανοῦ· Ἀπὸ Ἀδὰμ ...; Sync.² [AB] ... ἔτη δὲ ͵γφξγ′. Διαμαρτάνει ... (→ T33b)

2s → F16a; F16c

3 cf. Chron. Pasch. 114,6–11 (anno 3563)

2 τὴν < Sync.¹

T33a Georgius Syncellus (127,24–28 Mosshammer)

Τῷ ͵γχοβ′ ἔτει τοῦ κόσμου, ἤγουν τῷ ιβ′ τῆς ζωῆς Ἀμβραμ πατρὸς Μωυσέως, ἐτελεύτησεν Ἰωσὴφ ζήσας ἔτη ρι′, ὥς φησιν ἡ βίβλος τῆς Γενέσεως οὕτως· «καὶ ἐτελεύτησεν Ἰωσὴφ ὢν ἐτῶν ρι′», ἕως τούτου τοῦ ͵γχοβ′ κοσμικοῦ ἔτους ἱστορεῖ ἡ αὐτὴ θεόπνευστος πρώτη βίβλος. Ὁ μέντοι Ἀφρικανὸς ἔτη ρθ′ διαμαρτήσας κατ' ἔλλειψιν οὕτω γράφει· Ἀφρικανοῦ· ... (→ F33)

2 Gen 50,26a 2s cf. ps. Sym. f. 32ᵛ = Cedr. 62,16s

T33b Georgius Syncellus (122,4–7 Mosshammer)

(→ F33) ... Διαμαρτάνει προφανῶς ἔτη ρι′. τῷ γὰρ αὐτῷ ͵γφξγ′ ἔτει τοῦ κόσμου ἐγεννήθη Ἰωσήφ, ὡς ὑπόκειται. τῷ θ′ ἔτει τῆς ζωῆς τοῦ Λευὶ ἐγέννησε Ῥαχὴλ τὸν Ἰωσὴφ τῷ Ἰακώβ. ἦν δὲ τῆς ζωῆς Ἰακὼβ ἔτος ϙα′, κόσμου δὲ ͵γφξγ′.

2 → T28c,3s

1–3 cf. ps. Sym. f. 32ʳ ≈ Cedr. 59,20 – 60,3   2 cf. Chron. Pasch. 109,16s

[AB] 1 διαμαρτάνει B διαμαρτάνη A | αὐτῷ < B

F33 *The Date of Joseph's Death*[1]

From Africanus

From Adam, then, up to the death of Joseph and the end of this book,[2] there are 23 generations and 3563 years.[3]

T33a

In AM 3672, that is in the 12th year of the life of Amram the father of Moses, Joseph died, after living 110 years, as the book of Genesis says, 'And Joseph died when he was 110 years of age'. The historical record of the same divinely-inspired first book of the Scripture extends up to this year, AM 3672. Africanus, however, errs by omitting 109 years, and writes as follows: ... (→ F33)

T33b

(→ F33) ... He is manifestly in error by 110 years. For Joseph was born in this year AM 3563, as is shown below. In the ninth year of the life of Levi, Rachel give birth to Jacob's child Joseph. This was the 91st year of the life of Jacob, AM 3563.

---

1   Syncellus quotes this passage from Africanus twice, in each case faulting him for incorrectly calculating the duration of time from Adam to the death of Joseph (T33a.b).
2   The words "end of this book" could refer either to the end of the book of Genesis or to the end of the first book of Africanus' chronicle.
3   This date coincides with the chronology given in T45,18f: the birth of Abraham according to Africanus occurred in AM 3202. Isaac's birth 100 years later was in AM 3302 (Gen 21,5), Jacob's birth 60 years later in AM 3362 (Gen 25,26). By determining the birth of Joseph when Jacob was 91 years of age (= AM 3453, T28, esp. note to T28a), Africanus established that the death of Joseph at age 110 (Gen 50,26) occurred in AM 3563. For Syncellus' opposing date of the death of Joseph, see Adler/Tuffin 2002,149f, n. 6.

F34

Eus.: Eusebius, Praeparatio evangelica 10,10,1 – 10,23,6 (591,6 – 595,18 Mras/ des Places)
Sync.[1]: Georgius Syncellus (71,7 – 73,11 Mosshammer)
Sync.[2]: ibd. (173,15 – 174,10 Mosshammer)
Sync.[3]: ibd. (78,19s Mosshammer)

Μέχρι μὲν τῶν Ὀλυμπιάδων οὐδὲν ἀκριβὲς ἱστόρηται τοῖς Ἕλλησι, πάντων συγκεχυμένων καὶ κατὰ μηδὲν αὐτοῖς τῶν πρὸ τοῦ συμφωνούντων· αἱ δὲ ἠκρίβωνται πολλοῖς, τῷ μὴ ἐκ πλείστου διαστήματος, διὰ τετραετίας δὲ τὰς ἀναγραφὰς αὐτῶν ποιεῖσθαι τοὺς Ἕλληνας. οὗ δὴ χάριν τὰς ἐνδοξοτάτας καὶ μυθώδεις
5 ἐπιλεξάμενος ἱστορίας μέχρι τῆς πρώτης Ὀλυμπιάδος ἐπιδραμοῦμαι· τὰς δὲ μετὰ ταῦτα συζεύξας κατὰ χρόνον ἑκάστας, εἴ τινες ἐπίσημοι, ταῖς Ἑλληνικαῖς τὰς Ἑβραϊκάς, ἐξιστορῶν μὲν τὰ Ἑβραίων, ἐφαπτόμενος δὲ τῶν Ἑλληνικῶν, ἐφαρμόσω τόνδε τὸν τρόπον· λαβόμενος μιᾶς πράξεως Ἑβραϊκῆς ὁμοχρόνου πράξει ὑφ᾽ Ἑλλήνων ἱστορηθείσῃ καὶ ταύτης ἐχόμενος ἀφαιρῶν τε καὶ προστι-
10 θεὶς τίς τε Ἕλλην ἢ Πέρσης ἢ καὶ ὁστισοῦν τῇ Ἑβραίων συνεχρόνισεν ἐπισημειούμενος, ἴσως ἂν τοῦ σκοποῦ τύχοιμι.

Ἑβραίων μὲν οὖν ἡ μετοικία ἐπισημοτάτη, αἰχμαλωτισθέντων ὑπὸ Ναβουχοδονόσορ βασιλέως Βαβυλῶνος, παρέτεινεν ἔτη ἑβδομήκοντα, καθὰ προεφήτευσεν Ἱερεμίας. τοῦ δὴ Ναβουχοδονόσορ μνημονεύει Βηρωσσὸς ὁ Βαβυλώνιος.
15 μετὰ δὲ τὰ ο᾽ τῆς αἰχμαλωσίας ἔτη Κῦρος Περσῶν ἐβασίλευσεν, ᾧ ἔτει Ὀλυμπιὰς ἤχθη νε᾽, ὡς ἐκ τῶν Βιβλιοθηκῶν Διοδώρου καὶ τῶν Θαλλοῦ καὶ Κάστορος ἱστοριῶν, ἔτι δὲ Πολυβίου καὶ Φλέγοντος ἔστιν εὑρεῖν, ἀλλὰ καὶ ἑτέρων, οἷς ἐμέλησεν Ὀλυμπιάδων· ἅπασι γὰρ συνεφώνησεν ὁ χρόνος.

Κῦρος δ᾽ οὖν τῷ πρώτῳ τῆς ἀρχῆς ἔτει, ὅπερ ἦν Ὀλυμπιάδος νε᾽ ἔτος τὸ
20 πρῶτον, διὰ Ζοροβάβελ, καθ᾽ ὃν Ἰησοῦς ὁ τοῦ Ἰωσεδέκ, τὴν πρώτην καὶ μερι-

test.: 1 inc. Eus. [BIO(l.35–)(G)N(D)]: Ἀπὸ τοῦ τρίτου τῶν Ἀφρικανοῦ χρονογραφιῶν

1s ps. Iust., coh. Gr. 12,2 (38,14–18 Marcovich) Ἄλλως τε οὐδὲ τοῦτο ἀγνοεῖν ὑμᾶς προσήκει, ὅτι οὐδὲν Ἕλλησι πρὸ τῶν Ὀλυμπιάδων ἀκριβὲς ἱστόρηται, οὐδ᾽ ἔστι τι σύγγραμμα παλαιὸν Ἑλλήνων ἢ βαρβάρων σημαῖνον πρᾶξιν, μόνη δὲ ἡ τοῦ πρώτου προφήτου Μωυσέως προϋπῆρχεν ἱστορία, ἣν ἐκ θείας ἐπιπνοίας Μωυσῆς γέγραφεν τοῖς τῶν Ἑβραίων γράμμασι. Sync. (109,24–26 Moss.) Αἱ παρ᾽ Ἕλλησιν ἀρχαιολογίαι πᾶσαι μὲν ἀσύμφωνοι φέρονται παρὰ τοῖς συλλεξαμένοις αὐτὰς ἱστορικοῖς, ἐξαιρέτως δὲ αἱ πρὸ τῆς πρώτης Ὀλυμπιάδος. **19s** → F65,133s **19–22** → F73,3–6; F93,36–40

1s cf. Sync. 109,24–26 **12–14** cf. Ier 25,11 **14** Berossus Babylonius FGrHist 680 F8 **15–18** Diod. Sic. 9,21,1; Thallus FGrHist 256 F7; Castor FGrHist 250 F6; Polybius FGrHist 254 F3; Phleg. Trall. FGrHist 257 F8 **19–22** cf. I Esdr 2,1–11; 5,1–62

3 τῷ] τὸ G **7–20** τὰς…Ζοροβάβελ < B **7** τὰ IN τὰς G **15** δὲ τὰ < ND¹ (+ D⁴) **16** νε᾽] πεντεκοστῇ πέμπτῃ N πεντηκοστῇ D¹ (marg. νε᾽ D⁴) | Βιβλιοθηκῶν Διοδώρου I ~ GN **17** ἔτι δὲ] καὶ ND¹ (corr. D⁴) **17s** Φλέγοντος…Ὀλυμπιάδων] καὶ ἑτέρων ἐστὶν εὑρεῖν ND¹ (corr. D⁴) **19** δ᾽ < ND

Material from Book 3: From Moses to the First Olympiad

F34 *Synchronism of the Exodus and Ogygus*[1]

Until the time of the Olympiads, nothing accurate has been recorded by the Greeks in their histories, all their accounts before that time being muddled and in no point agreeing among themselves. The Olympiads, however, have been accurately recorded by many, because the Greeks kept registers of them that were not separated by a long span of time, but rather by an interval of four years. For this reason, I shall give a cursory treatment to my selection of the most notable of the legendary narratives up until the first Olympiad. But those narratives after that time, if any of them are noteworthy, I shall combine together chronologically one to the other, the Hebrew with the Greek, carefully investigating the affairs of the Hebrews while only touching upon those of the Greek. And I shall fit them together in the following manner: By taking up a single event in Hebrew history contemporary with an event recorded by the Greeks, and basing myself on it, and by either subtracting from or adding to it, I shall indicate what noteworthy person—whether Greek or Persian or whoever—was contemporary with the Hebrew event. And in this way I shall perhaps accomplish my objective.

So then, the resettlement of the Hebrews, when they were taken captive by Nebuchadnezzar king of Babylon, is a most noteworthy event, extending 70 years, in accordance with the prophecy of Jeremiah. Nebuchadnezzar is in fact mentioned by Berossus the Babylonian. After the 70 years of the Captivity, Cyrus became king of the Persians, in the year in which the 55th Olympic contest was held, as one may discover from the *Bibliothecae* of Diodorus, and the histories of Thallus and Castor, as well as those of Polybius and Phlegon, and from others too, who have made the Olympiads a subject of study. For in all of them, there is chronological agreement.

---

1 This important fragment, found at the beginning of book three of Africanus' chronicle, outlines his method for establishing a comparative chronology of Greek and Hebrew history from the Exodus down to the first year of the reign of Cyrus. Although the transmission of the text is complex (see the documentation provided in the fourth apparatus), the original wording can be reconstructed with confidence from the two main witnesses (for ps. Iust.'s dependence on Africanus, see Riedweg 1994,30–33). Syncellus, the more complete witness, quotes portions of the same passage in different places. Where he and Eusebius independently cite overlapping material, the level of concordance is very high. Since the formulaic expressions (e. g., "after a few words") used in two places to identify lacunae (ll. 37 and 74) imply that the omitted material is not extensive, we can assume that the entire text represents a single fragment.

κὴν ἀπόπεμψιν ἐποιήσατο τοῦ λαοῦ, πληρωθείσης τῆς ἑβδομηκονταετίας, ὡς ἐν τῷ Ἔσδρᾳ παρὰ τοῖς Ἑβραίοις ἱστόρηται. αἱ μὲν οὖν ἱστορίαι συντρέχουσι Κύρου τε βασιλείας καὶ αἰχμαλωσίας τέλους καὶ <τὰ> κατὰ τὰς Ὀλυμπιάδας οὕτως εἰς ἡμᾶς εὑρεθήσεται συμφωνήσαντα· τούτοις γὰρ ἑπόμενοι καὶ τὰς λοιπὰς
25 ἱστορίας κατὰ τὸν αὐτὸν λόγον ἀλλήλαις ἐφαρμόσομεν.

Τὰ δὲ πρὸ τούτων ὡδί πως τῆς Ἀττικῆς χρονογραφίας ἀριθμουμένης, ἀπὸ Ὠγύγου τοῦ παρ᾽ ἐκείνοις αὐτόχθονος πιστευθέντος, ἐφ᾽ οὗ γέγονεν ὁ μέγας καὶ πρῶτος ἐν τῇ Ἀττικῇ κατακλυσμός, Φορωνέως Ἀργείων βασιλεύοντος, ὡς Ἀκουσίλαος ἱστορεῖ, μέχρι πρώτης Ὀλυμπιάδος, ὁπόθεν Ἕλληνες ἀκριβοῦν
30 τοὺς χρόνους ἐνόμισαν, ἔτη συνάγεται χίλια εἴκοσιν, ὡς καὶ τοῖς προειρημένοις συμφωνεῖ καὶ τοῖς ἑξῆς δειχθήσεται. τὰ γὰρ Ἀθηναίων ἱστοροῦντες Ἑλλάνικός τε καὶ Φιλόχορος οἱ τὰς Ἀτθίδας, οἵ τε τὰ Σύρια Κάστωρ καὶ Θαλλός, καὶ τὰ πάντων Διόδωρος ὁ τὰς Βιβλιοθήκας, Ἀλέξανδρός τε ὁ Πολυΐστωρ καί τινες τῶν καθ᾽ ἡμᾶς ἀκριβέστερον ἐμνήσθησαν καὶ τῶν Ἀττικῶν ἁπάντων. εἴ τις οὖν
35 ἐν τοῖς χιλίοις εἴκοσιν ἔτεσιν ἐπίσημος ἱστορία τυγχάνει, κατὰ τὸ χρήσιμον ἐκλεγήσεται.
[…]
Φαμὲν τοίνυν ἐκ γε τοῦδε τοῦ συγγράμματος Ὤγυγον, ὃς τοῦ πρώτου κατακλυσμοῦ γέγονεν ἐπώνυμος πολλῶν διαφθαρέντων διασωθείς, κατὰ τὴν ἀπ᾽ Αἰ-
40 γύπτου τοῦ λαοῦ μετὰ Μωυσέως ἔξοδον γεγενῆσθαι, τόνδε τὸν τρόπον· ἐπὶ τὴν πρώτην Ὀλυμπιάδα τὴν προειρημένην ἀπὸ Ὠγύγου ἔτη δειχθήσεται ͵ακʹ. ἀπὸ δὲ αʹ Ὀλυμπιάδος ἐπὶ νεʹ, ἔτος πρῶτον, τουτέστιν ἐπὶ Κύρου βασιλείας ἔτος αʹ,

---

test.: Eus.   37 Eus.: καὶ μετὰ βραχέα ἐπιλέγει   38 inc. Sync.[1] [A]: κατὰ τὸν Ἀφρικανὸν ὧδέ πως ἐπὶ λέξεως γραφέντα et Sync.[2] [A]: ὁμοίως δὲ καὶ ἡ ἀπ᾽ Αἰγύπτου πορεία τοῖς Ἑλλήνων ἱστορικοῖς οὕτω φέρεται διαφόρως κατὰ τοὺς αὐτοὺς χρόνους τῷ ἐπὶ Ὠγύγου κατακλυσμῷ. συμφωνοῦσι δὲ τούτοις ἐν τούτῳ καὶ Ἰώσηπος καὶ Ἰοῦστος Ἰουδαῖοι ἱστορικοὶ καὶ τοῦ καθ᾽ ἡμᾶς λόγου Κλήμης ὁ στρωματεὺς καὶ Τατιανὸς καὶ Ἀφρικανός, οὗ καὶ χρῆσιν ἑξῆς παραθώμεθα. Ἀφρικανοῦ· ἐν τρίτῳ λόγῳ φησί 40 γεγενῆσθαι des. Sync.[2] (sequitur l. 71)

26-31 → T48b; F50,5-7   31-34 ps. Iust., coh. Gr. 9,2 (34,19–23 Marcovich) *Καὶ οἱ τὰ Ἀθηναίων δὲ ἱστοροῦντες, Ἑλλάνικός τε καὶ Φιλόχορος οἱ τὰς Ἀτθίδας, <οἵ τε τὰ Σύρια> Κάστωρ τε καὶ Θαλλός, καὶ Ἀλέξανδρος ὁ Πολυΐστωρ, ἔτι δὲ καὶ οἱ σοφώτατοι Φίλων τε καὶ Ἰώσηπος, οἱ τὰ κατὰ Ἰουδαίους ἱστορήσαντες, ὡς σφόδρα ἀρχαίου καὶ παλαιοῦ τῶν Ἰουδαίων ἄρχοντος Μωϋσέως μέμνηνται.*
38-40 → T55,20-24   40-42 → F54a,46-48; F65,133s; F73,1-6

26-33   Alex. Polyh. FGrHist 273 F101; Hellanicus FGrHist 4 F47; Philochorus FGrHist 328 F92; Castor FGrHist 250 F7; Thallus FGrHist 256 F5   26-29 Acusilaus FGrHist 2 F23b

21 ἐν < G   23 τὰ Routh   26 Τὰ Routh τὰς codd.   30 συνάγεται IG συνάγονται BN | χίλια εἴκοσιν I ͵ακʹ GN ͵αηʹ B | ὡς] ὃ Routh   31 συμφωνεῖν Routh | τὰ Gelzer[ms] (cf. ps. Iust.) ταῦτα codd. | γὰρ + οἱ τὰ Routh, Mras   32 οἱ] ὁ Routh   32-40 οἵ…Αἰγύπτου < B   32 καὶ[3] + ὁ Routh   33 τῶν βιβλιοθηκῶν ND | τινες] οἵτινες Routh τινες οἵ Mras   38 γε] δὲ Sync.[1] τε Eus. | τοῦ[1] < Sync.[1] | συγγράμματος] συνταγμάτος Sync.[2]   39 κατὰ] μετὰ Sync.[2]:A ante corr. κατὰ post corr. eadem manu | ἀπ᾽ < Eus.   40 γενέσεθαι Sync.[2] | τὸν < Sync.[1] | τὴν < Eus.:BIN   41 προειρημένην] πρώτην Eus.:B | ἀπὸ Ὠγύγου < Eus.:B   42 ἐπὶ[1] + τῆς Eus.

Cyrus, then, in the first year of his reign, which was the first year of the 55th Olympiad, brought about the first partial release of the people through Zorobabel, contemporary with whom was Jeshua the son of Jozadak, after the completion of the 70 years, as is recorded in the book of Ezra from the books of the Hebrews.[2] Therefore, the historical accounts of the reign of Cyrus and of the end of the Captivity coincide. And <events> dated according to the Olympiads will thus be found to agree down to our time. For by following them we shall also fit the other histories one to the other according to the same principle.

Now the Attic system of measuring time reckons the dates of the earlier events in something like the following way: From Ogygus, who was believed by them to be indigenous,[3] and in whose time the great first flood in Attica occurred, when Phoroneus was king of Argos, according to the historical record of Acusilaus, up to the first Olympiad, from which time the Greeks believed they were accurate in their chronology, there are altogether 1020 years. And this number also agrees with what has been stated before, and will be demonstrated in what follows. For the writers of Athenian history, both Hellanicus and Philochorus, authors of the *Atthides*; writers of Syrian history, Castor and Thallus; writers of universal history, Diodorus the author of the *Bibliothecae*, and Alexander Polyhistor; and some writers of our own[4] have recorded this chronology more accurately than even all the Attic historians. If, then, any noteworthy historical narrative comes to our attention in the 1020 years, it shall be selected in accordance with its value.

[...]

We assert, therefore, on the authority of this work, that Ogygus, who, having been saved when many perished,[5] has given his name to the first flood, lived at the time of the Exodus of the people with Moses from Egypt. This is the method of my calculation: 1020 years will be demonstrated from Ogygus up to the aforementioned first Olympiad. From the first Olympiad up to the first year of the 55th Olympiad (that is, to the first year of the reign of Cyrus, which was

---

2 Cyrus' accession to power in Persia occurred in 560 BC (= Ol. 55,1). When Cyrus conquered Babylon in 538 BC, he issued his decree releasing the Jews from captivity. Esdr 1,1, dating the decree of Cyrus to the "first year" of his rule, was likely the source of Africanus' assumption that the restoration of the Jews occurred when Cyrus first assumed power.
3 Africanus does not share the opinion of the Attic historiographers, according to whom Ogygus was the first indigenous king. Rather it was Cranaus (F54b), whereas Ogygus was an immigrant from Egypt (ll. 100f).
4 I. e. authors of the Jewish-Christian tradition.
5 For Africanus' chronology of Ogygus' rule after the flood, see F54c, n. 1. Later sources sometimes failed to take account of Africanus' assumption that Ogygus survived the flood by 17 years.

ὅπερ ἦν αἰχμαλωσίας τέλος, ἔτη σιε'. ἀπὸ Ὠγύγου τοίνυν ἐπὶ Κῦρον ἔτη ˏασλε'.
εἰ δὲ ἀναφέροι τις ἀναλογιζόμενος ἀπὸ τοῦ τέλους τῆς αἰχμαλωσίας τὰ ˏασλε'
45 ἔτη, κατὰ ἀναλογίαν εὑρήσει ταὐτὸν διάστημα ἐπὶ πρῶτον ἔτος τῆς ἀπ' Αἰγύπτου διὰ Μωυσέως ἐξόδου Ἰσραὴλ ὅσον ἀπὸ τῆς νε' Ὀλυμπιάδος ἐπὶ Ὤγυγον, ὃς ἔκτισεν Ἐλευσῖνα. ὅθεν ἐπισημότερόν ἐστι καταλαβεῖν τὴν Ἀττικὴν χρονογραφίαν.

Ὀλίγα δὲ τούτων ἐν Ἀσσυρίοις λόγοις ἀρχαιότερα μυθεύεται· πρῶτος ἦρξε
50 Νίνος ἁπάσης τῆς Ἀσίας, πλὴν Ἰνδῶν, ἔτεσι τριακοσίοις, οὐ πολὺ πρότερον Ὠγύγου. τοῦτον διεδέξατο Σεμίραμις ἡ διαβόητος, ἣ πολλαχοῦ τῆς γῆς ἤγειρε χώματα προφάσει μὲν διὰ τοὺς κατακλυσμούς, τὰ δ' ἦν ἄρα τῶν ἐρωμένων ζώντων κατορυσσομένων οἱ τάφοι, ὡς Κτησίας ἱστορεῖ· ὥστε οὐδὲν ἀξιομνημόνευτον Ἕλλησιν ἱστορεῖται πρὸ Ὠγύγου, πλὴν Φορωνέως τοῦ συγχρονίσαντος
55 αὐτῷ καὶ Ἰνάχου τοῦ Φορωνέως πατρός, ὃς πρῶτος Ἄργους ἐβασίλευσεν, ὡς Ἀκουσίλαος ἱστορεῖ. τούτου θυγάτηρ Ἰώ, ἣν Ἶσιν μετονομάσαντες σέβουσι.

Καὶ τοσαῦτα μὲν πρὸ Ὠγύγου. κατὰ δὲ τοὺς τούτου χρόνους ἐξῆλθε Μωυσῆς ἀπ' Αἰγύπτου. καὶ ὡς οὐκ ἄπιστον τότε ταῦτα συμβῆναι, δείκνυμεν οὕτως· ἀπὸ τῆς ἐξόδου Μωυσέως ἐπὶ Κῦρον, ὃς ἐβασίλευσε μετὰ τὴν αἰχμαλω-
60 σίαν, ἔτη ˏασλε'·

Μωυσέως γὰρ ἔτη τὰ λοιπὰ μ'.
Ἰησοῦ τοῦ μετ' ἐκεῖνον ἡγησαμένου κε'.
Πρεσβυτέρων ἔτη λ' τῶν μετὰ Ἰησοῦν.
Κριτῶν τῶν τε ἐν τῇ βίβλῳ τῶν Κριτῶν περιεχομένων ἔτη υϟ'.

test.: Eus. Sync.¹   48 des. Eus.   57 inc. Eus.: καὶ μεθ' ἕτερα   58 Αἰγύπτου des. Sync.¹ (sequitur l. 75)

43   ps. Io. Ant. fr. 1*,1–4 (556 Ro.) *Ὁ παρ' Ἕλλησιν ἀρχαῖος Ὤγυγος καὶ Φορωνεὺς ὁ υἱὸς Ἰνάχου κατὰ τὴν διὰ Μωυσέως ἀπ' Αἰγύπτου ἔξοδον τοῦ λαοῦ ἦσαν. ἀπὸ γὰρ Ὠγύγου μέχρι τῆς νε' Ὀλυμπιάδος, ἤγουν μέχρι τοῦ Κύρου τοῦ Περσῶν βασιλέως ἔτη ˏασλε'.*   **49–53**   → F24,7–9.17–19
51–53   ps. Io. Ant. fr. 28* (570 Ro.) *Σεμίραμις ἡ περιβόητος πολλαχοῦ τῆς γῆς ἤγειρε χώματα, προφάσει μὲν διὰ τοὺς κατακλυσμούς· τάδ' ἦσαν ἄρα τῶν ἐρωμένων ζώντων κατορυσσομένων οἱ τάφοι, <ὡς> Κτησίας ἱστορεῖ.*   **53–56**   → T48; F50,3s   **61–70**   → T6,9–14; F35,1; F58a,1–6; F59a,20–22; T77a,5s   **64** → T39a

51–53 Ctesias FGrHist 688 F1,1i   **53–56** Acusilaus FGrHist 2 F23c   **55s** cf. Eus., can.[Hier] 27,10–15
56 cf. Hdt. 2,41

43 τέλος] ἔτος Eus.:O | σιε' Sync.¹ σιζ' Eus. Routh Gelzer[ms] | Κύρου Sync.¹ | ˏασλε' Sync.¹ ps. Io. Ant. ˏασλζ' Eus. Routh Gelzer[ms]   **44** ἐπιλογιζόμενος Eus. | τὰ < Eus. | ˏασλε' Sync.¹ ps. Io. Ant. ˏασλζ' Eus. Routh Gelzer[ms]   **45** ἔτη < Eus.:ND¹ (+ D⁴) | ἀναλογίαν] ἀνάλυσιν Eus. | εὑρίσκεται Eus. | ταὐτὸν] αὐτὸν Sync.¹ | ἐπὶ + τὸ Eus.:IN   **46** Ὠγύγου Eus.:BN   **47** ἐστι καταλαβεῖν] ἐπικαταλαβεῖν Sync.¹ Ἀττικὴν] αὐτικὴν Sync.¹   **50** οὐ πολὺ] οὐ πλέοσι Gelzer[ms] ἢ πολὺ uel που Moss. (cf. etiam T59a)
51 διαβόητος] περιβόητος ps. Io. Ant.   **56** Ἰώ Di. ἰοῦς A   **58** Μωυσῆς ἀπ' Αἰγύπτου ~ Eus.:I | τότε < B | συμβαίνειν O   **60** ˏασλε' scripsimus (vide supra) ˏασλζ' Eus.   **61** Μωυσέως γὰρ ἔτη τὰ λοιπὰ O ~ I (Μ. γ. τὰ λ. ἔτη) ~ BN (ἔτη γ. Μ. τὰ λ.)   **62** ἡγησαμένου + ἔτη BN   **63** Ἰησοῦ IN

the year marking the end of the Captivity), there are 215 years.[6] Thus, from Ogygus up to Cyrus, there are 1235 years. If you trace back in your calculations the 1235 years from the end of the Captivity, you will discover that the chronological interval up to the first year of the Exodus of Israel from Egypt through Moses corresponds to the interval from the 55th Olympiad back to Ogygus, the founder of Eleusis; hence it is quite a noteworthy starting-point for Attic chronography.

Now in Assyrian documents a few stories are recorded that are even more ancient than this. Three hundred years earlier, not much before Ogygus, Ninus was the first to rule over all of Asia, with the exception of India. And he was succeeded by the celebrated Semiramis, who in many places erected earth embankments, professedly because of the floods. But in reality these embankments were tombs of her lovers being buried alive, as Ctesias records in his history. Nothing worthy of memory is thus recorded in history by the Greeks before Ogygus, with the exception of Phoroneus his contemporary and Inachus, the latter's father, who was the first king of Argos, as Acusilaus records in his history. His daughter was Io, whose name they changed to Isis and venerate.

So much for events before Ogygus. Around his time Moses came forth from Egypt. That there is no reason to doubt that this occurred at that time, we can demonstrate in the following manner: From the Exodus of Moses to Cyrus, who was king after the Captivity, there are 1235 years.[7]

For the remaining years of Moses were 40.

For Joshua, who became the leader after him: 25 years.

For the elders who came after Joshua: 30 years.

For the judges and what is included in the book of Judges: 490 years.[8]

---

6   The chronology found in Eusebius' version, and favored by Routh and Gelzer, assigns 217 years to the period from Ol. 1,1 to 1 Cyrus (Ol. 55,1). These additional two years lengthen the period from Ogygus to Cyrus from 1235 to 1237 years. Syncellus' reading is to be preferred for the following reasons: a) the number '1235' is independently attested in a fragment of ps. John of Antioch (fr. 1*,1–4 Ro.); b) this number also reflects the chronology of Hebrew history outlined in ll. 61–67 (on which, see also the following note). The numbering of years found in Eusebius is thus likely to be a correction, intended to bring the total years into agreement with the actual number of elapsed years from Ol. 1,1 to 55,1 (= 217, reckoning inclusively). A similar problem occurs in F93,54–59, see n. 6.

7   The chronology of Hebrew history given below illustrates the primacy of Hebrew chronology in Africanus' system of reckoning (see introduction p. XXII). The sum of the separate segments of Hebrew history from the Exodus to the end of the Captivity comes to 1235 (not 1237) years. For other witnesses confirming the accuracy of this number, see the supplementary references provided in the apparatus (especially T6).

8   This also includes the periods of anarchy and peace, cf. T6,11 and T39.

65   Ἱερέων δὲ Ἠλεὶ καὶ Σαμουὴλ ἔτη ρ'.
     Τῶν δ' ἑξῆς βασιλέων Ἑβραίων ἔτη τετρακόσια ρ'.
     <Τῆς δ' αἰχμαλωσίας ἑβδομήκοντα,> ἧς τὸ τελευταῖον ἔτος ἦν Κύρου βασιλείας ἔτος πρῶτον, ὡς προειρήκαμεν. ἐπὶ δὲ πρώτην Ὀλυμπιάδα ἀπὸ Μωυσέως ἔτη ,ακ', εἴπερ ἐπὶ πεντηκοστῆς πέμπτης ἔτος πρῶτον ἔτη ,ασλε', κἂν τοῖς
70   Ἑλληνικοῖς συνέδραμεν ὁ χρόνος.
     Μετὰ δὲ Ὤγυγον διὰ τὴν ἀπὸ τοῦ κατακλυσμοῦ πολλὴν φθορὰν ἀβασίλευτος ἔμεινεν ἡ νῦν Ἀττικὴ μέχρι Κέκροπος ἔτη ρπθ'. τὸν γὰρ μετὰ Ὤγυγον Ἀκταῖον ἢ τὰ πλασσόμενα τῶν ὀνομάτων οὐδὲ γενέσθαι φησὶ Φιλόχορος.
     [...]
75   Ἀπὸ Ὠγύγου τοίνυν ἐπὶ Κῦρον, ὁπόσα ἀπὸ Μωυσέως ἐπὶ τὸν αὐτὸν χρόνον, ἔτη ,ασλε'. ἀλλὰ καὶ Ἑλλήνων δέ τινες ἱστοροῦσι κατὰ τοὺς αὐτοὺς χρόνους γενέσθαι Μωυσέα. Πολέμων μὲν ἐν τῇ πρώτῃ τῶν Ἑλληνικῶν ἱστοριῶν λέγων· ἐπὶ Ἄπιδος τοῦ Φορωνέως μοῖρα τοῦ Αἰγυπτίων στρατοῦ ἐξέπεσεν Αἰγύπτου, οἳ ἐν

---

test.: Eus.   71 inc. Sync.²: καὶ μετ' ὀλίγα et Sync.³: (→ T55,3–14) ... ὡς αὐτὸς Ἀφρικανὸς μεμαρτύρηκεν ἐν ἀρχῇ τοῦ τρίτου λόγου εἰπών·   72 ρπθ' des. Sync.³: → T55,18s   74 Eus.: καὶ αὖθις, Sync.²: καὶ μεθ' ἕτερα   75 inc. Sync.¹ [AB^(l.94–)]: καὶ μετ' ὀλίγα

65   Petr. Alex. (190,34–39 Samodurova) Ἠλεὶ ὁ ἱερεὺς ἔτη κ'. ἡ κιβωτὸς ἐν γῇ τῶν ἀλλοφύλων μῆνας ζ'. ἡ κιβωτὸς ἐν οἴκῳ Ἀμιναδὰβ καὶ Σαμουὴλ δικάζων ἐν νεότητι τὸν λαὸν ἐν εἰρήνῃ διάγοντα ἔτη κ'. καὶ μετὰ ταῦτα τῶν ἀλλοφύλων ἐπαναστάντων τῷ λαῷ Σαμουὴλ ἐκπολεμήσας αὐτούς, ὡς ἔστι γνῶναι ἔκ τε τῶν γεγραμμένων Ἀφρικανῷ ἐν τῷ Χρονικῷ συγγράμματι καὶ ἑτέροις χρονογράφοις.
68–70 → F51a,19s   71s = F54b,2s; → F54a,4s; F54c; T55,16s; Eus., chron. (85,15–17 Karst) Und nach Ôgigos sei von wegen der großen Verwüstung durch die Sintflut ohne Königtum, *sagen sie*, gewesen das jetzt Attika *genannte* bis zu Kekrops 190 Jahre lang.   76–87   ps. Iust., coh. Gr. 9,2 (34,11–17 Marcovich) Ἐν γὰρ τοῖς χρόνοις Ὠγύγου τε καὶ Ἰνάχου, οὓς καὶ γηγενεῖς τινες τῶν παρ' ὑμῖν ὑπειλήφασι γεγενῆσθαι, Μωυσέως μέμνηνται ὡς ἡγεμόνος τε καὶ ἄρχοντος τοῦ τῶν Ἰουδαίων γένους. οὕτω γὰρ Πολέμων τε ἐν τῇ πρώτῃ τῶν Ἑλληνικῶν ἱστοριῶν μέμνηται καὶ Ἀππίων ὁ Ποσειδωνίου ἐν τῇ κατὰ Ἰουδαίων βίβλῳ καὶ ἐν τῇ τετάρτῃ τῶν ἱστοριῶν, λέγων κατὰ Ἴναχον Ἄργους βασιλέα, Ἀμώσιδος Αἰγυπτίων βασιλεύοντος, ἀποστῆναι Ἰουδαίους, ὧν ἡγεῖσθαι Μωυσέα.
77–80 → T48; F50,3–7; ps. Io. Ant. fr. 1*,10–14 (556 Ro.) Ὅτι δὲ Ὠγύγῳ συνήκμαζε Μωυσῆς, Πολέμων ἐν πρώτῳ Ἱστοριῶν Ἑλληνικῶν ἱστορεῖ λέγων· ἐπὶ Ἄπιδος τοῦ Φορωνέως μοῖρα τοῦ Αἰγυπτίων στρατοῦ ἐξέπεσεν Αἰγύπτου, οἳ ἐν τῇ Παλαιστίνῃ καλουμένῃ Συρίᾳ οὐ πόρρω Ἀραβίας ᾤκησαν. δῆλον δὲ ὅτι τούτους φησὶ τοὺς μετὰ Μωυσέως ἐξελθόντας ἐκεῖθεν Ἑβραίους.

71s   cf. Sym. Log. (Th. Mel. 26,27 – 27,2 = Leo Gr. 28,2–5); ps. Sym. f. 38ʳ = Cedr. 143,10–14; Ecl. Hist. 176,14–18   71–73 Philochorus FGrHist 328 F92   77–80 Polemo, Hellenica (Argolica) FHG 3 F13

65s Ἱερέων...ρ'² < B   67 Τῆς...ἑβδομήκοντα Vig.   68 πρῶτον < B | πρώτην IO πρώτης BN | Ὀλυμπιάδος BN   69 πεντηκοστῆς πέμπτης BN πεντηκοστῆς πέμπτου I νε' O | ,ασλε' scripsimus (vide supra) ,ασλζ' Eus.   71 Μετὰ δὲ] ἀπὸ μὲν Sync.³ | Ὠγύγου Sync.² Sync.³   72 μέχρι Κέκροπος < Sync.³ ἔτη] ἔτεσιν Sync.³ | γὰρ μετὰ Eus. μὲν γὰρ Sync.² | μετὰ + τὸν Eus.:B   73 φησὶ + ὁ Sync.²   75 Κύρου Sync.¹ | τὸν αὐτὸν χρόνον Eus. τῶν αὐτῶν χρόνων Sync.¹ τὸν αὐτοῦ χρόνον Sync.²   76 ,ασλε' Sync.¹ Sync.² ,ασλζ' Eus. Routh Gelzer^ms | ἀλλὰ < Eus. | αὐτοῦ Eus.:I   77 τῇ < Sync.² | λέγει Sync.¹   78 τοῦ²] τῶν Eus.:I | Αἰγυπτίων] Αἰγυπτιακοῦ Sync.¹ | Αἰγύπτου] ἐν Αἰγύπτῳ Sync.¹ | οἵ] ἡ Sync.²

For the priests Eli and Samuel: 90 years.

For the kings of the Hebrews who came next: 490 years.

<And for the Captivity: 70 years>, the last year of which was, as we have said before, the first year of the reign of Cyrus. From Moses up to the first Olympiad there are 1020 years, if, as is the case, there are 1235 years up to the first year of the 55th Olympiad: And the chronology in the Greek histories coincided.

After Ogygus, because of the great destruction wrought by the flood, what is now known as Attica remained without a king for 189 years until the time of Cecrops. For there never existed Actaeus, the successor to Ogygus, or those [other] fictitious names, so Philochorus asserts.

[...]

From Ogygus, then, to Cyrus, which are as many years as there are from Moses to the same time, there are 1235 years. And some of the Greeks also state in their histories that Moses lived about the same time. Polemon, for example, states in the first book of his *Hellenicae*: "At the time of Apis the son of Phoroneus, a portion of the Egyptian army was expelled from Egypt; they settled in

τῇ Παλαιστίνῃ καλουμένῃ Συρίᾳ οὐ πόρρω Ἀραβίας ᾤκησαν. οὗτοι δηλονότι οἱ
80 μετὰ Μωυσέως. Ἀπίων δὲ ὁ Ποσειδωνίου περιεργότατος γραμματικῶν ἐν τῇ
κατὰ Ἰουδαίων βίβλῳ καὶ ἐν τῇ τετάρτῃ τῶν ἱστοριῶν φησι κατὰ Ἴναχον Ἄργους βασιλέα, Ἀμώσιος Αἰγυπτίων βασιλεύοντος, ἀποστῆναι Ἰουδαίους, ὧν
ἡγεῖσθαι Μωυσέα. μέμνηται δὲ καὶ Ἡρόδοτος τῆς ἀποστασίας ταύτης καὶ Ἀμώσιος ἐν τῇ δευτέρᾳ, τρόπῳ δέ τινι καὶ Ἰουδαίων αὐτῶν, ἐν τοῖς περιτεμνομένοις
85 αὐτοὺς καταριθμῶν καὶ Ἀσσυρίους τοὺς ἐν τῇ Παλαιστίνῃ ἀποκαλῶν, τάχα δι'
Ἀβραάμ. Πτολεμαῖος δὲ ὁ Μενδήσιος τὰ Αἰγυπτίων ἀνέκαθεν ἱστορῶν ἅπασι
τούτοις συντρέχει· ὥστ' οὐδ' ἐπίσημος ἐπὶ πλέον ἡ τῶν χρόνων παραλλαγή.
σημειωτέον δὲ ὡς ὅ τι ποτὲ ἐξαίρετον Ἕλλησι δι' ἀρχαιότητα μυθεύεται, μετὰ
Μωυσέα τοῦθ' εὑρίσκεται· κατακλυσμοί τε καὶ ἐκπυρώσεις, Προμηθεύς, Ἰώ,
90 Εὐρώπη, Σπαρτοί, Κόρης ἁρπαγή, μυστήρια, νομοθεσίαι, Διονύσου πράξεις,
Περσεύς, ἆθλοι Ἡράκλειοι, Ἀργοναῦται, Κένταυροι, Μινώταυρος, τὰ περὶ
Ἴλιον, Ἡρακλειδῶν κάθοδος, Ἰώνων ἀποικία καὶ Ὀλυμπιάδες. ἔδοξε δή μοι τῆς
Ἀττικῆς βασιλείας τὸν προειρημένον ἐκτιθέναι χρόνον, παρατιθέναι μέλλοντι
ταῖς Ἑβραϊκαῖς ἱστορίαις τὰς Ἑλληνικάς. ἐξέσται γὰρ τῷ βουλομένῳ παρ' ἐμοῦ
95 τὴν ἀρχὴν κομιζομένῳ λογίζεσθαι τὸν ἀριθμὸν ὁμοίως ἐμοί.

Οὐκοῦν τῶν ͵α καὶ κ' ἐτῶν τῶν μέχρι πρώτης Ὀλυμπιάδος ἀπὸ Μωυσέως τε
καὶ Ὠγύγου ἐκκειμένων, πρώτῳ μὲν ἔτει τὸ Πάσχα καὶ τῶν Ἑβραίων ἔξοδος ἡ
ἀπ' Αἰγύπτου. ἐν δὲ τῇ Ἀττικῇ ὁ ἐπὶ Ὠγύγου γίνεται κατακλυσμός, καὶ κατὰ
λόγον. τῶν γὰρ Αἰγυπτίων ὀργῇ θεοῦ χαλάζαις τε καὶ χειμῶσι μαστιζομένων εἰ-

---

test.: Eus. Sync.¹ Sync.² 85 καταριθμῶν des. Sync.²

86s ps. Iust., coh. Gr. 9,2 (34,17s Marcovich) Καὶ Πτολεμαῖος δὲ ὁ Μενδήσιος τὰ Αἰγυπτίων <ἀνέκαθεν> ἱστορῶν ἅπασι τούτοις συντρέχει. **89** → infra ad l. 103s **90** → F50,17s; T61 **97-101** ps. Io. Ant. fr. 1*,5-9 (556 Ro.) Ὅτε τὸ Πάσχα καὶ ἡ τῶν Ἑβραίων ἔξοδος ἀπ' Αἰγύπτου ἐγένετο, ὁ ἐπὶ Ὠγύγου γέγονε κατακλυσμός. καὶ εἰκότως· τῶν γὰρ Αἰγυπτίων ὀργῇ θεοῦ χαλάζαις καὶ χειμῶνι μαστιζομένων, εἰκὸς ἦν μέρη τινὰ συμπάσχειν τῆς γῆς· ἔτι τε Ἀθηναίους τῶν αὐτῶν Αἰγυπτίοις ἀπολαύειν εἰκὸς ἦν, ἀποίκους ἐκείνων ὑπονοουμένους, ὥς φασιν.

80-83 Apion FGrHist 616 F2 **83-86** cf. Hdt. 2,162.104 **86s** Ptolem. Mendes. FGrHist 611 T2b **92** cf. Sync. 145,1-3; 190,16 - 191,12 **99-102** ps. Theopompus (= Anaximenes Lampsacenus), Tricaranus FGrHist 72 F20a

79 καλουμένη Sync.¹:Aᶜ λεγομένη ante corr. A | Ἀραβίας] Συρίας Eus.:B | οὗτοι Sync.¹ Sync.² ps. Io. Ant. αὐτοί Eus. **80** Ἀππίων Sync.¹ ps. Iust. **80-87** Ἀπίων…παραλλαγή < Eus.:B **80** ὁ Eus. ps. Iust. < Sync.¹ Sync.² | Ποσιδοννίου Sync.¹ Ποσιδωνίου Sync.² | τῇ] τοῖς Eus.:ND **81** βίβλῳ…ἱστοριῶν < Eus.:ND **82** Αἰγύπτου Sync.² **83** ἡγεῖσθαι Eus. ps. Iust. γίνεσθαι Sync.¹ Sync.² | ἀποστάσεως Eus.:ND¹ (corr. D⁴) **83s** καὶ²…δευτέρᾳ < Eus.:ND¹ (+ D⁴) **84** τινι < Sync.¹ | αὐτῶν < Sync.² **85** τοὺς < Sync.¹ | δι'] διὰ τὸν Sync.¹ **86** δὲ Eus. ps. Iust. τε Sync.¹ | ἔκαθεν Eus.:I | ἱστοριῶν Sync.¹ **87** ὥστ'] ὡς Sync.¹ | πλεῖον Sync.¹ **88** ὅ] εἴ Sync.¹ | μετὰ + γε Sync.¹ **89** τε < Sync.¹ Eus.:I **91** περσεῦ Sync.¹ < Eus.:ND¹ (+ D⁴) | ἄθλιοι Sync.¹ **91s** Ἀργοναῦται…Ἴλιον < Eus.:D¹ (+ D⁴) **91** Μινώταυροι Eus.:N **92** Ἴλιον] ἰανλίαν Sync.¹ **94** ἐξέσται Eus. ἐξέστω Sync.¹ **97** τὸ] τῷ Eus.:B **98s** καὶ κατὰ λόγον < Eus.:B **99** γὰρ Sync.¹:AᶜB Eus. παρ' ante corr. A | χειμῶνι Eus.:BN

the part of Syria called Palestine, not far from Arabia" (these are clearly those who went with Moses). And Apion son of Posidonius, the most painstaking of grammarians, states in his book *Adversus Judaeos* and in the fourth book of his *Historiae* that during the reign of Inachus king of Argos, when Amosis was king of the Egyptians, the Jews revolted, under the leadership of Moses. Herodotus also has made mention both of this revolt and of Amosis in his second book, and in a certain way of the Jews themselves, numbering them among those who practice circumcision and calling them Assyrians in Palestine, perhaps on account of Abraham. And Ptolemy of Mendes, who recorded the history of the Egyptians from the beginning, agrees with all of them, so that the variation in dates is not even worthy of further comment.

But it should be noted that if ever any remarkable story is recorded by the Greeks because of its antiquity, this will be found to have occurred after Moses: the floods and fires, Prometheus, Io, Europe, the Sparti, the rape of Kore, the mysteries, enactment of laws, the exploits of Dionysus, Perseus, the labors of Heracles, the Argonauts, the Centaurs, the Minotaur, the story of Troy, the return of the Heraclidae, the settlement of Ionia, and the Olympics.[9] So it seemed good to me to set out the aforementioned chronology of the Attic kingdom, since it is my intention to set out the Greek and Hebrew narratives side by side. And thus anyone who wishes to take his starting-point from me can reckon the number of years in the same way as I do.

So then, in the first year of the 1020 years extending from Moses and Ogygus up to the first Olympiad, the Passover and the Exodus of the Hebrews from Egypt took place. But in Attica the flood at the time of Ogygus occurred, and with good reason. For when the Egyptians were being scourged by the wrath of God with hailstones and tempests, it was fitting for certain parts of the earth to suffer along with them. For it was appropriate that the Athenians should exper-

---

[9] Portions of Africanus' catalogue of events of Greek history coincide with subjects treated in the surviving fragments of ps. John of Antioch (frs. 3*, 9*, 12*, 13*, 15*, 16*), an author known to have drawn on Africanus' chronicle. Africanus may thus have intended his summary to be a programmatic statement of topics subsequently treated in book three of the *Chronographiae*.

100 κὸς ἦν μέρη τινὰ συμπάσχειν τῆς γῆς· ἔτι τε Ἀθηναίους τῶν αὐτῶν Αἰγυπτίοις ἀπολαύειν εἰκὸς ἦν ἀποίκους ἐκείνων ὑπονοουμένους, ὥς φασιν ἄλλοι τε καὶ ἐν τῷ Τρικαράνῳ Θεόπομπος. ὁ δὲ μεταξὺ χρόνος παραλέλειπται, ἐν ᾧ μηδὲν ἐξαίρετον Ἕλλησιν ἱστορεῖται. μετὰ δὲ τέσσαρα καὶ ἐνενήκοντα ἔτη ἦν Προμηθεύς, ὥς τινες. ὃς πλάσσειν ἀνθρώπους ἐμυθεύετο· σοφὸς γὰρ ὢν εἰς παιδείαν αὐτοὺς
105 ἀπὸ τῆς ἄγαν ἰδιωτείας μετέπλασσε.

test.: Eus. Sync.[1]   **104** τινες des. Sync.[1]: Ταῦτα ὁ Ἀφρικανὸς ἐν τῷ τρίτῳ λόγῳ φιλαλήθως καὶ ἐμμαρτύρως ἱστορῶν ἀξιοπιστότερος εἶναί μοι δοκεῖ κατὰ πάντα Εὐσεβίου, ἐν τούτῳ τῷ κατὰ τὸν Μωυσέα καὶ τὴν ἀπ' Αἰγύπτου πορείαν λόγῳ ἔχων, ὡς προείρηται, καὶ τοὺς ἐκ περιτομῆς ὁμοφώνους καὶ τοὺς κατὰ Χριστὸν φιλοσοφήσαντας ἐξ Ἑλλήνων Κλήμεντα τὸν Στρωματέα καὶ Τατιανόν, ὡς αὐτὸς Εὐσέβιος ἐν τῷ προοιμίῳ τοῦ κανόνος ὧδέ πως γράφων συμμαρτυρεῖ... (→ T48a) **105** des. Eus.: Ταῦτα μὲν ὁ Ἀφρικανός. μεταβῶμεν δ' ἡμεῖς ἐφ' ἕτερον.

103-105 → F54a,6s; F56,2-5.10-13; Eus., can.[Hier] (35[e] Helm) Secundum quorundam opinionem *his temporibus* fuit Prometheus, a quo homines factos esse commemorant. *Et re vera.* Cum enim sapiens esset, *feritatem eorum et* nimiam imperitiam *ad humanitatem et* scientiam transfigurabat. Sync. (174,22s Moss.) Τούτοις τοῖς χρόνοις, ὥς φασι, Προμηθεὺς ἦν, ὃς ἐμυθεύετο πλάττειν ἀνθρώπους ἐξ ἀπαιδευσίας καὶ ἀλογίας εἰς παίδευσιν μετάγων. Sym. Log. (Leo Gr. [27,7-9 Bekker] = Th. Mel. [26,11-13 Tafel]) Κατὰ τούτους τοὺς χρόνους Προμηθεὺς μυθεύεται σοφὸς ὢν ἐν παιδείᾳ, ἐν ᾗ τοὺς ἀνθρώπους ἀπὸ ἰδιωτείας μετέπλασεν. Ecl. Hist. (188,4-6 Cramer) Καὶ Προμηθεὺς μὲν πλάττειν ἀνθρώπους ἐμυθεύετο· σοφὸς γὰρ ὢν ἀπὸ τῆς ἄγαν ἰδιωτίας μετέπλαττεν αὐτοὺς εἰς φιλοσοφίαν.

103-105 cf. Io. Mal. 4,3; Io. Ant. fr. 24.1; Exc. Barb. 228,6-9; Anon. Matr. 14,8-11

100 ἔτι τε ps. Io. Ant., sicut iam coniecerat Routh, quem secutus est Gelzer[ms] ὅτε γε Eus. ὅτε Sync.[1] **101** ἀπολαύειν εἰκὸς ἦν ~ Eus.:O (ε. ἦ. ἀ.)   **101-103** ἐν...ἦν < Eus.:B   **102** Τρικαράνῳ Eus.:IG (O incertus) Τρικαρήνω ND | δὲ < Sync.[1]   **105** μετέπλασσε I μετέπλασε O μετέπλαττε BN

F35 Symeon Logothetes (Leo Grammaticus [30,1-3 Bekker] = Theodosius Melitenus [28,10s Tafel])

Γίνεται τοίνυν ἀπὸ τῆς τελευτῆς Ἰησοῦ ἐπὶ τὴν τελευτὴν Σαμουὴλ ἔτη χι', ἀπὸ δὲ Νῶε καὶ τοῦ κατακλυσμοῦ ἔτη ͵βρκ', ἀπὸ Ἀδὰμ ἔτη ͵δτπβ'.

1s Iul. Pol. (104,12-14 Hardt) Γίνονται *οὖν* ἀπὸ Ἰησοῦ *τοῦ Ναυῆ ἕως Δαυὶδ* ἔτη φι'. ἀπὸ δὲ κτίσεως κόσμου ἔτη ͵δυ'.   **1** ἔτη χι' → T6,10-12; F34,63-65; F58a,5s   **2** ἔτη ͵βρκ' → T6,5-12; T45,10s (et saepe) | ἔτη ͵δτπβ' → T6,4-12; F34,65; T40,1s

2 βκ' Th. Mel. | ἀπὸ + δὲ Bekker

ience the same things the Egyptians did, since they are considered to be emigrants from them, as is stated, among others, by Theopompus in his *Tricaranus*. But the intervening period is ignored, in which no extraordinary event has been recorded by the Greeks in their history. After 94 years, there was Prometheus, according to some, who was said in legend to form men; for being a wise man he transformed them from their extreme crudeness into an educated condition.

F35 *The Chronology from Adam to Samuel*[1]

Then from the end of Joshua to the end of Samuel there are 610 years,[2] from Noah and the Flood 2120 years,[3] from Adam 4382 years.[4]

1   The numbers from this unattributed excerpt, which are given in larger print, accurately represent Africanus' system.
2   Africanus assigned 30 years to the elders after Joshua, 490 years to the judges, and 90 years to Samuel (30 + 490 + 90 = 610, see F34,63–65). In Africanus' system, the 90 years of Samuel end not with his death, but rather with the end of his leadership and the transfer of power to Saul (cf. 1 Sam 12,1–25). The reference in this passage to the "end of Samuel" suggests that its author failed to grasp the distinction.
3   For the basis of this calculation, see T6,5–12: 1015 (from Noah to Abraham's migration) + 430 (sojourn of Israel in Canaan and Egypt) + 40 (the period in the wilderness) + 25 (rule of Joshua) + 610 (see above) = 2120 years.
4   2262 (the year of the Flood) + 2120 (see previous note) = 4382. For Africanus' dating of the Flood in AM 2262, see T45,10f. For a different calculation see also T40,1f, which numbers 4292 years from Adam to Eli. The additional 90 years to the end of Samuel (F34,65) make a total of 4382 years.

T36 Georgius Syncellus (180,20-24 Mosshammer)

Ἑβδομηκοστῷ ἔτει τοῦ Ἀὼδ φησιν ὁ Ἀφρικανὸς τὸν ἐπὶ Δευκαλίωνος κατακλυσμόν. ἀλλ' οὐκ ἔστι τοῦτο ἀκριβῶς ἀποδεῖξαι τῶν παρ' Ἕλλησι πάντων χρόνων διασφαλλομένων ὅσοι πρὸ τῆς πρώτης Ὀλυμπιάδος ἱστόρηνται, πλὴν ὅτι τοῦ ἀληθοῦς ἐγγὺς ἐστοχάσατο, ἐπεὶ καὶ ἡμεῖς παραπλησίως, μὴ ἔχοντες ἄλλο τι περισσότερον δεῖξαι.

1s → T55; F34,89; Sym. Log. (Leo Gr. [28,2-5 Bekker] = Th. Mel. [26,27 - 27,2 Tafel] ≈ Cedr. [146, 17s Bekker]) *Τούτου* (sc. Aod) *ἐν ἔτει εἰκοστῷ ἑβδόμῳ ἐβασίλευσε τῆς Ἀττικῆς Κέκροψ ὁ διφυὴς διὰ τὸ δύο γλώσσαις λαλεῖν. ἐν δὲ τῷ οζ' ὁ κατακλυσμὸς ἐν Θεσσαλίᾳ καὶ Αἰθιοπίᾳ ὑπ' αὐτῶν μνημονεύεται.* Anon. Matr. (14,8-11 Bauer) *Ἀὼδ κριτὴς ἔτη π' ἐκ φυλῆς Ἐφραίμ. κατὰ τούτους Προμηθεὺς καὶ Ἐπιμηθεύς, Ἄτλας καὶ ὁ πανόπτης Ἄργος καὶ ὁ ἐπὶ Δευκαλίωνος κατακλυσμὸς ὑπὸ Ἑλλήνων μνημονεύεται.* Exc. Barb. (228,6-9 Frick) *In diebus Naoth* (sc. Aod) *et Semega filium eius iudicum in ipsis scribuntur fuisse Promitheus et Epimitheus et Atlas et prouidens Algus,* item Deucalios, et post eos diluuius *sub Gregorum.*

1 cf. Iud 3,15-30   1s cf. Eus., chron. 34,27-35,4; 86,20-22; Eus., can. armen 160; Io. Mal. 4,3; Ecl. Hist. 189,9-17; Anon. Matr. 14,3-5

[AB]   1 Ἑβδομηκοστῷ] οζ' Sym. Log.   1s κατακλυσμόν B κατακλοισμόν A

T37 Georgius Syncellus (186,20-24 Mosshammer)

Τοῦτον τὸν Ἀβιμέλεχ καὶ τοὺς ο' ἀδελφοὺς αὐτοῦ ἡ βίβλος τῶν κριτῶν πρῶτον μὲν τοῦ Γεδεὼν υἱοὺς λέγει τρανῶς, ἔπειτα δὲ τοῦ ἀδελφοῦ αὐτοῦ Ἱεροβαάλ, ὃς συνῴκησε τῷ Γεδεὼν περὶ τὰ τέλη αὐτοῦ, ὡς αὐτόθι γέγραπται, καὶ δοκεῖ πως ἄπορον εἶναι. Ἀφρικανὸς δὲ τοῦ Ἱεροβαὰλ αὐτοὺς λέγει πάντας.

1s cf. Iud 8,30s   2s cf. Iud 8,29; 8,35 - 9,2   3s cf. Iud 9,1s.5.24.28; II Regn 11,21

T38 Georgius Syncellus (193,9s Mosshammer)

Ἀβδὼν κριτὴς ἔκρινε τὸν Ἰσραὴλ ἔτη η'. Ἀφρικανὸς ἔτη κ' φησὶν οὐ καλῶς. τοῦ δὲ κόσμου ἦν ἔτος ,δσμβ'.

cf. Iud 12,14

[AB]   2 ,δσμβ' B ,δσκβ' A

T36 *Synchronism of Ehud and the Flood of Deucalion*[1]

Africanus says that in the seventieth[2] year of Ehud the flood at the time of Deucalion occurred. But this cannot be demonstrated precisely, since Greek chronology, to the extent that there is even a record of it before the 1st Olympiad, is in complete confusion. Nevertheless, his conjecture approximates the truth, since our conjecture also is close to his, and we lack any further information to bring to light.

T37 *The Family of Abimelech*

As for this Abimelech and his 70 brothers, the book of Judges initially states plainly that they were sons of Gideon; but it then says they were sons of his brother Jerubbaal, who came to live with Gideon around the end of his life, as it is written there. This appears to be somewhat problematic.[3] Now Africanus says that they were all sons of Jerubbaal.

T38 *Abdon the Judge*

Abdon acted as judge of Israel for eight years. Africanus incorrectly says that it was 20 years.[4] AM 4242.

---

1 See Gelzer 1,120, who suggests that Syncellus confused Deucalion's flood with a flood in Thessaly which Africanus dated to the time of Ehud. Africanus himself assigned Deucalion's flood to the time of Gothoniel. Note that Anon. Matr. gives both dates for Deucalion's flood (14,3–5: Gothoniel; 14,8–11: Ehud; see app.).

2 Following Symeon Logothete (see app.), Unger 1867,185 and 188, emends this to the 77th year of Ehud.

3 On the name of Abimelech's father, see Judges 8,31 (Gideon); 9,1 (Jerubbaal). On the identification of Jerubbaal with Gideon, see Judges 6,32 (MT); 7,1; 8,35. The confusion to which Syncellus refers may have arisen from Judges 8,29, which seems to distinguish between the two men.

4 The source of Africanus' 20-year chronology of Abdon's rule is unknown. Cf. Routh 442, who suggests that Syncellus knew a corrupted text of Africanus, which confused the Greek numerals 20 (κ′) and 8 (η′).

T39

T39a Georgius Syncellus (204,1–9 Mosshammer)

Τὰ μὲν Ἰησοῦ τοῦ Ναυῆ καὶ τῶν μετ' αὐτὸν πρεσβυτέρων ἡ γραφὴ παρεσιώπησεν, ἡ δὲ ἄγραφος συνήθεια τοῦ μὲν Ἰησοῦ κζ', τῶν δὲ πρεσβυτέρων ιη' παρέδωκε· καὶ οὕτω σχεδὸν πάντες ὁμοφωνοῦσιν. Εὐσέβιος δὲ μόνος ὁ Καισαρεὺς τὰ τῶν πρεσβυτέρων οὐ παρέλαβεν, ὁ δὲ Ἀφρικανὸς ἔτη λ' αὐτοῖς ἀπένειμεν, ᾧ πλεῖστα κατεγκαλεῖ ὁ Εὐσέβιος ὡς μεγάλα, φησί,
5 διαμαρτόντι καὶ τολμηροτάτῳ πράγματι ἐπικεχειρηκότι, πρὸς τούτοις ἄλλα ο' ἔτη, τὰ μ' μὲν τὰ τῆς ἀναρχίας, λ' δὲ τὰ τῆς εἰρήνης οἴκοθεν παρεμβαλόντι, τὰ ὅλα ρ'. ἀλλ' ὁ μὲν Ἀφρικανὸς περὶ τούτων ὡς διαφωνουμένων ἐν τέλει τοῦ ε' λόγου καθομολογεῖ.

3s → T6,10; F34,63; Ecl. Hist. (187,29 – 188,2 Cramer) *Πρεσβύτεροι δὲ μετὰ τὸν Ἰησοῦν προΐστανται τοῦ λαοῦ, ἐπὶ ἔτη κιη'* (fort. pro *ιη'*)· *τούτων τοὺς χρόνους Εὐσέβιος τῷ αὐτοῦ χρονικῷ κανονίῳ προσήρμοσεν· Ἀφρικανὸς δὲ λ' ἐνιαυτοὺς λέγει κρατῆσαι· ἔτεροι δὲ κδ', καὶ ἄλλοι κιη'* (fort. pro *ιη'*). *ἅτινα προκρίναντες, ἐκτεθείκαμεν διὰ τὴν καθ' ἡμᾶς παράδοσιν καλῶς συναρμόττουσαν.* Petr. Alex. (190,2s Samodurova) *Οἱ μετὰ τὸν Ἰησοῦν πρεσβύτεροι κατὰ τὸν ἀρχαιότατον Ἀφρικανὸν ἔτη λ'.* Mich. Syr. 3,8 (1,46 Chabot; cf. Barhebr. [15 Wallis Budge]; Hist. Dynast. [36 Pococke]) *L'Écriture ne fait pas connaître le nombre des années des Anciens qui dirigèrent le peuple après la mort de Josué; Africanus seul dit qu'ils gouvernèrent pendant 30 ans.* Sym. Log. (Leo Gr. [27,3–5 Bekker] = Th. Mel. [26,8–10 Tafel]) *Μετὰ Ἰησοῦν πρεσβύτεροι ἐκ τῆς Ἰούδα καὶ Συμεὼν φυλῆς, τοῖς ἀλλήλων σχοινίσμασιν ἀνὰ μέρος βοηθοῦντες, ἐπάρξαι τοῦ λαοῦ λέγονται ἔτη λ'.*   5s → T6,11; F34,64; Petr. Alex. (190,26–31 Samodurova) *Καὶ τὰ ἄλλα κ' ἔτη ἐκ τῆς ἀναρχίας κατὰ τὸν Ἀφρικανὸν καὶ ἑτέρους χρονογράφους. ... Ἀναρχίας τῆς προγεγραμμένης, καθ' ἣν καὶ ἡ Ροὺθ ἐγνωρίζετο, ἕτερα ἔτη κ'. εἰρήνης τῆς πρὸς τοὺς ἀλλοφύλους τῶν υἱῶν Ἰσραὴλ κατὰ Ἀφρικανὸν καὶ ἄλλους χρονογράφους ἔτη λ'.* Sym. Log. (Leo Gr. [29,10–16 Bekker] = Th. Mel. [27,26 – 28,3 Tafel] ≈ Iul. Pol. [102,17–21 Hardt]; cf. Cedr. [149,1–5 Bekker]) *Κατὰ τούτους τοὺς χρόνους Ἡρακλῆς ἐγνωρίζετο, ὁ τοὺς δώδεκα ἄθλους διανύσας. Σαμανὲς* (Σαμανῆ Th. Mel.) *ἡγήσατο τοῦ λαοῦ ἔτος ἕν* (ὁ τοὺς ... ἕν < Iul. Pol.), *ἀναρχίας γεγονυίας* (γ. ἀ. + *καὶ εἰρήνης* Iul. Pol.), *κατὰ τὰς Ἑβραϊκὰς παραδόσεις, ὅτε* (< Cedr.) *καὶ ἔπραττεν ἕκαστος ὅπερ ἐβούλετο* (ἠβούλετο Cedr.), *οἷα εἰκὸς ἐν ἀναρχίᾳ γίνεσθαι, ἔτη μ'* (< Th. Mel., οἷα ... ἔτη μ' < Iul. Pol.). (+ *καὶ τότε* Th. Mel.) *εἰρήνην ἔσχε πρὸς τοὺς ἀλλοφύλους ὁ λαὸς ἔτη λ'* (< Iul. Pol.), *Σαμανεὶ* (Σαμωνία Th. Mel. Iul. Pol. Σαμανῆ Cedr.) *αὐτοῦ* (< Cedr.) *ἡγουμένου.*

1 cf. Iud 2,7.16–19   **3** cf. Eus., chron. 52,12   **4–6** Eus., chron. (Ecl. Hist. et armen. = T41a,8–13)

[A] **1** αὐτὸν Goar αὐτῶν A   **4** ᾧ Goar ὡς A   **5** τὰ μ' Moss. τε μ' A μ' Goar^m

T39 *The Chronology after Joshua*

T39a

As to the chronology of Joshua son of Nun and the elders who succeeded him, Scripture has omitted any mention.[1] But the unwritten tradition has handed down 27 years for Joshua and 18 years for the elders. And on this there is almost universal agreement. But only Eusebius of Caesarea has not accepted the chronology for the elders, whereas Africanus assigned them 30 years. Eusebius censures him in the strongest terms for having been greatly in error, he says, and for having pursued an extremely reckless line of inquiry. Besides these 30 years, he criticizes him for inserting an additional 70 years—40 years for the interregnal period and 30 years of domestic peace—making a total of 100 years.[2] But Africanus in fact allows at the end of his fifth book that these matters are a subject of disagreement.

---

1 For the chronological problem caused by this gap, see Adler/Tuffin 2002, 252, n. 6; 253, n. 1.
2 For sources of the Byzantine chronographic tradition which draw upon Africanus' chronology of these undated epochs in biblical history, see app. The synchronism between Samson and Heracles found in the chronological notices of Sym. Log. et al. may also originate in Africanus (see also ps. Io. Ant. fr. 13* [562 Ro.]). For Eusebius' critique of Africanus' treatment of this period, see below T41.

T39b Annianus apud Georgium Syncellum (37,8–15 Mosshammer)

Ἔτι δὲ καὶ μετὰ τὴν τελευτὴν Σαμψὼν τοῦ κριτοῦ τῆς ἀναρχίας, ἤτοι εἰρήνης, τοῦ λαοῦ μ' ἔτη ἐν τῷ κατὰ πλάτος οὐκ ἔθηκεν (sc. Eusebius)· ὁ δὲ Ἀφρικανὸς αὐτῶν ἐμνημόνευσε καὶ τῇ τοῦ χρονογραφίου αὐτοῦ ὁμάδι συμψηφισάμενος ἥνωσε.

Ταῦτα Ἀννιανὸς ἐπὶ λέξεώς φησι μεμφόμενος Εὐσέβιον τὸν Παμφίλου δικαίως περὶ τῆς παρα-
5 λήψεως τῶν σρ' ἐτῶν. συνῳδὰ δὲ αὐτῷ καὶ Πανόδωρος περὶ τούτων ἐγκαλεῖ, οὗ τὰς χρήσεις περὶ τούτου παρέλκον ἡγούμεθα παραθέσθαι.

1–3 → T41a,11s; Exc. Barb. (234,13s Frick) *Et post obitum Sampson sine principem et pacem per annos XL.* Sync. (203,25 Moss.) ἀναρχίας καὶ εἰρήνης ἔτη μ'. Mich. Syr. 4,7 ([1,57 Chabot]; cf. Vardan Arawelcʻi [153a Thomson]) *Après Samson, les enfants d'Israël furent sans juge pendant 12 ans. Jean dit que Šamgar succéda à Samson, pendant 40 ans, comme il est aussi écrit dans l'hébreu; les LXX disent 20 ans, et Andronicus 10 ans seulement.* Africanus dit que les Anciens gouvernèrent pendant 40 ans, parce qu'on était en temps de paix et de tranquillité; et ils restèrent sans prince pendant 30 ans. Barhebr. ([16s Wallis Budge]; cf. Hist. Dynast. [42 Pococke]) After Samson the Elders ruled the people for forty years, according to what Africanus stateth, because there was peace and quietness, and there was no need for a man to stand at the head of an army. *Andronicus says ten years, and twenty years is written in the Septuagint, and others have written twelve.*

[A] **1** τῷ Di. τῷ δὲ A   **4** Ἀννιανὸς Di. αἰννιάνος A   **5** Πανόδωρος Di. παννόδωρος A

T40 Georgius Syncellus (205,17–23 Mosshammer)

Τὰ κατὰ Ἀφρικανὸν ἀπὸ Ἀδὰμ ἕως τέλους τῶν κριτῶν καὶ ἀρχῆς Ἠλεὶ τοῦ ἱερέως ἔτη ͵δσϟβ', κατὰ δὲ Εὐσέβιον τὸν Παμφίλου ͵δμδ', κατὰ δὲ τὴν ἀκριβῆ καὶ εὐαγγελικὴν παράδοσιν καὶ τόδε τὸ χρονογράφιον ͵δτνβ'. τὰ δὲ υν' ἔτη τῶν κριτῶν κατὰ τὸν θεῖον ἀπόστολον ἀπὸ τοῦ ͵γϡβ' ἔτους τοῦ κόσμου ἐπὶ τὸ πρῶτον ἔτος Ἠλεὶ πληροῦται, ἑνὸς ἔτους ὑπολειπομέ-
5 νου, ὅπερ Ἀφρικανὸς τὸν Σεμείγαρ λέγει κρατῆσαι τὸν Ἰσραὴλ τῆς γραφῆς οὐκ εἰπούσης χρόνον.

1s → T6,4–12; F34,61–64   **5s** Sym. Log. (Leo Gr. [29,11s Bekker] = Th. Mel. [27,28 Tafel]; cf. Cedr. [149,1s Bekker]) Σαμανὲς (Σαμανὴ γὰρ Th. Mel.) *ἡγήσατο τοῦ λαοῦ ἔτος ἕν.* Sulp. Sev., chron. 1,27,3 (de Senneville-Grave 161) *Huic Simmichar successit, de quo nihil amplius scripturae prodidit. ... Sed plerique qui de temporibus scripserunt, annum imerium eius annotauerunt.*

2 cf. Eus., chron. 53,25–31; Eus., can.[Hier] 70[a]   **2–4** cf. Io. Anag. f. 115[r]   **5s** cf. Iud 3,31; Hilarian., curs. temp. 164,5s

T39b

In addition, he [sc. Eusebius] did not include in his summation the 40 years after the death of Samson, the judge, when the people were without a government, that is, were at peace. **But Africanus did make mention of these years, and in the sum total of his chronography includes them in the reckoning.**[1]

This is verbatim what Annianus rightly says in his criticism of Eusebius [pupil] of Pamphilus, concerning the omission of 290 years. Panodorus also agrees with Annianus in charging Eusebius for these failings, excerpts from whom we deem it superfluous to quote regarding this matter.

T40 *The Chronology of the Judges and the One-year Rule of Shamgar*

According to Africanus, there are 4292 years from Adam up to the end of the judges and the rule of Eli the priest; according to Eusebius [pupil] of Pamphilus, there are 4044 years. But according to the reliable evangelical tradition and the present chronography, there are 4352 years. The 450 years of the judges according to the divine apostle encompass the period from AM 3902 up to the first year of Eli (minus one year, during which time Africanus says Shamgar ruled over Israel, even though Scripture does not discuss the date of his rule).

---

1 Syriac chroniclers transmit similar information about Africanus' treatment of biblical chronology after Joshua. Since Bar Hebraeus' report differs slightly from that of Michael Syrus, the apparatus includes both witnesses.

T41

T41a Eusebius, Chronica (Ecloga Historiarum [177,12 – 178,19 Cramer] ≈ armeniace [46,38 – 48,8 Karst])

Τὰ δὲ μετὰ Μωυσέως τελευτὴν ἐπὶ Σολομῶντα καὶ τὴν τοῦ ἱεροῦ κατασκευήν, ἑτέρως μὲν ἡ τῶν Κριτῶν γραφὴ λέγει, καὶ ὁ ἱερὸς ἀπόστολος, ἐν ταῖς πράξεσι τῶν ἀποστόλων· ἑτέρως δὲ ἡ τῶν βασιλειῶν ἱστορία, καὶ ἡ τῶν Ἑβραίων παρατήρησις παραδίδωσιν. εὖ δ᾽ ἂν ἔχοι ἕκαστα διελθεῖν, καὶ τὸν παριστάμενον ἀψευδῆ λόγον ἐπιγνῶναι.

5 Τοῦτό γε μὴν ἐν πρώτοις οὐκ ἀπαρατήρητον ἐατέον, ὡς καὶ Ἀφρικανὸς πέντε χρονογραφιῶν συνάξας βιβλία, τὰ μεγάλα μοι διαμαρτεῖν ἐν τοῖς προκειμένοις δοκεῖ. ἀπὸ γὰρ ἐξόδου Μωσέως ἐπὶ Σολομῶνα καὶ τὴν τοῦ ἱεροῦ οἰκοδομὴν ἐν Ἱεροσολύμοις συνάγει κατά τινα οἰκεῖον ἀριθμόν, ἔτη ψμδ'. τὰ πλεῖστα δὲ ἀμαρτύρως ἐκθέμενος, διήμαρτεν, <ὅτι> οὐ μόνον ταῖς θείαις γραφαῖς μαχόμενα εἴρηκεν, ἀλλ᾽ ὅτι καὶ τολμηροτάτῳ ἐπικεχείρηκε πράγματι, ὅλων ἑκατὸν ἐτῶν ἀριθμὸν ἀφ᾽ ἑαυτοῦ παρεμβαλών. τίθησι γὰρ περιττά, πρεσβυτέρων μὲν τῶν περὶ Ἰησοῦ ἔτη λ'. μετὰ δὲ Σαμψὼν ἀναρχίας ἔτη μ', καὶ πάλιν εἰρήνης ἔτη λ'.

Τοσαῦτα περιττὰ καὶ ἀμαρτύρως ἐκθέμενος ἀπερισκέπτως, πολὺ πλῆθος
15 ἐτῶν ἀφ᾽ ἑαυτοῦ συνήγαγε. μεταξὺ τῶν χρόνων Μωυσέως καὶ τῆς Σολομῶντος βασιλείας εἶναι γάρ, φησιν, ὑπὲρ τὰ ἔτη ψμ'.

Ταῦτα δὲ δέον λογίσασθαι τὰς ἐν μέσῳ διελθούσας γενεάς, πόσαι τίνες ἦσαν· ἀλλ᾽ ἐπ᾽ αὐτῶν τε συνιδεῖν τὸ ἀσύστατον τοῦ λόγου. εἰ γὰρ ἀπὸ Ἀβραὰμ ἕως Δαβὶδ γενεαὶ δεκατέσσαρες, ἤδη δὲ κατὰ Μωϋσέα ἐννάτη διελύθη γενεά, καθ᾽ ἣν Ναασὼν υἱὸς Ἀμιναδὰμ ἐγνωρίζετο ἄρχων φυλῆς
20 Ἰούδα· τελευτᾷ τε οὗτος ἐπὶ τῆς ἐρήμου· τῶν γὰρ ἀπ᾽ Αἰγύπτου προελθόντων, καὶ τῶν ἐπὶ τῆς πρώτης ἐξαριθμήσεως γεγονότων εἷς ἦν, δῆλον ὡς λοιπαὶ γενεαὶ ε' μετὰ Ναασὼν ἐλείποντο ἐπὶ Δαβὶδ ἀριθμούμεναι. Ναασὼν γὰρ ἐγέννησε τὸν Σαλμών, καὶ οὗτος τὸν Βοόζ, καὶ οὗτος τὸν Ὠβήδ, καὶ οὗτος τὸν Ἰεσσαί· καὶ οὗτος τὸν Δαβίδ.

Ποῖος οὖν λόγος ἐρεῖ ἐν πέντε γενεαῖς ταῖς μετὰ Μωυσέα ψ' ἐτῶν ἀριθμὸν συνεισάγεσθαι; ἵνα
25 γὰρ τὸν ἴσον τῶν κατὰ γενεὰν ἀνδρῶν ἑκάστῳ τίς ἀπονείμῃ χρόνον· εὑρεθήσεται ἔτη ρμ' γεγονὼς ἕκαστος πρὸ τῆς παιδοποιίας· τούτῳ δ᾽ οὐκ ἄν τις εὖ φρονῶν συνθήσεται. Μωυσῆς τὲ γὰρ αὐτὸς ρκ' ἐτῶν ἐτελεύτα, καὶ ὁ τούτου διάδοχος Ἰησοῦς, ρι'· καὶ πρὸ τούτων Ἰωσὴφ τὰ πάντα τῆς ζωῆς

---

8 → T42   11–13 → T39a,3–6   15s → Išodad Merv. (103,17s Eynde) Mais l'écrivain Africanus dit qu'il y a sept cent et quarante années depuis l'exode jusqu'à la construction.

2 cf. Act 7,45–47   8–15 cf. Sync. 204,4–8 = T39a,4–6   26s cf. Deut 31,2; 34,7   27s cf. Gen 50,26

3 παρατήρησις Cr. παρατήρασις cod.   8 ψμδ' armen. ψμα' Ecl. Hist.   9 ὅτι Gutschmid   12 Ἰησοῦ Cr. ἰνῶ cod.   16 τὰ Gutschmid (cf. Sync. in T41b) ταῦτα cod. < armen.   19 ἐννάτη] 11 armen. Ναασὼν Cr. Νασὼν cod. | Ἀμιναδὰμ Cr. ναδὰμ cod. *Aminadab* armen.   27 ρκ' armen. ρ' Ecl. Hist.

T41 *The Chronology from the Exodus to the Building of the Temple*

T41a

As for the chronology from after the death of Moses up to Solomon and the building of the Temple, both the book of Judges and the holy apostle in the Acts of the Apostles say one thing, whereas the history of the books of Kingdoms and the careful study of the Hebrews have a different tradition. It would be well to examine each of them in detail, and decide upon the account that is set forth accurately.

But first of all this point at least should not go unremarked: namely that when he compiled the five books of his *Chronographiae,* Africanus, in my opinion, was profoundly mistaken about the question at hand. For from the Exodus of Moses up to Solomon and the building of the Temple in Jerusalem, he reckons, according to some kind of calculation peculiar to him, a total of 744 years.[1] In making his case almost entirely without proof, he has gone completely astray, not only <because> he has said things in conflict with the divine Scriptures, but also because, by inserting on his own a full 100 years, he has embarked upon an extremely rash enterprise. For he assigns too many years: 30 years for the elders around the time of Joshua; after Samson 40 years for the period without a ruler; and again 30 years for the period of peace.

By setting forth so many excess years without proof and without due consideration, he on his own adds up a very large sum of years.[2] For between the time of Moses and the kingdom of Solomon, there are, he says, over 740 years.

It is therefore necessary to count how many generations elapsed in the intervening period, and based on this to comprehend the inconsistency of his argument. From Abraham up to David there were 14 generations, and the ninth generation was already passed at the time of Moses, during which time Nahshon, son of Amminadab, was becoming known as chief of the tribe of Judah. And he died in the wilderness. For he was one of those who departed from Egypt and were present at the first census. It is therefore clear that five more generations after Nahshon remain to be counted up to David. For Nahshon begot Salmon; and Salmon begot Boaz; and Boaz begot Obed; and Obed begot Jesse; and Jesse begot David.

What sort of reasoning would say, then, that for the five generations after Moses there is a total of 700 years? If one allots an equal time to each of these men by generation, each of them will be found to have lived 140 years before begetting a son. But no-one in his right mind would assent to this. Moses himself lived 120 years, and his successor Joshua 110 years. And before them Joseph—all the years of his life were 110 years. In addition to them, Jacob of ancient times, also known as Israel, the progenitor of all the Jews, completed 147 years in all. What kind of reasoning, then, will

---

1 The Armenian version of Eusebius (744 years) is to be preferred to the Greek text of the Ecl. Hist. (741 years). According to Africanus, the Exodus occurred in AM 3707 (see F34,68–70). The construction of Solomon's temple extended from the second to the eighth year of his reign (= AM 4451 to 4457 in Africanus' system, see T42). The length of time from the Exodus to the beginning of the Temple project would thus come to 744 years.

ἔτη ρι'. ἐπὶ τούτοις πάλαι Ἰακὼβ ὁ καὶ Ἰσραήλ, ὁ πάντων Ἰουδαίων ἀρχηγέτης, τὰ πάντα ἔστησεν ἔτη ρμζ'. ποῖος οὖν ἐρεῖ λόγος τοῖς κάτω καὶ μετὰ Μωυσέα τοσοῦτον τῆς ζωῆς ἐνδιδόναι χρόνον
30 ὁπόσος δεδήλωται; ἀλλ᾽ ὁ μὲν Ἀφρικανὸς τούτων διήμαρτε τῶν τρόπων.

28s cf. Gen 47,28

28 ρι' armen. ριζ' Ecl. Hist.   **29** ρμζ'] *145* armen.   **30** τούτον ... τὸν τρόπον Gutschmid, similiter etiam armen.

T41b Georgius Syncellus (204,21–28 Mosshammer)

Ἐὰν οὖν κατὰ τὸν ἀπόστολον τὰ τῶν κριτῶν υν' ἔτη καὶ τὰ ἐπὶ τῆς ἐρήμου μ' ἔτη Μωυσέως Ἰησοῦ τε κζ' καὶ τῶν μετὰ Ἰησοῦν πρεσβυτέρων ιη', καὶ ἔτι Ἡλεὶ τοῦ ἱερέως κ', Σαμουὴλ κ' καὶ Σαοὺλ μ', Δαβίδ τε μ' καὶ Σολομῶνος δ' συναριθμήσωμεν, ἔσται ὁ πᾶς ἀπὸ τῆς ἐξόδου χρόνος ἐπὶ τὴν τοῦ ναοῦ κατασκευὴν ἐτῶν χνθ', κατὰ δὲ Εὐσέβιον χ' καὶ κατὰ Ἀφρικανὸν ὑπὲρ τὰ ψμ'. καθ'
5 ἕκαστον δὲ τῶν τριῶν τούτων ἀριθμὸν αἵ τε ἐκ φυλῆς Ἰούδα αἵ τε ἐκ φυλῆς Λευὶ διαγενόμεναι γενεαὶ ἢ καὶ μεριζόμεναι ἀπίθανον ἕξουσι τὴν παιδοποιίαν.

4 → T41a,13s

1–3 cf. Act 13,16–23   **4** cf. Eus., chron. 48,24 – 49,29

[A] **2** Ἰησοῦν Moss. ιησοῦ A   **3** Σολομῶνος Di. σολομῶν A   **6** ἀπίθανον Di. ἀπείθανον A

T42 Georgius Syncellus (213,1–5 Mosshammer)

Σολομὼν τὸν ἐν Ἱερουσαλὴμ ναὸν ἀρξάμενος κτίζειν ἀπὸ δευτέρου ἔτους τῆς βασιλείας αὐτοῦ, ὅπερ ἦν ιδ' τῆς ζωῆς αὐτοῦ, ἐν ζ' ἔτεσιν ἐτελείωσεν ὀγδόῳ ἔτει τῆς βασιλείας αὐτοῦ, κ' δὲ ἔτει τῆς ζωῆς αὐτοῦ. εἰσὶν οὖν ἀπὸ Ἀδὰμ ἕως η' ἔτους αὐτοῦ ἔτη ͵δυοη', κατὰ δὲ τὸν Ἀφρικανὸν ͵δυνζ', κατὰ δὲ Εὐσέβιον ͵δρο'.

4 → F41a,8

1–3 cf. III Regn 6,1; Sym. Log. (Leo Gr. 31,22 – 32,1 = Th. Mel. 29,17–20 = Iul. Pol. 106,5–9)   **4** cf. Eus., can.[Hier] 70[a]

[AB] **2** ὅπερ...αὐτοῦ² < A

say that the number of years that we have just described is also the life span to be assigned to those both lower than and after Moses? Certainly Africanus has entirely gone astray of these logical inferences.

T41b

Suppose, then, we add up the 450 years of the judges according to the apostle and the 40 years of Moses in the wilderness, and the 27 years of Joshua and the 18 years of the elders after Joshua, in addition to the 20 years of the priest Eli, the 20 years of Samuel, and the 40 years of Saul, and the 40 years of Saul, the 40 years of David and the four years of Solomon. The entire period from the Exodus up to the building of the Temple will then come to 659 years, according to Eusebius 600 years, and according to Africanus over 740 years. And based on any one of these three calculations, if the generations both from the tribe of Judah and from the tribe of Levi are considered in their entirety or divided, the age at which they begot children will be implausibly high.

T42 *The Date of the Building of the Temple*

Solomon commenced his building of the Temple in Jerusalem from the second year of his reign, which was the 14th year of his life. He completed it in seven years, in the eighth year of his reign and the 20th year of his life. From Adam up to the eighth year of his reign, there are 4478 years, but according to Africanus 4457 years,[1] and according to Eusebius 4170.

---

1 See above T41a,8 and n. 1.

F43

F43a Excerpta Barbari (284,26 – 286,9 Frick)

F43b ps. Ioannes Antiochenus fr. 23* (568 Roberto)

Egyptiorum regnum inuenimus uetustissimum omnium regnorum. cuius initium sub Manethono dicitur memoramus scribere.
5 Primum deorum qui ab ipsis scribuntur faciam regna sic.

I. Ifestum dicunt quidam deum regnare in Aegypto annos sexcentos LXXX.

10 II. Post hunc Solem Ifesti ann. LXXVII.

III. Post istum Sosinosirim ann. CCCXX.

15 IIII. Post hunc Oron ptoliarchum ann. XXVIII.

V. Post hunc Tyfona ann. XLV.

Colliguntur deorum regna anni mille DL.

Αἰγύπτιοί φασιν ὡς Ἥφαιστος αὐτῶν ἐβασίλευσεν ἀπείρους τινὰς χρόνους.

μετὰ τοῦτον Ἥλιος ὁ Ἡφαίστου ἔτη ͵ζψοζ͵,

μετ' αὐτὸν Σῶς, ἤτοι Ἄρης,

μεθ' ὃν Κὴβ τοῦ Ἡλίου, ἤτοι Κρόνος.

1-4 → T45,5-9; F46,1; F15,1-7 10s Io. Mal. 2,1 (17,1s Thurn) Μετὰ καὶ τὴν τελευτὴν Ἡφαίστου ἐβασίλευσεν Αἰγυπτίων ὁ υἱὸς αὐτοῦ ὀνόματι Ἥλιος ἡμέρας ͵δυοζ͵, ὡς εἶναι ἔτη ιβ' καὶ ἡμέρας ϙζ'. 12-17 Io. Mal. 2,2 (18,23-26 Thurn) Μετὰ δὲ τὴν τελευτὴν Ἡλίου βασιλέως, υἱοῦ Ἡφαίστου, ἐβασίλευσεν τῶν Αἰγυπτίων Σῶσις, καὶ μετὰ τὴν βασιλείαν αὐτοῦ ἐβασίλευσεν Ὄσιρις, καὶ μετὰ Ὄσιριν ἐβασίλευσεν Ὧρος, καὶ μετὰ Ὧρον ἐβασίλευσεν Θοῦλις.

1-19 cf. Eus., chron. 63,23-27 (= Manetho FGrHist 609 F3a, p. 12); Io. Lyd., mens. 4,86; Sync. 19,1-8 (ps. Manetho); Sync. 56,24-26 (= Vetus Chronicon FGrHist 610 F2) 7-17 cf. Chron. Pasch. 82,12 - 84,14; Io. Ant. fr. 7.1-2; ps. Sym. f. 27ᵛ = Cedr. 36,1-10; Suda Ἥλιος H 235 (omnes ex Malala)

12 Sosinosirim] graece transtulit Frick Σῶσιν … Ὄσιριν ἔτ. τκ' et scripsit: *inter Σῶσιν et Ὄσιριν olim nonnulla fuerunt, quae tamen Barbarus non iam legisse videtur.*

11 ͵ξψοζ' V ͵ζψοξ' D corr. Mü.

F43 The Pre-History of Egypt[1]

F43a

F43b

We have discovered that the kingdom of the Egyptians is the most ancient of all the kingdoms. Its beginning, recounted by Manetho, we recall in writing.
First, I will set forth the reigns of the gods who are recorded by them, as follows:

I. Some say that the god Hephaestus was king in Egypt for 680 years.

The Egyptians say that Hephaestus was their king for countless number of years.

II. After him, Helios, son of Hephaestus, for 77 years.[2]

After him, Helios, son of Hephaestus, for 7777 years.

III. After him, Sosinosiris,[3] for 320 years.

After him, Sos (that is Ares),

after whom Keb (that is Cronus), son of Helius.

IIII. After him, Horus the prince, for 28 years.

V. After him, Typhon, for 45 years.

Altogether, the reigns of the Gods total 1550 years.[4]

---

1 Although the portion of Africanus' epitome of Manetho's *Aegyptiaca* preserved by Syncellus provides only the post-diluvian dynasties of Egyptian kings (F46), the list of Africanus must also have included the rulers for the earlier period. Syncellus would not have praised the quality of the Egyptian lists of both Africanus and Eusebius if one of them were incomplete in some way (59,12–14; see T45,7f). A reference at the beginning of Africanus' list to "the spirits of the dead and demigods" (F46,2) suggests that he, like Eusebius after him (chron. 63,17–65,2 Karst), also included in his chronicle the succession of earlier Egyptian rulers. While unattributed and corrupt in places, the lists of Egyptian mythic rulers preserved in the Exc. Barb. and ps. Io. Ant. are thus important supplements to Syncellus' text. Both writers draw upon Africanus elsewhere, and their record of Egyptian pre-history provides parallel and independent witnesses to the same tradition. It is unlikely that ps. Io. Ant., who uses Africanus as his authority for the post-Flood rulers of Egypt (F46; cf. Roberto 2005b), would have consulted another source for the earlier period. Whether or not Africanus' account of Egyptian pre-history originally belonged to book three of the *Chronographiae* cannot be determined. For the connection of these unattributed lists of the mythic rulers of Egypt with Africanus, see also Gelzer 1,192–196.

2 Cf. ps. Io. Ant.: 7777 years; Io. Mal.: 4777 days.

3 "Sosinosirim" conflates the names "Sosis" and "Osiris." Gr. (Frick): Μετὰ τοῦτον Σῶσιν … Ὄσιριν ἔτ. τκ'. See also Gelzer 1,193.

4 The total of the individual reigns actually comes to 1150 years.

F43c Excerpta Barbari (286,10–19 Frick)

Deinceps Mitheorum regna sic.

I. Prota Anubes †Amusim qui etiam Aegyptiorum scripturas conposuit ann. LXXXIII.
II. Post hunc Apiona grammaticus qui secundum Inachum interpraetatur quem
5 sub Argios initio regnauerunt ann. LXVII†.

I. Post hec Ecyniorum reges interpraetauit Imitheus uocans et ipsos <…> fortissimos uocans annos duo milia C.

4s → F50,3   6 → F46,2

1–3 cf. Sync. 56,26s (= Vetus Chronicon FGrHist 610 F2)   1–6 cf. Eus., chron. 63,31 – 64,7 (= Manetho FGrHist 609 F3a, p. 13); Sync. 19,9–17 (ps. Manetho)

2–5 ordo verborum corruptus   6 lacunam coni. Frick

F44 ps. Ioannes Antiochenus fr. 24* (568 Roberto)

Ὁ ἀπὸ Χάμ, τοῦ υἱοῦ Νῶε, Μεστρὲμ εἰς Αἴγυπτον ἀπῳκίσθη, καὶ ἀπ' αὐτοῦ ἐκλήθη ἡ χώρα· τὸ γὰρ Μεστρὲμ Ἑβραϊστὶ Αἴγυπτον δηλοῖ.

1s   Sym. Log. (Leo Gr. [27,17s Bekker] = Th. Mel. [26,21 Tafel] = Cedr. [27,1s Bekker]) Χὰμ γὰρ ὁ υἱὸς τοῦ Νῶε πατὴρ ἦν τοῦ Μεσραείμ, ἀφ' οὗ οἱ Αἰγύπτιοι.

1s   cf. Gen 10,6.13; Eus., chron. 64,11–14 (= Manetho FGrHist 609 F3a, p. 14); Ios., ant. Iud. 1,132; Io. Mal. 1,15; Sync. 38,21–25; 58,10–19; 102,17; 249,20–24; Iul. Pol. 68,17–20; ps. Sym. f. 23ʳ = Cedr. 21,14–17; Cedr. 23,2

F43c

Next, the reigns of the demigods,[1] as follows:[2]

I. First, Anubis for 83 years.

II. After him, <some say that> Amosis <was king>[3] for 67 years.[4] Apion the grammarian, who composed the annals of the Egyptians, explains <that he was> contemporary with Inachus, who was king at the time of the founding of Argos.[5]

I. After these, he set forth the kings of the spirits of the dead,[6] calling them also demigods[7] <…> calling them most powerful, for 2100 years.[8]

F44 *Mestrem, the Eponymous Father of the Egyptians*[9]

Mestrem, from Ham the son of Noah, migrated to Egypt, and from him the region received its name. For the word "Mestrem" means "Egypt" in Hebrew.

1 Gr. (Frick): Ἡμιθέων.
2 The Latin text is unreadable. The translation that follows is based on Frick's restoration of the underlying Greek text:
α'. Πρῶτα Ἄνουβις ἐτ. πγ'.
β' Μετὰ τοῦτον Ἄμουσιν <φασί τινες βασιλεῦσαι, ὃν> Ἀπίων ὁ γραμματικὸς ὁ καὶ τὰς Αἰγυπτίων γραφὰς συνθεὶς κατὰ Ἴναχον ἑρμηνεύει τὸν ἐπ' Ἀργείων ἀρχῆς βασιλεύσαντα ἔτη ξζ'.
3 In Africanus' list of Egyptian kings, Amos(is) was the first king of the 18th dynasty of human kings (see F46,132). During his reign, Moses led the Israelites from Egypt and Inachus was king of Argos. For unknown reasons, the *Excerpta* puts the entry concerning Amosis during the reigns of the demigods.
4 The 67 years most likely refer to the length of the reign of Amosis, not Inachus.
5 For Apion's dating of king Amosis during the time of Inachus, see F34,80–83.
6 *Ecyniorum reges* is a mistranslation of τὰς τῶν νεκύων βασιλείας ('the reigns of the spirits of the dead').
7 On the identification of the spirits of the dead as demigods, see F46,8 (= Sync. 59,28): Μετὰ νέκυας τοὺς ἡμιθέους. Cf. Eus. (in Sync. 61.1-2): Μετὰ νέκυας καὶ τοὺς ἡμιθέους.
8 The text is lacunose. The 2100 years do not refer to the reigns of the spirits of the dead, but rather to the dynasties of Egyptian human kings recorded in the first book of Manetho's *Aegyptiaca*; see Exc. Barb. 288,5–6 (2100 years in 10 dynasties); cf. F46,99 (2300 years in 11 dynasties).
9 The explanation of the origin of the word "Mestrem" provided here is widespread in Christian and Jewish sources, including Eusebius (chron. 64,11–14 Karst), see *loci similes*. For ps. Io. Ant.'s dependence on Africanus for this notice and his other reports about early Egyptian history, see above n. 1 to F43, and introduction, pp. XLI f.

T45 Georgius Syncellus (59,6–26 Mosshammer)

Ἐπειδὴ δὲ τῶν ἀπὸ Μεστραῒμ Αἰγυπτιακῶν ἐτῶν οἱ χρόνοι ἕως Νεκταναβῶ χρειώδεις τυγχάνουσιν ἐν πολλοῖς τοῖς περὶ τὰς χρονικὰς καταγινομένοις ζητήσεις, αὗται δὲ παρὰ Μανεθῶ ληφθεῖσαι τοῖς ἐκκλησιαστικοῖς ἱστορικοῖς διαπεφωνημένως κατά τε τὰς αὐτῶν προσηγορίας καὶ τὴν ποσότητα τῶν χρόνων τῆς βασιλείας ἐκδέδονται, ἐπὶ τίνος τε αὐτῶν Ἰωσὴφ ἡγεμόνευσε τῆς Αἰγύπτου καὶ μετ'
5 αὐτὸν ὁ θεόπτης Μωυσῆς τῆς τοῦ Ἰσραὴλ ἐξ Αἰγύπτου πορείας ἡγήσατο, ἀναγκαῖον ἡγησάμην δύο τῶν ἐπισημοτάτων ἐκδόσεις ἐκλέξασθαι καὶ ταύτας ἀλλήλαις παραθέσθαι, Ἀφρικανοῦ τέ φημι καὶ τοῦ μετ' αὐτὸν Εὐσεβίου τοῦ Παμφίλου καλουμένου, ὡς ἂν τὴν ἐγγίζουσαν τῇ γραφικῇ ἀληθείᾳ δόξαν ὀρθῶς ἐπιβάλλων καταμάθοι, τοῦτο πρό γε πάντων εἰδὼς ἀκριβῶς, ὅτι Ἀφρικανὸς μὲν κ' ἔτη προστί-
10 θησιν ἐν τοῖς ἀπὸ Ἀδὰμ ἕως τοῦ κατακλυσμοῦ χρόνοις, καὶ ἀντὶ ‚βσμβ' ‚βσξβ' ἔτη βούλεται εἶναι, ὅπερ οὐ δοκεῖ καλῶς ἔχειν. Εὐσέβιος δὲ ‚βσμβ' ὑγιῶς ἔθετο καὶ ὁμοφώνως τῇ γραφῇ.

Ἐν δὲ τοῖς ἀπὸ τοῦ κατακλυσμοῦ ἀμφότεροι διήμαρτον ἕως Ἀβραὰμ καὶ Μωυσέως ἔτεσι ρλ' τοῦ δευτέρου Καϊνᾶν υἱοῦ Ἀρφαξὰδ καὶ γενεᾷ μιᾷ, τῇ ιγ',
15 παρὰ τῷ θείῳ εὐαγγελιστῇ Λουκᾷ ἀπὸ Ἀδὰμ κειμένη. ἀλλ' ὁ μὲν Ἀφρικανὸς ἐν τοῖς ἀπὸ Ἀδὰμ προστεθεῖσιν αὐτῷ καὶ ἐπὶ τὸν κατακλυσμὸν ἔτεσιν κ' προαφήρπαξε ταῦτα, καὶ ἐν τοῖς τοῦ Καϊνᾶν καὶ τῶν μετέπειτα ρι' μόνα λείπεται. διὸ καὶ ἕως Ἀβραὰμ πρώτου ἔτους ‚γσβ' ἔτη ἐστοιχείωσεν. ὁ δὲ Εὐσέβιος ὁλοκλήρως τὰ ρλ' ὑφελών, ‚γρπδ' ἕως πρώτου ἔτους Ἀβραὰμ ἐξέδωκε.

5-9 → F46; T46a   9s → T22a,5; T22b,3s; T16g,1–4; T16o,6s   10s → T6,4; F16b; T16h; T16q
13-17 → T16i; T16l; T16m; T16o,5s; T16q; T47,1–3   17-19 → T16o,4–7

11s cf. Eus., chron. 42,32s   14s cf. Gen 11,10–13; Lc 3,36   18s cf. Eus., can.[Hier] 15,2–5

[AB]   1 ἐτῶν] δυναστειῶν Adler   11 ὑγιῶς A ὑγειῶς B   13 ἀβραὰμ B τοῦ ἀβραὰμ A   16s προαφήρπαξεν A προαφήρπαζεν B   18 ἔτη A ἔτει B

T45 *The Date of the Flood and the Date of Abraham*

Now the chronology of the Egyptian dynasties from Mestraim up to Nectanebo proves inadequate for many who have concerned themselves in chronological investigations. And these dynasties taken from Manetho have discrepancies in the versions presented by the ecclesiastical historians with regard to their name and the duration of their reigns, and also in whose reign Joseph was governor of Egypt, as subsequently in whose reign Moses the beholder of God led the Exodus of Israel from Egypt. For these reasons, I have thought it necessary to pick out the two most famous versions and set them side by side—I mean those of Africanus and his successor Eusebius, called [pupil] of Pamphilus—so that with proper application, one might know the opinion that more closely approaches scriptural truth.[1] But above all else, one must know full well that Africanus adds 20 years in his chronology from Adam up to the Flood, and instead of 2242 years wants there to be 2262 years,[2] which does not appear to be right. Eusebius, on the other hand, was correct in giving 2242 years, in harmony with Scripture.

But in the years from the Flood up to Abraham and Moses, both of them went wrong by omitting the 130 years of the second Kenan, the son of Arpachshad, one generation, representing the 13th position from Adam in the holy evangelist Luke. But since Africanus, by adding 20 years from Adam up to the Flood, had already removed 20 years for the period after the Flood, only 110 years are missing in his chronology of Kenan and his successors. Therefore, up to the first year of Abraham, he counted 3202 years. But Eusebius subtracted a full 130 years, and set forth 3184 years up to the first year of Abraham.

---

1   On the transmission of Manetho in Christian chronography, see Adler 1989,32–35 and 38–40.
2   On Africanus' dating of the Flood, see introduction, p. XXVII.

F46

Sync.¹: Georgius Syncellus (59,27 – 69,12 Mosshammer partim, vide app. test.)
Sync.²: ibd. (76,28 – 87,8 Mosshammer partim, vide app. test.)

Περὶ τῶν μετὰ τὸν κατακλυσμὸν Αἰγύπτου δυναστειῶν, ὡς ὁ Ἀφρικανός

α′ Μετὰ νέκυας τοὺς ἡμιθέους πρώτη βασιλεία καταριθμεῖται βασιλέων η′, ὧν
πρῶτος Μήνης Θεεινίτης ἐβασίλευσεν ἔτη ξβ′· ὃς ὑπὸ ἱπποποτάμου δι-
αρπαγεὶς διεφθάρη.
5 β′ Ἄθωθις υἱὸς ἔτη νζ′, ὁ τὰ ἐν Μέμφει βασίλεια οἰκοδομήσας· οὗ
φέρονται βίβλοι ἀνατομικαί, ἰατρὸς γὰρ ἦν.
γ′ Κενκένης υἱὸς ἔτη λα′.
δ′ Οὐενέφης υἱὸς ἔτη κγ′· ἐφ᾽ οὗ λιμὸς κατέσχε τὴν Αἴγυπτον μέγας.
οὗτος τὰς περὶ Κωχώμην ἤγειρε πυραμίδας.
10 ε′ Οὐσαφάιδος υἱὸς ἔτη κ′.
ς′ Μιεβιδὸς υἱὸς ἔτη κς′.
ζ′ Σεμέμψης υἱὸς ἔτη ιη′· ἐφ᾽ οὗ φθορὰ μεγίστη κατέσχε τὴν
Αἴγυπτον.
η′ Βιηνεχὴς υἱὸς ἔτη κς′.
15 Ὁμοῦ ἔτη σνγ′.
Τὰ τῆς πρώτης δυναστείας οὕτω πως καὶ Εὐσέβιος ὡς ὁ Ἀφρικανὸς ἐξέθετο.

Δευτέρα δυναστεία Θεινιτῶν βασιλέων θ′, ὧν
πρῶτος Βῶχος ἔτη λη′· ἐφ᾽ οὗ χάσμα κατὰ Βούβαστον ἐγένετο, καὶ ἀπ-
ώλοντο πολλοί.
20 β′ Καιέχως ἔτη λθ′· ἐφ᾽ οὗ οἱ βόες Ἆπις ἐν Μέμφει καὶ Μηνεὺς ἐν
Ἡλιουπόλει καὶ ὁ Μενδήσιος τράγος ἐνομίσθησαν εἶναι θεοί.

test.: 1 inc. Sync.¹ [AB] 1-28 59,27 – 60,24 Moss.

1-245 → T45,7-10 2-15 → F43c; Exc. Barb. (286,20s Frick) *II. Mineus et pronepotes ipsius* VII *regnauerunt* ann. CCLIII. 17-32 Exc. Barb. (286,22 Frick) *III. Bochus et aliorum octo* ann. CCCII.

2-242 cf. Manetho FGrHist 609 F2; Eus., chron. 65-69 (armeniace) et textum Graecum chronici Eusebii a Syncello Africano iuxtapositum; Eus., can.[armen] 156-197; Eus., can.[Hier] 20-124

1 δυναστειῶν A δυναστείας B 3 θεεινίτης AB Θεινίτης Scal. | ἱπποποτάμου Goar[m] ἱπποτάμου AB 12 σεμέμψης B σεμέμψις A 18 Βῶχος Eus. apud Sync. 61,22 *Bochus* Exc. Barb. Βοηθός AB | ἐφ᾽ B ἀφ᾽ A | χάσμα B φάσμα A 18s ἀπώλοντο B ἀπώλλοντο A 20 καιέχως B καὶ ἔχως A | Μέμφει Goar[m] μέμφι A μεμφὶ B | μηνεὺς AB Μνεῦις Scal. ex Eus. apud Sync. 61,24 21 ἡλιουπόλει B ἰλιοπόλει A

F46 *Dynasties of Egypt*[1]

Concerning the dynasties of Egypt after the Flood, according to Africanus

1. After the spirits of the dead, the demigods, the first royal line is numbered at eight kings.

   The first of them, Menes of This, reigned for 62 years. He was seized by a hippopotamus and perished.
   2. Athothis, his son, 57 years. He built the palace in Memphis. His books on anatomy are in circulation, for he was a physician.
   3. Kenkenes, his son, 31 years.
   4. Uenephes, his son, 23 years. During his reign, a great famine gripped Egypt. He erected the pyramids around Kochome.
   5. Usaphaidos, his son, 20 years.
   6. Miebidos, his son, 26 years.
   7. Semempses, his son, 18 years. During his reign, a vast pestilence gripped Egypt.
   8. Bieneches, his son, 26 years.

   Total of 253 years.

Eusebius also furnished the details of the first dynasty in somewhat the same way as Africanus.

Second dynasty of nine kings of This

   The first of them was Bochos, 38 years. During his reign, a chasm opened up in Bubastus, and many perished.
   2. Kaiechos, 39 years. During his reign, the bulls, Apis in Memphis and Meneus in Heliopolis, and the Mendesian goat were deemed to be gods.

---

[1] For two supplemental witnesses to Africanus' version of Manetho's list of post-diluvian Egyptian dynasties, see the parallel lists found in the *Excerpta Barbari* and ps. John of Antioch (in the third apparatus). Although the abridged list of the *Excerpta* provides only the sum of the years of each dynasty, this information is useful for confirming the numbers found in Syncellus. Comparison with the other witnesses to Africanus' list of Egyptian kings shows that the excerpts of ps. John of Antioch on the Egyptian kings also belong to the Africanus tradition. An entry about Semiramis (see F34,51–53) found within these excerpts also originates in Africanus' chronicle, but in a different context. For further discussion, see introduction, pp. XLI f. For Africanus' treatment of the mythical Egyptian rulers before the Flood (lacking in Syncellus), see F43.

γ' Βίνωθρις ἔτη μζ'· ἐφ' οὗ ἐκρίθη τὰς γυναῖκας βασιλείας γέρας ἔχειν.
δ' Τλὰς ἔτη ιζ'.
ε' Σεθένης ἔτη μα'.
ς' Χαίρης ἔτη ιζ'.
ζ' Νεφερχέρης ἔτη κε'· ἐφ' οὗ μυθεύεται τὸν Νεῖλον μέλιτι κεκραμένον ἡμέραις ἕνδεκα ῥυῆναι.
η' Σέσωχρις ἔτη μη'· ὃς ὕψος εἶχε πηχῶν ε', πλάτος γ'.
θ' Χενερὴς ἔτη λ'.
Ὁμοῦ ἔτη τβ'.
Ὁμοῦ πρώτης καὶ δευτέρας δυναστείας μετὰ τὸν κατακλυσμὸν ἔτη φνε' κατὰ τὴν δευτέραν ἔκδοσιν Ἀφρικανοῦ. [...]

Τρίτη δυναστεία Μεμφιτῶν βασιλέων θ'
α' ὧν πρῶτος Νεχερωφὴς ἔτη κη'· ἐφ' οὗ Λίβυες ἀπέστησαν Αἰγυπτίων καὶ τῆς σελήνης παρὰ λόγον αὐξηθείσης διὰ δέος ἑαυτοὺς παρέδοσαν.
β' Τόσορθρος ἔτη κθ'· οὗτος Ἀσκληπιὸς Αἰγυπτίοις κατὰ τὴν ἰατρικὴν νενόμισται, καὶ τὴν διὰ ξεστῶν λίθων οἰκοδομίαν εὕρατο, ἀλλὰ καὶ γραφῆς ἐπεμελήθη.
γ' Τύρεις ἔτη ζ'.
δ' Μέσωχρις ἔτη ιζ'.
ε' Σώϋφις ἔτη ις'.
ς' Τοσέρτασις ἔτη ιθ'.
ζ' Ἄχης ἔτη μβ'.
η' Σήφουρις λ'.
θ' Κερφέρης ἔτη κς'.
Ὁμοῦ ἔτη σιδ'.
Ὁμοῦ τῶν τριῶν δυναστειῶν κατὰ Ἀφρικανὸν ἔτη ψξθ'.

---

test.: Sync.[1]   29–33 62,5–9 Moss. (textum transposuit hoc e serie Eusebiana Moss.)   34–63 62,15 – 63,15 Moss.

22s   ps. Io. Ant. fr. 25* (568 Ro.) Ἐπὶ βινώριος βασιλέως Αἰγύπτου ἐκρίθη τὰς γυναῖκας γέρα ἔχειν βασίλεια   27s ps. Io. Ant. fr. 26* (570 Ro.) Ἐπὶ Νεφερχέρου βασιλέως Αἰγύπτου φασὶ τὸν Νεῖλον μέλιτι κεκραμένον ἡμέρας ἕνδεκα ῥυῆναι   34–48 Exc. Barb. (286,23 Frick) IV. Necherocheus et aliorum VII ann. CCXIIII.

27s κεκραμένον Di. κεκραμμένον AB   28 ἡμέραις Io. Ant. Eus. apud Sync. 62,3 ἡμέρας AB   29 πλάτος] παλαιστῶν Gelzer[ms] ex Eus. | πηχῶν A πειχῶν B   33 δευτέραν < Goar   35 α' ὧν α' B ὧν πρῶτος A | νεχερωφὴς B νεχερόφης A   38 κθ' + ἐφ' οὗ Ἰμούθης Sethe   41 τύρεις B τύρις A   46 σήφουρις B σίφουρις A   49 ἀφρικανὸν A ἀφρικανοῦ B

3. Binothris, 47 years. During his reign, it was decreed that women might possess the privilege of royalty.
4. Tlas, 17 years.
5. Sethenes, 41 years.
6. Chaires, 17 years.
7. Nephercheres, 25 years. There is a story that during his reign, the Nile flowed mixed with honey for 11 days.
8. Sesochris, 48 years. He was five cubits in height and three cubits wide.
9. Cheneres, 30 years.

Total of 302 years.

Total years of the first and second dynasties after the flood, 555 years according to the second edition of Africanus.[2]

Third dynasty of nine kings of Memphis
1. The first of them is Necherophes, 28 years. In his reign, the Libyans revolted from the Egyptians; when the moon waxed unexpectedly, they surrendered out of panic.
2. Tosorthros, 29 years. Among the Egyptians, he is considered an Asclepius in recognition of his medical skill. The inventor of the art of building with hewn stone, he also pursued the craft of writing.
3. Tyreis, 7 years.
4. Mesochris, 17 years.
5. Soyphis, 16 years.
6. Tosertasis, 19 years.
7. Aches, 42 years.
8. Sephuris, 30 years.
9. Kerpheres, 26 years.

Total of 214 years.

Total for these three dynasties, according to Africanus 769 years.

---

[2] Since the word δευτέρας appears in the preceding line, Syncellus' reference to the "second edition of Africanus" could be dittography (see Unger 1867,15; Gelzer 1,29f). It could also be Syncellus' way of distinguishing Africanus' list of Egyptian kings from the alternative edition of Manetho known to him through Eusebius' chronicle.

50 Τετάρτη δυναστεία Μεμφιτῶν συγγενείας ἑτέρας βασιλεῖς η΄
    α΄   Σῶρις ἔτη κθ΄.
    β΄   Σοῦφις ἔτη ξγ΄· ὃς τὴν μεγίστην ἤγειρε πυραμίδα, ἥν φησιν Ἡρό-
        δοτος ὑπὸ Χέοπος γεγονέναι. οὗτος δὲ καὶ ὑπερόπτης εἰς θεοὺς
        ἐγένετο καὶ τὴν ἱερὰν συνέγραψε βίβλον, ἥν ὡς μέγα χρῆμα ἐν
55   Αἰγύπτῳ γενόμενος ἐκτησάμην.
    γ΄   Σοῦφις ἔτη ξς΄.
    δ΄   Μενχέρης ἔτη ξγ΄.
    ε΄   Ῥατοίσης ἔτη κε΄.
    ς΄   Βίχερις ἔτη κβ΄.
60   ζ΄   Σεβερχέρης ἔτη ζ΄.
    η΄   Θαμφθὶς ἔτη θ΄.
    Ὁμοῦ ἔτη σοζ΄.
Ὁμοῦ τῶν δ΄ δυναστειῶν τῶν μετὰ τὸν κατακλυσμὸν ἔτη ͵αμς΄ κατ' Ἀφρικανόν. [...]

    Πέμπτη δυναστεία βασιλέων θ΄ ἐξ Ἐλεφαντίνης
65   α΄   Οὐσερχέρης ἔτη κη΄.
    β΄   Σεφρὴς ἔτη ιγ΄.
    γ΄   Νεφερχέρης ἔτη κ΄.
    δ΄   Σισίρης ἔτη ζ΄.
    ε΄   Χέρης ἔτη κ΄.
70   ς΄   Ῥαθούρης ἔτη μδ΄.
    ζ΄   Μενχέρης ἔτη θ΄.
    η΄   Τανχέρης ἔτη μδ΄.
    θ΄   Ὄννος ἔτη λγ΄.
    Ὁμοῦ ἔτη σμη΄.
75 Γίνονται σὺν τοῖς προτεταγμένοις ͵αμς΄ ἔτεσι τῶν δ΄ δυναστειῶν ἔτη ͵ασϥδ΄.

    Ἕκτη δυναστεία βασιλέων ἐξ Μεμφιτῶν
    α΄   Ὀθόης ἔτη λ΄· ὃς ὑπὸ τῶν δορυφόρων ἀνῃρέθη.

---

test.: Sync.[1] **64-90** 64,10 – 65,5 Moss.

54s → F98; Eus. apud Sync. (64,5s Moss.) ἥν ὡς μέγα χρῆμα *Αἰγύπτιοι περιέπουσι*. **62** Exc. Barb. (286,24 Frick) *V. Similiter aliorum XVII* ann. CCLXXVII. **76-85** Exc. Barb. (286,26 Frick) VII. *Othoi et aliorum VII* ann. CCIII.

52s Hdt. 2,124

52 ἥν < B **53** ὑπὸ Χέοπος Goar[m] ὑπὸ χέοττος AB | ὑπερόπτης B ὁ περόπτης A **55** ἐκτησάμην A ἐκτισάμην B **59** βίχερις B βίχερης A **62** σοζ΄ B Exc. Barb. σοδ΄ A **63** κατ' ἀφρικανόν in textu A κατ' ἀφρικανοῦ marg. B **64** θ΄ scripsimus η΄ Sync. < Scal. **68** σισίρης B σίσιρις A **70** ῥαθούρης B ῥαθουρὶς A **72** ταγχέρης B ταρχέρης A **73** ὄννος B ὄβνος A **76** δυναστεία B δυναστείων A **77** ὀθόης B ὀθώης A

Fourth dynasty of eight kings of Memphis from another line
1. Soris, 29 years.
2. Suphis, 63 years. He erected the Great Pyramid, which Herodotus says was built under Cheops. He also became disdainful of the gods, and composed the *Sacred Book*; this I acquired when I was in Egypt, because it was a great treasure.[3]
3. Suphis, 66 years.
4. Mencheres, 63 years.
5. Ratoises, 25 years.
6. Bicheris, 22 years.
7. Sebercheres, 7 years.
8. Thamphthis, 9 years.

Total of 277 years.

Total for the four dynasties after the flood, according to Africanus, 1046 years.

Fifth dynasty of nine kings from Elephantine
1. Userchres, 28 years.
2. Sephres, 13 years.
3. Nephercheres, 20 years.
4. Sisires, 7 years.
5. Cheres, 20 years.
6. Rhathures, 44 years.
7. Mencheres, 9 years.
8. Tancheres, 44 years.
9. Onnus, 33 years.

Total of 248 years.

Together with the aforementioned 1046 years of the first four dynasties, this makes 1294 years.

Sixth dynasty of six kings of Memphis
1. Othoës, 30 years. He was murdered by his bodyguard.

---

[3] The notice about the purchase of the *Sacred Book* is probably a comment from Africanus himself (cf. also Eusebius' version, given in the third app.). On Africanus' visit to Egypt, see F98.

β'   Φιὸς ἔτη νγ'.
γ'   Μεθουσουφὶς ἔτη ζ'.
δ'   Φίωψ ἑξαέτης ἀρξάμενος βασιλεύειν διεγένετο μέχρις ἐτῶν ρ'.
ε'   Μενθεσουφὶς ἔτος ἕν.
ς'   Νίτωκρις γεννικωτάτη τε καὶ εὐμορφοτάτη τῶν κατ' αὐτὴν γενομένη, ξανθὴ τὴν χροιάν, ἣ τὴν τρίτην ἤγειρε πυραμίδα· ἐβασίλευσεν ἔτη ιβ'.
Ὁμοῦ ἔτη σγ'.
Γίνονται σὺν τοῖς προτεταγμένοις ͵ασρδ'.
Τῶν ε' δυναστειῶν ἔτη ͵αυρζ'.

Ἑβδόμη δυναστεία Μεμφιτῶν βασιλέων ο', οἳ ἐβασίλευσαν ἡμέρας ο'.

Ὀγδόη δυναστεία Μεμφιτῶν βασιλέων κζ', οἳ ἐβασίλευσαν ἔτη ρμς'.
Γίνονται σὺν τοῖς προτεταγμένοις ἔτη ͵αχλθ' τῶν η' δυναστειῶν. [...]

Ἐνάτη δυναστεία Ἡρακλεοπολιτῶν βασιλέων ιθ', οἳ ἐβασίλευσαν ἔτη υθ', ὧν
  ὁ πρῶτος Ἀχθόης δεινότατος τῶν πρὸ αὐτοῦ γενόμενος τοῖς ἐν πάσῃ Αἰγύπτῳ κακὰ εἰργάσατο, ὕστερον δὲ μανίᾳ περιέπεσε καὶ ὑπὸ κροκοδείλου διεφθάρη.

Δεκάτη δυναστεία Ἡρακλεοπολιτῶν βασιλέων ιθ', οἳ ἐβασίλευσαν ἔτη ρπε'.

Ἑνδεκάτη δυναστεία Διοσπολιτῶν βασιλέων ις', οἳ ἐβασίλευσαν ἔτη μγ'. μεθ'
οὓς Ἀμμενέμης ἔτη ις'.
Μέχρι τοῦδε τὸν πρῶτον τόμον καταγήοχε Μανεθῶ.
Ὁμοῦ βασιλεῖς ρϟβ', ἔτη ͵βτ', ἡμέραι ο'.

         Δευτέρου τόμου Μανεθῶ

Δωδεκάτη δυναστεία Διοσπολιτῶν βασιλέων ἑπτά.
  α'   Σεσόγχωσις Ἀμμανέμου υἱὸς ἔτη μς'.
  β'   Ἀμμανέμης ἔτη λη'· ὃς ὑπὸ τῶν ἰδίων εὐνούχων ἀνῃρέθη.

test.: Sync.¹   91–114   65,26 – 66,21 Moss.

80   ps. Io. Ant. fr. 27* (570 Ro.) Φίωψ ἑξαέτης ἀρξάμενος βασιλεύειν διεγένετο μέχρις ἐτῶν ρ'
91   Exc. Barb. (288,3 Frick) VIIII. similiter et aliorum XX ann. CCCCVIIII.

82 γεννικωτάτη A γεννητικωτάτη B | τε < A   83 χροιάν A χροᾶν B   93 εἰργάσατο A ἠργάσατο B
93s κροκοδείλου Goar^m κορκοδείλου A κορκοδήλου B   98 καταγήοχε Μανεθῶ Di. καταγήωχε μανεθῶ B κατάγει ὁ κεμμανεθῶ A   99 ἔτη ͵βτ' ἡμέραι ο' B ἔτη ͵βτη', μέραι ο' A   101 δωδεκάτη δυναστεία διοσπολιτῶν B ιβ' δυναστεῖαι πολιτῶν A   102 Σεσόγχωσις Di. γέσων γώσης A γεσονγόσις B

2. Phius, 53 years.
3. Methusuphis, 7 years.
4. Phiops, whose reign began at the age of six, ruled continuously up to his 100th year.
5. Menthesuphis, 1 year.
6. Nitocris, the most noble and comely woman of her time, fair in complexion. She built the third pyramid and reigned for 12 years.

Total of 203 years.

Together with the aforementioned 1294 years of the first five dynasties, this makes 1497 years.

Seventh dynasty of 70 kings of Memphis: these reigned for 70 days.[4]

Eighth dynasty of 27 kings of Memphis: these reigned for 146 years.
Together with the aforementioned years, there are for these eight dynasties 1639 years.

Ninth dynasty of 19 kings of Heracleopolis: these reigned for 409 years.
> The first of them was Achthoes. Harsher than his predecessors, he caused hardship for the people of all Egypt. But he later succumbed to madness and was killed by a crocodile.

10th dynasty of 19 kings of Heracleopolis: these reigned for 185 years.

11th dynasty of 16 kings of Diospolis: these reigned for 43 years. Next after these, Ammenemes, 16 years.
At this point, Manetho concluded his first book.
Total 192 kings, 2300 years, 70 days.

From the second book of Manetho

12th dynasty of seven kings of Diospolis
1. Sesonchosis, son of Ammanemes, 46 years.
2. Ammanemes, 38 years. He was murdered by his personal eunuchs.

---

[4] It is not possible to emend the text on the basis of other witnesses. The parallel text in Eusebius gives 75 days (and five kings) for this dynasty.

γ΄ Σέσωστρις ἔτη μη΄· ὃς ἅπασαν ἐχειρώσατο τὴν Ἀσίαν ἐν ἐνιαυτοῖς θ΄ καὶ τῆς Εὐρώπης τὰ μέχρι Θράκης, πανταχόσε μνημόσυνα ἐγείρας τῆς τῶν ἐθνῶν σχέσεως, ἐπὶ μὲν τοῖς γενναίοις ἀνδρῶν, ἐπὶ δὲ τοῖς ἀγεννέσι γυναικῶν μόρια ταῖς στήλαις ἐγχαράσσων, ὡς ὑπὸ Αἰγυπτίων μετὰ Ὄσιριν πρῶτον νομισθῆναι.
δ΄ Λαχάρης ἔτη η΄· ὃς τὸν ἐν Ἀρσινοΐτῃ λαβύρινθον ἑαυτῷ τάφον κατεσκεύασε.
ε΄ Ἀμερὴς ἔτη η΄.
ς΄ Ἀμμενέμης ἔτη η΄.
ζ΄ Σκεμίοφρις ἀδελφὴ ἔτη δ΄.
Ὁμοῦ ἔτη ρξ΄. [...]

Τρισκαιδεκάτη δυναστεία Διοσπολιτῶν βασιλέων ξ΄, οἳ ἐβασίλευσαν ἔτη υνγ΄.

Τεσσαρεσκαιδεκάτη δυναστεία Ξοϊτῶν βασιλέων ος΄, οἳ ἐβασίλευσαν ἔτη ρπδ΄.

Πεντεκαιδεκάτη δυναστεία ποιμένων.
Ἦσαν δὲ Φοίνικες ξένοι βασιλεῖς ς΄, οἳ καὶ Μέμφιν εἷλον, ὧν
    πρῶτος Σαΐτης ἐβασίλευσεν ἔτη ιθ΄, ἀφ᾿ οὗ καὶ ὁ Σαΐτης νομός· οἳ καὶ ἐν τῷ Σεθροΐτῃ νομῷ πόλιν ἔκτισαν, ἀφ᾿ ἧς ὁρμώμενοι Αἰγυπτίους ἐχειρώσαντο.
β΄ Βνῶν ἔτη μδ΄.
γ΄ Παχνὰν ἔτη ξα΄.
δ΄ Σταὰν ἔτη ν΄.
ε΄ Ἄρχλης ἔτη μθ΄.
ς΄ Ἄφοβις ἔτη ξα΄.
Ὁμοῦ ἔτη σπδ΄.

Ἑξκαιδεκάτη δυναστεία ποιμένες ἄλλοι βασιλεῖς λβ΄. ἐβασίλευσαν ἔτη φιη΄.

---

test.: Sync.¹ 115–130 67,21 – 68,12 Moss.

104–107 ps. Io. Ant. fr. 29* (570 Ro.) Σέσωστρις ὁ βασιλεὺς Αἰγύπτου θ΄ ἔτεσι τὴν ἅπασαν Ἀσίαν ἐχειρώσατο καὶ τῆς Εὐρώπης τὰ μέχρι Θράκης καὶ μνημόσυνα πεποίηκε τῆς τῶν ἐθνῶν ἁλώσεως, ἐπὶ μὲν τοῖς γενναίοις ἀνδρῶν, ἐπὶ δὲ τοῖς ἀγεννέσι γυναικῶν [ταῖς στήλαις] ἐγχαράσσων μόρια. 117–127 → T46b,3.5s; T46c,15s 128–130 → T47,27s

104–108 cf. Hdt. 2,102

104 σέσωστρις A σεσόστρις B 105 πανταχόσε A πανταχόσαι B 106 ἐθνῶν B ἔθνος A | σχέσεως] κατασχέσεως Eus. ἁλώσεως ps. Io. Ant. 107 ἀγεννέσι B ἀγενέσι A | ἐγχαράστων A ἐνχαράσσων B ὡς Goarᵐ ὃς AB 108 ὄσιριν A ὄσιρην B 109 λαχάρης AB Λαμάρης Jacoby | ἐν Ἀρσινοΐτῃ Di. ἐναρσοίτῃ A ἐναρσοίτην B 111 ἀμερὴς B ἀμμερὴς A 112 Ἀμμενέμης Di. ἀμμενέμης A ἀμενέμης B 115s υνγ΄...ἔτη < A 120 σεθροΐτῃ A σαιθροίτῃ B | νομῷ πόλιν A νομοπόλιν B

3. Sesostris, 48 years. He subjugated all Asia in nine years, and the regions of Europe as far as Thrace, erecting everywhere monuments describing the character of the nations [that he subdued]. For the heroic nations, he engraved on pillars male genitalia; for the ignoble nations, female genitalia. As a result of his acts, he was considered by the Egyptians first in rank after Osiris.
4. Lachares, 8 years. He constructed the labyrinth in the nome of Arsinoë as a tomb for himself.
5. Ameres, 8 years.
6. Ammenemes, 8 years.
7. Scemiophris, his sister, 4 years.

Total of 160 years.

13th dynasty of 60 kings of Diospolis: these reigned for 453 years.

14th dynasty of 76 kings of Xoïs: these reigned for 184 years.

15th dynasty of shepherds
There were six foreign kings from Phoenicia, who also captured Memphis.

Their first king was Saïtes, who reigned for 19 years. The Salitis nome is named after him. They also built a city in the Sethroite nome, which they used as a base of operations when they subdued the Egyptians.
2. Bnon, 44 years.
3. Apachnan, 61 years.
4. Staan, 50 years.
5. Archles, 49 years.
6. Aphophis, 61 years.

Total of 284 years.

16th dynasty of 32 additional shepherd kings. They reigned for 518 years.

Ἑπτακαιδεκάτη δυναστεία ποιμένες ἄλλοι βασιλεῖς γ΄ καὶ Θηβαῖοι Διοσπολῖται γ΄.
Ὁμοῦ οἱ ποιμένες καὶ οἱ Θηβαῖοι ἐβασίλευσαν ἔτη ρνα΄. [...]

Ὀκτωκαιδεκάτη δυναστεία Διοσπολιτῶν βασιλέων ις΄, ὧν
πρῶτος Ἀμώς, ἐφ᾽ οὗ Μωυσῆς ἐξῆλθεν ἀπ᾽ Αἰγύπτου, ὡς ἡμεῖς ἀποδείκνυμεν.

Ὡς δ᾽ ἡ παροῦσα ψῆφος ἀναγκάζει, ἐπὶ τούτου τὸν Μωυσέα συμβαίνει νέον ἔτι εἶναι. [...]

Δεύτερος κατὰ Ἀφρικανὸν κατὰ τὴν ιη΄ δυναστείαν ἐβασίλευσε Χεβρὼς ἔτη ιγ΄.
Τρίτος Ἀμενωφθὶς ἔτη κα΄.
Τέταρτος Ἀμενσὶς ἔτη κβ΄.
Πέμπτος Μίσαφρις ἔτη ιγ΄.
Ἕκτος Μισφραγμούθωσις ἔτη κς΄· ἐφ᾽ οὗ ὁ ἐπὶ Δευκαλίωνος κατακλυσμός.
Ὁμοῦ ἀπ᾽ Ἀμὼς ἕως Μισφραγμουθώσεως ἀρχῆς κατὰ Ἀφρικανὸν γίνονται ἔτη ξθ΄. [...]
ζ΄ Τούθμωσις ἔτη θ΄.
η΄ Ἀμενῶφις ἔτη λα΄· οὗτός ἐστιν ὁ Μέμνων εἶναι νομιζόμενος καὶ φθεγγόμενος λίθος.
θ΄ Ὧρος ἔτη λζ΄.
ι΄ Ἀχερρῆς ἔτη λβ΄.
ια΄ Ῥαθῶς ἔτη ς΄.
ιβ΄ Χεβρὴς ἔτη ιβ΄.
ιγ΄ Ἀχερρῆς ἔτη ιβ΄.
ιδ΄ Ἀρμεσὶς ἔτη ε΄.
ιε΄ Ῥαμεσσῆς ἔτος α΄.
ις΄ Ἀμενωφὰθ ἔτη ιθ΄.
Ὁμοῦ ἔτη σξγ΄.

---

test.: Sync.¹ **131** inc. Sync.² [AB] **131–135** 69,9–12 Moss. = 76,28–31 Moss. **135** des. Sync.¹ **136–144** 77,24–78,5 Moss. **145–166** 80,3–24 Moss.

129s → T46b,6s **131–142** → F34,75–87.96–102; T46c,1–7; T47; T48b,4s; T55 **134s** → T46c,3–5; T47,3–8; T55,6–9.34s.41–44 **139** → T46g,3s **145–155** → T46g,5s **156** → T46d; T46e

132–135 cf. Tat., orat. 38 **146s** cf. Paus. 1,42,3

129 bis γ΄ scripsimus (vide T46b,6) μγ΄ AB **131** βασιλέων < Sync.² **132** ἐφ᾽] ἀφ᾽ Sync.²:A | ἀπ᾽ Sync.² ἐξ Sync.¹ **132s** ἀποδείκνυμεν Sync.² ἀποδεικνύωμεν Sync.¹:A ἀποδεικνύωμεν Sync.¹:B **138** κα΄ Goarᵐ κδ΄ AB **139** ἀμενσὶς B ἀμερσὶς A **141** ἔτη A ἔτι B **143** ἀπ᾽ Ἀμὼς ἕως Moss. ἀπὸ μωσέως AB ἐπὶ Ἀμώσεως τοῦ καὶ Di. **147** λίθος A λίθους B **153** ἀρμεσὶς B ἀρμεσῆς A **155** ἀμενωφὰθ B ἀμενώφ A

17th dynasty of three additional shepherd kings, and kings of Theban Diospolis, three in number.⁵

The total for the reigns of the shepherds and Theban kings is 151 years.

18th dynasty of 16 kings of Diospolis

    The first of them was Amos, during whose reign Moses went out from Egypt, as we can prove.

        But as our reckoning requires, it follows that in his reign Moses was still young.⁶

    According to Africanus, the second king of the 18th dynasty was Chebros, 13 years.

    The third was Amenhotep, 21 years.

    The fourth was Amensis, 22 years.

    The fifth was Misaphris, 13 years.

    The sixth was Misphragmuthosis, 26 years. During his reign, the flood at the time of Deucalion occurred.

    The total from Amos to the rule of Misphragmuthosis according to Africanus is 69 years.

    7.   Tuthmosis, 9 years.

    8.   Amenophis, 31 years. This is the one who is believed to be Memnon, a sounding stone.⁷

    9.   Orus, 37 years.

    10.   Acherres, 32 years.

    11.   Rathos, 6 years.

    12.   Chebres, 12 years.

    13.   Acherres, 12 years.

    14.   Armesis, 5 years.

    15.   Ramses, 1 year.

    16.   Amenophath, 19 years.

    Total of 263 years.

---

5   The manuscripts of Syncellus erroneously assign 43 shepherd kings and 43 kings of Theban Diospolis to the 17th dynasty. The emendation of both numbers to three is supported by Syncellus' subsequent comment accusing Eusebius of deliberately reducing the number of kings of Manetho's 17th dynasty (that is, Africanus' version of Manetho) from six to four (T46b).

6   According to Syncellus, Misphragmuthosis (the sixth king of the 18th dynasty in Africanus' list) was the ruler of Egypt at the time of the Exodus. Because this king was also known as Amosis or Amos, Syncellus supposed that Africanus mistakenly confused him with the first king of the 16th dynasty, thereby erring in his dating of the Exodus (see T46c). The comment that Moses was "still young" during the reign of Amos is thus a later gloss, presumably from Syncellus himself. Syncellus reports Africanus' notice about the reign of Amos twice, in both cases inexplicably adding the same gloss and in identical wording (69,11f; 76,30f). This raises the possibility that the remark about Africanus' erroneous dating of the Exodus already existed in the text of Africanus that Syncellus was transcribing.

7   For the attribution of this entry concerning Memnon to Africanus himself (not Manetho), see Routh 396.

Ἐννεακαιδεκάτη δυναστεία βασιλέων Διοσπολιτῶν ςʹ
    αʹ   Σέθως ἔτη ναʹ.
    βʹ   Ῥαψάκης ἔτη ξαʹ.
    γʹ   Ἀμενεφθῆς ἔτη κʹ.
    δʹ   Ῥαμεσσῆς ἔτη ξʹ.
    εʹ   Ἀμμενεμνῆς ἔτη εʹ.
    ςʹ   Θούωρις, ὁ παρ᾽ Ὁμήρῳ καλούμενος Πόλυβος, Ἀλκάνδρας ἀνήρ, ἐφ᾽ οὗ τὸ Ἴλιον ἑάλω, ἔτη ζʹ.
Ὁμοῦ ἔτη σθʹ.
Ἐπὶ τοῦ αὐτοῦ δευτέρου τόμου Μανεθῶ βασιλεῖς ϙςʹ ἔτη ͵βρκαʹ. [...]

Τρίτου τόμου Μανεθῶ

Εἰκοστὴ δυναστεία βασιλέων Διοσπολιτῶν ιβʹ, οἳ ἐβασίλευσαν ἔτη ρλεʹ

Πρώτη καὶ εἰκοστὴ δυναστεία βασιλέων Τανιτῶν ζʹ
    αʹ   Σμενδὴς ἔτη κςʹ.
    βʹ   Ψουσέννης ἔτη μςʹ.
    γʹ   Νεφελχερὴς ἔτη δʹ.
    δʹ   Ἀμενωφθὶς ἔτη θʹ.
    εʹ   Ὀσοχὼρ ἔτη ςʹ.
    ςʹ   Ψιναχῆς ἔτη θʹ.
    ζʹ   Ψουσέννης ἔτη ιδʹ.
Ὁμοῦ ἔτη ρλʹ.

Εἰκοστὴ δευτέρα δυναστεία Βουβαστιτῶν βασιλέων θʹ
    αʹ   Σέσωγχις ἔτη καʹ.
    βʹ   Ὀσορθὼν ἔτη ιεʹ.
    γʹδʹεʹ   ἄλλοι τρεῖς ἔτη κεʹ.
    ςʹ   Τακέλωθις ἔτη ιγʹ.
    ζʹηʹθʹ   ἄλλοι τρεῖς ἔτη μβʹ.
Ὁμοῦ ἔτη ρκʹ.

test.: Sync.² **167–198** 82,2 – 83,6 Moss.

164 → F50,26s

163 Hom., Od. 4,126

157 ςʹ Müller ζʹ AB   **160** ἀμενεφθῆς B ἀμμενεφθῆς A   **163** Πόλυβος Ἀλκάνδρας Di. πολύβους ςʹ ζʹ ἄλκανδρος A πολύβους ζʹ ἄλκανδρος B   **166** Μανεθῶ Di. μανεθῶθ AB   **167** μανεθῶ A μανεθῶθ B   **169** ζʹ B νζʹ A   **170** σμενδὴς B σμεδής A   **171** ψουσέννης B ψουσένης Aᶜ ψουνέσης ante corr. A | μςʹ AB μαʹ corr. Di.   **174** ὀσοχώρ B ὀσοχὼρ A   **176** ψυσεννὴς B σουσέννης A | ιδʹ AB λεʹ Di. ex Eus.   **178** βασιλέων] BᵃBᵃ A βασιλεῖς B   **179** σέσωγχις B Σεσώγχις A Σεσόγχωσις Di.   **180** ὀσορθῶν B ὀσωρθῶν A   **182** τακέλωθις B τακέλλωθις A

19th dynasty of six kings of Diospolis
1. Sethos, 51 years.
2. Rapsaces, 61 years.
3. Ammenepther, 20 years.
4. Ramesses, 60 years.
5. Ammenemnes, 5 years.
6. Thuoris, who in Homer is called Polybus, husband of Alcandra, and during whose reign Ilium was taken, 7 years.[8]

Total of 209 years.

In the above second book of Manetho, there is a total of 96 kings of 2121 years.

From the third book of Manetho

20th dynasty of twelve kings of Diospolis: these reigned for 135 years.

21st dynasty of seven kings of Tanis
1. Smendes, 26 years.
2. Psusennes, 46 years.
3. Nephelcheres, 4 years.
4. Amenophthis, 9 years.
5. Osochor, 6 years.
6. Psinaches, 9 years.
7. Psusennes, 14 years.

Total of 130 years.

22nd dynasty of nine kings of Bubastus
1. Sesonchis, 21 years.
2. Osorthon, 15 years.
3, 4, 5. Three others, 25 years.
6. Takelothis, 13 years.
7, 8, 9. Three others, 42 years.

Total of 120 years.

---

8 Although this notice about the fall of Troy is forward compatible with the date of the first Olympiad given later in the list (see the following note), it is not backward compatible with Africanus' chronology of the Exodus. According to Africanus, the Exodus occurred in the 55th year of the reign of Phoroneus (F50,6f), during the reign of the Egyptian king Amos (above, l. 132f). From 55 Phoroneus to the fall of Troy, Africanus counted 613 years (see F50,26f), a number far exceeding the length of time that Africanus' version of Manetho assigned to the period from Amos to Thuoris. The date given here probably preserves the version of the text from which Africanus copied.

185 Τρίτη καὶ εἰκοστὴ δυναστεία Τανιτῶν βασιλέων δ'
    α'   Πετουβάτης ἔτη μ'· ἐφ' οὗ Ὀλυμπιὰς ἤχθη.
    β'   Ὀσορχὼ ἔτη η', ὃν Ἡρακλέα Αἰγύπτιοι καλοῦσι.
    γ'   Ψαμμοῦς ἔτη ι'.
    †δ'   Ζὴτ ἔτη λα'. †
190 Ὁμοῦ ἔτη πθ'.

Τετάρτη καὶ εἰκοστὴ δυναστεία
    Βόχχωρις Σαΐτης ἔτη ϛ'· ἐφ' οὗ ἀρνίον ἐφθέγξατο, ἔτη Ϡϟ'.

Πέμπτη καὶ εἰκοστὴ δυναστεία Αἰθιόπων βασιλέων γ'
    α'   Σαβάκων, ὃς αἰχμάλωτον Βόχχωριν ἑλὼν ἔκαυσε ζῶντα, καὶ ἐβα-
195   σίλευσεν ἔτη η'.
    β'   Σεβιχὼς υἱὸς ἔτη ιδ'.
    γ'   Τάρκος ἔτη ιη'.
Ὁμοῦ ἔτη μ'. [...]

Ἕκτη καὶ εἰκοστὴ δυναστεία Σαϊτῶν βασιλέων θ'
200   α'   Στεφινάτης ἔτη ζ'.
    β'   Νεχεψὼς ἔτη ϛ'.
    γ'   Νεχαὼ ἔτη η'.
    δ'   Ψαμμήτιχος ἔτη νδ'.
    ε'   Νεχαὼ δεύτερος ἔτη ϛ'· οὗτος εἷλε τὴν Ἰερουσαλὴμ καὶ Ἰωάχαζ
205   τὸν βασιλέα αἰχμάλωτον εἰς Αἴγυπτον ἀπήγαγε.
    ϛ'   Ψάμμουθις ἕτερος ἔτη ϛ'.
    ζ'   Οὔαφρις ἔτη ιθ'· ᾧ προσέφυγον ἁλούσης ὑπὸ Ἀσσυρίων Ἱερου-
        σαλὴμ οἱ τῶν Ἰουδαίων ὑπόλοιποι.

test.: Sync.² **199–230** 84,11 – 85,14 Moss.

186 → F50,28s; F64; F65   **192–194** ps. Io. Ant. fr. 30* (572 Ro.) *Ἐπὶ βοκχορέως βασιλέως Αἰγύπτου ἀρνίον ἐλάλησεν ἀνθρωπίνῃ φωνῇ, ὃν Σαβάκων ὁ Αἰθιόπων βασιλεὺς αἰχμάλωτον λαβών, ζῶντα κατέκαυσεν· οἱ δέ φασιν ὡς ἐξέδειρεν.*   **204s** → F72   **207s** → T77a,5s

192 cf. Aelian., nat. animal. 12,3; Eus., chron. 68,34s; Eus., can.^armen 180; Eus., can.^Hier 86ⁱ; Constantinus Manasses, chron. 4854–4858   **204s** cf. II Par 36,2–4; IV Regn 23,33–35; Eus., can.^armen 186; Sync. 258,2–6; 259,25–29   **207s** cf. IV Regn 25,1–11; 25,25s; Hipp., chron. 679; Clem. Alex., strom. 1,21,127,1s; Eus., can.^armen 187; Sync. 268,18–25; Sym. Log. (Leo Gr. 44,12–15 = Th. Mel. 38,9–12 = Iul. Pol. 136,3s)

186 ἐφ' Goar^m ἀφ' AB | ἤχθη + πρώτη Routh   **189** δ' Α λδ' B | ζὴτ AB ζητεῖται Flinders-Petrie | λα' Α λδ' B   **192** ἔτη Ϡϟ'] fort. ἔτη ὁμοῦ ϟε'   **194** σαβάκων B σαββάκων A | βόχχωριν A βόχχωριν B   **196** σεβιχὼς B σεύηχος A   **199** σαϊτῶν B ἀσαϊτῶν A   **202** νεχαὼ A ναχαὼ B   **203** ψαμμήτυχος A ψαμμίτιχος B   **207** ὑπό A ἀπό B

23rd dynasty of four kings of Tanis
1. Petubates, 40 years. During his reign, the Olympic games were held.[9]
2. Osorcho, 8 years. The Egyptians call him Heracles.
3. Psammus, 10 years.
†4. Zet, 31 years.†[10]
Total of 89 years.

24th dynasty
Bochchoris of Saïs, 6 years. During his reign a lamb spoke, 990 years.[11]

25th dynasty of three Ethiopian kings
1. Sabacon, who, after taking Bochchoris captive, burned him alive. He reigned for 8 years.
2. Sebichos, his son, 14 years.
3. Tarcus, 18 years.
Total of 40 years.

26th dynasty of nine kings of Saïs
1. Stephinates, 7 years.
2. Nechepsos, 6 years.
3. Nechao, 8 years.
4. Psammetichus, 54 years.
5. Nechao II, 6 years. He captured Jerusalem and led king Joachaz captive into Egypt.
6. Another Psammuthis, 6 years.
7. Uaphris, 19 years. The remnant of the Jews fled to him when Jerusalem was captured by the Assyrians.

---

9   This notice about the staging of the first Olympic games during the reign of Petubates aligns with Africanus' reckoning. Following the conventional chronology established by Eratosthenes, Africanus numbered 407 years from the fall of Troy to Ol. 1,1 (F50,28). An earlier notice in his list of Egyptian kings dates the fall of Troy during the reign of Thouris (l. 164). From the end of his reign to 1 Petubates, the sum of the years given for the intervening dynasties (20, 21 and 22) totals 385. (Note, however, that the combined years of the individual kings of these dynasties come to only 365.) Depending on the year of Thouris' seven-year reign in which Troy fell, Ol. 1,1 would thus have occurred between 15 and 22 Petubates.
10 This is not a proper name. It is probably an abbreviation of ζητεῖται ("there is a question" or "he is missing"), intended to express some uncertainty about the 31 years.
11 The text must be corrupt here. For possible emendation, see app.; cf. Waddell 1940, 165 ad loc., who assumes a lacuna between 'a lamb spoke' and '990 years'.

η′   Ἄμωσις ἔτη μδ′.
θ′   Ψαμμεχερίτης μῆνας ς′.
Ὁμοῦ ἔτη ρν′ καὶ μῆνας ς′.

Ἑβδόμη καὶ εἰκοστὴ δυναστεία Περσῶν βασιλέων η′
α′   Καμβύσης ἔτει ε′ τῆς ἑαυτοῦ βασιλείας Περσῶν ἐβασίλευσεν Αἰγύπτου ἔτη ς′.
β′   Δαρεῖος Ὑστάσπου ἔτη λς′.
γ′   Ξέρξης ὁ μέγας ἔτη κα′.
δ′   Ἀρτάβανος μῆνας ζ′.
ε′   Ἀρταξέρξης ἔτη μα′.
ς′   Ξέρξης μῆνας δύο.
ζ′   Σογδιανὸς μῆνας ζ′.
η′   Δαρεῖος Ξέρξου ἔτη ιθ′.
Ὁμοῦ ἔτη ρκδ′, μῆνας δ′.

Εἰκοστὴ ὀγδόη δυναστεία
Ἀμύρτεος Σαΐτης ἔτη ς′.

Ἐνάτη καὶ εἰκοστὴ δυναστεία Μενδησίων βασιλέων δ′
α′   Νεφερίτης ἔτη ς′.
β′   Ἄχωρις ἔτη ιγ′.
γ′   Ψάμμουθις ἔτος α′.
δ′   Νεφορίτης μῆνας δ′.
Ὁμοῦ ἔτη κ′, μῆνας δ′. [...]

Τριακοστὴ δυναστεία Σεβεννυτῶν βασιλέων γ′
α′   Νεκτανέβης ἔτη ιη′.
β′   Τεὼς ἔτη β′.
γ′   Νεκτάνεβος ἔτη ιη′.
Ὁμοῦ ἔτη λη′.

Πρώτη καὶ τριακοστὴ δυναστεία Περσῶν βασιλέων γ′
α′   Ὦχος εἰκοστῷ ἔτει τῆς ἑαυτοῦ βασιλείας Περσῶν ἐβασίλευσεν Αἰγύπτου ἔτη β′.

test.: Sync.² **231–245** 86,22 – 87,8 Moss.

213s → T75a   **213–222** → F73,9–18   **236–241** → F73,19–21

215 ὑστάσπου B ὑστάπου A   **218** ἔτη B ἔτος A   **225** Μενδησίων βασιλέων Moss. μενδήσιοι βασιλέων A   μενδήσιοι Bᵃ Bᵃ B   Μενδήσιοι βασιλεῖς Di.   **226** νεφερίτης B νεφερείτης A   **228** ψάμμουθις A ψάμουθις B   **229** νεφορίτης B νεφορότις A   **231** βασιλέων A βασιλεῖς B   **236** βασιλέων A βασιλεῖς B

8. Amosis, 44 years.
9. Psammecherites, 6 months.
Total of 150 years, 6 months.

27th dynasty of eight Persian kings[12]
1. In the fifth year of his reign over the Persians, Cambyses became king of Egypt, ruling for 6 years.
2. Darius, son of Hystaspes, 36 years.
3. Xerxes the Great, 21 years.
4. Artabanus, 7 months.
5. Artaxerxes, 41 years.
6. Xerxes, 2 months.
7. Sogdianus, 7 months.
8. Darius, son of Xerxes, 19 years.
Total of 124 years, 4 months.

28th dynasty
Amyrteos of Saïs, 6 years.

29th dynasty of four kings of Mendes
1. Nepherites, 6 years.
2. Achoris, 13 years.
3. Psammuthis, 1 year.
4. Nepherites, 4 months.
Total of 20 years, 4 months.

30th dynasty of three kings of Sebennytos
1. Nectanebes, 18 years.
2. Teos, 2 years.
3. Nectanebus, 18 years.
Total of 38 years.

31st dynasty of three Persian kings
1. Ochus, in the 20th year of his reign over the Persians, became king of Egypt, ruling for 2 years.[13]

---

12 There are some slight differences between this list from Manetho and the list of the Persian kings in F73.
13 A total of 22 years for the reign of Ochus is not standard in ancient chronography, but rather a specific feature of Africanus' system, see F73,19.

      β'   Ἀρσῆς ἔτη γ'.
240   γ'   Δαρεῖος ἔτη δ'.
      Ὁμοῦ ἔτη ⟨θ'⟩.
γ' τόμου ,αν'.

Μέχρι τῶνδε Μανεθῶς.
Τὰ δὲ μετὰ ταῦτα ἐξ Ἑλληνικῶν συγγραφέων.
245 Μακεδόνων βασιλεῖς ιε'.

test.: Sync.²   **245** βασιλεῖς ιε' des. Sync.²

245 → T6,16; F86; F89,53–56; T84,2s

241 θ' scripsimus

T46a Georgius Syncellus (65,18–20 Mosshammer)

Σημειωτέον ὁπόσον ὁ Εὐσέβιος Ἀφρικανοῦ λείπεται ἀκριβείας ἔν τε τῇ τῶν βασιλέων ποσότητι καὶ ταῖς τῶν ὀνομάτων ὑφαιρέσεσι καὶ τοῖς χρόνοις, σχεδὸν τὰ Ἀφρικανοῦ αὐταῖς λέξεσι γράφων· [sequitur dynastia 7 secundum Eus.].

→ T45,7–12

1 cf. Eus., chron. 65–69

[AB]   **1** ὁ < A

2. Arses, 3 years.
3. Darius, 4 years.[14]
Total of <9> years.
In Book Three, 1050 [years].

Here ends the work of Manetho.[15]
Subsequent Egyptian chronology is based on Greek historians.
15 Macedonian kings.

T46a[16]

One should note the extent to which Eusebius falls short of Africanus' accuracy, in the number of kings, by the omission of names, and in dates. Yet he virtually reproduces Africanus verbatim, as follows: [seventh dynasty according to Eusebius].

---

14 There is no contradiction between this information (4 years for Darius III) and F73,21 (6 years). This dating is correct because it corresponds to the years for Darius as king of Egypt (336–333 BC). After the conquest of Egypt by Alexander, Darius was still king of Persia for about two years (333–331 BC).
15 The two lines that follow these words are from Africanus himself.
16 Syncellus gives the list of the kings of Egypt from Africanus, mixed with lists from Eusebius and other sources. Between these texts Syncellus comments on the names and the years of the various sources. The following *testimonia* are part of these introductions and comments.

T46b Georgius Syncellus (69,1-7 Mosshammer)

Σημειωτέον πῶς ὁ Εὐσέβιος πρὸς τὸν οἰκεῖον σκοπὸν τοὺς τῆς πεντεκαιδεκάτης δυναστείας παρὰ τῷ Ἀφρικανῷ φερομένους κατὰ τὴν ιζ' δυναστείαν γεγονέναι λέγει. ἐπὶ γὰρ πᾶσι συμπεφώνηται ὅτι ἐπὶ Ἀφώφεως ἦρξεν Ἰωσὴφ τῆς Αἰγύπτου. μὴ ἔχων ὁπωσοῦν ἐπὶ ἄλλου τινὸς αὐτὸν παραθέσθαι μετήγαγε τὸν Ἄφωφιν
5 ἀπὸ τῆς ιε' δυναστείας εἰς τὴν ιζ', κολοβώσας τὰ ἔτη αὐτοῦ ξα' ὑπάρχοντα εἰς λ', τὰ δὲ τῆς ὅλης δυναστείας ρνα' ργ' παραθεὶς καὶ ἀντὶ τῶν ἓξ βασιλέων δ' μόνους.

1-3 → F46,117-127; T47,28-30   3 → T46c,11s; F33   4-7 → F46,126s; T46c,15s   5-7 → F46,129s

1 cf. Eus., chron. 67,28 – 68,2; Sync. 68,21-30   3 cf. Ios., c. Ap. 1,80; Sync. 125,1-8

[AB]   3 Ἀφώφεως Goar ἀφῶφ ἕως A ἀφὼφ ἕως B   4 αὐτὸν B αὐτοῦ A

T46c Georgius Syncellus (77,1-23 Mosshammer)

Οἶμαι τὸν Ἀφρικανὸν ἀγνοεῖν ὅτι καὶ ὁ παρ' αὐτῷ Ἀμὼς Ἄμωσις ἐκαλεῖτο ὁ αὐτὸς καὶ Τέθμωσις υἱὸς Ἀσήθ, ὡς δηλωθήσεται· καὶ ὁ μετ' αὐτὸν ἕκτος Μισφραγμούθωσις ὁμοίως καὶ Ἄμωσις εὕρηται λεγόμενος. ἀλλὰ κατὰ μὲν τὸν πρῶτον Ἄμωσιν, ἤτοι Ἀμὼς παρ' αὐτῷ, ἢ πρὸ δ' τῆς ἀρχῆς αὐτοῦ ἐτῶν, Μωυσῆς γεγέ-
5 νηται, ὡς δεδήλωται, κατὰ τὸ ‚γψβ' ἔτος τοῦ κόσμου· κατὰ δὲ τὸν δεύτερον Ἄμωσιν, τὸν καὶ Μισφραγμούθωσιν, Μωυσῆς ἐξῆλθεν ἀπ' Αἰγύπτου σὺν τῷ λαῷ τῷ ‚γωιβ' ἔτει τοῦ κόσμου, π' δὲ αὐτοῦ.

Κατὰ Εὐσέβιον· Ὀκτωκαιδεκάτη δυναστεία Διοσπολιτῶν βασιλέων ιδ' ὧν πρῶτος Ἄμωσις ἔτη κε'.

1-7 → F46,131-141

8 cf. Eus., chron. 68,3s (= Manetho FGrHist 609 F3b, p. 37)

[AB]   2 τέθμωσις B τεθμωσῆς A   4s γεγένηται A γεγέννηται B   5 ὡς B ᾧ A | τὸ B τῷ A   6 τὸν καὶ A καὶ B   8 βασιλέων A βασιλεὺς B

T46b

It should be noted how Eusebius, to suit his own purpose, states that the kings who, according to Africanus' report, belonged to the 15th dynasty were part of the 17th dynasty. For it is agreed by all that Joseph was ruler of Egypt at the time of Aphophis. And as Eusebius was not at all able to put him during the reign of some other king, he transferred Aphophis from the 15th to the 17th dynasty. And he cut short the actual 61 years of his rule down to 30, presented the 151 years of the whole dynasty as 103 years, and instead of six kings gave only four.

T46c

I am of the opinion that Africanus was unaware that his 'Amos' was also known as 'Amosis', identical as well with Tethmosis the son of Aseth, as will be shown. And we find that Misphragmuthosis, the sixth king in succession after him, is likewise called Amosis. But during the reign of this first Amosis (that is, Ahmose according to Africanus), or four years before his rule, Moses was born, as has been shown, in AM 3732. During the reign of this second Amosis, also known as Misphragmuthosis, Moses went forth from Egypt with his people in AM 3812, his 80th year.

According to Eusebius: 18th dynasty of 14 kings of Diospolis. The first of them was Amosis, for 25 years.

Πρὸ τούτου τοῦ Ἀμώσεως τέταρτον καὶ τελευταῖον τῆς ιζ΄ δυναστείας Ἄφωφιν Εὐσέβιος παρέθετο παραλόγως, καθ᾽ ὃν πάντες ὁμολογοῦσι τὸν Ἰωσὴφ ἄρ-
ξαι Αἰγύπτου, ὃν ἐτῶν ιδ΄ φησὶ βασιλεῦσαι, πάντων ξα΄ ἔτη ὁμολογούντων αὐτὸν βεβασιλευκέναι τῶν πρὸ Εὐσεβίου. ὅσα γοῦν πόσοις ἔτεσι τὸν Ἄμωσιν προ-
γεγονέναι Μωυσέως καὶ τῆς ἐξόδου παρελογίσατο, ἵνα μὴ λέγω συνελογίσατο.
μαρτυρεῖ δὲ καὶ Ἀφρικανὸς ἕκτον βασιλέα Ἄφωφιν κατὰ τὴν ιε΄ δυναστείαν ἔτη
ξα΄ τῆς Αἰγύπτου βασιλεῦσαι. Εἰ δὲ τοῖς χρόνοις πεπλεονακέναι δοκεῖ ἀπὸ Ἀφώφεως ἐπὶ Ἄμωσιν, τοῦτο παρὰ τῆς Αἰγυπτίων ἔπαθεν ἀσυμφωνίας, οὕτω παρὰ
Μανεθῶ κείμενα εὑρών· πλείω γὰρ π΄ τῶν ἀπὸ Ἰωσὴφ ἐτῶν ἐπὶ Μωυσέα.

Οἱ λοιποὶ βασιλεῖς Αἰγύπτου τῆς ιη΄ δυναστείας μετὰ τὸν πρῶτον παρὰ Ἀφρικανῷ Ἀμώς.

11s → T46b,3   15s → F46,126; T46b

10s cf. Ios., c. Ap. 1,80

[AB]   10 πρὸ τούτου B πρώτου A   12 ὃν ἐτῶν B ὧν ἐτῶν A | ἔτη Di. ἔτος AB   12s αὐτὸν Goar^m
αὐτῶν AB   17 τοῦτο B τούτῳ A | ἀσυμφωνίας A ἀφωνίας B   18 εὑρών A εὗρον B   20 Ἀμώς
T46f,2 ἄμωσιν A ἄμουσιν B

T46d Georgius Syncellus (69,13–17 Mosshammer)

<Κατὰ Εὐσέβιον.> Ὀκτωκαιδεκάτη δυναστεία Διοσπολιτῶν βασιλέων ιδ΄, ὧν πρῶτος Ἄμωσις ἔτη
κε΄. Κἀνταῦθα Εὐσέβιος δύο βασιλεῖς περιέκρυψεν, ἔτη δὲ προσέθηκε πε΄, τμη΄
παραθεὶς ἀντὶ σξγ΄ τῶν παρ᾽ Ἀφρικανῷ.

3 → F46,156; T46e

1 Eus., chron. 68,3 (= Manetho FGrHist 609 F3b, p. 37)

[AB]   1 Κατὰ Εὐσέβιον suppl. Goar < AB | βασιλέων ιδ΄ B βασιλείων A | ἄμωσις B ἄμμωσης A
2 εὐσέβιος δύο βασιλεῖς περιέκρυψεν B δύο βασιλεῖς ὁ εὐσέβιος παρέκρυψεν A

T46e Georgius Syncellus (81,16–18 Mosshammer)

[dynastia 18 secundum Eus.] ὁμοῦ ἔτη τμη΄. προσέθηκεν ὑπὲρ τὸν Ἀφρικανὸν
ἔτη πε΄ Εὐσέβιος κατὰ τὴν ιη΄ δυναστείαν.

→ F46,156; T46d

Before this Amosis, Eusebius erroneously made Aphophis the fourth and last ruler of the 17th dynasty, during whose reign there is universal agreement that Joseph was ruler in Egypt. According to him, he was king for 14 years, even though all Eusebius' predecessors affirm that he reigned for 61 years. For by his illogical thinking—I dare not call it 'logic'—Amosis preceded Moses and the Exodus by as many years. And Africanus also attests that Aphophis, the sixth king in the 15th dynasty, reigned over Egypt for 61 years. Now if there is an apparent excess of years from Aphophis up to Amosis, this is the fault of disagreement among the Egyptians, since this is the way I found them in Manetho: for 80 years are more than the years from Joseph to Moses.

The remaining kings of the 18th dynasty of Egypt who succeeded Ahmose the first king, in Africanus.

T46d

<According to Eusebius:> 18th dynasty of 14 kings of Diospolis. The first of them was Amosis, for 25 years. Here as well Eusebius, while suppressing two kings, added on 85 years, providing 348 years instead of Africanus' 263 years.

T46e

[18th dynasty according to Eus.] Total, 348 years. At the 18th dynasty, Eusebius adds 85 years more than Africanus.

T46f Georgius Syncellus (76,22-26 Mosshammer)

Τετάχθωσαν δὲ ἡμῖν ἐφεξῆς αἱ λοιπαὶ δυναστεῖαι τῶν Αἰγύπτου βασιλέων ἀπὸ τῆς αὐτῆς ιη' καὶ τοῦ πρώτου βασιλέως αὐτῆς Ἀμὼς μὲν κατὰ Ἀφρικανόν, κατὰ δὲ Εὐσέβιον Ἀμώσιος, κατὰ δὲ τὸ παρὸν χρονογραφεῖον καὶ ἕτερα ἀκριβῆ, ὡς δειχθήσεται, δευτέρου τῆς αὐτῆς ιη' δυναστείας Ἀμώσιος.

2 → F46,132; T47,21-24

2s Eus., chron. 68,3s; Sync. 69,14s

T46g Georgius Syncellus (79,29 - 80,2 Mosshammer)

Ὁμοῦ ἀπὸ Ἀμώσεως τοῦ πρώτου τῆς προκειμένης ιη' δυναστείας ἕως Μισφραγμουθώσεως ἀρχῆς κατὰ Εὐσέβιον ἔτη γίνονται οα'. βασιλεῖς πέντε ἀντὶ τῶν ἕξ. τὸν γὰρ τέταρτον Ἀμενσὴν παραδραμών, οὗ Ἀφρικανός, ὡς καὶ οἱ λοιποί, μέμνηται, ἔτη κβ' αὐτοῦ ἐκολόβωσεν.
5 Οἱ λοιποὶ τῆς ιη' δυναστείας μετὰ τὸν Μισφραγμούθωσιν κατὰ Ἀφρικανὸν οὕτως· ... (→ F46,144-155)

3s → F46,139

1-4 Eus., chron. 68,4s; Sync. 79,23-28

[AB] 1 Ἀμώσεως Di. μωυσέως AB 3 οὗ Moss. ὁ AB 3s μέμνηται A μέμνηνται B

T47 Georgius Syncellus (69,18 - 71,7 Mosshammer)

Ἰδοὺ δὴ ὁ μὲν Ἀφρικανὸς βουληθεὶς κατὰ τὸ π' ἔτος Μωυσέως τὸν Ἄμωσιν ἐκθέσθαι διὰ τὴν ἔλλειψιν τῶν ρι' ἐτῶν ἣν ὑπέστη ἐκ τῆς ιγ' γενεᾶς τοῦ δευτέρου Καϊνᾶν υἱοῦ Ἀρφαξάδ, ὡς εἴρηται ἡμῖν καὶ ῥηθήσεται πολλάκις, πλὴν φιλαληθέστερος ὢν Εὐσεβίου καὶ εἰδὼς τὴν τῶν πολλῶν δόξαν οὕτω κρατοῦσαν, ὅτι
5 ἐπὶ Ἀμώσεως Φορωνεὺς Ἀργείων ἐβασίλευσε, καὶ πρό γε τούτου Ἴναχος ὁ τούτου πατήρ, ἐφ' οὗ Μωυσῆς γεννᾶται κατὰ τὸ μα' ἔτος, ἠναγκάσθη, καίπερ οὐ συμφωνούσης τῆς τοιαύτης ψήφου τελείως ταῖς ἀποδείξεσιν αὐτοῦ, πλὴν διὰ τὸ ἀληθὲς καὶ μᾶλλον τῇ τῶν πολλῶν ἐξηκολούθησε δόξῃ. οἵ τε γὰρ ἐκ περιτομῆς

1-3 → T16i,3-7; T16k,3s; T16l,3s; T16o,4-7; T16q 1-39 → F46,132-135 3s → F45,7-11; T46a
4-13 → F34,75-87; F48a,4-6; T48b,3-6; F50,3-7

1 cf. Eus., chron. 68,3 (= Manetho FGrHist 609 F3) 8-12 cf. Ios., c. Ap. 2,15-17; Iustus FGrHist 734 F2s

[AB] 1 ἄμωσιν B ἄμωσην A 2 ἐκ τῆς A < B 5 Ἀμώσεως Goar^m ἄμως ἕως AB | Φορωνεὺς Goar^m φορωνέως B φόρων ἕως A |'Ίναχος Goar^m ἰνάχωος AB 6 ἐφ' B ἀφ' A 8 δόξῃ A δόξει B

T46f

Now let us arrange in sequence the remaining dynasties of the kings of Egypt from the same 18th dynasty and its first king, called Amos according to Africanus and Amosis according to Eusebius. But in the present chronography, and in other accurate ones, as will be shown, the sequence will be arranged from Amosis as the second king of this 18th dynasty.

T46g

Altogether from Amosis, the first king of this 18th dynasty, down to the rule of Misphragmuthosis, there are, according to Eusebius, 71 years. And there are five kings instead of six. For by omitting the fourth king Amenses, mentioned by Africanus, as well as everyone else, he thereby cut out the 22 years of his reign.

Those remaining of the 18th dynasty after Misphragmuthosis, according to Africanus, as follows: ... (→ F46,144–155).

T47 *King Amosis and Moses*

Now notice that Africanus would set Amosis in the 80th year of Moses. This was because of his omission of the 110 years belonging to the 13th generation of the second Kenan, son of Arpachshad, as we have already said and shall say repeatedly. Nevertheless, Africanus, more committed to the truth than Eusebius, was aware of the dominant majority view that, during the reign of Amosis, Phoroneus was king of the Argives, as well as Inachus his predecessor and father, in the 41st year of whose reign Moses was born. And it was this that constrained him, even though such reckoning does not square entirely with his own arguments; but it was because of the truth that he preferred to align himself with the majority opinion. For all the historians of the circumcision, Josephus and

πάντες, Ἰώσηππός τε καὶ Ἰοῦστος, οἵ τε ἐξ Ἑλλήνων, Πολέμων φημὶ καὶ Ἀπίων,
10 Ποσειδώνιος καὶ Ἡρόδοτος, τὴν ἐξ Αἰγύπτου πορείαν τοῦ Ἰσραὴλ κατὰ Φορωνέα καὶ Ἆπιδα τοὺς Ἀργείων βασιλεῖς συνέγραψαν, Ἀμώσεως Αἰγυπτίων βασιλεύοντος, οὐ τούτου, ἀλλὰ τοῦ μετ' αὐτὸν τοῦ καὶ Μισφραγμουθώσεως καλουμένου· διώνυμοι γὰρ καὶ τριώνυμοι πολλαχοῦ τῶν Αἰγυπτίων οἱ βασιλεῖς εὕρηνται. ἀμέλει γοῦν καὶ ἐν τῇ θείᾳ γραφῇ κατὰ τὸ πλεῖστον Φαραὼ λέγονται, ὅπερ
15 ἦν τοῖς πᾶσι κοινόν τε καὶ προσηγορικὸν ὄνομα, καθάπερ ὁ ἐπὶ Ἀβραὰμ πρῶτος ἐν τοῖς λόγοις φερόμενος Φαραώ, οἵ τε μετέπειτα ἐπὶ Ἰωσὴφ καὶ Ἰακὼβ καὶ τῆς δουλείας τῶν υἱῶν Ἰσραὴλ ἐν Αἰγύπτῳ καὶ τῆς αὐτῶν ἐπὶ Μωυσέως ἐξόδου· καὶ σχεδὸν σπανίως ἔστιν εὑρεῖν κύριον αὐτῶν ὄνομα, πλὴν Σουσακεὶμ καὶ Νεχαὼ καὶ Οὐαφρί, παρ' ὅλην τὴν θείαν γραφήν· εἰ γὰρ καὶ ἦσαν ὀνόματα κύρια, οὐκ
20 ἂν τὰ πολλὰ περὶ αὐτοῦ διεφωνήθη.

Ἰστέον δὲ καὶ τοῦτον τὸν Ἄμωσιν τὸν πρῶτον ἐπὶ τῆς ιη' δυναστείας Αἰγύπτου βασιλεύσαντα ὁ Ἀφρικανὸς Ἄμωσιν ὀνομάζει, ὅτι διώνυμος ἦν Ἄμωσις, ὁ αὐτὸς καὶ Τέθμωσις καλούμενος υἱὸς Ἀσσήθ· ἡμεῖς δὲ δεύτερον αὐτὸν τῆς ιη' δυναστείας κατετάξαμεν ἔν τε ἄλλοις ἀντιγράφοις καὶ ἐν τοῖς πρὸς ἔλεγχον
25 Ἀπίωνος Ἰωσήππου δυσὶ λόγοις περὶ τῆς ἐξ Αἰγύπτου πορείας τοῦ λαοῦ, οὕτως αὐτὸν εὑρόντες. καὶ πρῶτον τὸν πατέρα αὐτοῦ Ἀσσήθ, οὗ μνήμην Ἀφρικανὸς καὶ Εὐσέβιος οὐ πεποίηνται, ἐπεὶ ὁ μὲν Ἀφρικανὸς τοὺς τῆς ἑξκαιδεκάτης καὶ ἑπτακαιδεκάτης δυναστείας ἀνωνύμως ἐξέδωκεν, ὁ δὲ Εὐσέβιος οὔτε τῷ Ἀφρικανῷ οὔτε τῷ Ἰωσήππῳ οὐδ' ἄλλῳ τινὶ συμφωνῶν, τὰ μὲν τῶν ὀνομάτων ἐκ
30 τῆς παρὰ τῷ Ἀφρικανῷ ιε' δυναστείας εἰς τὴν ιζ' μετήγαγε, τοὺς δὲ χρόνους περιέκοψε, σύγχρονον Μωυσέως δεῖξαι Κέκροπα τὸν διφυῆ ἐπειγόμενος, μαρτυρῶν καὶ αὐτὸς ἐν τῷ τοῦ κανόνος αὐτοῦ προλόγῳ τοὺς προλεχθέντας Ἰώσηππον μὲν καὶ Ἰοῦστον ἐκ περιτομῆς, Ἀφρικανὸν δὲ καὶ Κλήμεντα τὸν Στρωματέα καὶ Τατιανόν, τοῦ καθ' ἡμᾶς λόγου ἄνδρας ἐν παιδεύσει γνωρίμους πάντας, κα-
35 τὰ Ἴναχον καὶ Φορωνέα τὸν Ἰνάχου πρώτους Ἀργείων βασιλεῖς γενέσθαι Μωυσέα, ὧν σύγχρονος ἦν Ὤγυγος αὐτόχθων πρῶτος βασιλεὺς Ἀκτῆς τῆς νῦν Ἀττικῆς, καὶ ὁ κατ' αὐτὸν Ὤγυγον πρῶτος καὶ παλαιὸς ἱστορούμενος Ἕλλησι κατακλυσμὸς κατὰ τὸ π' ἔτος Μωυσέως, νε' δὲ Φορωνέως, κατὰ τὸν Ἀφρικανὸν ὧδέ πως ἐπὶ λέξεως γραφέντα· ... (→ F34,38–58)

21s → F46,132s; T46c   23s → T46f   27s → F46,128–130   28–31 → T46b; T46d   37s → T48a,6s

9s cf. Polemo FHG 3,119 F13; Apion FGrHist 616 F2; Posidonius FGrHist 87 F69; Hdt. 2,162
12s cf. Ios., c. Ap. 1,86   15s cf. Gen 12,15   16s cf. Gen 40,1; Exod 1,11   17 cf. Exod 13,17   18s cf. III
Regn 14,25; IV Regn 23,29   23–25 cf. Ios., c. Ap. 1,94 (= Manetho FGrHist 609 F9); 2,16 (= Apion
FGrHist 616 F4)   28–31 cf. Eus., chron. 67,28 – 68,2; Sync. 68,20 – 69,7   31–36 cf. Eus., can.[Hier]
7,11 – 10,4; Sync. 73,12–18   32s cf. Ios., ant. Iud. 1,16; Iustus Tib. FGrHist 734 F3   33s cf. Clem.
Alex., strom. 1,21,101,5s; Tat., orat. 38s

[AB]   9 πολέμων A πολέμῳ B   10 ποσειδώνιος A ποσιδώνιος B   12 Μισφραγμουθώσεως Goar[m] μὴ
φραγμουθώσεως A μηφραγμουθώσεως B   13s εὕρηνται A ηὕρηνται B   15 ὁ B < A   16 ἐπὶ B < A
19 καὶ[2] A < B   21 ἄμωσιν B ἄμωσην A   22 ἄμωσιν AB Ἀμὼς F46,132   23 ὁ αὐτὸς des. B
31s μαρτυρῶν Goar μαρτυρῶ A   38 Φορωνέως Goar φορονέως A

Justus, and those of the Greeks, I mean Polemon and Apion, Posidonius and Herodotus, have recorded the Exodus of Israel from Egypt at the time of Phoroneus and Apis the kings of the Argives; this was when Amosis was king of Egypt.[1] But it was not the above-mentioned Amosis, but rather the one who succeeded him, who was also known as Misphragmuthosis. For the kings of Egypt are often found to have two or three names. For example, in the divine Scripture they are generally called 'Pharaoh', which was an appellation they all shared. This is true of the 'Pharaoh' first mentioned in Scriptures at the time of Abraham, and of those who came afterwards during the times of Joseph, Jacob, the servitude of the sons of Israel in Egypt, and their exodus at the time of Moses. And it is only rarely that one finds their proper names (except for Sousakeim, Nechao, and Ouaphri) throughout all Scripture. Now if there had been proper names, there would not have been great disagreement about this matter.

It should also be known that this Amosis, the first king in the 18th dynasty of Egypt, Africanus calls Amos. This was because Amosis had two names; he was also called Tethmosis, son of Aseth. Now in our arrangement, we have made him the second king of the 18th dynasty, since this is the order in which we found him in other copies and in Josephus' two-volume work *Against Apion* concerning the Exodus of the people of Israel from Egypt. And we have put his father Aseth first, of whom neither Africanus nor Eusebius has made any mention; for whereas Africanus supplied the kings of the 16th and 17th dynasty without names, Eusebius agreed neither with Africanus nor with Josephus nor with anyone else. Instead, he transferred names from the 15th dynasty in Africanus to the 17th dynasty, and in his effort to prove that Moses was contemporary with Cecrops the Double-Natured, he cut short the chronology. But he himself witnesses in the prologue to the *Canons* that these aforementioned writers—Josephus and Justus of the circumcision, and Africanus, Clement, author of the *Stromata* and Tatian, men of our doctrine all well-known for their learning—say that Moses lived during the time of Inachus and his son Phoroneus, the first kings of the Argives. And their contemporary the indigenous Ogygus, was the first king of Acte, now called Attica. It was at the time of this Ogygus that what the Greeks report was the first flood of ancient times occurred in the 80th year of Moses, and the 55th year of Phoroneus. It is described by Africanus just about word for word as follows: ... (→ F34,38–58)

---

1 For Africanus' mention of Herodotus, see F34,83–86.

T48

T48a Eusebius, Canones (Georgius Syncellus [73,12–18 Mosshammer] = Hieronymus [7,10–17 Helm])

(→ F34,104) ... ὡς αὐτὸς Εὐσέβιος ἐν τῷ προοιμίῳ τοῦ κανόνος ὧδέ πως γράφων συμμαρτυρεῖ·

Μωυσέα γένος Ἑβραῖον, προφητῶν ἁπάντων πρῶτον, ἀμφὶ τοῦ σωτῆρος ἡμῶν, λέγω δὲ τοῦ Χριστοῦ, ἀμφί τε τῆς τῶν ἐθνῶν δι' αὐτοῦ θεογνωσίας χρησμοὺς καὶ λόγια θεῖα γραφῇ παραδεδωκότα, τοῖς χρόνοις ἀκμάσαι κατὰ Ἴναχον εἰρήκασιν ἄνδρες ἐν παιδεύσει γνώρι-
5 μοι, Κλήμης, Ἀφρικανός, Τατιανὸς τοῦ καθ' ἡμᾶς λόγου, τῶν τε ἐκ περιτομῆς Ἰώσηππος καὶ Ἰοῦστος, ἰδίως ἕκαστος τὴν ἀπόδειξιν ἐκ παλαιᾶς ὑποσχὼν ἱστορίας.

4s → F34,26–31.54–56.77–83; T47,4–8; F50,3s; T55,12–14; ps. Eust., in hex. (1,1–9 Allatius = PG 18,708A) = Georg. Mon. (40,17–19 de Boor/Wirth) ≈ Georg. Mon. cont. (29,10–13 Muralt = PG 110,84A) Κλήμης *μὲν οὖν, καὶ Ἀφρικανὸς καὶ πρὸς τούτοις Τατιανός, τῶν δὲ ἐκ περιτομῆς Ἰώσηπος, καὶ Ἰοῦστος κατὰ Ἴναχον ἀκμάσαι τὸν θεσπέσιον Μωϋσέα ἱστόρησαν, ἰδίως ἕκαστος ἐκ παλαιᾶς ἱστορίας ὑποσχὼν τὴν ἀπόδειξιν.*

4s cf. Sym. Log. (Leo Gr. 26,10–12 = Th. Mel. 25,19s ≈ Iul. Pol. 96,7–9); ps. Sym. f. 34ᵛ ≈ Cedr. 76,4s
5 cf. Clem. Alex., strom. 1,21,101,5; 1,21,136,3s | cf. Tat., orat. 38 **5s** cf. Ios., c. Ap. 2,15–17
6 Iustus Tib. FGrHist 734 F2

[AB] **2** Ἑβραῖον Scal. ἑβραίων AB | τοῦ σωτῆρος Scal. τοὺς πρὸ ἐξ AB *Domini Salvatoris* Hier.
3 θεῖα A θεία B θείᾳ Goar *divinas leges sacris litteris* Hier.

T48b Georgius Syncellus (140,9–15 Mosshammer)

Ἀλλ' ἡμῖν ἐπὶ Ἀμώσιος ἐπιλελόγισται ἔτη δύο αὐτοῦ κατὰ Ἴναχον πρῶτον Ἄργους βασιλέα, καθ' ὃν καὶ πάντες οἵ τε ἐκ περιτομῆς οἵ τε ἐκ χάριτος ἱστορικοί, Ἰώσηππος καὶ Ἰοῦστος, Κλήμης ὁ ἱερὸς στρωματεύς, Τατιανός τε καὶ Ἀφρικανὸς συνομολογοῦσι κατὰ Ἴναχον γεννηθῆναι Μωυσέα καὶ κατὰ Φορωνέα τὸν Ἰνάχου παῖδα καὶ Νιόβης ἀκμαῖον, κατὰ Ἄπιδα
5 δὲ τῆς ἐξ Αἰγύπτου πορείας τοῦ Ἰσραὴλ ἡγήσασθαι, τὰς ἀποδείξεις καὶ ἐκ τῶν παρ' Ἕλλησι δοκουμένων ὑποσχόντες ἱστορικῶν.

3s → F34,26–31.54–56.79–83; T47,4–8; F50,3s; T55,12–14

2 cf. Ios., c. Ap. 2,15–17 | cf. Iustus Tib. FGrHist 734 F3 **2s** cf. Clem. Alex., strom. 1,21,101,5; 1,21,136,3s **3** cf. Tat., orat. 38 **3s** cf. Sym. Log. (Leo Gr. 26,10–12 = Th. Mel. 25,19s ≈ Iul. Pol. 96,7–9); ps. Sym. f. 34ᵛ ≈ Cedr. 76,4s

[AB] **4** νιόβης A νηοβῆς B | ἀκμαῖον A ἀκμὰς B **6** ὑποσχόντες Di. ὑποσχόντι AB

T48 *Moses and Inachus*

T48a

Eusebius himself attests to this in the preface to his *Canons,* in something like the following words:

Moses, a Hebrew by lineage, the first of all the prophets, who committed to Scripture oracles and divine precepts about our Savior, I mean the Christ, and the knowledge of God made possible to the gentiles through him, flourished in the same time as Inachus. This is what is said by men who are well known for their learning—Clement, Africanus and Tatian, men of our doctrine,[1] as well as those of the circumcision, Josephus and Justus. Each of them separately produced proof from ancient history.

T48b[2]

But we have ascertained that the second year of Amosis' rule was at the time of Inachus, the first king of Argos. All the historians, both those of the circumcision and those living under grace—Josephus and Justus, the blessed Clement, author of the *Stromata,* and Tatian and Africanus—are in agreement that Moses was born at the time of Inachus, that he was in his prime at the time of Phoroneus, the son of Inachus and Niobe, and that at the time of Apis he was in command of Israel's Exodus from Egypt; the proof for this they also furnish from those historians who are held in repute among the Greeks.

---

1 I. e. Christians.
2 This information probably goes back to Eusebius as well. It is Syncellus' free rendering of the quotation given in T48a above.

T49

T49a Georgius Syncellus (145,4–13 Mosshammer)

Ἀρχὴ βασιλείας Ἀργείων

Ὧν πρῶτος βασιλεὺς Ἴναχος ἔτη νς'. τοῦ δὲ κόσμου ἦν ἔτος ‚γχοβ'. Οὔ μοι δοκεῖ καλῶς ὁ Ἀφρικανὸς ἐν γ' λόγῳ τῶν ἱστορικῶν αὐτοῦ φάναι τὴν Ἀργείων βασιλείαν τῷ σ' ἔτει τῆς Ἀσσυρίων βασιλείας ἄρξασθαι ἐπὶ Ἀρείου ε' βασιλέως Ἀσσυρίων. ἔσται
5 γὰρ κατὰ τοῦτο Μωυσῆς πρὸς τῷ τέλει τῆς ζωῆς Ἀβραὰμ τεχθείς, εἴ γε πάντες ὁμολογοῦσι τὸ πρῶτον ἔτος Ἀβραὰμ κατὰ τὸ μδ' ἔτος Νίνου τοῦ δευτέρου βασιλεύοντος μετὰ Βῆλον Ἀσσυρίων. Βήλου γὰρ νε', Νίνου μδ', Ἀβραὰμ ρα'. ἔσται ἄρα Μωυσῆς κατὰ τὸ ρα' ἔτος Ἀβραάμ, ὅπερ ἀδύνατον. ὁμολογεῖ δὲ αὐτὸν κατὰ Ἴναχον.

2–4 → F34,49–51; F50,3s; T57   8 → F34,53–58; T47,5–13; T48; T55,12–14

2   cf. Eus., chron. 83,28s (= Castor FGrHist 250 F3,30–33)   2–4   Eus., chron. 31,1; Eus., can.[Hier] 27,10–13; Chron. Synt. 84,8; Sync. 117,20; Exc. Barb. 282,12   8 cf. app. ad F50,3–7

[AB] 2 ἔτη νς'] 50 anni Eus., chron. | ἦν < B | ἔτος A ἔτη B   5 et infra constanter Ἀβραὰμ Goar ἄβραμ A ἄμβραμ B Di.   7 βήλου B βῆλον A

T49b Georgius Syncellus (217,18–20 Mosshammer)

Ἀθηναίων κς' ἐβασίλευσεν Ἀρίφρων Φερεκλέους ἔτη κ', κατὰ δὲ Ἀφρικανὸν ἔτη λα'. κατὰ τοῦτον τὸν Ἀρίφρονα ἡ τῶν Ἀσσυρίων κατελύθη ἀρχή, ὡς πάντες συμφωνοῦσι. τοῦ δὲ κόσμου ἦν ἔτος ‚δχνα'.

1 = T54e   1–3 = app. ad F54a,41

1   cf. Eus., chron. 88,7 (= Castor FGrHist 250 F4)   1–3   Eus., can.[Hier] 81[c]. 83[a-b]. 83,7–10; Chron. Synt. 84,48; Sync. 104,7–12; 193,20 – 194,2; Exc. Barb. 284,21–24

[AB] 2 τὸν < B | πάντες συμφωνοῦσι B πάντα συμφωνῶσι A

T49 *Chronology of the Assyrian Kingdom*[1]

T49a

Beginning of the Kingdom of the Argives

Their first king was Inachus, for 56 years, AM 3692. In my opinion, Africanus is not right when he states in the third book of his *Histories* that the kingdom of the Argives began in the 200th year of the Assyrian kingdom, during the reign of Areios, the fifth Assyrian king. For according to this reasoning, Moses will have been born near the end of the life of Abraham, since there is universal agreement that Abraham's first year coincides with the 43rd year of Ninus who succeeded Belos as the second king of the Assyrians. Belos ruled for 55 years, and Ninus for 44 years, and Abraham was 101 years old [in the 200th year of the Assyrian kingdom]. Then Moses will have been born in the 101st year of Abraham, which is impossible. For he [Africanus] admits that Moses was born at the time of Inachus.[2]

T49b

The 25th ruler of the Athenians was Pherecles' son Ariphron, for 20 years, according to Africanus 31 years.[3] During the reign of this Ariphron, the Assyrian empire was dissolved, as everyone agrees. This was AM 4651.

---

1 The various witnesses to Africanus' treatment of Assyrian chronology are not entirely consistent. According to F34,49–53 (following Ctesias), Ninus was the first king of Assyria, followed by Semiramis; but cf. F24,27–31, which makes Thuras the first king of Assyria. Although the list of Assyrian kings in the *Excerpta Barbari* (282,4 – 284,25 Frick) may include data from Africanus, it is mingled with material from other sources. For discussion, see Gelzer 1,209–215; Schwartz 1895,6–8.
2 For discussion of the chronological relationship between Moses and Inachus, see Adler/Tuffin 2002,182, n. 2.
3 The explicit reference to Africanus concerns the Athenians, and the text is given again below (see F54, especially F54e). However, the context suggests that "everyone (πάντες)" in the following sentence includes Africanus.

F50 Excerpta Barbari (288,18 – 292,3 Frick)

De regna autem, que in ceteris gentibus facta sunt et paulatim creuerunt, proferamus temporibus regni Argiuorum.

 I. Primus isargus Inachus regnauit ann. L.
  Quo tempore Moyses natus est.
 II. Post hunc Foroneus regnauit ann. LX.
  Quo anno quinquagesimo quinto ex Aegypto egressio Iudeorum per Moysen facta est.
 III. Post hunc Apius regnauit ann. XXXV.
 IIII. Post hunc Argius regnauit ann. LXX.
 V. Post hunc Criassus regnauit ann. LVI.
 VI. Post hunc Forbas regnauit ann. XXXV.
 VII. Post hunc Triopas regnauit ann. LXVI.

---

3 Sync. (145,4s Moss. = T49a,1s), cf. Eus., chron. (83,28 Karst) (= Castor FGrHist 250 F3) et can. (Hier. 27,10–13 Helm)
Ἀρχὴ βασιλείας Ἀργείων.
Ὦν πρῶτος βασιλεὺς Ἴναχος ἔτη νς' (50 Eus.). τοῦ δὲ κόσμου ἦν ἔτος ͵γχϱβ'... (→ T49a)
3s → F34,53–56.80–83; T47b,5–13; T48a,4–6; T48b,3s; T55,12–14; T57
5 Sync. (145,14 Moss.), cf. Eus., chron. (83,31s Karst) (= Castor FGrHist 250 F3) et can. (Hier. 29, 17s Helm)
Ἀργείων β' ἐβασίλευσε Φορωνεὺς ἔτη ξ' (60 Eus.). τοῦ δὲ κόσμου ἦν ἔτος ͵γψμη'.
5–7 → F34,26–31.77–80; F46,132–135; T48b,4–6 **8** Sync. (173,12 Moss.), cf. Eus., chron. (83,33 Karst) (= Castor FGrHist 250 F3) et can. (Hier. 32,7s Helm)
Ἀργείων γ' ἐβασίλευσεν Ἆπις ἔτη λε' (= Eus.). τοῦ δὲ κόσμου ἦν ἔτος ͵γωη'.
9s Sync. (174,19s Moss.), cf. Eus., chron. (84,1–3 Karst) (= Castor FGrHist 250 F3) et can. (armen. 156–158 Karst; Hier. 33,25s; 37,9s Helm)
Ἀργείων δ' ἐβασίλευσεν Ἄργος ἔτη ο' (= Eus.). τοῦ δὲ κόσμου ἦν ἔτος ͵γωμγ'.
Ἀργείων ε' ἐβασίλευσε Κρίασος ἔτη νε' (54 Eus.). τοῦ δὲ κόσμου ἦν ἔτος ͵γϡιγ'.
11–14 Sync. (178,5–9 Moss.), cf. Eus., chron. (84,4–9 Karst) (= Castor FGrHist 250 F3) et can. (armen. 158–162 Karst; Hier. 39,25s; 41,14s; 43,25s; 45,5s Helm)
Ἀργείων ς' ἐβασίλευσε Φόρβας ἔτη κε' (35 chron., can.[Hier], 34 can.[armen]). οὗτος Ῥόδου ἐκράτησε. τοῦ δὲ κόσμου ἦν ἔτος ͵γϡξη'.
Ἀργείων ζ' ἐβασίλευσε Τριόπας ἔτη λς' (46 chron., can.[Hier], 48 can.[armen]). τοῦ δὲ κόσμου ἦν ἔτος ͵γϡϙγ'.
Ἀργείων η' ἐβασίλευσε Κρότωπος ἔτη κδ' (21 Eus.). τοῦ δὲ κόσμου ἦν ἔτος ͵δκθ'.
Ἀργείων θ' ἐβασίλευσε Σθένελος ἔτη ια' (= Eus.). τοῦ δὲ κόσμου ἦν ἔτος ͵δνγ'.

3 cf. Sync. 144,5–12 **3–7** cf. Sym. Log. (Leo Gr. 26,10–12 = Th. Mel. 25,19s ≈ Iul. Pol. 96,7–9); ps. Sym. f. 34[v] ≈ Cedr. 76,4s; Ios., c. Ap. 2,15–17; Iustus Tib. FGrHist 734 F2s; Clem. Alex., strom. 1,21,101,5; 1,21,136,3s; Tat., orat. 38 **3–14** cf. Eus., chron. 84,10–13; Io. Mal. 4,1; Sync. 144,12–14; ps. Sym. f. 37[v] = Cedr. 143,3–6 **3–21** cf. Eus., reg. ser.[armen] 148; Eus., reg. ser.[Hier] 29; Sync. 144,15s
3–25 cf. Tat., orat. 39,1s **3–36** cf. Chron. Synt. 86,38 – 87,9

3 isargus] εἰς Ἄργος

F50 *The Kings of the Argives*[1]

From the kingdoms that came into being in the remaining nations and gradually grew in size, let us set forth the chronology of the kingdom of the Argives.

    1. The first to be king in Argos[2] was Inachus, for 50 years.
        At that time, Moses was born.
    2. After him, Phoroneus was king for 60 years.
        In his 55th year, the Exodus of the Jews through Moses took place.
    3. After him, Apis was king for 35 years.
    4. After him, Argus was king for 70 years.
    5. After him, Criassus was king for 56 years.
    6. After him, Phorbas was king for 35 years.
    7. After him, Triopas was king for 66 years.

---

1   For Africanus' treatment of Argive chronology, see also T49a. Several chronological notices in the unattributed list of Argive kings found in the *Excerpta Barbari* reveal its dependence on Africanus. The synchronism of the birth of Moses with the rule of Inachus and the dating of the Exodus to the 55th year of Phoroneus are distinctive features of Africanus' chronology (F34,53–58; T48). According to Exc. Barb., 1125 years elapsed from 1 Inachus to Ol. 1.1 (see below ll. 26–28). The Exodus, which occurred 105 years after the beginning of the Argive kingdom (50 Inachus + 55 Phoroneus, ll. 6f), would thus have preceded Ol. 1,1 by 1020 years. Boeck 1845,199 first observed that this is also the sum of years calculated by Africanus (F34,40f.96–98; T47,36–39). For reconstruction of Africanus' chronology of the individual Argive kings on the basis of the list in Exc. Barb., see Frick 1880,8; Gelzer 1,137–141.143.

2   Gr. (Frick): εἰς Ἄργος.

VIII. Post hunc Crotopus regnauit ann. XXI.
VIIII. Post hunc Sthenelus regnauit ann. XI.
X. Post hunc Danaus regnauit qui illas filias L ann. [...].
XI. Post hunc Lyggeus Aegyptius XLI.
    A quo Cadamus Aginorus ascendit Biotia Europissa ad exquirendum.
XII. Post hunc Abas regnauit ann. XXIII.
Post hunc Prytus regnauit ann. XXVII.
Post hunc Acrisius regnauit ann. XXXI.
Post hunc Pelops regnauit cum Nomaum ann. XXXVIII.
    A quo Peloponissus uocatur.
Post hunc Atreus et Thyestus ann. XLV.

---

15 Sync. (178,13–16 Moss.) ≈ Eus., can. (Hier. 46[f])
Ὁ αὐτὸς Δαναὸς διὰ τῶν λεγομένων Δαναΐδων (αὗται δὲ ἦσαν αὐτῷ θυγατέρες ν') τοὺς ν' υἱοὺς τοῦ ἀδελφοῦ αὐτοῦ Αἰγύπτου διεχρήσατο χωρὶς ἑνὸς τοῦ Λυγκέως, ὃς καὶ ἐβασίλευσε μετ' αὐτόν. οὐκ ἄπιστον δὲ ἐν βαρβάροις ἡ πολυτεκνία διὰ τὸ πλῆθος τῶν παλλακῶν.
15–21 Sync. (182,13–20 Moss.), cf. Eus., chron. (84,14–18 Karst) (= Castor FGrHist 250 F3) et can. (armen. 162–167 Karst; Hier. 45,22s; 48,8s; 50,9s; 51,13s; 52,9s Helm)
Ἀργείων ι' ἐβασίλευσε Δαναὸς ἔτη νη' (50 Eus.). τοῦ δὲ κόσμου ἦν ἔτος ͵δξδ'.
Ἀργείων ια' ἐβασίλευσε Λυγκεὺς ἔτη λε' (41 Eus.). τοῦ δὲ κόσμου ἦν ἔτος <͵δρκβ'.
Ἀργείων ιβ' ἐβασίλευσεν Ἄβας ἔτη λζ' (23 Eus.). τοῦ δὲ κόσμου ἦν ἔτος> ͵δρνζ'.
Ἀργείων ιγ' ἐβασίλευσε Προῖτος ὁ καὶ Περσεὺς ἔτη ιζ' (= Eus.). τοῦ δὲ κόσμου ἦν ἔτος ͵δρϙδ'.
Ἀργείων ιδ' ἐβασίλευσεν Ἀκρίσιος ἔτη λα' (= Eus.). τοῦ δὲ κόσμου ἦν ἔτος ͵δσια'.
22–24 Sync. (188,9–17 Moss.), cf. Eus., chron. (84,23–27 Karst) (= Castor FGrHist 250 F3) et can. (Hier. 54,1–6; 56,9–11 Helm)
Μυκηνῶν Ἀργείων ιε' ἐβασίλευσε Πέλοψ ἔτη λε' (59 can.[Hier]; - chron.). τοῦ δὲ κόσμου ἦν ἔτος ͵δσμδ'.
Τὸν Πέλοπα τινὲς οὐ μόνον Ἀργείων καὶ Μυκηνῶν ἱστοροῦσι βασιλεῦσαι, ἀλλὰ καὶ πάσης τῆς Πελοποννήσου. οὗτος Ὀλυμπίων προέστη καὶ στρατεύσας ἐπὶ Ἴλιον ἡττήθη ὑπὸ Δαρδάνου. ἀπ' αὐτοῦ Πελοπόννησος ὠνομάσθη. οὗτος Ἱπποδάμειαν ἔγημε. (cf. can.[Hier] 49[h]; 52[a]; 53[f])
Τινὲς δὲ νγ' ἔτη καὶ ἄλλοι ξγ' λέγουσιν αὐτὸν βασιλεῦσαι, καὶ ἕτεροι λε'.
Μυκηνῶν Ἀργείων ιϛ' ἐβασίλευσαν Ἀτρεὺς καὶ Θυέστης ἔτη λγ' κατὰ δὲ ἄλλους ἔτη ξε' (= Eus.), τοῦ δὲ κόσμου ἦν ἔτος ͵δσοθ'.

14s cf. Eus., can.[Hier] 45[h]   **15** cf. Eus., chron. 84,11–13; 86,24s; Eus., can.[Hier] 45[i]; Sync. 144,14s   **16–18** cf. Eus., chron. 87,3–5; Eus., can.[Hier] 55[e]; Ecl. Hist. 193,31; Io. Ant. fr. 10,15–19   **19–23** cf. Io. Mal. 4,13–14; Cedr. 212,16–18; 213,10   **22** cf. Sync. 144,17–24   **24s** cf. Sync. 144,25–27   **24–32** cf. Io. Mal. 4,16; Cedr. 214,3–7

13 XXI corr. man. prim. ex XXXI

8. After him, Crotopus was king for 21 years.
9. After him, Sthenelus was king for 11 years.
10. After him, Danaus was king, who had 50 daughters, for [...]³ years.
11. After him, Lynceus, son of Aegyptus,⁴ for 41 years.
>During his reign, Cadmus, son of Agenor, went up to Boeotia in search for Europa.⁵

12. After him, Abas was king for 23 years.

After him, Proetus was king for 27 years.

After him, Acrisius was king for 31 years.

After him, Pelops was king after Oenomaus⁶ for 38 years.
>From him, the Peloponnesus receives its name.

After him, Atreus and Thyestes, for 45 years.

---

3 Frick supplies 50 years for Danaus' reign; cf. Eusebius (50) and Syncellus (55).
4 Gr. (Frick): Λυγκεὺς Αἰγύπτου.
5 Gr. (Frick): ἐφ' οὗ Κάδμος Ἀγήνορος ἀνέβη Βοιωτίαν τῆς Εὐρώπης ἐπὶ ζήτησιν.
6 Gr. (Frick): μετ' Οἰνόμαον.

25   Post hos Agamemnus Atreus ann. XXXIII.

Colliguntur nunc ab Ichano rege usque ad desolationem solis quod est octauodecimo Agamemnonis anni septingenti XVIII.
A solis deuastatione usque ad primam olympiadam anni CCCCVII: et Porfyrius autem in historia philosofiae sic dixit.
30   Post autem solis deuastationem Agamemnonus reliquos annos XV.

Post hunc Egesthus regnauit ann. VII.
Post hunc Oresthus regnauit ann. XXVIII.
Post hunc Penthilus regnauit ann. XXII.

35 Et Argiorum regnum dissipatum est. Colliguntur uero Argiorum regna simul anni septingenti XC.

25-27 Sync. (198,27 – 199,4 Moss.), cf. Eus., chron. (84,28s Karst) (= Castor FGrHist 250 F3) et can. (Hier. 59,25s; 59ᵐ Helm)
Ἀργείων ιζ' ἐβασίλευσεν Ἀγαμέμνων ἔτη ιη' (30 chron., 35 can.^Hier), κατὰ δὲ ἄλλους ἔτη λε'. τοῦ δὲ κόσμου ἦν ἔτος ͵δτιβ'.
Τῷ η' ἔτει Ἀγαμέμνονος ὁ κατὰ τῆς Τροίας ἤρξατο πόλεμος διὰ τὴν Ἑλένης ὑπὸ Ἀλεξάνδρου τοῦ Πάριδος κλοπὴν υἱοῦ Πριάμου βασιλέως Ἰλίου, καὶ διήρκεσεν ἔτη ι' ἕως ἁλώσεως Ἰλίου, ἥτις τῷ ὑποκειμένῳ ιζ' ἔτει (18 Eus.) Ἀγαμέμνονος γέγονεν. Ἀγαμέμνονος Ἀργείων καὶ Μυκηνῶν βασιλεύοντος, Μενελάου δὲ τοῦ ἀδελφοῦ αὐτοῦ Λακεδαιμονίων, Πρίαμος υἱὸς Λαομέδοντος τῆς Τροίας καὶ Ἰλίου ἐβασίλευσε.
26-31 → F34,38–41; T57
32s Sync. (199,27 – 200,2 Moss.), cf. Eus., chron. (84,30–32 Karst) (= Castor FGrHist 250 F3) et can. (Hier. 62ᵈ; 62ᶠ Helm)
Μυκηνῶν Ἀργείων ιη' ἐβασίλευσεν Αἴγισθος ἔτη ε' (17 chron., - can.). τοῦ δὲ κόσμου ἦν ἔτος ͵δτλ'.
Μυκηνῶν Ἀργείων ιθ' ἐβασίλευσεν Ὀρέστης ἔτη κγ' (15 can.^Hier, - chron.). τοῦ δὲ κόσμου ἦν ἔτος ͵δτλε'.

26s cf. Clem. Alex., strom. 1,21,104,1 ≈ Tat., orat. 39,1   **28** cf. Clem. Alex., strom. 1,21,138,1s (= Eratosthenes FGrHist 241 F1); cf. Eus., praep. ev. 10,9,6; Eus., can.^Hier 60ᶜ; Sync. 211,16; Ecl. Hist. 188,27s   **28s** cf. Eus., chron. 89,4–8 = Exc. Eus. 140,5–16 (= Porphyrius FGrHist 260 F4)   **32** cf. Sync. 144,27   **33s** cf. Sync. 144,27s

26 solis] Ἰλίου

> After them, Agamemnon, son of Atreus,[7] for 33 years.

From king Inachus up to the destruction of Ilium,[8] which was in the 18th year of Agamemnon, there are, then,[9] 718 years in all.[10]
From the sack of Ilium[11] up to the first Olympiad there are 407 years: this is also what Porphyry says in his *Philosophic History*.[12]

> > After the sack of Ilium,[13] Agamemnon was king for another 15 years.

> After him, Aegisthus was king for 7 years.
> After him, Orestes was king for 28 years.
> After him, Penthilus was king for 22 years.

And the kingdom of the Argives came to an end. Altogether there are 790 years for the reigns of the Argives.

---

7   Gr. (Frick): Ἀγαμέμνων Ἀτρέως.
8   Gr. (Frick): ἕως ἐρημώσεως Ἰλίου.
9   Gr. (Frick): τοίνυν.
10 The years of the reigns of the individual Argive kings come to only 677 (assuming 50 years for Danaus).
11 Gr. (Frick): ἀπὸ τῆς Ἰλίου ἐκπορθήσεως. The chronological information given here shows that Africanus is in keeping with the mainstream chronology established by Eratosthenes.
12 Gr. (Frick): ἐν τῇ φιλοσόφῳ ἱστορίᾳ. This must be a later gloss. Obviously, Porphyry cannot be the author of the whole list, see the reference to Moses in ll. 4 and 7, and Porphyry's divergent dating, Eus., can.[Hier] 8,1–5; see also Gelzer 1,138f.
13 Gr. (Frick): Μετὰ δὲ Ἰλίου ἐκπόρθησιν.

F51

F51a Excerpta Barbari (292,4 – 296,2 Frick)

Siciniorum qui nunc Elladicorum uocantur reges et tempora

Proferamus iterum et Syciniorum qui nunc Elladici uocantur.
Disponamus regna a quibus initiata sunt temporibus, et in quibus diffinierunt manifestemus.
Africanus quidem dixit sic tenere eis omnes annos mille VII: a minuetate autem
5   eorum in primam olympiadam anni CCCXXVIIII, sicut numeratur ab initio
Sicyoniorum regna in primam olympiadam omnes anni mille CCCXXXVI.
Vicesimo nono autem anno patriarchae Iacob illum Syciniorum initiauit regnum sic:

    I. Egialeus ann. LII.
10   Anni autem Iacob XXVIIII, anni Isaac LXXXVIIII, anni Abraham CXIIII Ellada initiauerunt regna.
    II. Europs ann. XLV.
    III. Telchus ann. XX.
    IIII. Amfus ann. XXV.
15   V. Thelxius ann. LII.

4-6 → F64 9 Sync. (110,20s Moss.), cf. Eus., chron. (81,25 Karst) (= Castor FGrHist 250 F2)
Σικυωνίων πρῶτος ἐβασίλευσεν Αἰγιαλεὺς ἔτη νβ' (= chron.). τοῦ δὲ κόσμου ἦν ἔτος ͵γσλθ'.
10s → F16d,5s; T28a,1
12-15   Sync. (116,8-16 Moss.), cf. Eus., chron. (81,30 – 82,1 Karst) (= Castor FGrHist 250 F2) et can. (Hier. 20,1-5; 21,7s; 22,3s; 23,8s Helm)
Σικυωνίων δεύτερος ἐβασίλευσεν Εὔρωψ ἔτη με' (= Eus.). τοῦ δὲ κόσμου ἦν ἔτος ͵γσρα'.
   Κατὰ τὸ κ' (= chron., 22 can.[Hier]) ἔτος Εὔρωπος τούτου τοῦ δευτέρου βασιλέως Σικυωνίων, ἤτοι Πελοποννησίων, γεννᾶται ὁ παρ' Ἑβραίοις Ἀβραάμ. (...)
Σικυωνίων γ' ἐβασίλευσε Τελχὶν ἔτη κθ' (20 Eus.). τοῦ δὲ κόσμου ἦν ἔτος ͵γτλς'.
Σικυωνίων δ' ἐβασίλευσεν Ἆπις ἔτη κε' (= Eus.). τοῦ δὲ κόσμου ἦν ἔτος ͵γτξε'.
Σικυωνίων ε' ἐβασίλευσε Θελξίων ἔτη νβ' (= Eus.). τοῦ δὲ κόσμου ἦν ἔτος ͵γτρ'.

4-8 cf. Sync. 110,1-7   9 cf. Sync. 109,23-28; Eus., chron. 81,25-29 (= Castor FGrHist 250 F2); ps. Sym. f. 30ᵛ ~ Cedr. 144,5   9-39 cf. Eus., reg. ser.[armen] 146; Eus., reg. ser.[Hier] 26; Clem. Alex., strom. 1,21,102,5; Cyr., c. Iul. 1,10; Chron. Synt. 86 9-50 cf. Exc. Eus. 134,12 – 135,28

F51 *The Rulers of the Sicyonians*[1]

F51a

The kings and chronology of the Sicyonians who are now called Helladici.

Let us set forth again the Sicyonians who are now called Helladici.
Let us arrange their reigns from the time when they began, and let us explain when they came to an end.
Africanus in fact said the following, that they lasted for a total of 1007 years, and that from their dissolution up to the first Olympiad there are 329 years. From the beginning of the reigns of the Sicyonians up to the first Olympiad, the total number of years is thus 1336.[2]
In the 29th year of the patriarch Jacob, the kingdom of the Sicyonians began, as follows:

1. Aegialeus, 52 years.
   In the 29th year of Jacob, the 89th year of Isaac, and the 114th year of Abraham, the Helladic reigns began.[3]
2. Europs, 45 years.
3. Telchin, 20 years.
4. Apis, 25 years.
5. Thelxion, 52 years.

---

1. Although Malalas and the *Excerpta Barbari* report the duration of Sicyonian rule differently, both sources identify Africanus as their authority. The structure of the list in the Exc. Barb. exemplifies Africanus' historical method, as outlined in F34, see introduction, p. XXXVII. Sicyon was an ancient Greek kingdom belonging to the period that Africanus calls "mythical" (that is, pre-Olympiad) history. To secure the chronology of Sicyon, Africanus establishes the years of the beginning and end of the kingdom in relationship to Ol. 1,1 (ll. 5f.52f), and inserts into the list synchronistic notices from biblical history (ll. 7f.10f.19f).
2. The year of the beginning of the Sicyonian kingdom would therefore be AM 3391 (3391 + 1336 = AM 4727 = Ol. 1,1).
3. Lit.: "the 29 years of Jacob, 89 years of Isaac, 114 years of Abraham." In the manuscript text, these biblical synchronisms are arranged as a separate column. Since Abraham was 189 years of age when Isaac was 89, the number '114' must have been calculated from the date of Abraham's migration to the land of Canaan at age 75 (Gen 12,5). According to the reckoning of Africanus, this occurred in 3277 (F16d,5f), thereby confirming AM 3391 as the date of the beginning of the Sicyonian kingdom (AM 3277 + 114 + 1007 + 329 = AM 4727 = Ol. 1,1); see Routh 444, n. ad loc.; Gelzer 1,144.

VI. Egydrus ann. XXXIIII.
VII. Turimachus ann. XLV.
VIII. Leucippus ann. LIII.
    Anno quadragesimo tertio Leucippi egressio Iudeorum ex
    Aegypto.
VIIII. Mesapfus ann. XLVII.
X. Eratus ann. XLVI.
XI. Plammeus ann. XLVIIII.
XII. Ortopolus ann. LXV.
XIII. Marathus ann. XXX.
XIIII. Maratheus ann. XX.
XV. Echyrus ann. LV.
XVI. Corax ann. XX.
XVII. Epopeus ann. XXXV.
XVIII. Laomedus ann. XLIII.

16–22 Sync. (119,14–23 Moss.), cf. Eus., chron. (82,2–8 Karst) (= Castor FGrHist 250 F2) et can. (armen. 156 Karst; Hier. 25,18s; 27,2s; 29,5s; 31,12s; 33,18s Helm)
Σικυωνίων ς′ ἐβασίλευσεν Αἴγυδρος ἔτη λδ′ (= chron., can.^{Hier}, - can.^{armen}). τοῦ δὲ κόσμου ἦν ἔτος ‚γυμβ′.
Σικυωνίων ζ′ ἐβασίλευσε Θουρίμαχος ἔτη με′ (= chron., can.^{Hier}, - can.^{armen}). τοῦ δὲ κόσμου ἦν ἔτος ‚γυος′.
Σικυωνίων η′ ἐβασίλευσε Λεύκιππος ἔτη νγ′ (= chron., can.^{Hier}, - can.^{armen}). τοῦ δὲ κόσμου ἦν ἔτος ‚γφκα′.
Σικυωνίων θ′ ἐβασίλευσε Μέσαππος ἔτη μζ′ (= chron., can.^{Hier}, - can.^{armen}). τοῦ δὲ κόσμου ἦν ἔτος ‚γφοδ′.
Σικυωνίων ι′ ἐβασίλευσεν Ἔραστος ἔτη μς′ (= chron., can.^{Hier}, 43 can.^{armen}). τοῦ δὲ κόσμου ἦν ἔτος ‚γχκα′.
19s → F34,68–70.76–83
23s Sync. (125,25–28 Moss.), cf. Eus., chron. (82,9s Karst) (= Castor FGrHist 250 F2) et can. (armen. 156–159 Karst; Hier. 35,21s; 38,8s Helm)
Σικυωνίων ια′ ἐβασίλευσε Πλημναῖος ἔτη ν′, κατὰ δὲ ἄλλους μη′ (= chron., can.^{Hier}; 45 can.^{armen}). τοῦ δὲ κόσμου ἦν ἔτος ‚γχξζ′.
Σικυωνίων ιβ′ ἐβασίλευσεν Ὀρθόπολις ἔτη ξγ′ (= Eus.). τοῦ δὲ κόσμου ἦν ἔτος ‚γψιζ′.
25s Sync. (143,22–24 Moss.), cf. Eus., chron. (82,11–13 Karst) (= Castor FGrHist 250 F2) et can. (armen. 160s Karst; Hier. 41,5s; 42,16s Helm)
Σικυωνίων ιδ′ ἐβασίλευσε Μαραθώνιος ἔτη λ′ (= chron., can.^{Hier}, 28 can.^{armen}). τοῦ δὲ κόσμου ἦν ἔτος ‚γωλε′.
Σικυωνίων ιε′ ἐβασίλευσε Μαράθιος ἔτη κ′ (= Eus.). τοῦ δὲ κόσμου ἦν ἔτος ‚γωξε′.
27 Sync. (125,29s Moss.), cf. Eus., chron. (82,16 Karst) (= Castor FGrHist 250 F2) et can. (armen. 161–163 Karst; Hier. 43,20s Helm)
Σικυωνίων ιγ′ ἐβασίλευσεν Ἐχυρεὺς ἔτη νε′ (= Eus.). τοῦ δὲ κόσμου ἦν ἔτος ‚γψπ′.
28–30 Sync. (143,25 – 144,3 Moss.), cf. Eus., chron. (82,18–20 Karst) (= Castor FGrHist 250 F2) et can. (armen. 163–165 Karst; Hier. 46,21s; 48,8s; 50,1s Helm)
Σικυωνίων ις′ ἐβασίλευσε Κόραξ ἔτη λ′ (= Eus.). τοῦ δὲ κόσμου ἦν ἔτος ‚γωπε′.
Σικυωνίων ιζ′ ἐβασίλευσεν Ἐποπεὺς ἔτη λβ′ (35 Eus.). τοῦ δὲ κόσμου ἦν ἔτος ‚γϡιε′.
Σικυωνίων ιη′ ἐβασίλευσε Λαομέδων ἔτη μγ′ (40 Eus.). τοῦ δὲ κόσμου ἦν ἔτος ‚γϡμζ′.

6. Aegydrus, 34 years.
7. Thurimachus, 45 years.
8. Leucippus, 53 years.
   In the 43rd year of Leucippus, the Exodus of the Jews from Egypt.[4]
9. Mesappus, 47 years.
10. Erastus, 46 years.
11. Plemnaeus, 49 years.
12. Orthopolis, 65 years.
13. Marathonius, 30 years.
14. Marathius, 20 years.
15. Echyreus, 55 years.
16. Corax, 20 years.
17. Epopeus, 35 years.
18. Laomedon, 43 years.

---

4 The date of the Exodus in 43 Leucippus accurately represents Africanus' chronology. Exc. Barb. numbers 316 years from 1 Aegilaeus to 43 Leucippus, and 1336 years from 1 Aegialeus to Ol 1.1 (see ll. 5f and 52f). There are thus 1020 years from 43 Leucippus to Ol. 1.1 (1336 − 316= 1020). For Africanus' reckoning of 1020 years from the Exodus to Ol. 1,1, see F34,68–70.

<Σικυὼν ἔτη μβ'.>
<Polybus annos XLV.>
XVIIII. Inachus annos XLV.
XX. Festus annos L.
35 XXI. Adrastus annos IIII.
XXII. Polifidus annos XXXI.
XXIII. Pelastus annos XX.
XXIIII. Zeuxippus annos XXXV.
{XXV. Polybus annos XLV.}

40 Usque Zeuxippum tenuit Sicyoniorum regnum permanens annos quingentos LXXXI. Post Zeuxippum autem reges quidem non fuerunt, sed praeibant eis sacerdotes Carnii annos XXVIII.

Quem primus sacerdos Archelaus annum I.
Post hunc Automidus annum I.
45 Post hunc Methudutus annum I.
Post hunc Euneus annos IIII.
Post hunc Theonomus annum I.

31-37 Sync. (172,24 – 173,10 Moss.), cf. Eus., chron. (82,21–29 Karst) (= Castor FGrHist 250 F2) et can. (armen. 166–172 Karst; Hier. 51,26s; 54,7s; 56,4s; 58,11s; 58,23s; 59,3s; 62,6s Helm)
Σικυωνίων ιθ' ἐβασίλευσε Σικυὼν ἔτη μβ' (*44* can.^{armen}, *45* can.^{Hier}, - chron.). τοῦ δὲ κόσμου ἦν ἔτος ˏγϡϙ'.
Σικυωνίων κ' ἐβασίλευσε Πόλυβος ἔτη μγ' (*40* Eus.). τοῦ δὲ κόσμου ἦν ἔτος ˏδλβ'.
Σικυωνίων κα' ἐβασίλευσεν Ἴναχος ἔτη με' (*40* chron., *42* can.^{Hier}, can.^{armen}). τοῦ δὲ κόσμου ἦν ἔτος ˏδοε'.
Σικυωνίων κβ' ἐβασίλευσεν Ἥφαιστος ἔτη ι' (*8* Eus.). τοῦ δὲ κόσμου ἦν ἔτος ˏδρκ'.
Σικυωνίων κγ' ἐβασίλευσεν Ἄδραστος ἔτη ζ' (*4* Eus.). τοῦ δὲ κόσμου ἦν ἔτος ˏδρλ'.
Σικυωνίων κδ' ἐβασίλευσε Πολυφείδης ἔτη λα' (= Eus.). τοῦ δὲ κόσμου ἦν ἔτος ˏδρλζ'.
Σικυωνίων κε' ἐβασίλευσε Πελασγὸς ἔτη κ' (= Eus.). τοῦ δὲ κόσμου ἦν ἔτος ˏδρξη'.
38 Sync. (177,21s Moss.), cf. Eus., chron. (82,31 Karst) (= Castor FGrHist 250 F2) et can. (armen. 172s Karst; Hier. 63,8–10 Helm)
Σικυωνίων κς' ἐβασίλευσε Ζεύξιππος ἔτη λ' (*31* Eus.). τοῦ δὲ κόσμου ἦν ἔτος ˏδρπη'.
40s Sync. (178,3 Moss.), cf. Eus., chron. (82,32s Karst) et can. (Hier. 65,1–6 Helm)
Ὁμοῦ τὰ πάντα τῆς Σικυωνίων ἀρχῆς ἔτη χίλια (*959* chron., *962* can.^{Hier}).

32-38 cf. Sync. 110,4s (= ps. Apollodorus FGrHist 244 F86) (1000 anni regum); Sync. 110,8–13 (= Castor FGrHist 250 F2) = Eus., chron. 81,15–23 (959 anni regum / 33 anni sacerdotum); Exc. Eus. 135,16–19 (959 anni); ps. Sym f. 38^r = Cedr. 144,5–8 (980 anni regum) **41s** cf. Eus., chron. 82,33s (= Castor FGrHist 250 F2); Eus., can.^{Hier} 65,7–9; Sync. 178,1s **43-51** cf. Eus., chron. 82,33s; 83,1–9 (= Castor FGrHist 250 F2); Eus., can.^{Hier} 65,7–9; Exc. Eus. 135,20–26; Sync. 178,1s; Eus., chron. 83,1–9 (= Castor FGrHist 250 F2)

31 supplevimus e Eus. et Sync. **32** transposuimus e l. 39 cf. Sync. et Eus. **38** XXXV] *31* Io. Mal (= F51b,4) **39** vide l. 32 **40s** quingentos LXXXI] *noningentos LXXIX* Frick *985* Io. Mal. (= F51b,6)

<Sicyon, 42 years.>[5]
<Polybus, 45 years.>[6]
19. Inachus, 45 years.
20. Hephaestus, 50 years.
21. Adrastus, 4 years.
22. Polypheides, 31 years.
23. Pelasgus, 20 years.
24. Zeuxippus, 35 years.
{25. Polybus, 45 years.}

Up to Zeuxippus, the kingdom of the Sicyonians was in power, lasting for 581 years.[7] After Zeuxippus, however, there were not kings; rather priests of Carnius[8] were their leaders, for 28 years.

Of them,[9] the first was Archelaus, 1 year.
After him, Automedon, 1 year.
After him, Methudutus,[10] 1 year.
After him, Euneus, 4 years.
After him, Theonomus, 1 year.

---

5   The name and years of Sicyon are supplied from the parallel lists in Eusebius and Syncellus.
6   Transposed from l. 39, following Eusebius and Syncellus. Both errors (Sicyon and Polybius) might be explained by the fact that at this point the page in the manuscript changes.
7   Although the number is corrupt, it is difficult to restore the correct number of years from Aegialeus to Zeuxippus. According to l. 7, the combined rules of the kings and priests of Sicyon lasted 1007 years. Subtracting the 28 years of priestly rule (l. 42) from this total would leave 979 years for the kings. Frick emends accordingly. However, this corresponds neither to the sum of the reigns of the individual kings (1008 years including the 42-year reign of Sicyon) nor to the numbers transmitted in Malalas (see below n. 16).
8   Carneus, one of the epithets of Apollo.
9   Gr. (Frick): ὢν πρῶτος.
10 The name is unattested elsewhere; cf. Eus., chron.: Theoclitus.

>   Post hunc Amficyus annos VIIII.
>   Post hunc Charidus annum I.
> 50   Osuch sustinens cibaria fugiit.
>   A quo in prima olimpiada ut fertur scriptura anni CCCXXVIIII.
>
>   Fiunt uero omnes Sicioniorum regna ab Egialeo usque in prima olympiada anni mille CCCXXXVI.

51 CCCXXVIIII Frick (vide l. 5) *CCCXXVII* cod.

F51b Ioannes Malalas 4,1 (48,12–16 Thurn)

> Τῶν δὲ Σικυωνίων τῶν νυνὶ λεγομένων Ἑλλαδικῶν
>   ἐβασίλευσεν πρῶτος ὁ Αἰγιαλεὺς ἔτη νβ',
>   καὶ λοιπὸν ἄλλοι βασιλεῖς κς'
>   ἕως Ζευξίππου τοῦ βασιλεύσαντος αὐτῶν ἔτη λα'.
> 5 καὶ λοιπὸν οἱ ἱερεῖς αὐτῶν ἐδιοίκουν τὴν χώραν,
>   καὶ κατέσχεν ἡ βασιλεία αὐτῶν ἔτη ϡπε',
> καθὼς Ἀφρικανὸς ὁ σοφώτατος συνεγράψατο.

1–7 cf. ps. Sym. f. 38ʳ = Cedr. 144,5–8; Chron. Synt. 86,5–34; Exc. Eus. 135,16–19; Sync. (app. ad F51a) (omnes 26 reges)   **6** cf. Io. Ant. fr. 23.3

[OSl] **4** λα' Sl ps. Sym. Cedr. Exc. Eus. λβ' O *30* Sync. *35* Exc. Barb. (= F51a,38)   **6** ϡπε' O Io. Ant. *381* Sl *581* Exc. Barb. (= Fa,40s)

After him, Amphigyes, 9 years.[11]
After him, Charidemus, 1 year.
    Unable to bear the expense, he fled.[12]

From him up to the first Olympiad, as is reported in the written record,[13] 329 years.[14]

Altogether, then, the years of the reigns of the Sicyonians from Egialeus up to the first Olympiad come to a total of 1336.

F51b

Of the Sicyonians, who are now called Helladici,
    Aegialeus was their first king, for 52 years.
    And then the remaining 26 kings[15]
    up to Zeuxippus who was their king for 31 years.
    And then their priests managed the region.
And their kingdom was in power for 985 years,[16]
as Africanus, the most wise, has recorded.

---

11 To produce a total of 28 years, Gelzer 1,146 emends 9 to 19.
12 Gr. (Frick): ὃς οὐχ (= Lat. Osuch) ὑπομείνας τὴν δαπάνην ἔφυγεν.
13 Gr. (Frick): ὡς φέρεται γραφῇ.
14 Cod. 327; Frick's emendation is well-founded since the number transmitted in l. 5 is confirmed by the correct overall calculation (see ll. 4–6 and n. 2).
15 All other sources confirm the total number of kings as 26 (including Aegialeus and Zeuxippus).
16 985 is the number transmitted in Malalas' Greek text, cf. Slavonic: 381, Exc. Barb: 581 (in F51a,40f). The figure arrived at by collating the transmitted numbers would be 981, leaving 26 years for the priests (1007 − 981 = 26; see l. 4), but cf. the 28 years of priestly rule in F51a,42. Attempts at restoring the arithmetic of the whole list by means of single emendations (like Frick, see n. 7, or Gelzer, see n. 11) therefore seem problematic.

T52 Ioannes Lydus, De magistratibus populi Romani 1,2 (10,8–12 Bandy)

Ἀνύονται τοιγαροῦν ἐκ τῆς Αἰνείου ἐπὶ τὴν Ἰταλίαν παρόδου ἕως τοῦ πολισμοῦ τῆς Ῥώμης ἐνιαυτοὶ ἐννέα καὶ τριάκοντα καὶ τετρακόσιοι κατὰ Κάτωνα τὸν πρῶτον καὶ Βάρρωνα, τοὺς Ῥωμαίους· κατὰ δὲ Ἀφρικανὸν καὶ Κάστορα <καὶ Εὐσέβιον> τὸν Παμφίλου ἔτη ζ' καὶ ι' καὶ υ'.

3s → F53,2s; F65,53

3s cf. Eus., chron. 131,22–28; Eus., can.^Hier 62,1–10; Sync. 230,8–13; 230,18; 200,25 – 201,3; Exc. Barb. 302,14–17

3 καὶ Εὐσέβιον scripsimus καὶ Bandy

F53 Symeon Logothetes in codice Vaticano gr. 163, f. 9^v–10^r (≈ Leo Grammaticus [35,11–16 Bekker] et Theodosius Melitenus [31,30 – 32,2 Tafel])

Ἐν δὲ τῷ πρώτῳ ἔτει τῆς τούτου (sc. Achaz) βασιλείας Ἴφιτος τὰς Ὀλυμπιάδας συνέστησεν. ἐν δὲ τῇ αὐτῇ πρώτῃ Ὀλυμπιάδι Ῥῶμος καὶ Ῥωμύλος ἐγεννήθησαν, οἵτινες ἐν τῇ ἑβδόμῃ Ὀλυμπιάδι τὴν Ῥώμην ἤρξαντο κτίζειν.

Ἀφρικανὸς δέ φησιν ὁ σοφώτατος, ὅτι ἀπὸ Ῥωμύλου <βασιλεῖς> καὶ <ἀπὸ> τῶν
5 ὑπάτων κατέπαυσαν μέχρις Ἰουλίου Καίσαρος τῆς μοναρχίας, διαρκέσαντες ἐπὶ ἔτη διακοσία τεσσεράκοντα πέντε.

1 → F64a   1–3 → F65,47.53; T52   2s Sync. (230,8–10 Moss.) *Οὗτος ὁ Ῥωμύλος ἀνελὼν Ῥέμον τὸν ἀδελφὸν αὐτοῦ βασιλεύει μόνος καὶ κτίζει καὶ τειχίζει Ῥώμην κατὰ τὴν ζ' Ὀλυμπιάδα ἢ ὥς τινες κατὰ τὴν η', ἥτις τοῖς χρόνοις Ἄχαζ συντρέχει καὶ τῷ ,δψνβ' ἔτει τοῦ κόσμου.* 4s → F54d,8s

1–3 cf. Iul. Pol. 114,16–20   2s cf. Dion. Hal. 1,71,5; Eus., chron. 131,22–25; 136,30s (= Diod. Sic. 7,5,1s); Chron. Pasch. 204,2–5; Cedr. 189,12–19

1 δὲ¹ < Leo Gr. Th. Mel.   2 πρώτῃ < Th. Mel. | Ῥῆμος Th. Mel. | τῇ < Th. Mel.   4 Ἀφρικανὸς...ὅτι < Th. Mel. ἡ δὲ ἀριστοκρατία Leo Gr. | βασιλεῖς scripsimus | ἀπὸ² scripsimus   5 κατέπαυσαν] ἀρξαμένη κατέπαυσε Leo Gr. | Ἰουλίου...μοναρχίας ~ (τ. Ἰ. Κ. μ.) Leo Gr. | διαρκέσασα Leo Gr.

T52 *From Aeneas to the Foundation of Rome*

Now, from the arrival of Aeneas in Italy to the founding of Rome 439 years elapsed according to the Romans Cato the Elder and Varro, but 417 years according to Africanus, Castor, and <Eusebius>, [pupil] of Pamphilus.

F53 *The Kings of Rome*

In the first year of his (sc. Ahaz) reign, Iphitus instituted the Olympic games. In that same first Olympiad, Remus and Romulus were born; they started to build Rome in the seventh Olympiad.

The most learned Africanus says that from Romulus there were <kings>, and they ceased to exist <from> the consuls to the monarchy of Iulius Caesar, after a duration of 245 years.[1]

---

1   This tiny fragment is all that remains of Africanus' account of the early history of Rome. However, it is likely that he dealt with the matter in a more detailed way, probably giving a table of kings as he does with the other important monarchies (see the preceding and following fragments). In one preserved fragment, Africanus explicitly mentions the end of the early monarchy at the time of Brutus and the foundation of the consulship (F54d,8f).

F54

F54a Excerpta Barbari (296,3 – 300,12 Frick)

Athineorum reges

Nondum multo transacto tempore Aethineorum regnum <...> ab Aegypto populi egressio.
Anno enim ducentesimo octauo egressionis primus in Athinas regnauit Cec-
5 rops procerus et qui post eum, sicut manifestantur, sic.

> I. Cecrops procerus ann. L. Anno trecesimo quinto Cecropus Promitheus et Epimitheus et Atlas scribuntur, qui et Diu scribuntur.
> <Difyis autem uocatus est Cecrops, quoniam procer staturae fuit prae omnibus.>

4s → F54c,4s (206 anni); F54b,2s (189 anni); T57   **4s et 47s** → F34,40s   **6s** → F34,103s; F56,2–5. 10–13; T56a
6–9 Sync. (179,7–16 Moss.) (= Philochorus FGrHist 328 F93), cf. Eus., chron. (86,15s Karst) (= Castor FGrHist 250 F4) et can. (armen. 160 Karst; Hier. 41,6–9 Helm)
Ἀθηναίων α΄ ἐβασίλευσε Κέκροψ ὁ διφυὴς ἔτη ν΄ (= can., 5 chron.). τοῦ δὲ κόσμου ἦν ἔτος ͵γϡμε΄.
Κέκροψ ὁ διφυὴς τῆς τότε Ἀκτῆς, νῦν δὲ Ἀττικῆς, ἐβασίλευσεν ἔτη ν΄, διὰ μῆκος σώματος οὕτω καλούμενος, ὥς φησιν ὁ Φιλόχορος, ἢ ὅτι Αἰγύπτιος ὢν τὰς δύο γλώσσας ἠπίστατο. οὗτος ἀπὸ τῆς Ἀθηνᾶς τὴν πόλιν Ἀθήνας ὠνόμασεν. ἐπὶ αὐτοῦ ἡ ἐν τῇ ἀκροπόλει ἐλαία πρώτως ἐφύη. ἀπ᾽ αὐτοῦ δὲ Κεκροπία ἡ χώρα ἐκλήθη. οὗτος πρῶτος βοῦν ἐθυσίασε καὶ Ζῆνα προσηγόρευσεν, ὥς τινες. ἀπ᾽ αὐτοῦ ἐπὶ πρώτην Ὀλυμπιάδα βασιλεῖς ις΄, ἄρχοντες δὲ διὰ βίου ια΄, ἔτη δὲ ψ΄. κατὰ τούτους τὰ παρ᾽ Ἕλλησι θαυμαστὰ δοκοῦντα μυθολογεῖται.
6–10 → F54b,4s   **8s** Io. Ant. fr. 24.3,2s (58 Ro.) ... Κέκροψ, ὃς ἐκλήθη διφυὴς διὰ τὸ τοῦ σώματος μέγεθος ...

1–60 cf. Eus., chron. 85,3 – 88,24; Eus., can.[Hier] 41c; Chron. Synt. 87,24 – 88,12   **2–5** cf. Eus., can.[Hier] 9,19 – 10,4; 14,6–15; 41c   **6** (cum **27** et **45**) cf. Eus., can.[Hier] 41g   **6–9** cf. Eus., can.[Hier h-i]
6–60 cf. Eus., reg. ser.[armen] 148s; Eus., reg. ser.[Hier] 30s   **8s** cf. Eus., can.[armen] 159s; Eus., can.[Hier] 41h; Io. Mal. 4,5; Io. Ant. 24.3,2–4; Sym. Log. (Leo Gr. 28,3s = Th. Mel. 26,27 – 27,1); Cedr. 144,22 – 145,2

4 ducentesimo octauo] recte *206* cf. T54c,4s   **8s** transposuimus a l. 29s (cf. Sync., Eus., Io. Ant. supra in app.)

F54 *The Rulers of the Athenians*

F54a[1]

Kings of the Athenians

When not much time had yet elapsed, the kingdom of the Athenians <...> the Exodus of the people from Egypt.[2]

For in the 206th year from the Exodus,[3] Cecrops "the large" was the first to reign as king in Athens. Those who succeeded him to rule are the following, as they are shown below:

> 1. Cecrops "the large," 50 years. In the 35th year (of Cecrops), there are written records for Cecrops, Prometheus,[4] Epimethius and Atlas, who are also recorded for a long time.[5]
> <Now Cecrops was called "Double-natured," since he was larger in stature than everyone else.>[6]

---

1. Parallel witnesses with reference to Africanus point to the *Chronographiae* as being the likely source of this unattributed list of Athenian kings. According to Malalas (T54f,6), Africanus ascribed 907 years to the duration of Athenian rule (up to Creon), in agreement with the total years of the Athenian kingdom reported in the Excerpta (ll. 59f). Parts of the list also correspond with material credited to Africanus by Syncellus (F54b–e) and Eusebius (F64c). For further discussion, see Gelzer 1,152–155; De Sanctis 1912,99–106. Information about the Athenian kingdom preserved in Syncellus' chronicle and unattested in Eusebius is provided in the third apparatus as a possible additional witness to Africanus.
2. The Latin text is either lacunose or a misunderstanding of the Greek original. Gr. (Frick): Οὔπω πολλοῦ διεληλυθότος χρόνου τῆς ἐξ Αἰγύπτου τοῦ λαοῦ ἐξόδου ἡ Ἀθηναίων βασιλεία. ("When not much time had yet elapsed from the Exodus of the people from Egypt, the kingdom of the Athenians <arose>.")
3. Text: 208, emended to 206 (= John of Antioch). The *Excerpta* (see ll. 47f) numbers 814 years from 1 Cecrops to Ol. 1,1. The addition of 206 years from the Exodus to 1 Cecrops yields a total of 1020 years from the Exodus and the flood of Ogygus to Ol. 1,1. This sum corresponds precisely with Africanus' reckoning, see F34,40f.
4. Gr. (Frick): Ἔτει λε′ Κέκροπος Προμηθεύς ("in the 35th year of Cecrops").
5. Gr. (Frick): οἱ καὶ Διὸς γραφόμενοι ("who are also recorded as sons of Zeus"). According to F34,102–104, Africanus dated Prometheus 94 years after the flood of Ogygus, much earlier than the date given here. Africanus was aware of divergent traditions about the dates of Prometheus, Epimetheus and Atlas (see F56,10–13 and n. 1 ad loc.). The Greek text underlying the enigmatic Latin "qui et Diu scribuntur" may thus have meant: "who are also ascribed to a much earlier period."
6. The notice about Cecrops in angle-brackets has been transferred from ll. 29f of the *Excerpta*.

<Κραναὸς αὐτόχθων μετὰ Κέκροπα ἔτη θ'.>
II. Amifictryus ann. XL.
III. Ericthonius ann. X.
IIII. Pandius ann. L.
V. Erectheus ann. XL.
VI. Cecrops Erectheus ann. LIII.
VII. Pandius Cecropus ann. XLIII.
{VIII.} Temporibus Pandii Cecropi Cadmus Aginori litterarum uersos primus duxit ad Grecos.
VIIII. Egeus Pandionus annos XLVIII.

10-13 Sync. (184,6-24 Moss.) (= Philochorus FGrHist 328 F93), cf. Eus., chron. (86,23-29 Karst) (= Castor FGrHist 250 F4) et can. (armen. 160-165 Karst; Hier. 43,25s; 44,12s; 45,1s; 47,17s Helm)
Ἀθηναίων β' ἐβασίλευσε Κραναὸς αὐτόχθων ἔτη θ' (= Eus.). τοῦ δὲ κόσμου ἦν ἔτος ˏγϡρε'.

Κραναοῦ τούτου δευτέρου βασιλέως τῆς Ἀττικῆς θυγάτηρ ἦν Ἀτθίς, καθ' ἣν Ἀττικὴ ἡ χώρα ὠνομάσθη, πρότερον Ἀκτὴ λεγομένη. κατὰ τοῦτον τὸν Κραναὸν ὁ ἐπὶ Δευκαλίωνος κατακλυσμὸς ἐν Θεσσαλίᾳ (→ T55,10-14) καὶ ὁ ἐπὶ Φαέθοντος ἐμπρησμὸς ἐν Αἰθιοπίᾳ. πολλαὶ δὲ καὶ ἄλλαι γεγόνασιν Ἕλλησι τοπικαὶ φθοραί, ὡς Πλάτων ἐν Τιμαίῳ. ἀπὸ δὲ Ἕλληνος τοῦ Δευκαλίωνος Ἕλληνες οἱ Γραικοὶ καλοῦνται.

Ἀθηναίων γ' ἐβασίλευσεν Ἀμφικτύων ἔτη ι' (= can., 9 chron.), υἱὸς Δευκαλίωνος, γαμβρὸς Κραναοῦ. τοῦ δὲ κόσμου ἦν ἔτος ˏδδ'.

Κατὰ Ἀμφικτύωνα τὸν Δευκαλίωνος υἱόν τινές φασι Διόνυσον εἰς τὴν Ἀττικὴν ἐλθόντα ξενωθῆναι Σημάχῳ καὶ τῇ θυγατρὶ αὐτοῦ νεβρίδα δωρήσασθαι. ἕτερος δ' ἦν οὗτος ἐκ Σεμέλης.

Ἀθηναίων δ' ἐβασίλευσεν Ἐριχθόνιος ἔτη ν' (= can., - chron.). τοῦ δὲ κόσμου ἦν ἔτος ˏδιδ'.

Οὗτος Ἐριχθόνιος Ἡφαίστου ὁ παρ' Ὁμήρῳ Ἐρεχθεύς ἐστιν. Ἐριχθόνιος ἅρμα πρῶτος Ἕλλησιν ἐφεῦρεν. ἦν γὰρ παρὰ βαρβάρων.

Ἀθηναίων ε' ἐβασίλευσε Πανδίων ἔτη μ' (= Eus.). τοῦ δὲ κόσμου ἦν ἔτος ˏδξδ'.

Τούτου θυγατέρες Πρόκνη καὶ Φιλομήλα τοῦ Πανδίονος.

14-19 Sync. (188,24 - 189,6 Moss.), cf. Eus., chron. (86,30 - 87,8 Karst) (= Castor FGrHist 250 F4) et can. (armen. 165-169 Karst; Hier. 49,17s; 52,3s; 54,2s; 55,9-11 Helm)
Ἀθηναίων ϛ' ἐβασίλευσεν Ἐρεχθεὺς ἔτη ν' (= Eus.). τοῦ δὲ κόσμου ἦν ἔτος ˏδρδ'.

Ἐρεχθέως τούτου θυγατέρα Βορέας υἱὸς Ἀστραίου Θρὰξ ἥρπασεν Ὠριθυῖαν. ὁ δὲ μῦθος τὸν ἄνεμον, ὡς Φιλόχορος ἐν δευτέρᾳ φησίν. ἐπὶ τούτου δὲ καὶ τὰ λεγόμενα μυστήρια ἤρξαντο. (cf. can.[Hier] 50[b]; ps. Io. Ant. fr. 6*)

Ἀθηναίων ζ' ἐβασίλευσε Κέκροψ ἔτη μ' (= Eus.), ὁ δεύτερος Ἐρεχθέως ἀδελφός. τοῦ δὲ κόσμου ἦν ἔτος ˏδρνδ'.

Ἀθηναίων η' ἐβασίλευσε Πανδίων Ἐρεχθέως ἔτη κε' (= Eus.). τοῦ δὲ κόσμου ἦν ἔτος ˏδρϙδ'.

Ἀθηναίων θ' ἐβασίλευσεν Αἰγεὺς Πανδίονος ἔτη μη' (= Eus.). τοῦ δὲ κόσμου ἦν ἔτος ˏδσιθ'.

10 cf. Io. Mal. 4,6 **12** cf. Eus., can.[Hier] 12,19 **17s** cf. Eus., can.[Hier] 48[a]

10 restituimus e Sync. (78,21 Moss. = F54b,4), cf. etiam Sync. et Eus. supra in app., necnon Io. Mal. in app. ad F54b,4s

<Cranaus, native-born, reigned after Cecrops, 9 years.>[7]
2. Amphictyon, 40 years.
3. Erichthonius, 10 years.
4. Pandion, 50 years.
5. Erechtheus, 40 years.
6. Cecrops, son of Erechtheus, 53 years.
7. Pandion, son of Cecrops, 43 years.
>> In the time of Pandion son of Cecrops,[8] Cadmus, son of Agenor, first introduced the Greeks to rows of letters.[9]
9. Aigeus, son of Pandion, 48 years.

---

[7] The missing name of Cranaus and the nine years of his reign have been supplied from Syncellus, see also the other parallels in the app.
[8] Gr. (Frick): χρόνοις Πανδίονος Κέκροπος.
[9] The Latin translator may have confused γραμμάτων στοίχους with γραμμάτων στοιχεῖα, "letters of the alphabet" (Scal.).

X. Thiseus Egei ann. XXXI.
XI. Menestheus ann. XVIIII.
XII. Dimofus ann. XXXV.
XIII. Oxyntus ann. XIIII.
XIIII. Afydus ann. I.
XV. Thymytus ann. VIIII.
XVI. Melanthus ann. XXXVII.
XVII. Codrus ann. XXI.

A Cecropo procero usque Codrum anni quadringenti XCII. Post Codrum autem fuerunt sicut uixerunt principes. {Difyis autem uocatus est Cecrops, quoniam procer staturae fuit prae omnibus.}

20-24 Sync. (201,22 – 202,20 Moss.), cf. Eus., chron. (87,8-18 Karst) (= Castor FGrHist 250 F4) et can. (armen. 170-173 Karst; Hier. 57,21s; 59,13s; 62,1-3; 63,23s; 64,14s Helm)
Ἀθηναίων ι' ἐβασίλευσε Θησεὺς Αἰγέως ἔτη λα' (30 Eus.). τοῦ δὲ κόσμου ἦν ἔτος ‚δσξζ'.
  Θησεὺς Ἑλένην ἥρπασεν, ἣν αὖθις ἀπέλαβον οἱ ἀδελφοὶ αὐτῆς Κάστωρ καὶ Πολυδεύκης, τὴν μητέρα Θησέως αἰχμαλωτίσαντες ἀποδημοῦντος τοῦ Θησέως. Θησεὺς Ἀθηναίους κατὰ χώραν διεσπαρμένους εἰς ἓν συναγαγὼν ἤτοι εἰς μίαν πόλιν, πρῶτος ἐξωστρακίσθη, αὐτὸς πρῶτος θεὶς τὸν νόμον. Θησεὺς ἔφυγεν ἀπὸ Ἀθηνῶν.
Ἀθηναίων ια' ἐβασίλευσε Μενεσθεὺς Πετεῶ τοῦ Ὀρνέως τοῦ Ἐρεχθέως ἔτη λγ' (23 Eus.). τοῦ δὲ κόσμου ἦν ἔτος ‚δσϙη'.
  Ἐπὶ τούτου ὁ Τρωικὸς πόλεμος συνέστη ἕνεκα μήλου χρυσοῦ, ὃ κάλλους ἔπαθλον ἦν γυναικῶν τριῶν, ὑπὸ μιᾶς αὐτῶν προτεθείσης Ἑλένης τῷ κριτῇ. βουκόλος δ' οὗτος ἦν Ἰλιεύς, ὡς ἡ κωμῳδία. Μενεσθεὺς οὗτος Ἕλλησι κατὰ τῶν Τρώων συνεμάχησε. τούτου τῷ λγ' ἔτει Ἴλιον ἥλω ἐπανιὼν δὲ ἀπὸ Τροίας ἐν Μήλῳ τῇ νήσῳ τελευτᾷ.
Ἀθηναίων ιβ' ἐβασίλευσε Δημοφῶν Θησέως ἔτη κγ' (33 Eus.). τοῦ δὲ κόσμου ἦν ἔτος ‚δτλα'.
  Ἐπὶ τούτου τὰ περὶ Ὀδυσσέα καὶ Ὀρέστην. Αἰνείας τε ἐβασίλευσε Λαβινίου. τὰ κατὰ Ὀδυσσέα καὶ Σκύλλαν καὶ Χάρυβδιν καὶ Σειρῆνας. (cf. ps. Io.Ant. fr. 18*)
Ἀθηναίων ιγ' ἐβασίλευσεν Ὀξύντης Δημοφῶντος ἔτη ι' (12 Eus.). τοῦ δὲ κόσμου ἦν ἔτος ‚δτνδ'.
Ἀθηναίων ιδ' ἐβασίλευσεν Ἀφίδας ἔτος ἕν (= Eus.). τοῦ δὲ κόσμου ἦν ἔτος ‚δτξδ'.
25-27 Sync. (208,6-22 Moss.), cf. Eus., chron. (87,19-23 Karst) (= Castor FGrHist 250 F4) et can. (armen. 173-175 Karst; Hier. 64,17s; 65,3s; 66,23-25 Helm)
Ἀθηναίων ιε' ἐβασίλευσε Θυμοίτης ἔτη θ' (8 Eus.), Ἀφείδαντος ἀδελφός. τοῦ δὲ κόσμου ἦν ἔτος ‚δτξε'.
  Ἐπὶ τούτου ἡ τῶν Ἐρεχθειδῶν βασιλεία κατελύθη παρὰ Ἀθηναίοις Ἀττικῶν λεγομένη, καὶ μετῆλθεν εἰς ἕτερον γένος. Θυμοίτην γὰρ προσκαλεσαμένου Ξάνθου τοῦ Βοιωτίου καὶ μὴ ὑπακούσαντος τοῦ Θυμοίτου, Μέλανθος Ἀνδροπόμπου Πύλιος ἀναδεξάμενος ἐμονομάχησε καὶ νικήσας ἐβασίλευσεν. ἔνθεν Ἀθήνησιν ἡ τῶν Ἀπατουρίων ἑορτὴ ἄγεται διὰ τὸ σὺν ἀπάτῃ γενέσθαι τὴν νίκην. (cf. ps. Io.Ant. fr. 20*)
Ἀθηναίων ις' ἐβασίλευσε Μέλανθος Ἀνδροπόμπου Πύλιος ἔτη λζ' (= Eus.). τοῦ δὲ κόσμου ἦν ἔτος ‚δτοδ'.
Ἀθηναίων ιζ' ἐβασίλευσε Κόδρος Μελάνθου ἔτη κα' (= Eus.). τοῦ δὲ κόσμου ἦν ἔτος ‚δυια'.
  Ἐπὶ τούτου ἡ τῶν Ἡρακλειδῶν κάθοδος εἰς Πελοπόννησον γέγονεν, Ἴωνές τε εἰς Ἀθήνας κατέφυγον ἐκπεσόντες ἐξ Ἀχαΐας. Πελοποννήσιοι ἐστράτευσαν ἐπ' Ἀθήνας, οἷς ἑαυτὸν ἐξέδωκε διὰ χρησμὸν Κόδρος Μελάνθου, καὶ οὐκέτι βασιλεῖς, ἄρχοντες δὲ διὰ βίου τοῖς Ἀθηναίοις καθίσταντο.

25-28 cf. Eus., can.[Hier] 64[f]

29s transposuimus post l. 7 (cf. Sync. et Eus. supra in app.)

10. Theseus, son of Aigeus, 31 years.
11. Menestheus, 19 years.
12. Demophon, 35 years.
13. Oxyntes, 14 years.
14. Aphidas, 1 year.
15. Thymoites, 9 years.
16. Melanthus, 37 years.
17. Codrus, 21 years.

From Cecrops "the large" up to Codrus, there are 492 years. After Codrus, however, there were archons, just as they lived.[10]

---

10 Gr. (Frick): ἕως ἔζησαν ("for as long as they lived").

Principes diabii.
Post Codrum autem primus filius eius diabius factus est princeps Athineorum.

    I. Medrus Codri ann. XX.
    II. Acastus ann. XXXVIIII.
    III. Archippus ann. XIX.
    <Thersippus ann. XL.>
    IIII. Forbus ann. XXXIII.
    V. Megaclus ann. XXVIII.
    VI. Diognitus ann. XXVIII.
    VII. Fereclus ann. XV.
    VIII. Arifrus ann. XXX.

33s Sync. (208,23–29 Moss.), cf. Eus., chron. (87,27s Karst) (= Castor FGrHist 250 F4) et can. (armen. 175–177 Karst; Hier. 68,1–4; 69,7s Helm)

Ἀθηναίων ιη΄ ἐβασίλευσε Μέδων Κόδρου ἔτη κ΄ (= Eus.). οὗτος πρῶτός ἐστι τῶν διὰ βίου λεγομένων ἀρχόντων παρ᾽ Ἀθηναίοις. τοῦ δὲ κόσμου ἦν ἔτος ͵δυλβ΄.

Ἀθηναίων ιθ΄ ἄρχων β΄ Ἄκαστος Μέδοντος ἔτη λε΄ (36 Eus.). τοῦ δὲ κόσμου ἦν ἔτος ͵δυνβ΄.

Ἐπὶ Ἀκάστου Ἰώνων ἀποικία. καὶ Ὅμηρος ἱστορεῖται γεγονὼς παρ᾽ Ἕλλησιν, ὡς τινές, οἱ δὲ ὀλίγῳ πρότερον καὶ ἄλλοι ὕστερον.

35–41 Sync. (217,6–20 Moss.), cf. Eus., chron. (87,32 – 88,7 Karst) (= Castor FGrHist 250 F4) et can. (armen. 177–179 Karst; Hier. 71,8s; 72,8s; 74,22s; 76,25s; 80,15s; 81,18s Helm)

Ἀθηναίων κ΄ ἐβασίλευσεν Ἄρχιππος Ἀκάστου ἔτη ιθ΄ (= Eus.). τοῦ δὲ κόσμου ἦν ἔτος ͵δυπζ΄.

Ἀθηναίων κα΄ ἐβασίλευσε Θέρσιππος Ἀρχίππου ἔτη μ΄ (41 can.[armen], - chron., can.[Hier]). τοῦ δὲ κόσμου ἦν ἔτος ͵δφς΄.

Ἀθηναίων κβ΄ ἐβασίλευσε Φόρβας Θερσίππου ἔτη λ΄ (= chron., 31 can.[Hier]). τοῦ δὲ κόσμου ἦν ἔτος ͵δφμς΄.

Ἀθηναίων κγ΄ ἐβασίλευσε Μεγακλῆς Φόρβαντος ἔτη κη΄ (30 Eus.). τοῦ δὲ κόσμου ἦν ἔτος ͵δφος΄.

Ἀθηναίων κδ΄ ἐβασίλευσε Διόγνητος Μεγακλέους ἔτη κη΄ (= Eus.). τοῦ δὲ κόσμου ἦν ἔτος ͵δχδ΄.

Ἀθηναίων κε΄ ἐβασίλευσε Φερεκλῆς Διογνήτου ἔτη ιθ΄ (= Eus.). τοῦ δὲ κόσμου ἦν ἔτος ͵δχλβ΄.

Ἀθηναίων κς΄ ἐβασίλευσεν Ἀρίφρων Φερεκλέους ἔτη κ΄ (= chron., can.[Hier], can.[armen]), (→ T54e) κατὰ δὲ Ἀφρικανὸν ἔτη λα΄. κατὰ τοῦτον τὸν Ἀρίφρονα ἡ τῶν Ἀσσυρίων κατελύθη ἀρχή, ὡς πάντες συμφωνοῦσι. τοῦ δὲ κόσμου ἦν ἔτος ͵δχνα΄.

41 → T49b; T54e

31s cf. Eus., can.[Hier] 68,1–4 **33–45** Io. Mal. 4,5

35 XIX Sync. Eus. *XL* cod. **36** transposuimus a l. 44 (cf. numerum annorum in Sync. et Eus.)
41 XXX] *31* Sync. (T54e,2)

Archons for life.[11]
After Codrus, his son was the first to became archon of the Athenians for life.

    1. Medon, son of Codrus, 20 years.
    2. Acastus, 39 years.
    3. Archippus, 19 years.
    <Thersippus, 40 years.>
    4. Phorbas, 33 years.
    5. Megacles, 28 years.
    6. Diognetus, 28 years.
    7. Pherecles, 15 years.
    8. Ariphron, 30 years.[12]

---

11 Gr. (Frick): διὰ βίου.
12 Cf. Sync. (T54e), who states that Africanus assigned 31 years to Ariphron.

VIIII. Thispeus ann. XL.
X. Agamistor ann. XXVI.
{XI. Thersippus ann. XXIII.}
XII. Eschylus ann. <XIIII.>
     Eschylo anno secundo prima olympiada adducta est a Grecis.

Colliguntur uero ab initio regni Cecropi in prima olympiada anni octingenti XIIII.

Post Eschylum autem illi:

XIII. Almeus ann. X.
XIIII. Corops ann. X.
XV. Esimidus ann. X.
XVI. Celdicus ann. X.
XVII. Ippomenus ann. X.
XVIII. Leocratis ann. X.

42–46 Sync. (230,20 – 231,4 Moss.), cf. Eus., chron. (88,9–17 Karst) (= Castor FGrHist 250 F4) et can. (armen. 180–182 Karst; Hier. 82,24–26; 84,15s; 85,24s Helm)
Ἀθηναίων κζ' ἐβασίλευσε Θεσπιεὺς Ἀρίφρονος ἔτη κζ' (= can.[Hier], - chron., can.[armen]), κατὰ δὲ ἄλλους ἔτη μ'. τοῦ δὲ κόσμου ἦν ἔτος ͵δχοα'.
Ἀθηναίων κη' ἐβασίλευσεν Ἀγαμίστωρ Θεσπιέως ἔτη ιζ' (= chron., 20 can.[Hier], can.[armen]), κατὰ δὲ ἄλλους ἔτη κζ'. τοῦ δὲ κόσμου ἦν ἔτος ͵δχρη'.
(de Thersippo vide supra ad l. 36)
Ἀθηναίων κθ' ἐβασίλευσεν Αἰσχύλος ἔτη ιδ' (23 Eus.). τοῦ δὲ κόσμου ἦν ἔτος ͵δψιε'.
Αἰσχύλου τῷ β' ἔτει πληρουμένῳ καὶ ἀρχομένῳ τῷ γ' αὐτοῦ ἔτει,
ὃς ἦν κθ' βασιλεὺς Ἀθηναίων ἀπὸ τοῦ α' αὐτῶν Κέκροπος τοῦ διφυοῦς, ιβ' δὲ τῶν διὰ βίου ἀρχόντων, ἡ πρώτη Ὀλυμπιὰς ἤχθη κατὰ τὸ ͵δψκα' ἔτος ἀπὸ Ἀδάμ, Ἀζαρίου δὲ βασιλέως Ἰούδα ἔτει λθ', ὡς πρόκειται. **45s** → F64c.d

50–57 Sync. (250,21 – 251,16 Moss.), cf. Eus., chron. (88,20–24 Karst) (= Castor FGrHist 250 F4) et can. (armen. 182–184 Karst; Hier. 88,3s; 88,7s; 89,5s; 90,1s; 90,14s; 91,7s; 92,3s; 92,19s Helm)
Ἀθηναίων λ' ἐβασίλευσεν Ἀλκμαίων ἔτη β' (= Eus.). τοῦ δὲ κόσμου ἦν ἔτος ͵δψκθ'.
  Ἐπὶ τούτου Ἀθήνησιν ἡ διὰ βίου κατελύθη ἀρχή. μετὰ Ἀλκμαίωνα τὸν λ' βασιλέα Ἀθηναίων κατεστάθησαν ἄρχοντες δεκαετεῖς ζ'.
Ὧν πρῶτος ἄρχων δεκαετὴς Ἀθηναίων λα' Χάροψ Αἰσχύλου ἔτη ι' (= Eus.). οὗτος πρῶτος δεκαετής. τοῦ δὲ κόσμου ἦν ἔτος ͵δψλα'.
Ἀθηναίων λβ' ἐβασίλευσεν Αἰσιμίδης ἔτη ι' (= Eus.). τοῦ δὲ κόσμου ἦν ἔτος ͵δψμα'.
Ἀθηναίων λγ' ἐβασίλευσε Κλεόδικος ἔτη ι' (= Eus.). τοῦ δὲ κόσμου ἦν ἔτος ͵δψνα'.
Ἀθηναίων λδ' ἐβασίλευσεν Ἱππομένης ἔτη ι' (= Eus.). τοῦ δὲ κόσμου ἦν ἔτος ͵δψξα'.
Ἀθηναίων λε' ἐβασίλευσε Λεωκράτης ἔτη ι' (= Eus.). τοῦ δὲ κόσμου ἦν ἔτος ͵δψοα'.
Ἀθηναίων λς' ἐβασίλευσεν Ἄψανδρος ἔτη ι' (= Eus.). τοῦ δὲ κόσμου ἦν ἔτος ͵δψπα'.
Ἀθηναίων λζ' ἐβασίλευσεν Ἐρυξίας ἔτη ι' (= Eus.). τοῦ δὲ κόσμου ἦν ἔτος ͵δψρα'.

45–48 cf. Eus., can.[Hier] 85,24s; 86[b]

44 transposuimus post l. 35   **45** XIIII restituimus e Sync.

9. Thespieus, 40 years.
10. Agamestor, 26 years.
12. Aeschylus, <14>[13] years.
   In the second year of Aeschylus, the first Olympic games were celebrated by the Greeks.[14]

From the beginning of the reign of Cecrops up to the first Olympic games, there are therefore 814 years in all.[15]

After Aeschylus are the following:

13. Alcmaion, 10 years.
14. Charops, 10 years.
15. Aesimidus, 10 years.
16. Cleodicus, 10 years.
17. Hippomenes, 10 years.
18. Leocrates, 10 years.

---

13 The years of Aeschylus' reign are supplied from Sync. (see third app.); but cf. Eus. (F64c), who states that Africanus assigned 23 years to Aeschylus' reign. The figure of Syncellus is better suited to the overall chronology of the *Excerpta*'s list. Of the 907 total years of the Athenian kingdom (l. 59f and T54f), 814 belong to the period before the Olympiads (l. 47f). 80 of the 93 remaining years belong to the rule of the 10-year-archons, leaving 13 years for the reign of Aeschylus after the introduction of the Olympic games.
14 Latin literally: "… were introduced by the Greeks"; cf. Gr. (Frick): … πρώτη Ὀλυμπιὰς ἤχθη παρὰ τοῖς Ἕλλησιν.
15 The number 814 does not correspond exactly to the sum of the single figures. However, it fits well with Africanus' system, see above n. 3.

XVIIII. Apsandrus ann. X.
XX. Erygius ann. X.

Et cessauit regnum Athineorum in olympiada uicesima quarta. Fiunt uero omnem Athineorum fortitudinem a Cecropo usque Oxyrium ann. noningenti septem.

58 → F54d,4s 58-60 → T54f,5-7

58 cf. Eus., can.^Hier 93,12-16 (Ol. 24)

F54b Georgius Syncellus (78,18-25 Mosshammer)

Ὡς αὐτὸς Ἀφρικανὸς μεμαρτύρηκεν ἐν ἀρχῇ τοῦ τρίτου λόγου εἰπών·
 Ἀπὸ μὲν Ὠγύγου διὰ τὴν ἀπὸ τοῦ κατακλυσμοῦ πολλὴν φθορὰν ἀβασίλευτος ἔμεινεν ἡ νῦν Ἀττικὴ ἔτεσιν ρπθ'.
 Εἶτα Κέκροψ ὁ διφυὴς ἔτη ν'.
 Κραναὸς αὐτόχθων μετὰ Κέκροπα ἔτη θ'.
 Ὁμοῦ γίνονται ἀπὸ τοῦ ἐπὶ Ὠγύγου κατακλυσμοῦ ἐπὶ Κέκροπα πρῶτον βασιλέα Ἀθήνησι καὶ τὸν μετ' αὐτὸν δεύτερον Κραναὸν ἔτη σμη'. τὰ δ' αὐτὰ καὶ ἀπὸ τῆς ἐξόδου Μωυσέως καὶ Ἰσραὴλ ἐξ Αἰγύπτου ἕως τοῦ ἐπὶ Δευκαλίωνος κατακλυσμοῦ ἐν Θετταλίᾳ.

1-8 = T55,15-23 **2s** = F34,71s **2-5** → F54a,2-11; T57 **2s** Eus., chron. (85,15-17 Karst) Und nach Ogigos sei von wegen der großen Verwüstung durch die Sintflut ohne Königtum, *sagen sie*, gewesen das jetzt Attika *genannte bis zu Kekrops*, 190 (109 codd.) Jahre lang. → F54a,4s (206 anni) **4s** Io. Mal. 4,5 (51,70-72 Thurn) Ἐβασίλευσεν δὲ ὁ Κέκροψ τῶν Ἀθηναίων ἔτη ν', καὶ μετ' αὐτὸν ἐβασίλευσε Κραναὸς ἔτη θ'.

2-8 cf. Eus., chron. 85,15 - 86,23 (= Castor FGrHist 250 F4); Ecl. Hist. 176,14-18; Io. Ant. fr. 23.1; Io. Nic. 29; ps. Sym. f. 38^r = Cedr. 143,10-14 **6-8** cf. Sym. Log. (Leo Gr. 28,2-5 = Th. Mel. 26,27 - 27,2 ≈ Iul. Pol. 98,13s); ps. Sym. f. 25^v = Cedr. 26,15 - 27,2

[AB] **2** Μετὰ δὲ Ὠγυγον F34,71 **3** Ἀττικὴ + μέχρι Κέκροπος F34,72 | ἔτεσιν] ἔτη F34,72 **6** τοῦ < B | βασιλέα + ἐπὶ A

19. Apsandrus, 10 years.
20. Eryxias, 10 years.

The kingdom of the Athenians came to an end in the 24th Olympiad. Thus, for the entire rule[16] of the Athenians from Cecrops up to Eryxias,[17] there are 907 years.

F54b [18]

This Africanus himself has attested in the beginning of his third book:
> From the time of Ogygus, because of the great destruction wrought by the flood, what is now Attica remained without a king for 189 years.
> Then Cecrops the Double-Natured, 50 years.
> After Cecrops, indigenous Cranaus, 9 years.

Altogether from the flood at the time of Ogygus up to Cecrops the first king of Athens and Cranaus the second king after him, there are 248 years.[19] This same interval is also from the Exodus of Moses and Israel from Egypt up to the flood in Thessaly at the time of Deucalion.

---

16 Gr. (Frick): … γίνονται οὖν πάσης τῆς Ἀθηναίων δυναστείας…
17 Emended from Oxyrius.
18 This passage constitutes part of a longer discussion by Syncellus about the differing chronologies of the floods in Greece (T55). It is difficult to explain why the first two lines of this excerpt (ll. 2f) are identical to F34, 71f, even though they appear in a completely different context. The text in F34, which precedes a refutation of Philochorus, is independently supported by Eusebius and thus can be considered reliable. In the present text, Syncellus may have combined notices from two separate places in the *Chronographiae* (i.e. from the preface at the beginning of book 3, and then from the list of the Athenian rulers). It is also possible that the same notice about the 189 years without a king appeared twice in Africanus (in both instances based on the same source). In that case, one would have to assume that Syncellus' ascription of the notice to *the beginning* of his third book is erroneous. Since Africanus' treatment of the whole of Greek history came after Moses (F34,53–58), and hence after F34, it is hardly conceivable that the list of the Athenians preceded the material on the Argives, Sicyonians etc.
19 See below n. 1 to F54c and n. 1 to T55.

T54c Ioannes Malalas 3,11 (44,91–96 Thurn, ex quo Ioannes Antiochenus, fr. 23.1 [52 Roberto] et Ioannes Niciensis 29 [27,16–21 Charles])

Ἐν δὲ τοῖς χρόνοις Ἰησοῦ τοῦ Ναυῆ ἐκ τῆς φυλῆς τοῦ Ἰάφεθ ἐβασίλευσε τῆς Ἀττικῆς χώρας τὶς ὀνόματι Ὠγύγης, αὐτόχθων, ἔτη λβ'. καὶ γέγονε κατακλυσμὸς μέγας ἐν τῇ αὐτοῦ βασιλείᾳ, καὶ ἀπώλετο αὐτὸς καὶ πᾶσα ἡ χώρα ἐκείνη καὶ πᾶσα ψυχὴ οἰκοῦσα τὴν χώραν ἐκείνην τῆς Ἀττικῆς καὶ μόνης. καὶ ἔμεινεν ἐξ ἐκείνου ἔρημος καὶ ἀοίκητος ἡ αὐτὴ χώρα ἐπὶ ἔτη σς', καθὼς ἐν
5 τοῖς Ἀφρικανοῦ ἐμφέρεται συγγράμμασιν.

2–4 → F34,71s; F54b,2s; T55,16s   4 ἔτη σς' → F54a,4s

2–5   cf. Eus., chron. 85,15–17; Sym. Log. (Th. Mel. 26,27 – 27,2 = Leo Gr. 28,2–5); ps. Sym. f. 38ʳ = Cedr. 143,10–14; Ecl. Hist. 176,14–18

[OSl] 2   Ὠγύγης Chilm. Io. Ant. Γυγώγης O Γοιγύγης Sl Γύγης Cedr.   4 σς' Io. Ant. Io. Nic. σο' O σξ' Sl σ' Cedr.

F54d Georgius Syncellus (251,17–29 Mosshammer)

Ἕως τοῦδε τοῦ ͵δωα' ἔτους ἐξ Ἀδὰμ οἱ Ἀθηναίων βασιλεῖς πρῶτοι ιζ' καὶ μετ' αὐτοὺς οἱ διὰ βίου λεγόμενοι ἄρχοντες ιγ', ἔπειτα δεκαετεῖς ζ', ὁμοῦ πάντα λζ', κρατήσαντες τῆς Ἀθηναίων ἀρχῆς ἀπὸ τοῦ ͵γϡμε' κοσμικοῦ ἔτους ἐπαύσαντο, διαρκέσαντες ἐπὶ ἔτη ὅλα ͵ωνς'.

Μετὰ τούτους ἄρχοντες ἐνιαυσιαῖοι εὑρέθησαν ἐξ εὐπατριδῶν, ἐννέα τε ἀρχόντων Ἀθήνησιν
5 ἀρχὴ κατεστάθη· ἡ δὲ τῶν ἐνιαυσιαίων ἤρχθη τῷ ͵δωδ' ἔτει τοῦ κόσμου, Κρέοντος πρώτου ἄρχοντος ἡγησαμένου ἐπὶ τῆς ιθ' Ὀλυμπιάδος, οἱ δὲ ἐπὶ κε'. ἀφ' οὗ ἐπὶ σν' Ὀλυμπιάδα ἄρχοντες Ϡγ' μέχρι Φιλίνου, καθ' ὃν ὑπάτευον Γράτος Σαβινιανὸς Ῥωμαίων καὶ Σέλευκος ἀπὸ τῶν περὶ Βροῦττον μετὰ τοὺς βασιλεῖς ὑπατευσάντων ͵ψκε' καταριθμούμενοι ἐπὶ τὸ ͵εψκγ' ἔτος τοῦ κόσμου κατὰ τὸν Ἀφρικανόν, ὅπερ ἦν Ἀντωνίνου τοῦ
10 καὶ Ἀβίτου Ῥωμαίων βασιλέως ἔτος γ'.

2s → F54a,59s; T54f,5–7 (ambo 907 anni)   5s → F54a,58 (24 olym.)   6–10 → T11,5–7; F93,109s

5s cf. Eus., can.ᴴⁱᵉʳ 93,12–21 (Ol. 24); Eus., chron. 88,25–28 (= Castor FGrHist 250 F4) (Ol. 24)

[AB] 4   ἐνιαυσιαῖοι Moss. ἐνιαυσιαίων Di. ἐνιασίων AB   5   ἤρχθη B ἤρχθαι A | ͵δωδ'] ͵δωα' Gelzerᵐˢ   7 Ϡγ'] Ϡκγ' Goarᵐ | Σαβινιανὸς B σαβινιανοῦ A   8 ͵ψκε'] ͵ψκζ' Gelzer   9 τὸ B τῷ A
10 Ἀβίτου scripsimus Αὐγέντου AB Moss. Αὐγούστου Goar Αὐείτου Scal. Routh Gelzer

T54c

In the time of Joshua, the son of Nun, a man of the tribe of Japhet, named Ogygus, an original inhabitant of the country, reigned over the land of Attica for 32 years. In his reign a great flood occurred and Ogygus and all that land were destroyed, as was every soul living in that land of Attica, but only there. From that time the land remained barren and uninhabited for 206 years, as is related in the writings of Africanus.[1]

F54d[2]

Up to this year 4801 from Adam, the first kings of the Athenians numbered 17. After them came the 13 so-called archons for life, and then seven 10-year archons. Altogether there were 37 rulers, who ceased their rule after controlling the government of the Athenians from AM 3945, and lasting a total of 856 years.

After them, archons of one-year term were appointed from the aristocracy, and a government of nine archons was established at Athens. The government of annual archons was initiated in AM 4804, when Creon began his rule as the first archon in the 19th Olympiad. But some say it was in the 25th Olympiad. From him up to the 250th Olympiad, there were 903 archons extending to Philinus. Around his time, Gratus Sabinianus and Seleucus[3] were serving as consuls of the Romans. Beginning from those who around the time of Brutus served as consuls after the kings, 725 of them are counted up to AM 5723,[4] according to Africanus. This was the third year of Antoninus, also known as Avitus,[5] emperor of the Romans.[6]

---

1   The 189 years that F54b (= F34,71f) numbers from Ogygus to Cecrops probably begin with the death of Ogygus, and not with the flood in his time (according to F34,38f Ogygus did not die in the flood). If Malalas accurately adheres to Africanus' chronology, Ogygus would have survived the flood by 17 years.
2   Syncellus' account of Athenian rule from its inception up to the archonship of Philinus (preceding text in the 3rd app. to F54a) is a composite of Africanus and other sources. Africanus assigned 907 years to the Athenian kings and archons who ruled up to the time of Creon (= AM 3913 to AM 4820), see F54a,59f. According to ll. 1-6, the rule of the 37 Athenian kings and archons up to the archonship of Creon lasted 856 years, from AM 3945 to AM 4801. The ensuing description (ll. 6-10) of the rule of 903 one-year archons from Creon up to the third year of the reign of Antoninus Elagabalus (= AM 4820 to AM 5723) better reflects Africanus' reckoning.
3   C. Vettius Gratus Sabinianus and M. Flavius Vitellius Seleucus (AD 221).
4   Therefore, the rule of the consuls began in AM 4998. With the addition of the prior 245 years of the kings (F53), the founding of Rome would have occurred in AM 4753; for confirmation of this date, see F65,53, which states that Rome was founded in Ol. 7 = AM 4751-4754. Although Varro's (divergent) dating of the founding of Rome was widely accepted as a standard, Africanus did not follow it (see also T52).
5   Elagabalus, called M. Aurelius Antoninus, born as Varius Avitus (AD 218 May – AD 222 March).
6   The dates and names in ll. 6-10 are consistent with each other and with AD 221 (the year in which Africanus' *Chronographiae* ended and probably the date of its composition, see introduction, p. XVII).

T54e Georgius Syncellus (217,18s Mosshammer)

Ἀθηναίων κςʹ ἐβασίλευσεν Ἀρίφρων Φερεκλέους ἔτη κʹ, κατὰ δὲ Ἀφρικανὸν ἔτη λαʹ.

= T49b → F54a,41 (20 anni in Eus., cit. in app. ad F54a)

2 λαʹ] *30* F54a,41

T54f Ioannes Malalas 4,6 (51,76–84 Thurn)

Ἐν δὲ τοῖς χρόνοις τῶν ἀρχόντων ἐνομοθέτει Ἀθηναίους πρῶτος ὀνόματι Δράκων, καὶ μετ' αὐτὸν Σόλων, καὶ ἔλυσε τοὺς νόμους Δράκοντος Σόλων. καὶ πάλιν ἐνομοθέτησε Θαλῆς ὁ Μιλήσιος. καὶ πάλιν ἐβασίλευσεν αὐτῶν πρῶτος Αἰσχύλος ἔτη καʹ, καὶ μετὰ Αἰσχύλον ἐβασίλευσεν αὐτῶν Ἀκμαί-ων ἔτη δύο· περὶ οὗ Εὐριπίδης ὁ σοφώτατος δρᾶμα ἐξέθετο. καὶ μετὰ Ἀκμαίοντα ἐβασίλευσαν αὐ-
5 τῶν ἄλλοι ιηʹ ἕως Ἀρεξίωνος, ὃς ἐβασίλευσεν αὐτῶν ἔτη ιβʹ. **καὶ κατελύθη ἡ βασιλεία τῶν Ἀθηναίων, κρατήσασα ἔτη ⳨ζʹ, καθὼς Ἀφρικανὸς ὁ σοφώτατος χρονογράφος ἐξέθετο.**

2–5 → F64c   **5–7** → F54d,2s; Io. Ant. fr. 24.4,4 (60 Ro.) *καὶ ἐκράτησε* (sc. regnum Athenensium) *τὰ πάντα ἔτη ⳨πβʹ*

1s   cf. Clem. Alex., strom. 1,16,79,6; Eus., can.[Hier] 97g; 99g; Cyr., c. Iul. 1,15; Sync. 253,29; Suda Δράκων Δ 1495; Σόλων Σ 776   **1–4** cf. Exc. Eus. 139,12–18; Cedr. 145,17 – 146,1

[OSl]   **2** Θαλῆς Di. Θάλλης O   **3** ἔτη Chilm. ἔτος O | καὶ Ο ἓν καὶ μῆνας ιζʹ Cedr.   **3s** Ἀκμαίων OSl Ἀλκμαίων Sync. (in app. ad F54a,50)   **4** σοφώτατος + ποιητής Sl   **5** Ἀρεξίωνος O Σαροκσον Sl Ἐρυξίου Gelzer | ιβʹ O ιʹ Sl   **6** ⳨ζʹ] ⳨πβʹ Io. Ant.

T54e

The 26th ruler of the Athenians was Pherecles' son Ariphron, for 20 years, but according to Africanus 31 years.[1]

T54f

In the time of the archons, a man named Draco first enacted laws for the Athenians. Solon, who came after him, abolished Draco's laws. Thales the Milesian enacted laws once more, and Aeschylus was the first king to rule over them again, for 21 years. After Aeschylus, Acmaeon was their king, for two years. The most learned Euripides published a drama about him. After Acmaeon there were 18 others kings, up to Arexion, who was their king for 12 years. **The kingdom of the Athenians was abolished after lasting for 907 years, according to the exposition of Africanus, the most learned chronographer.**

---

1 The reference to Ariphron and the total years of his rule suggests that Africanus' chronicle included a complete list of Athenian rulers, see F54a, n. 1.

T55 Georgius Syncellus (78,4 – 79,22 Mosshammer)

(→ F46,143s) … Ὁμοῦ ἀπ' Ἀμὼς ἕως Μισφραγμουθώσεως ἀρχῆς κατὰ Ἀφρικανὸν γίνονται ἔτη ξθ', τοῦ γὰρ Ἀμὼς οὐδ' ὅλως εἶπεν ἔτη.

Εἰ δ' ἄρα γε κατὰ τὴν Εὐσεβίου στοιχείωσιν δῶμεν κε' ἔτη τοῦ Ἀμὼς καὶ κς' τοῦ Μισφραγμουθώσεως, ἢ κατὰ Ἀφρικανὸν καὶ Εὐσέβιον ἔσονται ἀπὸ ἀρχῆς
5 Ἀμὼς ἕως τέλους Μισφραγμουθώσεως ἔτη ρκ', ὅσα καὶ τῆς ζωῆς Μωυσέως πεπίστευται εἶναι. καὶ πῶς ἐστι δυνατὸν ἀπὸ τῆς ἀρχῆς Μωυσέως, εἴτουν τῆς ἐξ Αἰγύπτου πορείας, ἐὰν κατὰ τὸν Ἀμὼς δῶμεν αὐτὸν ἐξεληλυθέναι, ὡς Ἀφρικανῷ δοκεῖ, ἢ ἀπὸ τῆς νεότητος, ὡς αὐτὸς διαπορεῖ, ἕως τελευτῆς αὐτοῦ Μωυσέως τοὺς δύο κατακλυσμοὺς παρ' Ἕλλησι βεβοημένους γεγονέναι;
10 Λέγω δὴ τὸν πρῶτον ἐπὶ Ὠγύγου ἐν τῇ Ἀττικῇ καὶ τὸν ἐπὶ Δευκαλίωνος ἐν Θετταλίᾳ χρόνοις ὕστερον σμη', ἀναμφιλέκτως συμβάντα ἐπὶ Κραναοῦ αὐτόχθονος δευτέρου βασιλέως Ἀθήνησιν. ἵνα γὰρ ἐπὶ Ἀμὼς δῶμεν αὐτὸν γεγενῆσθαι, ὅπερ μᾶλλον συμφωνεῖ τοῖς Ἰνάχου χρόνοις, καὶ ἐπὶ Μισφραγμουθώσεως τετελευτηκέναι, διπλοῦς ὁ τῶν χρόνων πλείων πέφυκεν ἀριθμός.
15 Ὡς αὐτὸς Ἀφρικανὸς μεμαρτύρηκεν ἐν ἀρχῇ τοῦ τρίτου λόγου εἰπών·

Ἀπὸ μὲν Ὠγύγου διὰ τὴν ἀπὸ τοῦ κατακλυσμοῦ πολλὴν φθορὰν ἀβασίλευτος ἔμεινεν ἡ νῦν Ἀττικὴ ἔτεσιν ρπθ'.

Εἶτα Κέκροψ ὁ διφυὴς ἔτη ν'.

Κραναὸς αὐτόχθων μετὰ Κέκροπα ἔτη θ'.

20 Ὁμοῦ γίνονται ἀπὸ τοῦ ἐπὶ Ὠγύγου κατακλυσμοῦ ἐπὶ Κέκροπα πρῶτον βασιλέα Ἀθήνησι καὶ τὸν μετ' αὐτὸν δεύτερον Κραναὸν ἔτη σμη'. τὰ δ' αὐτὰ καὶ ἀπὸ τῆς ἐξόδου Μωυσέως καὶ Ἰσραὴλ ἐξ Αἰγύπτου ἕως τοῦ ἐπὶ Δευκαλίωνος κατακλυσμοῦ ἐν Θετταλίᾳ.

3-46 → F34; F46,131-144; T47   **4-9** → F34,75-86.96-102   **10-14** → T48; F50,3s; F54a,2-10
16s = F34,71s   **16-19** = F54b; → F54a,2-10; Eus., chron. (85,15-17 Karst) Und nach Ogigos sei von wegen der großen Verwüstung durch die Sintflut ohne Königtum, *sagen sie*, gewesen das jetzt Attika *genannte bis zu Kekrops*, 190 (109 codd.) Jahre lang.

10-12 cf. Marm. Par. FGrHist 239 A3s; Clem. Alex., strom. 1,21,136,4; Tat., orat. 39,2; Eus., can.[Hier] 42°; ps. Sym. f. 25[v] = Cedr. 26,15-27,2   **15-23** cf. Eus., chron. 85,15 - 86,23 (= Castor FGrHist 250 F4); Io. Nic. 29   **16s** cf. Ecl. Hist. 176,14-18; ps. Sym. f. 38[r] = Cedr. 143,10-14   **20-23** cf. Sym. Log. (Th. Mel. 26,27 - 27,2 = Leo Gr. 28,2-5 ~ Iul. Pol. 98,13s)

[AB] **1** ἀπ' Ἀμὼς ἕως Moss. ἀπὸ μωσέως AB ἐπὶ Ἀμώσεως τοῦ καὶ Di.   **2** εἶπεν Goar[m] εἰπεῖν AB   **3** τοῦ A τῷ B   **4** τοῦ A τῷ B | Μισφραγμουθώσεως Di. μισφραγμούθεως AB   **5** Μισφραγμουθώσεως Di. μισφραγμούθεος A μισφραγμούθεως B | ρκ' B κ' A   **6** εἴτουν Di. ἤτουν AB   **8** αὐτὸς Goar[m] αὔτως AB   **11** κραναόυ B κρανάο A   **13** Μισφραγμουθώσεως Goar[m] σφραγμούθεως A μισφραγμούθεως B   **16** Ἀπὸ μὲν Ὠγύγου] Μετὰ δὲ Ὤγυγον F34,71 | Ἀττικὴ + μέχρι Κέκροπος F34,72   **20** ἀπὸ τοῦ A ἀπὸ B   **21** ἀθήνησι B ἐπὶ ἀθήνησι A

T55 *The Chronology of the Floods among the Greeks*

(→ F46,143f) ... Total from Amos to the rule of Misphragmuthosis according to Africanus 69 years. Of the length of Amos' rule, he said nothing at all.

Let us, then following Eusebius' calculation, ascribe 25 years to Amos' reign and 26 years to Misphragmuthosis'. Following both Africanus and Eusebius, there will thus be 120 years from the beginning of Amos' rule up to the end of Misphragmuthosis'; this we are assured was the length of Moses' life. Now how can it be that from the beginning of Moses' rule—that is, from the Exodus out of Egypt, if we grant Africanus' opinion that he left during the reign of Amos, or from his youth (this is also a dilemma for Africanus)—up to the death of this same Moses, there occurred two famous floods among the Greeks?

I mean, of course, the first flood at the time of Ogygus in Attica and the one during the time of Deucalion in Thessaly, 248 years later—this later flood unquestionably occurring during the reign of the indigenous Cranaus, the second king of Athens. Let us grant that Moses was born at the time of Amos, which is roughly contemporary with the time of Inachus, and died at the time of Misphragmuthosis; then the elapsed period turns out to be more than double [his age at death].

This Africanus himself has attested in the beginning of his third book:

From the time of Ogygus, because of the great destruction wrought by the flood, what is now Attica remained without a king for 189 years.

Then Cecrops the Double-Natured, 50 years.

After Cecrops, indigenous Cranaus, 9 years.

Altogether from the flood at the time of Ogygus up to Cecrops the first king of Athens and Cranaus the second king after him, there are 248 years. This same interval is also from the Exodus of Moses and Israel from Egypt up to the flood in Thessaly at the time of Deucalion.[1]

---

1   This statement is not from Africanus, but from Syncellus. The sum of 248 years from the flood of Ogygus to the end of Cranaus does not fit with the information we have in F54a,4f, in T54c,4f (206 years from the flood of Ogygus to Cecrops + 50 years Cecrops + 9 years Cranaus = 267 years) and in F34,40f; see n. 3 to F54a and n. 1 to T54c. Syncellus may have arrived at the total of 248 years by confusing the date of the flood of Ogygus with the death of Ogygus 17 years later (189 + 50 + 9).

Ὅ τε γὰρ ἐπὶ Ὠγύγου κατακλυσμὸς ἐπὶ Φορωνέως καὶ τῆς ἀπ' Αἰγύπτου πορείας τοῦ λαοῦ ἱστορεῖται τῷ αὐτῷ Ἀφρικανῷ, καὶ ὁ ἐπὶ Δευκαλίωνος ἐπὶ Κραναοῦ δευτέρου βασιλέως Ἀθήνησιν, ὡς ἐκ τῶν αὐτοῦ συγγραμμάτων ἀποδέδεικται. οὐκ ἄρα καλῶς ἐπὶ Μισφραγμουθώσεως τὸν ἐπὶ Δευκαλίωνος λέγει κατακλυσμόν.

Ὁ γὰρ Μισφραγμούθωσις μετὰ τὸν Ἄμωσιν πρῶτον βασιλέα κατ' αὐτὸν καὶ
κατὰ τὸν Εὐσέβιον τῆς ιη' δυναστείας μόλις πε' χρόνοις ὕστερον καταλήγει.
ὑπολείπεται δὴ λοιπὸν ἡμῖν λογίζεσθαι τὸν ἐπὶ Ὠγύγου κατακλυσμὸν ἐπὶ Μισφραγμουθώσεως γεγονέναι μᾶλλον, ἐφ' οὗ καὶ Μωυσῆς καθ' ἡμᾶς καὶ ἄλλους
ἀκριβεστέρους ἐκπεπόρευται τῆς Αἰγύπτου σὺν τῷ λαῷ.

Ὅπερ Ἀφρικανός, συγγνώτω μοι, διαπορήσας ἀντὶ τοῦ ἐπὶ Ὠγύγου τὸν ἐπὶ
Δευκαλίωνος εἴρηκεν ἑαυτῷ ἀντιπίπτων. καὶ οὕτω μὲν ἐν τούτῳ διήμαρτεν οὐ
συλλογισάμενος ἀκριβῶς ὅτι Κέκροψ ὁ διφυὴς καὶ Κραναὸς οἱ πρῶτοι βασιλεῖς
Ἀθηναίων μετὰ Ὤγυγον, ἐφ' ὧν καὶ ὁ ἐπὶ Δευκαλίωνος γέγονε κατακλυσμὸς ἐν
Θετταλίᾳ, μετὰ Μισφραγμούθωσιν ἦσαν χρόνοις ὕστερον τοὐλάχιστον ρν', ὡς
αὐτὸς μαρτυρῶν ἀποδέδεικται.

Σαφῶς δὴ ἔκ τε τῶν Εὐσεβίου παραλογισμῶν πρὸς τοὺς βελτίονας αὐτοῦ,
οἷς ἀντιπίπτων ἀμαρτύρως τὰ δοκοῦντα αὐτῷ συνέγραψεν, ἔκ τε τῶν Ἀφρικανῷ λελεγμένων, ὀρθῶς μὲν ἐν οἷς ἐμμαρτύρως εἴρηκε κατὰ Ἴναχον καὶ Φορωνέα γενέσθαι Μωυσέα, διηπορημένως δὲ ἐν οἷς ἢ νέον αὐτὸν ἐπὶ Ἀμώσιος
εἶναι κατηναγκάσθη παρὰ τῆς ἀληθείας φάναι ἢ τῆς Αἰγύπτου ἐκπορευθῆναι,
παρέστη ἡμῖν ὅτι ἐπὶ Μισφραγμουθώσεως ἡγήσατο τοῦ λαοῦ, τοῦ καὶ Ἀμώσιος,
καὶ ὅτι ἐπ' αὐτοῦ καὶ ὁ ἐπὶ Ὠγύγου γέγονε κατακλυσμός.

24s → F34,26–29.38–40.96–102; T48; F50a,5–7   **27s** et **34s** → F46,141s   **29s** → F46,131–144
40–42 → T46a.b   **41–44** → F46,132–135   **45s** → T47,21–23

24s cf. Sync. 173,13–17   **24–28** cf. Eus., chron. 86,15–22; Eus., can.[Hier] 12,17s; Sync. 184,10s

27 μισφραγμουθώσεως A μισφραγμούθεως B   **30** πε' χρόνοις B κε' χρόνους A   **34s** ἐπὶ δευκαλίωνος B δευκαλίωνος A   **35** εἴρηκεν Goar[m] εἰρηκέναι AB | ἀντιπίπτων A ἀντιπίπτον B   **37** ὧν B ὂν A   **38** ἦσαν B ἤγουν A   **40** αὐτοῦ B αὐτῶν A   **42** λελεγμένων B λεγομένων A

It is recorded by this same Africanus that the flood at the time of Ogygus occurred during the reign of Phoroneus and the Exodus of the people from Egypt. And Deucalion's flood, he says, occurred during the reign of Cranaus, the second king of Athens, as has been shown from his own writings. Therefore, he is not correct in saying that Deucalion's flood occurred during the reign of Misphragmuthosis.

For after Amosis, who according to both Africanus and Eusebius was the first king of the 18th dynasty, Misphragmuthosis ended his rule scarcely 85 years later. The logical remaining conclusion, then, that we reach from this is that it was rather Ogygus' flood that occurred during the reign of Misphragmuthosis; and in our opinion and that of other more accurate historians, it was during his reign that Moses left Egypt with his people.

Thus, Africanus—may he excuse me for saying this—found himself in a dilemma and in a self-contradiction asserted that it was Deucalion's flood instead of Ogygus'. And in this particular matter, he thereby committed an error; for he did not draw the proper conclusion from the fact that Cecrops the Double-Natured and Cranaus, the first kings after Ogygus of the Athenians, in whose time Deucalion's flood did in fact occur in Thessaly, were, as he himself has attested, at least 150 years after Misphragmuthosis.[2]

So this is clear: (i) compared with his superiors, Eusebius' reasoning was defective, and in contradicting them he recorded opinions without evidence; (ii) what Africanus said is accurate, in that he has evidence in support of his statement that Moses was contemporary with Inachus and Phoroneus. But he found himself in a dilemma, in that he was forced by the truth to say that during the reign of Amosis, Moses was either still a youth, or that he left from Egypt. From these two points, we have demonstrated that Moses was leader of his people during the reign of Misphragmuthosis, also known as Amosis, and that it was during his reign that Ogygus' flood occurred.

---

2 On the synchronism of Deucalion's flood with the reign of Misphragmuthosis, see Africanus' version of Manetho (F46,141f). But cf. T36, where Syncellus states that Africanus dated Deucalion's flood in the 70th year of Ehud. For discussion of Africanus' dating of the flood of Deucalion, see above T36, n. 1; Gelzer 1,120.127f; Adler/Tuffin 2002,101, n. 1.

F56 Georgius Syncellus (175,3-15 Mosshammer)

Ἀφρικανοῦ·

Καλλίθυια Πείραντος ἐν Ἄργει πρῶτον ἱεράτευσε τῆς Ἥρας. τούτοις τοῖς χρόνοις Ἄτλας ὁ Προμηθέως ἀδελφὸς ἄριστος ἀστρολόγος διέλαμπεν, ὡς ἐπιστήμης ἕνεκεν τὸν οὐρανὸν αὐτὸν φέρειν πεφήμισται. Εὐριπίδης δὲ τὸν Ἄτλαν-
5 τα ὄρος εἶναί φησιν ὑπερνεφές.

Οὗτος κατὰ τοὺς χρόνους Γοθονιὴλ ἤκμαζεν, ὡς μαρτυροῦσι πάντες οἱ ἐκ τοῦ καθ' ἡμᾶς λόγου ἱστορικοί, ἐν οἷς καὶ Ἀφρικανός φησιν· οἱ ἀπὸ τῆς Κουρητείας τῆς νῦν Ἀκαρνανίας Κουρῆτες καὶ Κορύβαντες Κνωσσὸν ᾤκισαν, οἱ τὴν ἐν ὅπλοις εὔρυθμον κίνησιν εὑρόντες. τούτοις τοῖς χρόνοις Σύρος ἱστορεῖται γεγονέναι γηγενής, οὗ ἐπώνυ-
10 μος ἡ Συρία. ἄλλοι δὲ πρότερον ἔτεσιν ρ'. καὶ περὶ Προμηθέως δὲ καὶ Ἐπιμηθέως τὸ αὐτὸ διαφόρως ἱστοροῦσι καὶ Ἄτλαντος Ἄργου τε τοῦ Πανόπτου καὶ Ἰοῦς τῆς Προμηθέως θυγατρός. οἱ μὲν γὰρ ὅτι κατὰ Κέκροπα τὸν διφυῆ γεγόνασιν, οἱ δ᾽ ὅτι πρότερον ἔτεσιν ξ', ἄλλοι δὲ ρ'.

2 Eus., can.[Hier] (37ᶜ Helm) In Argis primus sacerdotio functus est Callithias, Pirantis *filius*. 2-5 Eus., can.[Hier] (37ᵈ Helm) Atlans, frater Promethei, praecipuus astrologus fuit. Qui ob eruditionem disciplinae etiam caelum sustinere dictus est. Euripides autem montem esse altissimum adfirmat, qui Atlans vocetur. Exc. Barb. (228,12-15 Frick) Atlas autem, Promitheus frater, amabilis astrologus fulgebat: per disciplinam eius et caelum illi fertur deponi. Euripidus autem poeta super nubes dixit Atlatum esse. Ecl. Hist. (188,7-9 Cramer) Ἄτλας δὲ *μέγιστος ἀστρολόγος διεφημίζετο· ἐπιστήμης δὲ ἕνεκα φέρειν αὐτὸν ἐπὶ τῆς κεφαλῆς τὸν οὐρανὸν ἱστοροῦσιν*. 6s = T56a 7-9 Eus., can.[Hier] (42ᵍ Helm) Curetes et Corybantes Cnosson condiderunt, qui modulatam et inter se concinentem in armis saltationem reppere. 9s Ecl. Hist. (187,28 Cramer) Κατὰ τοῦτον (sc. Iosue) *ἱστορεῖται γεγονέναι Σύρος, οὗ ἡ Συρία ἐπώνυμος*. Eus., can.[Hier] (38ᶜ Helm, ante Moysis tempora) *His regnantibus* Syrus fuisse perhibetur indigena, ex cuius vocabulo Syria nomen accepit. 10-13 → F34, 89.103s; Eus., can.[Hier] (40ᵉ Helm, in tempore infantiae Moysis) Quidam scribunt Prometheum et Epimetheum et Atlantem fratrem Promethei et Argum cuncta cernentem et Io filiam Promethei his fuisse temporibus, alii uero aetate Cecropis, nonnulli ante Cecropem annis LX siue nonaginta. 12 → F54a,6s

2 cf. Eus., praep. ev. 3,8,1 (= Plut., de Daed. Plat.) 2-4 cf. Diod. Sic. 3,60,2; Io. Mal. 4,3; Io. Ant. fr. 24.1 4s Euripides TGFr 1116 7-9 cf. Diod. Sic. 5,65,2-4 10-13 cf. Io. Mal. 4,3; Io. Ant. fr. 24.1; Ecl. Hist. 188,3s (ambo in tempore presbyterorum); Exc. Barb. 228,6-9; Anon. Matr. 14,8-11

[A B[(l. 7-13)]] 2 Καλλίθυια Πείραντος Goarᵐ καλλιθυσία σπείραντος A cf. *Callithias* Hier. | ἱεράτευσε Scal. ἱερατεῦσαι A 5 φησιν Scal. φασιν A 6 Γοθονιὴλ Di. γαθονιὴλ A 7 ἐν οἷς incipit B post unum folium omissum 8 Κνωσσὸν Di. κνώσον AB | ᾤκισαν Scal. ᾤκησαν AB 11 Ἄργου Scal. ἄργος A ἄργους B 11s Ἄργου…θυγατρός Routh ~ (Ἄ. τε καὶ Ἰ. τ. Π. θ. καὶ Π.) AB 13 οἱ δ᾽ B οὐδ᾽ A

F56 *Atlas and Prometheus*

From Africanus:

Peiras' daughter Callithuia began the priesthood of Hera in Argos. At this time, Atlas the brother of Prometheus achieved wide notice as an outstanding astrologer, so that on account of his knowledge it was reported that he carried the heaven itself. But Euripides states that Mount Atlas rises above the clouds.

This man was flourishing at the time of Gothoniel, as all the historians who belong to our doctrine attest, including Africanus, who says: The Curetes from Cureteia (now known as Acarnania) and the Corybantes inhabited Cnossus, and they discovered the art of co-ordinating the movement of men under arms. At this time, Syrus is reported to have been indigenously born, after whom Syria is named. Others say that it was 100 years earlier. There are similarly divergent reports about both Prometheus and Epimetheus, in addition to Atlas, as well as both all-seeing Argus and Io, the daughter of Prometheus. Some say that they were contemporary with Cecrops the Double-Natured; others that they were 60 years earlier, others 90 years earlier.[1]

---

1 Africanus reports conflicting traditions about the date of Prometheus. For Prometheus as a contemporary of Cecrops, see F54a,6f (with n. 5 ad loc.); the same notice puts the beginning of Cecrops' rule 206 years after the Exodus (= AM 3913). Elsewhere (F34,103f), Africanus mentions an opposing tradition dating Prometheus 94 years after the Exodus (= AM 3801). This date is consistent with l. 6f above, according to which Prometheus' brother Atlas was a contemporary of Gothoniel, the judge of Israel about 100 years after the Exodus.

T56a Georgius Syncellus (175,7s Mosshammer)

(→ F56,5) … Οὗτος (sc. Atlas) κατὰ τοὺς χρόνους Γοθονιὴλ ἤκμαζεν, ὡς μαρτυροῦσι πάντες οἱ ἐκ τοῦ καθ' ἡμᾶς λόγου ἱστορικοί, ἐν οἷς καὶ Ἀφρικανός φησιν· … (→ F56,7)

→ F34,103s

[AB²ˢ] **1** Γοθονιὴλ Di. γαθονιὴλ A   **2** ἐν οἷς incipit B post unum folium omissum

T57 Georgius Syncellus (75,13–15 Mosshammer)

Ἴναχος δὲ κατὰ τὴν Εὐσεβίου σύνθεσιν ἔτεσι τριακοσίοις προτερεύει Κέκροπος· οὕτω δὲ σχεδὸν καὶ κατὰ τὸν Ἀφρικανόν.

→ F34,53–56; F50,3s.26–31; F54a,4s.47

2 cf. Exc. Eus. 134,6–10; Eus., can.^Hier. 27,10–13; 41,6–9; Ecl. Hist. 175,17–23

F58

F58a Excerpta Barbari (304,1–24 Frick)

Tempora regni Lacedemoniorum

Regnauerunt et Lacedemonii per annos CCCXXV et defecerunt in prima olympiada quae facta est sub Achaz regem Iudae in diebus Esaiae prophetae, sicut scirent eorum initium ab Erystheum initiatum.
5   Anno uisesimo Sahul initiauerunt Lacedemoniorum reges, et defecerunt in anno primo Achaz rcgi Iude, in quo tempore prima olympiada a Grecis adducta est.

2–4 → F59a,5–7   **2s et 6** → F64a.b   **5** → F34,66; F35,1; F59a,20s; F59b,1s

5s cf. Eus., chron. 105,30s; 106,17s; Eus., can.^Hier 86^f

T56a

(→ F56,5) ... This man (sc. Atlas) was flourishing at the time of Gothoniel, as all the historians who belong to our doctrine attest, including Africanus, who says: ... (→ F56,7)

T57 *The Years from Inachus to Cecrops*

Now according to Eusebius' own system, Inachus preceded Cecrops by 300 years and in this calculation he roughly approximates Africanus.[1]

F58 *The Kings of the Lacedaemonians*

F58a[2]

The chronology of the kingdom of the Lacedaemonians

The Lacedaemonians reigned for 325 years, and came to an end in the first Olympiad,[3] which occurred during the reign of Ahaz, king of Judah, in the days of Isaiah the prophet. One can thus know that their rule began with Eurystheus.[4]

In the 20th year of Saul, the kings of the Lacedaemonians began their rule, and came to an end in the first year of Ahaz, king of Judah, at which time the first Olympiad was introduced by the Greeks.[5]

---

1 From the preserved material the time-span from Inachus to Cecrops can be calculated with precision: 105 years from 1 Inachus to 55 Phoroneus (= the date of the Exodus, F50,3–7) + 206 years from 55 Phoroneus to 1 Cecrops (F54a,4f) = 311 years.
2 This excerpt contains the characteristic elements of Africanus' system. For Africanus' synchronization of 1 Ahaz with Ol. 1.1 (l. 2), see also F64a.b. The 325-year duration of the Lacedaemonian kingdom found in l. 2 also reflects Africanus' reckoning, as it is reported in Malalas (F58b,6f). For other features of this list consistent with Africanus' chronology, see n. 5 below. For the attribution of this list to Africanus, see also Frick 1880,8f; Gelzer 1,141–144.
3 Since Ol. 1,1 is AM 4727, the date of the beginning of the Lacedaemonian kingdom 325 years earlier would be AM 4402.
4 The meaning of the Latin text is unclear. Cf. Gr. (Frick): ὡς εἰδέναι αὐτῶν ἀρχὴν ἀπὸ Εὐρυσθέως ἀρξαμένην.
5 This information reflects Africanus' chronology: From the Exodus, Africanus counts 675 years to the first year of the reign of Saul (40 years for Moses after the Exodus + 25 years for Joshua + 30 years for the elders after Joshua + 490 years for the judges + 90 years for Eli and Samuel, F34,61–65), therefore 695 years to 20 Saul. On the other hand, there are 1020 years from the Exodus to 1 Ahaz (= Ol. 1,1), F34,68f. The difference of 325 is the number given here for the duration of the Lacedaemonian kingdom.

{I.} Illa autem singillatim regnorum haec.
II. Erystheus ann. XLII.
III. Egeus ann. II.
IIII. Echestratus ann. XXXIIII.
Labotus ann. XXXVII.
V. Dorystheus ann. XXVIIII.
VI. Agisilaus ann. XXX.
VII. Cemenelaus ann. XLIIII.
VIII. Archelaus ann. LX.
VIIII. Celeclus ann. XL.
X. Alcamanus ann. XXVII.
{XI. Automedus ann. XXV.}

Simul reges Lacedemioniorum permanserunt in regno annos CCCL. Et Lacedemoniorum regnum dissipatum est.

8-12   Sync. (209,2-12 Moss.), cf. Eus., chron. (105,24-27 Karst) et can. (armen. 174-176 Karst; Hier. 66,9-11; 68,19s; 68,22s; 70,22s; 72,22s Helm)
Λακεδαιμονίων α' ἐβασίλευσεν Εὐρυσθεὺς ἔτη μβ' (= Eus.). τοῦ δὲ κόσμου ἦν ἔτος ͵δυκγ'.
Εὐρυσθεὺς καὶ Προκλῆς Σπάρτης ἐκράτησαν.
Λακεδαιμονίων β' ἐβασίλευσεν Ἆγις ἔτος α' (= Eus.). τοῦ δὲ κόσμου ἦν ἔτος ͵δυξε'.
Λακεδαιμονίων γ' ἐβασίλευσεν Ἐχέστρατος ἔτη λε' (= can.armen, 31 chron., can.Hier). τοῦ δὲ κόσμου ἦν ἔτος ͵δυξς'.
Λακεδαιμονίων δ' ἐβασίλευσε Λαβώτης ἔτη λζ' (= Eus.). τοῦ δὲ κόσμου ἦν ἔτος ͵δφα'.
Λακεδαιμονίων ε' ἐβασίλευσε Δόρυσθος ἔτη κθ' (= chron., can.Hier,- can.armen). τοῦ δὲ κόσμου ἦν ἔτος ͵δφλη'.
13-17   Sync. (217,22 - 218,7 Moss.), cf. Eus., chron. (105,28s Karst) et can. (armen. 178-180 Karst; Hier. 74,16s; 77,14s; 81,8s; 83,21-23 Helm)
Λακεδαιμονίων ς' ἐβασίλευσεν Ἀγησίλαος ἔτη μδ' (= Eus.). τοῦ δὲ κόσμου ἦν ἔτος ͵δφξζ'.
Λακεδαιμονίων ζ' ἐβασίλευσεν Ἀρχέλαος ἔτη ξ' (= Eus.). τοῦ δὲ κόσμου ἦν ἔτος ͵δχια'.
Λακεδαιμονίων η' ἐβασίλευσε Τήλεκλος ἔτη μ' (= Eus.). τοῦ δὲ κόσμου ἦν ἔτος ͵δχοα'.
Λακεδαιμονίων θ' ἐβασίλευσεν Ἀλκαμένης ἔτη λζ' (= can.Hier; 38 chron.; 37 can.armen). οὗτος τελευταῖός ἐστι τῆς πρώτης οἰκίας. τῆς δὲ δευτέρας οἰκίας κατὰ τοὺς αὐτοὺς χρόνους ἐβασίλευσαν ἐξ βασιλεῖς. τοῦ δὲ κόσμου ἦν ἔτος ͵δψια'.
Ἀπολλόδωρος Λυκούργου νόμιμα ἐν τῷ η' Ἀλκαμένους. ἐν Λακεδαιμονίᾳ πρῶτος ἔφορος κατεστάθη.

8-18   cf. Eus., reg. ser.armen 150; Eus., reg. ser.Hier 26s; Eus., chron. 106,7-16; Chron. Synt. 88; Diod. Sic. 7,8,1 = Apollodorus FGrHist 244 F62; Cedr. 215,23 - 216,2   19 cf. Mich. Syr. 4,15

14 Cemenelaus] καὶ Μενέλαος Gelzer 1,142   **18** delevimus, cf. Gelzer 1,141.146

{1.} Their reigns one after the other are the following:
2. Eurystheus, 42 years.
3. Agis, 2 years.
4. Echestratus, 34 years.
Labotes, 37 years.[6]
5. Dorystheus, 29 years.
6. Agesilaus, 30 years.
7. And Menelaus[7], 44 years.
8. Archelaus, 60 years.
9. Teleclus, 40 years.
10. Alcamenes, 27 years.
{11. Automedus, 25 years.}[8]

Altogether the kings of the Lacedaemonians remained in power for 350 years.[9] And the kingdom of the Lacedaemonians was destroyed.

6 The omission of a number for the reign of Labotus was probably intended to correct the error committed at the beginning of the list.
7 Cemenelaus is a misunderstanding of καὶ Μενέλαος.
8 The name Automedus, unknown in parallel lists of Lacedaemonian kings, has probably been mistakenly transferred from the list of the kings of Corinth (Automenus in F59a,10).
9 The number of 350 years can also be found in Eusebius (can.[armen] 181,1) and Syncellus (218,19f). However, it presupposes that the reign of the Lacedaemonians continued under king Alcamenes some time after Ol. 1,1, which is in contrast with Africanus' opinion (ll. 2f).

F58b Ioannes Malalas 4,20 (65,37–40 Thurn)

Ἐν αὐτοῖς δὲ τοῖς χρόνοις ἐβασίλευσεν τῶν Λακεδαιμονίων πρῶτος Εὐρυσθεὺς ἔτη μβ΄,
καὶ ἄλλοι βασιλεῖς μετ' αὐτὸν η΄, ὁμοῦ ἐβασίλευσαν ἔτη σμς΄,
καὶ ὁ Ἀλκαμένης ἔτη λζ΄.

5 Καὶ κατέσχεν ἡ βασιλεία Λακεδαιμονίων τὰ πάντα ἔτη τκε΄,
ὡς Ἀφρικανὸς ὁ σοφώτατος συνεγράψατο.

1–5 Iul. Pol. (102,10s Hardt) *Τῷ ιδ' ἔτει Φυλιστιαίων ἦρξεν ἡ Λακεδαιμονίων βασιλεία ἐπὶ ἔτη τκδ', ἧς πρῶτος ἐβασίλευσεν Ἐρυσθεύς.*

1–5 cf. Cedr. 215,23 – 216,2; Mich. Syr. 4,15

[OSl] **1–2** Εὐρυσθεὺς Cedr. Di. Ἐρυσθεὺς OSl   **3** η΄ OSl ζ΄ Di.   **4** Ἀλκαμένης Chilm. Gelzer Ἄλκμαινος O Ἀλκεμέων Sl   **5** τκε΄ OSl Exc. Barb. (= F58a,2) *350* Exc. Barb. (= F58a,20)

F59

F59a Excerpta Barbari (304,25 – 306,22 Frick)

Corinthinorum reges et tempora

Corinthinorum regnum stabilitum est secundo anno Erysthei regi Lacedemoniorum. Permansit autem per annos CCCXXIII. Eodem uero temporae Lacedemonii congregantes conmutauerunt illos trecentos XXIII annos, quos obtinu-
5 erunt Corinthinorum reges. Erystheo regnante Lacedemoniorum anno secundo regnauit autem Corinthinorum primus Alitus, et qui sequuntur post haec sic regnauerunt.

2–7 → F58a,2–4.9

1–22 cf. Eus., reg. ser.[armen] 150; Eus., reg. ser.[Hier] 30; Chron. Synt. 88; Cedr. 216,6–8; Mich. Syr. 4,15

3 CCCXXIII] *313* Io. Mal. (= F59b,7)

F58b

In these times, Eurystheus was the first king of the Lacedaemonians, for 42 years.

And there were another eight kings after him. Altogether they reigned for 246 years.

And Alcamenes was king for 37 years.

The kingdom of the Lacedaemonians lasted a total of 325 years,
as Africanus the most wise has recorded.

F59 *The Kings of the Corinthians*

F59a[1]

The kings and chronology of the Corinthians

The kingdom of the Corinthians was established in the second year of Eurystheus, king of the Lacedaemonians. It lasted for 323 years. Since, then, the Lacedaemonians were contemporaneous with them,[2] they completed the passage of these 323 years during the years when the Corinthian kings held power.[3] When Eurystheus was in the second year of his reign over the Lacedaemonians, Aletes was the first to become king of the Corinthians. And those who succeeded him to rule were the following:

---

1   The attribution to Africanus is not as certain as the previous list. However, the synchronization with Hebrew history at the end gives good reasons to think that it goes back to him as well, see below notes 3–5, cf. also Frick 1880,9f and Gelzer 1,146–150.
2   Gr. (Frick): τῷ αὐτῷ ... χρόνῳ συγχρονίσαντες.
3   In Africanus' chronology there are 696 years from the Exodus to 2 Eurystheus (see above F58, n. 5). Together with the 323 years of the Corinthians' kingdom, the end of their reign would be 1019 years after the Exodus—exactly one year before Ol. 1,1 (1020 years from the Exodus to Ol. 1,1, F34,68f), which was the last year of Jotham's reign, see below n. 5.

I. Alitus ann. XXXV.
II. Exius ann. XXXVII.
III. Agelaus ann. XXXIII.
IIII. Prymnus ann. XXXV.
V. Bacchus ann. XXXV.
VI. Agelas ann. XXXIIII.
VII. Eumidus ann. XXV.
VIII. Aristomidus ann. XXXV.
VIIII. Igemonius ann. XVI.
X. Alexander ann. XXV.
XI. Telestus ann. VIIII.
XII. Automenus ann. IIII.

Hii Corinthinorum reges sub anno tricesimo primo Sahulis regi Iudae initiauerunt, et defecerunt anno quinto decimo regni Ioatham fili Oziae, patri autem Achaz regis Iudae.

8-13   Sync. (210,25 – 211,5 Moss.), cf. etiam Eus., chron. (104,6–18; 104,35 – 105,4 Karst = Sync. 209,20–29; 210,10–16 Moss.) (= Diod. Sic. 7,9 = Apollodorus FGrHist 244 F331) et can. (armen. 174–178 Karst; Hier. 66,9–11; 68,8s; 70,10s; 72,12s; 74,16s; 76,25s Helm)
Κορινθίων α' ἐβασίλευσεν Ἀλήτης ἔτη λη' (= chron.; 35 can.). τοῦ δὲ κόσμου ἦν ἔτος ͵δυκγ'.
Κορινθίων β' ἐβασίλευσεν Ἰξίων ἔτη λη' (= chron., can.^Hier, 37 can.^armen). τοῦ δὲ κόσμου ἦν ἔτος ͵δυξα'.
Κορινθίων γ' ἐβασίλευσεν Ἀγέλας ἔτη λε' (37 Eus.). τοῦ δὲ κόσμου ἦν ἔτος ͵δυρθ'.
Κορινθίων δ' ἐβασίλευσε Πρύμνης ἔτη λε' (= chron., can.^Hier, 37 can.^armen). τοῦ δὲ κόσμου ἦν ἔτος ͵δφλδ'.
Κορινθίων ε' ἐβασίλευσε Βάκχις ἔτη λε' (= chron., can.^Hier, - can.^armen). ἀφ' οὗ οἱ μετὰ αὐτὸν βασιλεῖς ἐκλήθησαν Βακχίδαι. τοῦ δὲ κόσμου ἦν ἔτος ͵δφξθ'.
Κορινθίων ϛ' ἐβασίλευσεν Ἀγέλας ἔτη λ' (= Eus.). τοῦ δὲ κόσμου ἦν ἔτος ͵δχδ'.
14-19   Sync. (218,9–22 Moss.), cf. Eus. (Sync. [209,29 – 210,4 Moss.] ≈ Eus., chron. [104,19–26 Karst]) (= Diod. Sic. 7,9 = Apollodorus FGrHist 244 F331) et can. (armen. 178–184 Karst; Hier. 79,1s; 80,10s; 82,15s; 83,16s; 85,3s; 85,21-23 Helm)
Κορινθίων ζ' ἐβασίλευσεν Εὔδημος ἔτη κε' (= Eus.). τοῦ δὲ κόσμου ἦν ἔτος ͵δχλδ'.
Κορινθίων η' ἐβασίλευσεν Ἀριστομήδης ἔτη λε' (= Eus.). τοῦ δὲ κόσμου ἦν ἔτος ͵δχνθ'.
Κορινθίων θ' ἐβασίλευσεν Ἀγήμων ἔτη ιϛ' (= chron., can.^Hier, - can.^armen). τοῦ δὲ κόσμου ἦν ἔτος ͵δχοδ'.
Κορινθίων ι' ἐβασίλευσεν Ἀλέξανδρος ἔτη κε' (= Eus.). τοῦ δὲ κόσμου ἦν ἔτος ͵δψι'.
Κορινθίων ια' ἐβασίλευσε Τελέστης ἔτη ιβ' (= Eus.). τοῦ δὲ κόσμου ἦν ἔτος ͵δψλε'.
Κορινθίων ιβ' ἐβασίλευσεν Αὐτομένης ἔτος ἕν (= Eus.). τοῦ δὲ κόσμου ἦν ἔτος ͵δψμζ'.
Οἱ Λακεδαιμονίων βασιλεῖς καὶ οἱ Κορινθίων ἕως τοῦδε τοῦ χρόνου διήρκεσαν ἔτεσι τν', μεθ' οὓς ἐνιαύσιοι πρυτάνεις, ὡς μὲν τινές, ἐπὶ Αἰσχύλου ἄρχοντος καὶ τῆς πρώτης Ὀλυμπιάδος, ὡς δὲ ἕτεροι, μετὰ ταῦτα, ὡς πρόκειται.
20s → F34,66; F35,1; F58a,5 **21** → T64d,1s; T64e,1s

19 IIII] *1* Sync. Io. Mal. (= F59b,6) **25** Exc. Barb. (= F58a,18) **20** tricesimo primo] *uicesimo primo* Frick **21** quinto decimo] an *sexto decimo* legendum?

1. Aletes, 35 years.
2. Ixion, 37 years.
3. Agelas, 33 years.
4. Prymnes, 35 years.
5. Bacchis, 35 years.
6. Agelas, 34 years.
7. Eudemus, 25 years.
8. Aristomedes, 35 years.
9. Agemon, 16 years.
10. Alexander, 25 years.
11. Telestes, 9 years.
12. Automenes, 4 years.

These Corinthian kings begin their reign in the 31st year[4] of Saul, king of Judah. And they ceased their rule in the 15th year[5] of the reign of Jotham, son of Uzziah and father of Ahaz, king of Judah.

---

4 Emended by Frick to 21 Saul. According to l. 2, the kingdom of the Corinthians began in the second year of the reign of the Lacedaemonian king Eurystheus. If 1 Eurystheus = 20 Saul (see F58,4), the Lacedaemonian kingdom would have begun in the 21st year of Saul's reign.

5 More precisely, 16 Jotham. According to F 58a,2–6, the Lacedaemonian kingdom lasted 325 years from 20 Saul to 1 Ahaz (= Ol. 1,1). Beginning in 21 Saul, the 323 years of the Corinthian kingdom would thus have ended one year before the beginning of Ahaz' reign (= 16 Jotham, IV Regn 15,33), cf. Frick 1880,9.

F59b Ioannes Malalas 4,20 (65,41 – 66,46 Thurn)

Μετὰ δὲ Ἠλεὶ τὸν προφήτην τῶν Ἰουδαίων πρῶτος ἐβασίλευσεν τῶν Ἰουδαίων Σαοὺλ, ὁ τοῦ Κίς, ἐκ φυλῆς Βενιαμίν, ἔτη κ', ἐν Γαβαὼν τῇ πόλει.

Τῶν δὲ Κορινθίων μετὰ τοὺς Λακεδαιμονίους ἐβασίλευσε τότε Ἀλήτης ἔτη λε', καὶ ἄλλοι βασιλεῖς ια' ἔτη σοζ',
5 καὶ ὕστερον ἐβασίλευσεν <Αὐτομέδων> ἔτος α'.
Κατέσχεν δὲ ἡ βασιλεία Κορινθίων τὰ πάντα ἔτη τιγ'.

1s → F34,66; F35,1; F58a,5

1s   cf. Chron. Pasch. 155,20s; Georg. Mon. 165,15 – 166,4; Sym. Log. (Leo Gr. 30,4–8 = Th. Mel. 28,12–16 ≈ Iul. Pol. 104,2–5)   **3–6** cf. Cedr. 216,7s; Mich. Syr. 4,15

[OSl] **2** κ' Ο μ' Sl   **3** Ἀλήτης Sl Chilm. Ἀλέτης Ο   **5** Αὐτομέδων Sl < Ο Αὐτομένης Chilm. (sicut in Sync.) | α' OSl Sync. *4* Exc. Barb. (= F59a,19)   **6** τιγ' OSl 323 Exc. Barb. (= F59a,3)

F60 Ioannes Malalas 4,20 (66,47–53 Thurn)

Ἐν τοῖς χρόνοις τοῦ Σαοὺλ ἐπενόησαν πρῶτον ἀγῶνα οἱ Πισαῖοι Ὀλυμπίων, τότε τὴν ἑορτὴν ἐπιτελέσαντες τὴν κοσμικὴν τῷ Διὶ Ὀλυμπίῳ, περὶ ὧν ὁ σοφώτατος Ἀφρικανὸς ἐχρονογράφησεν.
   Ἐν αὐτῷ δὲ τῷ καιρῷ ἐγένετο ἱερεὺς τῶν Ἰουδαίων Σαμουὴλ ὁ προφήτης· καὶ προεβάλετο κατὰ
5 κέλευσιν θεοῦ βασιλέα τὸν Δαβὶδ τοῦ Ἰουδαϊκοῦ ἔθνους, τὸν υἱὸν τοῦ Ἰεσσαί.

1–3 → F34,91s; F65,11–13

1s cf. Cedr. 216,3–6 (e Malala)

[OSl] **1** Πισσαῖοι Ο corr. Di.   **2** κοσμικὴν Ο Ῥωμαϊκὴν Sl   **4** προεβάλλετο Ο corr. Di.

T61 Ioannes Malalas 2,17 (38,1–6 Thurn)

Καὶ ἐλύθη ἡ βασιλεία τῶν Θηβῶν, ἤτοι Βοιωτῶν, κατασχοῦσα ἔτη τξθ'. τὰ δὲ προγεγραμμένα ταῦτα πάντα ὁ σοφώτατος Παλαίφατος ἀληθῆ ἐξέθετο. ὁ γὰρ σοφώτατος Εὐριπίδης ποιητικῶς ἐξέθετο δρᾶμα περὶ τοῦ Οἰδίποδος καὶ τῆς Ἰοκάστης καὶ τῆς Σφιγγός. τὰ γὰρ τῶν Θηβῶν βασίλεια Ἀφρικανὸς ὁ σοφὸς χρονογράφος ἐξέθετο.

3s → F34,89s; F50,17s; F54a,17s

1–4   cf. ps. Sym. f. 30ᵛ = Cedr. 46,17–18; Sym. Log. (Leo Gr. 28,8–12 = Th. Mel. 27,6–9); Io. Ant. fr. 14–16; ps. Io. Ant. fr. 9*.12*

[OSl] **3** Ἰωκάστης Ο corr. Di.   **4** σοφὸς < Ο

F59b

After Eli the prophet of the Jews, the first to reign over the Jews was Saul, the son of Kish, from the tribe of Benjamin; he reigned for 20 years in the city of Gabaon.

> After the Lacedaemonians, Aletes was at that time king of the Corinthians, for 35 years.
> There were another 11 kings for 277 years.
> Subsequently, Automedon was king for one year.

The kingdom of the Corinthians lasted a total of 313 years.

F60 *The First Festival of Olympian Zeus*

In the time of Saul, the people of Pisa devised the first contest of the Olympic festival, celebrating at that time the universal festival of Olympian Zeus. The most learned Africanus wrote about this in his chronicle.

At that time Samuel the prophet became priest of the Jews. At God's command he appointed David, the son of Jesse, king of the Jewish people.

T61 *The Kings of Thebes*

So the kingdom of Thebes, or the Boeotians, which had lasted for 369 years, came to an end.[1] All that has been mentioned above the most learned Palaephatus has described truthfully. The most learned Euripides wrote a play in poetry about Oedipus, Jocaste and the Sphinx. Africanus, the learned chronographer, has also written about the kingdom of Thebes.[2]

---

1. This phrase could also originate in Africanus, although the mention of his name is separated by the notice on the Theban myth (summarized previously, τὰ προγεγραμμένα); for this myth in Malalas see D'Alfonso 2006,25–31.
2. Apart from a few small notices about Cadmus and Europa (see app.), Malalas is the only witness to Africanus' treatment of Theban chronology. For Africanus as the source of the 369-year chronology of the Theban kingdom, see Gelzer 1,140f and Huxley 1987.

F62 Excerpta Barbari (312,18 – 314,18 Frick)

Midorum regna et tempora

Midorum autem regnum obtinuit per annos CCLXVIIII. et haec Cyrus Persus destruens regnum eorum in Persida duxit in principio quinquagensimae quintae olympiadae. in ipsa nunc quinquagensima quarta olympiada fiunt CCXVI,
5 sicut pridem trium annorum primae olympiadae Midorum initium inuenimus esse regnum, quod est quinto decimo anno Oziae regis Iudae.

Quod uero CCLXVIIII annorum Midorum obtinuerunt tempora sic a principio Abbaci, qui primus regnauit in Midia, usque Artyagum, quem Cirus exterminans in Persida regnum migrauit.

10 I. Arbacus ann. XXVIII.
    II. Sosarmus ann. IIII.
    III. Mamythus ann. XL.
    IIII. Cardyceus ann. XXIII.
    V. Diycus ann. LIIII.
15 VI. Fraortus ann. XXIIII.
    VII. Cyaxarus ann. XXXII.

2–4 → F34,19s.40–47.67s; F65,133; F73,2s; F74; Sym. Log. (Leo Gr. [46,15–17 Bekker] = Th. Mel. [39,23s Tafel] = Iul. Pol. [140,10–12 Hardt] = Cedr. [257,7s Bekker]) Κῦρος ὁ Πέρσης καταλύσας τὴν Μήδων καὶ Ἀσσυρίων δυναστείαν, κρατήσας τε τῆς (< Th. Mel.) Ἀσίας ἁπάσης, ἐβασίλευσεν ἔτη λα'. 4–6 et 18s → F64
10–14 Sync. (233,19–27; 252,11s; 275,22s Moss.), cf. Eus., chron. (32,21–25 Karst), can. (armen. 183s Karst; Hier. 83,11s; 85,3s; 87,16s; 90,18s; 91,21s Helm) et Chron. Synt. (89 Schoene)
Μήδων α' ἐβασίλευσεν Ἀρβάκης, ὁ καταλύσας τὴν τῶν Ἀσσυρίων ἀρχήν, ἔτη κη' (= chron., can.^Hier, Chron. Synt., - can.^armen). τοῦ δὲ κόσμου ἦν ἔτος ‚δχος'.
Μήδων β' ἐβασίλευσε Μανδαύκης ἔτη κ' (= chron., can.^Hier, Chron. Synt., - can.^armen). τοῦ δὲ κόσμου ἦν ἔτος ‚δψδ'.
Μήδων γ' ἐβασίλευσε Σώσαρμος ἔτη λ' (= can.^Hier, 20 chron., 38 Chron. Synt., - can.^armen). τοῦ δὲ κόσμου ἦν ἔτος ‚δψκδ'.
Μήδων δ' ἐβασίλευσεν Ἄρτυκας ἔτη λ' (= chron., Chron. Synt., 13 can.^Hier, - can.^armen). τοῦ δὲ κόσμου ἦν ἔτος ‚δψνδ'.
Μήδων ε' ἐβασίλευσε Διοικής ἔτη νδ' (= Eus., Chron. Synt.). Διοικής ὁ Μήδων βασιλεὺς ἔκτισεν Ἐκβάτανα τὴν πόλιν μεγάλην καὶ διαβόητον. τοῦ δὲ κόσμου ἦν ἔτος ‚δψπδ'.
15s Sync. (252,11s Moss.), cf. Eus., chron. (32,26s Karst), can. (armen. 185–187 Karst; Hier. 95,8s; 96,21s Helm) et Chron. Synt. (90 Schoene)
Μήδων ς' ἐβασίλευσεν Ἀφραάρτης ἔτη να' (24 Eus., Chron. Synt.). τοῦ δὲ κόσμου ἦν ἔτος ‚δωλη'.
Μήδων ζ' ἐβασίλευσε Κυαξάρης ἔτη λβ' (= Eus., Chron. Synt.). τοῦ δὲ κόσμου ἦν ἔτος ‚δωπθ'.

2–17 cf. Eus., reg. ser.^armen 152; Eus., reg. ser.^Hier 28; Annianus apud Eliam Nisib. 16,27–35 6 cf. IV Regn 15,1; Sym. Log. (Leo Gr. 35,1s = Th. Mel. 31,16s = Iul. Pol. 112,16s)

5 post *pridem* spatium vacuum 4 versuum cod. | trium] *L* ante *trium* excidisse iam censuit Gelzer
11 IIII] XXX Frick

F62 *The Kings of the Medes*[1]

The reigns and chronology of the Medes

Now the kingdom of the Medes lasted for 269 years. Cyrus the Persian destroyed them and brought their kingdom to Persia in the beginning of the 55th Olympiad. In the 54th Olympiad, there were 216 <years>.[2] We thus find that the beginning of the kingdom of the Medes was three[3] years before the first Olympiad, which is in the 15th year of Ozias the king of Judah.

Thus there are 269 years for the Medes from the beginning of the reign of Arbacus, who was the first king in Media, up to Astyages. Cyrus eliminated him and transferred the kingdom to Persia.

1. Arbacus, 28 years.
2. Sosarmus, 4 years.
3. Mamythus, 40 years.
4. Cardyceus, 23 years.
5. Deioces, 54 years.
6. Aphraartes, 24 years.
7. Cyaxarus, 32 years.

---

1 The chronological notices about the beginning and the end of the Median kingdom reflect Africanus' system. According to ll. 4f and 18f, Arbacus (= 15 Ozias) began his rule 53 years before Ol. 1,1 (= 1 Ahaz). This is also the sum of the years that Africanus reckoned from 15 Ozias to 1 Ahaz (37 years remaining for Ozias + 16 years for Jotham). Africanus' dating of the beginning of Cyrus' rule in Ol. 55,1 (ll. 2–4) is also attested in F34,42f. For Africanus as the origin of this list, see also Frick 1880,11; Gelzer 1,215–219.
2 That is, from Ol. 1,1.
3 Cf. below, l. 19, which states more accurately that the kingdom of the Medes began 53 years before the first Olympiad; see Gelzer 1,216.

VIII. Astyagus ann. XXXVIII.

Haec Midorum regna permanserunt per annos CCLXVIIII, a quinto decimo anno Oziae regis Iuda, hoc est LIII annorum primae olympiadae. Finiit autem
20 quinquagensima quarta olympiada, anno tricensimo octauo regnante Astuago, quem exterminauit Cyrus Persus in quinquagensima quarta olympiada.
Et Lydorum et Midorum regna dissipata sunt sub Cyro Persarum.

17 Sync. (275,22s Moss.), cf. Eus., chron. (32,28 Karst) et can. (armen. 187 Karst; Hier. 99,9s Helm)
Μήδων η′ ἐβασίλευσεν Ἀστυάγης Δαρεῖος ἔτη λη′ (= Eus., Chron. Synt.). τοῦ δὲ κόσμου ἦν ἔτος ͵δκα′.

19 primae] πρὸ τῆς α′ Frick   **22** post *Persarum* spatium vacuum 5 versuum cod.

F63

F63a Excerpta Barbari (310,25 – 312,17 Frick)

Lydiorum regna et tempora

Et Lydiorum regnum tenuit per annos CCXXXII. incipiens ab Ardio primum regem Lydiorum sub Cryssum illum a Cyro Persarum dissipatum finiit in olympiada quinquagensima octaua. initium uero primae olympiadae inuenitur
5 exordium regni Lydiorum in anno primo Achaz. regnauit quidem et Lydiorum principatus per annos CCXXXII sic.

2–6 Sync. (287,21–26 Moss.), cf. Eus., can. (Hier. 103,13–18 Helm)
Κροῖσος κατὰ Κύρου στρατεύσας ἥλω σὺν τῇ Λυδῶν βασιλείᾳ διαρκεσάσῃ ἔτη σλβ′ (= can.^{Hier}). οὗτος θ′ βασιλεὺς Λυδῶν γεγονὼς ἔτη ιε′ ἐβασίλευσεν ἕως τοῦ ιδ′ ἔτους Κύρου. ἡ Λυδῶν βασιλεία ἀρξαμένη τῷ ͵δψλε′ ἔτει τοῦ κόσμου κατελύθη τῷ ͵δ⟆ξς′, ἤτοι Κύρου τοῦ Περσῶν ἔτει ιδ′, διαρκέσασα ἔτεσι σλβ′ (= can.^{Hier}) ἐν βασιλεῦσι θ′. **3s et 15** → F74,1–6 **4s et 16s** → F64a

3s cf. Io. Mal. 6,6.8–10; Cedr. 242,7–16; Georg. Mon. 20,6–17   **5s et 17s** cf. Georg. Mon. 20,19s

8. Astyagus 38 years.

These reigns of the Medians lasted for 269 years, from the 15th year of Ozias, the king of Judah, that is 53 years before the first Olympiad. It came to an end in the 54th Olympiad, in the 38th year of the reign of Astyages, whom Cyrus the Persian eliminated in the 54th Olympiad.

And the kingdoms of the Lydians and the Medes were destroyed by Cyrus, king of the Persians.

F63 *The Kings of the Lydians*[1]

F63a

The reigns and chronology of the Lydians

And the kingdom of the Lydians lasted for 232 years. Beginning from Ardysus, the first king of the Lydians, it came to an end in the 58th Olympiad, when it was dissolved by Cyrus of the Persians during the reign of Croesus. The beginning of the first Olympiad is thus found to coincide with the beginning of the kingdom of the Lydians in the first year of Ahaz. The kingdom of the Lydians thus held rule for 232 years,[2] as follows:

---

1 The lists of the Lydian kings found in the *Excerpta Barbara* and Malalas, which agree in all chronological particulars, independently attest the same tradition. Dependence on the *Chronographiae* is suggested by the correlation of 1 Ardysus with Africanus' foundational synchronism of 1 Ahaz with Ol. 1,1 (F63a,4f). For Malalas and Exc. Barb. as witnesses to Africanus' chronology of the Lydian kingdom, see also Frick 1880,11; Gelzer 1,219–222.

2 232 years from Ol. 1,1 would correspond to Ol. 59,1, but Cyrus actually defeated Croesus in Ol. 58,3, in the 14th year of Cyrus' rule. Gelzer 1,220 therefore suggests that Africanus dated the first year of the Lydian kingdom to AM 4725, two years before Ol. 1,1.

I. Ardirus ann. XXXVI.
II. Alyatus ann. XIIII.
III. Midus ann. XII.
IIII. Caudalus ann. XVII.
V. Gygus ann. XXXVI.
VI. Ardyssus ann. XXXVIII.
VII. Salyatus ann. XV.
VIII. Aliatus alius ann. XLVIIII.
VIIII. Cryssus ann. XV.

Haec Lydiorum regnum, incipiens a principio primae olympiadae in primo anno Achaz, regis Iudae. et cessauit in olympiada quinquagensima octaua. fiunt anni CCXXXII.

7–15 Sync. (287,11–20 Moss.), cf. Eus., chron. (32,35 – 33,7 Karst) et can. (armen. 181–189 Karst; Hier. 85,24s; 89,8s; 90,7; 90,26; 92,10s; 94,16s; 97,2s; 98,8s; 102,9s Helm)
α' Ἄρδυσος Ἀλυάτου ἔτη λς' (= Eus.)
β' Ἀλυάτης ἔτη ιδ' (= Eus.)
γ' Μίλης ἔτη ιβ' (= Eus.)
δ' Κανδαύλης ἔτη ιζ' (= Eus.)
ε' Γύγης ἔτη λς' (= can.^{armen}, 35 chron., 37 can.^{Hier})
ϛ' Ἄρδυσος ἔτη λη' (= can.^{armen}, 37 chron., can.^{Hier})
ζ' Σαδυάτης ἔτη ιε' (= can.^{Hier}, can.^{armen}, 5 chron.)
η' Ἀλυάτης ἔτη μθ' (= Eus.)
θ' Κροῖσος ἔτη ιε' (= Eus.).

7–15 cf. Eus., reg. ser.^{armen} 151; Eus., reg. ser.^{Hier} 30; Chron. Synt. 92

F63b Ioannes Malalas 6,2.5 (117,14-17; 119,54-58 Thurn)

Ἐν δὲ τοῖς αὐτοῖς χρόνοις οἱ Λυδοὶ ἔλαβον τὰς βασιλείας, ἤτοι τοπαρχίας, δυνάμει ἀπὸ τῶν πλησίον ὄντων ἄλλων ἐθνῶν.
Καὶ ἐβασίλευσε τῶν Λυδῶν πρῶτος ὁ Ἀρδεὺς ἔτη λϛ'. ὅστις καὶ ὑπέταξε τὰ πλησίον ἔθνη καὶ βασίλεια, καὶ διῆγεν ἐν ὑπερηφανίᾳ. [...]
Μετὰ δὲ τὴν βασιλείαν τοῦ Ἀρδέως ἐβασίλευσαν Λυδῶν ἄλλοι ὀκτὼ ἕως Κροίσου τοῦ ὑπερηφάνου. ἐβασίλευσε δὲ ὁ αὐτὸς Κροῖσος ἔτη ιε'.
Κατέσχεν οὖν ἡ βασιλεία Λυδῶν τὰ πάντα ἔτη σλβ'.

5–7 → F63a,7–18

5–7 cf. Cedr. 239,12–15   7 cf. Georg. Mon. 20,19s

[OSl] **1** πλησίον Chilm. πλησίων O   **5s** Κροίσου + τοῦ χρυσοῦ Sl   **6** Κροῖσος] ὁ χρυσοῦς Sl   **7** σλβ' O σλϛ' Sl

1. Ardysus, 36 years.
2. Alyates, 14 years.
3. Miles, 12 years.
4. Candaules, 17 years.
5. Gyges, 36 years.
6. Ardysus, 38 years.
7. Sadyates, 15 years.
8. Another Alyates, 49 years.
9. Croesus, 15 years.

This is the kingdom of the Lydians, starting from the beginning of the first Olympiad in the first year of Ahaz, king of Judah. It came to an end in the 58th Olympiad. Altogether there are 232 years.

F63b

At this same time the Lydians took by force the kingdoms, that is toparchies, from the other neighboring peoples.

And the first king of the Lydians was Ardeus, for 36 years. He made subjects of the neighboring peoples and kingdoms, and lived a life of arrogance. [...]

After the reign of Ardeus, there were another eight kings of the Lydians until Croesus the Proud. This same Croesus was king for 15 years.

The kingdom of the Lydians lasted, therefore, 232 years in all.

F64

F64a Georgius Syncellus (233,11–15 Mosshammer)

(→ T64e) ... Ὁ δὲ Ἀφρικανὸς μᾶλλον ἐναντιοῦται τῷ Εὐσεβίῳ, κατὰ τὸ α' ἔτος Ἄχαζ τὴν πρώτην Ὀλυμπιάδα φάσκων ἦρχθαι ἔν τε τῷ γ' καὶ ἐν τῷ δ' λόγῳ τῶν ἱστορικῶν αὐτοῦ τρανῶς, ἐν οἷς ὧδε γράφει·

Ἀναγραφῆναι δὲ πρώτην τὴν τεσσαρεσκαιδεκάτην, ἣν ἐνίκα Κόροιβος στά-
5 διον. τότε ἐβασίλευσεν Ἄχας ἐπὶ Ἱερουσαλὴμ ἔτος πρῶτον. ... (→ F64b)

1–5 = T64e,2–7   **4s** → F58a,2s.5s; F63a,4s.16s; F64b; F65,35–37; Eus., praep. ev. 10,14,5 (610s Mras) ... *Μεθ' ὃν Ἄχαζ ἔτη ις'· κατὰ τοῦτον ἡ πρώτη Ὀλυμπιὰς ἤχθη, ἣν ἐνίκα στάδιον Κόροιβος Ἠλεῖος.* Sym. Log. (Th. Mel. [31,27s Tafel] = Iul. Pol. [114,14s Hardt]) Ἐν τῷ πρώτῳ ἔτει *τῆς τούτου* (sc. Achaz; false Ioatham apud Leo. Gr. [35,10s Bekker]) *βασιλείας Ἴφιτος τὰς Ὀλυμπιάδας συνέστησεν.* Exc. Barb. (254,3–6 Frick) *Sub istius* (sc. Achaz) *regno anno undecimo illa prima olympiada uenit ad Grecis. Fiunt uero simul ab Adam usque initium olympiadae omnes anni IIII milia septingenti XLV. Est autem olympiada anni IIII.*

4s   cf. Callimachus fr. 433; Strabo 8,3,30; Paus. 5,8,5s; 8,26,3s; Phleg. Trall. FGrHist 257 F1; Mich. Syr. 4,20

[AB]   **4** τεσσαρεσκαιδεκάτην B   τεσσαρισκαιδεκάτην A | ἣν ἐνίκα scripsimus (cf. Exc. Eus. 189,13) ἡνίκα καὶ A   ἡνίκα καὶ B | Κόροιβος Di.   κόρυβος AB

F64b Georgius Syncellus (233,15–17 Mosshammer)

(→ F64a) ... Εἶτα ἐν τῷ τετάρτῳ φησίν (sc. Africanus)·

Ἦν δ' ἄρα τοῦ Ἄχας βασιλείας ἔτος πρῶτον, ᾧ συντρέχειν ἀπεδείξαμεν τὴν πρώτην Ὀλυμπιάδα.

2s cf. supra app. ad F64a

[AB]   **2** δ' ἄρα B   ἱάρα A | ᾧ Goar^m   ὡς AB | συντρέχειν B   συντρέχει A

F64 *The Date of the First Olympiad*

F64a[1]

(→ T64e) … But Africanus contradicts Eusebius, and states clearly in both the third and fourth books of his *Histories* that the 1st Olympiad was begun in the first year of Ahaz. There he states the following:

The 14th Olympiad was the first one that was registered, when Coroebus won the single-course race. At that time Ahaz was in the first year of his reign in Jerusalem. … (→ F64b)

F64b

(→ F64a) … Then in the fourth book he [sc. Africanus] says:

This then was the first year of the reign of Ahaz, with which we have shown the 1st Olympiad coincides.

---

1 In the quotation by Syncellus the two texts given on this page follow each other directly. However, in Africanus they certainly were at different places because the first belonged to the third book, and the second to the fourth. Therefore, they have to be considered as separate fragments.

F64c Eusebius, Canones (Chronicon Paschale [193,10–12 Dindorf] = Hieronymus [86^k Helm] = armeniace [181 Karst] = Michael Syrus 4,15 [1,79 Chabot])

Γράφει δὲ ὁ Ἀφρικανὸς ὧδε πρὸς λέξιν·
Αἰσχύλος ὁ Ἀγαμήστορος ἦρξεν Ἀθηναίων διὰ βίου ἔτη κγ΄, ἐφ' οὗ Ἰωαθὰμ ἐβασίλευσεν ἐν Ἱερουσαλήμ.

1–3 = T64d,12–14; → F54a,45s; T64e,1s

2 διὰ βίου < Hier.

T64d Eusebius, Canones (Hieronymus [86^{b–d,h,k} Helm] = armeniace [181 Karst] = Michael Syrus 4,15 [1,79 Chabot], a linea 8 = Chronicon Paschale [193,8–20 Dindorf])

Secundo anno Aeschyli Atheniensium iudicis prima Olympias acta, in qua Coroebus Eliensis extitit uictor.
    Elii agunt quinquennale certamen quattuor annis in medio expletis, in quibus principes annui constituuntur quattuor. Quam Olympiadem Ifitus, filius
5 Praxonidis siue <H>aemonis, primus constituit.
    Ab hoc tempore Graeca de temporibus historia uera creditur. Nam ante hoc, ut cuique uisum est, diuersas sententias protulerunt.
    Τὴν α΄ Ὀλυμπιάδα ὁ Ἀφρικανὸς κατὰ Ἰωαθὰμ Ἑβραίων τοῦ Ἰούδα βασιλέα συνάγει. καὶ ὁ ἡμέτερος δὲ κανὼν κατὰ τὸν αὐτὸν παρίστησιν. γράφει δὲ ὁ
10 Ἀφρικανὸς ὧδε πρὸς λέξιν·
    Αἰσχύλος ὁ Ἀγαμήστορος ἦρξεν Ἀθηναίων διὰ βίου ἔτη κγ΄, ἐφ' οὗ Ἰωαθὰμ ἐβασίλευσεν ἐν Ἱερουσαλήμ.
    Καὶ ὁ ἡμέτερος δὲ κανὼν {λέγει} ἐπὶ τῆς πρώτης Ὀλυμπιάδος τὸν Ἰωαθὰμ βασιλέα Ἰούδα συνείληφεν.

1 → T64e,1s 6s → T65,3s 11s = F64c

8–14 cf. supra app. ad F64a

1 *secundum annum* Hier.:O | *aescili* Hier.:L *aeschili* Hier.:BP *aescyli* Hier.:M | *iudicis*] ἄρχοντος armen. Mich. Syr. **2** *coebus* Hier.:M | *elius* Hier.:OL *selius* Hier.:B *heliensis* Hier.:M | *uictor* + στάδιον armen. Mich. Syr. **3** *aelii* Hier.:APN **4** *quattuor* < armen. Mich. Syr. **5** *saxonidis* Hier.:A *saxonides* Hier.:P *praxonides* Hier.:B *paxonidis* Hier.:M *Prach<s>ion* armen. | *Haemonis* Helm *aemonis* codd. *des Dimon* (probabiliter ex Αἴμονος) armen. | *primum* Hier.:L | *constituit posuit* Hier.:OB **11** διὰ βίου < Hier. **13** ὁ ἡμέτερος δὲ κανὼν] *nos* Hier. | λέγει Chron. Pasch. < armen. Hier. **14** βασιλέα Ἰούδα < armen. Hier.

F64c

This is what Africanus writes in the following words:

Aeschylus, son of Agamestor, ruled the Athenians for life. During his reign, Jotham was king in Jerusalem.[2]

T64d

In the second year of Aeschylus, archon of the Athenians, the first Olympic games were celebrated, in which Coroebus of Elis was the victor.

The Eleans celebrate the games every five years, after an interval of four years, during which four annual rulers are elected. Iphitus, son of Praxonides, also called Hemon, was the first to establish the Olympiad.

From this time, the dates of Greek chronography can be considered as reliable. For before this time, dates were variable, supplied according to individual preference.

Africanus puts the first Olympiad during the time of Jotham, king of the Hebrews of Judah.[3] Our canon presents it during the time of the same king. In the following words, this is what Africanus writes:

Aeschylus, son of Agamestor, ruled the Athenians for life. During his reign, Jotham was king in Jerusalem.

Our canon likewise puts Jotham, king of Judah, at the time of the first Olympiad.

2   Although Eusebius inserts this brief note into his discussion of Olympiad chronology (T64d), the excerpt has no direct bearing on this subject. For that reason, the citation from Africanus and its broader context in Eusebius' chronicle are provided separately as both a fragment and *testimonium*.

3   Eusebius misleadingly suggests that this quotation from Africanus confirms his own synchronism of the first Olympiad with the reign of Jotham. In Africanus' system, Ol. 1,1 coincides with the first year of Ahaz's reign and not the reign of his immediate predecessor Jotham. The second year of Aeschylus' archonship also occurred in Ol. 1,1 (F54a,45f); Aeschylus would thus have begun his rule one year before Ol. 1,1, during the final and 16th year of Jotham's reign (cf. IV Regn 15,33). See also F64e below, where Syncellus accuses Eusebius of misrepresenting Africanus for self-serving purposes.

T64e Georgius Syncellus (233,9–17 Mosshammer)

Εὐσέβιος δὲ τὴν πρώτην Ὀλυμπιάδα ἐπὶ Ἰωάθαμ συνάγει τοῦ μετὰ η' ἔτη βασιλεύσαντος τοῦ Ἰούδα καὶ τὸν Ἀφρικανὸν προφέρει συνάδοντα αὐτῷ ἐν τούτῳ. ὁ δὲ Ἀφρικανὸς μᾶλλον ἐναντιοῦται τῷ Εὐσεβίῳ, κατὰ τὸ α' ἔτος Ἄχαζ τὴν πρώτην Ὀλυμπιάδα φάσκων ἦρχθαι ἔν τε τῷ γ' καὶ ἐν τῷ δ' λόγῳ τῶν ἱστορικῶν αὐτοῦ τρανῶς, ἐν
5 οἷς ὧδε γράφει·

Ἀναγραφῆναι δὲ πρώτην τὴν τεσσαρεσκαιδεκάτην, ἣν ἐνίκα καὶ Κόροιβος στάδιον. τότε ἐβασίλευσεν Ἄχας ἐπὶ Ἱερουσαλὴμ ἔτος πρῶτον.

Εἶτα ἐν τῷ τετάρτῳ φησίν·

Ἦν δ' ἄρα τοῦ Ἄχας βασιλείας ἔτος πρῶτον, ᾧ συντρέχειν ἀπεδείξαμεν τὴν πρώτην Ὀλυμπιάδα.

1s → T64c; F64d 2–7 = F64a 8s = F64b

6s cf. supra app. ad F64a

[AB] **1** ἰωάθαμ A ἰώθαμ B | τοῦ² < A **6** τεσσαρεσκαιδεκάτην B τεσσαρισκαιδεκάτην A | ἣν ἐνίκα scripsimus (cf. Exc. Eus. 189,13) ἠνίκα καὶ A ἡνίκα καὶ B | Κόροιβος Di. κόρυβος AB **9** δ' ἄρα B ἰάρα A | ᾧ Goar^m ὡς AB | συντρέχειν B συντρέχει A

T64e

Eusebius computes the first Olympiad at the time of Jotham, who became king of Judah eight years later, and he cites Africanus as agreeing with him on this. But Africanus contradicts him, and states clearly in both the third and fourth books of his *Histories* that the first Olympiad was begun in the first year of Ahaz. There he states the following:

The 14th Olympiad was the first one that was registered, when Coroebus won the single-course race. At that time Ahaz was in the first year of his reign in Jerusalem.

Then in the fourth book he says:

This then was the first year of the reign of Ahaz, with which we have shown the 1st Olympiad coincides.

F65 Eusebius, Chronica (Excerpta Eusebiana [cod. Paris. gr. 2600, f. 204ʳ–210ᵛ = 140,17 – 153,21 Cramer = 190,33 – 220,8 Schoene] = armeniace [1,277–313 Aucher = 89,9 – 103,28 Karst])

Ἐνταῦθά μοι δοκεῖ καλῶς ἔχειν καὶ τὰς παρ᾽ Ἕλλησιν ἀναγραφομένας Ὀλυμπιάδας ἐπισυνάψαι τῷ λόγῳ.

Ἀπὸ γὰρ τούτων τὰ τῆς Ἑλλήνων χρονογραφίας, ἀκριβοῦς ἀναγραφῆς τετευχέναι δοκεῖ, τὰ πρὸ αὐτῶν, ὡς ἑκάστῳ φίλον ἦν, ἀπεφήναντο.

5   Περὶ τῆς θέσεως [τ]οῦ ἀγῶνος [τ]ῶν Ὀλυμπίων.

[Ὀ]λίγα δὲ ἀναγκαῖον περὶ τοῦ ἀγῶνος εἰπεῖν·

Ὡς οἱ μὲν πορρωτάτω τοῖς χρόνοις τὴν θέσιν αὐτοῦ προάγοντες πρὸ Ἡρακλέους αὐτὸν τεθῆναι φασίν, ὑπὸ ἑνὸς τῶν Ἰδαίων Δακτύλων· εἶτα ὑπὸ Ἀεθλίου ἐπὶ διαπείρᾳ τῶν αὐτοῦ παίδων· ἀφ᾽ οὗ καὶ οἱ ἀγωνισταὶ ἀθληταὶ
10   ἐκλήθησαν· μεθ᾽ ὃν τὸν υἱὸν αὐτοῦ Ἐπειόν, εἶτα Ἐνδυμίωνα, ἑξῆς δὲ Ἀλεξῖνον, εἶτα Οἰνόμαον προστῆναι τῆς θυσίας· μεθ᾽ ὃν Πέλοπα εἰς τιμὴν τῷ πατρίῳ Διὶ ἀγαγεῖν· εἶθ᾽ Ἡρακλέα τὸν Ἀλκμήνης καὶ Διός, ἀφ᾽ οὗ γενεὰς δέκα τυγχάνειν· οἱ δ᾽ ἑορτὰς τελείας τρεῖς φασιν, ἐπὶ Ἴφιτον τὸν ἀνανεωσάμενον τὸν ἀγῶνα. τοῦτον γὰρ Ἠλεῖον ὄντα, καὶ προνοούμενον τῆς Ἑλλάδος, βουλόμενόν τε
15   παῦσαι {τε} πολέμων τὰς πόλεις, ἐκ Πελοποννήσου πάσης στεῖλαι θεωροὺς

3s   → F34,1–4; T64d,6s   5s   → F34,92   8–37 Sync. (231,10 – 232,10 Moss.) *Ἄλλοι δὲ ὑπὸ Ἀεθλίου τεθῆναι τὸν ἀγῶνα κἀντεῦθεν ἀθλητὰς ὀνομάζεσθαι τοὺς ἀγωνιστάς, μεθ᾽ ὃν Ἐπειὸς παῖς αὐτοῦ· εἶτα Ἐνδυμίων, ἔπειτα Ἀλεξῖνος καὶ μετὰ τοῦτον Οἰνόμαος καὶ μετὰ τοῦτον, ὥς φασι, Πέλοψ εἰς τιμὴν τῇ πατρίδι προέστη τοῦ ἀγῶνος καὶ τῆς θυσίας. ἀριθμοῦσί τε ἀπὸ τοῦ Ἀλκμήνης Ἡρακλέους ἕως τοῦδε τοῦ χρόνου γενεὰς δέκα· ἄλλοι τρεῖς τελείας φασὶν Ὀλυμπιάδας ἐπὶ Ἴφιτον τὸν ἀνανεωσάμενον τὸν ἀγῶνα. τοῦτον γὰρ Ἠλεῖον ὄντα, καὶ προνοούμενον τῆς Ἑλλάδος, παῦσαί τε σπεύδοντα πολέμων τὰς πόλεις ἐκ πάσης Πελοποννήσου πέμψαι θεωροὺς τοὺς πευσομένους περὶ τῆς τῶν πολέμων ἀπαλλαγῆς, χρησμόν τε λαβεῖν Πυθικὸν τοῦτον· ὦ Πελοποννήσου ναέται, περὶ βωμὸν ἰόντες θύετε καὶ πείθεσθε, τά κεν μάντεις ἐνέπωσιν. Ἠλεῖοι πρόπολοι πατέρων νόμον ἰθύνοντες· τοῖς δὲ Ἠλείοις τάδε προαγορεῦσαι· τὴν αὐτῶν ῥύεσθε πάτραν, πολέμου δ᾽ ἀπέχεσθε, Κοινοδίκου φιλίας ἡγούμενοι <Ἕλλήνεσσι>, ἔστ᾽ ἂν ἑνὶ ξυνόδοις ἔλθῃ φιλόφρων ἐνιαυτός. τούτου χάριν Ἴφιτος κατήγγειλε τὴν ἐκεχειρίαν ἐπὶ ἡμέρῳ τροφῇ χρῆσθαι ὑπὸ Ἡρακλέους· καὶ χεῖρας ἀλλήλους οὐκ ἐπέφερον. τὸν δὲ ἀγῶνα τετέλεκεν Ἴφιτος Ἡρακλείδης σὺν Λυκούργῳ συγγενεῖ· ἑκάτεροι δὲ Ἡρακλεῖδαι. τότε δὲ ἀγὼν σταδίου μόνον ἦν καὶ οὐδεὶς ἀνεγράφετο νικηφόρος, ἀμελούντων ὡς τηνικάδε. ὀγδόῃ δὲ καὶ εἰκοστῇ Ὀλυμπιάδι Κόροιβος Ἠλεῖος ἀνεγράφη στάδιον νικήσας, καὶ ἡ κατ᾽ αὐτὸν Ὀλυμπιὰς πρώτη ἐτάχθη· ἀφ᾽ ἧς Ἕλληνες ἀριθμεῖν τι δοκοῦσιν ἀκριβῶς χρονικόν. ταῦτα Ἀριστόδημος ἱστορεῖ καὶ συνῳδὰ τούτῳ Πολύβιος. Καλλίμαχος δέ φησιν Ὀλυμπιάδας ιγ᾽ παρεῖσθαι μὴ ἀναγραφείσας· τῇ δὲ ιδ᾽ Κόροιβον Ἠλεῖον νικῆσαι.* **8–10** ps. Io. Ant. fr. 22* (568 Ro.) *Ἀπὸ τῆς ἁμίλλης τῶν Ἀεθλίου παίδων ἀθληταὶ ἐκλήθησαν οἱ ἀγωνισταί.*

6–29 cf. Strabo 8,3,30; Diod. Sic. 4,14,1s; Phleg. Trall. FGrHist 257 F1,1–10

2   λόγῳ + *Olympiaden der Griechen. Erste Olompias: in welcher siegte im Stadion Kuribos der Helier* armen. vide infra l. 41.44   **4**   πρὸ armen. περὶ P   **5**   τῶν Ὀλυμπίων + *das ist des Wettkampfes Übung* armen.   **10**   ὅν Scal. ὧν P   **11**   ὅν Scal. ὧν P   **15**   τε del. Gutschmid

Material from Book 4/5:
From the First Olympiad to the End of the *Chronographiae*

F65 *Victors in the Olympic Games*[1]

Here I think it would be good also to append to this discussion the Olympic games recorded by the Greeks.

For starting from them it is thought that the dates of Greek chronography have received accurate documentation, whereas before them dates were supplied according to individual preference.[2]

Concerning the institution of the Olympic contest.[3]

It is necessary to say a few things about the contest:

Those who trace its establishment to a very remote point in time say that it was established before Heracles by one of the Idaean Dactyls, and then held by Aëthlius as a test for his sons. From that point, the contestants were called "athletes." After him, his son Epeius, then Endymion, then Alexinus, and then Oenomaeus presided over the offering. After him, Pelops brought the offering in honor of his father Zeus, and then Heracles the son of Alcmene and Zeus; from him there were 10 generations (although some say there were three complete festivals) up to the time of Iphitus who renewed the contest. Since, as an Elean, he was mindful of the situation in Hellas and wanted to rid the cities of warfare, he sent envoys from all the Peloponnese to inquire about putting an end to the

---

1 Scholars since Scaliger 1606 have for the most part traced this unattributed list of Olympic victors to Africanus, see *inter alia* Rutgers 1863, Gilbert 1875, Gelzer 1,167–169. For recent discussion and arguments in favor of this origin, see introduction, p. XXXIII, and Wallraff 2006, 50–53.
2 These two lines express Africanus' opinion about Greek historiography for the archaic period (see F34,1–8). However, the word τούτων cannot come directly from Africanus, because it refers to the Olympiads previously mentioned by Eusebius. A similar formulation is used by Eusebius in T64d,6f.
3 For material similar to Eusebius' preliminary discussion of the Olympic games, see ps. John of Antioch and Syncellus. Since the latter two authors are both independent of Eusebius and in some cases reflect a better text (see below app. to ll. 25–27), all three writers probably drew on a common older source. Verbal similarities with material known to belong to Africanus' chronicle (cf. ll. 35–37 and F64a above) and the consistency of the discussion with Africanus' approach to disputed questions suggest that it originated in his chronicle.

τοὺς πευσομένους περὶ ἀπαλλαγῆς τῶν κατεχόντων πολέμων· τὸν δὲ θεὸν τοῖς μὲν Πελοποννησίοις χρῆσαι ταῦτα·

Ὦ Πελοποννήσου ναέται, περὶ βωμὸν ἰόντες
Θύετε καὶ πείθεσθε, τά κεν μάντεις ἐνέπωσιν.

20 [τ]οῖς δὲ Ἠλείοις τάδε προαγορεῦσαι·

Ἠλεῖοι πρόπολοι, πατέρων νόμον ἰθύνοντες·
[Τ]ὴν αὐτῶν ῥύεσθε πάτραν, πολέμου δ᾽ ἀπέχεσθε,
Κοινοδίκου φιλίας ἡγούμενοι Ἑλλήνεσσι,
[Ἔστ᾽ ἂν] ἐνὶ ξυνόδοις ἔλθῃ φιλόφρων ἐνιαυτός.

25 Τούτου χάριν Ἴφιτος κατήγγειλε τὴν ἐκεχειρίαν <ἐπὶ ἡμέρῳ τροφῇ χρῆσθαι ὑπὸ Ἡρακλέους· καὶ χεῖρας ἀλλήλους οὐκέτι ἐπέφερον>. καὶ τὸν ἀγῶνα ἐπετέλεσε <Ἴφιτος Ἡρακλείδης> σὺν Λυκούργῳ τῷ Λακεδαιμονίῳ συγγενεῖ τυγχάνοντι· ἀμφότεροι γὰρ ἀφ᾽ Ἡρακλέους. καὶ τότε μόνον ἦν σταδίου ὁ ἀγών· ὕστερον δὲ τὰ ἄλλα ἆθλα κατὰ μέρος προσετέθη.

30 Ἱστοροῦσι δὲ οἱ περὶ Ἀριστόδημον τὸν Ἠλεῖον, ὡς ἀπ᾽ εἰκοστῆς καὶ ἑβδόμης Ὀλυμπιάδος <ἀπ᾽ Ἰφίτου> ἤρξαντο οἱ ἀθληταὶ ἀναγράφεσθαι, ὅσοι δηλαδὴ νικηφόροι· πρὸ τοῦ γὰρ οὐδεὶς ἀνεγράφη, ἀμελησάντων τῶν πρότερον· τῇ δὲ εἰκοστῇ ὀγδόῃ τὸ στάδιον νικῶν Κόροιβος Ἠλεῖος, ἀνεγράφη πρῶτος. καὶ ἡ Ὀλυμπιὰς αὕτη πρώτη ἐτάχθη· ἀφ᾽ ἧς Ἕλληνες ἀριθμοῦσι τοὺς χρόνους. τὰ δ᾽
35 αὐτὰ τῷ Ἀριστοδήμῳ καὶ Πολύβιος ἱστορεῖ. Καλλίμαχος δὲ δεκατρεῖς Ὀλυμπιάδας ἀπὸ Ἰφίτου παρεῖσθαί φησι μὴ ἀναγραφείσας· τῇ δὲ τεσσαρεσκαιδεκάτῃ Κόροιβον νικῆσαι.

Πολλοὶ δὲ λέγουσιν ἀπὸ τῆς ὑπὸ Ἡρακλέους τοῦ Ἀλκμήνης τοῦ ἀγῶνος θέσεως ἐπὶ τὴν πρώτην ἀριθμουμένην Ὀλυμπιάδα, γενέσθαι ἔτη υνθ´. ἄγουσι δὲ
40 Ἠλεῖοι πενταετηρικὸν τὸν ἀγῶνα, τεσσάρων ἐτῶν μεταξὺ συντελουμένων.

[Ἑ]λλήνων Ὀλυμπιάδες
ἀπὸ τῆς πρώτης ἐπὶ τὴν σμζ´, καθ᾽ ἣν Ῥωμαίων ἐβασίλευσεν Ἀντωνῖνος υἱὸς Σεβήρου.

26-28 → F60,1s **35-37** → F64a **38-40** Sync. (231,5-10 Moss.) Ὀλυμπιὰς δέ ἐστι παρ᾽ Ἕλλησι τετραετηρικὸς χρόνος, οὗ κατὰ τὴν συμπλήρωσιν ἀρχομένου τοῦ ἔτους ὁ Ὀλυμπιακὸς ἀγὼν ἤγετο. τοῦτον Ἑλλήνων παῖδες ἀσυμφώνως ἱστοροῦσι καταδεδεῖχθαι. τινὲς γὰρ αὐτῶν ἀπὸ τῆς ὑπὸ Ἡρακλέους τοῦ Ἀλκμήνης τοῦ ἀγῶνος θέσεως τὸ πρῶτον ἤρχθαι τὸ τῆς Ὀλυμπιακῆς ἀθλήσεως εἶδός φασι πρὸ χ´ ἐτῶν τῆσδε τῆς πρώτης Ὀλυμπιάδος.

34s cf. Aristodemus FGrHist 414 F1; Polybius FGrHist 254 F2 **35s** Callimachus fr. 433

19 πείθεσθε Sync. armen. πύθεσθε P | ἐνέπωσιν Sync. ἐνέπουσιν P **20 et 21** ~ P Sync., recte armen. **22** αὐτῶν Sync. αὑτῶν P | ἀπέχεσθε Sync. ἐπέχεσθε P **24** Ἔστ᾽ ἂν Sync. armen., lacuna P Ἔστ᾽ … ξυνόδοις] εὖτ᾽ ἂν πενταετὴς Phleg. Trall. **25s** supplevimus e Sync. cf. etiam armen. **27** Ἴφιτος Ἡρακλείδης supplevimus e Sync. *Iphitos* armen. **31** ἀπ᾽ Ἰφίτου armen. **31s** νικηφόροι iteravit P **36** τῇ…τεσσαρεσκαιδεκάτῃ Sync. τῆς … -τῆς P

wars occupying them. The god delivered the following oracle to the Peloponnesians:

> Inhabitants of the Peloponnese, when you gather around the altar,
> make an offering, and follow whatever instructions the oracles give you.

And to the Eleans, the oracle proclaimed the following:[4]

> Eleans as devoted ministers, overseeing ancestral law:
> Rescue this country of your fathers, refrain from war,
> as leaders of a mutual alliance among the Greeks,
> [until] there comes a year of friendship at the festivals.

For this reason, Iphitus announced that an armistice <had been decreed in an oracle by Heracles to promote civilized conduct; and they no longer laid hands on one another.> And <Iphitus, a descendant of Heracles,> celebrated the contest, along with Lycurgus the Lacedaemonian, who happened to be his kinsman; for both were descended from Heracles. At that time there was only a single-course race. But later other contests were added on in turn.

Aristodemus of Elis[5] and his followers report that after the 27th Olympics <from Iphitus>, the names of athletes began to be registered, whoever, that is, that were prize-winners. Before that time, no-one was registered, since they were previously negligent about these matters. So at the 28th Olympics, Coroebus of Elis, the victor in the stadion race, was the first to be registered. And this was established as the first Olympics. From it the Greeks count their years. And what Polybius reports is in agreement with Aristodemus. But Callimachus says that 13 Olympics passed by unrecorded after Iphitus, and Coroebus was victor in the 14th Olympics.

Many say that from the establishment of the contest by Heracles, son of Alcmene, up to the first numbered Olympics, there are 459 years. And the Eleans celebrate the contest on every fifth year, when four intervening years have elapsed.

The Greek Olympics
From the first up to the 247th, at which time Antoninus son of Severus was Roman emperor.[6]

---

[4] The order of this and the following line, which is reversed in the Greek witnesses, has been corrected according to the Armenian version.

[5] Cf. Harpocration, *Lexicon*, s.v. Ἑλλανοδίκαι, who attributes to Aristodemus of Elis a report about the appointment of 10 head judges in the Olympic games. If this is the same Aristodemus mentioned here, he would have written sometime after the 108th Olympic games (= 348 BC), when the selection of 10 judges became accepted practice. Aristodemus of Elis could also be the one named below (l. 191) as the winner in wrestling at the 98th Olympic games (= 388 BC).

[6] I.e. Caracalla. The actual list continues up to Ol. 249, see introduction, p. XVIII.

	Πρώτη Ὀλυμπιάς, ἣν ἐνίκα Κόροιβος Ἠλεῖος	στάδιον.
45	τοῦτο γὰρ ἠγωνίζοντο μόνον ἐπὶ Ὀλυμπιάδων ιγ΄.	
	Δευτέρα. Ἀντίμαχος Ἠλεῖος	στάδιον.
	Ῥῶμος καὶ Ῥωμύλος ἐγεννήθησαν.	
	Τρίτη. Ἄνδροκλος Μεσήνιος	στάδιον.
	Τετάρτη. Πολυχάρης Μεσήνιος	στάδιον.
50	Πέμπτη. Αἰσχίνης Ἠλεῖος	στάδιον.
	Ἕκτη. Οἰβώτας Δυμαῖος	στάδιον.
	Ἑβδόμη. Διοκλῆς Μεσήνιος	στάδιον.
	Ῥωμύλος Ῥώμην ἔκτισε.	
	Ὀγδόη. Ἀντικλῆς Μεσήνιος	στάδιον.
55	Ἐννάτη. Ξενοκλῆς Μεσήνιος	στάδιον.
	Δεκάτη. Δωτάδης Μεσήνιος	στάδιον.
	Ἑνδεκάτη. Λεωχάρης Μεσήνιος	στάδιον.
	Δωδεκάτη. Ὀξύθεμις Κορωναῖος	στάδιον.
	Τρισκαιδεκάτη. Διοκλῆς Κορίνθιος	στάδιον.
60	Τεσσαρεσκαιδεκάτη. Δέσμων Κορίνθιος	στάδιον.
	προσετέθη καὶ δίαυλος, καὶ ἐνίκα Ὕπηνος Ἠλεῖος.	
	Πεντεκαιδεκάτη. Ὄρσιππος Μεγαρεὺς	στάδιον.
	προσετέθη δόλιχος· καὶ γυμνοὶ ἔδραμον· ἐνίκα Ἄκανθος Λάκων.	
	Ἑκκαιδεκάτη. Πυθαγόρας Λάκων	στάδιον.
65	Ἑπτακαιδεκάτη. Πῶλος Ἐπιδαύριος	στάδιον.
	Ὀκτωκαιδεκάτη. Τέλλις Σικυώνιος	στάδιον.
	προσετέθη πάλη, καὶ ἐνίκα Εὐρύβατος Λάκων.	
	προσετέθη καὶ πένταθλος, καὶ ἐνίκα Λάμπις Λάκων.	
	Ἐννεακαιδεκάτη. Μένος Μεγαρεὺς	στάδιον.
70	Εἰκοστή. Ἀθηράδας Λάκων	στάδιον.
	Εἰκοστὴ α΄. Παντακλῆς Ἀθηναῖος	στάδιον.
	Εἰκοστὴ β΄. ὁ αὐτὸς τὸ δεύτερον.	{στάδιον}

---

44 → F64a   47 → F53,1s   53 → T52; F53,2s

44 cf. Strabo 8,3,30; Paus. 5,8,5s; 8,26,3s; Phleg. Trall. FGrHist 257 F1; Philostr., gym. 12 (142,14–19 Jü.); Mich. Syr. 4,20   46 cf. Phleg. Trall. FGrHist 257 F4   49 cf. Paus. 4,4,5   51 cf. Paus. 6,3,8; 7,17,6.13   52 cf. Dion. Hal. 1,71,5; Phleg. Trall. FGrHist 257 F1,11   59 cf. Arist., Pol. 1274a,34   60 cf. Paus. 4,13,7   61 cf. Paus. 5,8,6; Philostr., gym. 12 (142,19s Jü.)   62 cf. Paus. 1,44,1   63 cf. Dion. Hal. 7,72,3; Paus. 5,8,6; Philostr., gym. 12 (142,20s Jü.)   64 cf. Plut., Numa 1,3; Dion. Hal. 2,58,3   67s cf. Paus. 5,8,7; Philostr., gym. 12 (142,21–24 Jü.)   72 SIG³ 1056,17s

45 Ὀλυμπιάδων ιγ΄ armen. -πιακῶν ἀγώνων P   51 Οἰβώτας armen. Paus. Οἰβώλας P   52 διοκλῆς P Daikles armen.   61 δίαυλον P corr. Rutgers   67 Εὐρύβατος] ibaton armen.

1st Olympics,[7] in which Coroebus of Elis was the victor   stadion race.
   For 13 Olympics, this was the only event that they contested.
2nd. Antimachus of Elis   stadion race.
   Romulus and Remus were born.
3rd. Androclus of Messenia   stadion race.
4th. Polichares of Messenia   stadion race.
5th. Aeschines of Elis   stadion race.
6th. Oebotas of Dyme   stadion race.
7th. Diocles of Messenia   stadion race.
   Romulus founded Rome.
8th. Anticles of Messenia   stadion race.
9th. Xenocles of Messenia   stadion race.
10th. Dotades of Messenia   stadion race.
11th. Leochares of Messenia   stadion race.
12th. Oxythemis of Coronea   stadion race.
13th. Diocles of Corinth   stadion race.
14th. Desmon of Corinth   stadion race.
   A double-course race was added, and Hypenus of Elis was the victor.
15th. Orsippus of Megara   stadion race.
   A long-course race was added, and they ran naked. Acanthus of Laconia was the victor.
16th. Pythagoras of Laconia   stadion race.
17th. Polus of Epidauris   stadion race.
18th. Tellis of Sicyon   stadion race.
   Wrestling was added, and Eurybatus of Laconia was the victor.
   The pentathlon was also added, and Lampis of Laconia was the victor.
19th. Menos of Megara   stadion race.
20th. Atheradas of Laconia   stadion race.
21st. Pantacles of Athens   stadion race.
22nd. The same man, for a second time.

---

[7] Unfinished rubrication is responsible for the frequent omission of the initial letter in the numbering of the Olympic games in the Paris manuscript of the *Excerpta Eusebiana*. The missing letters have been tacitly restored in this edition.

Εἰκοστὴ γ΄. Ἰκάριος Ὑπηρεσιεὺς στάδιον.
προσετέθη πυγμή, καὶ Ὀνομαστὸς Σμυρναῖος ἐνίκα, ὁ καὶ τῇ πυγμῇ νόμους
75   θέμενος.
Εἰκοστὴ δ΄. Κλεοπτόλεμος Λάκων στάδιον.
Εἰκοστὴ ε΄. Θάλπις Λάκων στάδιον.
προσετέθη τέθριππον, καὶ ἐνίκα Πάγων Θηβαῖος.
Εἰκοστὴ ς΄. Καλλισθένης Λάκων στάδιον.
80   Φιλόμβροτος δὲ Λάκων πένταθλος τρισὶν Ὀλυμπιάσιν ἐνίκησε.
Κάρνεια ἐτέθη πρῶτον ἐν Λακεδαίμονι κιθαρῳδῶν ἀγών.
Εἰκοστὴ ζ΄. Εὔρυβος Ἀθηναῖος στάδιον.
Εἰκοστὴ η΄. Χάρμις Λάκων στάδιον.
ὃς σύκοις ξηροῖς ἤσκει. ταύτην ἦξαν Πισαῖοι,
85   Ἠλείων ἀσχολουμένων διὰ τὸν πρὸς Δυμαίους πόλεμον.
Εἰκοστὴ θ΄. Χίονις Λάκων, οὗ τὸ ἄλμα ποδῶν ἦν νβ΄, στάδιον.
Τριακοστή. ὁ αὐτὸς τὸ δεύτερον.
Πισαῖοι Ἠλείων ἀποστάντες ταύτην τε ἦξαν, καὶ τὰς ἑξῆς κβ΄.
Τριακοστὴ α΄. Χίονις Λάκων, τὸ τρίτον, στάδιον.
90   Τριακοστὴ β΄. Κρατῖνος Μεγαρεὺς στάδιον.
ὅτε καὶ πυγμὴν Κομαῖος τρίτος ἀδελφῶν ἀγωνισάμενος ἐνίκα.
Τριακοστὴ γ΄. Γύλις Λάκων στάδιον.
προσετέθη παγκράτιον καὶ ἐνίκα Λύγδαμις Συρακούσιος ὑπερμεγέθης, ὃς
στάδιον ἐξεμέτρησε τοῖς αὑτοῦ ποσί, μόνας ἑξακοσίας παραθέσεις ποιησά-
95   μενος.
προσετέθη κέλης καὶ ἐνίκα Κραξίλας Θεσσαλός.
Τριακοστὴ δ΄. Στόμας Ἀθηναῖος στάδιον.
Τριακοστὴ ε΄. Σφαῖρος Λάκων στάδιον.
καὶ δίαυλον Κύλων Ἀθηναῖος ὁ ἐπιθέμενος τυραννίδι.
100 Τριακοστὴ ς΄. Φρύνων Ἀθηναῖος,
ὃς Πιττακῷ μονομαχῶν ἀνῃρέθη, στάδιον.

86 ps. Io. Ant. fr. 34* (574 Ro.) Χιόνου τοῦ Λάκωνος τὸ ἄλμα ποδῶν ἦν νβ΄.

73 cf. Paus. 4,15,1; Phleg. Trall. FGrHist 257 F5   **74s** cf. Paus. 5,8,7; Philostr., gym. 12 (142,24–32 Jü.)   **78** cf. Paus. 5,8,7   **82** cf. Dion. Hal. 3,1,3; Paus. 2,24,7   **83** cf. Paus. 3,14,3; 4,23,4.10; 8,39,3   **93–95** cf. Paus. 5,8,8; Philostr., gym. 12 (142,32 – 144,2 Jü.); Sol. 1,74   **98** cf. Dion. Hal. 3,36,1   **99** cf. Hdt. 5,71; Thuc. 1,126,3   **100s** cf. Hipp. Rheg. FGrHist 554 F3; Diog. Laert. 1,74

76 Κλεοπτόλεμος] *Kleoptilomeos* armen.   **85** Δυμαίους Scal. δυσμαίους P *Westländer* (δυσμικούς) armen.   **86** νβ΄ P ps. Io. Ant. κβ΄ armen.   **96** κέλης armen. καὶ et lacuna P   **100** Τριακοστὴ ς΄ + Ἀρυτάμας Λάκων στάδιον· παγκράτιον Rutgers ex Hipp. Rheg. et Diog. Laert.   **101** Πιττακῷ] *auf der Insel Kos* (ἐπὶ τῇ Κῷ) armen. | στάδιον < Rutgers

23rd. Icarius of Hyperesia   stadion race.
   Boxing was added, and Onomastus of Smyrna was the victor. He also established rules for boxing.
24th. Cleoptolemus of Laconia   stadion race.
25th. Thalpis of Laconia   stadion race.
   A four-horse chariot race was added, and Pagon of Thebes was the victor.
26th. Callisthenes of Laconia   stadion race.
   Philombrotus of Laconia, a pentathlete, was the victor in three Olympics.
   The Carnean games, a contest for cithara players, were first established in Lacedaemonia.
27th. Eurybus of Athens   stadion race.
28th. Charmis of Laconia   stadion race.
   He used to train on a diet of dried figs. The people of Pisa held these games, since the Eleans were occupied with the war with the Dymaeans.
29th. Chionis of Laconia, whose leap was 52 feet,[8]   stadion race.
30th. The same man, for a second time.
   The people of Pisa revolted from the Eleans, and held these and the next 22 games.
31st. Chionis of Laconia, for the third time   stadion race.
32nd. Cratinus of Megara   stadion race.
   At these games, Comaeus was the third of brothers to win in boxing.
33rd. Gylis of Laconia   stadion race.
   A pancration was added, and the victor was Lygdamis of Syracuse, an enormous man who measured out the stadion with his feet in only 600 paces.
   A horse race was added, and the victor was Craxilas of Thessaly.
34th. Stomas of Athens   stadion race.
35th. Sphaerus of Laconia   stadion race.
   Cylon of Athens, who later attempted to set himself up as tyrant, was the victor in the double-course race.
36th. Phrynon of Athens,[9]
   who was killed in single combat with Pittacus,   stadion race.

---

8   Cf. armen.: 22 feet. The number 52, while implausibly high, is attested in both P and ps. John of Antioch, and is thus to be preferred to the Armenian text. The Armenian translator either intentionally reduced the number to a more credible 22 feet or mistakenly copied this numeral from the succeeding entry (l. 88 of the Greek text); see also Moretti 1953,27f.
9   On the basis of parallel notices from Hippys of Rhegium and Diogenes Laertius, Rutgers' emendation names Arytamas as the stadion victor and Phrynon as the victor in the pancration (see app.). Although this restoration is plausible, it is uncertain whether it represents Africanus' original text.

Τριακοστὴ ζ'. Εὐρυκλείδας Λάκων στάδιον.
προσετέθη στάδιον παίδων, καὶ ἐνίκα Πολυνίκης Ἠλεῖος.
προσετέθη καὶ παίδων πάλη καὶ ἐνίκα Ἱπποσθένης Λάκων, ὃς διαλιπὼν μίαν
105   τὰς ἑξῆς πέντε Ὀλυμπιάδας ἀνδρῶν πάλην ἐνίκησε.
Τριακοστὴ η'. Ὀλυνθεὺς Λάκων στάδιον.
προσετέθη παίδων πένταθλος, καὶ ἠγωνίσαντο τότε μόνον·
ἐνίκα Δευτελίδας Λάκων.
Τριακοστὴ θ'. Ῥιψόλαος Λάκων στάδιον.
110 Τεσσαρακοστή. Ὀλυνθεὺς Λάκων τὸ δεύτερον στάδιον.
Τεσσαρακοστὴ α'. Κλεώνδας Θηβαῖος στάδιον.
προσετέθη παίδων πυγμή, καὶ ἐνίκα Φιλώτας Συβαρίτης.
Τεσσαρακοστὴ β'. Λυκώτας Λάκων στάδιον.
Τεσσαρακοστὴ γ'. Κλέων Ἐπιδαύριος στάδιον.
115 Τεσσαρακοστὴ δ'. Γέλων Λάκων στάδιον.
Τεσσαρακοστὴ ε'. Ἀντικράτης Ἐπιδαύριος στάδιον.
Τεσσαρακοστὴ ς'. Χρυσόμαξος Λάκων στάδιον,
καὶ Πολυμήστωρ Μιλήσιος παίδων στάδιον, ὃς αἰπολῶν λαγὼν κατέλαβε.
Τεσσαρακοστὴ ζ'. Εὐρυκλῆς Λάκων στάδιον.
120 Τεσσαρακοστὴ η'. Γλύκων Κροτωνιάτης στάδιον.
Πυθαγόρας Σάμιος ἐκκριθεὶς παίδων πυγμήν, καὶ ὡς θῆλυς χλευαζόμενος,
προβὰς εἰς τοὺς ἄνδρας, ἅπαντας ἑξῆς ἐνίκησε.
Τεσσαρακοστὴ θ'. Λυκῖνος Κροτωνιάτης στάδιον.
Πεντηκοστή. Ἐπιτελίδας Λάκων στάδιον.
125   οἱ ἑπτὰ σοφοὶ ὠνομάσθησαν.
Πεντηκοστὴ α'. Ἐρατοσθένης Κροτωνιάτης στάδιον.
Πεντηκοστὴ β'. Ἆγις Ἠλεῖος στάδιον.
Πεντηκοστὴ γ'. Ἄγνων Πεπαρήθιος στάδιον.
Πεντηκοστὴ δ'. Ἱππόστρατος Κροτωνιάτης στάδιον.
130 Ἀρηχίων Φιγαλεὺς τὸ τρίτον νικῶν παγκράτιον ψιλωθεὶς ἀπέθανε, καὶ νεκρὸς ἐστέφθη, φθάσαντος ἀπείπασθαι τοῦ ἀνταγωνιστοῦ, κλωμένου αὐτῷ τοῦ ποδὸς ὑπ' ἐκείνου.

118 ps. Io. Ant. fr. 35* (574 Ro.) Πολυμήστωρ ὁ Μιλήσιος λαγὼν *ἐκ ποδῶν* κατέλαβε.   **121s** Sync. (287,1s Moss.) Πυθαγόρας ὁ Σάμιος Ὀλυμπίασιν ἐκκριθεὶς παίδων πυγμῇ ὡς *ἁπαλὸς προσβὰς τοὺς ἄνδρας* ἐνίκα.   **130–132** Sync. (287,2–5 Moss.) Κατὰ τὴν νδ' Ὀλυμπιάδα Ἀρριχίων Φιγαλεὺς τὸ τρίτον νικῶν παγκράτιον *ψιλισθεὶς* ἀπέθανε, νεκρός τε ἐστέφθη, φθάσαντος ἀπείπασθαι τοῦ ἀνταγωνιστοῦ, κλωμένου τοῦ ποδὸς ὑπ' αὐτοῦ.

103–105 cf. Paus. 3,13,9; 5,8,9; Philostr., gym. 1 (134,14–16 Jü.)   **107s** cf. Paus. 5,9,1; 6,15,8; Philostr., gym. 13 (144,3–5 Jü.); SIG³ 1056,1s **111** cf. Dion. Hal. 3,46,1; Philostr., gym. 13 (144,8–11 Jü.)   **112** cf. Paus. 5,8,9; SIG³ 1056,5s   **118** cf. Philostr., gym. 13 (144,5–8 Jü.); 43 (168,18–24 Jü.); Sol. 1,97   **120** cf. Paus. 10,7,4   **121s** cf. Eratosthenes FGrHist 241 F11a   **124** cf. Diod. Sic. 5,9,2; Dion. Hal. 4,1,1   **130–132** cf. Paus. 8,40,1; Philostr., gym. 21 (150,5–9 Jü.); Philostr., imag. 2,6,1

112 Συβαρίτης armen. συκαρίτης P

37th. Eurycleidas of Laconia stadion race.
A stadion race for boys was added, and the victor was Polynices of Elis.
A wrestling contest for boys was also added. The victor was Hipposthenes of Laconia, who starting with the Olympics after the next one, was the victor in the men's wrestling contest five times in a row.

38th. Olyntheus of Laconia stadion race.
A pentathlon for boys was added, but this was the only time that they competed in the contest. The victor was Deutelidas of Laconia.

39th. Rhipsolaus of Laconia stadion race.
40th. Olyntheus of Laconia for a second time stadion race.
41st. Cleondas of Thebes stadion race.
Boxing for boys was added, and the victor was Philotas of Sybaris.

42nd. Lycotas of Laconia stadion race.
43rd. Cleon of Epidaurus stadion race.
44th. Gelon of Laconia stadion race.
45th. Anticrates of Epidaurus stadion race.
46th. Chrysomaxus of Laconia stadion race.
Polymestor of Miletus was the victor in the boys' stadion race. While he was tending goats, he caught a hare.

47th. Eurycles of Laconia stadion race.
48th. Glycon of Croton stadion race.
Pythagoras of Samos, after he was rejected from boys' boxing and mocked for being womanish, advanced to men's boxing and defeated everyone one after the other.

49th. Lycinus of Croton stadion race.
50th. Epitelidas of Laconia stadion race.
The seven sages were designated.

51st. Eratosthenes of Croton stadion race.
52nd. Agis of Elis stadion race.
53rd. Hagnon of Peparethus stadion race.
54th. Hippostratus of Croton stadion race.
Arichion of Phigaleia, the victor in the pancration for the third time, died defenseless. Even though he was dead, he was crowned as the victor, because his opponent had already given up after his foot was broken by him.

Πεντηκοστὴ ε΄. Ἱππόστρατος ὁ αὐτὸς τὸ δεύτερον.
ὅτε Κῦρος ἐβασίλευε Περσῶν.
135 Πεντηκοστὴ ϛ΄. Φαῖδρος Φαρσάλιος στάδιον.
Πεντηκοστὴ ζ΄. Λάδρομος Λάκων στάδιον.
Πεντηκοστὴ η΄. Διόγνητος Κροτωνιάτης στάδιον.
Πεντηκοστὴ θ΄. Ἀρχίλοχος Κερκυραῖος στάδιον.
Ἑξηκοστή. Ἀπελλαῖος Ἠλεῖος στάδιον.
140 Ἑξηκοστὴ α΄. Ἀγάθαρχος Κερκυραῖος στάδιον.
Ἑξηκοστὴ β΄. Ἐρυξίας Χαλκιδεὺς στάδιον.
Μίλων Κροτωνιάτης πάλην· ὃς νικᾷ Ὀλύμπια ἑξάκις, Πύθια ἑξάκις, Ἴσθμια δεκάκις, Νέμεα ἐννάκις.
Ἑξηκοστὴ γ΄. Παρμενίδης Καμαριναῖος στάδιον.
145 Ἑξηκοστὴ δ΄. Μένανδρος Θεσσαλεὺς στάδιον.
Ἑξηκοστὴ ε΄. Ἀνοχᾶς Ταραντῖνος στάδιον.
Προσετέθη ὁπλίτης, καὶ ἐνίκα Δαμάρητος Ἡραιεύς.
Ἑξηκοστὴ ϛ΄. Ἰσχυρὸς Ἱμεραῖος στάδιον.
Ἑξηκοστὴ ζ΄. Φανᾶς Πελληνεύς·
150 πρῶτος ἐτρίσσευσεν, στάδιον, δίαυλον, ὅπλον.
Ἑξηκοστὴ η΄. Ἰσόμαχος Κροτωνιάτης στάδιον.
Ἑξηκοστὴ θ΄. ὁ αὐτὸς τὸ δεύτερον.
Ἑβδομηκοστή. Νικέας Ὀπούντιος στάδιον.
Ἑβδομηκοστὴ α΄. Τισικράτης Κροτωνιάτης στάδιον.
155 Ἑβδομηκοστὴ β΄. ὁ αὐτὸς τὸ δεύτερον.
Ἑβδομηκοστὴ γ΄. Ἀστύαλος Κροτωνιάτης στάδιον.
Ἑβδομηκοστὴ δ΄. ὁ αὐτὸς τὸ δεύτερον.
Ἑβδομηκοστὴ ε΄. ὁ αὐτὸς τὸ τρίτον.
Ἑβδομηκοστὴ ϛ΄. Σκάμανδρος Μιτυληναῖος στάδιον.
160 Ἑβδομηκοστὴ ζ΄. Δάνδης Ἀργεῖος στάδιον.
Ἑβδομηκοστὴ η΄. Παρμενίδης Ποσειδωνιάτης στάδιον.

134 → F34,19s.41–48.67s; F62,2–4; F73,5s; F74 **142s** ps. Io. Ant. fr. 36* (574 Ro.) Μίλων ὁ Κροτωνιάτης ἐνίκησεν Ὀλύμπια ἑξάκις, Ἴσθμια δεκάκις, Νέμεα ἐννάκις.

137 cf. Paus. 10,5,13 **140** cf. Dion. Hal. 4,41,1 **141** cf. Iambl., vit. Pythag. 7,35 **142** cf. Simonides in Anth. Graeca 16,24; Diod. Sic. 12,9,5; Strabo 6,1,12; Paus. 6,14,5; Philostr., gym. 1 (134,14–19 Jü.) **144** cf. Diod. Sic. 1,68,6 **146** cf. Paus. 6,14,11 **147** cf. Paus. 5,8,10; 6,10,4; 8,26,2;10,7,7; Philostr., gym. 13 (144,11–13 Jü.); SIG³ 1056,7s **151** cf. Dion. Hal. 5,1,1 **152** cf. Dion. Hal. 5,37,1 **153** cf. Dion. Hal. 5,50,1 **154** cf. Dion. Hal. 6,1,1 **155** cf. Dion. Hal. 6,34,1; Paus. 6,9,5 **156** cf. Dion. Hal. 8,1,1; Plin., nat. hist. 34,8,19; Paus. 6,13,1; Clem. Alex., strom. 3,6,50 **157** cf. Dion. Hal. 8,77,1 **158** cf. Diod. Sic. 11,1,2; Dion. Hal. 9,1,1 **159** cf. Diod. Sic. 11,48,1; Dion. Hal. 9,18,1 **160** cf. Simonides in Anth. Graeca 13,14; Diod. Sic. 11,53,1; Dion. Hal. 9,37,1 **161** cf. Diod. Sic. 11,65,1; Dion. Hal. 9,56,1

145 Μένανδρος armen. εὔανδρος P **147** Ἡραιεύς armen. Paus. ἡρακλείδης P **153** Νικέας armen. Dion. Hal. νικαίστας P **159** Σκάμανδρος armen. Dion. Hal. σκαμάνδριος P Diod. Sic.

55th. The same Hippostratus for a second time   stadion race.
  At that time Cyrus became king of the Persians.
56th. Phaedrus of Pharsalus   stadion race.
57th. Ladromus of Laconia   stadion race.
58th. Diognetus of Croton   stadion race.
59th. Archilochus of Corcyra   stadion race.
60th. Apellaeus of Elis   stadion race.
61st. Agatharchus of Corcyra   stadion race.
62nd. Eryxias of Chalcis   stadion race.
  Milon of Croton was the victor in wrestling. He was the victor six times at the Olympic games, six times at the Pythian games, ten times at the Isthmian games, and nine times at the Nemean games.
63rd. Parmenides of Camarina   stadion race.
64th. Menander of Thessaly   stadion race.
65th. Anochas of Tarentum   stadion race.
  A race of men in full armor was added, and Damaretus of Heraea was the victor.
66th. Ischyrus of Himera   stadion race.
67th. Phanas of Pellene.
  He was the first to be the victor in three races: the stadion race, the double-course race and the race in full armor.
68th. Isomachus of Croton   stadion race.
69th. The same man, for a second time
70th. Niceas of Opus   stadion race.
71st. Tisicrates of Croton   stadion race.
72nd. The same man, for a second time.
73rd. Astyalus of Croton   stadion race.
74th. The same man, for a second time.
75th. The same man, for a third time.
76th. Scamander of Mytilene   stadion race.
77th. Dandes of Argos   stadion race.
78th. Parmenides of Poseidonia   stadion race.

Ἑβδομηκοστὴ θ'. Ξενοφῶν Κορίνθιος στάδιον.
Ὀγδοηκοστή. Τορύμμας Θεσσαλὸς στάδιον.
πάλην Ἀμησινᾶς Βαρκαῖος, ὃς βουκολῶν ταύρῳ ἐγυμνάζετο· ὃν καὶ εἰς Πί-
165 σαν ἀγαγὼν συνεγυμνάσθη.
Ὀγδοηκοστὴ α'. Πολύμναστος Κυρηναῖος στάδιον.
Ὀγδοηκοστὴ β'. Λύκος Λαρισσαῖος στάδιον.
Ὀγδοηκοστὴ γ'. Κρίσσων Ἱμεραῖος στάδιον.
Ὀγδοηκοστὴ δ'. ὁ αὐτὸς τὸ δεύτερον.
170 Ὀγδοηκοστὴ ε'. ὁ αὐτὸς τὸ τρίτον.
Ὀγδοηκοστὴ ς'. Θεόπομπος Θεσσαλὸς στάδιον.
Ὀγδοηκοστὴ ζ'. Σώφρων Ἀμβρακιώτης στάδιον.
ἐν ᾧ ὁ Πελοποννησιακὸς πόλεμος συνεκροτήθη.
Ὀγδοηκοστὴ η'. Σύμμαχος Μεσσήνιος στάδιον.
175 Ὀγδοηκοστὴ θ'. ὁ αὐτὸς τὸ δεύτερον.
Ἐννενηκοστή. Ὑπέρβιος Συρακούσιος στάδιον.
Ἐννενηκοστὴ α'. Ἐξάγεντος Ἀκραγαντῖνος στάδιον.
Ἐννενηκοστὴ β'. ὁ αὐτὸς τὸ δεύτερον.
Ἐννενηκοστὴ γ'. Εὔβατος Κυρηναῖος στάδιον.
180 παγκράτιον Πολύδαμας Σκοτουσσαῖος ὑπερμεγέθης, ὃς ἐν Πέρσαις παρὰ
Ὤχῳ γενόμενος λέοντας ἀνῄρει, καὶ ὡπλισμένους γυμνὸς κατηγωνίσατο·
ἵστη δὲ καὶ ἅρματα ἐλαυνόμενα κατὰ κράτος.
προσετέθη συνωρίς, καὶ ἐνίκα Εὐαγόρας Ἠλεῖος.
Ἐννενηκοστὴ δ'. Κροκίνας Λαρισσαῖος στάδιον.
185 Ἐννενηκοστὴ ε'. Μίνων Ἀθηναῖος στάδιον.
Ἐννενηκοστὴ ς'. Εὐπόλεμος Ἠλεῖος στάδιον.
προσετέθη σαλπιγκτής, καὶ ἐνίκα Τίμαιος Ἠλεῖος.
προσετέθη καὶ κῆρυξ, καὶ ἐνίκα Κράτης Ἠλεῖος.

172s → F81a,2-5   **180-182** Sync. (306,15-17 Moss.) *Τότε δὴ καὶ* Πολυδάμας Σκοτουσαῖος *παγκράτιον νικήσας παρ᾽ Ὤχῳ τῷ Περσῶν βασιλεῖ γέγονε μετὰ χρόνους, λέοντας διαχρώμενος καὶ ὡπλισμένοις γυμνὸς πολεμῶν, παμμεγέθης ὑπάρχων καὶ ἀλκιμώτατος.*   **187** Sync. (310,15 Moss.) Σαλπιγκτῶν <καὶ> κηρύκων ἀγὼν προσετέθη ἐν Ὀλυμπίᾳ.

162 cf. Pind., Olymp. 13; Diod. Sic. 11,70,1; Dion. Hal. 9,61,1; Paus. 4,24,5   **163** cf. Diod. Sic. 11,77,1; Dion. Hal. 10,1,1   **164s** cf. Philostr., gym. 43 (168,18-23 Jü.)   **166** cf. Diod. Sic. 11,84,1; Dion. Hal. 10,26,1   **167** cf. Dion. Hal. 10,53,1   **168** cf. Diod. Sic. 12,5,1; Dion. Hal. 11,1,1; 10,61,1; Paus. 5,23,4; Clem. Alex., strom. 3,6,50   **169** cf. Diod. Sic. 12,23,1   **170** cf. Diod. Sic. 12,29,1   **171** cf. Diod. Sic. 12,33,1   **172** cf. Diod. Sic. 12,37,1   **174** cf. Diod. Sic. 12,49,1; Paus. 6,2,10   **175** cf. Diod. Sic. 12,65,1; Paus. 6,2,10   **176** cf. Diod. Sic. 12,77,1   **177** cf. Diod. Sic. 12,82,1; Aelian., varia hist. 2,8   **178** cf. Diod. Sic. 13,34,1; 13,82,7   **179** cf. Diod. Sic. 13,68,1; Paus. 6,8,3   **180-182** cf. Paus. 6,5,1s   **183** cf. Diod. Sic. 13,75,1; Paus. 5,8,10; SIG³ 1056,10s   **184** cf. Diod. Sic. 14,3,1   **185** cf. Diod. Sic. 14,35,1   **186** cf. Diod. Sic. 14,54,1; Paus. 6,3,7; 8,45,4

174 Μεσσήνιος armen. μερλήνιος P   **179** Εὔβατος Diod. Sic. *Eurōtos* armen. εὔκατος P   **185** Μίνων armen. μένων P Μίνως Diod. Sic.

79th. Xenophon of Corinth   stadion race.
80th. Torymmas of Thessaly   stadion race.
   Amesinas of Barce was the victor in wrestling. He trained with a bull while he was tending cattle. He even brought it to Pisa and trained with it.
81st. Polymnastus of Cyrene   stadion race.
82nd. Lycus of Larissa   stadion race.
83rd. Crisson of Himera   stadion race.
84th. The same man, for a second time.
85th. The same man, for a third time.
86th. Theopompus of Thessaly   stadion race.
87th. Sophron of Ambracia   stadion race.
   At this time, the Peloponnesian war broke out.
88th. Symmachus of Messenia   stadion race.
89th. The same man, for a second time.
90th. Hyperbius of Syracuse   stadion race.
91st. Exagentus of Acragas   stadion race.
92nd. The same man, for a second time.
93rd. Eubatus of Cyrene   stadion race.
   Polydamas of Scotussa, a huge man, was the victor in the pancration. When he was at the court of Ochus among the Persians, he killed lions and fought unarmed against armed men; he even stopped chariots advancing at top speed.
   A race was added for chariots drawn by a pair of horses, and Evagoras of Elis was the victor.
94th. Crocinas of Larissa   stadion race.
95th. Minon of Athens   stadion race.
96th. Eupolemus of Elis   stadion race.
   A trumpet contest was added, and Timaeus of Elis was the victor.
   A herald contest was added, and Crates of Elis was the victor.

Ἐννενηκοστὴ ζ'. Τεριναῖος Ἠλεῖος στάδιον.
190 Ἐννενηκοστὴ η'. Σώσιππος Δελφὸς στάδιον.
Ἀριστόδημος Ἠλεῖος πάλην· οὗ μέσα οὐδεὶς ἔλαβεν.
Ἐννενηκοστὴ θ'. Δίκων Συρακούσιος στάδιον.
προσετέθη τέθριππον πωλικόν, καὶ ἐνίκα Εὐρύβατος Λάκων.
Ἑκατοστή. Διονυσόδωρος Ταραντῖνος στάδιον.
195 Ἑκατοστὴ α'. Δάμων Θούριος στάδιον.
Ἑκατοστὴ β'. ὁ αὐτὸς τὸ δεύτερον.
Ἑκατοστὴ γ'. Πυθόστρατος Ἐφέσιος στάδιον.
Ἑκατοστὴ δ'. Φωκίδης Ἀθηναῖος στάδιον.
αὕτη ὑπὸ Πισαίων ἐτέθη.
200 Ἑκατοστὴ ε'. Πῶρος Κυρηναῖος στάδιον.
Ἑκατοστὴ ς'. ὁ αὐτὸς τὸ δεύτερον.
Ἑκατοστὴ ζ'. Μικρίνας Ταραντῖνος στάδιον.
Ἑκατοστὴ η'. Πολυκλῆς Κυρηναῖος στάδιον.
Ἑκατοστὴ θ'. Ἀριστόλοχος Ἀθηναῖος στάδιον.
205 <Ἑκατοστὴ ι'. Ἀντικλῆς Ἀθηναῖος στάδιον.>
Ἑκατοστὴ ια'. Κλεόμαντις Κλειτόριος στάδιον.
Ἑκατοστὴ ιβ'. Εὐρύλας Χαλκιδεὺς στάδιον.
Ἀλέξανδρος Βαβυλῶνα κατέσχε, Δαρεῖον καθελών.
Ἑκατοστὴ ιγ'. Κλίτων Μακεδὼν στάδιον.
210 Ἀγεὺς Ἀργεῖος δόλιχον, ὃς ἐν Ἄργει τὴν ἑαυτοῦ νίκην
αὐθημερὸν ἀνήγγειλεν.
Ἑκατοστὴ ιδ'. Μικίνας Ῥόδιος στάδιον.
Ἀλέξανδρος ἐτελεύτησε· μεθ' ὃν εἰς πολλοὺς διαιρεθείσης τῆς ἀρχῆς, Αἰγύπτου καὶ Ἀλεξανδρείας ἐβασίλευσε Πτολεμαῖος.
215 Ἑκατοστὴ ιε'. Δαμασίας Ἀμφιπολίτης στάδιον.
Ἑκατοστὴ ις'. Δημοσθένης Λάκων στάδιον.
Ἑκατοστὴ ιζ'. Παρμενίδης Μιτυληναῖος στάδιον.

208 → F73,22–24; F82,34   213s → F82,35; F86,1–3

189 cf. Diod. Sic. 14,94,1   190 cf. Diod. Sic. 14,107,1   191 cf. Paus. 6,3,4   192 cf. Diod. Sic. 15,14,1; Paus. 6,3,11; Anth. Graec. 13,15   193   cf. Paus. 5,8,10; SIG³ 1056,12s   194   cf. Diod. Sic. 15,23,1   195 cf. Diod. Sic. 15,36,1; Paus. 7,25,4   196 cf. Diod. Sic. 15,50,1; Paus. 4,27,9; 6,5,3; 8,27,8   197 cf. Diod. Sic. 15,71,1   198s cf. Diod. Sic. 15,78,1; Paus. 6,22,3   200 cf. Diod. Sic. 16,2,1; Paus. 10,2,3   201 cf. Diod. Sic. 16,15,1   202 cf. Diod. Sic. 16,37,1   203 cf. Diod. Sic. 16,53,1; Paus. 10,3,1   204 cf. Diod. Sic. 16,69,1   205 cf. Diod. Sic. 16,77,1   206 cf. Diod. Sic. 16,91,1   207 cf. Diod. Sic. 17,40,1   209 cf. Diod. Sic. 17,82,1   212 cf. Diod. Sic. 17,113,1   216 cf. Diod. Sic. 19,17,1; Paus. 6,16,8   SIG³ 1069   217 cf. Diod. Sic. 19,77,1

190 Δελφὸς armen. ἀδελφὸς P   191 μέσα Scal. μέσας P   198 στάδιον armen. (cf. etiam Diod. Sic. 15,78,1) πάλη P πάλην Scal.   200 Πῶρος armen. Paus. Diod. Sic. παῦρος P   205 restituimus ex armen. | Ἀντικλῆς Diod. Sic. Anikles armen.

97th. Terinaeus of Elis   stadion race.
98th. Sosippus of Delphi   stadion race.
    Aristodemus of Elis was the victor in wrestling. No-one could hold him around the middle.
99th. Dicon of Syracuse   stadion race.
    A four-horse chariot race was added, and Eurybatus of Laconia was the victor.
100th. Dionysodorus of Tarentum   stadion race.
101st. Damon of Thurii   stadion race.
102nd. The same man, for a second time.
103rd. Pythostratus of Ephesus   stadion race.
104th. Phocides of Athens   stadion race.
    The contest was held by the people of Pisa.
105th. Porus of Cyrene   stadion race.
106th. The same man, for a second time.
107th. Micrinas of Tarentum   stadion race.
108th. Polycles of Cyrene   stadion race.
109th. Aristolochus of Athens   stadion race.
<110th. Anticles of Athens   stadion race.>
111th. Cleomantis of Cleitor   stadion race.
112th. Eurylas of Chalcis   stadion race.
    Alexander captured Babylon and killed Darius.
113th. Cliton of Macedonia   stadion race.
    Ageus of Argos was the victor in the long race. On the very same day, he personally announced his victory in Argos.
114th. Micinas of Rhodes   stadion race.
    Alexander died, and his kingdom was subsequently divided among many. Ptolemy became king of Egypt and Alexandria.
115th. Damasias of Amphipolis   stadion race.
116th. Demosthenes of Laconia   stadion race.
117th. Parmenides of Mytilene   stadion race.

Ἑκατοστὴ ιη΄. Ἀνδρομένης Κορίνθιος στάδιον.
Ἀντήνωρ Ἀθηναῖος ἢ Μιλήσιος, παγκράτιον, ἀκόντιον, περιοδονίκης ἄλειπτος ἐν ταῖς τρισὶν ἡλικίαις.
Ἑκατοστὴ ιθ΄. Ἀνδρομένης Κορίνθιος στάδιον.
Ἑκατοστὴ κ΄. Πυθαγόρας Μάγνης <ἀπὸ Μαιάνδρου> στάδιον.
πάλην Κερᾶς Ἀργεῖος, ὃς χηλὰς ἀπέσπα βοός.
Ἑκατοστὴ κα΄. Πυθαγόρας τὸ δεύτερον.
Ἑκατοστὴ κβ΄. Ἀντίγονος Μακεδὼν στάδιον.
Ἑκατοστὴ κγ΄. ὁ αὐτὸς τὸ δεύτερον.
Ἑκατοστὴ κδ΄. Φιλόμηλος Φαρσάλιος στάδιον.
Ἑκατοστὴ κε΄. Λάδας Αἰγιεὺς στάδιον.
Ἑκατοστὴ κς΄. Ἰδαῖος ἢ Νικάτωρ Κυρηναῖος στάδιον.
Ἑκατοστὴ κζ΄. Περιγένης Ἀλεξανδρεὺς στάδιον.
Ἑκατοστὴ κη΄. Σέλευκος Μακεδὼν στάδιον.
Ἑκατοστὴ κθ΄. Φιλῖνος Κῷος στάδιον.
Ἑκατοστὴ λ΄. ὁ αὐτὸς τὸ δεύτερον.
Ἑκατοστὴ λα΄. Ἀμμώνιος Ἀλεξανδρεὺς στάδιον.
Ἑκατοστὴ λβ΄. Ξενοφάνης Αἰτωλὸς <ἐξ Ἀμφίσσης> στάδιον.
Ἑκατοστὴ λγ΄. Σιμύλος Νεαπολίτης στάδιον.
Πάρθοι Μακεδόνων ἀπέστησαν, καὶ πρῶτος ἐβασίλευσεν Ἀρσάκης, ὅθεν Ἀρσακίδαι.
Ἑκατοστὴ λδ΄. Ἀλκίδας Λάκων στάδιον.
Ἑκατοστὴ λε΄. Ἐράτων Αἰτωλὸς στάδιον.
πυγμὴν Κλεόξενος Ἀλεξανδρεὺς περιοδονίκης ἀτραυμάτιστος.
Ἑκατοστὴ λς΄. Πυθοκλῆς Σικυώνιος στάδιον.
Ἑκατοστὴ λζ΄. Μενεσθεὺς Βαρκυλίτης στάδιον.
Ἑκατοστὴ λη΄. Δημήτριος Ἀλεξανδρεὺς στάδιον.
Ἑκατοστὴ λθ΄. Ἰολαΐδας Ἀργεῖος στάδιον.
Ἑκατοστὴ μ΄. Ζώπυρος Συρακούσιος στάδιον.
Ἑκατοστὴ μα΄. Δωρόθεος Ῥόδιος στάδιον.
Ἑκατοστὴ μβ΄. Κράτης Ἀλεξανδρεὺς στάδιον.
Κάπρος Ἠλεῖος πάλην καὶ παγκράτιον ἐνίκα μεθ᾽ Ἡρακλέα καὶ ἀναγράφεται δεύτερος ἀφ᾽ Ἡρακλέους.
Ἑκατοστὴ μγ΄. Ἡράκλειτος Σάμιος στάδιον.

218 cf. Diod. Sic. 20,37,1   **221** cf. Diod. Sic. 20,91,1   **228** cf. Paus. 3,21,1; 10,23,14   **229** cf. Paus. 6,12,2   **232s** cf. Paus. 6,17,2   **249s** cf. Paus. 6,15,3.10; Lucian., verae hist. 2,22

219 ἀκόντιον] ἀκονιτί Rutgers ἀγωνιστής (?) armen.   **222** ἀπὸ Μαιάνδρου armen.   **223** πάλην < armen.   **232** Κῷος + hinzügefugt ward das Füllen-Zweigespann, und es siegte Philiasticos des Maketos armen.   **234** Ἀλεξανδρεὺς + hinzügefügt ward das Füllen-Einpferd, und es siegte Ippokrates des Ordthesalos armen.   **235** ἐξ Ἀμφίσσης armen.   **240** Αἰτωλὸς Scal. αἰτώλιος P   **249** Κάπρος Paus. κάρος P Κάπος armen.

118th. Andromenes of Corinth   stadion race.
Antenor of Athens or Miletus, in the pancration, javelin, and undefeated victor in all the major games in three age groups.
119th. Andromenes of Corinth   stadion race.
120th. Pythagoras of Magnesia <on the Maeander>   stadion race.
Ceras of Argos was the victor in wrestling. He tore the hooves off a cow.
121st. Pythagoras, for a second time.
122nd. Antigonus of Macedonia   stadion race.
123rd. The same man, for a second time.
124th. Philomelus of Pharsalus   stadion race.
125th. Ladas of Aegium   stadion race.
126th. Idaeus or Nicator of Cyrene   stadion race.
127th. Perigenes of Alexandria   stadion race.
128th. Seleucus of Macedonia   stadion race.
129th. Philinus of Cos   stadion race.
130th. The same man, for a second time.
131st. Ammonius of Alexandria   stadion race.
132nd. Xenophanes of Aetolia <from Amphissa>   stadion race.
133rd. Simylus of Neapolis   stadion race.
The Parthians revolted against the Macedonians; the first to be their king was Arsaces, whence the Arsacids.
134th. Alcidas of Laconia   stadion race.
135th. Eraton of Aetolia   stadion race.
Cleoxenus of Alexandria, winner in all the major games without injury, was the victor in boxing.
136th. Pythocles of Sicyon   stadion race.
137th. Menestheus of Barcyla   stadion race.
138th. Demetrius of Alexandria   stadion race.
139th. Iolaïdas of Argos   stadion race.
140th. Zopyrus of Syracuse   stadion race.
141st. Dorotheus of Rhodes   stadion race.
142nd. Crates of Alexandria   stadion race.
Caprus of Elis was the victor both in wrestling and the pancration, next after Heracles; and he was registered as "second after Heracles".
143rd. Heracleitus of Samos   stadion race.

Ἑκατοστὴ μδ′. Ἡρακλείδης Σαλαμίνιος <ἐκ Κύπρου>   στάδιον.
Ἑκατοστὴ με′. Πυρρίας Αἰτωλὸς   στάδιον.
παίδων πυγμὴν Μόσχος Κολοφώνιος· μόνος παιδικὴν περίοδον.
255   προσετέθη παίδων παγκράτιον, καὶ ἐνίκα Φαίδιμος Ἀλεξανδρεύς.
Ἑκατοστὴ μς′. Μικίων Βοιώτιος   στάδιον.
Ἑκατοστὴ μζ′. Ἀγέμαχος Κυζικηνὸς   στάδιον.
πάλην Κλειτόστρατος Ῥόδιος· ὃς τραχηλίζων ἀπελάμβανεν.
Ἑκατοστὴ μη′. Ἀρκεσίλαος Μεγαλοπολίτης   στάδιον.
260   Ἑκατοστὴ μθ′. Ἱππόστρατος Σελευκεὺς <ἐκ Πιερίας>   στάδιον.
Ἑκατοστὴ ν′. Ὀνησίκριτος Σαλαμίνιος   στάδιον.
Ἑκατοστὴ να′. Θυμίλος Ἀσπένδιος   στάδιον.
Ἑκατοστὴ νβ′. Δημόκριτος Μεγαρεὺς   στάδιον.
Ἑκατοστὴ νγ′. Ἀρίστανδρος Λέσβιος <ἐξ Ἀντίσσης>   στάδιον.
265   Ἑκατοστὴ νδ′. Λεωνίδας Ῥόδιος τριαστὴς   στάδιον.
Ἑκατοστὴ νε′. ὁ αὐτὸς τὸ δεύτερον.
Ἑκατοστὴ νς′. ὁ αὐτὸς τὸ τρίτον.
<Ἀριστομένης> Ῥόδιος τρίτος ἀφ᾽ Ἡρακλέους πάλην ὁμοῦ καὶ παγκράτιον.
Ἑκατοστὴ νζ′. Λεωνίδας τὸ τέταρτον στάδιον, μόνος δὲ καὶ πρῶτος ἐπὶ
270   τέσσαρας Ὀλυμπιάδας στεφάνους Ὀλυμπιακοὺς ἔχει δώδεκα.
Ἑκατοστὴ νη′. Ὄρθων Συρακούσιος   στάδιον.
Ἑκατοστὴ νθ′. Ἄλκιμος Κυζικηνὸς   στάδιον.
Ἑκατοστὴ ξ′. Ἀγνόδωρος Κυζικηνὸς   στάδιον.
Ἑκατοστὴ ξα′. Ἀντίπατρος Ἠπειρώτης   στάδιον.
275   Ἑκατοστὴ ξβ′. Δάμων Δελφὸς   στάδιον.
Ἑκατοστὴ ξγ′. Τιμόθεος Τραλλιανὸς   στάδιον.
Ἑκατοστὴ ξδ′. Βοιωτὸς Σικυώνιος   στάδιον.
Ἑκατοστὴ ξε′. Ἀκουσίλαος Κυρηναῖος   στάδιον.
Ἑκατοστὴ ξς′. Χρυσόγονος Νικαεὺς   στάδιον.
280   Ἑκατοστὴ ξζ′. ὁ αὐτὸς τὸ δεύτερον.
Ἑκατοστὴ ξη′. Νικόμαχος Φιλαδελφεὺς   στάδιον.
Ἑκατοστὴ ξθ′. Νικόδημος Λακεδαιμόνιος   στάδιον.
Ἑκατοστὴ ο′. Σιμμίας Σελευκεὺς ἀπὸ Τίγριος   στάδιον.
Ἑκατοστὴ οα′. Παρμενίσκος Κερκυραῖος   στάδιον.

269s ps. Io. Ant. fr. 33* (572 Ro.) Λεωνίδης μόνος καὶ πρῶτος ἐπὶ τέσσαρας Ὀλυμπιάδας στεφάνους ἔσχε δώδεκα.

255 cf. Paus. 5,8,11; Philostr., gym. 13 (144,13–17 Jü.)   **257** cf. Paus. 6,13,7   **258** cf. Suda τραχηλίζων T 921   **268** cf. Paus. 5,21,10   **269s** cf. Paus. 6,13,4; Philostr., gym. 33 (158,18–20 Jü.)   **273** cf. Paus. 7,16,10

252 ἐκ Κύπρου armen.   **253** Αἰτωλὸς Scal. αἰτώλιος P   **254** παιδικὴν Scal. παιδὶ τὴν P   **259** Ἀρκεσίλαος armen. ἀκεσίλαος P   **260** ἐκ Πιερίας armen.   **264** ἐξ Ἀντίσσης armen.   **268** Ἀριστομένης Paus. *Aristosenes* armen.   **273** Ἀγνόδωρος Gutschmid *Anōdōros* armen. ἀνώδωκος P

144th. Heracleides of Salamis <from Cyprus>   stadion race.
145th. Pyrrhias of Aetolia   stadion race.
   Moschus of Colophon was the victor in boys' boxing. He was the only boy who was the victor in all the major games. A boys' pancration was introduced, and Phaedimus of Alexandria was the victor.
146th. Micion of Boeotia   stadion race.
147th. Agemachus of Cyzicus   stadion race.
   Cleitostratus of Rhodes was the victor in wrestling. By twisting their necks, he overcame his opponents.
148th. Arcesilaus of Megalopolis   stadion race.
149th. Hippostratus of Seleucia <in Pieria>   stadion race.
150th. Onesicritus of Salamis   stadion race.
151st. Thymilus of Aspendus   stadion race.
152nd. Democritus of Megara   stadion race.
153rd. Aristander of Lesbos <from Antissa>   stadion race.
154th. Leonidas of Rhodes, three times victor   stadion race.
155th. The same man, for a second time.
156th. The same man, for a third time.
   <Aristomenes> of Rhodes was the third from Heracles to be the victor both in wrestling and the pancration.
157th. Leonidas, victor for the fourth time   stadion race.
   He was the first and only man to obtain 12 Olympic crowns over four Olympics.
158th. Orthon of Syracuse   stadion race.
159th. Alcimus of Cyzicus   stadion race.
160th. Hagnodorus of Cyzicus   stadion race.
161st. Antipater of Epirus   stadion race.
162nd. Damon of Delphi   stadion race.
163rd. Timotheus of Tralles   stadion race.
164th. Boeotus of Sicyon   stadion race.
165th. Acusilaus of Cyrene   stadion race.
166th. Chrysogonus of Nicaea   stadion race.
167th. The same man, for a second time.
168th. Nicomachus of Philadelphia   stadion race.
169th. Nicodemus of Lacedaemon   stadion race.
170th. Simmias of Seleuceia on the Tigris   stadion race.
171st. Parmeniscus of Corcyra   stadion race.

285 Ἑκατοστὴ οβ΄. Εὔδαμος Κῷος στάδιον.
   Πρωτοφάνης Μάγνης <ἀπὸ Μαιάνδρου> πάλην καὶ παγκράτιον, τέταρτος ἀφ' Ἡρακλέους.
   Ἑκατοστὴ ογ΄. Παρμενίσκος Κερκυραῖος τὸ δεύτερον στάδιον.
   <Ἑκατοστὴ οδ΄. Δαμόστρατος Λαρισαῖος στάδιον.>
290 Ἑκατοστὴ οε΄. στάδιον παίδων. Ἐπαινετὸς Ἀργεῖος·
   ἄνδρες γὰρ οὐκ ἠγωνίσαντο, Σύλλα πάντας εἰς Ῥώμην μεταπεμψαμένου.
   Ἑκατοστὴ ος΄. Δίων Κυπαρισσεὺς στάδιον.
   Ἑκατοστὴ οζ΄. Ἑκατόμνως Ἠλεῖος στάδιον.
   Ἑκατοστὴ οη΄. Διοκλῆς Ὑπεπηνὸς στάδιον.
295 Στρατόνικος Κορράγου Ἀλεξανδρεύς, πάλην καὶ παγκράτιον πέμπτος ἀφ' Ἡρακλέους· ὃς Νεμέᾳ τῇ αὐτῇ ἡμέρᾳ παίδων καὶ ἀγενείων τέσσαρας στεφάνους ἔσχεν †...†.
   Ἑκατοστὴ οθ΄. Ἀνδρέας Λακεδαιμόνιος στάδιον.
   Ἑκατοστὴ π΄. Ἀνδρόμαχος Ἀμβρακιώτης στάδιον.
300 Ἑκατοστὴ πα΄. Λάμαχος Ταυρομενίτης στάδιον.
   Ἑκατοστὴ πβ΄. Ἀνθεστίων Ἀργεῖος στάδιον.
   Μαρίων Μαρίωνος Ἀλεξανδρεὺς πάλην καὶ παγκράτιον ἕκτος ἀφ' Ἡρακλέους.
   Ἑκατοστὴ πγ΄. Θεόδωρος Μεσήνιος στάδιον.
   Ἰούλιος Καῖσαρ ἐμονάρχησε Ῥωμαίων.
305 Ἑκατοστὴ πδ΄. ὁ αὐτὸς τὸ δεύτερον.
   Αὔγουστος Ῥωμαίων ἐβασίλευε.
   Ἑκατοστὴ πε΄. Ἀρίστων Θούριος στάδιον.
   Ἑκατοστὴ πς΄. Σκάμανδρος Ἀλεξανδρεὺς <τῆς Τρῳάδος> στάδιον.
   Ἑκατοστὴ πζ΄. Ἀρίστων Θούριος στάδιον.
310 Ἑκατοστὴ πη΄. Σώπατρος Ἀργεῖος στάδιον.
   Ἑκατοστὴ πθ΄. Ἀσκληπιάδης Σιδώνιος στάδιον.
   Ἑκατοστὴ ϟ΄. Αὐφίδιος Πατρεὺς στάδιον.
   Ἑκατοστὴ ϟα΄. Διόδοτος Τυανεὺς στάδιον.
   Ἑκατοστὴ ϟβ΄. Διοφάνης Αἰολεὺς στάδιον.
315 Ἑκατοστὴ ϟγ΄. Ἀρτεμίδωρος Θυατείριος στάδιον.
   Ἑκατοστὴ ϟδ΄. Δημάρατος Ἐφέσιος στάδιον.
   Ἑκατοστὴ ϟε΄. ὁ αὐτὸς τὸ δεύτερον.
   Ἑκατοστὴ ϟς΄. Παμμένης Μάγνης ἀπὸ Μαιάνδρου στάδιον.

306 → F89,56s; F93,51–53

286–288 cf. Paus. 1,35,6; 5,21,10   **291** cf. App., bell. civ. 1,99   **293** cf. Phleg. Trall. FGrHist 257 F12,1   **295–297** cf. Paus. 5,21,9; 7,23,5; Aelian., varia hist. 4,15   **302** cf. Paus. 5,21,10

286 ἀπὸ Μαιάνδρου armen. | πάλην καὶ < armen.   **289** restituimus ex armen.   **297** ἔσχεν + ալա, զմերկանալսս մարտին առաջս ձեռս վարելոյ. եւ այս ըստ շնորհաց զճակատան, կամ՝ ի բարեկամին, կամ՝ ի թագաւորս զրեէ. ուսաի և վարեէ իսկ չեավարեցուն: armen.   **299** Ἀμβρακιώτης Scal. ἀμιρακιώτης P der Lakedämonier armen.   **308** τῆς Τρῳάδος armen.

172nd. Eudamus of Cos — stadion race.
Protophanes of Magnesia <on the Maeander> was the victor in wrestling and the pancration, the fourth from Heracles to do so.
173rd. Parmeniscus of Corcyra, for a second time — stadion race.
<174th. Damostratus of Larissa — stadion race.>
175th. Epaenetus of Argos, boys' — stadion race.
Male athletes did not compete in the stadion race, because Sulla had summoned all of them to Rome.
176th. Dion of Cyparissus — stadion race.
177th. Hecatomnos of Elis — stadion race.
178th. Diocles Hypepenus — stadion race.
Stratonicus of Alexandria, son of Corragus, was the victor in wrestling and the pancration, the fifth from Heracles to do so; at the Nemean games, he obtained four crowns on the same day in the contests for boys and youths †…†.[10]
179th. Andreas of Lacedaemon — stadion race.
180th. Andromachus of Ambracia — stadion race.
181st. Lamachus of Tauromenium — stadion race.
182nd. Anthestion of Argos — stadion race.
Marion of Alexandria, son of Marion, was the victor in wrestling and the pancration, the sixth from Heracles to do so.
183rd. Theodorus of Messenia — stadion race.
Iulius Caesar became sole ruler of the Romans.
184th. The same man, for a second time.
Augustus became Roman emperor.
185th. Ariston of Thurii — stadion race.
186th. Scamander of Alexandria <of Troas> — stadion race.
187th. Ariston of Thurii — stadion race.
188th. Sopater of Argos — stadion race.
189th. Asclepiades of Sidon — stadion race.
190th. Auphidius of Patrae — stadion race.
191st. Diodotus of Tyana — stadion race.
192nd. Diophanes of Aeolia — stadion race.
193rd. Artemidorus of Thyateira — stadion race.
194th. Demaratus of Ephesus — stadion race.
195th. The same man, for a second time.
196th. Pammenes of Magnesia on the Maeander — stadion race.

---

10 The text of Eus., chron.armen is insufficiently clear to enable a restoration of the lacunose Greek text. It could be rendered as follows: "… for winning (lit. 'conducting') the gymnastic combats without horse, and by the grace it happened that this was attributed (lit. 'written') either to friends or to kings, so [those deeds] were not even considered to have taken place (lit. 'conducted')" (transl. courtesy of Aram Topchyan). On the problems in the Armenian text, see Karst, p. 257, n. 165.

Ἑκατοστὴ ϙζ'. Ἀσιατικὸς Ἁλικαρνασεὺς στάδιον.
Ἑκατοστὴ ϙη'. Διοφάνης Προυσαεὺς <ἀπ' Ὀλύμπου> στάδιον.
Ἀριστέας Στρατονικεὺς ἢ Μαιάνδριος, πάλην καὶ παγκράτιον ἕβδομος ἀφ' Ἡρακλέους.
Τιβέριος Ῥωμαίων ἐβασίλευσεν.
Ἑκατοστὴ ϙθ'. Αἰσχίνης Μιλήσιος ὁ Γλαυκίας στάδιον.
ἀπεδόθη τῶν ἵππων ὁ δρόμος πάλαι κωλυθεὶς καὶ ἐνίκα <Γερμανικὸς Καῖσαρ ὁ> Τιβερίου Καίσαρος τέθριππον.
Διακοσιοστή. Πολέμων Πετραῖος στάδιον.
Διακοσιοστὴ α'. Δαμασίας Κυδωνιάτης στάδιον.
Διακοσιοστὴ β'. Ἑρμογένης Περγαμηνὸς στάδιον.
Διακοσιοστὴ γ'. Ἀπολλώνιος Ἐπιδαύριος στάδιον.
Διακοσιοστὴ τετάρτη. Σαραπίων Ἀλεξανδρεὺς στάδιον.
[Νεικό]στρατος Αἰγεάτης πάλην καὶ παγκράτιον ὄγδοος <ἀφ' Ἡρακλέους, μεθ' ὃν μέχρι ἡμῶν οὐδεὶς ἐγένετο> ἀφ' Ἡρακλέους ἔτι, παραβραβευόντων τῶν Ἠλείων τοὺς δυναμένους.
<Γάιος Ῥωμαίων ἐβασίλευε.>
Διακοσιοστὴ ε'. Εὐβουλίδας Λαοδικεὺς στάδιον.
Κλαύδιος Ῥωμαίων ἐβασίλευε.
Διακοσιοστὴ ϛ'. Οὐαλέριος Μιτυληναῖος στάδιον.
Διακοσιοστὴ ζ'. Ἀθηνόδωρος Αἰγιεὺς στάδιον.
Διακοσιοστὴ η'. ὁ αὐτὸς τὸ δεύτερον.
Νέρων Ῥωμαίων ἐβασίλευε.
Διακοσιοστὴ θ'. Καλλικλῆς Σιδώνιος στάδιον.
Διακοσιοστὴ ι'. Ἀθηνόδωρος Αἰγιεὺς τὸ δεύτερον στάδιον.
Διακοσιοστὴ ια'.
οὐκ ἤχθη, Νέρωνος ἀναβαλλομένου εἰς τὴν ἑαυτοῦ ἐπιδημίαν.
μετὰ δὲ ἔτη δύο ἀχθείσης αὐτῆς, στάδιον μὲν Τρύφων Φιλαδελφεὺς ἐνίκα, Νέρων δὲ κηρύκων ἀγῶνα ἐστεφανοῦτο, τραγῳδούς, κιθαρῳδούς, ἅρμα πωλικόν, καὶ τὸ τέλειον καὶ δεκάπωλον.
Διακοσιοστὴ ιβ'. Πολίτης Κεραμίτης στάδιον.
Οὐεσπασιανὸς Ῥωμαίων ἐβασίλευε.
Διακοσιοστὴ ιγ'. Ῥόδων Κυμαῖος, ἢ Θεόδοτος, στάδιον.

323 → F93,57s

321s cf. Paus. 5,21,10   332–334 cf. Paus. 5,21,9; Tac., dial. 10,5; Quintil., instit. orat. 2,8,14   344s cf. Paus. 10,36,9; Philostr., VA 5,7; Suet., Nero 23,1   346–348   cf. Philostr., VA 4,24; Cass. Dio 63,14; Zon. 11,12; Suet., Nero 23,1; 24,4   349 cf. Paus. 6,13,3

320 ἀπ' Ὀλύμπου armen.   321 Μαιάνδριος Scal. μένανδρος P   325 ἀπεδόθη] ἀνενεώθη Rutgers ex armen.   325s Γερμανικὸς Καῖσαρ ὁ Gelzer   332 Νεικόστρατος armen.   332s ἀφ'…ἐγένετο suppl. Rutgers ex armen.   335 Γάιος…ἐβασίλευε armen.   347 ἐστεφανοῦτο Scal. ἐστεφανοῦ P

197th. Asiaticus of Halicarnassus	stadion race.
198th. Diophanes of Prusa <by Mt. Olympus>	stadion race.

Aristeas of Stratoniceia or Maeander was the victor in wrestling and the pancration, the seventh from Heracles to do so.

Tiberius became Roman emperor.

199th. Aeschines Glaucias of Miletus	stadion race.

The horse race, which had been stopped a long time ago, was reinstated, and <Germanicus Caesar, the son of> Tiberius Caesar, was the victor in the four-horse chariot race.[11]

200th. Polemon of Petra	stadion race.
201st. Damasias of Cydonia	stadion race.
202nd. Hermogenes of Pergamum	stadion race.
203rd. Apollonius of Epidaurus	stadion race.
204th. Sarapion of Alexandria	stadion race.

Nicostratus of Aegae was the victor in wrestling and the pancration, the eighth <from Heracles> to do so. From Heracles <up to our time, there was no one> else to do so <after him>, because the Eleans wrongly denied the crown to those qualified to receive it.

<Gaius became Roman emperor.>

205th. Eubulidas of Laodicea	stadion race.

Claudius became Roman emperor.

206th. Valerius of Mytilene	stadion race.
207th. Athenodorus of Aegium	stadion race.
208th. The same man, for a second time	stadion race.

Nero became Roman emperor.

209th. Callicles of Sidon	stadion race.
210th. Athenodorus of Aegium, for a second time	stadion race.

211th. This contest was not held, because Nero postponed it until the time of his visit. It was held two years later, and Tryphon of Philadelphia was the victor in the stadion race. Nero was awarded the crown in the contests for heralds, performers of tragedy and cithara-players; and also in the races for chariots drawn by foals, full-grown horses and 10 foals.

212th. Polites of Ceramus	stadion race.

Vespasian became Roman emperor.

213th. Rhodon of Cyme, or Theodotus	stadion race.

---

11 The text is emended by Gelzer 1,168 on the basis of an inscription in Olympia (Γερμανικὸν Καίσαρα, αὐτοκράτορος Τιβερίου Καίσαρος Σεβαστοῦ υἱόν, νικήσαντα Ὀλύμπια τεθρίππῳ τελεί[ῳ]..., Dittenberger/Purgold 1896, no. 221).

Διακοσιοστὴ ιδ'. Στράτων Ἀλεξανδρεὺς στάδιον.
Τίτος Ῥωμαίων ἐβασίλευε.
Διακοσιοστὴ ιε'. Ἑρμογένης Ξάνθιος στάδιον.
Δομιτιανὸς Ῥωμαίων ἐβασίλευε.
Διακοσιοστὴ ις'. Ἀπολλοφάνης, ὁ καὶ Πάπις, Ταρσεὺς στάδιον.
Διακοσιοστὴ ιζ'. Ἑρμογένης Ξάνθιος τὸ δεύτερον στάδιον.
Διακοσιοστὴ ιη'. Ἀπολλώνιος Ἀλεξανδρεὺς ἢ Ἡλιόδωρος στάδιον.
Διακοσιοστὴ ιθ'. Στέφανος Καππάδοξ στάδιον.
Νερούας Ῥωμαίων ἐβασίλευε, μεθ᾽ ὃν <Τραϊανός>.
Διακοσιοστὴ κ'. Ἀχιλλεὺς Ἀλεξανδρεὺς στάδιον.
Διακοσιοστὴ κα'. Θεωνᾶς, ὁ καὶ Σμάραγδος, Ἀλεξανδρεὺς στάδιον.
Διακοσιοστὴ κβ'. Κάλλιστος Σιδήτης στάδιον.
<ἀνενεώθη τῶν ἵππων ὁ δρόμος.>
Διακοσιοστὴ κγ'. Εὔστολος Σιδήτης στάδιον.
Διακοσιοστὴ κδ'. Ἰσαρίων Ἀλεξανδρεὺς στάδιον.
Ἁδριανὸς Ῥωμαίων ἐβασίλευε.
Διακοσιοστὴ κε'. Ἀριστέας Μιλήσιος στάδιον.
Διακοσιοστὴ κς'. Διονύσιος ὁ Σαμευμὺς Ἀλεξανδρεὺς στάδιον.
Διακοσιοστὴ κζ'. ὁ αὐτὸς τὸ δεύτερον.
Διακοσιοστὴ κη'. Λουκᾶς Ἀλεξανδρεὺς στάδιον.
Διακοσιοστὴ κθ'. Ἐπίδαυρος ὁ καὶ Ἀμμώνιος, Ἀλεξανδρεὺς στάδιον.
Ἀντωνῖνος Εὐσεβὴς Ῥωμαίων ἐβασίλευε.
Διακοσιοστὴ λ'. Δίδυμος <Κλιδεὺς> Ἀλεξανδρεὺς στάδιον.
Διακοσιοστὴ λα'. Κραναὸς Σικυώνιος στάδιον.
Διακοσιοστὴ λβ'. Ἀττικὸς Σαρδιανὸς στάδιον.
Σωκράτης πάλην καὶ παγκράτιον ἀπογραψάμενος, ὑπὸ Ἠλείων παρεβραβεύθη ὑπὲρ Διονυσίου Σελευκέως.
Διακοσιοστὴ λγ'. Δημήτριος Χῖος στάδιον.
Διακοσιοστὴ λδ'. Ἡρᾶς Χῖος στάδιον.
Διακοσιοστὴ λε'. Μνασίβουλος Ἐλατεὺς στάδιον.
Ἀντωνῖνος Μάρκος Πίος καὶ Λούκιος Βῆρος Ῥωμαίων ἐβασίλευον.
Διακοσιοστὴ λς'. Ἀειθαλὴς Ἀλεξανδρεὺς στάδιον.
Διακοσιοστὴ λζ'. Εὐδαίμων Ἀλεξανδρεὺς στάδιον.
Διακοσιοστὴ λη'. Ἀγαθόπους Αἰγινήτης στάδιον.
Διακοσιοστὴ λθ'. ὁ αὐτὸς τὸ δεύτερον.
Κόμοδος Ῥωμαίων ἐβασίλευεν.
Διακοσιοστὴ μ'. Ἀνουβίων ὁ καὶ Φεῖδος, Ἀλεξανδρεὺς στάδιον.

354 cf. Paus. 6,13,3   **375** cf. Paus. 2,11,8   **381** cf. Paus. 10,34,5

360 Τραϊανός armen.   **362** Ἀλεξανδρεὺς armen. ἀλέξανδρος P   **364** ἀνενεώθη…δρόμος armen.   **374** Κλιδεὺς armen.   **378** ὑπὲρ Gutschmid ὑπὸ P   **381** Ἐλατεὺς armen. ἐρατεὺς P   **388** Ἀνουβίων… Φεῖδος armen. ἀνουβί … φειδούς P

214th. Straton of Alexandria stadion race.
  Titus became Roman emperor.
215th. Hermogenes of Xanthus stadion race.
  Domitian became Roman emperor.
216th. Apollophanes, also known as Papis, of Tarsus stadion race.
217th. Hermogenes of Xanthus, for a second time stadion race.
218th. Apollonius of Alexandria, or Heliodorus stadion race.
219th. Stephanus of Cappadocia stadion race.
  Nerva became Roman emperor, and after him <Trajan>.
220th. Achilleus of Alexandria stadion race.
221st. Theonas, also known as Smaragdus, of Alexandria stadion race.
222nd. Callistus of Side stadion race.
  <The horse race was reinstated.>
223rd. Eustolus of Side stadion race.
224th. Isarion of Alexandria stadion race.
  Hadrian became Roman emperor.
225th. Aristeas of Miletus stadion race.
226th. Dionysius Sameumys of Alexandria stadion race.
227th. The same man, for a second time.
228th. Lucas of Alexandria stadion race.
229th. Epidaurus, also known as Ammonius, of Alexandria stadion race.
  Antoninus Pius became Roman emperor.
230th. Didymus <Clydeus> of Alexandria stadion race.
231st. Cranaus of Sicyon stadion race.
232nd. Atticus of Sardis stadion race.
  Socrates was registered as the victor in both wrestling and the pancration, but he was unfairly denied the crown by the Eleans, in favor of Dionysius son of Seleucus.
233rd. Demetrius of Chios stadion race.
234th. Eras of Chios stadion race.
235th. Mnasibulus of Elateia stadion race.
  Marcus Antoninus Pius and Lucius Verus became Roman emperors.
236th. Aeithales of Alexandria stadion race.
237th. Eudaemon of Alexandria stadion race.
238th. Agathopus of Aegina stadion race.
239th. The same man, for a second time.
  Commodus became Roman emperor.
240th. Anubion, also known of Pheidus, of Alexandria stadion race.

Διακοσιοστὴ μα΄. Ἥρων Ἀλεξανδρεὺς στάδιον.
390 Διακοσιοστὴ μβ΄. Μάγνος <Λίβυς> Κυρηναῖος στάδιον.
Διακοσιοστὴ μγ΄. Ἰσίδωρος <ὁ καὶ Ἀρτεμίδωρος> Ἀλεξανδρεὺς στάδιον.
  Περτίναξ, εἶτα Σεβῆρος, Ῥωμαίων ἐβασίλευσαν.
Διακοσιοστὴ μδ΄. ὁ αὐτὸς τὸ δεύτερον.
Διακοσιοστὴ με΄. Ἀλέξανδρος Ἀλεξανδρεὺς στάδιον.
395 Διακοσιοστὴ μς΄. Ἐπινίκιος Κυζικηνός, ὁ καὶ Κυνᾶς, στάδιον.
Διακοσιοστὴ μζ΄. Σατορνίλος Κρὴς Γορτύνιος στάδιον.
  Ἀντωνῖνος, ὁ καὶ Καράκαλλος, Ῥωμαίων ἐβασίλευε.
Διακοσιοστὴ μη΄. Ἡλιόδωρος, ὁ καὶ Τρωσιδάμας, Ἀλεξανδρεὺς στάδιον.
Διακοσιοστὴ μθ΄. ὁ αὐτὸς τὸ δεύτερον.
400 τέλος.
Μέχρι τούτου τὴν τῶν Ὀλυμπιάδων ἀναγραφὴν εὕρομεν.

390 Λίβυς armen.   **391** ὁ καὶ Ἀρτεμίδωρος armen.

F66 Georgius Syncellus (238,21–24 Mosshammer)

Τούτοις τοῖς χρόνοις προεφήτευσεν Ὠσηέ, Ἀμώς, Ἰωνᾶς, Ναούμ, ἡνίκα καὶ Ἰωνᾶς ἐκπεμφθεὶς εἰς Νινευὶ εἰς Θαρσεῖς φεύγει καὶ ὑπὸ κήτους καταποθεὶς τριήμερος ἀνεμεῖται. Θαρσεῖς δὲ Ῥόδον καὶ Κύπρον Ἀφρικανὸς λέγει εἶναι.

2s ps. Sym. f. 51ᵛ *Ὅτι ἡ Θαρσὶς λεγομένη χώρα ἐν ᾗ Ἰωνᾶς ἔφυγεν ἡ Ῥόδος καὶ ἡ Κύπρος ἐστίν, ὡς Ἀφρικανὸς λέγει.*

1s cf. Ion 1,1–3; 2,1; Ios., ant. Iud. 9,208–214; Eus., praep. ev. 10,14,5; Eus., can.[Hier 84a]; Chron. Pasch. 190,12; Anon. Matr. 22,14s; Georg. Mon. 251,4; Io. Anag. f. 115ᵛ; Sym. Log. (Leo Gr. 35,3–6 = Th. Mel. 31,18–20); Iul. Pol. 114,2–4; 118,9s; Cedr. 186,2s; 187,4s; 189,9s; Mich. Syr. 4,16

[AB] **1s** καὶ…φεύγει < B   **2** καταποθεὶς B καταπωθεὶς A   **3** καὶ AB ἢ Goar

T67 Georgius Syncellus (239,8s Mosshammer)

Τοῦ Ἰσραὴλ ις΄ ἐβασίλευσε Φακεσίας υἱὸς Μαναὴμ ἔτη ι΄. Ἀφρικανὸς δὲ ἔτη β΄. τοῦ δὲ κόσμου ἦν ἔτος ͵δψκδ΄.

1 Sym. Log. (Leo Gr. [42,6s Bekker] = Th. Mel. [36,23s Tafel] = Iul. Pol. [132,2s Hardt] = Cedr. [187,9s Bekker]) *Φαλκίας* (*Φαλκείας* Iul. Pol.) *ὁ τοῦ Μαναεὶμ υἱὸς τὸν πατέρα διαδεξάμενος ἐβασίλευσεν ἔτη β΄* (+ *ἐν ἄλλῳ ι΄* Iul. Pol.)

1 cf. IV Regn 15,23 (ann. 10 cod. A, ann. 2 cett. et textus hebraicus); Georg. Mon. 262,12–14

[AB] **2** ͵δψκδ΄ Gelzer ͵δψλγ΄ AB

241ˢᵗ. Heron of Alexandria	stadion race.
242ⁿᵈ. Magnus <the Libyan> of Cyrene	stadion race.
243ʳᵈ. Isidorus, <also known as Artemidorus,> of Alexandria	stadion race.
Pertinax, and then Severus, became Roman emperors.	
244ᵗʰ. The same man, for a second time	stadion race.
245ᵗʰ. Alexander of Alexandria	stadion race.
246ᵗʰ. Epinicius of Cyzicus, also known as Cynas	stadion race.
247ᵗʰ. Satornilus of Crete, from Gortyn,	stadion race.
Antoninus, also known as Caracalla, became Roman emperor.	
248ᵗʰ. Heliodorus, also known as Trosidamas, of Alexandria	stadion race.
249ᵗʰ. The same man, for a second time	stadion race.

The end.

This is the end point of the registry of the Olympic games that we have found.

F66 *The Prophet Jonah*[1]

At this time, Hosea, Amos, Jonah, and Nahum began to prophesy, at which time Jonah, upon being sent out to Nineveh, fled to Tarshish. Swallowed by a huge fish, he was disgorged on the third day. Africanus states that **Tarshish is Rhodes or Cyprus.**

T67 *Pekahiah, King of Israel*

The 16ᵗʰ king of Israel was Menahem's son Pekahiah, for 10 years. **But Africanus says it was two years.** AM 4724.

---

[1] It is not possible to decide whether the whole text belongs to Africanus. The evidence provided by ps. Symeon is too scanty to resolve the problem. Probably, there was some chronological and biographical information about the prophets in the *Chronographiae*.

T68 Georgius Syncellus (239,12-19 Mosshammer)

Τοῦ Ἰσραὴλ ιζ' ἐβασίλευσε Φακεὲ υἱὸς Ῥωμελίου ἔτη κη' κατὰ τὸν ἀκριβῆ λόγον. τοῦ δὲ κόσμου ἦν ἔτος ͵δψλδ'. οὕτω γὰρ εὑρεθήσεται τὸ θ' ἔτος τοῦ ιη' καὶ τελευταίου βασιλέως τῶν ι' φυλῶν Ὡσηὲ συντρέχον τῷ ς' ἔτει Ἐζεκίου βασιλέως Ἰούδα κατὰ τὴν γραφὴν καὶ {οὐ} καλῶς, καθ' ὃ γέγονεν ἡ πρώτη τοῦ Ἰσραὴλ αἰχμαλωσία. εἰσὶ μέντοι τινὰ τῶν ἀντιγράφων κ' ἔχοντα ἔτη τοῦ
5 Φακεέ, ὡς καὶ Ἀφρικανὸς καὶ Εὐσέβιος, καὶ ἕτερα ιη', ἀλλ' οὐ χρὴ πείθεσθαι διὰ τὴν εἰρημένην ἀναγκαίαν αἰτίαν.

4s Sym. Log. (Leo Gr. [42,7s Bekker] = Th. Mel. [36,25 Tafel] = Iul. Pol. [132,3-5 Hardt] ≈ Cedr. [187,10s Bekker]) Φακεέ ὁ τοῦ Ῥομελίου τὸν Φαλκίαν ἀνελὼν ἐβασίλευσε ἔτη κ' (η' Cedr.).

4s cf. IV Regn 15,27; Eus., can.[Hier] 86,22; Georg. Mon. 262,16-18; Sync. 240,2-31

[AB] **1** ῥωμελίου A ῥωμελείου B   **2** ͵δψλδ' Gelzer ͵δψμγ' AB   **3** συντρέχον Goar[m] συντρέχων AB οὐ del. Di. | οὐ καλῶς AB εἰκότως Moss.

T69 Georgius Syncellus (241,28 - 242,3 Mosshammer)

Διήρκεσε δὲ ἡ αὐτὴ τῶν ι' φυλῶν βασιλεία ἐν Σαμαρείᾳ ἀπὸ τοῦ α' βασιλέως αὐτῶν Ἱεροβωὰμ δούλου Σολομῶντος ἐν βασιλεῦσι ιη', ἔτεσι δὲ σξ'. ἀπὸ γὰρ τοῦ κοσμικοῦ ͵δφιγ' ἀρξαμένη εἰς τὸ ὑποτεταγμένον ͵δψοα' ἔληξε, κατὰ δὲ Ἀφρικανὸν ͵δψν', κατὰ δὲ Εὐσέβιον ͵δυνε'.

2 cf. III Regn 14,20; Sync. 221,16s   **3** cf. IV Regn 18,9-12; Hipp., chron. 668; Eus., can.[Hier 88e]; Chron. Pasch. 200,13 - 201,10; Sync. 241,15-25; Chron. Synt. 94,30

[AB] **1** ἱεροβωὰμ B ἱερωβοὰμ A

F70 Ioannes Damascenus, Sacra parallela (recensio secundum alphabeti litteras disposita, quae tres libros conflat), secundum codicem Vaticanum gr. 1236, f. 158[r] (463C Lequien = PG 95,1436C)

Ἱστόρηται παρὰ Ἀφρικανῷ, ὅτι ἐν τῷ λέγειν τὴν ᾠδὴν τὸν Μανασσῆ, τὰ δεσμὰ διερράγη σιδηρᾶ ὄντα, καὶ ἔφυγεν.

Iul. Pol. (116,22 - 118,8 Hardt) *Μανάσσης υἱὸς Ἐζεκίου ἐβασίλευσεν ἔτη νε'. οὗτος παρανομώτατος ὑπὲρ παντὸς γενόμενος, ἐν εἰδωλομανίᾳ καὶ αἱματοχυσίᾳ δικαίων αἱμάτων, δέσμιος κατὰ θείαν ὀργὴν παρελήφθη παρὰ Μαροδὰχ τοῦ Ἀσσυρίων βασιλέως, καὶ δεσμοῖς πεπεδήμενος σιδηροῖς, καὶ ἐν ἀγάλματι χαλκῷ εἰργμένος, δέησιν ἀνέτεινε μετανοίας, δι' ἧς ὁ θεὸς ἱκετευθείς, διέρρηξεν τοὺς δεσμοὺς αὐτοῦ, καὶ τῇ ἰδίᾳ γῇ καὶ βασιλείᾳ ἀποκατέστησεν.*

cf. IV Regn 21,18; II Par 33,11-13; OrMan; Ios., ant. Iud. 10,39-43; Io. Ant. fr. 50; Chron. Pasch. 220,8s; Georg. Mon. 235,10 - 237,2; Sync. 254,7-20; Sym. Log. (Leo Gr. 36,10-12 = Th. Mel. 32,13-15); Anon. Matr. 25,4-15

T68 *Pekah, King of Israel*

The 17th king of Israel was Remaliah's son Pekah, for 28 years, based on an accurate calculation. AM 4734. In this way we shall find that the ninth year of Hoshea, the 18th and final king of the 10 tribes of Israel, corresponds with the sixth year of Hezekiah, king of Judah. This is both reasonable and in accordance with the Scripture. In that year Israel's first captivity occurred. There are, however, some manuscripts that assign 20 years for Pekah,[1] as do Africanus and Eusebius, wheras others assign 18 years. But there is no need to heed them, based on the compelling reason already cited.

T69 *The End of the Northern Kingdom*

The kingdom of the 10 tribes in Samaria extended from their first king Jeroboam, servant of Salomon, over a period of 18 kings and 260 years. It began in AM 4513 and ended in the year demonstrated, AM 4771. According to Africanus, this was the year 4750,[2] and according to Eusebius, the year 4455.

F70 *Manasseh's Supplication and Liberation*[3]

It is stated by Africanus that while Manasseh was reciting his song, his bonds, which were made of iron, were broken and he escaped.[4]

---

1. While the majority of manuscript witnesses to the Greek text of IV Regn 15,27 supply "20" years for Pekah's reign, the numbers "28" and "30" are also attested, see Brooke/McLean 1917, ad loc.
2. According to Africanus, 1 Ahaz = Ol. 1,1, corresponding to AM 4727 (F64). After the 16 years of his rule (IV Regn 16,2), the Northern Kingdom ended in the sixth year of the reign of his successor Hezekiah (IV Regn 18,10). This would correspond with AM 4748 (4727 + 15 + 6 = 4748). AM 4750 can, however, be independently verified from Africanus' dating of the completion of Solomon's temple. Africanus dated the completion of the Temple in AM 4457 (= 8 Solomon, T42,4), meaning that Solomon's 40-year reign ended in AM 4489. Beginning in the following year (= AM 4490), the kingdom of Israel lasted 260 years up to AM 4750.
3. The transmission of John of Damacus' *Hiera* is complex and much of it is not yet published. For the *florilegium* of Vat. gr. 1236, see Richard 1964,480f. In the two consulted Vatican codices this text has a marginal note in red ink saying "σχόλιον". However, this does not necessarily mean that the text is a scholion to John of Damascus. It seems more plausible to assume that it is an explanation of the preceding biblical texts (immediately preceding is II Par 33,11–13); it may well go back to John of Damascus. Cf. also Routh 463, n. ad loc.
4. An apparent reference to the Prayer of Manasseh, a work recounting Manasseh's prayer of contrition after his imprisonment by the Assyrians. It is included in some manuscripts of the Septuagint in a section called Odes.

T71 Michael Syrus 4,15 (4, 53c,20 – 54a,15 Chabot)

1s cf. IV Regn 22,4; Ier 1,1s; Sus 2 θ; Hipp., chron. 741; Eus., can. [Hier 96a]; Sync. 255,8; Sym. Log. (Leo Gr. 36,22s = Th. Mel. 32,24s)   4–8   cf. IV Regn 22,8–13; 23,4–24; II Par 34,9ss; 35,8.19; Chron. Pasch. 224,11–13; Sync. 255,18s; 256,16s; 260,23–25; Sym. Log. (Leo Gr. 36,20 – 37,7 = Th. Mel. 32,23 – 33,4)

4 ܕܥܒܼܕܘ scripsimus pro ܕܒܥܘ

F72 Georgius Syncellus (257,13–18 Mosshammer)

Εἶτα καὶ ἔλαβεν ὁ λαὸς τῆς γῆς τὸν Ἰωάχαζ υἱὸν Ἰωσίου, καὶ ἔχρισαν αὐτὸν καὶ κατέστησαν αὐτὸν εἰς βασιλέα ἀντὶ τοῦ πατρὸς αὐτοῦ. εἴκοσι τριῶν ἐτῶν Ἰωάχαζ ἐν τῷ βασιλεύειν αὐτὸν καὶ τρίμηνον ἐβασίλευσεν ἐν Ἰερουσαλήμ. καὶ ἔδησεν αὐτὸν Φαραὼ Νεχαὼ ἐν Δεβλαθὰ ἐν γῇ Αἰμὰθ τοῦ μὴ βασιλεύειν ἐν Ἰερουσαλήμ. καὶ ἤγαγεν αὐτὸν εἰς Αἴγυπτον, καὶ ἐπέβαλε φόρον ἐπὶ τὴν γῆν ρ΄ τάλαντα
5   ἀργυρίου καὶ τάλαντον χρυσίου.

Nota marginalis ad l. 4s [AB]: τότε πρῶτον ὑπόφορος ἐγένετο ἡ γῆ ὥς φησιν Ἀφρικανός.

→ F46,204s; F84

1–5 cf. II Par 36,1–4; I Esdr 1,32–35; Eus., can.[armen] 186; Sync. 258,2–6; 259,25–29

[AB]   3 αἰμὰθ II Par[A]   ἐμὰθ AB   Ἰεμὰθ II Par[V]

T71 *The High Priest Hilkiah*

This priest Hilkiah, who according to some was the father of the prophet Jeremiah, lived in the time of Amon, Josiah and Jehoiakim, kings of Judah, as we have stated above. He administered his office for 30 years. Concerning him there exist numerous witnesses in the sacred Scriptures, as well as what these chroniclers who inform us about the history of time have revealed about him. For they speak at length about the high priest Hilkiah, a righteous and famous man—this according to the report of Andronicus, Africanus and John, who [follows] Eusebius.

F72 *King Jehoahaz and the first Tribute*

Then the people of the land received Josiah's son Jehoahaz and anointed him and make him king in place of his father. Jehoahaz was 23 years old when he began to reign, and ruled for three months in Jerusalem. Pharaoh Neco bound him in Deblatha in the land of Aemath that he might not reign in Jerusalem, led him to Egypt, and imposed a tribute on the land of 100 talents of silver and one talent of gold.

Nota marginalis: At that time, the land was for the first time subject to tribute, as Africanus says.

F73 Excerpta Barbari (314,19 – 316,18 Frick)

Tempora regni Persarum

Cyrus Persarum rex dissipans regna Lydorum et Midorum regnauit Olympiadas VII et dimidiam. In anno autem primo regni ipsius, in quo contigit consumari septuaginta annos depredicationi genti Iudeorum, relaxauit multitudinem
5 filiorum Israhel remeare ad propriam habitationem. In quo anno fuit initium quinquagensimae quintae Olympiade. Tenuit autem Persarum regnum usque Darium, quem occidit Alexander Macedo et conditor, annos CCXXX sic:

I. Cirus Persus ann. XXX.
II. Cambysus ann. VIIII.

2-6 → F34,19s.41-47.67s; F62,3s.21s; F65,133s; F74; Sym. Log. (Leo Gr. [46,15-20 Bekker] = Th. Mel. [39,23-28 Tafel] = Iul. Pol. [140,10-12.17-21 Hardt] = Cedr. [252,7-12 Bekker])
Κῦρος ὁ Πέρσης καταλύσας τὴν Μήδων καὶ Ἀσσυρίων δυναστείαν, κρατήσας τε τῆς (< Th. Mel.) Ἀσίας ἁπάσης, ἐβασίλευσεν ἔτη λα'. τούτου (τούτῳ Th. Mel.) τῷ πρώτῳ ἐνιαυτῷ ἑβδομηκονταετὴς χρόνος τῆς μετοικεσίας συμπληροῦται. ἐν δὲ τῷ ἐχομένῳ (ἐρχομένῳ Leo Gr. ἐπομένῳ Cedr.) ἔτει συγχωρεῖ τοὺς δυναμένους τῶν Ἑβραίων οἰκίζειν ἀνελθόντας τὰ (εἰς Cedr.) Ἱεροσόλυμα, καὶ τὸν ναὸν ἀνοικοδομηθῆναι προσέταξε.
3-5 → F34,12-18; F77   6s vide infra app. ad l. 22-24   9 → T75
9-14   Sym. Log. (Leo Gr. [47,8-20 Bekker] = Th. Mel. [40,5-18 Tafel] = Iul. Pol. [142,10s; 142,15 - 144,4 Hardt])
Καμβύσης ὁ καὶ Ἀρταξέρξης (ὁ αὐτὸς δέ ἐστιν ὁ καὶ ἐν τῷ Ἔσδρᾳ λεγόμενος Ἀρθασασθά) τὸν Κῦρον ὁ υἱὸς διαδεξάμενος ἐβασίλευσεν ἔτη ὀκτώ (Κ. ὁ καὶ Ναβουχοδονόσορ υἱὸς Κύρου ἐ. ἔ. η' Iul. Pol.).
Σφενδάτις καὶ Κιμάρδιος (Σφενδάτης καὶ Κιμέρδιος Th. Mel. σπέρδιος μάγος σὺν τῷ ἀδελφῷ αὐτοῦ Iul. Pol.) ἀδελφοὶ μάγοι (< Iul. Pol.), Μῆδοι τῷ γένει, ἐπιθέμενοι βασιλεύουσι (βασιλεῦσι Iul. Pol.) μῆνας ἑπτά.
Δαρεῖος ὁ Κύρου μὲν ἀπόγονος, Ὑστάσπου δὲ υἱός, τοῖς μάγοις ἐπιθέμενος καὶ κρατήσας ἐβασίλευσε μέχρι συμπληρώσεως Ἱερουσαλὴμ ἔτη ἓξ καὶ πρὸς τούτοις ἄλλα τριάκοντα, ὥστε βεβασιλευκέναι ἔτη λϛ' (ὦ. β. ἔ. λϛ' < Iul. Pol.). κατὰ τούτους τοὺς χρόνους Πυθαγόρας ὁ φιλόσοφος ἐτελεύτησε καὶ Ἱπποκράτης ὁ (< Iul. Pol.) ἰατρὸς ἐγνωρίζετο.
Ξέρξης ὁ Δαρείου υἱὸς ἐβασίλευσεν ἔτη κ'.
Ἀρτάβανος ἐβασίλευσε μῆνας ζ'.
Ἀρταξέρξης ὁ Ξέρξου ὁ μακρόχειρ (καὶ οὗτος ἐν τῷ Ἔσδρᾳ Ἀρπασασθὰ [Ἀρθασασθά Th. Mel. ὁ αὐτὸς δέ ἐστι ὁ ἐν τῷ Ἔσδρᾳ λεγόμενος Ἀρσασθὰ Iul. Pol.] κέκληται [< Iul. Pol.]) ἐβασίλευσεν ἔτη μα'.
9-21 → F46,212-222.236-241 (e Manethone)

2-6 cf. Io. Mal. 6,11   4s cf. Georg. Mon. 20,18s   7 et 22s cf. Hipp., Dan. 4,3.24; Eus., can.[Hier] 124[a]; Sync. 314,16-24   8   cf. Sync. 278,20 - 283,24   8-21   cf. Hipp., chron. 702-715; Eus., chron. 33, 10-29; Eus., reg. ser.[armen] 152; Io. Mal. 6,13.28; Exc. Barb. 261,27 - 268,23; Sync. 247,16-28; 278, 9-18; 288,24 - 289,10; 295,15; 300,28 - 302,6; 306,7 - 308,6; Chron. Synt. 92s; 99; Anon. Matr. 29,14 - 30,9; 35,5 - 38,11; Cedr. 243,7-12; 249,20 - 252,6; 252,21 - 256,20; Sulp. Sev., chron. 2,8,1 - 17,1

9 VIIII] VIII Gelzer e Sym. Log.

F73 *The Kings of the Persians*[1]

Chronology of the kingdom of the Persians

After dissolving the kingdoms of the Lydians and Medes, Cyrus, king of the Persians, reigned for 7 ½ Olympiads. In the first year of his reign, when it came to pass that the 70 years of the captivity of the Jewish people were completed, he allowed the host of the sons of Israel to return to their own homeland. In this year, it was the beginning of the 55th Olympiad.[2] Up until Darius, whom Alexander of Macedon, the Founder, slew, the kingdom of the Persians lasted 230 years, as follows:

    I. Cyrus the Persian, for 30 years.
    II. Cambyses, for 9 years.

---

[1] The fragment should be attributed to Africanus for the following reasons: a) At l. 2–6 there is a mention of the synchronism 1 Cyrus = Ol. 55,1 = last year of the Babylonian Captivity. This synchronism is well-attested in Africanus (F34,19f.41–47.67f). b) 230 years for the total of the Persian reign correspond to Africanus' system (T6,14; F93,51). c) The name *conditor* ('the Founder') for Alexander is attested elsewhere in Africanus (F84,2). d) F93,40f states that Nehemiah was allowed to rebuild Jerusalem in the 20th year of Artaxerxes Longarm; this was the 115th year from the beginning of the Persian reign. If Africanus' dates of the single Persian kings are summed up to 20 Artaxerxes, the total is exactly 115 years: 30 (Cyrus) + 8 (Cambyses, emended) + 7 months (Smerdes) + 36 (Darius) + 20 (Xerxes) + 7 months (Artabanus) = 95 years and 2 months + 20 Artaxerxes = 115. e) The list gives 22 years for king Ochus, which is peculiar to Africanus, see F46,237. The *communis opinio* (including Eusebius) assigns 26 years to this king, see the chronicle material given in Helm 1956,362, note on p. 120, ll. 19–21. See also Gelzer 1,103–105.

[2] On Africanus' dating of the end of the Babylonian captivity in Ol. 55,1, see the previous note.

III. Serdius <mens.> VII.
IIII. Darius iuuenis ann. XXXVI.
V. Xerxes maior ann. XX.
VI. Artabanus <mens.> VII.
VII. Artaxerxes minor ann. XL.
VIII. Xerxes iunior mens. II.
<VIIII>. Sogdianus mens. VII.
<X>. Darius Stultus ann. XVIIII.
<XI>. Artaxerxes Memoratus ann. XLII.
<XII>. Ochus filius Artaxerxi ann. XXII.
<XIII>. Alsus filius Ochi ann. IIII.
<ιδ′ Δαρεῖος ὁ Ἀρσάμου ἔτη ς′>.

14 → T78b,3s; F79; F81b; F93,31–43.54–58 (annus 20 Artaxerxis = 115 a primo anno Cyri).79s
15–24 Sym. Log. (Leo Gr. [48,15 – 49,4 Bekker] = Th. Mel. [41,4–19 Tafel] = Iul. Pol. [144,22 – 146,16 Hardt])
Ξέρξης ὁ Ἀρταξέρξου υἱὸς τὴν ἀρχὴν διαδεξάμενος βασιλεύει μῆνας δύο.
Σογδιανὸς (Σουγδιανὸς Leo Gr. Σογδιανὸς τὸν Ξέρξην διαδεξάμενος Iul. Pol.) βασιλεύει μῆνας ἑπτά.
Δαρεῖος ὁ Ξέρξου (< Iul. Pol.) ὁ ἐπικληθεὶς Νόθος ἀνελὼν τὸν (< Iul. Pol.) Σογδιανὸν (Σουγδιανὸν Leo Gr.) ἐβασίλευσε Περσῶν (< Iul. Pol.) ἔτη ιθ′. Ἀρταξέρξης ὁ Δαρείου καὶ Παρυσάτιδος τὸν πατέρα διαδεξάμενος ἐβασίλευσεν ἔτη μβ′. κατὰ τούτους τοὺς χρόνους Πλάτων ὁ φιλόσοφος καὶ Ἀριστοτέλης ἐγνωρίζετο (ἐπὶ τούτου Σωκράτης ὁ φιλόσοφος, ὡς φαυλίσας τοὺς Ἑλλήνων νόμους, θανατοῦται, κωνείον πίνων ἐν τῷ δεσμωτηρίῳ. ἐπὶ αὐτοῦ Θουκυδίδης, καὶ Ξενοφῶν ἱστορικοί, καὶ Πλάτων ὁ φιλόσοφος, μαθητὴς Σωκράτους καὶ Ἀρίστιππος Iul. Pol.).
Ἀρταξέρξης ὁ ἐπικληθεὶς Ὦχος ἐβασίλευσεν ἔτη κβ′ (< Iul. Pol.).
Ναρσῆς (Νασῆς Iul. Pol.) τοῦτον διαδεξάμενος ἐβασίλευσεν ἔτη δ′. Δαρεῖος ὁ Ἀρσάμου ἐβασίλευσε μετὰ τὸν Ναρσῆν ἔτη ς′ (Δαρεῖος ἐβασίλευσε μ. τ. Ν. ἔ. ἔξ, ὁ Ἀρσάμου Th. Mel.).
Ἀλεξάνδρου δὲ τοῦ Μακεδόνος Πέρσαις ἐπικειμένου, Δαρεῖον οἱ περὶ τὸν Βῆσσον ἀναιροῦσιν ἐν Βάκτροις, καὶ καταλύεται ἡ Περσῶν βασιλεία, ἐφ᾽ ὅλοις παρατείνασα ἔτεσι τριακοσίοις, τὰ μὲν τῆς μετοικεσίας ο′, τὰ δὲ ἑξῆς σλ′, καὶ μεταπίπτει εἰς Μακεδόνας ἡ βασιλεία (τοῦτον Ἀλέξανδρος ὁ Φιλίππου καὶ Ὀλυμπιάδος υἱὸς βασιλεὺς Μακεδόνων χειρωσάμενος καθεῖλεν τῆς ἀρχῆς, καὶ καταλύεται ἡ Περσῶν δυναστεία καὶ μεταπίπτει εἰς Μακεδόνας ἡ βασιλεία Iul. Pol.).
19 → F46,237; Sync. (307,12s.18s Moss.)
Περσῶν ιβ′ ἐβασίλευσεν Ὦχος ὁ καὶ Ἀρταξέρξου παῖς ἔτη ε′, κατὰ δὲ τινὰς κ′. (...) Οὗτος ὁ Ὦχος κρατήσας Αἰγύπτου β′ ἔτη ἀναιρεῖται ὑπὸ Βαγώου τινὸς Πέρσου τῶν ἐν τέλει.
Anon. Matr. (37,8 Bauer)
Ὦχος ὁ καὶ Ἀρταξέρξης ἔτη κβ′.

10 mens. scripsimus   **11** λς′ Sym. Log. Gelzer Frick VI cod.   **13** mens. scripsimus   **14** ante VII in cod. vocabulum erasum ut vidit Schoene   **16** VIIII] X cod.   **17** X] XI cod. | XVIIII Sym. Log. Frick VIIII cod.   **18** XI] XII cod.   **19** XII] XIII cod.   **20** XIII] XIIII cod.   **21** supplevimus e Sym. Log., cf. supra l. 7

III. Smerdes, for 7 <months>.
IIII. Darius the youth,³ for 36 years.
V. Xerxes the Great, for 20 years.
VI. Artabanus, for 7 <months>.
VII. Artaxerxes the lesser, for 40 years.
VIII. Xerxes the younger, for 2 months.
<VIIII>. Sogdianus, for 7 months.
<X>. Darius the fool, for 19 years.
<XI>. Artaxerxes Mnemon, for 42 years.
<XII>. Ochus, son of Artaxerxes, for 22 years.
<XIII>. Arses, son of Ochus, for 4 years.
<XIIII. Darius, son of Arsamus, for 6 years.>⁴

---

3   Gr. (Frick): Δαρεῖος ὁ Νόθος ("Darius, the illegitimate").
4   The missing reign of Darius III has been restored from the text of Symeon Logothete, which, following the generally accepted tradition, assigns six years to his reign (= 336–331 BC). With the addition of these years, the sum of the years of the reigns of the individual Persian kings comes to 230 (see l. 7, cf. T6,15). It is possible, however, that Africanus counted only the four years of Darius' reign in Egypt and excluded his remaining two years as king of Persia. For the four years of Darius' rule in Egypt, see Africanus' version of Manetho's list of Egyptian kings (F46,240 and n. 14 ad loc.). According to Africanus' chronology, the beginning of the Persian kingdom began in AM 4942, 70 years after the Babylonian captivity (= AM 4872; see F76,3f). The end of the Persian kingdom 230 years later would thus have occurred in AM 5172. Since, by Africanus' calculations, the 300-year reign of the Ptolemies ended in AM 5472 (see T6,16 and F89,56f), the Ptolemaic kingdom began in the same year; this would mean that, for Africanus, Alexander's conquest of Egypt marked the end of the Persian kingdom.

Alexander Macedo et conditor exterminans Persarum regnum traduxit in Macedonia regnum permanentem annos CCXXX, sub Olympiada centesima duodecima.

22s → F93,47–54; T6,15; Sym. Log. (Leo Gr. [49,12s Bekker] = Th. Mel. [42,1s Tafel]) Ἀλέξανδρος ὁ Μακεδὼν τὴν Περσῶν καταλύσας ἀρχὴν περιῆγεν εἰς Μακεδονίαν (Μακεδόνας Th. Mel.); Sync. (314,21–24 Moss.) Τῷ αὐτῷ ἔτει ἡ ἐν Ἀρβήλοις τῆς Μηδικῆς ἤχθη μάχη, καθ᾽ ἣν Δαρεῖος μὲν ὑπὸ τῶν περὶ Βῆσσον ἀνῃρέθη τῶν Βακτριανῶν, Ἀλέξανδρος δὲ τὴν Περσικὴν βασιλείαν σὺν τῇ Βαβυλῶνι καὶ Σουσᾶν προσηγάγετο, διαρκέσασαν ἀπὸ Κύρου ἕως Δαρείου ἔτη σλ'. Cedr. (256,20 – 257,1 Bekker) Ἀλεξάνδρου δὲ τοῦ Μακεδόνος, περὶ οὗ ἐν ταῖς βασιλείαις εἰρήσεται πλατύτερον, Πέρσαις ἐπικειμένου Δαρεῖον οἱ περὶ τὸν Βῆσσον ἀναιροῦσιν ἐν Βάκτροις. καὶ καταλύεται ἡ Περσῶν βασιλεία, ἐφ᾽ ὅλοις παρατείνασα ἔτεσι τριακοσίοις, ὧν τὰ μὲν τῆς μετοικεσίας ο', τὰ δὲ ἑξῆς σλ'.
22–24 → F65,207s; F82,34

F74 Ioannes Malalas 6,12 (122,65 – 123,72 Thurn)

Μετὰ δὲ τὸ ἀπολέσθαι τὴν βασιλείαν τῶν Λυδῶν οἱ Σάμιοι θαλασσοκρατήσαντες ἐβασίλευσαν τῶν μερῶν ἐκείνων. καὶ ἀκούσας μετὰ χρόνους Κῦρος ὁ βασιλεὺς Περσῶν νικήσας Κροῖσον ἐπεστράτευσε κατ᾽ αὐτῶν, καὶ συμβαλὼν αὐτοῖς ναυμαχίᾳ πολεμήσας ἡττήθη καὶ ἔφυγε, καὶ ἐλθὼν εἰς τὴν χώραν αὐτοῦ ἐσφάγη·
5 περὶ οὗ πολέμου Κύρου καὶ τῶν Σαμίων ὁ σοφώτατος Πυθαγόρας ὁ Σάμιος συνεγράψατο· ὅστις καὶ εἶπεν αὐτὸν Κῦρον τεθνάναι εἰς τὸν πόλεμον. ταῦτα δὲ πάντα καὶ ὁ σοφὸς Ἀφρικανὸς ἐχρονογράφησεν.

1–6 → F62,22; F63a,2–4; F63b,5s; F73,2s

1 cf. Hdt. 3,36; Eus., chron. 33,8s; 189; Eus., can.[Hier] 103,13–18; Sync. 281,13s; 287,21–26   **1–6** cf. Cedr. 242,24 – 243,6 (e Malala)   **1s** cf. Eus., chron. 107,9 (e Diodoro Siculo); can.[armen] 189 (anno 30 regni Cyri)   **4** cf. Hdt. 1,214; Eus., chron. 189; Eus., can.[Hier] 104[b]; Sync. 282,18s

[OSl] **3** νικήσας Κροῖσον Sl < O   **4** ναυμαχίᾳ O σὺν πολλαῖς ναυσὶν Sl   **6** σοφὸς O σοφώτατος Sl

After annihilating the kingdom of the Persians, Alexander of Macedon, the 'Founder,' transferred power to Macedonia, which lasted for 230 years, up to the 112th Olympiad.

F74 *Cyrus and the Samians*[1]

After the kingdom of the Lydians was destroyed, the people of Samos gained control of the sea and reigned over those parts. After a while, Cyrus, king of the Persians, heard about this and upon defeating Croesus went to war against them. He engaged with them, fought a battle with them at sea, but was defeated and fled; upon reaching his own land he was murdered. The most learned Pythagoras of Samos composed an account of the war between Cyrus and the people of Samos. He was the one who also stated that Cyrus himself died in the conflict. Also the learned Africanus has recorded the chronology of all these events.

---

1 The historical information given in the first four lines of this fragment is probably derived from Africanus. It should be noted that Eusebius (chron. 106f) has a list of Greek thalassocracies taken from Diodorus Siculus and that the Samians are mentioned there. The technical term θα-λασσοκρατήσαντες also suggests that Malalas took it from a source, which would have to be Africanus, since the mention of Pythagoras in this context does not seem to be helpful. We have no evidence that Pythagoras dealt with the history of Samos. The notice for him could originate in either Malalas or Africanus.

T75

T75a Georgius Syncellus (282,18 – 283,2 Mosshammer)

Κῦρος στρατεύσας ἐπὶ Μασσαγέτας ὑπὸ Τομύριδος γυναικὸς βασιλίδος αὐτῶν διεφθάρη. μεθ' ὃν Καμβύσης παῖς κρατεῖ Περσῶν ἔτη η'. τοῦτον οἴονταί τινες εἶναι Ναβουχοδονόσωρ β' τὸν κατὰ Ὀλοφέρνην καὶ τὴν Ἰουδήθ, ὡς καὶ Ἀφρικανός, ὅπερ ἀδύνατον, πρῶτον μὲν ὅτι ὀκτωκαιδεκάτῳ ἔτει αὐτοῦ γέγραπται ἐν τῇ Ἰουδὴθ ἐξαπεστάλθαι Ὀλοφέρνης κατὰ Συρίας καὶ
5 Παλαιστίνης καὶ Αἰγύπτου, οὗτος δὲ η' μόνα ἔτη ἐβασίλευσε καὶ πῶς τῷ ὀκτωκαιδεκάτῳ ἔτει αὐτοῦ ἐξέπεμψεν Ὀλοφέρνην; ἔπειτα ὅτι ἐπὶ Ἰωακεὶμ τοῦ μεγάλου ἀρχιερέως, ὃς ἦν υἱὸς Ἰησοῦ τοῦ Ἰωσεδέκ, γέγραπται πεπρᾶχθαι τὰ κατὰ Ἰουδὴθ καὶ Ὀλοφέρνην· ὁ δὲ Ἰωακεὶμ μετὰ τὴν Καμβύσου τελευτὴν ἀρχιεράτευσεν εἰς ἔτη κ'.

2s → F73,9; ps. Io. Ant. fr. 37* (574 Ro.) Ὁ Ὀλοφέρνης τοῦ δευτέρου Ναβουχοδονόσορ, ὃν Ἕλληνες Καμβύσην καλοῦσιν, ἦν στρατηγός. Sync. (289,5s Moss.) Τὸν Καμβύσην τινὲς Ναβουχοδονόσωρ νομίζουσι τὸν κατὰ τὴν Ἰουδήθ· *οὐκ ἔστι δέ, ὡς προδέδεικται καὶ ἐν τοῖς μετὰ ταῦτα δειχθήσεται*. Georg. Mon. 274,20s Μετὰ δὲ Κῦρον ἐβασίλευσε Καμβύσης υἱὸς αὐτοῦ ὁ καὶ Ναβουδονόσωρ κληθεὶς ἔτη ιη'.

1 cf. Hdt. 1,214; Eus., can.^Hier 104^b   **1s** cf. Eus., chron. 15,13; 33,12 (ann. 8, ita astr. can. et eccl. can.); Hdt. 3,66 (ann. 7, menses 5)   **2s** cf. Eus., chron. (Chron. Pasch. 270,2 = Eus., can.^Hier 104^c); Io. Mal. 6,13s; Georg. Mon. 20,21–22; Suda Ἰουδήθ I 431; Anon. Matr. 30,4–6; Sym. Log. (Leo Gr. 47,8–10 = Th. Mel. 40,5–7 = Iul. Pol. 142,10s); Sulp. Sev., chron. 2,14,1   **4** cf. Idt 2,1   **6s** cf. Idt 4,8

[AB] **1** Τομύριδος Di. τοῦ μύριδος A τουμύριδος B | ὃν B ὧν A   **4** γέγραπται B ἐγέγραπτο A ἐξαπεστάλθαι A ἐξαπεστάλθη B   **7** τὰ < B

T75b Suda Ἰουδήθ I 430 (2,641 Adler)

Ἰουδήθ· ὅτι ἐπὶ Ξέρξου, τοῦ βασιλέως Περσῶν, οἱ τῶν Αἰθιόπων βασιλεῖς ἐπανίστανται Πέρσαις, καὶ τοῦ βασιλέως κατ' ἐκείνων στρατεύσαντος, οἱ Ἰουδαῖοι πρὸς ἀπόστασιν εἶδον καὶ καταφρονήσαντες αὐτοῦ ἐπὶ τὴν Ἱερουσαλὴμ ἀνῆλθον. οὗτος δὲ περιγενόμενος τῶν Αἰθιόπων ἐπὶ τοὺς Ἰουδαίους στρατεύει Ὀλοφέρνῃ τὸν κατ' αὐτῶν πόλεμον ἐπιτρέψας. πολιορκοῦντος τοίνυν Ὀλοφέρνου τὴν
5 Ἱερουσαλήμ, γυνή τις, ὄνομα Ἰουδήθ, προσποιησαμένη τὴν φιλοῦσαν αὐτόν, ὡς ἐκάθευδε, νυκτὸς ἀπέτεμεν αὐτοῦ τὴν κεφαλὴν καὶ ἀνασκολοπίσασα ταύτην ἐπὶ τοῦ τείχους φυγεῖν παρεσκεύασε τοὺς Πέρσας· οὕτω τε τῆς πολιορκίας λυθείσης ἀπηλλάγησαν οἱ Ἰουδαῖοι τοῦ φόβου. ὁ δὲ τῶν Ἰουδαίων ἱερεὺς Νεμεσίας παρρησίαν ἔχων πρὸς αὐτὸν ἔπεισεν αὐτὸν εἰρήνην σπείσασθαι πρὸς αὐτοὺς καὶ συγχωρῆσαι αὐτοῖς ἀνακτίσασθαι τὴν Ἱερουσαλήμ, Ἔσδρα προηγουμένου αὐτῶν. Ἰούλιος δὲ
10 Ἀφρικανὸς λέγει, ὅτι Ναβουχοδονόσωρ, ὁ καὶ Καμβύσης, ἀναιρεῖται ὑπ' αὐτῆς.

[AGIFVM] **1** τοῦ < A   **6–10** καὶ…αὐτῆς < F   **7** τε ex VM solis   **8** Νεμεσίας Wolf   **8s** πρὸς²…ἀνακτίσασθαι < V   **9** ἀνακτήσασθαι GIM

T75 The Identification of Cambyses and Nebuchadnezzar II

T75a

When Cyrus launched a campaign against the Massagetae, he was killed by a woman named Tomyris, their queen. After him, his son Cambyses ruled the Persians for eight years. **Some, such as Africanus, think that he was Nebuchadnezzar II, who was at the time of Holofernes and Judith.**[1] But this is impossible, first because it is written in Judith that in his 18th year, Holofernes was sent out against Syria, Palestine and Egypt. But this Cambyses was king for only eight years, so how did he dispatch Holofernes in his 18th year? Secondly, it is written that it was during the time of Joiakim the great high priest, who was son of Jeshua, the son of Jozadak, that the events involving Judith and Holofernes occurred. Now Joiakim began his service as high priest 20 years after the death of Cambyses.

T75b

Judith: During the reign of Xerxes the king of the Persians, the kings of the Ethiopians rose up in rebellion against the Persians. When the king went to war against them, the Jews turned their attention to revolt and in their contempt for him returned to Jerusalem. When Xerxes arrived from the Ethiopians, he went to war against the Jews, entrusting the battle against them to Holofernes. And so as Holofernes was setting siege to Jerusalem, a certain woman named Judith feigned affection for him, and while he was sleeping cut off his head at night. After impaling his head on the city-wall, she put the Persians to flight. When the siege was lifted, the Jews were in this way relieved of their fear. Now Nehemiah, the priest of the Jews, dealt boldly with him and persuaded him to conclude a peace with them and allow them to rebuild Jerusalem, with Ezra as their leader. **Iulius Africanus states that Nebuchadnezzar, who was also known as Cambyses, was killed by her.**[2]

---

1 On this identification in Africanus, see Gelzer 1,109–111. It should be noted that Eusebius reports this information and attributes it to 'Hebrew authors', Eus., can. ^Hier 104^c (*ab Hebraeis*); Chron. Pasch. 270,2 (παρ' Ἑβραίοις). On the other hand, it is interesting to observe that ps. John of Antioch, fr. 37*, mentions this information through a perspective which is not Greek: Ὀλοφέρνης ... ὃν Ἕλληνες Καμβύσην καλοῦσιν (i.e. the author does not consider himself as Ἕλλην); on the text see also Roberto 2005b,287f.
2 Cf. Idt 13,6–8, according to which Judith slew Holofernes, Nebuchadnezzar's general. The sentence in its present form must be a misunderstanding of Africanus, either by the lexicographer or his source. About Africanus it does not provide more than the identification of Cambyses (therefore considered *testimonium*).

F76 Symeon Logothetes (Leo Grammaticus [38,17-22 Bekker] = Theodosius Melitenus [34,4-8 Tafel] = Georgius Monachus continuatus [180,1-6 Muralt = PG 110,304BC])

Συνάγεται τοίνυν ἀπὸ πρώτου ἔτους Ἄχαζ καὶ πρώτης Ὀλυμπιάδος μέχρι τῆσδε τῆς μετοικήσεως ἔτη ρμδ', ἀπὸ δὲ Σαοὺλ τοῦ πρώτου βασιλεύοντος Ἑβραίων ἔτη υϙ', ἀπὸ δὲ τῆς τελευτῆς Ἰησοῦ τοῦ Ναυῆ ἔτη ͵αρ', ἀπὸ δὲ Νῶε καὶ τοῦ κατακλυσμοῦ ἔτη ͵βχι', ἀπὸ δὲ Ἀδὰμ ἔτη ͵δωοβ'.

1 → F64   2 → F34,66   3 → F34,63-66   3s → T40,1s + F34,65s   4 Sym. Log. (Leo Gr. [43,16-20 Bekker] = Th. Mel. [37,24-27 Tafel]) *Ἀκόλουθον λοιπὸν ἐπιδραμεῖν τοῖς ἐν τοῖς ο' τῆς αἰχμαλωσίας ἔτεσιν ἡγησαμένοις. ἄχρι τούτου τοῦ τελευταίου Ἰωακεὶμ συνάγονται ἀπὸ Ἀδὰμ ͵δωοβ' ἔτη. λοιπὸν οὖν τοὺς ἐφεξῆς χρόνους ἀπὸ τοῦ πρώτου ἔτους Σεδεκίου δεῖ ψηφίζειν.*

2 μετοικεσίας Leo Gr. | ρμδ' Th. Mel. (cod.) Georg. Mon. ρμα' Leo Gr. sed lege ρμε' | υϙ' Th. Mel. (cod.) υς' Leo Gr. υζ' Georg. Mon. cont. (Muralt)   3 ͵βχι' Th. Mel. ͵βχ' Leo Gr.

T77

T77a
Sync.¹: Georgius Syncellus (265,29 - 266,8 Mosshammer)
Sync.²: Georgius Syncellus (261,14-19 Mosshammer)

Ἐκ ταύτης τῆς αἰχμαλωσίας ἦν Δανιὴλ ἅμα τοῖς σὺν αὐτῷ Ἀνανίᾳ, Ἀζαρίᾳ, Μιζαήλ. οὗτος ὁ Δανιὴλ παιδευθεὶς τὴν παιδείαν εὐάρεστος ἐγένετο τῷ βασιλεῖ Ναβουχοδονόσωρ. **ταῦτα καὶ ὁ Ἀφρι-**

test.: 1 inc. Sync.¹[AB]

1 cf. Eus., can.[Hier] 98[b]   1s cf. Dan 4,1-5   2-4 cf. Hipp., Dan. 1,6,1s; Hipp., chron. 679; Sync. 260,20s

F76 *The Chronology from Adam to the Babylonian Captivity*[1]

From the first year of Ahaz and the first Olympiad up to this captivity, there are, therefore, 144 years[2] in all; from Saul the first king of the Hebrews, 490 years;[3] from the death of Joshua, son of Nun, 1100 years,[4] from Noah and the Flood, 2610 years;[5] from Adam, 4872 years.[6]

T77 *Daniel and the Captivity*[7]

T77a

Daniel, together with his companions Ananias, Azarias and Mizaël, was part of this captivity. Well-educated, this Daniel proved pleasing to King Nebuchadnezzar. This is what Africanus also

---

1 The chronological information found in this unattributed text is for the most part an accurate representation of Africanus' reckoning. See also Gelzer 1,94 and Schwartz 1895,32.
2 More precisely, 145 years. Africanus numbered 215 years from Ol. 1,1 to the end of the 70 years of the Babylonian captivity in 1 Cyrus (= Ol. 55,1), see F34,41–43. The subtraction of 70 years from this total would produce 145 years for the period of time from Ol. 1,1 to the beginning of the captivity (or 147 with the variant reading of 217 years, see F34, n. 6).
3 For the 490 year chronology from Saul to the captivity, see F34,66.
4 For Africanus' calculation of this sum, see F34,63–66: 30 (the years of the elders) + 490 (the judges) + 90 (Eli and Samuel) + 490 (the kings) = 1100 years.
5 According to T40,1f, Africanus counted 4292 years from Adam to the end of the rule of the judges. Since the period of time from the end of the judges to the captivity lasted 580 years (F34, 65f), the years from Adam to the captivity total 4872. The number of years from the Flood (= AM 2262, T45,10) to the captivity would thus come to 2610 (4872 – 2262 = 2610).
6 See previous note.
7 The repetition of ll. 5–7 of this text in two differing contexts and in identical wording suggests either that his knowledge of Africanus was indirect or that he was drawing upon previously recorded notes.

κανὸς μαρτυρῶν, ὅτι ἐκ τῆς β' αἰχμαλωσίας Ἰούδα ἦν ὅ τε Δανιὴλ καὶ οἱ τρεῖς παῖδες. Πανόδωρος δὲ καὶ ἕτεροι τῶν ἱστορικῶν ἐκ τῆς ἐν Σαμαρείᾳ ὑπὸ Σαλμανασὰρ αἰχμαλω-
5 σίας. τοῦ Ἰούδα κ' ἐβασίλευσε Σεδεκίας ἔτη ια'. τοῦ δὲ κόσμου ἦν ἔτος ͵δωϛ'. Ἀφρικανὸς ἀπὸ τοῦ α' ἔτους Σεδεκίου τὰ ο' ἔτη τῆς αἰχμαλωσίας ἀριθμεῖ. τῷ ε' ἔτει Σεδεκίου, κόσμου δὲ ͵δϡ', ἤρξατο προφητεύειν ὁ μέγας προφήτης Ἰεζεκιήλ.

test.:Sync.[1] 5 τοῦ Ἰούδα inc. Sync.[2] [AB]

3s Sym. Log. (Leo Gr. [45,1–12 Bekker] = Th. Mel. [38,21–30 Tafel]) *Οὗτος ὁ Ναβουχοδονόσορ τρίτον ἐπόρθησε τὰ Ἱεροσόλυμα, πρῶτον μὲν ὅτε ἐν τῷ τρίτῳ ἔτει Ἐλιακεὶμ ἀνῆλθε καὶ ἔλαβεν αὐτόν τε Ἰεχονίαν καὶ τὴν τούτου μητέρα καὶ σὺν τῷ ἄλλῳ πλήθει τὸν προφήτην Ἰεζεχιήλ, ἔτος ἄγων τῆς βασιλείας πρῶτον· δεύτερον δὲ ὅτε ἐν τῷ τρίτῳ μηνὶ Ἰεχονίου, τοῦ καὶ Ἰωακείμ, ἀνῆλθε καὶ ἔλαβε σὺν ἑτέροις τὸν Δανιὴλ καὶ Ἀνανίαν καὶ Μισαὴλ καὶ Ἀζαρίαν* (Ἀζάτον Th. Mel.), *ἔτος ἄγων αὐτὸς ὄγδοον τῆς βασιλείας* (< Th. Mel.). *τὸ δὲ τρίτον ὅτε ἐν τῷ ἑνδεκάτῳ ἔτει τοῦ Σεδεκίου ἀνῆλθε, καὶ τὸν μὲν ναὸν ἐνέπρησε, τὸν δὲ Σεδεκίαν ἐξετύφλωσε, καὶ τοὺς υἱοὺς αὐτοῦ σὺν ἑτέροις κατέσφαξε, καὶ τὸ λοιπὸν πλῆθος ἀπήγαγεν εἰς αἰχμαλωσίαν, ἔτος ἄγων αὐτὸς τῆς βασιλείας ἐννεακαιδέκατον.* Exc. Barb. (258,1–5 Frick) *Et hunc iterum adduxit Nabugodonosor rex Babylonis ad se ligatum catenis et multitudinem populi filiorum Israhel, in quibus et Danihelem et qui cum eo erant Annaniam et Hiezechielem captiuos duxit in Babylonia.* Cedr. (198,7–17 Bekker) *Ἀθετήσαντος δὲ τὴν φορολογίαν Ἰωακεὶμ ἦλθε πάλιν εἰς Ἱερουσαλὴμ Ναβουχοδονόσορ, καὶ τοῦτον χειρωσάμενος καὶ ἀνελὼν καὶ ἀπὸ τοῦ τείχους ῥιφῆναι κελεύσας ἄταφον ἐπὶ πολὺν κατέλιπε χρόνον, βασιλεύσαντα ἔτη ἕνδεκα. περὶ οὗ φησὶν Ἱερεμίας τάδε λέγει κύριος ἐπὶ Ἰωακεὶμ υἱὸν Ἰωσίου· οὐαὶ ἐπὶ τὸν ἄνδρα τοῦτον. οὐ μὴ κόψονται αὐτόν, ὦ ἀδελφέ, οὐδὲ μὴ κλαύσονται αὐτόν, οἴ μοι, κύριε, καὶ οἴ μοι, ἀδελφέ· ἀλλὰ ταφὴν ὄνου ταφήσεται, καὶ συμψηφισθεὶς ῥιφήσεται ἐπέκεινα τῆς πύλης Ἱερουσαλήμ. τότε καὶ Δανιὴλ ἀπήχθη καὶ οἱ τρεῖς παῖδες καὶ ἄλλοι τοῦ λαοῦ πλεῖστοι καὶ μέρος τῶν σκευῶν κυρίου εἰς Βαβυλῶνα.* **5s** →
T6,14; F34,19–24.67; F46,207s; F76; Sym. Log. (Leo Gr. [43,16–20 Bekker] = Th. Mel. [37,24–27 Tafel]) *Ἀκόλουθον λοιπὸν ἐπιδραμεῖν τοῖς ἐν τοῖς ο' τῆς αἰχμαλωσίας ἔτεσιν ἡγησαμένοις. ἄχρι τούτου τοῦ τελευταίου Ἰωακεὶμ συνάγονται ἀπὸ Ἀδὰμ ͵δωϟβ' ἔτη. λοιπὸν οὖν τοὺς ἐφεξῆς χρόνους ἀπὸ τοῦ πρώτου ἔτους Σεδεκίου δεῖ ψηφίζειν.*

3s cf. Dan 1,1–6 **5s** cf. IV Regn 24,18 – 25,21; II Par 36,11–21; I Esdr 1,44; Clem. Alex., strom. 1,21,127,1s; Hipp., Dan. 1,3,4–8; Sym. Log. (Leo Gr. 44,22 – 46,18 = Th. Mel. 38,18–27); Iul. Pol. 134,16 – 140,19 **6s** cf. Ez 1,2

4 ἐκ Β ἐν Α 5 κ' Sync.[2] κε' Sync.[1] | ἦν ἔτος < Sync.[1]:Α 6 τῷ ο' ἔτει Sync.[2]:Α | ἀριθμεῖ τῆς αἰχμαλωσίας Sync.[2]:Α

T77b Michael Syrus 4,21 (4, 65a,15–26 Chabot)

[Syriac text]

5 Barhebr. (26–27 Wallis Budge) And Clemens reckons from the burning [of the temple] the seventy years of the Captivity until the second year of Darius … and Africanus from the beginning [of the reign of] Zedekiah.

attests, namely that Daniel and the three young men were from the second captivity of Judah. But Panodorus and other historians say that they belonged to the captivity of Samaria under Salmanasar. The twentieth king of Judah was Sedekias, 11 years, AM 4896. **Africanus numbers the seventy years of the captivity from the first year of Sedekias.**[8]
In the fifth year of Sedekias, AM 4900, the great prophet Ezekiel began to prophesy.

T77b

The sum of years from the burning of the Temple to its reconstruction is 70 years, and from the first year of Cyrus who returned the captives, 44 years. If someone asks why the Hebrews say that it was built in 46 years, this difference of two years arises from the fact that some reckon from the beginning of the prophecy of Jeremiah, others from the third year of Joachim, others from the burning of the Temple. **Africanus counts from the beginning of the reign of Sedekias;** Daniel, from Jeremiah; Clement, from the time of the burning of the Temple.

---

8   For Africanus' division of these 70 years according to the years of individual rulers, see Sym. Log. (Leo Gr. [44,22 – 46,18 Bekker] = Th. Mel. [38,18–27 Tafel]): 11 years Zedekiah + 25 years Nebuchadnezzar + 12 years Marodach + 4 years Baltasar + 17 Darius + 1 Cyrus. On the problem, see also Gelzer 1,100f. For the Logothete group as a witness to Africanus, see more generally Wallraff 2006,56–58.

F78 Chronicon Paschale (307,15 – 308,9 Dindorf)

[praecedit Dan 9,24–27 θ] Ἐντεῦθεν οὖν Ἀφρικανὸς ἐξαριθμεῖ τὸν ἐν τῇ αὐτῇ προφητείᾳ τῶν ἑβδομήκοντα ἑβδομάδων ἀριθμόν, συντείνοντα οὐ μόνον ἐπὶ τὴν τοῦ σωτηρίου κηρύγματος παρουσίαν, ἀλλὰ γὰρ καὶ εἰς ἔτη υρ', αἵ παρὰ τῷ Δανιὴλ προφητευθεῖσαι ο' τῶν ἐτῶν ἑβδομάδες τὴν ἀρχὴν ἔλαβον, καὶ συμπληροῦνται εἰς τὸ κβ' ἔτος τῆς ἡγεμονίας
5 Τιβερίου Καίσαρος, ἤγουν δ' ἔτος σα' Ὀλυμπιάδος, καὶ τῶν μὲν ξθ' ἑβδομάδων πληρουμένων εἰς τὸ ιδ' ἔτος τῆς ἡγεμονίας Τιβερίου Καίσαρος καὶ πρῶτον ἔτος σβ' Ὀλυμπιάδος, ἐν ᾧ ἡ παρουσία ἡ ἐπὶ τὸ βάπτισμα καὶ ἡ ἀρχὴ τοῦ σωτηρίου κηρύγματος τοῦ μεγάλου θεοῦ καὶ σωτῆρος ἡμῶν Ἰησοῦ Χριστοῦ. τῆς δὲ λοιπῆς μιᾶς ἑβδομάδος, ἥτις δυναμώσει διαθήκην πολλοῖς, πληρουμένης, ὡς εἴρηται, κατὰ τὸ κβ' ἔτος τῆς Τιβερίου Καίσαρος μοναρχίας. τὸ δὲ ἥμισυ τῆς ἑβδομάδος, ἐν ᾧ φησιν ὁ προφήτης,
10 Ἀρθήσεταί μου θυσία, φθάνει κατὰ τὸ ιθ' ἔτος τῆς Τιβερίου μοναρχίας, ἤγουν τέταρτον ἔτος σβ' Ὀλυμπιάδος, καθ' ὃ τὸν ἑκούσιον καὶ ζωοποιὸν ὑπέμεινε σταυρὸν Χριστὸς ὁ ἀληθινὸς θεὸς ἡμῶν.

1–3   → F93,19s.22–25.31–33.54–69.78–83.100–103; Exc. Barb. (264,16–18 Frick) (→ cf. app. ad F79,2–4) Post haec et Africanus dinumerans ipsam prophetiam septem ebdomadarum et septuagesimum numerum extendens ad Christi aduentum.

3s cf. Dan 9,24–27   9 cf. Dan 9,27 θ

[V] 4 ο' τῶν transposuimus τῶν ο' V   5 σα' V recte probabiliter σγ'   10 οβ' V corr. Di.

T78a Eusebius, Chronica (Chronicon Paschale [311,3–9 Dindorf])

Ἐντεῦθεν Ἀφρικανὸς ἀριθμεῖ κατὰ τὴν τοῦ Δανιὴλ προφητείαν τὸν τῶν ο' ἑβδομάδων ἀριθμόν, συντείνοντα εἰς ἔτη υρ'. καὶ εὕροι τις αὐτὰς περαιουμένας μετὰ τὴν τοῦ Χριστοῦ ἀνάληψιν ἐπὶ τὴν ἀρχὴν Νέρωνος Ῥωμαίων αὐτοκράτορος, καθ' ὃν ἡ πόλις ἀρξαμένη πολιορκεῖσθαι δευτέρῳ ἔτει τοῦ μετ' αὐτὸν βασιλεύσαντος Οὐεσπασιανοῦ καὶ δευτέρῳ σιβ' Ὀλυμ-
5 πιάδος τὴν ἐσχάτην ἅλωσιν, ἤγουν αἰχμαλωσίαν, ὑπέμεινε.

1s cf. supra app. ad F78,1–3   1–5 Eus., can.[Hier] (114[f] Helm) Neemiam, qui muros Hierusalem construxit, consummasse opus XXXII anno Artaxerxis regis Persarum Ezras memorat. Si quis autem ab hoc tempore LXX <h>ebdomadas a Danihelo scriptas numeret, quae faciunt annos CCCCXC, repperiet eas in regno Neronis expletas, sub quo obsideri Hierusalem coepta secundo postea Vespasiani anno capitur. Eus., can.[armen] (194 Karst) Und wenn man von da an zählt die 70 Wochen, die bei Daniel vorkommenden, welche ausmachen 490 Jahre, so wird man finden, daß unter Neron dem Selbstherrscher vollendet worden sind die Wochen, unter welchem der Beginn der Belagerung der Stadt ward; nach Neron, im zweiten Jahre des Vespianos, erlitt sie dann vollends die letzte Zerstörung. Sync. (299,25–30 Moss.) (→ T80d) Τὰς μέντοι ο' ἑβδομάδας παρὰ τῷ Δανιὴλ ἕως Χριστοῦ ἡγουμένου ἐντεῦθεν ἀριθμεῖσθαι δεῖ κατὰ τὸν Ἀφρικανὸν ἔτη υρ'. Εὐσέβιος δὲ ὁ Καισαρεὺς φησιν ὅτι εἴ τις ἐντεῦθεν ἀριθμήσειε τὰ παρὰ τῷ Δανιὴλ ο' ἑβδομάδας, <αἵ> γίνονται ἔτη υρ', εὕροι ἄν αὐτὰς ἐπὶ Νέρωνα Ῥωμαίων αὐτοκράτορα περαιουμένας, καθ' ὃν πολιορκεῖσθαι ἀρξαμένη ἡ πόλις μετὰ Νέρωνα ἔτους β' Οὐεσπασιανοῦ τὴν ἐσχάτην ἅλωσιν ὑπέμεινεν. Mich. Syr. 5,1 (1,108,3s Chabot) C'est de cette époque d'Artaxerxès qu'Africanus commence à compter les semaines indiquées par Daniel (cf. etiam l. 5–10 Chabot).

[V] 5 ὑπομεῖναι V corr. Di.

F78 *The Seventy Weeks of Daniel*[1]

From this point on,[2] therefore, Africanus enumerates the number of years in the same prophecy of the 70 'weeks', a number which extends not only up to the *parousia* of the proclamation of salvation, but also for 490 years.[3] From this point, the 'weeks' of 70 years prophesied in Daniel took their beginning and are completed in the 22nd year of the rule of Tiberius Caesar, that is the fourth year of the 201st Olympiad.[4] For the 69 weeks are completed in the 14th year of the rule of Tiberius Caesar and the first year of the 202nd Olympiad, at the time of the *parousia* at his baptism, and the beginning of the proclamation of salvation of the great God and our Savior Jesus Christ. And the remaining one week, which 'will strengthen a covenant for many', is completed, as has been said, in the 22nd year of the reign of Tiberius Caesar. And the half of the week, in which the prophet says, 'My offering will be taken away', is completed in the 19th year of the reign of Tiberius, that is the fourth year of the 202nd Olympiad, at which time Christ, our true God, underwent of his own will the life-giving Crucifixion.

T78a[5]

From that point,[6] Africanus numbers the 70 'weeks' according to the prophecy of Daniel, extending to 490 years. And one would find them completed after the Resurrection of Christ during the reign of the Roman emperor Nero. During his reign the city began to be besieged, and endured the final capture, that is the captivity, in the second year of Vespasian, the emperor who succeeded him, and the second year of the 212th Olympiad.

1. For a parallel text in Latin independent of the *Chronicon Paschale*, see the *Excerpta Barbari* (in app. to ll. 1–3). Close verbal similarities between the two witnesses and terminology typical of Africanus suggest that this is a direct quotation from his chronicle. See, for example, the use of παρουσία (l. 5) (= *aduentus*); for Africanus' use of the word in connection with the beginning of Jesus' ministry, see F93,24.29.83.108 (and n. 18 ad loc.); F94,1f. Note also the use of ἐξαριθ-μέω (= very literally *dinumerans*). Because the reference from Eusebius that follows (T78a) is more of a paraphrase, it has been classified as *testimonium*.
2. That is, in the context of the *Chronicon Paschale*, Ol. 81,3. Cf. F93,57, according to which the starting point of the prophecy in Africanus was Ol. 83,4.
3. The explanation of the chronology of the 70 weeks in Daniel that follows differs from Africanus' own interpretation. Africanus assigned only one year to the period between Christ's baptism and the Crucifixion. The endpoint of Daniel's prophecy by his reckoning was 16 Tiberius = Ol. 202,2; see F93,57f.
4. Text: σα' (201). The more accurate Olympiad number would be σγ' (203). 490 years from Ol. 81,3 would be Ol. 203,4 (reckoning inclusively).
5. In the *Chronicon Paschale*, the text is not explicitly attributed to Eusebius; see, however, the parallels in the apparatus of secondary witnesses, in particular Syncellus.
6. In Ol. 90,1, according to the *Chronicon Paschale*. Cf. Eus., can.[armen] 194: Ol. 87,1; Eus., can.[Hier] 114[f]: Ol. 86,4.

T78b Georgius Syncellus (277,12–19 Mosshammer)

Μαρδοχαῖος δὲ διὰ τῆς Ἐσθὴρ τὸν βασιλέα ἔπεισεν ἀναιρεθῆναι τὸν Ἀμάν. τινὲς μὲν οὖν τὰς ο΄ ἑβδομάδας ἀπὸ τοῦδε τοῦ χρόνου βούλονται ἀριθμεῖσθαι, ἕτεροι δέ, ὡς καὶ Ἀφρικανός, ἀπὸ Νεεμίου καὶ τελείας ἀνοικοδομῆς τοῦ ναοῦ καὶ τῆς πόλεως, ἥτις γέγονε κατὰ τὸ κ΄ ἔτος Ἀρταξέρξου τοῦ καὶ Μακρόχειρος, ὅπερ ἦν κόσμου ͵εξη΄. ἕτεροι ἀπὸ τῆς
5 οἰκοδομῆς τοῦ ναοῦ τῆς διὰ Ζοροβάβελ καὶ Ἰησοῦ τοῦ υἱοῦ Ἰωσεδέκ, τῷ β΄ ἔτει Δαρείου, ἀριθμοῦσι τὰς αὐτὰς ο΄ ἑβδομάδας.

2–4 → F93,33–45.54–57.79s

1 cf. Est 7,1–10   1s cf. Hipp., chron. 685   2–4 cf. II Par 36,22s; I Esdr 2; 5,1 – 7,5; II Esdr 12,17 – 13,37; 15,14; Hipp., chron. 684; Eus., can.[Hier] 160[a]

F79 Georgius Syncellus (298,12–19 Mosshammer)

Ἀφρικανοῦ περὶ τοῦ Ἔσδρα ἑπτακαιδεκάτου ἀπὸ Ἀαρὼν τοῦ πρώτου ἱερέως·

Συγχωρήσαντος Ἀρταξέρξου τοὺς ὑπολοίπους τῆς Ἰουδαίων αἰχμαλωσίας ἤθροισεν Ἔσδρας τά τε λείψανα τῶν σκευῶν τοῦ ναοῦ ἦλθεν ἔχων εἰς Ἰερουσαλὴμ καὶ τὸν νόμον ἐδίδασκεν. ὡς δὲ ἐπύθετο κατ' ἐπιγαμίας αὐτοὺς ἀναμεμίχθαι
5 τοῖς ἔθνεσιν, ἠνάγκαζε τοὺς οὐχ ὁμοεθνεῖς ἔχοντας ἐξεῶσαι ἕκαστον τὴν γυναῖκα τὴν ἑαυτοῦ. οἱ δ' ὑπήκουον καὶ τοῦ χειμῶνος ἐπειγομένου τὸ ἔργον ἐπετελεῖτο.

2–4 → F93,31–45; Sym. Log. (Leo Gr. [47,22 – 48,1 Bekker] = Th. Mel. [40,20s Tafel] = Iul. Pol. [144,6–8 Hardt]) *Συγχωρήσαντος Ἀρταξέρξου Ἔσδρας ὁ ἱερεὺς τοὺς ὑπολοίπους ἀναγαγὼν εἰς Ἰερουσαλὴμ (Ἰσραὴλ Leo Gr.) τὸν νόμον ἐξεπαίδευεν (ἐξεπαίδευσεν Iul. Pol.).* Exc. Barb. (264,13s Frick) *Eo tempore Hesdras ascendens in Hierusalem legem docebat …* (→ F78, app. ad l. 1–3). Io. Mal. 6,15 (124,25–30 Thurn) *Ὁ δὲ αὐτὸς Ἀρταξέρξης παρακληθεὶς ὑπό τινων τῆς συγκλήτου αὐτοῦ, καὶ τοὺς ὑπολοίπους Ἰουδαίους ἀπέλυσεν, καὶ εἴ τις ἐὰν ἠβουλήθη τότε ἀνελθεῖν εἰς τὴν Ἰερουσαλήμ, ἀνῆλθε μετὰ Ἔσδρα τοῦ προφήτου καὶ ἡγουμένου· ᾧτινι καὶ τὰ ἱερὰ σκεύη ἔδωκεν καὶ τὰς βίβλους τὰς ἱερατικὰς τὰς εὑρεθείσας· ὁ δὲ αὐτὸς Ἔσδρας τῶν μὴ εὑρεθέντων βιβλίων ἀπὸ ὑπομνήσεως αὐτοῦ γράφεσθαι τὰ ὑπομνήματα ἐποίησεν.*

2–4   cf. Eus., can.[Hier] 111[g]; Sync. 298,21–26   2–7   cf. II Esdr 7–10; 23,23–31; Ios., ant. Iud. 11,121–153

[AB] 1 ἀφρικανοῦ περὶ τοῦ ἔσδρα habet in margine A ut ἑπτακαιδεκάτος … ἱερέως ad textum praecedentem pertinere uideatur. Moss. transposuit auctore B et II Esdr 7,1–5, et corr. in ἑπτακαιδεκάτου

T78b

But through Esther, Mordecai persuaded the king to kill Haman. There are those, then, who would reckon the 70 weeks from this date, whereas others, such as Africanus, reckon them from Nehemiah and the final building of the Temple and the city, which occurred in the 20th year of Artaxerxes, also known as 'Longarm.' This was AM 5068. And still others count the 70 weeks from the building of the Temple under Zorobabel and Jeshua the son of Josedek in the second year of Darius.

F79 *Ezra the Priest*

From Africanus, concerning Ezra, the 17th priest from Aaron, the first priest:

With the permission of Artaxerxes, Ezra collected the remnant of the Jewish captivity and with what was left of the Temple vessels came to Jerusalem and taught the law. When he learned that they had mixed with the gentiles through intermarriage, he forced each of the men married to foreign women to get rid of his wife. They complied, and the matter was completed with the approach of winter.

T80

T80a Eusebius, Canones (Hieronymus [113ᵃ Helm])

Hucusque Hebraeorum diuinae scripturae annales temporum continent. Ea uero, quae post haec aput eos gesta sunt, exhibebimus de libro Macchabaeorum et Iosephi et Africani scriptis, qui deinceps uniuersam historiam usque ad Romana tempora persecuti sunt.

T80b Eusebius, Canones (armeniace [2,120,16–19 Aucher = 193 Karst])

Մինչև ցայսվայր ունին եբրայեցւոց մարգարէականն գիրք։ Եւ որ ինչ յետ այսորիկ գործեցաւ 'ի նոցանէ, 'ի գրոցն որ մակաբայեցւոց կոչին՝ կարգեցից, և 'ի յովսեպայ և յափրիկանոյ, որ զևս յառաջ զամենայն պատմութիւնն մինչև 'ի Հռոմայեցւոց ժամանական իշուցին:

5–7 → T6,17–21; T11,4–7

1–7 Mich. Syr. 5,2 (1, 109 Chabot; cf. Barhebr. 35 Wallis Budge) A partir d'ici, nous pouvons trouver la série des années et les événements qui s'y passèrent dans les livres des Macchabées, dans ceux de Josèphe et du chroniqueur Africanus.

T80c Eusebius, Chronica (armeniace [1, 106,14–19 Aucher = 34,10–13 Karst])

Զեբրայեցւոցն աղբիւմեր կարգեցաք 'ի մուխէ, և որ յետ նորա որ 'ի մէջ Հեբրայեցւոց գիրք կրին. և 'ի փղատոս յովսեպեայ 'ի Հրէական նախնեացն պատմութենէ, և յափրիկանոսի ժամանակագրութեանցն:

T80d Georgius Syncellus (299,19–24 Mosshammer)

Ἕως μὲν οὖν Ἔσδρα καὶ Νεεμίου αἱ ἐνδιάθετοι Ἑβραϊκαὶ γραφαὶ ἐκκλησιάζεσθαι παρεδόθησαν ὑπὸ τῶν μακαρίων ἀποστόλων καὶ μαθητῶν τοῦ κυρίου καὶ θεοῦ καὶ σωτῆρος ἡμῶν Ἰησοῦ Χριστοῦ καὶ τῶν ἁγίων πατέρων καὶ διδασκάλων ἡμῶν, τὰ δὲ μετὰ ταῦτα συμβάντα ἢ πραχθέντα ἕως τῆς θείας σαρκώσεως τοῖς Ἰουδαίοις Ἰώσηππος ἐν τοῖς Μακκαβαϊκοῖς ἱστορεῖ καὶ Ἀφρικανὸς μετ' αὐτὸν ἐν ἐπιτόμῳ ... (→ T78a, app.)

3–5 → T6,17–21; T11,4–7; F89; T92,3s

T80 *Africanus as a Source for post-biblical Jewish History*

T80a

The divine Scriptures of the Hebrews contain chronological records up to this point. Events, however, that happened among them afterwards, we will set forth from the book of the Maccabees, and the writings of Josephus and Africanus, who have continued universal history after that up to Roman times.

T80b

The prophetic books of the Hebrews have [passed down the tradition] to this point. And what has been done by them afterwards, I will arrange from the writings which are called 'of the Maccabees', and from Josephus and Africanus, who have continued universal history after that up to Roman times.

T80c

In what follows we have arranged the chronography of the Hebrews from Moses and from those books that are handed down among the Hebrews after him, and from the *Jewish Antiquities* of Flavius Josephus, and from Africanus' *Chronographiae*.

T80d

The canonical Hebrew books up to Ezra and Nehemiah, then, were handed down for use in the churches by the blessed apostles and disciples of the Lord God, our Savior Jesus Christ, and the holy fathers and our teachers; but as to what subsequently happened to or was done by the Jews up until the divine Incarnation, Josephus recounts this in his Maccabaean histories, and after him Africanus in summary form.

F81

F81a Georgius Syncellus (309,8–19 Mosshammer)

Πλάτων πρὸς Σωκράτην ἐφοίτα· Σιμίας καὶ Κέβης καὶ οἱ λοιποὶ Σωκρατικοί. Ἀφρικανοῦ·
Ὀλυμπιὰς πζ'·
  ὁ Πελοποννησίων καὶ Ἀθηναίων πόλεμος ζ' καὶ εἰκοσαετής, ὃν Θουκυδίδης συνέγραψε, δι' Ἀσπασίας πόρνας β' καὶ στήλας κατὰ Μεγαρέων ἀστυγειτό-
5 νων Ἀθηναίοις συνέστη.
Ὀλυμπιὰς πη'·
  Βακχυλίδης μελοποιὸς ἐγνωρίζετο.
  Ἀθηναίους ἐπίεσεν ὁ λοιμός.
  Σωκράτης φιλόσοφος καθαρτικὸς ἤνθει.
10 Εὔπολις καὶ Ἀριστοφάνης κωμικοί, Σοφοκλῆς τε ὁ τραγῳδοποιὸς ἐγνωρί-
ζετο.
  Γοργίας καὶ Ἱππίας καὶ Πρόδικος, ὡς δὲ τινές, καὶ Ζήνων καὶ Παρμενίδης κατὰ τούτους ἤκμαζον.
  Πῦρ ἐκ τῆς Αἴτνης ἐν τοῖς κατὰ Σικελίαν τόποις ἐρράγη.

3–5 → F65,172s; Sync. (304,10–13 Moss.) *Τότε καὶ ὁ Πελοποννησιακὸς συνέστη πόλεμος διὰ τὸ γεγονὸς ὑπὸ Περικλέους ψήφισμα μὴ κοινωνεῖν Μεγαρεῦσι τοὺς Ἀθηναίους, ὡς ὑβρίσασιν Ἀσπασίαν τὴν γαμετὴν αὐτοῦ, καὶ διὰ τὴν τοιαύτην αἰτίαν προσθεμένων τῶν Μεγαρέων τοῖς Λακεδαιμονίοις.* Eus., can.[Hier] (114[g] Helm) Initium belli Peloponnesiaci **7s** Eus., can.[Hier] (114[h]–115[a] Helm; sed Ol. 87) Bacchylides carminum scriptor agnoscitur. Athenienses pestilentia laborant. Eus., can.[armen] (194 Karst) Olomios überzeugte die Athener. **9–13** → F81b,7s **10s** Eus., can.[Hier] (115[d] Helm) Eupolis et Aristofanes scriptores comoediarum agnoscuntur. **12s** Eus., can.[Hier] (114[d] Helm; sed Ol. 86) *Democritus Abderites et Empedocles et Hippocrates medicus* Gorgias Hippiasque et Prodicus et Zeno et Parmenides *philosophi insignes habentur.* **14** Eus., can.[Hier] (115[e] Helm) Ex Aetna monte ignis erupit. Cedr. (255,13s Bekker) *Ἐν τούτοις τοῖς χρόνοις ἐρράγη ἐν Σικελίᾳ τὸ Αἰτναῖον ὄρος καὶ ἐξῆλθε πῦρ.*

1 cf. Suda Σωκράτης Σ 829 **3–5** cf. Thuc. 2,2,1; Diod. Sic. 12,37,2; Iul. Afr., cest. I 2,55 **4s** cf. Ar., Ach. 519–527 **6s** cf. Suda Διάγορας ὁ Μήλιος Δ 523 (Ol. 78) **8** cf. Thuc. 2,47,3; Diod. Sic. 12,45,2 **9** cf. Plut., Plat. quaest. 1.999 E, 1000 C

[AB] **1** Σιμίας Di. σημίας A σημεία B | non liquet ex libris manuscriptis utrum Ἀφρικανοῦ solum ad lemmata sequentia pertineat an etiam ad praecedentia; in duobus codicibus scriptum est in fine lineae post σωκρατικοί **3** ὃν B ὧν A **4** στήλας B στείλας A **4s** ἀστυγειτόνων Scal. ἀστυγείτων AB **8** ἔπεισεν ὁ λιμός AB corr. Moss.

F81 The Beginning of the Peloponnesian War

F81a

Plato studied with Socrates. Simias and Cebes and the remaining Socratics. From Africanus.

The 87th Olympiad.

    The 27-year-long war between the Peloponnesians and the Athenians, which Thucydides wrote about, broke out because of two of Aspasia's prostitutes and columns erected against the Megarians, neighbors to the Athenians.

The 88th Olympiad.

    Bacchylides, the lyric poet, was becoming known.
    The plague oppressed the Athenians.
    Socrates, the cathartic philosopher, was flourishing.
    Eupolis and Aristophanes, comic poets, and Sophocles the tragic poet were becoming known.
    Gorgias, Hippias and Prodicus, according to some, and Zeno and Parmenides as well, were flourishing at this time.
    Fire from Mount Etna burst forth over the regions of Sicily.[1]

---

[1] Routh gives only ll. 2–5 as Africanus' text. However, the list in the *Excerpta Barbari* (F81b) gives some of the names in ll. 7–14. Therefore, the whole text should be attributed to Africanus, see also Gelzer 1,180f.

F81b Excerpta Barbari (266,1–14 Frick)

Post Darium autem regnauit filius eius Artarxerxis secundus qui uocatur Memoratus annos XLII: fiunt simul anni V milia XCVIII. Fuit autem sub istum princeps sacerdotum in Hierusalem Heliasibus. Filosofi autem cognoscebantur temporibus Artarxersis Sofoclus, et Traclitus, et Anaxagorus, et Hirodotus, et Melissus, et Euripidus cantoconpositor,
5 et Protagorus, et Socrator ritor, et Fideas statuasconpositor, et Theetitus artifex, et Dimocritus Abderitus, et Ippocratis medicus, et Thucudidus ritor, et Empedoclus, et Gorgias, et Zinon, et Parmenidus, et Socratus Athineus, et Periclus, et Eupolus, et Aristofanus architector. Hii omnes cognoscebantur: unde et Africanus sub Artarxerxe rege dinumerat filosofos.

4–7   Eus., can.[Hier] (113c–114e Helm) Herodotus *cum Athenis libros suos in concilio legisset, honoratus est.* Melissus *physicus agnoscitur.* Euripides tragoediarum scriptor *clarus habetur* et Protagoras *sophista, cuius libros decreto publico Athenienses combusserunt. Romae rursum consules creati.* Fidias *eburneam Mineruam facit. Fidenates contra Romanos rebellant.* Theaetetus mathematicus *agnoscitur, Aristofanes clarus habetur et Sofocles poeta tragicus. Gens Campanorum in Italia constituta.* Democritus Abderites et Empedocles et Hippocrates medicus Gorgias *Hippiasque et Prodicus et* Zeno et Parmenides *philosophi insignes habentur.* Socrates *plurimo sermone celebratur.*   4–6   Sync. (297, 11–15 Moss.) Ἡρόδοτος ἱστορικὸς ἐτιμήθη παρὰ τῆς Ἀθηναίων βουλῆς ἐπαναγνοὺς αὐτοῖς τὰς βίβλους. Εὐριπίδης τραγῳδοποιὸς ἐγνωρίζετο. Πρωταγόρας ὁ σοφιστὴς ἤκμαζε. τούτου Ἀθηναῖοι τὰς βίβλους ἐψηλάφησαν τοῦ καῦσαι. Sync. (297,18 – 298,3 Moss.) Μέλισσος φυσικὸς ἐγνωρίζετο. Φειδίας πλάστης καὶ ἀγαλματοποιὸς ἐγνωρίζετο, ὃς τὴν ἐλεφαντίνην Ἀθηνᾶν ἐποίησε. Θεαίτητος μαθηματικὸς ἤνθει. ἐν Ἰταλίᾳ Καμπανῶν ἔθνος συνέστη. Δημόκριτος Ἀβδηρίτης φυσικὸς φιλόσοφος ἤκμαζεν. ...Ἱπποκράτης Κῷος ἰητρῶν ἄριστος ἐγνωρίζετο Ἀσκληπιάδης τὸ γένος.   6–8   → F81a,9–13; Eus., can.[Hier] (115c.d Helm) Pericles *moritur.* Eupolis et Aristofanes scriptores comoediarum agnoscuntur.

3–9   cf. Eus., can.[Hier] 115b; Eus., praep. ev. 10,14,15; Io. Mal. 6,27s; Sync. 304,18–23; Anon. Matr. 36,15 – 37,7; Mich. Syr. 5,1; Iul. Pol. 147,2–8

F82 Excerpta Barbari (306,23 – 310,24 Frick)

Macedoniorum reges et tempora

Macedoniorum autem regnum non silendum est. et enim Romeis obtinentibus fortitudinem nondum longinquo tempore sub Ozia regem Iudeorum anno tricensimo tertio nouimus eam sustentare. et regnauit per annos DCXLVII, cessa-
5 uit autem annos unusquisque in quinquagesima tertia Olympiada. regnauit autem Ozias in Hierusalem et in Iuda annos LII.

4 cf. Io. Mal. 7,19

F81b[1]

After Darius, his son Artaxerxes II, called Mnemon, was king for 42 years. Altogether there are 5098 years. During his reign, the high priest in Jerusalem was Eliashib. In the time of Artaxerxes, there were becoming known the philosophers Sophocles, Heraclitus,[2] Anaxagoras, Herodotus, Melissus, Euripides the tragic poet,[3] Protagoras, Isocrates the rhetor,[4] Phidias the sculptor,[5] Theatetus the grammarian,[6] Democritus of Abdera, Hippocrates the physician, Thucydides the rhetor, Empedocles, Gorgias, Zeno, Parmenides, Socrates the Athenian, Pericles, Eupolis and Aristophanes the comic poet.[7] All these men were becoming known, whence Africanus reckons the dates of the philosophers during the time of king Artaxerxes.

F82 *The Kings of the Macedonians*[8]

The kings and chronology of the Macedonians

But we should not fail to mention the kingdom of the Macedonians. For seeing that the Romans did not become powerful for a long time yet,[9] we have learned that this kingdom was established at the time of king Uzziah, in his 33rd year. And their kingdom[10] lasted 647 years, and came to an end in the 153rd Olympiad.[11] Now Uzziah was king in Jerusalem and Judah for 52 years.[12]

---

1 For discussion, see Gelzer 1,177f.
2 Gr. (Frick): Ἡράκλειτος.
3 Gr. (Frick): Εὐριπίδης ὁ τραγῳδοποιός.
4 Gr. (Frick): Ἰσοκράτης ὁ ῥήτωρ.
5 Gr. (Frick): Φειδίας ὁ ἀγαλματοποιός.
6 Gr. (Frick): Θεαίτητος ὁ τεχνικός.
7 Gr. (Frick): Ἀριστοφάνης ὁ κωμῳδός.
8 Africanus must be the source of this list for two reasons: a) The chronological data (see below n. 12) is consistent with Africanus' system. b) The synchronization with Hebrew kings is typical of his historical method. For further discussion, see also Frick 1880,10; Gelzer 1,155–160; Trieber 1892,334f; Schwartz 1895, 75–92.
9 Although obscure, the statement may mean that in the succession of world empires, the Romans achieved supremacy only after the end of Macedonian rule.
10 Gr. (Frick): αὐτήν, in reference to βασιλεία (l. 2).
11 Gr. (Frick): ἐν τῇ ἑκατοστῇ πεντηκοστῇ τρίτῃ Ὀλυμπιάδι.
12 If Uzziah was king of Judah for 52 years and his successor Jotham ruled for 16 years (cf. IV Regn 15,2.33), a total of 35 years would have elapsed from 33 Uzziah (= 1 Cranaus) to 1 Ahaz (= AM 4727 = Ol. 1,1; cf. F64). From Ol. 1,1, the Macedonian kingdom would thus have lasted 612 years (647–35). Translated into Olympiad dating, the last year of the Macedonian kingdom would be Ol. 154,1 (not Ol. 153 as given here and below, ll. 54f). Converted into universal years, the entire 647-year duration of the Macedonian kingdom would have extended from AM 4692 (= 33 Uzziah) to AM 5339 (= Ol. 154,1). On this problem, see Gelzer 1,158.

Sub tricensimo tertio autem anno Oziae Macedonorum regnum ordinatum est, Cranaus primus in Macedonia regnans, sicut numerus manifestat, sic.

I. Cranaus ann. XXVIII.
II. Cynus ann. XII.
III. Tyrimmus ann. XXXVIII.
IIII. Perdicus ann. LI.
V. Argeus ann. XXXVIII.
VI. Filippus ann. XXVI.
VII. Aeropus ann. XXXVIII.
VIII. Alcetus ann. XXVIIII.
VIIII. Amyntus ann. L.
X. Alexander ann. XLIII.
XI. Perdicus ann. XXVIII.
XII. Arcelaus ann. XXIIII.
XIII. Orestus ann. III.
XIIII. Arceclaus alius ann. unum et dimidium.
XV. Amyntus ann. III.
XVI. Pausanius ann. I et dimidium.
<XXIII. Amyntus alius ann. VI.>
XVII. Argeus ann. III.

9–26 Eus., reg. ser.[armen.] (150s Karst) ≈ Eus., reg. ser.[Hier] (27 Schoene), cf. Chron. Synt. (90 Schoene)
Im dritten Jahre der Regierung Alexanders des Korintherkönigs regiert über die Makedonier als erster:
1. Karanos Jahre 28 (= Hier., Chron. Synt.)
2. Koindos Jahre 12 (= Hier., Chron. Synt.)
3. Tirimmas Jahre 38 (= Hier., Chron. Synt.)
4. Perdikas Jahre *51* (= Hier., Chron. Synt.)
5. Argeos Jahre 38 (= Hier., Chron. Synt.)
6. Philipos Jahre *38* (= Hier., *39* Chron. Synt.)
7. Aëropos Jahre *26* (= Hier., *25* Chron. Synt.)
8. Alketas Jahre 29 (= Hier., *22* Chron. Synt.)
9. Amintas Jahre 50 (= Hier., Chron. Synt.)
10. Alexandros Jahre 43 (= Hier., Chron. Synt.)
11. Perdikas Jahre 28 (= Hier., Chron. Synt.)
12. Archelaos Jahre *23* (*24* Hier. = Chron. Synt.)
13. Orestes Jahre 3 (= Hier., Chron. Synt.)
14. Archelaos Jahre 6 (*4* Hier. = Chron. Synt.)
15. Amintas Jahre *1* (= Hier., Chron. Synt.)
16. Pausanias Jahre *1* (= Hier., Chron. Synt.)
17. Amintas Jahre 6 (= Hier., Chron. Synt.)
18. Argeos Jahre *2* (1 Hier., - Chron. Synt.)

9–52 cf. Eus., chron. 107,17 – 109,7 (= Diod. Sic. 7,15,1s); 109,8 – 114,17 (= Porphyrius FGrHist 260 F3); Exc. Eus. 133,11–28; Sync. 234,1–18; 252,14–20; 285,25 – 286,4; 296,1–13; 304,25–28; 313,9 – 324,28; 325,17 – 327,6; 340,20 – 341,10

25 transposuimus e l. 32 (cf. Eus., reg. ser. supra in app.) **26** III] *II* Frick

During the 33rd year of Uzziah, the kingdom of the Macedonians was established. Cranaus was the first to be king in Macedonia, as the following sequence demonstrates:

1. Cranaus, 28 years.
2. Coenus, 12 years.
3. Tyrimmas, 38 years.
4. Perdiccas,[13] 51 years.
5. Argaeus, 38 years.
6. Philip,[14] 26 years.
7. Aeropas,[15] 38 years.
8. Alcetas, 29 years.
9. Amyntas,[16] 50 years.
10. Alexander, 43 years.
11. Perdiccas,[17] 28 years.
12. Archelaus, 24 years.
13. Orestes, 3 years.
14. Another Archelaus,[18] 1 ½ years.
15. Amyntas,[19] 3 years.
16. Pausanias, 1 ½ years.
<23. Another Amyntas,[20] 6 years.>
17. Argaeus, 3 years.

[13] Perdiccas I.
[14] Philip I.
[15] Aeropas I.
[16] Amyntas I.
[17] Perdiccas II.
[18] Archelaus II.
[19] Amyntas II.
[20] Amyntas III.

XVIII. Amyntus alius ann. XVIII.
XVIIII. Alexander alius ann. II.
XX. Ptolemeus ann. III.
XXI. Perdicus alius ann. VI.
XXII. Filippus ann. XXVI.
{XXIII. Amyntus alius ann. VI.}
XXIIII. Alexander alius ann. XIII.

Alexander omnia regna tenens Macedonorum regno coniunxit.
Post Alexandrum autem conditorem in principes eius rebus uenerunt.
Et Macedonorum principato successit Filippus frater Alexandri, et sic secundum ordinem.

XXV. Filippus frater ann. VII.
XXVI. Casandrus ann. XVIIII.
XXVII. Pedes Casandrus ann. IIII.
XXVIII. Dimitrius ann. V.
XXVIIII. Pyrrus mens. XI.
XXX. Lysimachus ann. V.

27–33 Eus., reg. ser.^{armen.} (151 Karst) ≈ Eus., reg. ser.^{Hier} (27 Schoene), cf. Chron. Synt. (90 Schoene)
19. Amintas Jahre 18 (= Hier., Chron. Synt.)
20. Alexandros Jahre *1* (*4* Hier., Chron. Synt.)
21. Ptlomeos der Alorite Jahre 3 (= Hier., Chron. Synt.)
22. Perdikas Jahre 6 (= Hier., Chron. Synt.)
23. Philipos Jahre *25* (26 Hier., *27* Chron. Synt.)
24. Alexandros des Philipos *Jahre 12 Monate 6* (*12* Hier. = Chron. Synt.)
34 → F65,208; F73,22–24; T6,16   35 → F65,213
35–52 Io. Mal. 8,5 (148,71–82 Thurn) Μετὰ οὖν τὴν τελευτὴν Ἀλεξάνδρου τοῦ Μακεδόνος ἐμερίσθησαν εἰς τέσσαρας τοπαρχίας, ἤτοι βασιλείας, αἱ χῶραι ἃς ὑπέταξεν ὁ αὐτὸς Ἀλέξανδρος ἅμα τοῖς συμμάχοις αὐτοῦ· καὶ ἐβασίλευσαν αὐτῶν οἱ Μακεδόνες οἱ συνασπισταὶ τοῦ αὐτοῦ Ἀλεξάνδρου καθὼς διετάξατο οὕτως. τῆς Μακεδονίας καὶ τῆς Εὐρώπης πάσης κρατεῖν καὶ βασιλεύειν Φίλιππον τὸν ἀδελφὸν αὐτοῦ τὸν ἴδιον τὸν μείζονα. καὶ ἐβασίλευσεν ὁ Φίλιππος, καὶ μετὰ Φίλιππον ἐβασίλευσε Κάσσανδρος, καὶ μετὰ Κάσσανδρον ἐβασίλευσαν οἱ παῖδες τοῦ αὐτοῦ Κασσάνδρου, καὶ μετ' αὐτοὺς ἐβασίλευσε Δημήτριος, καὶ μετὰ Δημήτριον ἐβασίλευσεν ὁ Ἠπειρώτης Πύρρος, καὶ μετὰ Πύρρον τὸν Ἠπειρώτην ἐβασίλευσε Μελέαγρος καὶ ἄλλοι βασιλεῖς ἐξ ἐβασίλευσαν ἕως τῆς βασιλείας Περσέως τοῦ Ἠπειρώτου. καὶ ἐκράτησεν ἡ βασιλεία αὐτῶν μετὰ τὴν τελευτὴν Ἀλεξάνδρου ἔτη ρνζ'.
38–43 Eus., reg. ser.^{armen} (151 Karst) ≈ Eus., reg. ser.^{Hier} (27 Schoene), cf. Chron. Synt. (90 Schoene)
25. Philipos, Brüder Alexanders Jahre 7 (= Hier., Chron. Synt.)
26. Kassandros Jahre 19 (= Hier., Chron. Synt.)
27. Söhne Kassanders Jahre 4 (= Hier., Chron. Synt.)
28. Demetrios Jahre *6* (= Hier., Chron. Synt.)
29. Phireus Monate *7* (- Hier., Chron. Synt.)
30. Lysimachos Jahre 5 (= Hier., *6* Chron. Synt.)

31 XXII Frick *XII* cod.   **33** XIII] *XII* Frick

18. Another Amyntas, 18 years.
19. Another Alexander, 2 years.
20. Ptolemy, 3 years.
21. Another Perdiccas,[21] 6 years.
22. Philippus,[22] 26 years.

24. Another Alexander,[23] 13 years.

Alexander, in control of all the kingdoms, joined them to the Macedonian kingdom.
After Alexander, the Founder, affairs of state fell to his governors.
Alexander's brother Philip succeeded to the rule of the Macedonians, and the succession of rulers is as follows:

25. Philip,[24] his brother, 7 years.
26. Casander, 19 years.
27. The sons of Casander,[25] 4 years.
28. Demetrius,[26] 5 years.
29. Pyrrhus, 11 months.
30. Lysimachus, 5 years.

---

21 Perdiccas III.
22 Philip II.
23 Alexander III.
24 Philip III.
25 Gr. (Frick): παῖδες Κασάνδρου.
26 Demetrius I.

XXXI. Ptolomeus Ceraunus ann. II.
XXXII. Meleagrus mens. VII.
XXXIII. Antipatrus mens. II.
XXXIIII. Sosthenus ann. II.
XXXV. Antigonus Gonata ann. XXXV.
XXXVI. Dimitrius ann. X.
XXXVII. Antigonus alius ann. XV.
XXXVIII. Filippus alius ann. XLV.
XXXVIIII. Perseus ann. X.

Haec Macedonorum regna regnantes ab anno Oziae regis Iudae tricensimo tertio obtinuerunt per annos DCXLVII et cessauerunt in Olympiada centesima LIII.

44–55 Eus., reg. ser.^{armen} (151 Karst) ≈ Eus., reg. ser.^{Hier} (27 Schoene), cf. Chron. Synt. (90s Schoene)
31. Ptlomeos Keraunos Jahre *1* (= Hier., Chron. Synt.)
32. Mel<e>agros Monate *2* (- Hier., Chron. Synt.)
33. Antipatros *Tage 45* (- Hier., Chron. Synt.)
34. Sosthenes Jahre *2* (= Hier., Chron. Synt.)
35. Antigonos Gonatos Jahre *36* (= Hier. *15* Chron. Synt.)
36. Demetrios Jahre *10* (= Hier., Chron. Synt.)
37. Antigonos Jahre *15* (= Hier., Chron. Synt.)
38. Philipos Jahre *42* (= Hier., Chron. Synt.)
39. Perseus Jahre *10* (= Hier., Chron. Synt.)
Jahre *647, Monate 3, Tage 45*. Anhebend im Jahre 1204 haben sie aufgehört in der 150. Olympiade.

51 XLV] *XLII* Frick

T83 Michael Syrus 5,4 (4, 74a,21 – 75b,3 Chabot)

3s Barhebr. (40 Wallis Budge) From Adam to Seleucus, according to Africanus, is 5083 years.

1 cf. Eus., chron. (can.^{Hier} 126^h = Chron. Pasch. 323,17); Sync. 330,1–8

31. Ptolemy Ceraunus, 2 years.
32. Meleager, 7 months.
33. Antipater, 2 months.
34. Sosthenes, 2 years.
35. Antigonus[27] Gonatas, 35 years.
36. Demetrius,[28] 10 years.
37. Another Antigonus,[29] 15 years.
38. Another Philip[30], 45 years.
39. Perseus, 10 years.

These reigns of the Macedonians, which began in the 33rd year of Uzziah, king of Judah, lasted for 647 years and came to an end in the 153rd Olympiad.

T83 *From Adam to Seleucus I*[31]

Starting with the first year of his [sc. Seleucus' I] reign, in which he founded Antioch, the reckoning of the years of the Greeks begins, of which we also make use. From Adam to Seleucus, Eusebius counts 4889 years;[32] Andronicus 5072 years; Annianus 5181 years; Africanus 5083 years;[33] George 5085 years; some among the Greeks 5197 years; Jacob [of Edessa] 5149 years. The Syrians are accustomed to accept 5180 years.

---

27 Antigonus II.
28 Demetrius II.
29 Antigonus III.
30 Philip V. Frick emends his years from 45 to 42 (following Eusebius), in order to arrive at the correct sum, as given below. Along with his other emendations (ll. 26 and 33), the sum of the individual reigns would come to 646 years and 8 months (489 years + 157 years, 8 months).
31 Africanus probably had some information on the Seleucid era. Almost nothing else of his treatment of Seleucid chronology survives, see F84, n. 2.
32 The calculation of Michael is based on the following dates in Eusebius: 2242 years from Adam to the Flood, 942 from the Flood to the birth of Abraham (Hier., can. 15,2–5); 1705 years from the birth of Abraham to 1 Seleucus (Hier., can. 126,21). Therefore, from Adam to 1 Seleucus in Eusebius there are 2242 + 942 + 1705 = 4889 years. This calculation confirms that Michael's information is accurate.
33 In the case of Africanus the number is corrupt. Because of the lack of clear information in the preserved fragments, it is difficult to suggest a correct number; it must have been at least 100 years more than the figure in the text (according to F65,213f Alexander's death occurred in Ol. 114, i.e. in AM 5179–82).

F84 Georgius Syncellus (334,1-15 Mosshammer)

<Ἰουδαίων ιδ' ἀρχιεράτευσεν Ὀνείας υἱὸς Σίμωνος ἔτη ζ'.> τοῦ δὲ κόσμου ἦν ἔτος ͵ετη'.

Κατὰ Ἀφρικανὸν ἀπὸ τῶν Ἀλεξάνδρου τοῦ κτιστοῦ χρόνων ὑποδύντες Ἰουδαῖοι τῇ Μακεδόνων ἀρχῇ ποτὲ μὲν Πτολεμαίοις, ποτὲ δὲ τοῖς Ἀντιόχοις ἐτέλουν ὑπόφοροι, ἕως Ὀνείου τοῦ ἀρχιερέως ἀντὶ βασιλέων ὑπὸ τῶν ἀρχιερέ-
5 ων διεπόμενοι τὰ πολλὰ μετ' εἰρήνης. ἐπὶ δὲ τοῦ ιδ' Ὀνείου τοῦδε Σίμων τις προστάτης τοῦ ἐν Ἱεροσολύμοις ναοῦ προσφεύγει Ἀπολλωνίῳ στρατηγῷ Φοινίκης, τὴν ἀρχιερωσύνην ἑαυτῷ περιποιούμενος καὶ τὰ τοῦ ἱεροῦ χρήματα προδίδειν ὑπισχνούμενος· ἅτινα μαθὼν ὁ Σέλευκος διὰ τοῦ Ἀπολλωνίου πέμπει Ἡλιόδωρον τὸν ἐπὶ τῶν πραγμάτων, ὃς θείαις μάστιξι παιδευθεὶς κενὸς ἐπανῆλθεν· Ὀνείας δὲ ὁ ἀρχιερεὺς διαπράττεται φυγαδευθῆναι τὸν Σίμωνα. καὶ ἐν τούτοις θνήσκει
10 Σέλευκος ὁ καὶ Φιλοπάτωρ βασιλεύσας ἔτη ιβ', μεθ' ὃν Ἀντίοχος ὁ Ἐπιφανὴς ἀδελφὸς τοῦ αὐτοῦ Σελεύκου, υἱὸς δὲ Ἀντιόχου τοῦ μεγάλου, ὃς καὶ ἦν ὁμηρεύων ἐν Ῥώμῃ. βασιλεύει δὲ Συρίας ἔτη ια'.

2-4 → F72

1 cf. Chron. Pasch. 357,16s; 390,20s; Chron. Synt. 95,28   5-9 cf. II Mac 3,4-7.22-28; 4,4-6; Eus., can.^Hier 137^e (hinc Chron. Pasch. 336,2)   9-11 cf. I Mac 1,10; II Mac 4,7

[AB] 1 suppl. Moss.   2 κατὰ ἀφρικανόν in textu B marg. A   4 et infra ὀνείου et ὀνείας B ὀνίου et ὀνίας A   4s τοῦ…Ὀνείου < B   6 ἀρχιερωσύνην A ἀρχιεροσύνην B

F85 Eusebius, Chronica (Excerpta Eusebiana [cod. Paris. gr. 2600, f. 213^r = 159,10s Cramer = 130,11-13 Schoene] = armeniace [61,11s Karst] ≈ Hieronymus [145,25s Helm])

Μετὰ δὲ Σίμωνα Ἰουδαίων ἡγεῖται, καθὼς Ἀφρικανὸς καὶ Ἰώσηππος ἱστορεῖ, Ἰωνάθης ὁ καὶ Ὑρκανὸς ἔτη κς'.

1s cf. Ios., ant. Iud. 12,249-299 (31 anni); Eus., can.^armen 204 (19 anni); Eus., dem. ev. 8,2,73 (29 anni)

1 καθὼς Scal. καθω P | Ἰωνάθης armen. Ἰωανάθης P

T85a Georgius Syncellus (348,29 - 349,4 Mosshammer)

Ἰωάννης υἱὸς Σίμωνος σφόδρα διαπρέπων, ἡγησάμενος τοῦ ἔθνους Ἰουδαίων ἐν ἱερωσύνῃ, καὶ πολέμοις καὶ πλούτῳ, τρισμυρίων ταλάντων ἐκ τῶν πατρῴων Δαβὶδ καὶ Σολομῶνος τάφων ἀνελόμενος, ἄλλοις τε πολλοῖς κατορθώμασι καὶ τροπαίοις κατὰ τῶν πλησιοχώρων καὶ Σαμαρείας εὐδοκιμήσας, ἐν τῷ θορύβῳ τῶν β' βασιλέων Ἀντιόχων πρὸς ἀλλήλους τοῦ Γρυποῦ καὶ τοῦ Κυζι-
5 κηνοῦ ἀναιρεθεὶς τελευτᾷ ἀρχιερατεύσας ἔτη λ', **κατὰ δὲ Ἀφρικανὸν κζ'.**

5 cf. Chron. Pasch. 346,9; 358,1; 391,7 (27 anni)

[AB] 2 τάφων B τάφον A

F84 *The Jews under Greek Domination*

<The 14th high priest of the Jews was Simon's son Onias, for 7 years.> AM 5308.

According to Africanus,[1] beginning from the time of Alexander, the Founder, the Jews, having submitted to Macedonian rule, at one time paid taxes to the Ptolemies and then to the Antiochids; up to the high priest Oneias, they were peacefully guided for the most part by high priests instead of kings. But at the time of the 14th high priest, the aforementioned Onias, a certain Simon, captain of the Temple in Jerusalem, fled to Apollonius, the governor of Phoenicia, claiming the high priesthood for himself and promising to hand over the Temple treasury. Upon learning of this through Apollonius, Seleucus sent Heliodorus, who was in charge of administrative affairs; but after having been disciplined by the scourges of God, he returned empty-handed. And Onias, the high priest, arranged to have Simon banished. During this time, Seleucus, also known as Philopator, died after a reign of 12 years. His successor was Antiochus Epiphanes. He was brother of this Seleucus, and son of Antiochus the Great, and was serving as a hostage in Rome. He reigned over Syria for 11 years.[2]

F85 *Jonathan, Simon's son, the High Priest*

After Simon, Jonathan, also known as Hyrcanus, ruled the Hebrews for 26 years, according to Africanus and Josephus.

T85a[3]

Simon's son John was truly extraordinary, leading the Jewish nation in the office of priest. Through wars and riches (having removed 30,000 talents from the tombs of his forefathers David and Solomon), he gained honor for his many other achievements, but especially for his trophies of war against the neighboring peoples and Samaria. A casualty of the internecine turmoil caused by the two Antiochid kings, Grypus and Cyzicenus, he died after holding the high-priesthood for 30 years. According to Africanus, it was 27 years.

---

1   The material from Africanus may extend beyond the single sentence designated in large print.
2   According to Gelzer 1,275, ll. 9–11 are the only surviving parts of Africanus' list of the Seleucid kings.
3   Gelzer 1,256 attributes the whole text to Africanus.

F86 Ioannes Malalas 8,6–8 (148,83 – 149,14 Thurn)

Τῆς δὲ Αἰγύπτου πάσης καὶ τῆς Λιβύης ἣν διαταξάμενος ὁ αὐτὸς Ἀλέξανδρος κρατεῖν καὶ βασιλεύειν Πτολεμαῖον τὸν Λάγου τὸν ἀστρονόμον· ὃς ἐβασίλευσεν Αἰγυπτίων ἐν τῷ τῶν Μακεδόνων κράτει ἔτη μβ'.

Δεύτερος δὲ βασιλεὺς Πτολεμαῖος ὁ υἱὸς αὐτοῦ.
5 Ἐπὶ δὲ τῆς αὐτοῦ βασιλείας τοῦ αὐτοῦ Πτολεμαίου τοῦ υἱοῦ Λάγου ἡρμηνεύθησαν αἱ βίβλοι τῶν Ἰουδαίων Ἑλληνιστὶ παρὰ τῶν οβ' διδασκάλων διὰ ἡμερῶν οβ'. ἦσαν γὰρ γεγραμμέναι Ἑβραϊστί· οἷα τοῦ αὐτοῦ Πτολεμαίου βουληθέντος ἀναγνῶναι δι' Ἑλληνικῆς φράσεως τὴν δύναμιν τῶν Ἰουδαϊκῶν βίβλων.
Μετὰ δὲ τὴν βασιλείαν αὐτοῦ ἐβασίλευσε τρίτος Πτολεμαῖος ὁ Φιλάδελφος ἔτη λζ'.
10 Καὶ μετ' αὐτὸν ἐβασίλευσε τέταρτος Πτολεμαῖος ὁ Εὐεργέτης ἔτη κε',
καὶ μετ' αὐτὸν ἐβασίλευσε ε' Πτολεμαῖος ὁ Φιλοπάτωρ ἔτη ιζ',
καὶ μετ' αὐτὸν ἐβασίλευσεν ϛ' Πτολεμαῖος ὁ Ἐπιφανὴς ἔτη κε',
καὶ μετ' αὐτὸν ἐβασίλευσε ζ' Πτολεμαῖος ὁ Φιλομήτωρ ἔτη ια',
καὶ ἕτεροι Πτολεμαῖοι βασιλεῖς πέντε ἐβασίλευσαν ἔτη ϙβ',
15 Δωδέκατος δὲ Πτολεμαῖος ἐβασίλευσεν ὀνόματι Διόνυσος ἔτη κθ'. ὃς ἔσχεν θυγατέρα ὀνόματι Κλεοπάτραν καὶ υἱὸν ὀνόματι Πτολεμαῖον.
Καὶ λοιπὸν τρισκαιδέκατος πειράζεται Διόνυσος.
Ἐγένετο δὲ βασίλισσα Κλεοπάτρα· ἐβασίλευσε δὲ ἡ αὐτὴ Κλεοπάτρα ἡ θυγάτηρ τοῦ αὐτοῦ Διονύσου ἔτη κβ'.

1–3 → F65,213s; F84,2s 13 → T86a,3

1–22 cf. Hipp., chron. 742–756; Eus., chron. 75,19 – 80,6 (= Porphyrius FGrHist 260 F2); Exc. Eus. 120,3 – 125,29; Eus., reg. ser.^armen 152s; Eus., reg. ser.^Hier 29; Exc. Barb. 276–280; Sync. 321,23–31; 327,7 – 329,10; 341,11 – 342,33; 349,10 – 350,6; Sym. Log. (Leo Gr. 49,21 – 52,17; 54,20 – 55,13 = Th. Mel. 42,9 – 45,30); Iul. Pol. 148,9 – 156,27; Chron. Synt. 100; Cedr. 284,14; 289,17–23; 290,12 – 292,7; 291,1–3

[OSl] 3 μβ' O μ' Gelzer   12 ἔτη κε' Thurn ex Sl < O   14 ϙβ' O ρϙ' Sl   15 Διόνυσος Di. Διονύσιος OSl (cf. Cedr. 284,22)   17s τρισκαιδέκατος ... ἐγένετο δὲ Sl (cf. Cedr. 292,2s) τρισκαιδεκάτη βασίλισσα τῶν Πτολεμαίων O   19 Διονύσου Di. Διονυσίου OSl | κβ' O κθ' Sl

F86 *The Ptolemies*[1]

This Alexander appointed Ptolemy son of Lagus, the astronomer, to take possession of all of Egypt and Libya and reign over it. **He was king of the Egyptians** in the dominion of the Macedonians **for 42 years.**

> The second king was his son Ptolemy.[2]
>> During the reign of this Ptolemy son of Lagus, the Scriptures of the Jews were translated into Greek by the 72 teachers over the course of 72 days. For they had been composed in Hebrew and this Ptolemy wanted to read the meaning of the Jewish Scriptures expressed in Greek.
>
> After his reign, the third to be king was **Ptolemy Philadelphus, for 37 years.**
> And after him, the fourth to be king was **Ptolemy Euergetes, for 25 years.**
> And after him, the fifth to be king was **Ptolemy Philopator, for 17 years.**
> And after him, the sixth to be king was **Ptolemy Epiphanes, for 25 years.**[3]
> And after him, the seventh to be king was **Ptolemy Philometor, for 11 years.**[4]
> And five other Ptolemaic kings reigned **for 92 years.**[5]
> The twelfth to be king was **Ptolemy named Dionysus, for 29 years.** He had a daughter named Cleopatra and a son named Ptolemy.
> And then the thirteenth to be put to the test was **Dionysus.**[6]
> Cleopatra became queen. This **Cleopatra, the daughter of Dionysus, was queen for 22 years.**

---

1 Portions of Malalas' account of the Ptolemaic dynasty are unique to the Africanus tradition, including his 300-year chronology of the Ptolemies (see l. 22). While the rules of individual kings are also dependent on Africanus (see n. 4), Malalas' enumeration is confused and contradictory in places (see nn. 2 and 5–7). For reconstruction of Africanus' chronology of the Ptolemaic dynasty, see Gelzer 1,272–274. Contra Frick 1880,13f, the list of Ptolemaic kings found in the Exc. Barb. draws upon Eusebius, not Africanus, see Gelzer 1,274, n. 2.
2 That is, Ptolemy II Philadelphus. But cf. l. 9, where Malalas also identifies Ptolemy III as Philadelphus. Because of confusion in Malalas' enumeration of the Ptolemies, the numbering of the reigns beginning with Ptolemy III is given in small print.
3 The 25 years of the reign of Ptolemy Epiphanes, lacking in the Greek text, have been supplied from the Slavonic version of Malalas.
4 For Africanus' attribution of 11 years to the reign of Ptolemy Philometor see T86a,3.
5 With the addition of these five unnamed kings, the succeeding king should be number 13, not 12.
6 The sense of this sentence (πειράζεται) is unclear. It is missing in codex Baroccianus (O).

20 Ἐβασίλευσαν οὖν οἱ ιγ´ Πτολεμαῖοι οἱ Μακεδόνες τῆς Αἰγυπτιακῆς χώρας ἁπάσης ἀπὸ τοῦ Πτολεμαίου τοῦ Λάγου ἕως Κλεοπάτρας τῆς Διονύσου θυγατρὸς ἔτη τ´ ἕως τοῦ ιε´ ἔτους τῆς βασιλείας Αὐγούστου Καίσαρος τοῦ καὶ Ὀκταβιανοῦ Σεβαστοῦ ἰμπεράτορος τοῦ νικήσαντος τὸν Ἀντώνιον καὶ τὴν αὐτὴν Κλεοπάτραν ἐν τῇ Ἠπείρῳ χώρᾳ ναυμαχίᾳ εἰς τὸν Λευκάτην τόπον καὶ φονεύσαντος αὐτοὺς καὶ ὑποτάξαντος τὴν Αἴγυπτον
25 πᾶσαν, καθὼς Εὐσέβιος ὁ Παμφίλου καὶ Παυσανίας οἱ χρονογράφοι συνεγράψαντο.

20 → F46,245 (15 reges); Cedr. (284,19–22 Bekker) *Διαιροῦνται δὲ τὴν βασιλείαν οἱ μεγιστᾶνες αὐτοῦ, καὶ βασιλεύουσι Πτολεμαῖος μὲν ὁ Λάγου Αἰγύπτου καὶ καθεξῆς Πτολεμαῖοι ιγ´ ἕως Κλεοπάτρας θυγατρὸς Διονυσίου.* **22** → T6,16; F89,53–57 (ann. 14 Augusti); F93,52s; Sync. (314,16 Moss.) *Ἀπὸ ζ´ ἔτους Ἀλεξάνδρου ἕως κβ´ Κλεοπάτρας ἔτη τ´.* Sync. (375,4–6 Moss.) *Διαγεγόνασι δὲ ἀπὸ τῆς Ἀλεξάνδρου τοῦ Φιλίππου τελευτῆς, ἥτις γέγονε κατὰ τὸ ροζ´ ἔτος τῆς τῶν ὑπάτων ἀρχῆς, μέχρι τῆς Αὐγούστου καὶ Ἀντωνίου βασιλείας Ὀλυμπιάδες οε´, ἔτη δὲ σύνεγγυς τ´.* **23–25** → F89,39–52

25 Eus., can.[Hier] 163[f]; 163,17–19; Eus.,can.[armen] 210

20 ιγ´ O κ´ Sl sed legendum ιε´ (cf. F46,245)   **23** Ἠπείρῳ Sl ἐπὶ O   **25** καθὼς + σοφώτατος Sl

T86a Georgius Syncellus (349,10–18 Mosshammer)

Αἰγύπτου καὶ Ἀλεξανδρείας βασιλεῖς·
   Αἰγύπτου καὶ Ἀλεξανδρείας ς´ ἐβασίλευσε Πτολεμαῖος ὁ Φιλομήτωρ ἔτη λε´. τοῦ δὲ κόσμου ἦν ἔτος ˏετιδ´. Ἀφρικανὸς ἔτη ια´ μόνα λέγει τοῦ Φιλομήτορος. Πτολεμαῖος ὁ Φιλομήτωρ πρῶτον Ἀλεξάνδρῳ τὴν θυγατέρα Κλεοπάτραν δοὺς πρὸς γάμον, ἔπειτα διὰ τὴν Ἀμμωνίου τοῦ
5 στρατηγοῦ αὐτοῦ ἐπιβουλὴν συμμαχεῖ Δημητρίῳ κατ᾽ αὐτοῦ. καὶ ὁ μὲν κατὰ τὴν μάχην ἐκπεσὼν τοῦ ἵππου τιτρώσκεται, Ἀλεξάνδρου δὲ τὴν κεφαλὴν ἐκκοπεῖσαν ψυχορραγῶν δέχεται.

3 → F86,13

2 cf. Eus., chron. 76,2 (= Porphyrius FGrHist 260 F2)   **3** cf. Eus., chron. 75,18 (= Porphyrius FGrHist 260 F2)   **3–6** I Mac 10,58; 11,9–18; Ios., ant. Iud. 13,82.106–108.116–118

[AB] **1** titulus marg. A | αἰγύπτου A[m] αἰγυπτίων B   **2s** ἦν ἔτος < A   **3** λέγει τοῦ B ~ A   **4** ἀλεξάνδρῳ B ἀλέξανδρον A | ἀμμωνίου A ἀμωνίου B

Thus, the 13 Macedonian Ptolemies[7] reigned over all the land of Egypt from the time of Ptolemy son of Lagus up to Cleopatra, daughter of Dionysus, for 300 years, until the 15th year of the reign of Augustus Caesar, also known as Octavian Augustus Imperator. In a naval battle at Epirus in the place known as Leucates, he defeated Antony and this Cleopatra, slew them and subjugated all of Egypt, just as the chronographers Eusebius [disciple] of Pamphilus and Pausanias have recorded.[8]

T86a

Kings of Egypt and Alexandria
    The sixth to be king of Egypt and Alexandria was Ptolemy Philometor, for 35 years. This was AM 5314. Africanus states that the years of Philometor were only 11. Ptolemy Philometor initially gave his daughter Cleopatra to Alexander in marriage; but because of the plot of Ammonius his general, he then allied with Demetrius against him. He fell from his horse in battle and was wounded; but as he was breathing his last, he received the decapitated head of Alexander.

---

7   With the inclusion of "Ptolemy III Philadelphus" and "Ptolemy XII Dionysius", Malalas' actual list names 15, not 13, rulers from Ptolemy I to Cleopatra. Africanus' own chronology of the 300 years of Macedonian rule in Egypt also enumerated 15 rulers, but unlike Malalas included the six-year reign of Alexander, see F46,245, F89,53–55 and F93,53.
8   The story in this form is found neither in Eusebius nor in Africanus (their versions of the story are completely different, cf. Eus, can.^{Hier} 163^{f}; Africanus, F89,39–49). Since little is known about the historian Pausanias apart from Malalas' references to him (see Jeffreys 1990,188f), the source of Malalas' own embellishments of the tradition cannot be determined.

F87

F87a Eus.¹: Eusebius, Historia ecclesiastica 1,6,2s (48,12–19 Schwartz)
Eus.²: Eusebius, Eclogae propheticae 3, 26 (cod. Vind. theol. gr. 29, f. 41ʳ = 158,5–8 Gaisford)

F87b Georgius Syncellus (356,23 – 357,4 Mosshammer)

Ἐντεῦθεν δέος καὶ λύπη τοῖς Ὑρκανοῦ φίλοις ἐπιπίπτει παρ' ἐλπίδα κρατήσαντος Ἀριστοβούλου, καὶ μάλιστα Ἀντιπάτρῳ τινί, Ἡρώδου πατρὶ τοῦ βασιλεύσαντος ἔπειτα Ἰουδαίων, ὃς ἦν

5 Φασὶν οἱ τὰ κατ' αὐτὸν ἀκριβοῦντες Ἀντίπατρον (τοῦτον δ' εἶναι αὐτῷ πατέρα) Ἡρῴδου τινὸς Ἀσκαλωνίτου τῶν περὶ τὸν νεὼ τοῦ Ἀπόλλωνος

ἀλλόφυλος Ἰδουμαῖος κατὰ Ἰώσηππον, κατὰ δὲ 5
Ἀφρικανὸν Ἀσκαλωνίτης, υἱός τινος ἱεροδούλου καλουμένου Ἡρώδου τῶν περὶ τὸν νεὼν τοῦ Ἀπόλλωνος τεταγ-

test.: **1** inc. Sync.[AB]   **5** inc. Eus.¹Eus.²[ATERBDMΣΛ]: Ἀτελῆ γέ τοι τὰ τῆς προρρήσεως ἦν καθ' ὃν ὑπὸ τοῖς οἰκείοις τοῦ ἔθνους ἄρχουσι διάγειν αὐτοῖς ἐξῆν χρόνον, ἄνωθεν ἐξ αὐτοῦ Μωυσέως καταρξαμένοις καὶ εἰς τὴν Αὐγούστου βασιλείαν διαρκέσασιν, καθ' ὃν πρῶτος ἀλλόφυλος Ἡρώδης τὴν κατὰ Ἰουδαίων ἐπιτρέπεται ὑπὸ Ῥωμαίων ἀρχήν, ὡς μὲν Ἰώσηπος παραδίδωσιν, Ἰδουμαῖος ὢν κατὰ πατέρα τὸ γένος Ἀράβιος δὲ κατὰ μητέρα, ὡς δ' Ἀφρικανός (οὐχ ὁ τυχὼν δὲ καὶ οὗτος γέγονε συγγραφεύς) et Eus.²: ὡς δ' ὁ Ἀφρικανός, οὐ μικρῷ πρόσθεν ἐμνήσθημεν

5-12 Iul. Afr., ep. Arist. (60,15 – 61,1 Reichardt = Eus., h.e. 1,7,11[1,58,15–22 Schwartz]) Τοῦ γοῦν σωτῆρος οἱ κατὰ σάρκα συγγενεῖς, εἴτ' οὖν φανητιῶντες, εἴθ' ἁπλῶς ἐκδιδάσκοντες, πάντως δὲ ἀληθεύοντες, παρέδοσαν καὶ ταῦτα, ὡς Ἰδουμαῖοι λῃσταί, Ἀσκάλωνι πόλει τῆς Παλαιστίνης ἐπελθόντες, ἐξ εἰδωλείου Ἀπόλλωνος, ὃ πρὸς τοῖς τείχεσιν ἵδρυτο, Ἀντίπατρον Ἡρώδου τινὸς ἱεροδούλου παῖδα πρὸς τοῖς ἄλλοις σύλοις αἰχμάλωτον ἀπῆγον· τῷ δὲ λύτρα ὑπὲρ τοῦ υἱοῦ καταθέσθαι μὴ δύνασθαι τὸν ἱερέα ὁ Ἀντίπατρος τοῖς τῶν Ἰδουμαίων ἔθεσιν ἐντραφεὶς ὕστερον Ὑρκανῷ φιλοῦται τῷ τῆς Ἰουδαίας ἀρχιερεῖ. ps. Ath. fr. (PG 26,1253A) Ὁ δὲ Ἀφρικανὸς καὶ οἱ κατ' αὐτὸν ἀκριβοῦντες Ἀντιπάτρου μὲν εἶναι υἱόν· τὸν δὲ Ἀντίπατρον ἐσχηκέναι πατέρα Ἡρώδην Ἀσκαλωνίτην, ἱερόδουλον τοῦ νεὼ τοῦ Ἀπόλλωνος. τὸν δὲ Ἀντίπατρον τὸν υἱὸν αὐτοῦ, παιδίον ὄντα, αἰχμαλωτισθῆναι παρὰ τῶν λῃστῶν Ἰδουμαίων· τὸν δὲ πατέρα αὐτοῦ Ἡρώδην μὴ δυνηθῆναι δοῦναι λύτρα ὑπὲρ αὐτοῦ· ἐντραφεὶς οὖν τοῖς τῶν Ἰδουμαίων ἔθεσιν, Ἰδουμαῖος ἐνομίσθη εἶναι, ὧν Ἀσκαλωνίτης.   **7-9** Eus., dem. ev. 8,1,44 (360,4–8 Heikel) Ἦν γοῦν ὁ Ἡρώδης Ἀντιπάτρου παῖς, ὁ δ' Ἀντίπατρος Ἀσκαλωνίτης, ἔκ τινος τῶν περὶ τὸν νεὼν τοῦ Ἀπόλλωνος ἱεροδούλων καλουμένων, ὃς δὴ Κυπρίνην ὀνόματι, τὸ γένος τῶν ἐξ Ἀραβίας, γυναῖκα πρὸς γάμον ἀγαγόμενος τὸν Ἡρώδην ποιεῖται.

1-6 cf. Ios., bell. Iud. 1,123   **6-9** cf. Iust., dial. 52,3,1–12; Eus., chron. 61,25–27; Eus., can.^Hier 153ᶠ; Sulp. Sev., chron. 2,27,1; Chron. Pasch. 358,13–15; 362,2–4; Anon. Matr. 46,4–6; Exc. Barb. 324,11–13   **6-16** cf. Epiph., haer. 1,224,17 – 225,13 (ordo narrationis valde similis); Exp. off. 1,8; Sym. Log. (Leo Gr. 52,23 – 53,6 = Th. Mel. 44,14–19 ≈ Iul. Pol. 152,11–18) = ps. Sym. f. 74ʳ,39 – 74ᵛ,5 = Cedr. 293,11–18

5 a: Φασὶν] ὡς φασὶν Eus¹:ATEΣ   **6 a:** Ἀντίπατρον] ἀντιπάτρου Eus¹:A | αὐτῷ Eus¹:BDMΣ Eus² αὐτὸν Eus¹:TER   **7-9 b:** τῶν...τεταγμένων Goarᵐ τῷ...τεταγμένῳ AB   **8 a+b:** νεὼ Eus¹ Sync.:B νεὼν Eus² Sync.:A Gelzerᵐˢ

F87 The Father of Herod[1]

F87a

F87b

Those with an accurate knowledge concerning him say that Antipater (he was his father) was son of a certain Herod an Ashkelonite, one of those who are known as temple-servants in the temple of Apollo; captured as a child

Thus as a result of Aristobulus' unexpected victory, fear and grief descended upon the allies of Hyrcanus, especially a certain Antipater, the father of the Herod who subsequently became king of the Jews. Antipater was a foreigner, an Idumean according to Josephus. But according to Africanus, he was an Ashkelonite, the son of Herod, known as one of the temple slaves appointed in Ashkelon in the temple of Apollo. Idumean bandits

---

1   For discussion of this fragment, see Gelzer 1,258-60. Elsewhere, the excerpts from Africanus' chronicle preserved independently in both Syncellus and Eusebius represent fairly faithful witnesses to the text of his chronicle, see F34 and F93. Pronounced differences between the two versions found here, however, suggest that neither author is quoting verbatim from Africanus. A parallel account of Herod's background reported in Epiph., haer. 1,224,17–225,13 may also have drawn either upon Africanus or his source; on the influence of Africanus' chronicle on Epiphanius, see Adler 1990.

ἱεροδούλων καλουμένων γεγονέναι· ὃς Ἀντίπατρος ὑπὸ Ἰδουμαίων λῃστῶν παιδίον αἰχμαλωτισθεὶς σὺν ἐκείνοις ἦν, διὰ τὸ μὴ δύνασθαι τὸν πατέρα πτωχὸν ὄντα καταθέσθαι ὑπὲρ αὐτοῦ, ἐντραφεὶς δὲ τοῖς ἐκείνων ἔθεσιν ὕστερον Ὑρκανῷ τῷ Ἰουδαίων ἀρχιερεῖ φιλοῦται.

μένων ἐν Ἀσκαλῶνι. τοῦτον Ἰδουμαῖοι λῃσταὶ τὸν Ἀντίπατρον εἶχον αἰχμαλωτίσαντες ἐν αὐτοῖς λῃστεύοντα, λαβεῖν ἐλπίζοντες ἐκ τοῦ πατρὸς αὐτοῦ Ἡρώδου λύτρα. διὰ δὲ τὸ πτωχὸν εἶναι τὸν αὐτοῦ πατέρα καὶ λύτρα δοῦναι ἀπορεῖν ἐχρόνισε συλληστεύων καὶ τοῖς αὐτῶν ἐντρεφόμενος ἤθεσιν. οὗτος ὕστερον Ὑρκανῷ φιλωθεὶς πλούτῳ καὶ δόξῃ τῶν πολλῶν προεῖχεν ἐντρεχείας χάριν καὶ τῆς περὶ τὰ κοινὰ πράγματα δεινότητος· ὃς ἀναπείθει τὸν Ὑρκανὸν Ἀρέτᾳ τῷ τῶν Ἀράβων προσφυγόντα βασιλεῖ τὴν Ἰουδαίων ἀρχὴν ἀνακτήσασθαι.

test.: Eus.[1] Eus.[2] Sync. 9 γεγονέναι· des. Eus.[2] 16 φιλοῦται des. Eus.[1]: τούτου γίνεται ὁ ἐπὶ τοῦ σωτῆρος ἡμῶν Ἡρῴδης. post Ἡρῴδης addidit Rufinus: haec Africanus 22 ἀνακτήσασθαι des. Sync.

9 a: καλουμένων < Eus[2] 11 b: αἰχμαλωτίσαντες Α αἰχμαλωτήσαντες Β 13 a: πτωχὸν Eus[1]:TERBDM πένητα Eus[1]:A 14 a: ἔθεσιν Eus[1]:A (cf. Iul. Afr., ep. Arist., supra in app.) ἤθεσιν Eus[1]:TERBDM 15 a: τῷ Eus[1]:TERM τῶ τῶν Eus[1]:A τῶν Eus[1]:BD | Ἰουδαίων] ἰδουμαίων Eus[1]:M b: ἐχρόνισε Α ἐχρόνησε Β

T88 Moses Chorenensis, Historia Armeniorum 2,10 (120,3–16 Abelean/Yarut'iwnean)

Սկիզբն արասցուք պատմել քեզ 'ի Հնդերորդ գրոցն Ափրիկանոսի ժամանակագրի, որում վկայէ Յովսեպոս և Հիպողիտայ և այլ բազումք 'ի Յունաց: Քանզի նա բովանդակ փոխադրեաց որ ինչ 'ի քարտէս դիւանին Եդեսիայ, որ է Ուռհայ, որ յաղագս թագաւորացն մերոց պատմէր. որ
5 մատեանքն 'ի Մծբնայ էին փոխեալ ամէր և 'ի Սինոպայ Պոնտոս 'ի մեծէնականն պատմութեանն: Մի ոք անհաւատասցի, քանզի և մեզէն իսկ ականատես եղաք այսմ դիւանի: Եւ վկայ քեզ 'ի մտոյ երաշխաւորեսցէ Եկղեսիաստէ գիրք Եւսերի կեսարացւոյ, զոր եւս թարգմանել երանելի վարդապետն մեր Մաշտոցի 'ի Հայ լեզու: Խնդիր արասցես 'ի Դեղարդունի 'ի գաւառն Անձևաց, և զգոյս յայտնի Հաղբերդգութեանն
10 յերկրպաստաններդ թուին, զի վկայ Յեդեսիայ դիւանին վկել ամէնայն գործոց սուշտող թագաւորացն մերոց մինչև ցԱրդար, և զնի Արգարու մինչև զԵրուանդ: Որ և այժմ կարդեմ գտանի պահեալ 'ի նոյն քաղաքի:

3–6 cf. Mos. Choren. 2,38 9s cf. Eus., h.e. 1,13

by Idumean bandits, Antipater stayed with them because his father being poor, was unable to pay the ramsom for him. Raised in their customs, he was later befriended by Hyrcanus, the high priest of the Jews.	captured this Antipater and were keeping him as a bandit among them, hoping to receive a ransom from his father Herod. But because his father was poor and unable to pay ransom, he grew up as one of their accomplices, and was brought up in their customs. Later befriended by Hyrcanus, he assumed a role of leadership over the populace by means of his wealth and honor, and by virtue of his aptitude and acuity in public affairs. He persuaded Hyrcanus to flee to Aretas, king of the Arabs, and recover the kingdom of the Jews.

T88 *Africanus and the Archive of Edessa*[1]

We shall begin our narrative for you from the fifth book of Africanus, the chronographer, to which Josephus and Hippolytus and many other Greeks lend [corroborative] witness. For he transcribed everything from the charters of the archive of Edessa,[2] that is, Urha, which concerned the history of our kings. These books had been transported there from Nisibis and from the temple histories of Sinope in Pontus. Let no one doubt this, for we have seen that archive with our own eyes. And as a closer witness the *Ecclesiastical [History]* of Eusebius of Caesarea is a guarantee, which our blessed teacher Mashtots' had had translated into Armenian. If you search in Gełark'uni in the province of Siunik' you will find in book one, chapter 13, that he bears witness that in the Edessene archive are to be found all the acts of our first kings down to Abgar and from Abgar down to Eruand. I think that these are preserved today in the same city.

---

1   The translation is taken from Thomson 1978,145f. For Africanus' well-documented connection with the Edessene court see his *Cesti* 1,20, which describes his experiences in the court of Abgar VIII (176–213), also F29 (on the preservation of Jacob's tent in Edessa). On the basis of this text it has been claimed that much of the following material in Moses comes from Africanus (Topchyan 2001). However, this cannot be proved and the hypothesis has been rightly criticized (Terian 2001/02). The material of Moses should be considered only where Greek parallels are available (e. g. F89), see also Topchyan 2006 and Wallraff 2006,49f.
2   On the archive of Edessa, see Inglebert 2001,185–187.

F89 Georgius Syncellus (371,1 – 373,10 Mosshammer)

Ἀφρικανοῦ περὶ τῶν Ὑρκανῷ καὶ Ἀντιγόνῳ συμβάντων καὶ περὶ Ἡρώδου τοῦ τε Σεβαστοῦ καὶ Ἀντωνίου καὶ Κλεοπάτρας ἐν ἐπιτόμῳ·

Ὀκταούιος ὁ Σεβαστός, ὃν Αὔγουστον καλοῦσι Ῥωμαῖοι, θετὸς ὢν υἱὸς αὐτοῦ (sc. Caesar), ἀπὸ Ἀπολλωνιάδος τῆς Ἠπείρου, ἔνθα ἐπαιδεύετο, εἰς Ῥώ-
5 μην ἐπανελθὼν τῶν ἐν τέλει τῆς ἡγεμονίας εἴχετο. Ἀντώνιος δὲ ὕστερον τὴν τῆς Ἀσίας καὶ ἐπέκεινα ἀρχὴν ἔλαχεν. ἐπὶ τούτου Ἡρώδου κατηγόρουν Ἰουδαῖοι. ὁ δὲ τοὺς πρέσβεις ἀποκτείνας Ἡρώδην ἐπὶ τὴν αὐτοῦ κατῆξεν ἀρχήν. ὕστερον δὲ ἅμα Ὑρκανῷ καὶ Φασαΐλῳ τῷ ἀδελφῷ ἐξεώθη καὶ προσφυγὼν Ἀντωνίῳ κατῆλθε. μὴ δεχομένων δὲ αὐτὸν Ἰουδαίων μάχη γίνεται καρτερά. μετ᾽
10 οὐ πολὺ δὲ καὶ Ἀντίγονον κατιόντα ἐκδιώκει μάχῃ, Ἀντίγονος δὲ προσφυγὼν Ὀρώδῃ τῷ τῶν Πάρθων βασιλεῖ διὰ Πακόρου τοῦ υἱοῦ κατῆλθεν ἐπὶ χρυσοῦ ταλάντοις χιλίοις. καὶ ὁ μὲν Ἡρώδης φεύγει, Φασάιλος δὲ ἐν τῇ μάχῃ ἀναιρεῖται, Ὑρκανὸς δὲ Ἀντιγόνῳ παρεδόθη ζῶν· ὁ δὲ Πάρθοις αὐτὸν ἔδωκεν ἄγειν, ἀποτεμὼν αὐτοῦ τὰ ὦτα, ὡς μηκέτι ἱερῷτο· ᾐδέσθη γὰρ αὐτὸν ὡς οἰκεῖον
15 ἀποκτεῖναι. Ἡρώδης δὲ ἐκπεσὼν τὸ μὲν πρῶτον Μαλίχῳ τῷ τῶν Ἀράβων βασιλεῖ προσφεύγει· ὡς δ᾽ οὐ προσήκατο αὐτὸν φόβῳ τῶν Πάρθων, εἰς Ἀλεξάνδρειαν παρὰ Κλεοπάτραν ἀπῆλθεν.

7–16 Sync. (367,23 – 368,5 Moss.) *Διωχθεὶς δὲ πάλιν τῆς ἀρχῆς σὺν τῷ Ὑρκανῷ προσφεύγει Ἀντωνίῳ, καὶ μὴ δεχθεὶς παρὰ τῶν Ἰουδαίων καρτερῶς μάχεται, αὐτὸν δὲ ἐκδιώκει Ἀντίγονον. ὁ δὲ Ἀντίγονος ἀπογνοὺς τῆς Ῥωμαίων βοηθείας Ἡρώδῃ προσφεύγει Περσῶν βασιλεῖ μαχομένῳ Ῥωμαίοις, καὶ κατάγεται διὰ Πακόρου παιδὸς Ἡρώδου εἰς τὴν Ἰουδαίαν, ὑποσχόμενος χρυσοῦ χίλια τάλαντα Πέρσαις. Ὑρκανόν τε ζῶντα παραλαμβάνει· τοῖς ὀδοῦσιν ἐκκόψας αὐτοῦ τὰ ὦτα, ὡς μηκέτι ἱερατεύειν· καὶ τοῦτον προὔδωκεν αὖθις Πέρσαις ἄγειν μεθ᾽ ἑαυτῶν. Ἡρώδης δὲ φυγὰς ἧκε πρὸς Μάλιχον Ἀράβων βασιλέα.* **13–17** Sync. (369,14–23 Moss.) *Τῷ γὰρ λα΄ ἔτει Ὑρκανοῦ καταχθεὶς ὑπὸ Πάρθων εἰς τὴν ἀρχὴν τῶν Ἰουδαίων, κρατεῖ μὲν αὐτῆς ζῶντα τὸν Ὑρκανὸν χειρωσάμενος καὶ τοῖς ὀδοῦσιν ἀποτεμὼν αὐτοῦ τὰ ὦτα, ὡς ἂν μὴ τὸ λοιπὸν ἱερατεύοι, καὶ Πάρθοις ἐκδίδωσιν ἄγειν εἰς τὴν Περσικήν. ἀναιρεῖ δὲ Φασάιλον ἀδελφὸν Ἡρώδου καὶ φυγαδεύει τοῦτο, πολλὰ καταδραμόντων αὐτοῦ Πάρθων ἐπὶ τὴν Ἰουδαίαν μετὰ μητρὸς καὶ τῆς συγγενείας. φεύγοντος Ἡρώδου καὶ τούτους πολλάκις πολέμῳ τρεπομένου, καὶ κατασφαττόμενος, ὃς πολλάκις πρὸς Μάλιχον Ἀράβων βασιλέα θαρρῶν καταφεύγει, ἤδη προευεργετημένον, οὐ προσδεχθεὶς δὲ φόβῳ τῶν Πάρθων εἰς Ἀλεξάνδρειαν ἔρχεται πρὸς Κλεοπάτραν.*

3–57 cf. Sym. Log. (Leo Gr. 54,20 – 55,13 = Th. Mel. 45,17–30); Iul. Pol. 155,15 – 157,27   **5–7** cf. Ios., bell. Iud. 1,242–247; Ios., ant. Iud. 14,302s.326s   **10–12** cf. Ios., bell. Iud. 1,248; Ios., ant. Iud. 14,331   **12–17** cf. Ios., bell. Iud. 1,269–278; Ios., ant. Iud. 14,366–370   **13s** cf. Leu 21,18

[ABt = x (= COTV) + z (= MPQRS)] **1** τε < B   **1s** ἀντωνίου ABVP^cQMRS ἀντωνίῳ COT et ante corr. P   **5** τῶν ἐν ABV τῷ COTz | τὴν < OTz   **8** ἐξεώθη Bt ἐξεώθει A   **9** αὐτὸν At αὐτῶν B   **11** Ὀρώδῃ scripsimus Ὑρώδῃ Gelzer^ms Ἡρώδῃ codd. | πακόρου CV πακόρου ABOT πακούρου z   **13** αὐτὸν < A   **14** ἱερῷτο ABx ἱερατεύει PRMS ἱερατεύοι Q

F89 *Herod and Cleopatra*

From Africanus, on Hyrcanus and Antigonus' fate, and on Herod, Augustus, Antony and Cleopatra, in summary form:[1]

As his (sc. Caesar's) adopted son, Octavius Sebastus, whom the Romans call Augustus, returned to Rome from Apollonias of Epirus, where he was being educated, and took over the principate from those in power. Subsequently Antony obtained as his portion rule of Asia and the regions beyond. During his rule, the Jews brought charges against Herod. But Antony killed their envoys and restored Herod to rule. Later he, as well as Hyrcanus and his brother Phasaël, were ousted and returned in flight to Antony for refuge. But since the Jews would not accept him, there arose a violent struggle. Not long thereafter he also banished Antigonus, who was on his way back, after defeating him in battle. Now Antigonus fled to the Parthian king Orodes[2] and returned to Judaea with the aid of Orodes' son Pacorus, which he got in exchange for 1000 talents of gold. So now Herod took flight, and Phasaël was killed in battle. Hyrcanus was delivered up alive to Antigonus, and after cutting off his ears to disqualify him from the priesthood, he gave him to the Parthians to take him with them. For insofar as he was a relative, Antigonus recoiled from executing him. Herod escaped and first sought refuge with Malichus, king of the Arabs. But when he would not receive him for fear of the Parthians, Herod departed for Cleopatra in Alexandria.

---

1 For the use of the word ἐπιτομή in connection with the *Chronographiae,* see also F100. While Syncellus' characterization of this excerpt as ἐν ἐπιτόμῳ may be intended as a general description of the abbreviated style of Africanus' chronicle, it more likely points to the editorial work of a later epitomator. The excerpt that follows is either an abridgement of a longer passage (see Gelzer 1,264) or a composite of material culled from various places in Africanus' chronicle. For further discussion, see introduction, p. XIX.

2 The spelling Ἡρώδης in Syncellus is corrupt for Ὀρώδης (see also Sync. 367,26 – 368,1). For this latter spelling see Cass. Dio 40,28,3; Iustin. 42,4,1–5.

Ἦν Ὀλυμπιὰς ρπε΄.

Κλεοπάτρα τὸν συμβασιλεύσαντα αὐτῇ ἀδελφὸν ἀποκτείνασα πρὸς ἀπολογίαν ὑπ᾽ Ἀντωνίου εἰς Κιλικίαν μεταπεμφθεῖσα τὴν τῆς ἀρχῆς ἐπιμέλειαν ἐπέτρεψεν Ἡρώδῃ, καὶ ὡς οὐδὲν ἠξίου πιστεύεσθαι ἔστ᾽ ἂν καταχθῇ εἰς τὴν ἑαυτοῦ ἀρχήν, ἔχουσα αὐτὸν ᾔει παρὰ Ἀντώνιον. ὡς δὲ ἁλώκει τῆς γυναικὸς ἔρωτι, τὸν Ἡρώδην ἀπέστειλεν εἰς Ῥώμην κατὰ τὸν Σεβαστὸν Ὀκταούιον, ὃς διά τε Ἀντίπατρον τὸν Ἡρώδου πατέρα καὶ δι᾽ αὐτὸν Ἡρώδην διά τε τὸ ὑπὸ Πάρθων καθεστάσθαι τὸν Ἀντίγονον βασιλέα ἐπέστειλε τοῖς ἐν Παλαιστίνῃ καὶ Συρίᾳ στρατηγοῖς κατάγειν αὐτὸν ἐπὶ τὴν ἀρχήν. καὶ ἅμα Σωσίῳ διεπολέμει πρὸς τὸν Ἀντίγονον χρόνῳ πολλῷ καὶ παντοίαις μάχαις. τότε καὶ Ἰώσηπος ἀδελφὸς Ἡρώδου ἀποθνήσκει στρατηγῶν. Ἡρώδου δὲ πρὸς Ἀντώνιον ἐλθόντος <...> τρία ἔτη τὸν Ἀντίγονον ἐξεπολιόρκησαν καὶ ζῶντα ἀπεκόμισαν Ἀντωνίῳ. Ἀντώνιος δὲ Ἡρώδην μὲν καὶ αὐτὸς ἀνηγόρευσε βασιλέα, προσέθηκε δὲ αὐτῷ πόλεις Ἵππον, Γάδαρα, Γάζαν, Ἰόππην, Ἀνθηδόνα καὶ τῆς Ἀραβίας τόν τε Τράχωνα καὶ τὴν Αὐρανῖτιν καὶ Σακίαν καὶ Γαυλάνην, πρὸς δὲ καὶ τῆς Συρίας ἐπιτροπήν.

Ἡρώδης ὑπὸ τῆς συγκλήτου καὶ Ὀκταουίου τοῦ Σεβαστοῦ βασιλεὺς Ἰουδαίων ἀνηγορεύθη καὶ ἐβασίλευσεν ἔτη λδ΄.

Ἀντώνιος ἐπὶ Πάρθους στρατεύειν μέλλων Ἀντίγονον τὸν Ἰουδαίων ἀπέκτεινε βασιλέα καὶ Ἀραβίαν Κλεοπάτρᾳ παρέδωκε, διαβάς τε ἐπὶ Πάρθους ἔπταισε μεγάλως τὸ πλεῖστον ἀποβαλὼν τοῦ στρατοῦ.

18-22 Sync. (375,12-16 Moss.) *Τῆς οὖν ρπε΄ Ὀλυμπιάδος περιελθούσης Ἀντώνιος ἐκστρατεύει μὲν ἐπὶ Πέρσας, Ἡρώδου τοῦ Περσῶν βασιλέως φονευθέντος ὑπὸ Φραάρτου τοῦ μετ᾽ αὐτὸν βασιλεύσαντος, συναντήσας δὲ τῇ Κλεοπάτρᾳ πρὸς τῇ Κιλίκων Ταρσῷ καὶ τῷ κάλλει ταύτης ἁλοὺς οὐδὲν ἀξιόλογον πράττει κατὰ Περσῶν.* Sync. (369,6-9 Moss.) *Οὗτος ἐλθὼν ἐν Κιλικίᾳ καὶ Κλεοπάτραν μεταστειλάμενος ἁλίσκεται τῷ ταύτης ἔρωτι.* **20-29** Sync. (369,23 - 370,5 Moss.) *Δεξιωθεὶς οὖν παρ᾽ αὐτῆς καὶ τὴν ἐπιμέλειαν τῆς ὑπ᾽ αὐτὴν ἔχειν ἀρχῆς ἀνεβάλλετο διὰ τὴν πρὸς Ἀντώνιον ἐπὶ Ῥώμην καὶ Αὔγουστον πορείαν, ὡς Ἰώσηππος, ὡς δὲ Ἀφρικανός, σὺν αὐτῇ πρὸς Ἀντώνιον ἦλθε, κἀκεῖνος παρὰ τὸν Σεβαστὸν Ὀκταούιον εἰς Ῥώμην αὐτὸν ἔστειλεν. ὁ δὲ διὰ τὸ τὸν Ἀντίγονον ὑπὸ Πάρθων ἐχθρῶν ὄντων Ῥωμαίοις κρατῆσαι τῆς ἀρχῆς, διά τε τὸν αὐτοῦ πατέρα Ἀντίπατρον συμμαχήσαντα Ῥωμαίοις καὶ αὐτὸν Ἡρώδην, γράφει τοῖς κατὰ Συρίαν στρατηγοῖς κατάγειν Ἡρώδην ἐπὶ τὴν βασιλείαν Ἰουδαίων, Σωσίου τὸν πρὸς Ἀντίγονον πόλεμον ἐπιτραπέντος ὑπὸ τοῦ Καίσαρος, ὃς ἔτεσι τρισὶν ἐπεκράτησεν.* **23s** → F87 **33s** → T89a; Anon. Matr. (34,3s Bauer; cf. etiam 46,2) *Ἡρώδης ἀλλόφυλος ἔτη λδ΄, ὑπὸ Ῥωμαίων τὴν τῶν Ἰουδαίων βασιλείαν ἐγχειρίζεται.* **36** Sync. (365,12 Moss.) *Ἀντώνιος Ἀραβίαν Κλεοπάτρᾳ προὔδωκε.*

20-22 cf. Ios., bell. Iud. 1,279; Ios., ant. Iud. 14,376 **22-26** cf. Ios., bell. Iud. 1,282-284; Ios., ant. Iud. 14,379-389 **27s** cf. Ios., bell. Iud. 1,323s; Ios., ant. Iud. 14,448s **28s** cf. Ios., bell. Iud. 1,343; Ios., ant. Iud. 14,449s; Mos. Choren. 2,21 **29** cf. Ios., bell. Iud. 1,357; Ios., ant. Iud. 14,481 **33s** cf. Ios., bell. Iud. 1,284s; Ios., ant. Iud. 14,388s; Mos. Choren. 2,20 **35-37** cf. Ios., bell. Iud. 1,357. 361-363; Ios., ant. Iud. 14,490; 15,8s.88 **36** cf. Ios., ant. Iud. 15,92-94; Eus., can.[Hier] 162[e]

19 αὐτῇ ABC αὐτὴν OTVz **20** τῆς ἀρχῆς Bt ταύτης ἀρχὴν A **22** ᾔει AOTz ἴη BCV **24** τὸν < t **25** Συρίᾳ] συρίας Oz **28** post ἐλθόντος Routh lacunam coniecit sicut iam Goar **31** ἀνθηδόνα ABC[c] ἀνθηδόνα CV ἀνθιδῶνα OTz **32** αὐρανῖτιν A αὐρανίτην Bt **35** ἀντίγονον Bt ἀντώνιον A **36** τε AB δὲ t

This was the 185th Olympiad.

Now since Cleopatra had killed her brother, who had shared the throne with her, Antony summoned her to Cilicia to defend her actions. For this reason, she consigned the supervision of her realm to Herod. But because he would not consent to be entrusted with anything until he was restored to his own rule, she took him with her to Antony. And since he had been overcome by passionate love for the woman, Antony sent Herod off to Octavius Augustus in Rome. For the sake of Herod's father Antipater and of Herod himself, and because it was the Parthians who had installed Antigonus as king, Augustus ordered the governors in Palestine and Syria to restore him (sc. Herod) to power. Alongside Sosius, he carried on the war against Antigonus for a long time and in manifold battles. At that time too, Herod's brother Josephus, a general in his command, died. And after Herod came to Antony <...>,[3] besieged Antigonus for three years and took him alive as a captive to Antony. Antony himself also proclaimed Herod king, and delivered to him the cities of Hippos, Gadara, Gaza, Joppe, Anthedon, and in Arabia Trachon, Auranites, Sacia, and Gaulane, and in addition to this, the procuratorship of Syria.

Herod was declared king of the Jews by the Senate and Octavius Augustus, and he reigned for 34 years.

When Antony was about to launch an invasion against the Parthians, he executed Antigonus, the king of the Jews, and handed over Arabia to Cleopatra. And when he crossed over to the Parthians, he suffered a major setback, losing the greater part of his army.

---

3   At this point, Goar suggests a lacuna; see also Routh 469, ad loc. Josephus states that after Antigonus had killed Herod's brother, Antony appointed Sosius as governor of Syria and ordered him to assist Herod in the war against Antigonus.

Ἦν Ὀλυμπιὰς ρπςʹ.

Ὁ Σεβαστὸς Ὀκταούιος τὴν ἐξ Ἰταλίας καὶ πάσης ἑσπέρας δύναμιν ἐπ᾽
Ἀντώνιον ἦγεν, οὐ βουλόμενον εἰς Ῥώμην ἐπανελθεῖν δέει τῶν ἐν Πάρθοις ἐπ-
ταισμένων καὶ Κλεοπάτρας ἔρωτι. Ἀντώνιος δὲ αὖ τὴν ἐκ τῆς Ἀσίας ἔχων δύναμιν ὑπηντίαζεν. ὁ δὲ Ἡρώδης οἷα δεινὸς καὶ τῶν ἰσχυόντων θεραπευτὴς διπλᾶς
ἐξέπεμψεν ἐπιστολὰς καὶ νηὶ τὸν στρατόν, ἐντειλάμενος τοῖς ἡγουμένοις καρα-
δοκεῖν τὸ ἀποβησόμενον. ὡς δ᾽ ἐκρίθη τε ἡ νίκη καὶ δυσὶ ναυμαχίαις ἡττηθεὶς ὁ
Ἀντώνιος ἔφυγεν εἰς Αἴγυπτον ἅμα τῇ Κλεοπάτρᾳ, οἱ κομίζοντες ἀπέδοσαν τὰς
πρὸς τὸν Σεβαστὸν ἐπιστολάς, ἃς πρὸς Ἀντώνιον εἶχον ἀποκρύψαντες. ἔπιπτε
δ᾽ εὖ Ἡρώδῃ. Κλεοπάτρα ἐν τῷ μαυσωλείῳ ἑαυτὴν διεχρήσατο ἀσπίδι τῷ θηρίῳ
καθ᾽ ἑαυτῆς ὅπλῳ χρησαμένη. τότε Κλεοπάτρας υἱοὺς Ἥλιον καὶ Σελήνην ἐπὶ
Θηβαΐδα φυγόντας συνέλαβεν ὁ Σεβαστός.

Νικόπολις ἡ κατὰ Ἀκτίαν ἐκτίσθη καὶ Ἄκτια ὁ ἀγὼν ἐτέθη. Ἀλεξανδρείας
εἰλημμένης πρῶτος ἡγεμὼν Αἰγύπτου πέμπεται Γάλλος Κορνήλιος, ὃς τῶν
ἀποστάντων Αἰγυπτίων καθεῖλε τὰς πόλεις.

Μέχρι τοῦδε οἱ Λαγίδαι, καὶ <ὁ> σύμπας τῆς Μακεδονικῆς ἡγεμονίας {μετὰ}
ἔτη τʹ <ἀπὸ> τῆς Περσῶν καθαιρέσεως {δυοῖν δέοντα}· συνάγονται τοίνυν οἱ
χρόνοι ἀπὸ μὲν τῆς Μακεδόνων ἀρχῆς ἕως καταλύσεως κατὰ Πτολεμαίους καὶ
τὴν τελευταίαν Κλεοπάτραν, ὃ γίνεται τῆς Ῥωμαίων μοναρχίας ἡγεμονίας ἔτος
ιδʹ, Ὀλυμπιάδος δὲ ρπζʹ ἔτος δʹ. τὰ σύμπαντα ἔτη ἀπὸ Ἀδὰμ ͵ευοβʹ.

44-49 Leo Gr. (55,8-13 Bekker) Ἀντώνιος *καὶ φεύγει μετὰ τῆς Κλεοπάτρας εἰς Αἴγυπτον. καὶ ὁ μὲν Ἀντώνιος ἑαυτὸν διαχειρίζει, ἡ δὲ Κλεοπάτρα εὐλαβουμένη τὸν ἐν τῇ Ῥώμῃ θρίαμβον καὶ συσχεθεῖσα, ἀσπίδα τὸ θηρίον ἑαυτῇ προσενεγκαμένη τελευτᾷ. Ἥλιος καὶ Σελήνη τὰ ταύτης τέκνα συσχεθέντα προήχθη ἐν τῷ θριάμβῳ Ῥώμης.* **47-54** Sync. (365,13-15 Moss.) *Κλεοπάτρα ἡ τελευταία τῶν Λαγιδῶν ἀπόγονος ἐπὶ τῷ φόνῳ τοῦ ἀδελφοῦ, Ἀντωνίου μοιχευθεῖσα, τούτῳ καὶ αὐτὴ γέγονεν ἀπωλείας αἴτιος, ἀσπίδι καθ᾽ ἑαυτῆς ὅπλῳ θανάτου χρησαμένη.* **48s** Sync. (375,24-26 Moss.) *Τοὺς δὲ Κλεοπάτρας παῖδας φεύγοντας λαβὼν Ἥλιον καὶ Σελήνην κατῆξεν εἰς Ῥώμην, θρίαμβον ἐπ᾽ αὐτοῖς ἥδιστον Ῥωμαίοις ἐνδειξάμενος.* **53-57** → F46,245; F86,20-25; F93,51s; T6,16; F65,306

50-52 cf. Eus., can.[Hier] 163[f]; 162[h]   **53s** cf. Sync. 314,16; 375,4-6   **54-57** cf. Eus., can.[Hier] 163[a] (Ol. 187,4, ann. 15 Augusti; sed post annos 295 Lagidarum regni); Eus., can. [armen] 210

41 αὖ τὴν Di. αὐτὴν ABt   **43** νηὶ τὸν] νῄτην Gelzer[ms]   **44** τὸ ἀποβησόμενον Bt τὰ ἀποβησόμενα A ὁ < t   **46s** ἔπιπτε δ᾽ εὖ Ἡρώδῃ Κλεοπάτρα Gelzer[ms] ἐπιπίπτει δὲ ἡρώδῃ κλεοπάτρα ABt ἐπιπίπτει δὲ Ἡρώδης Κλεοπάτρᾳ Moss.   **47** μαυσωλείῳ Gelzer[ms] (cf. Plut., de proverbis Alexandrinorum 45,10 πρὸ τοῦ μνήματος τῆς Κλεοπάτρας, ὃ καλεῖται Μαυσώλειον) μεσαιολίῳ ABt | διεχρήσατο Scal. δὲ ἐχρήσατο ABt   **48** υἱοὺς Bt υἱὸς A   **49** Θηβαΐδα B θηβαίδι A θηβαΐδος t   **53** ὁ Gelzer[ms]   **53s** μετὰ…καθαιρέσεως] μετὰ τὴν Περσῶν καθαίρεσιν ἔτη τʹ Routh   **54** δυοῖν δέοντα < Routh, cf. F86,20-23; F93,52; T6,16; Sync. (314,16 Moss., textus supra in app. ad F86,22s), aliter Sync. (365,15 Moss.) | δέοντα TVz δὲ ὄντα ABCO   **55** ἕως Goar[m] καὶ ABt   **56** μοναρχίας] μοναρχικῆς Scal.   **57** ιδʹ Scal. Routh Gelzer[ms] ιαʹ ABt ιεʹ F86,22

This was in the 186th Olympiad.

Octavius Augustus led his army from Italy and the entire West against Antony, who, out of fear resulting from his failures in Parthia and because of his love for Cleopatra, was unwilling to return to Rome. Antony in turn began moving to meet him with his army from Asia. But Herod, as clever as he was, and as one who waited on the powerful, sent out both a double set of letters and his army by ship, ordering his commanders to wait and see the way things would turn out. When the victory was decided, and Antony, defeated in two naval battles, fled to Egypt with Cleopatra, those carrying the letters delivered the ones for Augustus, but hid those they were holding for Antony. And Herod attacked Cleopatra. She killed herself in the mausoleum, using a wild asp as the instrument of death. Then Augustus arrested Cleopatra's children Helios and Selene, who had fled to the Thebaïd.

Nicopolis was founded near Actia and the Actian games were instituted. When Alexandria was captured, Gallus Cornelius was sent as the first prefect of Egypt; he destroyed the cities of the Egyptians that were in revolt.

Up to this time, the Lagids were in control, and the entire duration of the Macedonian empire after the conquest of the Persians was 300 years {less two}.[4] So then, this is the entire chronology from the beginning of the Macedonians to their dissolution during the time of the Ptolemies and Cleopatra their last ruler, which occurred in the 14th year[5] of the supremacy of the Roman empire, the fourth year of the 187th Olympiad. Altogether there are 5472 years from Adam.[6]

---

4   For Africanus' 300-year chronology of the Macedonian kingdom, see app. to l. 54. The words "less two (δυοῖν δέοντα)" are an addition by Syncellus who intended to harmonize the text of Africanus with his own 298-year chronology of the Macedonian kingdom, cf. Sync. 365,15: ἀπὸ Ἀλεξάνδρου ἔτη σϙη'. For discussion, see further Routh 471f ad loc. and Gelzer 1,268f.

5   The numeral "11" (ια') in the manuscripts of Syncellus is corrupt. Scaliger, Routh and Gelzer[ms] emended it to "14" (ιδ', but cf., differently, Gelzer 1,277f, n. 5). This emendation is both necessary and probably correct. Necessary, because 11 years before the death of Cleopatra (30 BC) no historical event is attested which is fundamental for the beginnings of the Roman monarchy, whereas 14 years lead to the death of Caesar (44 BC) and the events immediately thereafter. Correct, because 14 years align with Africanus' system: Africanus counted 74 years from 1 Augustus to the Resurrection of Christ (= 16 Tiberius, T6,17f) and 60 years from the death of Cleopatra to 16 Tiberius (F93,52f). The date of Cleopatra's death would thus be 14 Augustus.

6   The equation Ol. 187,4 with AM 5472 is inconsistent with other witnesses to Africanus' chronology. Probably the text ought to be corrected to Ol. 187,2. If AM 5723 = Ol. 250,1 (F54d), then AM 5472 would equate to Ol. 187,2, see Mosshammer 2006,84–86. This would also be compatible with the dating of the Resurrection in AM 5532 = Ol. 202,2, see F93, n. 18. Cf. also Trieber 1880,66, Gelzer 1,46, Adler/Tuffin 2002,444, n. 6, who opt for an emendation to Ol. 187,3.

Μετὰ Ἀλεξανδρείας ἅλωσιν Ὀλυμπιὰς ἤχθη ρπη΄.

Ἡρώδης ἐπικτίσας τῶν Γαβινίων πόλιν τήν ποτε Σαμάρειαν, Σεβαστὴν αὐ-
60 τὴν προσηγόρευσε· τὸ δὲ ἐπίνειον αὐτῆς τὸν Στράτωνος πύργον πολίσας ἀπὸ
τοῦ αὐτοῦ Καισάρειαν ἐκάλεσεν, ἐφ' ἑκάτερα ναὸν ἐγείρας Ὀκταουίῳ. ὕστερον
δὲ καὶ Ἀντιπατρίδα κτίζει ἐν τῷ Λυδῷ πεδίῳ ἀπὸ τοῦ ἑαυτοῦ πατρός, καὶ τοὺς
περὶ τὴν Σεβαστὴν οἰκοῦντας, ὧν ἀφείλατο τὴν γῆν, ἐγκατῴκισεν ἐν αὐτῇ. ἔκ-
τισε δὲ καὶ ἑτέρας πόλεις, καὶ τοῖς μὲν Ἰουδαίοις βαρὺς ἦν, τοῖς δὲ ἄλλοις ἔθνεσι
65 δεξιώτατος.

Ἦν Ὀλυμπιὰς ρπθ΄, ἥτις πρὸ ἓξ καλανδῶν Μαρτίων, κατὰ Ἀντιοχεῖς κδ΄, ἤχθη, δι' ἧς ἐπὶ
τῶν ἰδίων ὅρων ἔστη ὁ ἐνιαυτός.

59s   Sync. (379,24s Moss.) *Ἡρώδης τὴν πάλαι Σαμάρειαν ἔρημον οὖσαν ἐκ θεμελίων ἤγειρε, Σεβαστὴν εἰς τιμὴν τοῦ Καίσαρος ὀνομάσας.*   **60s**   Sync. (380,2–5 Moss.) *Ἡρώδης τὸν πάλαι Στράτωνος
πύργον Καισάρειαν εἰς τιμὴν τοῦ Καίσαρος ἐπικτίσας ὠνόμασεν. ὁ αὐτὸς Ἀνθηδόνα ἐπέκτισεν
Ἀγριππίναν μετονομάσας, ἔτι τε Παρσανάβαν εἰς τιμὴν Ἀντιπάτρου τοῦ πατρὸς αὐτοῦ Ἀντιπατρίδα
ὠνόμασε.*

59s cf. Ios., bell. Iud. 1,403; Ios., ant. Iud. 15,292.296.363; Eus., can.[Hier] 166[a]   **60s** cf. Ios., ant. Iud.
15,293.331; Ios., bell. Iud. 1,408; Eus., can.[Hier] 167[d]   **61s**   cf. Ios., ant. Iud. 16,142s; Ios., bell. Iud.
1,417; Eus., can.[Hier] 167[e]   **62s** cf. Ios., ant. Iud. 15,296

59 Γαβηνῶν Gelzer[ms]   **60** ἐπίνειον A πίνιον C ἐπίνηον BOTVz | τὸν] τοῦ A τῶν C | πολίσας A
πολήσας Bt   **63** ὧν Bt ὂν A | ἐγκατῴκισεν Di. ἐγκατῴκησεν AB ἐγκατῴκησας t

T89a Georgius Syncellus (373,11–16 Mosshammer)

Ἀφρικανὸς ἐάσας εἰπεῖν πόσα ἔτη Ὑρκανὸς ἡγήσατο Ἰουδαίων διὰ τὸ ἀντιπίπ-
τειν τῇ ἐκδόσει αὐτοῦ τὰ λδ΄ ἔτη Ὑρκανοῦ, πρὸς τούτοις ἔτη γ΄ τῆς Ἡρώδου βασιλείας ἐκολόβωσεν, ἀντὶ λζ΄ ἐτῶν μόνα λδ΄ στοιχειώσας· ὅπερ εἰ δῶμεν ἀληθεύειν,
εὑρεθήσεται θνήσκων Ἡρώδης κατὰ τὸ πρῶτον ἔτος τῆς ἐνανθρωπήσεως τοῦ κυρίου καὶ θεοῦ καὶ
5 σωτῆρος ἡμῶν Ἰησοῦ Χριστοῦ, ὅπερ ἄτοπον κατὰ τὰς εὐαγγελικὰς παραδόσεις.

After the conquest of Alexandria, the 188th Olympiad began.

Herod re-established the city of the Gabinians, which was formerly called Samaria, giving it the name Sebaste. After building its seaport, Straton's Tower, into a city, he called it Caesarea after the same person, and erected in each city a temple to Octavius. Later, he built Antipatris in the Lydian plain, named after his father; those dwelling around Sebaste, whose land he had taken, he resettled in this city. He also built other cities, and while oppressive to the Jews, he was extremely benevolent to the other nations.

The 189th Olympiad began, which included the additional sixth day before the Calends of March, in the 24th year according to the Antiochenes. Through this means, the course of the year was established with fixed limits.[7]

T89a

Africanus fails to say how many years Hyrcanus was ruler of the Jews, because the 34 years of Hyrcanus' rule contradicts his exposition. In addition to this, he cut off three years from Herod's rule, assigning him only 34 years instead of 37. Now if we grant this as true, Herod will be found to have died in the first year of the Incarnation of the Lord and God, our Savior Jesus Christ, which is totally at odds with the teachings of the gospels.

---

7   Since Africanus' *Chronographiae* does not as a rule use the Antiochene era, Unger 1867,36f suggests that the words given here in small print were a later insertion by a Syrian chronicler, see further Adler/Tuffin 2002,445, n. 2.

F90

F90a Ioannes Chrysostomus, in: Catena in Matthaeum 1,17 (9,6–16 Cramer)

Περὶ τούτων οὖν τῶν τριῶν βασιλέων (sc. Ὀχοζίας, Ἰωάς, Ἀζαρίας) φησὶν ὁ Ἀφρικανὸς ἐν πέμπτῳ βιβλίῳ τῶν Χρονικῶν αὐτοῦ, ὅτι διὰ τὴν ἄγαν δυσσέβειαν αὐτῶν, παρέδραμε τούτους ὁ εὐαγγελιστής· ἔθος γάρ, φησι, τῇ γραφῇ τοὺς οὐκ ἀξίους μνήμης παραλιμπάνειν, <ὡς> τὸν Συμεών, καὶ ἄλλοτε ἄλλως ἀλλαχόθεν πολλούς· τούτους μὲν οὖν
5 τοὺς τρεῖς βασιλεῖς διὰ τοῦτο παρέδραμεν ὁ εὐαγγελιστής· ἐν δὲ τῇ ἐσχάτῃ μερίδι καθεὶς γενεὰς δεκατέσσαρας αὐτὰς εἶναι ἔφησεν, ὅτι τὸν χρόνον τῆς αἰχμαλωσίας εἰς γενεὰν ἔταξεν· ἔτι δὲ καὶ αὐτὸν τὸν Χριστόν, πανταχόθεν συνάπτων ἡμῖν αὐτόν.

2–4 Barhebr., Hor. Myst. (105 Carr) *Africanus reckons fifty persons from Abraham to Christ. And in all the codices of Luke, which are read in the holy Church, there are fifty and six, and so from Adam to our Lord seventy and six. And as the natural genealogy of the Gospel of Matthew from Abraham to Joseph is forty persons, so the book of the Kings has forty and four, that is to say, when Ahaziah and Joash and Amaziah and Eliakim who is the same as Jehoiakim are added.* Dionysius Bar Salibi, Commentarii in Evangelia (44,7–26 Sedláček) *Africanus et Eusebius tertium ponunt Melchi; quomodo etiam Matthan tertius sit ante Iosephum? scriptum est: 'Iosephi, filii Heli, filii Melchi.' in exemplaribus autem syriacis Lucae quae habemus, quintum ponunt eum: 'Iosephi, filii Heli, filii Mathat, filii Levi, filii Melchi.' et rursus Africanus quinquaginta personas ponit in Luca ab Abrahamo ad Iosephum; in exemplaribus autem syriacis Lucae quinquaginta sex sunt. et opus est ut verum inquiramus. Gregorius Theologus dicit septuaginta et septem generationes esse ab Adamo usque ad Christum, secundum genealogiam Lucae, qui retrograditur. et Iacobus Batnanensis dicit in epistula ad Maronem: ab Abrahamo usque ad Christum XLII generationes sunt, sicut scripsit Matthaeus, et secundum Lucam LVII. si vero secundum verbum praedictorum doctorum, et secundum exemplaria Evangelii quae habebant, LXXVII generationes sunt ab Adamo usque ad Christum, restant nobis LVII ab Abrahamo ad Christum, sicut dixit Mār Iacobus. et si detrahimus e LVII unum, h.e. Christum, remanent LVI ab Abrahamo ad Iosephum, non autem L, sicut dixit Africanus; et genuina sunt exemplaria syriaca, quae sunt apud nos, et non est verax Africanus eo quod L tantum personas posuit.*

1 cf. III Regn 22,52–54; IV Regn 1,1–16; 12,20–22; 15,1–7; 24; II Par 20,35; 26,16–23; Sync. 220,20 – 221,6; 224,16–23; 235,18–20   **2–4** Io. Chrys., hom. 4 in Mt. (PG 57,39,33–41)   **3** cf. Mt 1,8; I Par 3,10–12   **4** cf. Deut 33,6–25; Gen 34,15–31

[CB] **1** πέμπτῳ] ἕκτῳ B   **4** ὡς scripsimus ὥσπερ ἀμέλει καὶ ὁ θεσπέσιος Μωυσῆς πεποίηκεν ἐν ταῖς εὐλογίαις παραλιπῶν B | πολλούς Routh πολλοί CB

F90 *Omissions in Jesus' Genealogy*

F90a[1]

Concerning these three kings (Ahaziah, Joash, Azariah), then, Africanus states in the fifth book of his *Chronicae* that because of their extreme impiety the evangelist omitted them. For it is customary of Scripture, he says, to omit those who are not worthy of mention, <such as> Symeon and many others elsewhere in different places. As for these three kings, then, this is why the evangelist omitted them. But as he proceeded down in the last part, he said that these were 14 generations, because he arranged the period of the captivity as a generation, as well as Christ himself, in this way joining him to us in every way.

---

1   For this type of the Catena on Mt and its manuscript tradition, see Reuss 1941,42–45 (die "auf der Grundform aufgebaute Katene"), in particular pp. 43f for cod. Coisl. gr. 23, and pp. 46f on the quality of Cramer's edition of the codex ("Unter Berücksichtigung der genannten Fehler ist die Ausgabe Cramers immerhin wissenschaftlich verwendbar"). Chrysostom's citation of the fifth book of the *Chronographiae* makes it clear that he is not referring to Africanus' discussion of Jesus' genealogy in the fragmentarily preserved *Epistle to Aristides*. It is difficult to know, however, whether Syriac excerpts from Africanus' treatment of Jesus' genealogy that are not attributed to a specific work refer to the *Chronographiae* or to a part of the epistle that does not survive elsewhere. Citations bearing close resemblances to Chrysostom's notice are provided in the third apparatus. Excerpts from Africanus' treatment of Jesus' genealogy that are not attested in the surviving portions of the epistle are given here as separate fragments (F90b.c).

F90b Gregorius Barhebraeus, Horreum Mysteriorum (3,9–12 Carr)

ܘܐܦܪܝܩܢܘܣ ܕܐܡܐܘܣ ܘܩܕܝܫܐ ܣܐܘܪܐ ܐܡܪܝܢ ܕܠܗܠܝܢ ܬܠܬܐ ܟܕ
ܡܢ ܟܬܠܝܐ ܫܘܬܗ ܕܐܚܒ ܗܘ، ܕܐܦ ܒܪܬ ܐܝܟܝܠ ܒܪܘܫܟܡܗ ܐܫܬܪܪܬ
ܡܬܡܠܟܝܢ ܥܩܡ ܐܢܘܢ ܐܘܢܓܠܣܛܐ. ܘܐܠܘ ܗܟܢܐ ܗܘ ܐܝܟܢܐ ܠܐܚܝ
ܘܠܡܟܢܫܐ ܕܬܪܬ ܒܢܫܝܢ ܐܬܟܡܗ.

4 → F70

F90c Gregorius Barhebraeus, Horreum Mysteriorum (134,13–18; 136,4–6 Carr)

ܘܐܦܪܝܩܢܘܣ ܡܫܒܠܢܐ ܕܫܪ̈ܒܬܐ ܐܡܪ ܕܗܠܝ ܒܪ ܡܛܬܬ ܘܝܥܩܘܒ ܒܪ
ܡܬܢ ܐܚ̈ܐ ܡܢ ܐܡܐ ܕܫܡܗ ܐܣܬܐ ܘܒܚܝܫܐ ܐܣܬܪ ܐܬܝܗܒܬܗ
ܗܘܘ ܘܟܕ ܡܝܬ ܗܠܝ ܕܠܐ ܒܢ̈ܝܐ ܢܣܒܗ ܝܥܩܘܒ ܐܚܘܗܝ، ܠܐܢܬܬܗ ܐܝܟ
ܢܡܘܣܐ ܠܡܩܡܬ ܒܢ̈ܝܐ ܘܐܘܠܕ. ܡܢܗ ܠܝܘܣܦ ܘܡܢ ܗܪܟܐ ܝܘܣܦ ܒܪܐ
ܗܘ ܟܝܢܝܐ ܕܝܥܩܘܒ ܐܝܟ ܕܐܡܪ ܡܬܝ، ܘܒܪܐ ܢܡܘܣܝܐ ܕܗܠܝ ܐܝܟ
ܕܐܡܪ ܠܘܩܐ. …
ܐܦܪܝܩܢܘܣ ܐܡܪ ܕܐܝܟ ܡܫܠܡܢܘܬܐ ܕܡܠܟ ܡܢ ܡܫܒ̈ܠܝ ܫܪ̈ܒܬܐ
ܕܒܢ̈ܝܐ ܕܗܠܝ ܘܡܛܬܬ ܠܘ، ܐܚ̈ܐ ܐܢܘܢ ܬܪ̈ܝܢ ܡܠܟܝ ܘܠܘ ܐܝܟ ܕܐܡܪ
ܠܘܩܐ ܗܠܝ ܒܪ ܡܛܬܬ ܘܡܛܬܬ ܒܪ ܠܘܝ.

1–9 cf. ep. Arist. (59–62 Reichardt); Dionys. Sal., comm. Ev. (37,5–26 Sedláček); Exp. off. 1,8 2 cf. Aug., retract. 2,7,2

F90b[1]

And Africanus of Emmaus and Saint Severus say that these three the Evangelist omitted because they derived their descent from Athaliah the sister of Ahab, who also for her wickedness was called the daughter of Jezebel. But if it be so, why does he mention Ahaz and Manasseh who were more wicked?

F90c

And Africanus, a compiler of genealogies, says that Eli the son of Matthat and Jacob the son of Mathan were brothers on the side of the mother whose name was Estha, and in one codex Esther. When Eli died without sons, Jacob his brother took her to wife according to the law for the provision of sons, and begot from her Joseph. Hence Joseph was the natural son of Jacob, as Matthew says, and the legal son of Eli, as Luke says. […]

Africanus says that according to the tradition which he received from the Hebrew genealogists, Eli, Matthat and Levi were brothers, sons of Melchi, and not, as Luke says—Eli the son of Matthat, and Matthat the son of Levi.

---

1 The translations are taken from Carr 1925.

T91 Agapius Mabbugensis, Historia universalis (PO 11/1, 132,10 – 133,3 Vasiliev)

واما ملك الفرس ذلك الذي بعث المجوس فانه كان اسمه فرنسون فجاووا اوليك المجوس الى المسيح في سنة اربعة واربعين من سني اوغسطس اذ المسيح ابن سنتين على ما ذكر اناس فاما قريلس وافرقيانس مع اخرين فذكروا ان المسيح كان ابن سبعة ايام حيث جاووا المجوس وكذلك يشبه ان يكون لانا قد وجدنا فى الصور والمثالات فى كنايس كثيرة
5 المجوس والرعاة مصورين الى جانب المسيح ومريم امّه

1 cf. Cyr., Os.-Mal. 2,133s; Cyr., fr. Mt. 12

[ABC] **2** *Des gens racontent que le Christ était âgé de deux ans. Quant aux savants, aux philosophes et à l'auteur de ce livre, ils disent qu'au moment de l'arrivée des Mages, le Christ avait sept jours* A

T92 Paschale Campanum anno 464–599, Epitoma temporum et indiculum Pascae (745,7–18 Mommsen)

Iosephus igitur, qui XX antiquitatum edidit libros, ab exordio mundi usque ad quartum decimum annum Domitiani Caesaris annos V̄DCV scribsit.

Iulius Africanus, cuius quinque de temporibus extant volumina, a primo homine usque ad domini incarnationem annos V̄D stilo terminavit.

5 Prosper presbyter usque ad annum XV Tiberi Caesaris, id est duobus Geminis, quo dominus Iesus Christus passus est, annos V̄CCXXVIII exponit.

In chronica Eusebi Caesariensis episcopi, quam beatus Hieronymus in Latinam linguam vertit et nonnulla quae omissa videbantur, adiecit, a principio mundi usque ad XIIII Valentis annum, id est usque ad consulatum eius sextum et Valentiniani iterum, annos V̄DLXXVIIII legimus.

10 Orosius presbyter in septimo ad Augustinum libro ab initio mundi usque ad tempora Honori annos V̄DCXVIII adserit.

3s → T11,4s; T13a,2s; F14; F15,12–15; T80d,3–5; T93c,8–10

1s Ios., ant. Iud. 20,267   **3s** cf. Hipp., Dan. 4,23,3   **5s** Prosp., chron. 386–388   **7–9** Eus., can.[Hier] 250,24–26   **10s** Oros., hist. 7,43,19

[VW] **1** Iosephus V iosippus W   **2** annum…annos V Domitiani Caesaris ann. W   **3** quinque V cumque W   **4** incarnationem W incarnatione V | annos Mom. < V anni W   **5** Prosper W Prosperius V | quo V quod W   **7** Eusebi] eusevi V eusebii W   **8** adiecit Mom. adiecta VW   **9** iterum V tercium W

T91 *The Arrival of the Magi*

As to the king of the Persians who had sent the Magi, he was named Faransun. In the 44th year of Augustus,[1] these Magi came to Christ, who, according to the statement of some, was already two years of age. But Cyril and Africanus together with some others report that Christ was seven days old when the Magi arrived. This opinion seems to be more probable, since in the pictures and images in many churches, we have found the Magi and the shepherds depicted at the side of Christ and his mother Mary.

T92 *The Date of the Incarnation*

Josephus, then, who published the *Antiquities* in 20 books, recorded 5605 years from the beginning of the world up to the 14th year of Domitian Caesar.

Iulius Africanus, whose five volumes on chronology are in circulation, established in his writing 5500 years from the first man to the Incarnation of the Lord.[2]

Prosper the presbyter sets forth 5228 years up to the 15th year of Tiberius Caesar, that is in the consulship of the two Gemini, at which time the Lord Jesus Christ underwent the Passion.

In the chronicle of Eusebius bishop of Caesarea, which blessed Jerome translated into the Latin language and to which he added some material that appeared to be left out, we read 5579 years from the beginning of the world up to the 14th year of Valens, that is up to his sixth consulship and the second of Valentinian.

In his seventh book to Augustine, Orosius the presbyter affirms 5618 years from the beginning of the world up to the times of Honorius.

---

1   For 42 Augustus as the date of Jesus' birth, see *inter alia* Eus., h.e. 1,5,2; Eus., can.[Hier] 169[c]; Epiph., haer. 2,288,19–23. Africanus' chronology also presupposes this date (and he seems to be the first to establish it). According to F89,56f, 14 Augustus corresponds to AM 5472; hence, 42 Augustus = AM 5500. For the visitation of the magi two years after Jesus' birth, see Epiph., haer. 2,288,7–9.
2   The fact that the description of the other chronicles and histories encompasses their entire chronological scope may mean that the author believed that Africanus' *Chronographiae* extended only as far as the Incarnation in AM 5500. Although the Incarnation does mark an important event in Africanus' reckoning, the *Chronographiae* continued well beyond this point, to the reign of Elagabalus, see introduction, p. XVII.

F93

Eus.¹: Eusebius, Eclogae propheticae 3,26 (cod. Vind. theol. gr. 29, f. 39ᵛ–40ʳ = 151,10 – 153,11 Gaisford)
Eus.²: Eusebius, Demonstratio evangelica 8,2,46–54 (374,28 – 377,9 Heikel), unde Hieronymus, Commentaria in Danielem 3,9,24 (145–223 Glorie)
Sync.: Georgius Syncellus (391,1 – 393,30 Mosshammer)

Τὸ δὲ καθ᾽ ἕκαστον τῶν πράξεων αὐτοῦ καὶ θεραπειῶν σωμάτων καὶ ψυχῶν καὶ τῶν τῆς γνώσεως ἀποκρύφων, ἀναστάσεώς τε τῆς ἐκ νεκρῶν αὐταρκέστατα τοῖς πρὸ ἡμῶν μαθηταῖς τε καὶ ἀποστόλοις αὐτοῦ δεδήλωται. καθ᾽ ὅλου τοῦ κόσμου σκότος ἐπήγετο φοβερώτατον, σεισμῷ τε αἱ πέτραι διερρήγνυντο καὶ
5 τὰ πολλὰ Ἰουδαίας τε καὶ τῆς λοιπῆς γῆς κατερρίφη.
Τοῦτο τὸ σκότος ἔκλειψιν τοῦ ἡλίου Θάλλος ἀποκαλεῖ ἐν τρίτῃ τῶν ἱστοριῶν, ὡς ἐμοὶ δοκεῖ, ἀλόγως. Ἑβραῖοι γὰρ ἄγουσι τὸ πάσχα κατὰ σελήνην ιδ′, πρὸ δὲ μιᾶς τοῦ πάσχα τὰ περὶ τὸν σωτῆρα συμβαίνει. ἔκλειψις δὲ ἡλίου σελήνης ὑπελθούσης τὸν ἥλιον γίνεται· ἀδύνατον δὲ ἐν ἄλλῳ χρόνῳ πλὴν ἐν τῷ
10 μεταξὺ μιᾶς καὶ τῆς πρὸ αὐτῆς κατὰ τὴν σύνοδον αὐτὴν ἀποβῆναι. πῶς οὖν ἔκλειψις νομισθείη κατὰ διάμετρον σχεδὸν ὑπαρχούσης τῆς σελήνης ἡλίῳ; ἔστω δή, συναρπαζέτω τοὺς πολλοὺς τὸ γεγενημένον καὶ τὸ κοσμικὸν τέρας ἡλίου ἔκλειψις ὑπονοείσθω ἐν τῇ κατὰ τὴν ὄψιν <πλάνῃ>.

test.: 1 inc. Sync. [AB x=COTV Par. 1336]: Ἀφρικανοῦ περὶ τῶν κατὰ τὸ σωτήριον πάθος καὶ τὴν ζωοποιὸν ἀνάστασιν·

3–19 Cedr. (331,16 – 332,8 Bekker) *Καὶ Ἀφρικανὸς δὲ ἱστορεῖ κατ᾽ αὐτὴν τὴν ἡμέραν τοῦ πάθους σκότος καθ᾽ ὅλου τοῦ κόσμου φοβερώτατον γενέσθαι. σεισμῷ τε αἱ πέτραι διερρήγνυντο, καὶ πολλὰ τῆς γῆς κατερρίφη. τοῦτο τὸ σκότος ἔκλειψιν ἡλίου οἱ Ἰουδαῖοι καλοῦσιν, ἀλόγως, ὡς ἐμοὶ καὶ τῇ ἀληθείᾳ δοκεῖ· Ἑβραῖοι γὰρ ἄγουσι τὸ πάσχα κατὰ σελήνην, πρὸ δὲ τῆς μιᾶς τοῦ πάσχα τὰ περὶ τὸν σωτῆρα συνέβη. ἔκλειψις δὲ ἡλίου τῆς σελήνης αὐτὸν ὑπελθούσης γίνεται, ἀδύνατον δὲ ἐν ἄλλῳ χρόνῳ πλὴν ἐν τῷ μεταξὺ νουμηνίας καὶ τῆς πρὸ αὐτῆς κατὰ τὴν σύνοδον αὐτὴν ἀποβῆναι· πῶς οὖν ἔκλειψις νομισθείη κατὰ διάμετρον σχεδὸν ὑπαρχούσης τῆς σελήνης ἡλίῳ; ἔστω δὲ συναρμόζον πολλοῖς τὸ γεγενημένον, καὶ κοσμικὸν τέρας ἡλίου ἔκλειψις ὑπονοείσθω ἔκ γε τῆς κατὰ τὴν ὄψιν πλάνης. τίς δὲ ἡ κοινωνία σεισμῷ καὶ ἐκλείψει πέτραις τε ῥηγνυμέναις καὶ ἀναστάσει νεκρῶν, τοσαύτη τε κίνησις κοσμική; ἐν γοῦν τῷ μακρῷ χρόνῳ τοιοῦτόν τι συμβὰν οὐ μέμνηταί τις. ἀλλ᾽ ἦν σκότος θεοποίητον, διότι τῇδε τῇ ἡμέρᾳ τὸν κύριον συνέβη παθεῖν.*

2 cf. Col 2,3   3–5 cf. Mt 27,45.51   6s Thallus FGrHist 256 F1   7 cf. Exod 12,6   8 cf. Io 19,31

1 θεραπειῶν Ax θεραπιῶν B   2 γνώσεως] γνώμης T   2s αὐταρκέστατα τοῖς x αὐταρκεστάτοις AB   4 ἐπήγετο C ἐπείγετο ABOTV ἐγένετο Paris. 1336 γενέσθαι Cedr. | τε Bx δὲ A   5 τε < AB κατερρίφη Ax Cedr. κατερρίφθη B κατερρήφθει Paris. 1336   6 τοῦ < x   7 δοκεῖ < C   8 πάσχα + ἡμέρας Paris. 1336   10 μιᾶς ABx Paris. 1336 νουμηνίας Cedr. | πρὸ...αὐτὴν ABx Cedr. πρώτης κατὰ τὴν σύνοδον αὐτῆς Paris. 1336   11 ὑπαρχούσης ABx Cedr. ὑποχωρούσης Paris. 1336   11s ἔστω...πολλοὺς ABx ἔστω δὲ συναρμόζον πολλοῖς Cedr. < Paris. 1336   13s ὑπονοείσθω...ἔκλειψιν < A, + eadem manu Aᵐ   13 ἐν τῇ Bx ἔν τι A | πλάνη cf. Cedr. (textus supra in app.)

F93 *The Passion and Resurrection of the Savior*[1]

Concerning each of his deeds and his cures, both of bodies and souls, and the secrets of knowledge, and his resurrection from the dead, this has been explained with complete adequacy to his disciples and apostles before us. A most terrible darkness fell over all the world, the rocks were torn apart by an earthquake, and many places both in Judaea and the rest of the world were thrown down.

In the third book of his *Histories*, Thallus calls this darkness a solar eclipse. In my opinion, this is nonsense.[2] For the Hebrews celebrate the Passover on Luna 14, and what happened to the Savior occurred one day before the Passover. But an eclipse of the sun takes place when the moon passes under the sun. The only time when this can happen is in the interval between the first day [of the new moon] and the preceding day, when they are in conjunction. How then could one believe an eclipse took place when the moon was almost in opposition to the sun? So be it. Let what had happened beguile the masses, and let this wonderful sign all over the world be considered a solar eclipse through an <error> due to the optical illusion.

---

1   The central parts of this fragment are very well attested by the two independent witnesses Eusebius and Syncellus. It therefore seems likely that the quality of the transmission is high also in the initial and final parts of the text which are known from one source only (mostly Syncellus).
2   For discussion of early Christian and non-Christian accounts of the darkness during Jesus' passion, see Xeres 1989.

Φλέγων ἱστορεῖ ἐπὶ Τιβερίου Καίσαρος ἐν πανσελήνῳ ἔκλειψιν ἡλίου γεγονέναι τελείαν ἀπὸ ὥρας ϛ' μέχρις θ', δῆλον ὡς ταύτην. τίς δ᾽ ἡ κοινωνία σεισμῷ
καὶ ἐκλείψεσι, πέτραις τε ῥηγνυμέναις καὶ ἀναστάσει νεκρῶν, τοσαύτῃ τε κινήσει κοσμικῇ;
Ἐν γοῦν τῷ μακρῷ χρόνῳ τοιοῦτόν τι συμβὰν οὐ μνημονεύεται, ἀλλ᾽ ἦν
σκότος θεοποίητον, διότι τὸν κύριον συνέβη παθεῖν, καὶ λόγος αἱρεῖ ὅτι ο' ἑβδομάδες εἰς τοῦτον συναιροῦνται τὸν χρόνον ἐν τῷ Δανιήλ.
[...]
Ἡ μὲν οὖν περικοπὴ οὕτω πῶς ἔχουσα πολλά τε καὶ παράδοξα σημαίνει· νῦν
δ᾽ ὧν χρεία περί τε τοὺς χρόνους καὶ τὰ τούτοις συντείνοντα τὸν λόγον ποιησό-
μεθα. ὅτι μὲν οὖν περὶ τῆς τοῦ Χριστοῦ παρουσίας λέγεται ταῦτα μετὰ ἑβδομάδας ο' μέλλοντος ἐπιφαίνεσθαι, δῆλον· ἐπὶ γὰρ τοῦ σωτῆρος ἢ ἀπὸ τούτου τά
τε παραπτώματα παλαιοῦται, καὶ αἱ ἁμαρτίαι συντελοῦνται διὰ τὴν ἄφεσιν αἵ τε
ἀνομίαι ἐξιλασμῷ μετὰ τῶν ἀδικιῶν ἐξαλείφονται, δικαιοσύνη τε αἰώνιος κατ-
αγγέλλεται παρὰ τὴν ἐκ νόμου· ὁράσεις τε καὶ προφητεῖαι μέχρις Ἰωάννου·
χρίεται δὲ ἅγιος ἁγίων. πρὸ γὰρ τῆς τοῦ σωτῆρος ἡμῶν παρουσίας οὐκ ὄντα
ταῦτα προσεδοκᾶτο μόνον.
Ἄρξασθαι δὴ τῶν ἀριθμῶν, τοῦτ᾽ ἔστιν τῶν ο' ἑβδομάδων, ἅ ἐστιν ἔτη υϟ', ὁ
ἄγγελος ὑποτίθεται ἀπὸ ἐξόδου λόγου τοῦ ἀποκριθῆναι καὶ τοῦ οἰκοδομῆσαι

test.: Sync.   20 des. Sync. (sequitur l. 54)   22 inc. Eus.[1]: τῶν εἰς τὰς προκειμένας ἑβδομάδας ἐπιβε-
βληκότων μόνον ἴσμεν Ἀφρικανὸν ἀκριβέστατα καὶ μᾶλλον παρὰ τοὺς λοιποὺς ἐπιτετευγμένως τε-
θεωρηκότα· καὶ δή μοι δοκεῖ ἀναγκαῖον εἶναι πρῶτον αὐτοῦ τὴν εἰς τοὺς τόπους διήγησιν εἰς μέσον
ἀγαγεῖν, εἶθ᾽ οὕτως ἐπισκέψασθαι, εἴ τι ἄρα καὶ αὐτοὶ δυναίμεθα συμβαλέσθαι τῷ λόγῳ. γράφει δὴ
οὖν ἐν πέμπτῳ τῶν χρονογραφιῶν κατὰ λέξιν οὕτως. et Eus.[2]: καὶ ἐπειδὴ προσήκει συγχρῆσθαι μὲν
εὐγνωμονοῦντας τοῖς καλῶς ὑφ᾽ ἑτέρων εἰρημένοις, μὴ μὴν ἀποστερεῖν τοὺς πατέρας τῶν ἐκγόνων
μηδὲ τοὺς πρώτους φύ<σα>ντας τῶν οἰκείων σπερμάτων, τὰς αὐτοῦ παραθήσομαι λέξεις. φέρονται
δὲ αὗται Ἀφρικανοῦ ἐν τῷ πέμπτῳ τῶν Χρονογραφιῶν, τοῦτον ἔχουσαι τὸν τρόπον·

14s → T93a   22-25 → F78   25-29 Leo Gr. (46,11-14 Bekker) ὅτε παλαιοῦται τὸ παράπτωμα καὶ
συντελεῖται ἡ ἁμαρτία *καὶ σφραγίζεται ὅραμα καὶ προφητεύει καὶ χρίεται ἅγια ἁγίων, τουτέστιν ἐπὶ
τὴν τοῦ Χριστοῦ παρουσίαν καὶ τὴν λοιπὴν πραγματείαν.*   **31-34 → F78; F79   31-35** Leo Gr.
(46,4-9 Bekker) *Καὶ εἴ τις ἀκριβῶς τῶν ἑβδομάδων ἐξετάσαι βουληθείη τὸν λόγον καὶ διαριθ-
μήσασθαι τοὺς χρόνους,* ἀρξάμενος ἀπὸ ἐξόδου λόγου *κατὰ τὸν προφήτην* τοῦ οἰκοδομηθῆναι
Ἰερουσαλήμ, *τουτέστιν ἀπὸ Νεεμίου υἱοῦ Ἀχελῆ, τοῦ ἀρχιοινοχόου Ἀρταξέρξου, ὃς ἀξιώσας καὶ
ἐπιτραπεὶς ἄνεισιν οἰκοδομήσων τὰ Ἱεροσόλυμα.*

14s Phleg. Trall. FGrHist 257 F16   **26-29** cf. Dan 9,24   **28** cf. Lc 16,16 par   **31-33** Dan 9,25 θ

14 φλέγων Bx φλέγον A   **15** μέχρις AB ἄχρις x   **16** πέτραις τε Cedr. καὶ πέτραις Paris. 1336 πέτραις
ABx   **16s** κινήσει Routh κίνησις Sync.   **19** σκότος θεοποίητον AB Cedr. Paris. 1336 ~ x   **19s** ἑβδομάδες εἰς < C   **22** περικοπὴ...ἔχουσα *capitulum, quod in Daniele de septuaginta hebdomadibus legi-
mus* Hier. | σημαίνει + *quae nunc longum est dicere* Hier.   **23** τε < Eus.[2]   **26** τε[1] < Eus.[1] | διὰ + δὲ
Eus.[2]   **27** ἐξαλείφονται Eus.[2] ἀπαλείφονται Eus.[1] (cf. Dan. 9,24 ἀπαλεῖψαι)   **28** παρὰ < Eus.[1] | ὁρά-
σεις...Ἰωάννου] *et impleta est uisio et prophetia quia lex et prophetae usque ad Ioannis baptisma*
Hier.   **29** δὲ < Eus.[1] | ἡμῶν < Eus.[1]   **31** δὴ] δὲ Eus.[2]

Phlegon records that during the reign of Tiberius Caesar there was a complete solar eclipse at full moon from the sixth to the ninth hour; it is obvious that he is talking about this one.[3] But what have eclipses to do with an earthquake, rocks breaking apart with the resurrection of the dead, and a universal disturbance of this nature?

Certainly an event of such magnitude has not been recalled for a long time. But it was a darkness created by God, because it happened that the Lord experienced his passion at that time. And reason proves that the 70 hebdomads mentioned in Daniel were completed in this time.

[…][4]

What the section thus expressed means is both abundant and out of the ordinary. But here we will make the necessary examination of the times and the matters connected with them. It is clear that concerning the *parousia* of the Christ it states this, that it is due to appear after 70 hebdomads. For in the time of our Savior, or after him, transgressions are annulled and sins ended by remission, iniquities are blotted out by a propitiation together with unrighteousness, eternal righteousness is proclaimed surpassing that of the law—visions and prophecies until John—, and the Holy of holies is anointed. For before our Savior's *parousia*, these things did not exist but were only expected.

And the angel explains we must begin counting, that is to say the 70 hebdomads, which are 490 years, from the going forth of the word of answer and

---

3 Contra Routh, ad loc., the identification of Phlegon's eclipse with the darkness at noon at the time of the Crucifixion (Mt 27,45–54) need not be treated as a later gloss. Africanus accepts the idea, commonly held by early Christian writers (see, for example, Origen, Cels. 2,33), that Phlegon and Matthew's gospel described the same event. But he rejects Phlegon's characterization of it as a naturally recurring phenomenon.

4 The continuation of the analysis of Dan 9,24–27 after the lacuna suggests that the portion of Africanus' text apparently lost in the gap between Syncellus' excerpt (ll. 1–20) and Eusebius' (ll. 22–53) could not have been substantial.

Ἰερουσαλήμ· συνέβη δὲ ταῦτα ἐπὶ Ἀρταξέρξου τοῦ Περσῶν βασιλεύοντος εἰκοστῷ ἔτει. Νεεμίας γὰρ ὁ τούτου οἰνοχόος δεηθεὶς ἀποκρίσεώς τε ἔτυχεν οἰκο-
35 δομηθῆναι Ἰερουσαλήμ, καὶ λόγος ἐξῆλθεν κελεύων ταῦτα· μέχρι γὰρ ἐκείνου τοῦ χρόνου ἡ πόλις ἠρήμωτο. Κύρου γὰρ μετὰ τὴν ἑβδομηκονταετίαν τῆς αἰχμαλωσίας τῶν βουλομένων ἕκαστον ἑκουσιαστὶ καταπέμψαντος, οἱ μετὰ Ἰησοῦ τοῦ μεγάλου ἱερέως καὶ Ζοροβάβελ κατελθόντες, καὶ οἱ ἐπὶ τούτοις ἅμα Ἔζρᾳ, τὸν νεὼν οἰκοδομεῖν ἐκωλύοντο τὰ πρῶτα, καὶ τεῖχος τῇ πόλει περιβαλεῖν, ὡς
40 οὐ κεκελευσμένου τούτου. ἔμεινεν οὖν ἕως Νεεμίου καὶ βασιλείας Ἀρταξέρξου εἰκοσαετοῦς, Περσῶν δὲ ἡγεμονίας ἔτους πεντεκαιδεκάτου καὶ ἑκατοστοῦ, ἀπὸ δὲ τῆς ἁλώσεως Ἰερουσαλὴμ ρπε΄ ἔτη. καὶ τότε βασιλεὺς Ἀρταξέρξης ἐκέλευσεν οἰκοδομηθῆναι τὴν πόλιν. Νεεμίας δὲ καταπεμφθεὶς τοῦ ἔργου προέστη, ἡ δὲ οἰκοδομὴ πλατεῖα καὶ περίτειχος, ὡς προεφητεύθη. κἀκεῖθεν ἀριθμοῦσιν ἡμῖν ο΄
45 ἑβδομάδες εἰς τὸν Χριστὸν συντελοῦνται.

Εἰ γὰρ ἄλλοθέν ποθεν ἀριθμεῖν ἀρξαίμεθα καὶ οὐκ ἐντεῦθεν, οὔτε ὁ χρόνος συνδραμεῖται, καὶ πλεῖστα ἄτοπα ἀπαντήσει· ἐάν τε γὰρ ἀπὸ Κύρου καὶ τῆς πρώτης καταπομπῆς τὴν ἀρχὴν ποιησώμεθα τῆς ἀριθμήσεως τῶν ο΄ ἑβδομάδων, ἔτη ρ΄ καὶ προσέτι περισσεύει, πλείων δὲ χρόνος, εἰ ἀφ᾿ ἧς ἡμέρας τῷ Δα-
50 νιὴλ ὁ ἄγγελος προεφήτευσεν, πολλῷ δὲ πλείων, εἰ ἀπ᾿ ἀρχῆς τῆς αἰχμαλωσίας. εὑρίσκομεν γὰρ τὴν Περσῶν βασιλείαν ἔτεσιν σλ΄ περιγραφομένην, τήν τε Μακεδόνων εἰς ἔτη τ΄ παρατείνουσαν, κἀκεῖθεν ἐπὶ τὸ Τιβερίου Καίσαρος ἔτος ἐκκαιδέκατον {εἰς} ἔτη ξ΄·

Ἀπὸ δὲ Ἀρταξέρξου αἱ ο΄ ἑβδομάδες εἰς τὸν ἐπὶ Χριστοῦ συντελοῦνται χρό-
55 νον κατὰ τοὺς Ἰουδαίων ἀριθμούς. ἀπὸ γὰρ Νεεμίου, ὃς ὑπ᾿ Ἀρταξέρξου τὴν Ἰε-

test.: Eus.¹ Eus.² **54** inc. Sync. [AB x=COTV z^(l.86-)=PQMRS t=xz]: καὶ μεθ᾿ ἕτερα·

43s Sync. (299,13s Moss.) Ἡ δὲ ᾠκοδομήθη πλατεῖα καὶ περίτειχος *κατὰ τὴν πρόρρησιν Δανιὴλ τοῦ προφήτου.* **51** → T6,15 **51s** → T6,16; F86,22s; F89,53s

33s cf. II Esdr 12,1 **34–36** cf. II Esdr 12,5–9 **36–40** cf. II Par 36,22s; I Esdr 2; 5,1–7,5 **42–44** cf. II Esdr 12,5 **43s** cf. Dan 9,25 **47s** cf. I Esdr 2,1–11 **51s** Sync. 314,16-24 **54–66** cf. Aldhelmus Malmesbiriensis, de metris 69,19–24

33 τοῦ < Eus.¹ **34** οἰνοχόος + *sicut in Ezrae libro legimus* Hier. | τε < Eus.² **35** μέχρι + μὲν Eus.² **36** ἠρήμωτο] *vicinarum gentium patebat incursibus* Hier. **40** ἔμεινεν + *imperfectum opus* Hier. οὖν + ἀτελὲς Heikel (cf. Eus., dem. ev. 8,2,62), + οὕτως Routh **41** εἰκοσαετοῦς] καὶ τῆς Eus.² | δὲ < Eus.² | ἔτους...ἑκατοστοῦ] πεντεκαιδεκάτῳ καὶ ἑκατοστῷ Eus.¹ **42** ἔτη + γίνεται Eus.² **43** δὲ¹] τε Eus.¹ **44** οἰκοδομὴ] ᾠκοδομήθη Eus.² | περίτειχος] περὶ τεῖχος Eus.¹ | ὡς προεφητεύθη < Hier. **47s** καὶ²...καταπομπῆς] *et prima eius indulgentia, qua Iudaeorum est laxata captiuitas* Hier. **48s** ἑβδομάδων + εἰς Eus.² **52** τ΄] τριακόσια ἑβδομήκοντα Eus.² | παρατείνουσαν] παρατείνασαν Eus.¹ **52s** Τιβερίου...ἐκκαιδέκατον + *quando passus est Christus* Hier. **52s** ἔτος ἐκκαιδέκατον ~ Eus.², *annum quintum decimum* Hier. **53** εἰς delevimus (sicut Heikel) εἰσὶ Routh | ἔτη ξ΄ + *qui simul faciunt annos quingentos nonagenos, ita ut centum supersint anni* Hier. **54** αἱ < Sync.:A Eus.¹ **55** κατὰ...ἀριθμούς] *iuxta lunarem Hebraeorum supputationem, qui menses non iuxta solis sed iuxta lunae cursum numerant* Hier. **55s** ἀπὸ...βασιλείας] *nam a centesimo et quinto decimo anno regni Persarum* Hier.

from the building of Jerusalem. This took place in the 20th year of Artaxerxes, king of Persia. For Nehemiah his cup-bearer made the request, and received the answer that Jerusalem should be rebuilt, and the order went forth to carry it out. For until that date the city lay desolate. For when Cyrus after the 70th year of the Captivity allowed every one who wished to return voluntarily, those with Jeshua the high priest and Zerubbabel went back, and those afterwards with Ezra, and were at first prevented from building the Temple, and from surrounding the city with a wall, as no order had been given for it; and so there was a delay until Nehemiah and the 20th year of the reign of Artaxerxes and the 115th year of the Persian Empire. And this was 185 years from the taking of Jerusalem. It was then that King Artaxerxes gave the order for the city to be built. And Nehemiah was sent to take charge of the work, and the building was in large scale and surrounded by walls, as it had been prophesied. And from that date to [the coming of] Christ, the 70 hebdomads are completed in our numbering.

For if we begin to count from any other point but this, not only the dates will not agree, but very many absurdities arise. If, for instance, we begin counting the 70 hebdomads from Cyrus and the first Mission, the period will be too long by more than a century, if from the day the angel prophesied to Daniel still longer, and longer still if we start from the beginning of the captivity. For we find the length of the Persian Empire to be 230 years, and of the Macedonians 300, and from then to the 16th year of Tiberius Caesar 60 years.[5]

According to the calculations of the Jews, the 70 hebdomads are completed from Artaxerxes up to the time of Christ. For from Nehemiah, who was sent by

---

5   This calculation shows that the time-span from the proposed *terminus a quo* is roughly correct: 115 years Persians (230–115) + 300 Macedonians + 60 Romans = 475 years. In what follows, Africanus explains the difference between these 475 years and the number 490 ("70 hebdomads") which one would expect from the prophecy. On this problem and the intricate calculations deriving from it, see Fraidl 1883; Schwartz 1895,25–27; Burgess 2006,39–42; Mosshammer 2006,86–89.

ρουσαλὴμ ἀνοικίσων ἐπέμφθη ἔτει τῷ ιε' καὶ ρ' τῆς Περσῶν βασιλείας, αὐτοῦ δ'
Ἀρταξέρξου κ' ἔτει, Ὀλυμπιάδος πγ' ἔτει δ', ἐπὶ τοῦτον τὸν χρόνον, ὃς ἦν
Ὀλυμπιάδος σβ' ἔτος δεύτερον, Τιβερίου δὲ Καίσαρος ἡγεμονίας ἔτος ις', ἔτη
συνάγεται υοε', ἅπερ Ἑβραϊκὰ υρ' ἔτη γίνεται, κατὰ τὸν σεληνιαῖον μῆνα τοὺς
60 ἐνιαυτοὺς ἐκείνων ἐξαριθμουμένων, ὅς ἐστι, ὡς πρόχειρον εἰπεῖν, ἡμερῶν κθ' ∪·
τοῦ κυκλικοῦ ἐνιαυτοῦ τοῦ καθ' ἥλιον ὑπάρχοντος ἡμερῶν τξε' δ', τὴν κατὰ σελήνην δωδεκάμηνον παραλλάσσειν ἡμέρας ια' καὶ δ'.

Διὰ τοῦτο καὶ Ἕλληνες καὶ Ἰουδαῖοι τρεῖς μῆνας ἐμβολίμους ἔτεσιν η' παρ-
εμβάλλουσιν. ὀκτάκις γὰρ τὰ ια' δ' ποιεῖ τρίμηνον. τὰ τοίνυν υοε' ἔτη ὀκταετίαι
65 μὲν γίνονται νθ' καὶ {μῆνες} γ', ὡς τριμήνου ἐμβολίμου τῇ ὀκταετίᾳ γινομένης,
ἔτη συνάγεται ιε'· ταῦτα δὲ πρὸς τοῖς υοε' ἔτεσιν, αἱ ο' ἑβδομάδες συντελοῦνται.

Μὴ δή τις ἡμᾶς τῶν κατ' ἀστρονομίαν ἀριθμῶν ἀπείρους εἶναι νομιζέτω,
τξε' ἡμερῶν καὶ δ' προτεταχέναι αὐτήν. οὐδὲ γὰρ ἀγνοίᾳ τἀληθοῦς, διὰ δὲ τὴν
λεπτολογίαν τὸ ψηφιζόμενον συνετέμομεν.

70 Τοῖς δὲ ἐπ' ἀκριβὲς πάντα πειρωμένοις ἐξετάζειν καὶ τοῦθ' ὡς ἐν βραχεῖ πα-
ρακείσθω. τὸ μὲν ἔτος ἐπίπαν ἕκαστόν ἐστιν ἡμερῶν τξε', καὶ ἡμέρας καὶ νυκτὸς
εἰς ἐννεακαιδέκατον διαιρεθείσης μέρη τούτων τὰ ε'. μεταξὺ δὲ τοῦ λήγειν τὸν
ἐνιαυτὸν ἡμερῶν τξε' δ' καὶ τὸν ἀπὸ ιθ' τῆς νυχθημέρου μερῶν ε' εἰς τὰ υοε'
ἡμέραι τὸ παράλληλόν εἰσιν ϛ' καὶ δ'. ἔτι γε μὴν τὸν τῆς σελήνης μῆνα κατὰ
75 τὴν ἀκριβῆ λεπτολογίαν εὑρίσκομεν κθ' ∪, ἡμέρας καὶ νυκτὸς διαιρεθείσης εἰς
μέρη σλε'. τούτων τὰ ζ' ∪, ἃ γίνεται ἐνενηκοστοτέταρτα τρία. καὶ ταῦτα περὶ
ὀλίγων χρόνων καταγίνεται.

---

test.: Eus.¹ Eus.² Sync.   66 des. Eus.¹: ταῦτα μὲν ὁ προδηλωθεὶς ἀνὴρ εἰς τοὺς τόπους ἐπιβέβληκεν et Eus.²: ταῦτα μὲν οὖν Ἀφρικανός.

59-64 cf. ps. Sym. f. 61ᵛ = Cedr. 343,18-23

56 ἀνοικίσων Eus.¹ sic Di. ἀνοικοδομήσων Eus.² ἀνοικήσων Sync.:Bx ἐνοικήσων Sync.:A | ἔτει τῷ] ἐπὶ τῷ (τὸ AB) Sync. | τῷ < Eus.¹ Eus.² | δ'] τε Eus.¹ Eus.²   **57** Ἀρταξέρξου + βασιλείας Eus.¹ Eus.² κ' ἔτει Sync.:BOTV κ' ἔτη Sync.:AC | ἔτει¹ + καὶ Eus.¹ Eus.² | τούτων τῶν χρόνων Sync.   **58** σβ'] οβ' Sync. | ἔτος¹...ἡγεμονίας < Sync.:T | Τιβερίου δὲ ~ Sync. | ις'] *quintum decimum* Hier.   **59** ἔτη < Eus.² | γίγνονται Sync.:C | σεληνιαῖον Eus.² Sync.:AB σεληναῖον Eus.¹ Sync.:x | μῆνα] δρόμον Eus.²   **60** ὅς ἔστι ὡς Eus.¹ Eus.² ὡς ἔστι Sync. | κθ' ∪] τριακοσίων πεντήκοντα τεσσάρων Eus.²   **61** τοῦ¹] οὕτως τοῦ Eus.¹ | κυκλικοῦ...ἥλιον Sync. τοῦ κύκλου Eus.¹ τοῦ ἡλιακοῦ κύκλου Eus.² | δ' τὴν] διὰ τὸ τὴν Sync.:T | τὴν + γὰρ Eus.²   **62** ἡμέραις Eus.¹   **63** καὶ¹ < Eus.² | ἐμβολίμους ἔτεσιν] ἐμβολιμός ἐστιν Sync.:C   **64** ὀκτάκι Eus.¹ | ποιεῖ τρίμηνον cf. Hier.: *nonaginta dies, hoc est tres menses, efficies* ὀκταετηρίδες Eus.¹ Eus.²   **65** μὲν < Eus.¹ Eus.² | μῆνες γ'] μῆνες delevimus μῆνες γ' Eus.¹ μῆνες τρεῖς Eus.² Sync. ἔτη τρία Routh | τριμήνου + δὲ Eus.¹ Eus.² | γινομένης] γίνονται Eus.¹   **66** συνάγεται < Eus.¹ Eus.² | ιε' ὀλίγων ἡμερῶν ἀποδέοντα γίνεται Eus.¹ ὀλίγων ἡμερῶν ἀποδεόντων γίγνονται Eus.² *plus minusve* Hier. | δὲ] τε Sync. | υοε'] οε' Eus.¹ | αἱ < Sync. | συντελοῦνται < Sync.   **70** ἐπ' ἀκριβὲς] ἀκριβῶς C | βραχεῖ BCOV βραχὺ T γραφῇ A   **72** εἰς Ax καὶ εἰς B | λήγειν Moss. λέγειν ABx   **73** τὸν Moss. τῶν ABx   **76** σλε' Schwartz σε' ABx | ζ' Schwartz ο' ABx | ἃ < x

Artaxerxes to resettle Jerusalem in the 115th year of the Persian empire, the 20th year of Artaxerxes, the fourth year of the 83rd Olympiad, until this time, which was the second year of the 202nd Olympiad, the 16th year of the reign of Tiberius Caesar, there is a total of 475 years.[6] This represents 490 Hebrew years, since they number their years according to the lunar month, which is commonly said to be 29 ½ days. For the cycle of the solar year is 365 ¼ days, and the twelve-month lunar cycle is 11 ¼ days less.[7]

For this reason, both the Greeks and the Jews insert three intercalary months every eight years. For 11 ¼ multiplied by 8 makes a period of three months.[8] Therefore, 475 years come to 59 eight-year periods, remainder three;[9] since there are three intercalary months in an octaeteris, this adds up to 15 years.[10] Added to the 475 years, they make 70 hebdomads.

So let no-one consider us unversed in astronomical calculation for having postulated a calculation of 365 ¼ days. And it is not out of ignorance of the truth, but because of the complexity of the argument, that we have condensed the calculation.

For those who seek to examine everything in rigorous detail, the following will serve as a brief summary.[11] Each year consists of a total of 365 days, and an additional $5/19$ of a day, if we divide day and night into 19 parts. Over a period of 475 years, the difference between the year of 365 ¼ days in length and that of 365 $1/19$ days comes to 6 ¼ days.[12] We find further that a lunar month, according to the most minute computation, is 29 ½ days and an additional fraction of 7 ½ divided by 235 which represents $3/94$ of a day.[13] And this is a matter of a short duration of time.

---

6   There would be 474 years from Ol. 83,4 to Ol. 202,2. The difference is usually explained by the hypothesis that Africanus is counting "inclusively", i.e. including the first *and* the last year. However, this is not normally Africanus' way of calculating. It seems more plausible to assume that he did his calculations on the basis of years from Adam rather than Olympiads: AM 5532 – AM 5057 = 475. For the year AM 5057 as the date of the rebuilding of Jerusalem, see the chronological system in the appendix and the introduction, p. XXIX.
7   Africanus tries to explain the difference between 475 and 490 with the hypothesis that the prophet uses a Hebrew lunar year for his calculation. This year is shorter than the usual solar year. It consists of 12 months, 29 ½ days each, i.e. 354 days; that is 11 ¼ days less than the solar year of 365 ¼.
8   11 ¼ × 8 = 90 days = 3 months.
9   The word μῆνες, attested in all witnesses, must be an early corruption. The original had either nothing (as suggested in the text) or ἔτη (as suggested by Routh). The sense must be that 475 years ÷ 8 = 59, remainder 3 (sc. years).
10 The precise calculation would be: 59 leap years with 3 additional months each = 177 months, which are 14.75 years. In addition, there would be 33.75 days of the remaining three years, which would lead to ca. 14.85 years.
11 In what follows, Africanus confirms his finding by repeating the same calculation, this time on the basis of the 19-year Metonic cycle. For the specifics, see Adler/Tuffin 2002,468f, n. 2.
12 The calculation is correct: $5/19 - 1/4 = 1/76$, and $1/76 × 475 = 6 ¼$.
13 The (correct) equation $7.5/235 = 3/94$ presupposes Schwartz' emendations (see app.; the manuscripts read $70.5/205$ for the first fraction). Over 475 years this would lead to a difference of about 15 days.

Συμβαίνει δὲ τοίνυν ἀπὸ Ἀρταξέρξου βασιλείας ἔτους κ', ὡς ἐν τῷ Ἔσδρᾳ παρ' Ἑβραίοις, ὅπερ καθ' Ἕλληνας ἦν Ὀλυμπιάδος ὀγδοηκοστῆς <τρίτης>
80 τέταρτον ἔτος, μέχρις ϛ' καὶ ι' Τιβερίου Καίσαρος, ὅπερ ἦν Ὀλυμπιάδος σβ' ἔτος β', ἐπισυνάγεσθαι τὰ προειρημένα υοε', ἃ γίνεται καθ' Ἑβραίους ἔτη υϙ', ὡς προείρηται, τοῦτ' ἔστιν ἑβδομάδες ο', καθὰ προεφητεύθη τῷ Δανιὴλ ὑπὸ τοῦ Γαβριὴλ ἡ Χριστοῦ παρουσία.

Εἰ δέ τῳ δοκεῖ τὰ ιε' ἔτη τὰ Ἑβραϊκὰ πλάνην ἐγγεννᾶν, μετ' ἐκεῖνα εἰς ἡμᾶς
85 ἔτη σ' ἐγγὺς καὶ οὐδὲν ἐν μέσῳ παράδοξον ἱστόρηται. δύναται δὲ καὶ ἡ μία καὶ <ἡ> ἡμίσεια ἑβδομάς, ἣν ἐπὶ συντελείᾳ παραλαμβάνεσθαι δεῖν ὑπονοοῦμεν, παρηγορεῖν τὸν ἐπιζητούμενον τῶν ιε' ἐτῶν καὶ κουφίζειν χρόνον. ὅτι τε συμβολικώτερον αἱ προφητεῖαι ἐξενηνεγμέναι τυγχάνουσι δῆλον. ὁπόσον δὲ ἐφ' ἡμῖν, ὀρθῶς οἶμαι τὴν γραφὴν ἐδεξάμεθα, ἐπεὶ καὶ συναιρεῖσθαί πως <ἡ> ἡγου-
90 μένη τῆς ὀπτασίας περικοπὴ δοκεῖ, ἧς ἡ ἀρχή· ἐν ἔτει τρίτῳ τῆς βασιλείας Βαλτάσαρ, ἔνθα περὶ τῆς καθαιρέσεως τῆς Περσῶν ἀρχῆς ὑφ' Ἑλλήνων προδηλοῖ, ἣν διὰ τοῦ κριοῦ καὶ τοῦ τράγου προδηλοῖ· ἡ θυσία, φησίν, ἡ ἀρθεῖσα καὶ τὰ ἅγια ἐρημωθήσεται εἰς καταπάτημα, ἅπερ εἰς ͵βτ' ἡμέρας περιγραφήσεται. εἰ γὰρ εἰς μῆνα τὴν ἡμέραν λογισαίμεθα, ὡς ἀλλαχοῦ κατὰ προφητείαν εἰς ἐνιαυ-
95 τοὺς αἱ ἡμέραι παραλαμβάνονται καὶ ἄλλως ἀλλαχόθι, ἀναλύσαντες ὁμοίως τοῖς πρὸ τούτου εἰς μῆνας τοὺς Ἑβραϊκούς, εὕροιμεν ἂν κ' τῆς Ἀρταξέρξου βασιλείας ἀπὸ τῆς ἁλώσεως Ἱερουσαλὴμ συντελούμενον τὸν χρόνον. ἔτη γὰρ συνάγονται ρπε' καὶ ἐνιαυτὸς εἷς, ἐν ᾧ τὴν πόλιν ἐτείχισεν ὁ Νεεμίας. τοὺς οὖν ρπϛ' ἐνιαυτοὺς μῆνας εὑρίσκομεν ͵βτ' Ἑβραϊκούς, τῆς ὀκταετίας ἀκολούθως τοὺς
100 πρὸς τούτοις ἐμβολίμους τρεῖς μῆνας προσλαμβανούσης. ἀπὸ δὲ Ἀρταξέρξου, ὅθεν ὁ λόγος ἐξῆλθεν οἰκοδομηθῆναι Ἱερουσαλήμ, ο' ἑβδομάδες συντελοῦνται. ἰδίᾳ δὲ περὶ τούτων καὶ ἀκριβέστερον ἐν τῷ περὶ ἑβδομάδων καὶ τῆσδε τῆς προφητείας ἀπεδείξαμεν.

Θαυμάζω δὲ Ἰουδαίων μὲν μήπω φασκόντων ἐληλυθέναι τὸν κύριον, τοὺς
105 ἀπὸ Μαρκίωνος δὲ ἀπὸ τῶν προφητειῶν μὴ προηγορεῦσθαι, οὕτω γυμνῶς ὑπ' ὄψιν τῶν γραφῶν δεικνυουσῶν.

test.: Sync.

78s cf. II Esdr 11,1   81–83 cf. Dan 9,24–27   85–87 cf. Dan 9,27 (?)   90–93 cf. Dan 8,1.5–7.11–14

78 τοίνυν Moss. τῶν ABx   79 τρίτης scripsimus ὀγδοηκοστῆς τέταρτον Scal. ὀγδοηκοστῷ τετάρτῳ AB ὀγδοηκοστοτέταρτον CT ὀγδοηκοστὸν τέταρτον (δ' V) OV   80s   σβ' ἔτος β' AB σβ' ἔτος x   82 δανιηλ ABTCᶜ δᾱδ OV et ante corr. C   84 ἐγγεννᾶν Bx ἐνγεννᾶν A   85 σ' Bx ι' A   85s ἡ μία καὶ ἡ ἡμίσεια ἑβδομάς scripsimus ἡ μία καὶ ἡμίσεια AB α' καὶ ∪ OV α' καὶ κ' T ια' καὶ ἥμισυ C   87 χρόνον ABC χρόνους OTVz   89 ἡ Moss.   91 ὑφ' Bt ἐφ' A   92 ἣν…προδηλοῖ < Oz | κριοῦ CTV κυρίου AB   93 περιγραφήσεται A περιγράφεται Bt   95 ἄλλως TVz ἄλλος ABCO   96 εὕροιμεν Scal. εὕρομεν At εὕρωμεν B | κ' ABC κατὰ OTVz   98 ἐν ᾧ post rasuram C ἐν ᾧ εἰς ABt   99 τοὺς BCV τοῖς AOTz   105 τῶν < At | προηγορεῦσθαι Bt προηγορέσθαι A | γυμνῶς BTV γυμνὸς ACOz

Therefore, it turns out that from the 20th year of Artaxerxes' reign, as it is described in the Hebrews' book of Ezra (which according to the Greeks was the fourth year of the 83th Olympiad[14]) until the 16th year of Tiberius Caesar (which was the second year of the 202nd Olympiad), there are altogether the aforementioned 475 years. As we stated previously, these are 490 years according to the Hebrews, that is 70 hebdomads, in accordance with the *parousia* of Christ as it was prophesied to Daniel by Gabriel.

But if it is someone's opinion that these 15 Hebrew years produce an error, after these events up to our time, nearly 200 years have elapsed and nothing out of the ordinary has been recorded in the interim. However, the one as well as the half-week, which we suppose must be added on to complete the number, could also resolve and allay the chronological problem of the 15 years.[15] For it is clear that the prophecies are put forth in a somewhat symbolic way. As far as we are concerned, however, I believe that we have correctly grasped the Scripture, especially since the preceding section of the vision seems somehow to fit together, the beginning of which is: 'In the third year of the reign of Baltasar', where he foretells the subjugation of the Persian empire by the Greeks, which he clearly alludes to by the ram and the goat: 'The offering', he says, 'having been removed, and the holy places shall be made desolate, so as to be trodden underfoot, which events will be determined in 2300 days.' Now if we reckoned the day as a month (since elsewhere in prophecy days are taken as years, and elsewhere in a different way), and if we converted the days to Hebrew months in like manner as we have done before, we should discover that the period was completed in the 20th year of the reign of Artaxerxes from the conquest of Jerusalem. Altogether the years come to 185 and one additional year, in which year Nehemiah built the wall of the city. Therefore, we discover that these 186 years are 2300 Hebrew months, since the eight-year period consistently receives an additional three intercalary months.[16] Then from the time of Artaxerxes, when the decree went out that Jerusalem was to be rebuilt, the 70 hebdomads are completed. We have proved this separately in more detail in what we have written about the hebdomads and this prophecy.[17]

But I am amazed at the Jews who claim that the Lord has not yet arrived, and that the followers of Marcion deny that he was foretold by the prophecies, seeing that the Scriptures point to this in a way that is obvious to the eyes.

---

14 The manuscripts read Ol. 80,4, which must be emended to 83,4, see above l. 57.
15 This passage remains somewhat obscure (possibly even for Africanus himself: see the remark on the symbolic understanding). Probably, he is dealing with competing explanations where Dan 9,27 (one week, then half a week) played some role.
16 2300 months would be 191.66 years. However, if 69 of them were considered additional months in leap years (23 periods of 8 years, 3 months each), the remaining 2231 months would come almost exactly to 186 years.
17 This could refer to a separate work that Africanus wrote on Dan 9,24–27.

Καὶ μετ' ὀλίγα·
Συνάγονται δὲ τοίνυν οἱ χρόνοι ἐπὶ τὴν τοῦ κυρίου παρουσίαν ἀπὸ Ἀδὰμ †καὶ τῆς ἀναστάσεως† ἔτη ‚εφλα'. ἀφ' οὗ χρόνου ἐπὶ Ὀλυμπιάδα σν' ἔτη ρϙβ',
110 ὡς ἐν τοῖς πρόσθεν ἡμῖν ἀποδέδεικται.

test.: Sync.   110 des. Sync.

108s → T11,7; F54d,9; T93b.c; F94,1–3

108 δὲ < t   109 καὶ τῆς ἀναστάσεως sive delendum quia glossa, sive scribendum καὶ τὴν ἀνάστασιν (cf. Routh et F94)

T93a Ioannes Scythopolitanus (ps. Maximus Confessor), Scholion in Dionysii Areopagitae ep. 7 (97 Cordier = PG 4,544B)

Μέμνηται μὲν καὶ Φλέγων ὁ Ἑλληνικὸς χρονογράφος ἐν τρισκαιδεκάτῳ χρονογραφιῶν ἐν τῇ σγ' Ὀλυμπιάδι, τῆς ἐκλείψεως ταύτης, παρὰ τὸ εἰωθὸς αὐτὴν λέγων γενέσθαι· οὐ μὴν τὸν τρόπον ἀνέγραψε. καὶ Ἀφρικανὸς δὲ ὁ ἡμέτερος ἐν πέμπτῳ χρονογραφιῶν, καὶ Εὐσέβιος ὁ Παμφίλου ἐν ταῖς αὐταῖς μέμνηται τῆς αὐτῆς ἐκλείψεως.

T93b Georgius Syncellus (394,23 – 395,2 Mosshammer)

Φλάκκος Ἀσύλαιος τῆς Ἀλεξανδρείας καὶ Αἰγύπτου ἐπίτροπος ὑπὸ Τιβερίου ἐκπέμπεται. πολλὰ δὲ τοῦ Ἰουδαίων ἔθνους ἐπεβούλευσεν. ὅτι μὲν ‚εφλα', οὐχὶ δὲ ‚εφλγ' ὁ Ἀφρικανὸς λέγων δύο σφάλλεται ἔτη κατὰ τὴν ἀψευδῆ τῶν εὐαγγελίων ὑφήγησιν. πρόδηλον γὰρ ὅτι τῷ λ' ἔτει ἀρχομένῳ που ἢ μικρῷ πρὸς ἢ ἔλαττον διὰ τὸ εἰρημένον, Ἰησοῦς
5 δὲ ἦν ὡσεὶ ἐτῶν λ' παρὰ τῷ μεγάλῳ εὐαγγελιστῇ Λουκᾷ ἐβαπτίσθη καὶ ἐδίδαξε καὶ ἐθεράπευσε πᾶσαν νόσον καὶ πᾶσαν μαλακίαν ἐπὶ τρία ἔτη.

[AB t = x (= COTV) + z (= PQMRS)]   **2** τοῦ...ἔθνους AB τὸ ... ἔθνος t   **3s** πρόδηλον...πρὸς < V, + altera manu V^m **4** τῷ ABCT τὸ Oz | ἀρχομένῳ Bt ἀρχομένου A | εἰρημένον] εἰρημένῳ Oz | Ἰησοῦς Goar^m ῑσ V σι' ABCOz διακοσιοστὸν δέκατον T

And after a few words:

Therefore, from Adam there are altogether 5531 years up to the *parousia* of the Lord [and of the Resurrection],[18] from which time to the 250th Olympiad there are 192 years,[19] as has been demonstrated by us above.

T93a

Phlegon the Greek chronographer also mentioned this eclipse in the 13th book of his *Chronographiae*, in the 203rd Olympiad, saying that it did not occur in the usual way, though he did not record in what respect this was so. **Moreover, our Africanus in the fifth book of his *Chronographiae* recorded this eclipse**, as also did Eusebius [disciple] of Pamphilus.

T93b

Flaccus Asylaeus was dispatched by Tiberius as governor of Alexandria and Egypt. He devised many intrigues against the Jewish nation. **In asserting that it was 5531 and not 5533, Africanus commits an error of two years, according to the inerrant guidance of the gospels. For it is abundantly clear that starting about the beginning of his 30th year – more or less, because of the statement by the great evangelist Luke, 'Jesus was about 30 years of age' – he was baptized and began to teach and treat every disease and every infirmity over a period of three years.**[20]

---

18 The words καὶ τῆς ἀναστάσεως have to be either emended or deleted; in the transmitted form they do not fit in grammatically. If they are not to be corrected in the way suggested by Routh, they might have been a marginal gloss, in an attempt at explaining the word *parousia*, which is typical for Africanus but whose sense was obscure to later generations. Note that "advent" (*parousia*) does not necessarily imply Crucifixion and Resurrection (as Syncellus understood it, see also T93b.c, similarly F94); rather it might mean the beginning of Jesus' public ministry. The Resurrection would then have been one year later (see T93b), that is in AM 5532 = Ol. 202,2 (as attested in T93d, and accepted by most modern scholars, see introduction, p. XXVI).
19 5531 + 192 = AM 5723 (= Ol. 250,1), which is the final year of the *Chronographiae*, attested also elsewhere (see app.), probably the time of its writing.
20 The "short" chronology of Jesus' life (one year of public ministry, according to the synoptic tradition) is also indirectly attested in F22.

T93c Georgius Syncellus (395,8 – 396,4 Mosshammer)

Εἰ δέ τις ἀπιστεῖ τοῖς λεγομένοις περὶ τῆς αὐτῆς πολλαχοῦ λεγομένης, ὅτι ἐν αὐτῇ τὸν θάνατον πατήσας ὁ κύριος ἡμῶν πρωτοκτίστῳ ἡμέρᾳ ζωὴν ἡμῖν ἐκ νεκρῶν ἐπήγασε, σκοπείτω εἰς τὴν ια΄ περίοδον τῶν φλβ΄ κυκλικῶν ἐτῶν κατὰ τὸ σιγ΄ ἔτος τῆς αὐτῆς περιόδου τὴν ιδ΄ τοῦ παρ᾽ Ἑβραίοις πάσχα, καὶ εὑρήσει κατὰ τὴν κγ΄ τοῦ αὐτοῦ Μαρτίου μηνὸς ἐν ἡμέρᾳ παρασκευῇ καταντῶσαν ἐπὶ τὸ
5   σωτήριον πάθος, ὃ ὑπὲρ ἡμῶν ἑκουσίως ὑπέστη, καὶ ταφεὶς ὑπὸ Ἰωσὴφ τοῦ ἐξ Ἀριμαθαίας καὶ Νικοδήμου ἀνέστη τῇ μετὰ τὴν αὐτὴν παρασκευὴν ἐπιφωσκούσῃ τρίτῃ ἡμέρᾳ, μιᾷ σαββάτων, πρώτῃ δὲ τοῦ παρ᾽ Ἑβραίοις Νισὰν πρώτου μηνός, ἥτις ἀεὶ τῇ κε΄ Μαρτίου μηνὸς μία καὶ ἡ αὐτή ἐστιν. ὁ μὲν οὖν Ἀφρικανὸς συμφώνως τῇ ἀποστολικῇ παραδόσει τῷ ͵εφ΄ ἔτει τὴν θείαν χρονολογήσας σάρκωσιν, περὶ τὸ πάθος καὶ τὴν σωτήριον ἀνάστασιν
10 δυσὶν ἔτεσι διήμαρτε, κατὰ τὸ ͵εφλα΄ ἔτος τοῦ κόσμου ταύτην συναγαγών. Εὐσέβιος δὲ ὁ Παμφίλου τὰ ἀπὸ Ἀδὰμ ἕως Ἀβραὰμ γενέσεως, ἢ κατὰ τοὺς χρόνους Νίνου καὶ Σεμιράμεως τῶν Ἀσσυρίων βασιλέων ὡμολόγηται, συντεμὼν ἔτη ͵γρπδ΄ ἐστοιχείωσε τῷ Ἑβραϊκῷ ἐξακολουθήσας καὶ τὸν δεύτερον Καϊνὰν ἔτη ρλ΄ ζήσαντα πρὸ τῆς τεκνώσεως μὴ στοιχειώσας, οὗ ὁ θεῖος εὐαγγελιστὴς Λουκᾶς μέμνηται ἐν τῇ κατ᾽ αὐτὸν γενεαλογίᾳ, ὡς καὶ ἀλλαχοῦ λέλεκται. τὸ δὲ
15 καθ᾽ ἡμᾶς τοῦτο χρονογράφιον ἀπὸ Ἀδὰμ ἕως γενέσεως Ἀβραὰμ ἔτη ͵γλβ΄ περιέχει συμφώνως τῇ θείᾳ Μωυσέως γραφῇ καὶ ταῖς γενεαῖς τοῦ κατὰ Λουκᾶν εὐαγγελίου.

8s → F15,10–14   8–10 → T92,3s

[AB t = x (= COTV) + z (= PQMRS)] **1** περὶ…λεγομένης < Q et Scorialensis 233 | τῆς < z   **2** ἡμῖν < A   **3** φλβ΄ t ,ελβ΄ AB | ιδ΄] ιγ΄ C   **4** εὑρήσει post rasuram C εὑρήσεις ABCOVz εὑρήσης T   **5** ἀριμαθαίας AB ἀριμαθείας t   **6** ἐπιφωσκούσῃ…μιᾷ ABOVz ἐπιφωσκούσης τρίτης ἡμέρας μιᾶς CT | σαββάτων ABT σαββάτῳ COVz   **7** Νισὰν Di. νισσὰν A νησὰν B νησᾶν t   **10** τὸ Bt τῷ A ͵εφλα΄] ͵εφα΄ O | ἔτος Bt ἔτει A   **11** δὲ < AB | ἢ Di. ἡ ABt   **12** βασιλέων AB βασιλέως t | ͵γρπδ΄ ABx ͵γρπα΄ z   **13** ἔτη < AB   **14** αὐτὸν Bt αὐτῶν A   **15** ͵γλβ΄] ͵γτιβ΄ Goar^m cf. p. 105, 6 Moss.

T93d Michael Syrus 5,10 (4, 90b,14–38 Chabot, cf. Barhebraeus [49 Wallis Budge])

9 ܐܟܬܒ scripsimus pro ܐܟ

T93c

Now there may be those who do not believe what we have said about this day in our frequent discussions about it: that on it our Lord trampled upon death, and on the first-begotten day brought forth life for us from the dead. If so, let them examine the 11th revolution of the 532-year cycle in the 213th year of this same cycle, and consider Luna 14 of the Hebrew Passover. And they will discover that on the 23rd of this month of March, on this day of preparation, it corresponds with the Passion of the Savior, which he willingly endured on our behalf. And after his burial by Joseph of Arimathea and Nicodemus, he arose from the dead at dawn of the third day after this day of preparation, on the first day of the week, on the 1st day of the first Hebrew month of Nisan, which is forever one and the same day as 25 March. **So Africanus, in conformity with apostolic tradition, reckoned the divine Incarnation in the 5500th year, but he was in error by two years in dating the Passion and the Resurrection of the Savior, calculating this in AM 5531.**[21] But Eusebius, [pupil of] Pamphilus cut short the years from Adam up to the birth of Abraham, which, as he allows, was at the time of Ninus and Semiramis. In concert with the Hebrew tradition, he computed 3184 years, and did not include in his calculation the second Kenan who lived 130 years before begetting a child; of him, Luke the divine evangelist makes mention in his genealogy, as has been stated elsewhere. But our chronography encompasses 3032 years from Adam up to the birth of Abraham, in harmony with the divine writing of Moses and the generations recorded in the gospel according to Luke.

T93d

From Adam up to the year in which our Savior suffered, there is a total of 5539 years. That year began on a Sunday. If one counts the years from Adam, there are different calculations of which we are aware, and which are neither in agreement among themselves, nor with the years transmitted by the prophets and the Maccabees. Some assign 5500 years from Adam up to the birth of our Savior. Hippolytus, John and Mar Jacob agree with this number of years. And indeed we find that Eusebius accepts it. In another place, he says that there were 5232 years from Adam up to the Passion of our Savior. Others say 5320; **Africanus 5532;** the Hebrews 4000; the Samaritans 4365; the Syrians 4156; and according to the chronological order accepted by many, 5519. Andronicus says that Christ suffered the Passion in the 342nd year[22] of the Greeks; according to others in the 19th year, the first year of the 203rd Olympiad.

---

21 For an explanation of Syncellus' apparently imprecise statement that Africanus dated the Resurrection in AM 5531 (and not 5532), see n. 18 above.
22 The manuscript reads 340, which must be a scribal error (see Chabot 1, 142, n. 3). 342 is confirmed by Bar Hebraeus; Michael himself uses the number 342 a few lines later.

F94 ps. Eustathius Antiochenus, Commentarius in Hexaemeron (55,17–34 Allatius = PG 18,757D)

Γίνεται οὖν ἀπὸ Ἀδὰμ ἐπὶ τὴν τελευτὴν Φαλὲκ ἔτη τρισχίλια. ἐπὶ δὲ τὴν τοῦ κυρίου παρουσίαν καὶ ἀνάστασιν ἔτη πεντακισχίλια καὶ πεντακόσια τριάκοντα ἕν, ὡς λείπειν τετρακόσια πεντήκοντα ἐννέα ἔτη τῆς ἕκτης χιλιάδος. ἔστι δὲ τῆς τοῦ κόσμου συντελείας σημεῖον τὸ σάββατον· καὶ εἰκότως ἐπ᾽ ἐσχάτων τῶν ἡμερῶν ὁ Κύριος ἐπιδημήσας τῷ κόσμῳ ἐν
5 παρασκευῇ πέπονθεν, ἥτις ἐστὶν ἡμέρα ἕκτη, καὶ ταύτης τῆς ἡμέρας ὥρα ἦν ὡσεὶ ἕκτη, ἡνίκα ἐσταυρώθη, τοῦ λόγου σημαίνοντος διὰ τοῦ τῆς ἕκτης χιλιάδος τὸ ἥμισυ· καὶ διὰ τοῦτο ὡρισμένως οὐκ εἶπεν ὥρα ἕκτη, ὑπεμφαίνοντος τοῦ λόγου ὀλίγῳ πλείω τοῦ ἀριθμοῦ ὑπερπαίειν.

1 → F16c,8   1–3 → F93,108s

1 cf. Io. Mal. 2,10; Cat. Gen. 860,1; Proc. G., in Gen. 11 (PG 87/1,315C); Cedr. 28,4–7   1–3 cf. Io. Mal. 10,2   5 cf. Mt 27,62; Mc 15,42; Lc 23,54 | cf. Lc 23,44

F95 Ioannes Malalas 11,2 (204,7–11 Thurn)

Ἕως δὲ τοῦ δευτέρου ἔτους τῆς βασιλείας αὐτοῦ (sc. Traianus) ἦν φαινόμενος καὶ διδάσκων ἐν Ἐφέσῳ, ἐπίσκοπος καὶ πατριάρχης ὤν, ὁ ἅγιος Ἰωάννης ὁ ἀπόστολος καὶ θεολόγος· καὶ ἀφανῆ ἑαυτὸν ποιήσας οὐκέτι ὤφθη τινὶ καὶ οὐδεὶς ἔγνω, τί ἐγένετο, ἕως τῆς νῦν, καθὼς Ἀφρικανὸς καὶ Εἰρηναῖος οἱ σοφώτατοι
5 χρονογράφοι συνεγράψαντο.

1–5 cf. Eus., h.e. 3,23,3s; Chron. Pasch. 470,2–19; Sync. 424,15s; Niceph., chron. syn. 93,12–14; Iul. Pol. 204,5–17; Anon. Matr. 49,10   4s Iren., haer. 2,22,5; 3,3,4

[O] 5 χρονογράφοι O < Chilm. Di.

F96 Georgius Syncellus (439,21s Mosshammer)

Ἀφρικανὸς Αὔγαρόν φησιν ἱερὸν ἄνδρα τοῦ πρώην Αὐγάρου ὁμώνυμον βασιλεύειν Ἐδέσσης κατὰ τούτους τοὺς χρόνους.

1s Eus., can.armen (224,971 Karst) Über Urrha regierte Abgarios, ein ausgezeichneter Mann, *wie Aphricanos berichtet*. Eus., can.Hier (214c Helm; hinc Anon. Matr. 52,3s) Abgarus uir sanctus regnauit Edessae, *ut uult Africanus*. Mich. Syr. 5,6 (1,120,20s Chabot) Eusèbe ne fait point mention de ces choses, mais il dit en abrégé ceci: «A Édesse régna Abgar, homme probe, *comme dit Africanus*.»

1s cf. Cass. Dio 79,16,2

[At = x (= COTV) + z (= MPQRS)] 2 ἐδέσσης post corr. C ἐδέσης ATV αἰδέσης COz | χρόνους ἐποίησεν t

F94 The Millennialist Framework of History[1]

From Adam to the death of Peleg there are, then, 3000 years. Up to the *parousia* of the Lord and his resurrection there are 5531 years; 459 years[2] thus remain of this sixth millennium. The Sabbath is a sign of the consummation of the world. And fittingly the Lord, who came into the world in the final days, suffered the Passion on the day of preparation, which is the sixth day. And it was around the sixth hour when he was crucified, with Scripture signifying by this half of the sixth millennium. Hence, it did not say 'sixth hour' exactly, Scripture indicating that it exceeds the number by a little more.

F95 John the Apostle in Ephesus

Until the second year of his (Trajan's) reign, Saint John, the apostle and theologian, was seen teaching in Ephesus, serving as bishop and patriarch. And after removing himself from sight, he no longer appeared to anyone and up to this day no-one knows what happened, just as Africanus and Irenaeus, the most learned chronographers, have written.

F96 Abgar VIII, King of Edessa[3]

Africanus says that Abgar, a holy man, who bore the same name as the earlier Abgar, was king in Edessa at this time.

---

1 The present text is not directly attributed to Africanus. The specific use of the term *parousia* indicates that the text belongs to the tradition which goes back to Africanus (see F93, 24.29.83. 108). The death of Peleg in AM 3000 and the dating of the *parousia* in AM 5531 are part of Africanus' chronological system (F16c; F25; F93,109f), see Gelzer 1,24f.66f.280; Adler/Tuffin 2002,471, n. 2; Mosshammer 2006,86. Whether the millennialist interpretation of the chronology of the Crucifixion in the final part of the passage (ll. 3–7) originated in Africanus' chronicle is uncertain.
2 Obviously this should read 469.
3 Abgar VIII (AD 177–212).

F97 Symeon Logothetes (cod. Vat. gr. 163, f. 20ʳ ≈ Leo Grammaticus [71,2-11 Bekker] = Theodosius Melitenus [54,6-14 Tafel]) et ps. Symeon f. 79ᵛ-80ʳ = Georgius Cedrenus (441,3-12 Bekker)

Κόμοδος υἱὸς Μάρκου ἐβασίλευσε ἔτη ιβ' μῆνας ε'. [...] ὥς φησιν Ἀφρικανὸς ὁ σοφώτατος· ἐπὶ τούτου Κλήμης ὁ στρωματεὺς ἐν Ἀλεξανδρείᾳ ἐγνωρίζετο· Κλήμεντος δὲ φοιτητὴς Ὠριγένης ἐγένετο. ἀλλὰ καὶ Μοντανὸς αἱρεσιάρχης τότε ἦν, ὃς ἑαυτὸν παράκλητον ἔλεγεν εἶναι.

1-3   Iul. Pol. (226,19 - 228,3 Hardt) *Κατὰ τούτους τοὺς χρόνους Κλήμης ὁ στρωματεὺς ἐπ' Ἀλεξανδρείᾳ ἐγνωρίζετο. κατὰ δὲ τὴν Φρυγίαν αἱρέσεις ξενὰς αὖθις ὁ μισόκαλλος καὶ φιλοπόνηρος δαίμων ἐπιφύεσθαι τῇ ἐκκλησίᾳ ἐνεργεῖ. Μοντανὸν γάρ τινα ἐπήγειρεν λέγειν ἑαυτὸν παράκλητον.* Georg. Mon. cont. (PG 110, 532B) Ἐφ' οὗ (sc. Commodus) *Θεόδοτος, ὁ καὶ πρῶτος τῆς κατὰ Παῦλον τὸν Σαμοσατέα καὶ Νεστόριον πλάνης ἀρξάμενος, καὶ Θεοδοτίων, οἱ αἱρεσιάρχαι, ἐγνωρίζοντο. καὶ Κλήμης ὁ Στρωματεὺς ἐν Ἀλεξανδρείᾳ ἦν. Κλήμεντος δὲ φοιτητὴς Ὠριγένης ἐγένετο. ἀλλὰ καὶ Μοντανὸς αἱρεσιάρχης τότε ἦν, ὃς ἑαυτὸν παράκλητον ἔλεγεν εἶναι.*

1 Κόμοδος + ὁ V | Μάρκου + ζήσας ἔτη λη' ps. Sym. | ε' V Leo Gr. Th. Mel. θ' ps. Sym. Cedr. | ὥς φησιν Ἀφρικανὸς ὁ σοφώτατος marg. Leo Gr. ὡς φησὶ δὲ Ἀ. ὁ σ. ὅτι V Ἀ. δέ φησιν ὅτι ps. Sym. Ἀ. δέ φησιν ὁ χρονογράφος ὅτι Cedr. < Th. Mel.   **2**   τούτου V ps. Sym. Cedr. Κομόδου Leo Gr. Th. Mel. | δὲ < ps. Sym.   **3** ἔλεγεν εἶναι ~ V

F98 Eusebius, Historia ecclesiastica 6,31,2 (586,2-7 Schwartz)

Τοῦ δ' αὐτοῦ Ἀφρικανοῦ καὶ ἄλλα τὸν ἀριθμὸν πέντε Χρονογραφιῶν ἦλθεν εἰς ἡμᾶς ἐπ' ἀκριβὲς πεπονημένα σπουδάσματα· ἐν οἷς φησιν ἑαυτὸν **πορείαν στείλασθαι ἐπὶ τὴν Ἀλεξάνδρειαν διὰ πολλὴν τοῦ Ἡρακλᾶ φήμην**, ὃν ἐπὶ λόγοις φιλοσόφοις καὶ τοῖς ἄλλοις Ἑλλήνων μαθήμασιν εὖ μάλα διαπρέψαντα, τὴν ἐπισκοπὴν τῆς αὐτόθι ἐκκλησίας ἐγχειρισθῆναι ἐδηλώσαμεν.

1-4 = T3a,5-9   **2s** → F46,54s

4 cf. Eus., h.e. 6,26; 6,29,4; 6,35; Eus., can.^Hier 215^h (sub anno 231 p. Chr. n.)

[ATERBDMΣ^arm Λ]   **1** πεποιημένα M   **3** ἑλλήνων ATERM τῶν ἑλλήνων TER Graecorum Λ < Σ^arm

T99 Georgius Syncellus (123,10-12 Mosshammer)

Ἡ ποιμενικὴ σκηνὴ τοῦ Ἰακὼβ ἐν Ἐδέσῃ σωζομένη κατὰ τοὺς χρόνους Ἀντωνίνου Ῥωμαίων βασιλέως διεφθάρη κεραυνῷ, ὥς φησιν ὁ Ἀφρικανός, ἕως τῶν χρόνων αὐτοῦ Ἀντωνίνου ἱστορήσας.

1s = F29,2-4   **2** → T6,20s; T11,5-7

[AB]   **1** Ῥωμαίων βασιλέως B ~ A

F97 Clement of Alexandria

Commodus, son of Marcus, reigned for 12 years, 5 months[1] [...] As the most learned Africanus says:[2] During his reign, Clement, author of the *Stromata*, was becoming known in Alexandria. Origen became a pupil of Clement. Montanus, the heresiarch, was also living at that time. He claimed that he himself was [the] paraclete.

F98 Africanus' Journey to Alexandria

From the same Africanus, there has also come to us the *Chronographiae*, five books in number, a project that was pursued with painstaking accuracy. In this work, he states that he himself set out on a journey to Alexandria because of the great fame of Heraclas.[3] As we stated, Heraclas, very well-known for his discourses in philosophy and other branches of Greek learning, was entrusted with the oversight of the church there.

T99 The End of the Chronographiae[4]

The shepherd's tent of Jacob preserved in Edessa was destroyed by a thunderbolt around the time of Antoninus the emperor of the Romans, as Africanus states, who has written his history up to the time of this Antoninus.[5]

---

1 Lucius Aurelius Commodus (17 March 180 – 31 December 192).
2 It is unlikely that this phrase in Sym. Log., starting with ὡς, refers to the preceding text rather than to the notice on Clement. The previous sentence is different in both relevant witnesses (Leo Gr.: hardships in Rome under Commodus; V: violent death of Commodus). This and the position of the marginal note in the Paris manuscript that was used for the Leo Gr. edition (Paris. gr. 854, fol. 352ᵛ), leaves no doubt that the reference is to Clement (contra Bekker). Ps. Symeon and Cedrenus also understood the text in this sense (continuing with ὅτι).
3 Africanus' visit to Heraclas preceded the latter's service as bishop of Alexandria (232–248), see also introduction, p. XIV, n. 14.
4 This text is both a fragment with information about the tent of Jacob (F29) and a *testimonium* about the end of the *Chronographiae* (given here).
5 For the reign of Elagabalus (218–222) as the endpoint of Africanus' chronicle, see introduction, p. XVII. Since Africanus spent time in Edessa during the reign of Abgar VIII (the Great, see T88, n. 1), it is possible that his original reference to Antoninus was to Caracalla (211–217); both emperors were officially called Marcus Aurelius Antoninus.

F100 Basilius Caesariensis, De spiritu sancto 29,73 (508,20–27 Pruche)

Ἀλλ' οὐδὲ Ἀφρικανὸν τὸν ἱστοριογράφον τὸ τοιοῦτον εἶδος τῆς δοξολογίας παρέλαθε. φαίνεται γὰρ ἐν τῷ πέμπτῳ τῆς τῶν χρόνων ἐπιτομῆς, οὕτω καὶ αὐτὸς λέγων·

Ἡμεῖς γὰρ οἱ κἀκείνων τῶν ῥημάτων τὸ μέτρον ἐπιστάμενοι καὶ τῆς πίστεως οὐκ ἀγνοοῦντες τὴν χάριν, εὐχαριστοῦμεν τῷ παρασχομένῳ τοῖς ἰδίοις ἡμῖν
5 πατρὶ τὸν τῶν ὅλων σωτῆρα καὶ κύριον ἡμῶν Ἰησοῦν Χριστόν· ᾧ ἡ δόξα, μεγαλωσύνη σὺν ἁγίῳ πνεύματι εἰς τοὺς αἰῶνας.

[ACFGKM] **4** εὐχαριστοῦμεν + τῷ πατρὶ KM   **5** πατρὶ < KM

F100 *Final Doxology*

But this form of the doxology was not unknown to Africanus, the historian. For it appears in the fifth book of his chronological epitome, where he states the following:

Those of us who know the weight of those words and are not ignorant of the grace of faith, give thanks to the Father, who granted to us who belong to him Jesus Christ the Savior of the universe and our Lord, to whom be the glory and majesty with the Holy Spirit, for ever.

INDICES

1. Index textuum adhibitorum et locorum citatorum

•• = textus e quibus fragmenta vel testimonia hausta sunt
• = textus qui in tertio apparatu adhibentur (vide p. LVI)

1.1. Biblia sacra

Vetus Testamentum
   (secundum ordinem LXX)
Gen
   1,1–23   F14a
   1,26s   F14a
   2,7   F14a
   4,17–19   F22
   4,25   F18
   4,26   F19
   5,3   F18
   5,3–29   F16a
   5,9   T16f
   5,21   T22a
   5,25   T22a
   5,27   F22
   6,1s   F23,1s
   6,3   F23,11–14
   7,6   F16b
   7,6–16   F23,15–18
   8,4   F23,18s
   8,13–19   F23,20–23
   10,6   F44
   10,13   F44
   10,21   F16d
   10,21s   F24,2s
   10,25   F16c,5s
   11,10–13   T16l; T45
   11,10–26   F16c,2–12
   11,12   T16n
   12,6s   F30
   12,10   F26,2s
   12,11–17   F26,3–5
   12,15   T47,15s
   13,1–11   F26,5–10
   14,1–10   F26,10–13
   14,13   F16d
   18,1–15   F30
   20,1   T27
   29,30   T28c
   33,18–20   F30
   34,15–31   F90a
   34,30–35,5   F30
   35,28   F29
   35,29   F29
   40,1   T47,16s
   41,46   T28b
   41,46s   T32
   41,46–49   T28c
   45,6   T28b; T28c; T32
   47,8s   T28b; T28c
   47,9   T32
   47,28   T41a,28s
   50,25   F30
   50,26   T32; T41a,27s
   50,26a   T33a
Exod
   1,11   T47,16s
   12,6   F93,7
   13,17   T47,17
   13,19   F30
Leu
   21,18   F89,13s

Deut
    31,2   T41a,26s
    33,6–25   F90a
    34,7   T41a,26s
Ios
    24,32   F30
Iud
    2,7   T39a
    2,16–19   T39a
    3,15–30   T36
    3,31   T40
    8,29   T37
    8,30s   T37
    8,35 – 9,2 T37
    9,1s   T37
    9,5   T37
    9,24   T37
    9,28   T37
    12,13   T38
II Regn
    11,21   T37
III Regn
    6,1   T42
    14,20   T69
    14,25   T47,18s
    22,52–54   F90a
IV Regn
    1,1–16   F90a
    12,20–22   F90a
    15,1   F62,6
    15,1–7   F90a
    15,23   T67
    15,27   T68
    18,9–12   T69
    21,18   F70
    22,4   T71
    22,8–13   T71
    23,4–24   T71
    23,29   T47,18s
    23,33–35   F46,204s
    24,18 – 25,21 T77a,5s
    25,1–11   F46,207s
    25,25s   F46,207s
I Par
    3,10–12   F90a
II Par
    20,35   F90a
    26,16–23   F90a
    33,11–13   f70
    34,9ss   T71
    35,8   T71
    35,19   T71
    36,1–4   F72
    36,2–4   F46,204s
    36,11–21   T77a,5s
    36,22s   T78b; F93,36–40
I Esdr
    1,32–35   F72
    1,44   T77a,5s
    2   T78b; F93,36–40
    2,1–11   F34,19–22; F93,47s
    5,1–62   F34,19–22
    5,1–7,5   T78b; F93,36–40
II Esdr
    7–10   F79
    11,1   F93,78s
    12,1   F93,33s
    12,5s   F93,42–44
    12,5–9   F93,34–36
    12,17–13,37 T78b
    15,14   T78b
    23,23–31   F79
Est
    7,1–10   T78b
Idt
    2,1   T75a
    4,8   T75a
I Mac
    1,10   F84
    10,58   T86a
    11,9–18   T86a
II Mac
    3,4–7   F84
    3,22–28   F84

4,4–6	F84	1,16	T7b
4,7	F84	27,45	F93,3–5
Ion		27,51	F93,3–5
1,1–3	F66	27,62	F94
2,1	F66	Mc	
Ier		15,42	F94
1,1s	T71	Lc	
25,11	F34,12–14	3,23–38	T2b
Ez		3,35s	T16n
1,2	T77a,6s	3,36	T16i; T16k; T16m; T16o; T45
Sus			
2 θ	T71	16,16	F93,28
Dan		23,44	F94
1,1–6	T77a,3s	23,54	F94
4,1–5	T77a,1s	24,13	T2d
8,1	F93,90–93	Io	
8,5–7	F93,90–93	19,31	F93,8
8,11–14	F93,90–93	Act	
9,24	F93,26–29	7,16	F30
9,24–27	F78; F93,81–83	7,45–47	T41a
9,25	F93,43s	13,16–23	T41b
9,25 θ	F93,31–33	I Cor	
9,27 θ	F78	15,47	F14a
		Col	
Novum Testamentum		2,3	F93,2
Mt		2,9	F20
1,1–17	T2b		
1,8	F90a		

1.2. Textus antiquitatis et medii aevi

Acusilaus (FGrHist 2)
    F23b   F34,26–29
    F23c   F34,53–56
Aelianus, nat. animal.
    12,3   F46,192
Aelianus, varia hist.
    2,8   F65,177
    4,15   F65,295–297

Agapius Mabbugensis, Historia universalis, ed. Vasiliev
    (PO 5/4, 587,8s V.) ••
        F18
    (PO 7/4, 526,1s V.) ••
        T3b
    (PO 11/1, 132,10 – 133,3 V.) ••
        T91

Aldhelmus Malmesbiriensis, De metris
 69,19–24 F93,54–67

Alexander Polyhistor (FGrHist 273)
 F19a T28a; T28b; T28c; F31
 F101 F34,26–33

Anaximenes Lampsacenus
 → ps. Theopompus

Annianus
 (e Sync.) •• T39b
 (e Elia Nisib.) T16f; T16i; F62,2–17

Anonymus Matritensis, ed. Bauer
 2,12s F16b
 3,6 – 4,4 •• T16m
 9,4 T28b
 14,3–5 T36
 14,8–11 F34,103–105; F56
 14,8–11 • T36
 22,14s F66
 25,4–15 F70
 29,14 – 30,9 F73,8–21
 30,4–6 T75a
 34,3s • F89,33s
 35,5 – 38,11 F73,8–21
 36,15 – 37,7 F81b
 37,8 • F73,19
 46,2 F89,33s
 46,4–6 F87,6–9
 49,10 F95
 52,3s • F96

Anthologia Graeca
 13,14 F65,160
 13,15 F65,192
 16,24 F65,142

Apion (FGrHist 616)
 F2 F34,80–83; T47,9s
 F4 T47,23–25

Apollodorus (FGrHist 244)
 F33 F59a,8–13
 F62 F58a,8–18
 F331 F59a,14–19

ps. Apollodorus (FGrHist 244)
 F86 F51a,32–38

Appianus, bell. civ.
 1,99 F65,291

Aristeas (FGrHist 725)
 F1 F31

Aristodemus (FGrHist 414)
 F1 F65,34s

Aristophanes, Ach.
 519–527 F81a

Aristoteles, Pol.
 2,1274a,34 F65,59

ps. Athanasius fr. (PG 28, 1252–1257)
 1253A • F87,5–12

ps. Athanasius, pass.
 208,5–8 T17

Augustinus, retract.
 2,7,2 T7b; F90c

Aurelius Victor, Caes.
 20,1 T1a

Barhebraeus
 → Gregorius Barhebraeus

Basilius, De spiritu sancto
 29,73 •• F100

Basilius, hex.
 1,5 F14b
 2,8 F22

ps. Basilius, enarratio in proph. Isaiam
 5,141,13 T17

Berossus Babylonius (FGrHist 680)
 F4c F23,19
 F8 F34,14

Callimachus
 fr. 433 F64a; F65,35s

Cassius Dio
 63,14 F65,346–348
 74,1,1s T1a
 79,16,2 F96

Castor (FGrHist 250)
   F2   F51a,9.12–15.16–
               22.23s.25s.27.28–
               30.31–37.32–38.38.
               41s.43–51
   F3   F50,3.5.8.9s.11–14.
               15–21.22–24.25–
               27.32s
   F3,30–33   T49a
   F4   T49b; F54a,6–9.
               10–13.14–19.20–
               24.25–27.33s.35–
               41.42–46.50–57;
               F54b; F54d; T55,
               15–23
   F6   F34,15–18
   F7   F34,26–33

Catena in Genesim, ed. Petit
   574   F19
   699   F16b
   860,1   F16c,8; F94
   865   F16b

Catena in Matthaeum, ed. Cramer
   → Ioannes Chrysostomus

Catena in Ioannem in codice Parisino gr. 209
   2,105 Montfaucon = PG 26,
   1321B ••   T17

Cedrenus → Georgius Cedrenus

Chronicon Epitomon, ed. Pusch
   10,16–26 ••   T16n
   11,1–4   F16c,5s

Chronicon Paschale, ed. Dindorf
   34,17–35,10   F16a
   36,10–16   F16a
   36,17–21 ••   T16g
   43,3–13   F16c,2–12
   64,19 – 65,16 F24,2–10
   65,19 – 66,3 F24,15–20
   66,5–11   F24,10–14
   66,11–13   F24,38–43
   66,15 – 67,3 F24,21–26
   68,1–11   F24,27–31
   80,1–10   F24,24–26
   80,11–16   F24,32–37
   82,12 – 84,14 F43
   86,18 – 87,5 F16c,2–12
   106,21 – 107,3 T28a
   107,14s   T28b; T28c
   109,16s   T33b
   109,17s   T28c
   114,6–11   F33
   155,20s   F59b
   190,12   F66
   193,8–20 ••   T64d
   193,10–12 •• F64c
   200,13 – 201,10
               T69
   204,2–5   F53
   220,8s   F70
   224,11–13   T71
   270,2   T75a
   307,15 – 308,9 ••
               F78
   311,3–9 ••   T78a
   323,17   T83
   336,2   F84
   346,9   T85a
   357,16s   F84
   358,1   T85a
   358,13–15   F87,6–9
   362,2–4   F87,6–9
   390,20s   F84
   391,7   T85a
   403,13   F16b; T16g
   470,2–19   F95
   499,5–7 ••   T2a
   526,7   F16b
   526,7   T16g

Chronographeion Syntomon, ed. Schoene
   84,8   49a
   84,48   T49b
   86   F51a,9–39

86,38 – 87,9	F50,3–36	Cyrillus, fr. Mt	
86,5–34	F51b	12	T91
87,24 – 88,12	T54a,1–60	Cyrillus, Os.-Mal.	
88	F58a,8–18; F59a,1–22	2,133s	T91
		Demetrius (FGrHist 722)	
89	F62,10–14	F1,1	T28a
90	F62,15s; F82,9–26.27–33.38–43.44–55	F1,1–3	T28b
		F1,1–5	T28c
92	F63a,7–15	Didymus Caecus, in Gen., ed. Nautin	
92s	F73,8–21		
94,30	T69	59,2–5	F14a
95,30	F84	144,27 – 145,8 •	
99	F73,8–21		F19
100	F86,1–22	Diodorus Siculus, ed. Vogel	

Cicero, div.

1,19	F15	1,26,1–5	F15

Clemens Alexandrinus, paed., ed. Marcovich/van Winden

		1,68,6	F65,144
		3,60,2	F56
1,12,98,2s	F14a	4,14,1s	F65,6–29

Clemens Alexandrinus, strom., ed. Stählin/Früchtel/Treu

		5,9,2	F65,124
		5,65,2–4	F56
		7,5,1s	F53
1,16,79,6	T54f	7,8,1	F58a,8–18
1,21,101,5	T48a; T48b; F50,3–7	7,9	F59a,8–13.14–19
		7,15,1s	F82,9–52
1,21,101,5s	T47,33s	9,21,1	F34,15–18
1,21,102,5	F51a,9–39	11,1,2	F65,158
1,21,104,1	F50,26s	11,48,1	F65,159
1,21,127,1s	F46,207s; T77a,5s	11,53,1	F65,160
1,21,136,3s	T48a; T48b; F50,3–7	11,65,1	F65,161.175
		11,70,1	F65,162
1,21,136,4	T55,10–12	11,77,1	F65,163
1,21,138,1s	F50,28	11,84,1	F65,166
2,22,131,6	F14a	12,5,1	F65,168
3,6,50	F65,156.168	12,9,5	F65,142

Constantinus Manasses, chron.

		12,23,1	F65,169
4854–4858	F46,192	12,29,1	F65,170

Ctesias Cnidius (FGrHist 688)

		12,33,1	F65,171
F1,1i	F34,51–53	12,37,1	F65,172

Cyrillus, c. Iul.

		12,37,2	F81a
1,10	F51a,9–39	12,45,2	F81a
1,15	T54f	12,49,1	F65,174
		12,77,1	F65,176

12,82,1	F65,177	4,1,1	F65,124
13,34,1	F65,178	4,41,1	F65,140
13,68,1	F65,179	5,1,1	F65,151
13,75,1	F65,183	5,37,1	F65,152
13,82,7	F65,178	5,50,1	F65,153
14,3,1	F65,184	6,1,1	F65,154
14,35,1	F65,185	6,34,1	F65,155
14,54,1	F65,186	7,72,3	F65,63
14,94,1	F65,189	8,1,1	F65,156
14,107,1	F65,190	8,77,1	F65,157
15,14,1	F65,192	9,1,1	F65,158
15,23,1	F65,194	9,18,1	F65,159
15,36,1	F65,195	9,37,1	F65,160
15,50,1	F65,196	9,56,1	F65,161
15,71,1	F65,197	9,61,1	F65,162
15,78,1	F65,198s	10,1,1	F65,163
16,2,1	F65,200	10,26,1	F65,166
16,15,1	F65,201	10,53,1	F65,167
16,37,1	F65,202	10,61,1	F65,168
16,53,1	F65,203	11,1,1	F65,168
16,69,1	F65,204		
16,77,1	F65,205		
16,91,1	F65,206		
17,40,1	F65,207		
17,82,1	F65,209		
17,113,1	F65,212		
19,17,1	F65,216		
19,77,1	F65,217		
20,37,1	F65,218		
20,91,1	F65,221		

Ecloga Chronicarum, ed. Cramer
    233,9–11   F23,18–20

Ecloga Historiarum, ed. Cramer
    170,17s   F16b
    174,22s   T28c
    174,27   T32
    174,30–32   T32
    175,17–23   T57
    176,14–18   F34,71s; F54b; T54c; T55,16s
    177,12 – 178,19 ••   T41a
    187,28 •   F56
    187,29 – 188,2 •   T39a
    188,3s   F56
    188,4–6 •   F34,103–105
    188,27s   F50,28
    189,9–17   T36
    193,31   F50,16–18

Diogenes Laertius
    1,74   F65,100s

Dionysius Bar Salibi, Commentarii in Evangelia, ed. Sedláček
    37,5–26   F90c
    44,7–26 •   F90a

Dionysius Halicarnassensis
    1,71,5   F53; F65,52
    2,58,3   F65,64
    3,1,3   F65,82
    3,36,1   F65,98
    3,46,1   F65,111

Elias Nisibenus, ed. Brooks
    7,35   T16f

8,7–16	T16i	174–178	F59a,8–13
16,27–35	F62,2–17	175–177	F54a,33s

Epiphanius, anc., ed. Holl

110,5	T28b	177–179	F54a,35–41
		178–180	F58a,13–17

Epiphanius, haer., ed. Holl/Dummer

1,224,17 – 225,13		178–184	F59a,14–19
		180	F46,192
	F87,6–16	180–182	F54a,42–46
1,173,16s	F16b	181 ••	F64c; T64d
1,175,18	F23,19	181–189	F63a,7–15
1,180,19 – 181,2		182–184	F54a,50–57
	F31	183s	F62,10–14
2,208,15 – 209,10		185–187	F62,15s
	T17	186	F72

Eratosthenes (FGrHist 241)

		186	F46,204s
F1	F50,28	187	F46,207s; F62,17
F11a	F65,121	189	F74

Euripides

		193 ••	T80b
TGFr 1116	F56	194 •	T78a

Eusebius, Canones

		194 •	F81a
••	T2a; T48a; F64c;	204	F85
	T64d; T80a; T80b,	210	F86,25
vide locos singulos sub can.[armen]		210	F89,54–57
et can.[Hier]		224 ••	T2a
		224,971 •	F96

Eusebius, can.[armen], ed. Karst		Eusebius, can.[Hier], ed. Helm	
156	F51a,16–22	7,10–17 ••	T48a
156–158	F50,9s	7,11 – 10,4	T47,31–36
156–159	F51a,23s	9,19 – 10,4	T54a,2–5
156–197	F46,2–242	12,17s	T55,24–28
158–162	F50,11–14	12,19	T54a,12
159	T54a,8s	14,6–15	T54a,2–5
160	T36; F54a,6–9	15,2–5	T45
160s	F51a,25s	15,4s	F16b; T16h
160–165	F54a,10–13	20–124	F46,2–242
161–163	F51a,27	20,1–5	F51a,12–15
162–167	F50,15–21	21,7s	F51a,12–15
163–165	F51a,28–30	22,3s	F51a,12–15
165–169	F54a,14–19	23,8s	F51a,12–15
166–172	F51a,31–37	25,18s	F51a,16–22
170–173	F54a,20–24	27,2s	F51a,16–22
172s	F51a,38	27,10–13	T49a; F50,3; T57
173–175	F54a,25–27	27,10–15	F34,55s
174–176	F58a,8–12		

29,5s	F51a,16–22	48ᵃ	T54a,17s
29,17s	F50,5	48,8s	F50,15–21;
30ᵉ	T28a		F51a,28–30
31ᵃ	T28b	49,17s	F54a,14–19
31ᵈ	T28c	50ᵇ	F54a,14–19
31,12s	F51a,16–22	50,1s	F51a,28–30
32,7s	F50,8	50,9s	F50,15–21
33ᵃ	T32	51,13s	F50,15–21
33ᵈ	T32	51,26s	F51a,31–37
33,18s	F51a,16–22	52,3s	F54a,14–19
33,25s	F50,9s	52,9s	F50,15–21
35ᵉ •	F34,103–105	54,1–6	F50,22–24
35,21s	F51a,23s	54,2s	F54a,14–19
36ᶜ	T32	54,7s	F51a,31–37
37ᶜ •	F56	55ᵉ	F50,16–18
37ᵈ •	F56	55,9–11	F54a,14–19
37,9s	F50,9s	56,4s	F51a,31–37
38ᶜ •	F56	56,9–11	F50,22–24
38,8s	F51a,23s	57,21s	F54a,20–24
39,25s	F50,11–14	58,11s	F51a,31–37
41ᶜ	T54a,1–60.2–5	58,23s	F51a,31–37
41ᵍ	T54a,6.27.45	59ᵐ	F50,25–27
41ʰ	T54a,6–9.8s	59,3s	F51a,31–37
41ⁱ	T54a,6–9	59,13s	F54a,20–24
41,5s	F51a,25s	59,25s	F50,25–27
41,6–9	F54a,6–9; T57	60ᶜ	F50,28
41,14s	F50,11–14	62ᵈ	F50,32s
42ᵍ •	F56	62ᶠ	F50,32s
42ᵒ	T55,10–12	62,1–3	F54a,20–24
42,16s	F51a,25s	62,1–10	T52
43,20s	F51a,27	62,6s	F51a,31–37
43,25s	F50,11–14;	63,8–10	F51a,38
	F54a,10–13	63,23s	F54a,20–24
44,12s	F54a,10–13	64ᶠ	T54a,25–28
45ʰ	F50,14s	64,14s	F54a,20–24
45ⁱ	F50,15	64,17s	F54a,25–27
45,1s	F54a,10–13	65,1–6	F51a,40s
45,5s	F50,11–14	65,3s	F54a,25–27
45,22s	F50,15–21	65,7–9	F51a,41s.43–51
46ᶠ	F50,15	66,9–11	F58a,8–12; F59a,8–
46,21s	F51a,28–30		13
47,17s	F54a,10–13	66,23–25	F54a,25–27

68,1–4	T54a,31s; F54a,33s	86ⁱ	F46,192
68,8s	F59a,8–13	86ᵏ ••	F64c; T64d
68,19	F58a,8–12	86,22	T68
68,22	F58a,8–12	87,16s	F62,10–14
69,7s	F54a,33s	88ᵉ	T69
70ᵃ	F16b; T40; T42	88,3s	F54a,50–57
70,10s	F59a,8–13	88,7s	F54a,50–57
70,15s	T16h	89,5s	F54a,50–57
70,22	F58a,8–12	89,8s	F63a,7–15
71,8s	F54a,35–41	90,14s	F54a,50–57
72,8s	F54a,35–41	90,18s	F62,10–14
72,12s	F59a,8–13	90,1s	F54a,50–57
72,22	F58a,8–12	90,7	F63a,7–15
74,16s	F58a,13–17; F59a,8–13	90,26	F63a,7–15
		91,7s	F54a,50–57
74,22s	F54a,35–41	91,21s	F62,10–14
76,25s	F54a,35–41; F59a,8–13	92,3s	F54a,50–57
		92,10s	F63a,7–15
77,14s	F58a,13–17	92,19s	F54a,50–57
79,1s	F59a,14–19	93,12–21	F54a,58; F54d
80,10s	F59a,14–19	94,16s	F63a,7–15
80,15s	F54a,35–41	95,8s	F62,15s
81ᶜ	T49b	96ᵃ	T71
81,8s	F58a,13–17	96,21	F62,15s
81,18s	F54a,35–41	97ᵍ	T54f
82,15s	F59a,14–19	97,2s	F63a,7–15
82,24–26	F54a,42–46	98ᵇ	T77a,1
83ᵃ⁻ᵇ	T49b	98,8s	F63a,7–15
83,7–10	T49b	99ᵍ	T54f
83,11s	F62,10–14	99,9s	F62,17
83,16s	F59a,14–19	102,9s	F63a,7–15
83,21–23	F58a,13–17	103,13–18	F63a,2–6; F74
84ᵃ	F66	104ᵇ	F74; T75a
84,15s	F54a,42–46	104ᶜ	T75a
85,3s	F59a,14–19; F62,10–14	111ᵍ	F79
		113ᵃ ••	T80a
85,21–23	F59a,14–19	113ᶜ–114ᵉ •	F81b
85,24	F63a,7–15	114ᵈ •	F81a
85,24s	F54a,42–46.45–48	114ᶠ •	T78a
86ᵇ	T54a,45–48	114ᵍ •	F81a
86ᵇ⁻ᵈ,ʰ ••	T64d	114ʰ–115ᵃ •	F81a
86ᶠ	F58a,5s	115ᵇ	F81b

115ᶜ •	F81b	32,28	F62,17
115ᵈ •	F81a; F81b	32,35 – 33,7	F63a,7–15
115ᵉ •	F81a	33,8s	F74
124ᵃ	F73,7.22	33,10–29	F73,8–21
126ʰ	T83	33,12	T75a
137ᵉ	F84	34,10–13 ••	T80c
145,25s ••	F85	34,27 – 35,4	T36
153ᶠ	F87,6–9	38,7 – 39,21	F16a
160ᵃ	T78b	38,22–26	F22
162ᵉ	F89,36	38,31–34	F16b
162ʰ	F89,50–52	39,18s	F22
163,17–19	F86,25	39,28	T16h
163ᵃ	F89,54–57	40,21 – 41,4	F16a
163ᶠ	F86,25; F89,50–52	41,1s	F22
166ᵃ	F89,59s	41,10	T16h
167ᵈ	F89,60s	41,33 – 42,28	F16c,2–12
167ᵉ	F89,61s	42,1	T16i; T16k; T16l; T16m
174,5	F16b		
174,5	T16h	42,1s	T16i
211ᵃ	T1a	42,32s	T45
212ᶜ	T1a	42,33	T16o
212ᵍ	T1a	43,4–22	F16c,2–12
212ˡ	T1a	43,6	T16i; T16k; T16l; T16m
214ᶜ •	F96		
214ʰ ••	T2a	43,29 – 44,13	F16c,2–12
215ʰ	T3a; F98	43,31	T16i; T16k; T16l; T16m
250,23	T16h		
250,23s	F16b	45,20–22	T16o
250,24–26	T92	45,20–28	F16d; T16h
		46,29	T28b

Eusebius, Chronica
  ••   T41a; F65; T78a; T80c; F85,
vide locos singulos sub chron., ed. Karst, necnon Ecl. Hist., Exc. Eus., Chron. Pasch.

Eusebius, chron., ed. Karst

4,8 – 6,12	F15	46,38 – 48,8 ••	T41a
11,35 – 12,2	F23,19	47,22 – 48,8	T16k
15,13	T75a	48,24 – 49,29	T41b
31,1	49a	52,12	T39a
32,21–25	F62,10–14	53,25–31	T40
32,26s	F62,15s	61,11s ••	F85
		61,25–27	F87,6–9
		63,23–27	F43
		63,31 – 64,7	F43c
		64,11–14	F44
		65–69	F46,2–242; T46a
		67,28 – 68,2	T46b; T47,28–31

68,3	T46d; T47,1
68,3s	T46c; T46f
68,4s	T46g
68,34s	F46,192
75,18	T86a
75,19 – 80,6	F86,1–22
76,2	T86a
81,15–23	F51a,32–38
81,25	F51a,9
81,25–29	F51a,9
81,30 – 82,1	F51a,12–15
82,2–8	F51a,16–22
82,9s	F51a,23s
82,11–13	F51a,25s
82,16	F51a,27
82,18–20	F51a,28–30
82,21–29	F51a,31–37
82,31	F51a,38
82,32s	F51a,40s
82,33s	F51a,41s.43–51
83,1–9	F51a,43–51
83,28	F50,3
83,28s	49a
83,31s	F50,5
83,33	F50,8
84,1–3	F50,9s
84,4–9	F50,11–14
84,10–13	F50,3–14
84,11–13	F50,15
84,14–18	F50,15–21
84,23–27	F50,22–24
84,28s	F50,25–27
84,30–32	F50,32s
85,3 – 88,24	T54a,1–60
85,15–17 •	F34,68–70; F54b; T55,16–23
85,15–17	T54c
85,15 – 86,23	F54b; T55,15–23
86,15s	F54a,6–9
86,15–22	T55,24–28
86,20–22	T36
86,23–29	F54a,10–13
86,24s	F50,15
86,30 – 87,8	F54a,14–19
87,3–5	F50,16–18
87,8–18	F54a,20–24
87,19–23	F54a,25–27
87,27s	F54a,33s
87,32 – 88,7	F54a,35–41
88,7	T49b
88,9–17	F54a,42–46
88,20–24	F54a,50–57
88,25–28	F54d
89,4–8	F50,28s
89,9 – 103,28 ••	F65
104,6–18	F59a,8–13
104,19–26	F59a,14–19
104,35 – 105,4	F59a,8–13
105,24–27	F58a,8–12
105,28s	F58a,13–17
105,30s	F58a,5s
106,7–16	F58a,8–18
106,17s	F58a,5s
107,9	F74
107,17 – 109,7	F82,9–52
109,8 – 114,17	F82,9–52
131,22–25	F53
131,22–28	T52
136,30s	F53

Eusebius, dem. ev., ed. Heikel

5,9,7 •	F30
8,1,44 •	F87,7–9
8,2,46–54 ••	F93
8,2,73	F85

Eusebius, ecl. proph., ed. Gaisford

3,26 (151,10–153,11 G.) ••	F93
3,26 (158,5–8 G.) ••	F87a

Eusebius, fr. Lc. (PG 24,529–606)
   540D   F31
Eusebius, h.e., ed. Schwartz
   1,6,2s ••   F87a
   1,7   T7b
   1,7,1   T2c
   1,7,11 •   F87,5–12
   1,13,5   T88
   3,23,3s   F95
   6,16,4 –17 T1b
   6,26   T3a; F98
   6,29,4   T3a; F98
   6,31,1–3 •• T3a
   6,31,2 •• F98
   6,35   T3a; F98
Eusebius, onomasticon, ed. Klostermann
   1,1   F23,19
   237   F30
Eusebius, praep. ev., ed. Mras/des Places
   3,8,1   F56
   9,11   F23,19
   9,21,1–3   T28b
   9,21,1–5   T28c
   9,21,1s   T28a
   9,25,1   F31
   10,9,6   F50,28
   10,10,1 – 10,23, 6 ••
             F34
   10,14,5   F66
   10,14,5 • F64a
   10,14,15   F81b
Eusebius, reg. ser.^{armen}, ed. Karst
   146   F51a,9–39
   148   F50,3–21
   148s   T54a,6–60
   150   F58a,8–18; F59a,1–22
   150s •   F82,9–26
   151   F63a,7–15
   151 •   F82,27–33.38–43. 44–55
   152   F62,2–17; F73,8–21
   152s   F86,1–22
Eusebius, reg. ser.^{Hier}, ed. Schoene
   26   F51a,9–39
   26s   F58a,8–18
   27   F82,9–26.27–33. 38–43.44–55
   28   F62,2–17
   29   F50,3–21; F86,1–22
   30   F59a,1–22; F63a,7–15
   30s   T54a,6–60
Eusebius, v. C.
   3,53   F30
Eusebius Emesenus
             F19
ps. Eustathius, in hex., ed. Allatius (= PG 18,708–793)
   708A •   T48a
   757D ••   F94
   761B–D   F26,7–22
   761C •   F26,13–15
   777D–780A ••
             F30b
Excerpta Barbari, ed. Frick
   191,13–15 F16c,5s
   205,24   F16d
   222,17–19 T28b
   228,6–9   F34,103–105; F56
   228,6–9 • T36
   228,12–15 • F56
   234,13s • T39b
   234,25 – 236,3
             F24,15–20
   236,4–22   F24,21–26
   238,3–5   F24,32–37
   254,3–6 • F64a
   258, 1–5 • T77a,3s
   261,27 – 268,23

	F73,8–21	135,16–19	F51a,32–38; F51b
264,13s •	F79	135,20–26	F51a,43–51
264,16–18 •	F78	139,12–18	T54f
266,1–14 ••	F81b	140,5–16	F50,28s
276–280	F86,1–22	140,17 - 153,21 ••	
282,12	49a		F65
284,21–24	T49b	159,10s ••	F85
284,26 - 286,9 ••			

Excerptor anonymus in calce chronici Hieronymiani

	F43a	••	T6
286,10–19 ••	F43c		

Expositio officiorum ecclesiae

286,20s •	F46,2–15	1,8	F87,6–16; F90c
286,22 •	F46,17–32		

Florilegium anonymum in codice Parisino gr. 1115

286,23 •	F46,34–48	f. 224^v–225^r ••	F14a
286,24 •	F46,62		

Georgius Cedrenus, ed. Bekker

286,26 •	F46,76–85	7,2–21 •	F14b
288,3 •	F46,91	16,16	F18
288,18 - 292,3 ••		17,9–12	F19
	F50	18,11–13	T17
292,4 - 296,2 ••		20,18s •	F23,18–20
	F51a	21,14–17	F44
296,3 - 300,12 ••		22,4	F16c,8
	F54a	23,2	F44
302,14–17	T52	26,15 - 27,2	F54b; T55,10–12
304,1–24 ••	T58a	27,1s •	F44
304,25 - 306,22 ••		27,21	T16h
	F59a	27,21–23	F16b
306,23 - 310,24 ••		28,4–6 •	F16c,8
	F82	28,4–7	F94
310,25 - 312,17 ••		28,20 - 29,12 ••	
	F63a		F24b
312,18 - 314,18 ••		36,1–10	F43
	F62	46,17–18	T61
314,19 - 316,18		49,11–13 •	F16d
	F73	51,1s	T27
324,11–13	F87,6–9	51,5–14 •	F26,7–15

Excerpta Eusebiana, ed. Cramer

120,3 - 125,29		51,14–23 •	F26,16–22
	F86,1–22	59,15 - 60,3	T28c
133,11–28	F82,9–52	59,17–19	T28a
134,12 - 135,28		59,20 - 60,3	T33b
	F51a,9–50	62,8–10	F29
134,6–10	T57		

62,12–14	T32
62,16	T32
62,16s	T33a
76,4s	T48a; T48b; F50,3–7
76,23 – 77,3 ••	F31
126,8–11	F31
143,3–6	F50,3–14
143,10–14	F34,71s; F54b; T54c; T55,16s
144,5	F51a,9
144,5–8	F51a,32–38; F51b
144,22 – 145,2	T54a,8s
145,17 – 146,1	T54f
146,17s •	T36
149,1s	T40
149,1–5	T39a
186,2s	F66
187,4s	F66
187,9s •	T67
187,10s •	T68
189,9s	F66
189,12–19	F53
198,7–17 •	T77a,3s
212,16–18	F50,19–23
213,10	F50,19–23
214,3–7	F50,24–32
215,23 – 216,2	F58a,8–18; F58b
216,3–6	F60
216,6–8	F59a,1–22
216,7s	F59b
239,12–15	F63b
242,7–16	F63a,3s
242,24 – 243,6	F74
243,7–12	F73,8–21
249,20 – 252,6	F73,8–21
252,7–12 •	F73,2–6
252,21 – 256,20	F73,8–21
255,13s •	F81a
257,7s •	F62,2–4
284,14	F86,1–22
284,19–22 •	F86,20
289,17–23	F86,1–22
290,12 – 292,7	F86,1–22
291,1–3	F86,1–22
293,11–18	F87,6–16
331,16 – 332,8 •	F93,3–19
343,18–23	F93,59–64
441,3–12 ••	F97
441,17–21 ••	T1b

Georgius Monachus, ed. de Boor/ Wirth

10,5	F18
11,17 – 12,8	F24,2–10
13,4–10	F24,27–31
20,6–17	F63a,3s
20,18s	F73,4s
20,19s	F63a,5s.17s; F63b
20,21–22	T75a
40,17–19 •	T48a
43,16s •	T17
47,15–18	F23,19
112,11s	T28a
115,17	T28b
165,15 – 166,4	F59b
235,10 – 237,2	F70
251,4	F66
262,12–14	T67
262,16–18	T68
274,20s •	T75a

Georgius Monachus continuatus, ed. Muralt

29,10–13 = PG 110,84A •	T48a

180,1–6 = PG 110,304BC ••
            F76
PG 110,532B •
            F97
PG 110,545B •
            T3a
360,4–6 = PG 110, 552C ••
            T4a
Georgius Syncellus, ed. Mosshammer
    3,1–18 ••   F14b
    10,7–11 ••   F19
    17,28 – 18,10 ••
                   F15
    18,11–20   F15
    19,1–8   F43
    19,9–17   F43c
    19,24 – 20,4 ••F23
    20,5–13 ••   T22a
    20,29s (not. marg.) ••
                   F21
    21,1–8 ••   F22
    21,27 – 22,10 ••
                   F23
    31,28 – 32,1   F23,19
    36,29s   T16k
    37,8–15 ••   T39b
    38,21–25   F44
    40,26–31   F15
    56,24–26   F43
    56,26s   F43c
    58,10–19   F44
    59,6–26 ••   T45
    59,27 – 69,12 ••
                   F46
    64,5s •   F46,54s
    65,18–20 ••   T46a
    68,20 – 69,7   T47,28–31
    68,21–30   T46b
    69,1–7 ••   T46b
    69,13–17 ••   T46d
    69,14s   T46f

69,18 – 71,7 •• T47
71,7 – 73,11 •• F34
73,12–18 ••   T48a
73,12–18   T47,31–36
75,13–15 ••   T57
76,22–26 ••   T46f
76,28 – 87,8 ••F46
77,1–23 ••   T46c
78,4 – 79,22 ••T55
78,18–25 ••   F54b
78,19s ••   F34
79,23–28   T46g
79,29 – 80,2 ••T46g
81,16–18 ••   T46e
89,28 – 90,7 ••T16k
91,1–11••   T16e
91,23 – 92,4 ••F16a
92,8–26   F16a
92,22s   F22
92,30 – 93,14   F16a
93,13s   F22
93,17–34   F16a
93,31s   F22
94,4–14 ••   T16h
94,15–17 ••   F16b
94,20–23   F16b
96,13–18 ••   T16l
97,4–15 ••   F16c
97,16–18 ••   F16d
97,20 – 98,13   F16c,2–12
97,22   T16i; T16k; T16l;
                T16m
97,22s   T16i
98,17   T16o
98,20 – 99,6   F16c,2–12
98,22   T16i; T16k; T16l;
                T16m
99,12–30   F16c,2–12
99,14   T16i; T16k; T16l;
                T16m
100,32–34   T16o
100,32 – 101,3 F16d; T16h

102,17	F44	143,25 – 144,3 •	
104,7–12	T49b		F51a,28–30
104,16–23 ••	T16o	144,5–12	F50,3
105,3–5 ••	T16p	144,12–14	F50,3–14
109,23–28	F51a,9	144,14s	F50,15
109,24–26	F34,1s	144,15s	F50,3–21
109,24–26 •	F34,1s	144,17–24	F50,22
110,1–7	F51a,4–8	144,25–27	F50,24s
110,4s	F51a,32–38	144,27	F50,32
110,8–13	F51a,32–38	144,27s	F50,33s
110,20s •	F51a,9	145,1–3	F34,92
112,16–21 ••	F16d	145,4s •	F50,3
112,22 – 113,2 ••		145,4–13 ••	T49a
	T16q	145,14 •	F50,5
113,25s ••	T27	172,24 – 173,10 •	
114,1–24 ••	F26		F51a,31–37
116,8–16 •	F51a,12–15	173,12 •	F50,8
117,20	T49a	173,13–17	T55,24s
119,14–23 •	F51a,16–22	173,15 – 174,10 ••	
120,18–21 ••	T28a		F34
120,22	T28a	174,19s •	F50,9s
121,8–13 ••	T28b	174,22s •	F34,103–105
122,1–3 ••	F33	175,3–15 ••	F56
122,4–7 ••	T33b	175,7–8 ••	T56a
123,8–12 ••	F29	176,4–6	F30
123,10–12 ••	T99	177,21s •	F51a,38
123,13–21 ••	F30a	178,1s	F51a,41s; F51a,43–51
125,1–8	T46b		
125,25–28 •	F51a,23s	178,3 •	F51a,40s
125,29s •	F51a,27	178,5–9 •	F50,11–14
126,10–17 ••	T32	178,13–16 •	F50,15
127,24–28 ••	T33a	179,7–16 •	F54a,6–9
128,1–3 ••	F33	180,20–24 ••	T36
131,7–16 ••	T22b	182,13–20 •	F50,15–21
132,15–22 ••	T16i	184,6–24 •	F54a,10–13
133,23 – 134,28		184,10s	T55,24–28
	T28a	186,20–24 ••	T37
134,2–13 ••	T28c	188,9–17 •	F50,22–24
134,14–28	T28c	188,24 – 189,6 •	
140,9–15 ••	T48b		F54a,14–19
143,22–24 •	F51a,25s	190,16 – 191,12	
			F34,92

193,9s ••	T38	231,10 – 232,10 •	
193,20 – 194,2			F65,8–37
	T49b	233,9–17 ••	T64e
198,27 – 199,4 •		233,11–15 ••	F64a
	F50,25–27	233,15–17 ••	F64b
199,27 – 200,2 •		233,19–27 •	F62,10–14
	F50,32s	234,1–18	F82,9–52
200,25 – 201,3		235,18–20	F90a
	T52	238,21–24 ••	F66
201,22 – 202,20 •		239,8s ••	T67
	F54a,20–24	239,12–19 ••	T68
203,25 •	T39b	240,2–31	T68
204,1–9 ••	T39a	241,15–25	T69
204,4–8	T41a,8–15	241,28 – 242,3 ••	
204,21–28 ••	T41b		T69
205,17–23 ••	T40	247,16–28	F73,8–21
208,6–22 •	F54a,25–27	249,20–24	F44
208,23–29 •	F54a,33s	250,21 – 251,16 •	
209,2–12 •	F58a,8–12		F54a,50–57
209,20–29	F59a,8–13	251,17–29 ••	F54d
209,29 – 210,4		252,11s •	F62,10–14; F62,15s
	F59a,14–19	252,14–20	F82,9–52
210,10–16	F59a,8–13	253,29	T54f
210,25 – 211,5 •		254,7–20	F70
	F59a,8–13	255,8	T71
211,16	F50,28	255,18s	T71
213,1–5 ••	T42	256,16s	T71
217,6–20 •	F54a,35–41	257,13–18 ••	F72
217,18s ••	T54e	258,2–6	F46,204s; F72
217,18–20 ••	T49b	259,25–29	F46,204s; F72
217,22 – 218,7 •		260,20s	T77a,2–4
	F58a,13–17	260,23–25	T71
218,9–22 •	F59a,14–19	261,14–19 ••	T77a
220,20 – 221,6	F90a	265,29 – 266,8 ••	
221,16s	T69		T77a
224,16–23	F90a	268,18–25	F46,207s
230,8–10 •	F53	275,22s •	F62,10–14; F62,17
230,8–13	T52	277,12–19 ••	T78b
230,18	T52	278,9–18	F73,8–21
230,20 – 231,4 •		278,20 – 283,24	
	F54a,42–46		F73,8
231,5–10 •	F65,38–40	281,13s	F74

282,18 – 283,2 ••		325,17 – 327,6	
	T75a		F82,9–52
282,18s	F74	327,7 – 329,10	
285,25 – 286,4			F86,1–22
	F82,9–52	330,1–6	T83
287,1s •	F65,121s	334,1–15 ••	F84
287,1s	F65,121	340,20 – 341,10	
287,2–5 •	F65,130–132		F82,9–52
287,2–5	F65,130–132	341,11 – 342,33	
287,11–20 •	F63a,7–15		F86,1–22
287,21–26 •	F63a,2–6	348,29 – 349,4 ••	
287,21–26	F74		T85a
288,24 – 289,10		349,10–18 ••	T86a
	F73,8–21	349,10 – 350,6	F86,1–22
289,5s •	T75a	356,23 – 357,4 ••	
295,15	F73,8–21		F87b
296,1–13	F82,9–52	365,12 •	F89,36
297,11–15 •	F81b	365,13–15 •	F89,47–54
297,18 – 298,3 •		367,23 – 368,5 •	
	F81b		F89,7–16
298,12–19 ••	F79	369,6–9 •	F89,18–22
298,21–26	F79	369,14–23 •	F89,13–17
299,13s •	F93,43s	369,23 – 370,5 •	
299,19–24 ••	T80d		F89,20–29
299,25–30 •	T78a	371,1 – 373,10 ••	
300,28 – 302,6	F73,8–21		F89
304,10–13 •	F81a	373,11–16 ••	T89a
304,18–23	F81b	375,4–6	F89,53s
304,25–28	F82,9–52	375,4–6 •	F86,22s
306,7 – 308,6	F73,8–21	375,12–16 •	F89,18–22
306,15–17 •	F65,180–182	375,24–26 •	F89,48s
307,12s •	F73,19	379,24s •	F89,59s
307,18s •	F73,19	380,2–5 •	F89,60s
309,8–19 ••	F81a	391,1 – 393,30 ••	
310,15 •	F65,187		F93
313,9 – 324,28	F82,9–52	394,23 – 395,2 ••	
314,16	F89,53s		T93b
314,16 •	F86,22s	395,8 – 396,4 ••	
314,16–24	F73,7.22; F93,51s		T93c
314,21–24 •	F73,22s	424,15s	F95
321,23–31	F86,1–22	434,11–21 ••	T1a
		439,15–20 ••	T2d

439,21s ••	F96
445,27 – 446,7 ••	
	T5

Gregorius Barhebraeus, Chronographia, ed. Wallis Budge

15	T39a
16s •	T39b
26–27 •	T77b
35	T80
40 •	T83
49 ••	T93d
59 •	T2a

Gregorius Barhebraeus, Historiae Dynastiarum, ed. Pococke

36	T39a
42	T39b

Gregorius Barhebraeus, Horreum Mysteriorum, ed. Carr

3,9–12 ••	F90b
105 •	F90a
134,13–18 ••	F90c
136,4–6 ••	F90c

ps. Gregorius Nyssenus, hom. 1 de creatione hominis

28,13 – 31,5	F14a

ps. Gregorius Nyssenus, imag.

1328BC	F14a

Herodotus

1,214	F74; T75a
2,41	F34,56
2,102	F46,104–108
2,104	F34,83–86
2,124	F46,52s
2,162	F34,83–86; T47,9s
3,36	F74
3,66	T75a
5,71	F65,99

Hellanicus Lesbius (FGrHist 4)

F47	F34,26–33

Hieronymus, Canones
→ Eusebius, Chronica et Canones

Hieronymus, Commentaria in Danielem, ed. Glorie

3,9,24 ••	F93

Hieronymus, Commentaria in Matheum, ed. Hurst

9,46–56 ••	T7b

Hieronymus, Epistulae, ed. Hilberg

70,4 ••	T7a

Hieronymus, De uiris illustribus, ed. Ceresa-Gastaldo

63 ••	T2b

Hieronymus Aegyptius (FGrHist 787)

F2	F23,19

Hilarianus, curs. temp.

164,5s	T40

Hippolytus, chron., ed. Bauer/Helm

23–32	F16a
34s	F16b
35	T16h
36–41	F16c,2–6
38s	T16i
616–619	F16c,7–12
621	F16d
668	T69
679	F46,207s; T77a,2–4
684	T78b
685	T78b
698	F15
702–715	F73,8–21
741	T71
742–756	F86,1–22

Hippolytus, Dan.

1,3,4–8	T77a,5s
1,6,1s	T77a,2–4
4,3	F73,7; F73,22
4,23,3	F15; T92
4,24	F73,7; F73,22

Hippolytus, haer.

285,11	T28b

Hippys Rheginus (FGrHist 554)

F3	F65,100s

Homerus, Od.
 4,126   F46,163
Iamblich, vit. Pythag.
 7,35   F65,141
Ioannes Anagnostes (cod. Athen. Bibl. Nat. 2492, f.108^v–116^r)
 f. 109^r F14b
 f. 115^r T40
 f. 115^v F16d; F66
Ioannes Antiochenus, Historia chronica, ed. Roberto
 fr. 1 (app.) • T10
 fr. 1,13s F18
 fr. 2,17–23 F23,18–20
 fr. 2,18s F16b
 fr. 4,1–19 F24,2–10
 fr. 4,20–22 F24,15–20
 fr. 4,22–26 F24,10–14
 fr. 4,26–28 F24,38–43
 fr. 4,29–32 F24,21–26
 fr. 6.1   F24,27–31
 fr. 6.2,4–13 F24,24–26
 fr. 6.2,14–24 F24,32–37
 fr. 7.1–2 F15; F43
 fr. 10,15–19 F50,16–18
 fr. 14–16 T61
 fr. 18,8s F16d
 fr. 23.1 •• T54c
 fr. 23.1   F54b
 fr. 23.3   F51b
 fr. 24.1   F34,103–105; F56
 fr. 24.3,2–4 T54a,8s
 fr. 24.3,2s • F54a,8s
 fr. 24.4,4 • T54f
 fr. 50   F70
ps. Ioannes Antiochenus, ed. Roberto
 fr. 1*,1–4 • F34,43
 fr. 1*,5–9 • F34,97–101
 fr. 1*,10–14 • F34,77–80
 fr. 6 *   F54a,14–19
 fr. 9*   T61
 fr. 12*   T61

 fr. 18*   F54a,20–24
 fr. 20*   F54a,25–27
 fr. 22* • F65,8–10
 fr. 23* •• F43b
 fr. 24* •• F44
 fr. 25* • F46,22s
 fr. 26* • F46,27s
 fr. 27* • F46,80
 fr. 28* • F34,51–53
 fr. 29* • F46,104–107
 fr. 30* • F46,192–194
 fr. 33* • F65,269s
 fr. 34* • F65,86
 fr. 35* • F65,11
 fr. 36* • F65,142s
 fr. 37* • T75a
Ioannes Chrysostomus, in: Catena in Matthaeum, ed. Cramer
 1,17 (9,6–16 C.) ••
     F90a
Ioannes Chrysostomus, hom. in Gen.
 21 (PG 53,181,23–25)
     T22a
Ioannes Chrysostomus, hom. in Mt.
 4 (PG 57,39,33–41)
     F90a
Ioannes Chrysostomus, hom. in Io.
 85 (PG 59,459)
     T17
Ioannes Damascenus, Sacra parallela, recensio secundum cod. Vat. gr. 1236
 PG 95,1436C ••
     F70
Ioannes Lydus, De magistratibus populi Romani, ed. Bandy
 1,2 ••   T52
Ioannes Lydus, mens.
 3,5   F15
 4,86   F43

Ioannes Malalas, ed. Thurn
  pr. (3,4–11 Th.) ••
              T10
  1,1 •   F18
  1,4 •   F23,18–20
  1,4   F16b
  1,5   F16d
  1,7   F24,2s
  1,8 •   F24,2–10
  1,9 (10,66–71 Th.) •
              F24,15–20
  1,9 (10,71–76 Th.) •
              F24,10–14
  1,9 (10,75–78; 11,86 Th.) •
              F24,38–43
  1,10 (11,89–97 Th.) •
              F24,21–25
  1,12–14 (12,19 – 14,56 Th.) •
              F24,27–37
  1,13 (13,45 – 14,52 Th.) •
              F24,25s
  1,15   F15; F44
  2,1 •   F43
  2,1   F15
  2,2 •   F43
  2,10 •   F16c,7s
  2,10   F94
  2,17 ••   T61
  3,3   F16d
  3,11 ••   T54c
  4,1 ••   F51b
  4,1   F50,3–14
  4,3   F34,103–105; T36; F56
  4,5 •   F54b
  4,5   T54a,8s.33–45
  4,6 ••   T54f
  4,6   T54a,10
  4,13–14   F50,19–23
  4,16   F50,24–32
  4,20 (65,37–40 Th.) ••
              F58b
  4,20 (65,41 – 66,46 Th.) ••
              F59b
  4,20 (66,47–53 Th.) ••
              F60
  6,2 ••   F63b
  6,5 ••   F63b
  6,6   F63a,3s
  6,8–10   F63a,3s
  6,11   F73,2–6
  6,12 ••   F74
  6,13   F73,8–21
  6,13s   T75a
  6,15 •   F79
  6,27s   F81b
  6,28   F73,8–21
  7,19   F82,4
  8,5 •   F82,35–52
  8,6–8 ••   F86
  10,2   F94
  11,2 ••   F95
Ioannes Niciensis, tr. Charles
  6,1–3   F24,2–10
  29 ••   T54c
  29   F54b; T55,15–23
Ioannes Scythopolitanus (ps. Maximus Confessor), Scholia in Dionysii Areopagitae epistulas, ed. Cordier (= PG 4,527–576)
  531B ••   F20
  544B ••   T93a
Ioannes Zonaras
  → Zonaras
Iordanes, Rom., ed. Mommsen
  279 (36 Mommsen) •
              T2a
Iosephus, ant. Iud., ed. Niese
  1,16   T47,32s
  1,73s   F23,2–7
  1,93–95   F23,19
  1,132   F44
  1,146   F16d
  1,162–164   F26,3–5

1,170	F26,5–10	1,361–363	F89,35–37
1,171–175	F26,10–13	1,403	F89,59s
9,208–214	F66	1,408	F89,60s
10,39–43	F70	1,417	F89,61s
11,121–153	F79	4,533	F30
12,249–299	F85		

Iosephus, c. Ap., ed. Reinach

13,82	T86a	1,80	T46b; T46c
13,106–108	T86a	1,86	T47,12s
13,116–118	T86a	1,94	T47,23–25
14,302s	F89,5–7	2,15–17	T47,8–12; T48a; T48b; F50,3–7
14,326s	F89,5–7		
14,331	F89,10–12	2,16	T47,23–25

Irenaeus, haer.

14,366–370	F89,12–17	2,22,5	F95
14,376	F89,20–22	3,3,4	F95
14,379–389	F89,22–26		

Isidorus Hispalensis, chron.

14,388s	F89,33s	1 (424,1–4) •• T9	

Išodad Mervensis, ed. Eynde

14,448s	F89,27s	103,17s •	T41a,15s
14,449s	F89,28s		

Itinerarium Burdigalense

14,481	F89,29	587,5 – 588,6	F30

Iubilaeorum (liber)

14,490	F89,35–37	2,2-23	F14b,5–13
15,8s	F89,35–37	13,10	F26,2s
15,88	F89,35–37	13,13	F26,3-5
15,92–94	F89,36	13,14-17	F26,5–10
15,292	F89,59s	13,22	F26,10-13
15,293	F89,60s	29,13	T28a,1

Iulius Africanus, cest., ed. Vieillefond

15,296	F89,59s; F89,62s		T3a, T11; T12
15,331	F89,60s	I 2,55	F81a

Iulius Africanus, ep. Arist., ed. Reichardt

15,363	F89,59s		T3a; T7b; T11
16,142s	F89,61s	59 – 62	F90c
20,267	T92	60,15 – 61,1 •	F87,5–12

Iosephus, bell. Iud., ed. Michel/ Bauernfeind

Iulius Africanus, ep. Orig.

			T3a; T11; T12

Iulius Pollux, ed. Hardt

1,123	F87,1–6	58,2 – 60,18 •	F16a
1,242–247	F89,5–7	58,6–9 •	T17
1,248	F89,10–12	58,13–15	F19
1,269–278	F89,12–17		
1,279	F89,20–22		
1,282–284	F89,22–26		
1,284s	F89,33s		
1,323s	F89,27s		
1,343	F89,28s		
1,357	F89,29; F89,35–37		

60,18 – 62,4 •	F23,1–10	155,15 – 157,27	
60,18 – 64,20	F23,1–23		F89,3–57
62,7–22	F23,1–7	164,6–21 •	F15
64,18 – 66,1 •	F16b	204,5–17	F95
66,1 – 80,6 •	F16c,2–6	226,19 – 228,3 •	
68,7–11	F16d		F97
68,17–20	F44	228,23 – 230,3	
80,11 – 82,20 •	F16c,7–12		T1b
86,9–11	F16d	236,3s	T3a

Iustinus, dial., ed. Marcovich
52,3,1–12   F87,6–9

ps. Iustinus, coh. Gr., ed. Marcovich
9,2 (34,11–17 M.) •
            F34,76–87
9,2 (34,17s M.) •
            F34,86s
9,2 (34,19–23 M.) •
            F34,31–34
12,2 (38,14–18 M.) •
            F34,1s

92,2s	T28b		
96,7–9	T48a; T48b; F50,3–7		
98,13s	F54b; T55,20–23		
102,17–21 •	T39a		
102,10s •	F58b		
104,2–5	F59b		
104,12–14 •	F35		
106,5–9	T42		
112,16s	F62,6		
114,2–4	F66		
114,14s •	F64a		
114,16–20	F53		
116,22 – 118,8 •			
	F70		

Iustus Tiberiensis (FGrHist 734)
F2   T48a
F2s   T47,8–12; F50,3–7
F3   T47,32s; T48b

Leo Grammaticus, ed. Bekker

118,9s	F66	8,22 – 10,20 •	F16a
132,2s •	T67	9,4–7 •	T17
132,3–5 •	T68	9,13–15	F19
134,16 – 140,19		9,22 – 10,1 •	F18
	T77a,5s	10,21 – 11,3 •	F23,1–10
136,3s	F46,207s	10,21 – 12,5	F23,1–23
140,10–12 •	F62,2–4; F73,2–6	12,3–5 •	F16b
140,17–21 •	F73,2–6	12,6 – 14,12 •	F16c,2–6
142,10s	T75a	13,4–7	F16d
142,10s •	F73,9–14	14,4 – 19,10 •	F16c,7–12
142,15 – 144,4 •		15,5 – 16,3 ••	F24a
	F73,9–14	20,16–20 ••	F25
144,6–8 •	F79	20,18–20 •	F16d
144,22 – 146,16 •		21,16–18	T28a
	F73,15–24	23,3s	T28b
147,2–8	F81b	24,22 – 25,4	T32
148,9 – 156,27	F86,1–22	25,4s	T32
152,11–18	F87,6–16		

26,10–12	T48a; T48b; F50, 3–7	57,8–12 •	F15
		71,2–11 ••	F97
27,3–5 •	T39a	71,16–18 ••	T1b
27,7–9 •	F34,103–105	75,17s •	T3a
27,17s •	F44	76,14 – 77,1 ••	T4a
28,2–5 •	T36	Liber Genealogus	
28,2–5	F34,71s; F54b; T54c; T55,20–23	352s	F30
		Lucianus, verae hist.	
28,3s	T54a,8s	2,22	F65,249s
28,8–12	T61	Manetho (FGrHist 609)	
29,10–16 •	T39a	F2	F46,2–242
29,11s •	T40	F3, p. 36s	T46c; T46d; T47,1
30,1–3 ••	F35	F3a, p. 12	F43
30,4–8	F59b	F3a, p. 13	F43c
31,22 – 32,1	T42	F3a, p. 14	F44
35,1s	F62,6	F9	T47,23–25
35,3–6	F66	ps. Manetho	
35,11–16 ••	F53		F43; F43c
36,10–12	F70	Marmor Parium (FGrHist 239)	
36,20 – 37,7	T71	A3s	T55,10–12
36,22s	T71	ps. Maximus Confessor	
38,17–22 ••	F76	→ Ioannes Scythopolitanus	
42,6s •	T67	Michael Psellus, hist. synt., ed. Aerts	
42,7s •	T68	34	T1b
43,16–20 •	F76; T77a,5s	44 ••	T4b
44,12–15	F46,207s	Michael Syrus, Descriptio temporum, ed. Chabot	
44,22 – 46,18	T77a,5s		
45,1–12 •	T77a,3s	pr. (2,4–15 Sawalaneancʻ 1871) •• T13a	
46,4–9 •	F93,31–35		
46,11–14 •	F93,25–29	1,3 ••	T16f
46,15–17 •	F62,2–4	1,4	F18
46,15–20 •	F73,2–6	2,1	F23,18–20
47,8–10	T75a	3,8 •	T39a
47,8–20 •	F73,9–14	4,7 •	T39b
47,22 – 48,1 •	F79	4,15 ••	F64c; T64d
48,15 – 49,4 •	F73,15–24	4,15 ••	T71
49,12s •	F73,22s	4,15	F58a,19; F58b; F59a,1–22; F59b
49,21 – 52,17	F86,1–22		
52,23 – 53,6	F87,6–16	4,16	F66
54,20 – 55,13	F86,1–22; F89,3–57	4,20	F64a; F65,44
		4,21 ••	T77b
55,8–13 •	F89,44–49	5,1 •	T78a

5,1	F81b	Paschale Campanum…, ed. Mommsen	
5,2 •	T80		
5,4 ••	T83	745,7–18 ••	T92
5,6 •	F96	Pausanias	
5,10 ••	T93d	1,35,6	F65,286–288
6,7 •	T2a	1,42,3	F46,146s
6,7	T3a	1,44,1	F65,62
10,20 ••	T13b	2,11,8	F65,375

Moses Chorenensis, Historia Armeniorum

		2,24,7	F65,82
		3,13,9	F65,103–105
2,10 ••	T88	3,14,3	F65,83
2,20	F89,33s	3,21,1	F65,228
2,21	F89,28s	4,4,5	F65,49
2,38	T88	4,13,7	F65,60

Nicephorus Callistus Xanthopulus, Excerpta ex historia ecclesiastica in codice Barocciano 142

		4,15,1	F65,73
		4,23,4	F65,83
		4,23,10	F65,83
f. 212^r ••	T2c	4,24,5	F65,162

Nicephorus, chron. syn., ed. de Boor

		4,27,9	F65,196
81,7 – 83,2	F16a	5,21,9	F65,295–297; F65,332–334
83,21–84,15	F16c,2–12		
83,25–28	T16i; T16m	5,21,10	F65,268; F65,286–288; F65,302; F65,321s
84,5–7	F16c,5s		
85,1	T28b 0		
93,12–14	F95	5,23,4	F65,168

Nicolaus Damascenus (FGrHist 90)

		5,8,5s	F64a; F65,44
F72	F23,19	5,8,6	F65,61; F65,63

Nota in margine codicis Parisini gr. 1711 (= Sync., cod. A)

		5,8,7	F65,67; F65,74s; F65,78
p. 13 ••	F21	5,8,8	F65,93–95

OrMan

		5,8,9	F65,103–105; F65,112
	F70		

Origenes, Cels.

		5,8,10	F65,147; F65,183; F65,193; F65,255
5,55,1–9	F23,2–7		

Origenes, comm. in Gen.

		5,9,1	F65,107s
PG 12,113,9s	F16d	6,2,10	F65,174; F65,175

Origenes, comm. in Mt.

		6,3,4	F65,191
265	T17	6,3,7	F65,186

Origenes, sel. in ps.

		6,3,8	F65,51
118,164	F22	6,3,11	F65,192

Orosius, hist.

		6,5,1s	F65,180–182
7,43,19	T92	6,5,3	F65,196

6,8,3	F65,179	
6,9,5	F65,155	
6,10,4	F65,147	
6,12,2	F65,229	
6,13,1	F65,156	
6,13,3	F65,349; F65,354	
6,13,4	F65,269s	
6,13,7	F65,257	
6,14,5	F65,142	
6,14,11	F65,146	
6,15,3	F65,249s	
6,15,8	F65,107s; F65,216	
6,15,10	F65,249s	
6,17,2	F65,232s	
6,22,3	F65,198s	
7,16,10	F65,273	
7,17,6	F65,51	
7,17,13	F65,51	
7,23,5	F65,295–297	
7,25,4	F65,195	
8,26,2	F65,147	
8,26,3s	F64a; F65,44	
8,27,8	F65,196	
8,39,3	F65,83	
8,40,1	F65,130–132	
8,45,4	F65,186	
10,2,3	F65,200	
10,3,1	F65,203	
10,5,13	F65,137	
10,7,4	F65,120	
10,7,7	F65,147	
10,23,14	F65,228	
10,34,5	F65,381	
10,36,9	F65,344s	

Petrus Alexandrinus, Ekthesis chronon, ed. Samodurova
   190,2s •   T39a,3s
   190,26–31 •   T39a,5s
   190,34–39 •   F34,65

Philippus Sidensis, Christiana historia, cf. Heyden 2006
   frg. 4.1   T2c

Philo, post.
   40s   F22

Philo, migr. Abr.
   20   F16d

Philo, op.
   29–33   F14b

Philochorus (FGrHist 328)
   F92   F34,26–33.71–73
   F93   F54a,6–9.10–13

Philostratus, gym., ed. Jüthner
   1 (134,14–16 Jü.)
            F65,103–105
   1 (134,14–19 Jü.)
            F65,142
   12 (142,14–19 Jü.)
            F65,44
   12 (142,19s Jü.)
            F65,61
   12 (142,20s Jü.)
            F65,63
   12 (142,21–24 Jü.)
            F65,67
   12 (142,24–32 Jü.)
            F65,74s
   12 (142,32 – 144,2 Jü.)
            F65,93–95
   13 (144,11–13 Jü.)
            F65,147
   13 (144,13–17 Jü.)
            F65,255
   13 (144,3–5 Jü.)
            F65,107s
   13 (144,5–8 Jü.)
            F65,118
   13 (144,8–11 Jü.)
            F65,111
   21 (150,5–9 Jü.)
            F65,130–132
   33 (158,18–20 Jü.)
            F65,269s
   43 (168,18–23 Jü.)
            F65,164s

43 (168,18-24 Jü.)
       F65,118
Philostratus, imag.
  2,6,1   F65,130-132
Philostratus, Vita Apollonii
  4,24   F65,346-348
  5,7   F65,344s
Phlegon Trallianus (FGrHist 257)
  F1   F64a; F65,44
  F1,1-10   F65,6-29
  F1,11   F65,52
  F4   F65,46
  F5   F65,73
  F8   F34,15-18
  F12,1   F65,293
  F16   F93,14s
Photius, bibl.
  34,7a7-24 •• T11
Pindarus, olymp.
  13   F65,162
Plato, Ti.
  23E   F15
  35C2-36A6   F14a
Plinius, nat. hist.
  34,8,19   F65,156
Plutarchus, de Daed. Plat.
               F56
Plutarchus, Numa
  1,3   F65,64
Plutarchus, Plat. quaest.
  999 E   F81a
  1000 C   F81a
Polemo (FHG)
  3 F13   F34,77-80
  3,119 F13   T47,9s
Polybius (FGrHist 254)
  F2   F65,34s
  F3   F34,15-18
Porphyrius (FGrHist 260)
  F2   F86,1-22; T86a
  F3   F82,9-52
  F4   F50,28s

Posidonius (FGrHist 87)
  F69   T47,9s
Procopius Gazaeus, in Gen., ed Mai
(= PG 87/1,21-512)
  6 (265C - 268C)
               F23,2-7
  8 (285A) •   F23,19
  11 (315C)   F16c,8; F94
Prosper Tiro, chron.
  386-388   T92
Ptolemaeus Mendesius (FGrHist 611)
  T2b   F34,86s
Quintilianus, instit. orat.
  2,8,14   F65,332-334
SIG³
  1056,1s   F65,107s
  1056,5s   F65,112
  1056,7s   F65,147
  1056,10s   F65,183
  1056,12s   F65,193
  1056,17s   F65,72
  1069   F65,216
Simonides → Anthologia Graeca
Socrates, h. e.
  2,34,10s •• T8a
Solinus
  1,74   F65,93-95
  1,97   F65,118
Sozomenus, h. e.
  1,1,12 ••   T8b
  2,4   F30
  5,21,5   T2a
Strabo
  6,1,12   F65,142
  8,3,30   F64a; F65,6-29.44
Suda, ed. Adler
  Ἀφρικανός Λ 4647,1-5 ••
               T12
  Διάγορας ὁ Μήλιος Δ 523
               F81a
  Δράκων Δ 1495
               T54f

Ἥλιος Η 235	F43	42,11 ••	F53
Ἰουδήθ Ι 430 ••		42,11 •	F64a
	T75b	42,20 ••	F76
Ἰουδήθ Ι 431	T75a	44,17 •	T67
Κεστός Κ 1428		44,18 •	T68
	T12	45,1 •	F76; T77a,5s
Μωυσῆς Μ 1348,15s		45,8 •	T77a,3s
	T28b	46,1 •	F62,2–4
Σόλων Σ 776	T54f	46,1s •	F73,2–6
Σωκράτης Σ 829		46, 4–9 •	F73,9–14
	F81a	46,9 •	F79
Σωσάννα Σ 856 •		46,11–18 •	F73,15–24
	T12	47,1 •	F73,22s
τραχηλίζων Τ 921		50,8 •	F15
	F65,258	66,2 ••	F97

Suetonius, Nero
   23,1   F65,344s.346–348
   24,4   F65,346–348

67,2 ••	T1b
75,2 •	T3a
77,2 ••	T4a

Sulpicius Severus, chron., ed. Senne-ville-Grave
1,27,3 •	T40
2,8,1 – 17,1	F73,8–21
2,14,1	T75a
2,27,1	F87,6–9

Symeon Logothetes, vide locos singulos sub Leo Gr., Theod. Mel., Iul. Pol.
nunc ed. Wahlgren, vide supra p. VI
24,3–10 •	F16a
24,4 •	T17
24,7 •	F18
24,11 •	F23,1–10
25,5 •	F16b
26,1–32,5 •	F16c,2–6.7–12
28,2–5 ••	F24a
33,5 ••	F25
33,5 •	F16d
37,2 •	F34,103–105
37,3 •	F44
37,4 •	T36
37,11 •	T40
37,14 ••	F35

Symeon Logothetes in cod. Vat. gr. 163
   f. 9^v–10^r •• (= 42,11 Wahlgren)
                                F53

ps. Symeon (cod. Par. gr. 1712, f. 18 – f. 271)
f. 19^r •	F14b
f. 20^v •	F23,18–20
f. 21^v	F18
f. 22^r	F19
f. 23^r	F44
f. 25^v	F54b; T55,10–12
f. 26^r •	F16c,8
f. 26^r	F16b; T16h
f. 26^v – 27^r ••	F24b
f. 27^v	F43
f. 30^v •	F16d
f. 30^v	F51a,9; T61
f. 31^r •	F26,7–15
f. 31^r	T27
f. 31^r–31^v •	F26,16–22
f. 32^r	T28a; T28c; T33b
f. 32^v	F29; T32; T33a

f. 34ᵛ	T48a; T48b; F50,3–7	23,20	T28b
		24,23 – 25,1	T32
f. 37ᵛ	F50,3–14	25,1s	T32
f. 38ʳ	F34,71s; F51a,32–38; F51b; F54b; T54c; T55,16s	25,19s	T48a; T48b; F50,3–7
		26,8–10 •	T39a
f. 51ᵛ •	F66	26,11–13 •	F34,103–105
f. 61ᵛ	F93,59–64	26,21 •	F44
f. 74ʳ,39–74ᵛ,5	F87,6–16	26,27 – 27,2 •	T36
f. 79ᵛ–80ʳ ••	F97	26,27 – 27,1	T54a,8s
f. 80r	T1b	26,27 – 27,2	F34,71s; F54b; T54c; T55,20–23

Syncellus
→ Georgius Syncellus

		27,6–9	T61
Tacitus, dial.		27,26 – 28,3 •	T39a
10,5	F65,332–334	27,28 •	T40
Tatianus, orat., ed. Whittaker		28,10s ••	F35
27,1	F24,24–26	28,12–16	F59b
38	F46,132–135; T48a; T48b; F50,3–7	29,17–20	T42
		31,16s	F62,6
38s	T47,33s	31,18–20	F66
39,1	F50,26s	31,27s •	F64a
39,1s	F50,3–25	31,30 – 32,2 ••	F53
39,2	T55,10–12	32,13–15	F70

Thallus (FGrHist 256)

		32,23 – 33,4	T71
F1	F93,6s	32,24s	T71
F5	F34,26–33	34,4–8 ••	F76
F7	F34,15–18	36,23s •	T67

Theodosius Melitenus, ed. Tafel

		36,25 •	T68
14,2 – 15,7 •	F16a	37,24–27 •	F76; T77a,5s
14,5–7 •	T17	38,9–12	F46,207s
14,11–14	F19	38,18 – 27	T77a,5s
14,20s •	F18	38,21–30 •	T77a,3s
15,8–13 •	F23,1–10	39,23–28 •	F73,2–6
15,8 – 16,12	F23,1–23	39,23s •	F62,2–4
16,11s •	F16b	40,5–7	T75a
16,13 – 17,31 •	F16c,2–6	40,5–18 •	F73,9–14
17,5–7	F16d	40,20s •	F79
18,15 – 19,2 ••	F24a	41,4–19 •	F73,15–24
20,13 – 21,7 •	F16c,7–12	42,1s •	F73,22s
22,1–3 ••	F25	42,9 – 45,30	F86,1–22
22,1–3 •	F16d	44,14–19	F87,6–16
22,20–22	T28a	45,17–30	F89,3–57

46,31–34 •	F15	Thucydides	
54,6–14 ••	F97	1,126,3	F65,99
54,18–20 ••	T1b	2,2,1	F81a
56,14 •	T3a	2,47,3	F81a

56,25 – 57,2 ••T4a

Theodorus Lector, epitome
   1   T8b

Theophilus Antiochenus, Autol.
   1,10,12s   F24,24–26
   3,19,21s   F23,19

ps. Theopompus (Anaximenes Lampsacenus), Tricaranus (FGrHist 72)
   F20a   F34,99–102

Vardan Arawelcʻi, ed. Thomson
   153a   T39b

Vetus Chronicon (FGrHist 610)
   F2   F43; F43c

Zonaras, ed. Dindorf
   11,12   F65,346–348
   12,17 •   T3a

2. Index nominum propriorum

Ἀαρών F79,1
Ἄβας F50,19
Ἄβγαρος vide Αὔγαρος
Ἀβδών T38,1
Ἀβιμέλεχ T37,1
Ἀβίτος· vide Ἐλαγάβαλος
Ἀβραάμ T6,5; F15,11; T16c,12;
　T16d,1.3.5; T16e,4.9; T16o,1s.4;
　T16p,1; F25,1; F26,2.5.7; T27,1;
　F30a,14.16; F30b,3.16; F34,86;
　T41a,18; T45,13.19; T47,15;
　T49a,5-7; F51a,10; ad F90a,2-4;
　T93c,11.15
Ἀγάθαρχος Κερκυραῖος F65,140
Ἀγαθόπους Αἰγινήτης F65,385
Ἀγαμέμνων F50,25.27.30
Ἀγαμήστωρ F54a,43
Ἀγέλαος F59a,10
Ἀγέλας F59a,13
Ἀγέμαχος Κυζικηνός F65,257
Ἀγεύς Ἀργεῖος F65,210
Ἀγήμων F59a,16
Ἀγησίλαος F58a,13
Ἆγις F58a,9
Ἆγις Ἠλεῖος F65,127
Ἀγνόδωρος Κυζικηνός F65,273
Ἄγνων Πεπαρήθιος F65,128
Ἀγριππίνα urbs Palaestinae
　ad F89,60s
Ἀδάμ T6,4; T10,6; T13a; F14b,12;
　T16a,2.4; T16b,3; T16c,8;
　T16d,6; T16e,2.8; T16h,1.7;
　T16i,6s; T16k,7; T16o,2-4;
　T16q,3; T17,1; F18; F19,1;
　F25,3; F33,2; F35,2; T40,1;
　T42,3; T45,10.15s; ad F54a,42-
　46; T54c,1; ad F64a,4s; F76,3;
　ad T77a,5s; F83; F89,57; F93,
　108; T93c,11.15; T93d; F94,1
Ἄδαμα F26,9

Ἀδιαβηνοί ad F23,18-20
Ἄδραστος F51a,35
Ἀδριανός F65,367
Ἀδωνίδης Ἀθηναῖος ad F24,38-43
Ἀέθλιος F65,9
Ἀειθαλής Ἀλεξανδρεύς F65,383
Ἀέροπος F82,15
Ἀέτιος T8,1
Ἀζαρίας (1) ad F54a,42-46; F90a,1
Ἀζαρίας (2) T77a,1
Ἀζουρά ad T16a,2-13
Ἀθανάσιος T17,2
Ἀθηνᾶ ad F54a,6-9; ad F81b,4-7
Ἀθῆναι F54a,4; ad F81b,4-7
Ἀθηναῖοι F34,31; F34,100; T49b,1;
　F54a,1.2.32.58s; F54b,6;
　T54c,1.2.4; T54e,1; T54f,1.6;
　T55,12.21.26.37; F64c,2;
　F64d,1.11; F81a,3.5.8; ad
　F81b,4-7
Ἀθηνόδωρος Αἰγιεύς F65,339.343
Ἀθηράδας Λάκων F65,70
Ἄθωθις F46,5
Αἰγεύς F54a,19.20
Αἰγιαλεύς F51a,9.52; F51b,2
Αἴγισθος F50,32
Αἴγυδρος F51a,16
Αἰγύπτιοι F14b,4; F15,1s.6; F26,4;
　F34,78.82.86.99s; F43a,1;
　F43b,7; F43c,2; F46,35.38.
　108.120.187; T46c,17;
　T47,11.13; ad F54a,6-9; F86,2;
　F89,52
Αἴγυπτος F26,2; T28b,3; T28c,5;
　F30b,1; T32,2.5; F34,39.45.59.
　78.98; T41a,20; F43a,8; F44,1s;
　T45,4.5; F46,1.8.13.55.92.132.
　205.214.237; T46b,3; T46c,6.
　12.16.19; T46f,1; T47,10.17.21.
　25; T48b,5; F50,6; F51a,20;

F54a,2; F54b,8; T55,7.22.24.33s;
F65,213; F72,4; ad F73,19;
T75a,5; F86,1.24; T86a,1s;
F89,45.51; T93b,1
Αἰθίοπες F46,193; T75b,1.3
Αἰθιοπία ad T36,1s; ad F54a,10–13
Αἰλάμ (Ἰλάμ) F26,11
Αἰμάθ F72,3
Αἰνείας T52,1; ad F54a,20–24
Αἰσιμίδης F54a,52
Αἰσχίνης Ἠλεῖος F65,50
Αἰσχίνης Μιλήσιος ὁ Γλαυκίας F65,324
Αἰσχύλος (1) ὁ Ἀγαμήστορος F54a,45s.49; ad F59a,14–19; F64c,2; F64d,1.11
Αἰσχύλος (2) T54f,3
Αἴτνη F81a,14
Ἄκανθος Λάκων F65,63
Ἀκαρνανία F56,7
Ἄκαστος F54a,34
Ἀκμαίων T54f,3s
Ἀκουσίλαος F34,29.56
Ἀκουσίλαος Κυρηναῖος F65,278
Ἀκρίσιος F50,21
Ἀκταῖος F34,72
Ἀκτή vide Ἀττική
Ἄκτια F89,50
Ἀλεξάνδρεια T1a,2.6.8; T3a,7; T5,6; F65,214; T86a,1s; F89,17.50.58; F97,2; T93b,1; F98,2
Ἀλεξανδρεῖς T6,2.16
Ἀλέξανδρος Ἀλεξανδρεύς F65,394
Ἀλέξανδρος coniux Cleopatrae T86a,4.6
Ἀλέξανδρος imperator Romanus T2d,2.5
Ἀλέξανδρος ὁ Πάρις ad F50,25–27
Ἀλέξανδρος ὁ Πολυΐστωρ F34,33

Ἀλέξανδρος rex Corinthiorum F59a,17
Ἀλέξανδρος I. rex Macedoniae F82,18
Ἀλέξανδρος II. rex Macedoniae F82,28
Ἀλέξανδρος III. Magnus, rex Macedoniae F65,208.213; F73,7.22; F82,33–36; F84,2; F86,1
Ἀλεξῖνος F65,10
Ἀλήτης F59a,6.8; F59b,3
Ἀλκαμένης F58a,17; F58b,4
Ἀλκάνδρα F46,163
Ἀλκέτας F82,16
Ἀλκίδας Λάκων F65,239
Ἄλκιμος Κυζικηνός F65,272
Ἀλκμαίων F54a,50
Ἀλκμήνη F65,12
Ἀλυάτης (1) F63a,8
Ἀλυάτης (2) F63,14
Ἀμαζίας ad F90a,2–4
Ἀμάν T78b,1
Ἄμβραμ T33a,1
Ἀμενεφθῆς F46,160
Ἀμενσίς F46,139; T46g,3
Ἀμενωφάθ F46,155
Ἀμενωφθίς (1) F46,138
Ἀμενωφθίς (2) F46,173
Ἀμενῶφις F46,146
Ἀμερής F46,111
Ἀμησινᾶς Βαρκαῖος F65,164
Ἀμιναδάμ T41a,19
Ἀμμανέμης (1) F46,102
Ἀμμανέμης (2) F46,103
Ἀμμενέμης (1) F46,97
Ἀμμενέμης (2) F46,112
Ἀμμενεμνῆς F46,162
Ἀμμώνιος Ἀλεξανδρεύς F65,234
Ἀμμώνιος dux Aegypti T86a,4
Ἄμουσις F43c,2

Ἀμύντας I. rex Macedoniae
  F82,17
Ἀμύντας II. rex Macedoniae
  F82,23
Ἀμύντας III. rex Macedoniae
  F82,25.32
Ἀμύντας IV. rex Macedoniae
  F82,27
Ἀμύρτεος Σαΐτης F46,224
Ἀμφιγύης F51a,48
Ἀμφικτύων F54a,11
Ἀμφίσση F65,235
Ἀμών T71
Ἀμώς propheta F66,1
Ἀμώς rex Aegypti F46,132.143;
  T46c,1.20; T46f,2; T55,1–3.5.
  7.12
Ἀμώσιος vide Ἄμωσις
Ἄμωσις rex Aegypti F34,82s;
  F46,209; T46c,1.3.4.6.9s.13.17;
  T46d,1; T46f,3s; T46g,1; T47,1.
  5.11.21s; T48b,1; T55,29.43.45
Ἀνανία T77a,1
Ἀναξαγόρας F81b,4
Ἀνδρέας Λακεδαιμόνιος F65,298
Ἄνδροκλος Μεσήνιος F65,48
Ἀνδρόμαχος Ἀμβρακιώτης
  F65,299
Ἀνδρομένης Κορίνθιος
  F65,218.221
Ἀνδρόνικος T13b; ad T39b,1–3;
  T71; F83; T93d
Ἀνδρόπομπος ad F54a,25–27
Ἀνθεστίων Ἀργεῖος F65,301
Ἀνθηδών F89,31
Ἀννιανός T13a; T13b; T39b,4; F83
Ἄνουβις F43c,2
Ἀνουβίων ὁ καὶ Φεῖδος,
  Ἀλεξανδρεύς F65,388
Ἀνοχᾶς Ταραντῖνος F65,146
Ἀντήνωρ Ἀθηναῖος ἢ Μιλήσιος
  F65,219

Ἀντίγονος Μακεδών F65,225
Ἀντίγονος rex Iudaeorum
  F89,1.10.13.25s.29.35
Ἀντίγονος I. Gonata, rex
  Macedoniae F82,48
Ἀντίγονος II. rex Macedoniae
  F82,50
Ἀντικλῆς Ἀθηναῖος F65,205
Ἀντικλῆς Μεσήνιος F65,54
Ἀντικράτης Ἐπιδαύριος F65,116
Ἀντίμαχος Ἠλεῖος F65,46
Ἀντιόχεια F83
Ἀντιοχεῖς F89,66
Ἀντίοχοι F84,3; T85a,4
Ἀντίοχος III. ὁ Μέγας F84,11
Ἀντίοχος IV. ὁ Ἐπιφανής F84,10
Ἀντίπατρος Ἠπειρώτης F65,274
Ἀντίπατρος pater Herodis
  F87a,6.10; F87b,3.10; F89,24.62
Ἀντίπατρος rex Macedoniae
  F82,46
Ἀντωνῖνος vide Ἐλαγάβαλος
Ἀντωνῖνος Εὐσεβής (Pius)
  F65,373
Ἀντωνῖνος Μάρκος Πίος (Marcus
  Aurelius) F65,382; F97,1
Ἀντωνῖνος (Caracalla sive
  Elagabalus) T9,2; T99,1.2
Ἀντωνῖνος ὁ καὶ Καράκαλλος
  F65,397
Ἀντώνιος triumvir F86,23;
  F89,1.5.9.20.22.28s.35.40s.45s
Ἀπάμεια (vide etiam Κελαιναί) ad
  F23,18–20
Ἀπελλαῖος Ἠλεῖος F65,139
Ἆπις deus F46,20
Ἆπις rex Sicyoniorum F51a,14
Ἆπις rex Argivorum F34,78;
  T47,11; T48b,4; F50,8
Ἀπίων F43c,4; T47,9
Ἀπολλοφάνης ὁ καὶ Πάπις
  Ταρσεύς F65,356

Ἀπολλωνιάς urbs Epiri F89,4
Ἀπολλώνιος Ἀλεξανδρεύς
    F65,358
Ἀπολλώνιος Ἐπιδαύριος F65,330
Ἀπολλώνιος στρατηγός F84,6.8
Ἀπόλλων F87a,8; F87b,8
Ἄραβες F87b,20; F89,15
Ἀραβία F34,79; ad F87b,7-9;
    F89,31.36
Ἀραράτ F23,19
Ἀρβάκης F62,8.10
Ἀργαῖος (1) F82,13
Ἀργαῖος (2) F82,26
Ἀργεῖοι F34,28; T47,5.11.35;
    T49a,1.3; F50,2.35
Ἀργοναῦται F34,91
Ἄργος rex Argivorum F50,9
Ἄργος urbs Graeciae F34,55.81;
    T48b,1; F56,2; F65,210
Ἄργος ὁ Πανόπτης ad T36,1s;
    F56,11
Ἀρδεύς F63a,2.7; F63b,3.5
Ἄρδυσος F63a,12
Ἄρειος T49a,4
Ἀρεξίων T54f,5
Ἀρέτας F87b,20
Ἄρης F24a,28; F24b,28; F43b,12
Ἀρηχίων Φιγαλεύς F65,130
Ἀρίστανδρος Λέσβιος F65,264
Ἀριστέας Μιλήσιος F65,368
Ἀριστέας Στρατονικεὺς ἢ
    Μαιάνδριος F65,321
Ἀριστείδης T2b,7; T2c,1; T3a,10;
    T11,12
Ἀριστίππος ad F73,15-24
Ἀριστόβουλος F87b,2
Ἀριστόδημος Ἠλεῖος F65,191
Ἀριστόδημος F65,30.35
Ἀριστόλοχος Ἀθηναῖος F65,204
Ἀριστομένης Ῥόδιος F65,268
Ἀριστομήδης F59a,15
Ἀριστοτέλης ad F73,15-24

Ἀριστοφάνης F81a,10; F81b,8
Ἀρίστων Θούριος F65,307.309
Ἀρίφρων T49b,1s; F54a,41; T54e,1
Ἀρκεσίλαος Μεγαλοπολίτης
    F65,259
Ἀρμενία ad F23,18-20
Ἀρμένιοι ad F23,18-20
Ἀρμεσίς F46,153
Ἀρπασασθά vide Ἀρταξέρξης ὁ
    καὶ Μακρόχειρ
Ἀρράν T16c,12
Ἀρσάκης F65,237
Ἀρσακίδαι F65,238
Ἀρσῆς F46,239; F73,20
Ἀρσινοΐτης F46,109
Ἀρτάβανος F46,217; F73,13
Ἀρταξέρξης ὁ καὶ Μακρόχειρ
    F46,218; F73,14; ad F73,9-14;
    ad T78a,1-5; T78b,4; F79,2;
    F93,33.40.42.54s.57.78.96.100
Ἀρταξέρξης Μνήμων F73,18;
    F81b,1.3.9
Ἀρτεμίδωρος Θυατείριος F65,315
Ἄρτυκας F62,13
Ἀρφαξάδ F16c,2s; T16i,1.3.6;
    T16l,1; T16n,1.2.5; T16o,2.5;
    T45,14; T47,3
Ἀρχέλαος rex Lacedaemoniorum
    F58a,15
Ἀρχέλαος I. rex Macedoniae
    F82,20
Ἀρχέλαος II. rex Macedoniae
    F82,22
Ἀρχέλαος sacerdos Sicyoniorum
    F51a,43
Ἀρχίλοχος Κερκυραῖος F65,138
Ἄρχιππος F54a,35
Ἄρχλης F46,125
Ἀσήθ T46c,2; T47,23.26
Ἀσία F34,50; F46,104; ad F62,2-4;
    F89,6; F89,41
Ἀσιατικὸς Ἁλικαρνασεύς F65,319

Ἀσκάλων T27,1; F87b,9
Ἀσκληπιάδης Σιδώνιος F65,311
Ἀσκληπιός F46,38
Ἀσπασία F81a,4
Ἀσσήθ vide Ἀσήθ
Ἀσσύριοι F24a,6.18.21.27.30;
 F24b,6.22.27.29; F34,85;
 F46,207; T49a,4.6; T49b,2; ad
 F54a,35–41; ad F62,2–4; ad F70;
 ad F73,2–6; T93c,12
Ἀστραῖος Θρᾴξ ad F54a,14–19
Ἀστυάγης F62,8.17
Ἀστύαλος Κροτωνιάτης F65,156
Ἀστυνόμη F24a,13; F24b,13
Ἄτλας ad T36,1s; F54a,7;
 F56,3.4.11; T56a,1
Ἀτρεύς F50,24
Ἀττική F34,26.28.47.77.93.98; ad
 T36,1s; T47,36; ad F54a,6–9;
 F54b,3; T54c,1.3; T55,10.16
Ἀττικὸς Σαρδιανός F65,376
Αὔγαρος T88; F96,1
Αὔγουστος (Καῖσαρ) ad F15,12–
 14; F65,306; F86,22; ad F87b,5
 (test.); F89,3.24.33.39.46.49; T91
Αὐρανῖτις F89,32
Αὐτομέδων rex Corinthiorum
 F58a,18; F59b,5
Αὐτομέδων sacerdos Sicyoniorum
 F51a,44
Αὐτομένης F59a,19
Αὐφίδιος Πατρεύς F65,312
Ἀφίδας F54a,24
Ἄφοβις F46,126
Ἀφραάρτης F62,15
Ἀφροδίτη F24a,14; F24b,14;
 F24b,38
Ἄφροι F24b,12
Ἄφρος F24a,11; F24b,11s
Ἄφωφις T46b,3s; T46c,10.15s
Ἀχαάβ F90b

Ἄχαζ F53,1; F58a,3.6; F59a,22;
 F63a,5.17; F64a,1.5; F64b,2;
 T64e,3.7.9; F76,1; F90b
Ἀχελῆ ad F93,31–35
Ἀχερρῆς F46,149.152
Ἄχης F46,45
Ἀχθόης F46,92
Ἀχιλλεὺς Ἀλεξανδρεύς F65,361
Ἄχωρις F46,227
Ἄψανδρος F54a,56
Ἀώδ T36,1

Βάαλ/Βήλ F24a,30; F24b,30
Βαβυλών F34,13; F65,208; ad
 T77a,3s
Βαγώας ad F73,19
Βαιθήλ F30a,8
Βάκτροι ad F73,15–24
Βάκχις F59a,12
Βακχυλίδης F81a,7
Βαλτάσαρ F93,90
Βάρρων T52,2
Βενιαμίν F59b,2
Βῆλος ad F24,21–25; T49a,6s
Βηρωσσὸς ὁ Βαβυλώνιος F34,14
Βῆσσος ad F73,15–24
Βινεχής F46,14
Βίνωθρις F46,22
Βίχερις F46,59
Βνῶν F46,122
Βοιωτία F50,17
Βοιωτοί T61,1
Βοιωτὸς Σικυώνιος F65,277
Βορέας ad F54a,14–19
Βουβαστιταί F46,178
Βούβαστος F46,18
Βόχχωρις Σαΐτης F46,192.196
Βοώζ T41a,22
Βροῦττος T54d,8
Βῶχος F46,18

Γαβαών F59b,2
Γαβινίοι F89,59
Γαβριήλ F93,83
Γάδαρα F89,31
Γάζα F89,31
Γάιος Caligula F65,335
Γάλλος Κορνήλιος F89,51
Γαυλάνη F89,32
Γεδεών T37,1.2
Gełark'uni T88
Γέλων Λάκων F65,115
Γέραρα T27,1
Γεώργιος historiographus T13b; F83
Γλύκων Κροτωνιάτης F65,120
Γοθονιήλ F56,6; T56a,1
Γόμορρα F26,9
Γοργίας F81a,12; F81b,7
Γορδιανὸς Αὔγουστος T3a,1; T3b,1
Γράτος Σαβινιανός F54d,7
Γρηγόριος ὁ θαυματουργός T4a,2
Γρηγόριος vide Θεόδωρος
Γρυπός T85a,4
Γύγης F63a,11
Γύλις Λάκων F65,92

Δαβίδ ad F35,1s; T41a,18.21.23; T41b,3; F60,5; T85a,2
Δαμάρητος Ἡραιεύς F65,147
Δαμασίας Ἀμφιπολίτης F65,215
Δαμασίας Κυδωνιάτης F65,328
Δαμνώ ad F24,2–10
Δαμόστρατος Λαρισαῖος F65,289
Δάμων Δελφός F65,275
Δάμων Θούριος F65,195
Δαναός F50,15
Δανιήλ T3a,3; T12,5; T77a,1.3; T77b; F78,3; T78a,1; F93,20. 49.82
Δάρδανος ad F50,22–24

Δαρεῖος I. rex Persarum F46,215; F73,11
Δαρεῖος II. rex Persarum F46,221; F73,17; F81b,1
Δαρεῖος III. rex Persarum F46,240; F65,208; F73,7.21; T78b,5
Δαυίδ vide Δαβίδ
Δεβλαθά F72,3
Δέκιος T4a,1; T4b,1
Δέσμων Κορίνθιος F65,60
Δευκαλίων T36,1; F46,141; ad F54a,10–13; F54b,8; T55,10.22. 25.35.37
Δευτελίδας Λάκων F65,108
Δημάρατος Ἐφέσιος F65,316
Δημήτριος Ἀλεξανδρεύς F65,244
Δημήτριος I. rex Macedoniae F82,41
Δημήτριος II. rex Macedoniae F82,49
Δημήτριος rex Syriae T86a,5
Δημήτριος Χῖος F65,379
Δημόκριτος Ἀβδηρίτης F81b,6
Δημόκριτος Μεγαρεύς F65,263
Δημοσθένης Λάκων F65,216
Δημοφῶν F54a,22
Δίδυμος T10,2s
Δίδυμος Κλιδεὺς Ἀλεξανδρεύς F65,374
Δίκων Συρακούσιος F65,192
Διόγνητος F54a,39
Διόγνητος Κροτωνιάτης F65,137
Διόδοτος Τυανεύς F65,313
Διόδωρος T10,3; ad F24,25s; F34,16.33
Διοικής (Diycus) F62,14
Διοκλῆς Κορίνθιος F65,59
Διοκλῆς Μεσήνιος F65,52
Διοκλῆς Ὑπεπηνός F65,294
Διονύσιος Ἀλεξανδρείας T5,5

Διονύσιος ὁ Σαμευμὺς
  Ἀλεξανδρεύς F65,369
Διονύσιος Σελευκεύς F65,378
Διονυσόδωρος Ταραντῖνος
  F65,194
Διόνυσος deus F34,90; ad
  F54a,10-13
Διόνυσος rex Aegypti F86,17.19
Διοσπολῖται F46,96.101.115.129.
  131.157.168; T46c,8; T46d,1
Διοφάνης Αἰολεύς F65,314
Διοφάνης Προυσαεύς F65,320
Δίων Κυπαρισσεύς F65,292
Δομιτιανός F65,355; T92,2
Δομνῖνος T10,3
Δόρυσθος F58a,12
Δράκων T54f,1.2
Δυμαῖος F65,85
Δωρόθεος Ῥόδιος F65,247
Δωτάδης Μεσήνιος F65,56

Ἕβερ T16c,4s; T16d,1.4
Ἑβραῖοι T1b,1; T6,1.13; F14b,3;
  T16d,2; T16e,6; T16h,6; ad
  F19,1-4; F34,7.10.12.22.66.97;
  T41a,3; T48a,2; ad F51a,4-6;
  F64d,8; ad F73,2-6; F76,2;
  T77b; T80a,1; T80b; T80c;
  F93,7.79.81; T93c,3.7; T93d
Ἔδεσσα F29,2; T88; F96,2; T99,1
Ἔδνα ad T16c,7s
Ἑζεκίας T68,3; ad F70
Ἔζρα F93,38
Εἰρηναῖος F95,4
Ἑκατόμνως Ἠλεῖος F65,293
Ἑλαγάβαλος (Marcus Aurelius Antoninus) ad T2a,1-3; T2b,2;
  T6,16; T9,2; F29,3s; T54c,9s;
  F65,42
Ἐλευσίς F34,47
Ἐλεφαντίνη F46,64
Ἑλιακείμ ad T77a,3s

Ἑλιακίμ ad F90a,2-4
Ἑλιάσιβος F81b,2
Ἑλλάς F51a,11; F65,14
Ἑλλαδικοί F51a,1s
Ἕλληνες (Graeci) T3a,8; T6,1;
  T8b,4; F34,1.4.9s.29.54.76.
  88.103; T36,2; T47,9.37; T48b,6;
  ad F50,25-27; ad F54a,6-9.
  18.46; T55,9; F58a,6; ad
  F64a,4s; F65,1s.23.34.41; ad
  F73,15-24; ad T75a,2s; F83;
  T88; F93,63.91; T93d; F98,3
Ἐμμά ad T16a,2-13
Ἐμμαοῦς T2a,1; T2b,3; T2c,4;
  T2d,1
Ἐμπεδοκλῆς F81b,6
Ἐνδυμίων F65,10
Ἐνώς T16a,4-6; T16f,1; F19,1.3
Ἐνώχ T16a,9s; F21,1; F22,7;
  T22a,1; T22b,6
Ἐξάγεντος Ἀκραγαντῖνος F65,177
Ἐπαινετὸς Ἀργεῖος F65,290
Ἐπειός F65,10
Ἐπίδαυρος ὁ καὶ Ἀμμώνιος,
  Ἀλεξανδρεύς F65,372
Ἐπιμηθεύς ad T36,1s; F54a,7;
  F56,10
Ἐπινίκιος Κυζικηνός, ὁ καὶ Κυνᾶς
  F65,395
Ἐπιτελίδας Λάκων F65,124
Ἐποπεύς F51a,29
Ἔραστος F51a,22
Ἐρατοσθένης Κροτωνιάτης
  F65,126
Ἐράτων Αἰτωλός F65,240
Ἐρεχθεῖδαι ad F54a,25-27
Ἐρεχθεύς F54a,14s
Ἐριχθόνιος F54a,12
Ἑρμῆς F24a,34; F24b,34
Ἑρμογένης Ξάνθιος F65,354.357
Ἑρμογένης Περγαμηνός F65,329
Eruand T88

Ἐρυξίας   F54a,57.59
Ἐρυξίας Χαλκιδεύς   F65,141
Ἔσδρα   F34,22; F79,1.3; T80d,1
Ἐσθήρ   T78b,1; F90c
Εὐαγόρας Ἠλεῖος   F65,183
Εὔβατος Κυρηναῖος   F65,179
Εὐβουλίδας Λαοδικεύς   F65,336
Εὐδαίμων Ἀλεξανδρεύς   F65,384
Εὔδαμος Κῶος   F65,285
Εὔδημος   F59a,14
Εὔνεος   F51a,46
Εὐπόλεμος Ἠλεῖος   F65,186
Εὔπολις   F81a,10; F81b,8
Εὐριπίδης   T54f,4; F56,4; T61,2; F81b,4
Εὐρύβατος Λάκων   F65,67.193
Εὔρυβος Ἀθηναῖος   F65,82
Εὐρυκλείδας Λάκων   F65,102
Εὐρυκλῆς Λάκων   F65,119
Εὐρύλας Χαλκιδεύς   F65,207
Εὐρυσθεύς   F58a,4.8; F58b,1; F59a,2.5
Εὐρώπη (1)   F34,90; F50,17
Εὐρώπη (2)   F46,105; ad F82,35–52
Εὔρωψ   F51a,12
Εὐσέβιος (ὁ Παμφίλου)   T1a,9; T1b,1; T5,1; T7b,6; T8b,4; T9,3; T10,2; T13a; T13b; T16c,8; T16e,4s; T16h,1.7; T16i,1.4; T16k,2.6; T16l,3; T16m,2; T16o,1.6; ad F23,18–20; T28b,2; T28c,3; T39a,3s; T39b,2.4; T40,2; T41b,4; T42,4; T45,7.11.18; F46,16; T46a,1; T46b,1; T46c,8.11.13; T46d,1s; T46e,1s; T46f,3; T46g,2; T47,4.27s; T48a,1; T52,3; T55,3s.30.40; T57,1; F64a,1; T64e,1.3; T68,5; T69,3; T71; ad T78a,1–5; F83; F86,25; T88; ad F90a,2–4; T92,7; T93a,3; T93c,11; T93d; ad F96,1s
Εὐστάθιος   T10,3
Εὔστολος Σιδήτης   F65,365
Εὐφράτης   T16d,3
Ἔφεσος   F95,2
Ἐφραίμ   ad T36,1s
Ἐχέστρατος   F58a,10
Ἐχυρεύς   F51a,27

Ζάμης   ad F24,27–37
Ζαρέθ   F31,2
Ζεύξιππος   F51a,38.40s; F51b,4
Ζεύς   ad F54a,6–9
Ζεύς   F24a,9.16s.21.32; F24b,9.16.21.32; F60,2; F65,11s
Ζήνων philosophus   F81a,12; F81b,7
Ζήνων imperator Romanus   T10,6
Ζήτ   F46,189
Ζοροβάβελ   F34,20; T78b,5; F93,38
Ζώπυρος Συρακούσιος   F65,246

Ἡγήσιππος   T8b,2; T13a
Ἠλεί (Ἠλί)   T16k,4; F34,65; T40,1.4; T41b,2; F59b,1
Ἠλεῖοι   F64d,3; F65,20s.40.85. 88.334.377
Ἠλί   T7b,2; ad F90a,2–4; F90c
Ἡλιόδωρος (1)   F65,358
Ἡλιόδωρος (2)   F84,8
Ἡλιόδωρος, ὁ καὶ Τρωσιδάμας, Ἀλεξανδρεύς   F65,398
Ἥλιος filius Cleopatrae   F89,48
Ἥλιος deus   F43a,10; F43b,10.14
Ἡλιούπολις   F46,21
Ἤπειρος   F86,24; F89,4
Ἥρα   F24a,10; F24b,10; F56,2
Ἡρακλεῖδαι   ad F54a,25–27
Ἡρακλείδης Σαλαμίνιος   F65,252
Ἡράκλειτος   F81b,3

Ἡράκλειτος Σάμιος F65,251
Ἡρακλεοπολῖται F46,91.95
Ἡρακλῆς T3a,7; ad T39,5s;
    F46,187; F65,8.12.26.28.38.249s.
    268.287.296.302.322.332s; F98,3
Ἡρᾶς Χῖος F65,380
Ἡρόδοτος F34,83; F46,52; T47,10;
    F81b,4
Ἡρώδης ad F15,12-14; F87a,7;
    F87b,3.5.7.13; F89,1.6s.12.15.
    21.23s.28.30.33.42.47.59;
    T89a,2.4
Ἥρων Ἀλεξανδρεύς F65,389
Ἠσαίας F58a,3
Ἠσαῦ F29,2; F31,1
Ἥφαιστος rex Sicyoniorum
    F51a,34
Ἥφαιστος deus F43a,7.10;
    F43b,7.10;

Θαλῆς ὁ Μιλήσιος T54f,2
Θαλλός F34,16.32; F93,6
Θάλπις Λάκων F65,77
Θαμφθίς F46,61
Θάρα T16c,11.12
Θαρσίς F66,2
Θεαίτητος F81b,5; ad F81b,4-7
Θεινιταί F46,17
Θελξίων F51a,15
Θεόδοτος F65,351
Θεόδωρος (Γρηγόριος) T7a,1
Θεόδωρος Μεσήνιος F65,303
Θεόνομος F51a,47
Θεόπομπος Θεσσαλός F65,171
Θεόφιλος T10,3
Θέρσιππος F54a,36.44
Θεσπιεύς F54a,42
Θετταλία ad T36,1s; ad F54a,10-
    13; F54b,8; T55,11.23.38
Θεωνᾶς ὁ καὶ Σμάραγδος,
    Ἀλεξανδρεύς F65,362
Θῆβαι T61,1.4

Θηβαῖοι F46,129s
Θηβαΐς F89,49
Θησεύς F54a,20
Θουκυδίδης ad F73,15-24; F81a,3;
    F81b,6
Θοῦλις ad F43a,12-17
Θούρας (vide etiam Ἄρης)
    F24a,28; F24b,28
Θουρίμαχος F51a,17
Θούωρις F46,163
Θράκη F46,105
Θυέστης F50,24
Θυμίλος Ἀσπένδιος F65,262
Θυμοίτης F54a,25

Ἰακώβ Edessenus F83
Ἰακώβ T7b,1s; F14b,12; T28a,1.3;
    T28b,2s; T28c,3s.6; F29,1s;
    F30a,1; F30b,5; T32,1-3.5;
    T33b,2s; T41a,28; T47,16;
    F51a,7.10; F90c; T99,1
Ἰάρεδ T16a,8s; T22b,1
Ἰάφεθ ad T16a,2-13; T54c,1
Ἰδαῖος F65,229
Ἰδουμαῖοι F87a,10; F87b,9
Ἰεζάβελ F90b
Ἰεζεκιήλ T77a,7
Ἰερεμίας F34,14; T71; ad T77a,3s;
    T77b
Ἰεροβαάλ, T37,2.3
Ἰεροβωάμ T69,1
Hieronymus T9,3; T92,7
Ἰερουσαλήμ T6,14; ad T17,1;
    T41a,8; T42,1; F46,204.207;
    F64a,5; F64c,3; F64d,12; T64e,7;
    F72,3.4; F73,2-6; T75b,3.5.9; ad
    T77a,3s; ad T78a,1-5; F79,3;
    F81b,2; F82,6; F84,6; F93,33.35.
    42.55.97.101
Ἰεσσαί T41a,23; F60,5
Ἰεχονίας ad T77a,3s

Ἰησοῦς ὁ υἱὸς Ἰωσεδέκ T75a,6; T78b,5
Ἰησοῦς ὁ τοῦ Ναυῆ T16k,4; ad F35,1s; F39a,1; T54c,1; F76,3
Ἰησοῦς ὁ μέγας ἱερεύς F93,37
Ἰκάριος Ὑπηρεσιεύς F65,73
Ἴλιον F34,92; F46,164; ad F50,22–24; ad F50,25–27; ad F54a,20–24
Ἴναχος F34,55.81; F43c,4; T47,5.35; T48a,4; T48b,1.3s; T49a,2.8; F50,3.26; F51a,33; T55,13.42; T57,1
Ἰνδοί F34,50
Ἰξίων F59a,9
Ἰοκάστη T61,3
Ἰολαΐδας Ἀργεῖος F65,245
Ἰόππη F89,31
Ἰορδάνης F26,19
Ἰούδα ad T39,3s; T41a,20; T41b,5; ad F54a,42–46; F58a,3.6; F59a,20.22; F62,6.19; F63a,17; F64d,8.14; T64e,1; T68,3; T71; T77a,3.5; F82,6.53
Ἰουδαῖοι T13a; F15,10; F34,81.82.84; ad F34,31–34; T41a,28; F46,208; F50,6; F51a,19; F59,1; F60,4; F73,4; T75b,2s.7; F79,2; F82,3; F84,1.3; F85,1; T85a,1; F86,6; F87a,15; F87b,4.21; F89,7.9.33.35.64; T89a,1; F93,55.63.104; T93b,2
Ἰουδήθ T75a,3s.7; T75b,1.5
Ἰουλιανός (Iulianus Augustus) T7b,1
Ἰούλιος Καῖσαρ F53,5; F65,304; F89,4
Ἰοῦστος historiographus ad F34,38; T47,9.33; T48a,6; T48b,2
Ἱππίας F81a,12
Ἱπποδάμεια ad F50,22–24

Ἱπποκράτης ad F73,9–14; F81b,6
Ἱππόλυτος T5,5; T88; T93d
Ἱππομένης F54a,54
Ἵππος F89,30
Ἱπποσθένης Λάκων F65,104
Ἱππόστρατος Κροτωνιάτης F65,129.133
Ἱππόστρατος Σελευκεύς F65,260
Ἰσαάκ F29,1; F30a,14; F51a,10
Ἰσαρίων Ἀλεξανδρεύς F65,366
Ἰσίδωρος ὁ καὶ Ἀρτεμίδωρος Ἀλεξανδρεύς F65,391
Ἶσις F34,56
Ἰσοκράτης ὁ ῥήτωρ F81b,5
Ἰσόμαχος Κροτωνιάτης F65,151
Ἰσραήλ (1) T6,7; F34,46; T38,1; ad T39b,1–3; T40,6; T45,5; T47,10; T48b,5; F54b,7; T55,22; T67,1; T68,1.4; F73,5
Ἰσραήλ (2) (vide etiam Ἰακώβ) T28c,6; T41a,28
Ἰσχυρὸς Ἱμεραῖος F65,148
Ἰταλία F24a,20.24; F24b,17.24; T52,1; ad F81b,4–7; F89,39
Ἴφιτος F53,1; F64d,4; F65,13.25.27.31.36
Ἰώ F34,56.89; F56,11
Ἰωάθαμ F59a,21; ad F64a,4s; F64c,2; F64d,8.11.13; T64e,1
Ἰωακείμ rex Iudae T71; ad F76,4; ad T77a,3s; T77b; ad F90a,2–4
Ἰωακείμ summus sacerdos T75a,6s
Ἰωάννης Ἀντιοχεύς (1) ad T10,1–4
Ἰωάννης Ἀντιοχεύς (2) T13b
Ἰωάννης ὁ ἀπόστολος F95,2
Ἰωάννης υἱὸς Σίμωνος T85a,1
Ἰωάς F90a,1
Ἰωάχαζ F46,204; F72,1s
Ἰώβ F31,2
Ἰωνάθης (Ὑρκανός) F85,1
Ἰωνᾶς F66,1

Ἴωνες F34,92; ad F54a,25-27
Ἰωσεδέκ F34,20; T78b,5
Ἰώσηππος ἀδελφὸς Ἡρώδου
    F89,27
Ἰώσηππος (Flavius Iosephus)
    T13a; T13b; ad F23,18-20; ad
    F34,38; T47,9.29.32; T48a,6;
    T48b,2; F79,4; T80b; T80c;
    T80d,4; F85,1; F87b,5; T88;
    T92,1
Ἰωσήφ (1) T7b,1s; T28a,2;
    T28b,2.4; T28c,4; F30b,1;
    T32,2-4; F33,2; T33a,1s;
    T33b,2; T41a,27; T45,4; T46b,3;
    T46c,11.18; T47,16
Ἰωσήφ (2) ad F90a,2-4; F90c
Ἰωσὴφ ὁ ἐξ Ἀριμαθαίας T93c,5
Ἰωσίας T71; F72,1; ad T77a,3s

Καάθ T32,1.6
Κάδμος F50,17; F54a,17
Καιέχως F46,20
Κάιν F22,7; F23,5
Καϊνᾶν (1) T16a,6s
Καϊνᾶν (2) ad T16c,2-6; T16i,3.5;
    T16k,1.4; T16l,2s; T16m,1s;
    T16n,1.5.7; T16o,2.5; T16q,2;
    T45,14.17; T47,3; T93c,13
Καισάρεια F89,61
Καλλίθυια F56,2
Καλλικλῆς Σιδώνιος F65,342
Καλλίμαχος F65,35
Καλλισθένης Λάκων F65,79
Κάλλιστος Σιδήτης F65,363
Καμβύσης rex Persarum F46,213;
    F73,9; T75a,2.7; T75b,10
Καμπανοί ad F81b,4-7
Κανδαύλης F63a,10
Κάπρος Ἠλεῖος F65,249
Κάρνειος F51a,42
Κάσσανδρος F82,39.40

Κάστωρ frater Pollucis
    ad F54a,20-24
Κάστωρ historiographus
    F34,16.32; T52,3
Κάτων T52,2
Κέβης F81a,1
Κέκροψ (1) F34,72; ad T36,1s;
    T47,31; F54a,4s.8.10.28s.47.59;
    F54b,4-6; T55,18-20.36;
    F56,12; T57,1
Κέκροψ (2) F54a,15s
Κελαιναί F23,19
Κενκένης F46,7
Κένταυροι F34,91
Κερᾶς Ἀργεῖος F65,223
Κερφέρης F46,47
Κήβ F43b,14
Κίλικες ad F89,18-22
Κιλικία F89,20
Κιμάρδιος ad F73,9-14
Κίνυρος F24b,40
Κίς F59b,1
Κλαύδιος F65,337
Κλειτόστρατος Ῥόδιος F65,258
Κλεόδικος F54a,53
Κλεόμαντις Κλειτόριος F65,206
Κλεόξενος Ἀλεξανδρεύς F65,241
Κλεόπας T2c,5
Κλεοπάτρα regina Aegypti
    F86,16.18.21.23; F89,2.17.19.36.
    41.45.47s.56
Κλεοπάτρα filia Ptolemaei
    Philometoris T86a,4
Κλεοπτόλεμος Λάκων F65,76
Κλέων Ἐπιδαύριος F65,114
Κλεώνδας Θηβαῖος F65,111
Κλήμης (ὁ στρωματεύς) T1a,2;
    T4a,1; T4b,1; T5,5; T8a,3;
    T8b,2; T10,3; ad F34,38;
    T47,33; T48a,5; T48b,2; T77b;
    F97,2
Κλίτων Μακεδών F65,209

Κνωσσός F56,8
Κόδρος F54a,27s.32s
Κοῖνος F82,10
Κομαῖος F65,91
Κόμοδος F65,387; F97,1
Κόραξ F51a,28
Κόρη F34,90
Κορίνθιοι F59a,1s.5s.20; F59b,3.6
Κόροιβος Ἠλεῖος F64a,4; F64d,2; F64e,6; F65,33.44
Κορύβαντες F56,8
Κουρητεία (vide etiam Ἀκαρνανία) F56,7
Κουρῆτες F56,8
Κραναὸς Σικυώνιος F65,375
Κραναός rex Macedoniae F82,8s
Κραναός rex Atheniensium F54a,10; F54b,5.7; T55,11.19.21.25.27.36
Κραξίλας Θεσσαλός F65,96
Κράτης Ἀλεξανδρεύς F65,248
Κράτης Ἠλεῖος F65,188
Κρατῖνος Μεγαρεύς F65,90
Κρέων T54c,5
Κρήτη F24a,26; F24b,26
Κρίασος F50,10
Κρίσσων Ἱμεραῖος F65,168
Κροῖσος F63a,3.15; F63b,5s; F74,3
Κροκίνας Λαρισσαῖος F65,184
Κρόνος F24a,4.10.15; F24b,4.10.15; F43b,14
Κρότωπος F50,13
Κτησίας F34,53
Κυαξάρης F62,16
Κύλων Ἀθηναῖος F65,99
Κυπρίνη ad F87b,7-9
Κύπρος F65,252; F66,3
Κύριλλος T91
Κῦρος F34,15.19.22.42s.59.67.75; F62,2.8.21.22; F63a,3; F65,134; F73,2.8; F74,2.5s; T75a,1; T77b; F93,36.47

Κωνστάντιος T8a,5
Κωσταντῖνος T13a
Κωχώμη F46,9

Λάβαν F30b,5
Λαβίνιος ad F54a,20-24
Λαβώτης F58a,11
Λαγίδαι F89,53
Λάγος F86,2.5
Λάδας Αἰγιεύς F65,228
Λάδρομος Λάκων F65,136
Λακεδαιμόνιοι ad F50,25-27; F58a,1s.5.19; F58b,1.5; F59a,2s.5; F59b,3; ad F81a,3-5
Λακεδαίμων F65,81
Λακερία ad F24,10-14
Λάμαχος Ταυρομενίτης F65,300
Λάμεχ T16a,12s; T16g,4; F22,8; T22a,2s
Λάμπις Λάκων F65,68
Λάνδης Ἀργεῖος F65,160
Λαομέδων ad F50,25-27; F51a,30
Λαχάρης F46,109
Λεῖα T28c,1
Λευί T28b,1; T28c,2.3; F30a,1; T32,1; T33b,2; T41b,5; F90c
Λευκάτης F86,24
Λεύκιππος F51a,18s
Λεωκράτης F54a,55
Λεωνίδας Ῥόδιος F65,265.269
Λεωνίδης T1a,6; T1b,4
Λεωχάρης Μεσήνιος F65,57
Λίβυες F46,35
Λιβύη F24a,12; F86,1
Λικίνιος T8b,6
Λοῦκας Ἀλεξανδρεύς F65,371
Λούκιος Βῆρος F65,382
Λύγδαμις Συρακούσιος F65,93
Λυγκεύς F50,16
Λυδοί F62,22; F63a,1s.5.16; F63b,1.3.5.7; F73,2; F74,1
Λυκῖνος Κροτωνιάτης F65,123

Λύκος Λαρισσαῖος F65,167
Λυκούργος F65,27
Λυκώτας Λάκων F65,113
Λυσίμαχος F82,43
Λώτ F26,7.8

Μάγνος Λίβυς Κυρηναῖος F65,390
Μαθουσάλα T16a,10.12; T16g,4;
  T16o,6; T16q,4; F22,1.7;
  T22a,1s.6; T22b,4s
Μαίανδρος F65,222.286.318
Μακεδόνες T6,2.16; F46,245;
  F65,237; F82,1s.7.34.36.53;
  F84,3; F86,2; F89,55; F93,51
Μακεδονία F73,22; F82,8
Μακρῖνος T2b,2; T11,6
Μαλελεήλ T16a,7.8
Μάλιχος F89,15
Μαναήμ T67,1
Μανασσῆ F70,1; F90b
Μανδαύκης F2,12
Μανέθων F43a,3; T45,2; F46,98.
  100.166s.243; T46c,18
Μαράθιος F51a,26
Μαραθώνιος F51a,25
Μαρδοχαῖος T78b,1
Μαρία T91
Μαρίων Μαρίωνος Ἀλεξανδρεύς
  F65,302
Μαρκίων F93,105
Μάρκος Αὐρήλιος Ἀντωνῖνος vide
  Ἐλαγάβαλος
Μαροδὰχ ad F70
Mashtots‛ T88
Μασσαγέται T75a,1
Ματθάν ad F90a,2–4; F90c
Ματθάτ F90c
Μεγακλῆς F54a,38
Μεγαρεῖς F81a,4
Μέδων F54a,33
Μεθουσουφίς F46,79
Methudutus F51a,45

Μέλανθος F54a,26
Μελέαγρος F82,45
Μέλισσος F81b,4
Μελχί ad F90a,2–4; F90c
Μέμνων F46,146
Μέμφις F46,5.20.118
Μεμφῖται F46,34.50.76.88s
Μένανδρος Θεσσαλεύς F65,145
Μενδήσιοι F46,225
Μενέλαος ad F50,25–27; F58a,14
Μενεσθεύς F54a,21
Μενεσθεὺς Βαρκυλίτης F65,243
Μενθεσουφίς F46,81
Μένος Μεγαρεύς F65,69
Μενχέρης (1) F46,57
Μενχέρης (2) F46,71
Μέσαππος F51a,21
Μεσοποταμία T28a,1
Μεστραΐμ F44,1s; T45,1
Μέσωχρις F46,42
Μηδία F62,8
Μῆδοι F62,1s.5.7.18.22; F73,2
Μῆλος ad F54a,20–24
Μήνης Θεεινίτης F46,3.20
Μιεβιδός F46,11
Μιζαήλ T77a,1
Μικίνας Ῥόδιος F65,212
Μικίων Βοιώτιος F65,256
Μικρίνας Ταραντῖνος F65,202
Μίλης F63a,9
Μίλων Κροτωνιάτης F65,142
Μίνων Ἀθηναῖος F65,185
Μινώταυρος F34,91
Μίσαφρις F46,140
Μισφραγμούθωσις F46,141.143;
  T46c,2.6; T46g,1.5; T47,12;
  T55,1.4s.13.27.29.31.38.45
Μνασίβουλος Ἐλατεύς F65,381
Μοντανός F97,3
Moricauitus vide Ἐλαγάβαλος
Μόσχος Κολοφώνιος F65,254
Μουσιανός T1a,7

Μυκῆναι ad F50,22-24
Μωυσῆς T7b,4; T10,1; F14b,12;
  F15,12; T16c,7s; T33a,1; F34,40.
  46.58.59.61.68.75.77.80.83.89.
  96; T41a,1.7.15.19.24.26.29;
  T41b,1; T45,5.14; F46,132.134;
  T46c,4.6.14.18; T47,1.6.17.31.
  35.38; T48a,2; T48b,4; T49a,5.7;
  F50,4.7; F54b,7; T55,5s.8.22.
  32.43; T80c; ad F87b,5 (test.);
  T93c,16

Ναασών T41a,19.21s
Ναβουχοδονόσωρ F34,12.14; ad
  F73,9-14; T75a,2; T75b,10;
  T77a,2
Ναούμ F66,1
Ναρσῆς ad F73,15-24
Ναυάτος T4b,2
Ναχώρ T16c,10-12
Νεεμίας T78b,3; ad T78a,1-5;
  T80d,1; F93,34.40.43.55.98
Νεικόστρατος Αἰγεάτης F65,332
Νεῖλος F46,27
Νεκτανέβης F46,232
Νεκτάνεβος T45,1; F46,234
Νεμεσίας T75b,8
Νερούας F65,360
Νέρων F65,341.345.347; T78a,3
Νεφελχερής F46,172
Νεφερίτης F46,226
Νεφερχέρης (1) F46,27
Νεφερχέρης (2) F46,67
Νεφορίτης F46,229
Νεχαώ (1) F46,202
Νεχαώ (2) F46,204; T47,18; F72,3
Νεχερωφής F46,35
Νεχεψώς F46,201
Νικασίας Ὀπούντιος F65,153
Νικάτωρ Κυρηναῖος F65,229
Νικόδημος Λακεδαιμόνιος
  F65,282

Νικόδημος T93c,6
Νικόμαχος Φιλαδελφεύς F65,281
Νικόπολις urbs Graeciae F89,50
Νικόπολις urbs Palaestinae T2a,1;
  T2b,3; T2c,6; T2d,2
Νινευί F66,2
Νίνος F24a,17.27; F24b,12.27;
  F34,50; T49a,6.7; T93c,11
Νιόβη T48b,4
Nisibis T88
Νίτωκρις F46,82
Νῶε T6,4; T16a,13; T16b,2.3;
  T16d,5; T16g,1; T22a,4;
  F23,15.16.18; ad F24,2-10;
  F35,1; F44,1; F76,3

Ξάνθος ὁ Βοιώτιος ad F54a,25-27
Ξενοκλῆς Μεσήνιος F65,55
Ξενοφάνης Αἰτωλός F65,235
Ξενοφῶν ad F73,15-24
Ξενοφῶν Κορίνθιος F65,162
Ξέρξης I. rex Persarum F46,216;
  F73,12
Ξέρξης II. rex Persarum
  F46,219.221; F73,15; T75b,1
Ξοῖται F46,116

Ὀδυσσεύς ad F54a,20-24
Ὀζίας F59a,21; F62,6.19;
  F82,3.6s.53
Ὀθόης F46,77
Οἰβώτας Δυμαῖος F65,51
Οἰδίπους T61,3
Οἰνόμαος F50,22; F65,11
Ὀκταβιανός/ Ὀκταούιος vide
  Αὔγουστος
Ὀλοφέρνης T75a,3s.6s; T75b,4
Ὄλυμπος F65,320
Ὀλυνθεὺς Λάκων F65,106.110
Ὅμηρος F46,163; ad F54a,10-13
Ὀνείας F84,1.4.5.9
Ὀνησίκριτος Σαλαμίνιος F65,261

Ὄννος F46,73
Ὀνομαστὸς Σμυρναῖος F65,74
Ὀνώριος T92,10
Ὀξύθεμις Κορωναῖος F65,58
Ὀξύντης F54a,23
Ὀρέστης rex Argivorum F50,33; ad F54a,20–24
Ὀρέστης rex Macedoniae F82,21
Ὀρθόπολις F51a,24
Ὄρθων Συρακούσιος F65,271
Ὄρσιππος Μεγαρεύς F65,62
Ὀρώδη F89,11
Ὄσιρις ad F43,12–17; F46,108
Ὀσορθών F46,180
Ὀσορχώ F46,187
Ὀσοχώρ F46,174
Οὐαλέριος Μιτυληναῖος F65,338
Οὐάλης T92,8
Οὔαφρις F46,207; T47,19
Οὐενέφης F46,8
Οὐεσπασιανός F65,350; T78a,3
Οὐσαφάιδος F46,10
Οὐσερχέρης F46,65
Ὀχοζίας F90a,1

Πάγων Θηβαῖος F65,78
Πάκορος F89,11
Παλαιστίνη T2a,1; T2c,4; T2d,1; F34,79.85; T75a,5; ad F87b,5–12; F89,25
Παλαίφατος T61,2
Παμμένης Μάγνης F65,318
Πανδίων (1) F54a,13
Πανδίων (2) F54a,16s
Πανόδωρος T39b,6; T77a,4
Πανόπτης F56,11
Πάνταινος T1a,4
Παντακλῆς Ἀθηναῖος F65,71
Παπίας ad T10,1–4
Παρθία F23,19
Πάρθοι ad F23,18–20; F65,237; F89,11.13.16.24.35s.40

Παρμενίδης F81a,12; F81b,7
Παρμενίδης Καμαριναῖος F65,144
Παρμενίδης Μιτυληναῖος F65,217
Παρμενίδης Ποσειδωνιάτης F65,161
Παρμενίσκος Κερκυραῖος F65,284.288
Παρσανάβας ad F89,60s
Παρύσατις ad F73,15–24
Παυσανίας rex Macedoniae F82,24
Παυσανίας historiographus T10,2; F86,25
Παχνάν F46,123
Πείρας F56,2
Πελασγός F51a,37
Πελοποννήσιοι ad F51a,12–15; F81a,3
Πελοπόννησος F50,23; ad F54a,25–27; F65,15.18
Πέλοψ F50,22; F65,11
Πένθιλος F50,34
Πέργαμος ὁ Παμφύλιος ad F23,18–20
Περδίκκας I. rex Macedoniae F82,12
Περδίκκας II. rex Macedoniae F82,19
Περδίκκας III. rex Macedoniae F82,30
Περιγένης Ἀλεξανδρεύς F65,230
Περικλῆς ad F81a,3–5; F81b,7
Πέρσαι T6,2.15; F34,10.15; F46,212s.237; F62,22; F63a,3; F65,134.180; F73,1s.6.22; F74,3; T75a,2; T75b,1.7; ad T78a,1–5; ad F89,18–22; F89,54; T91; F93,33.41.51.56.91
Περσεύς rex Macedoniae F82,52
Περσεύς heros F34,91
Περσίς ad F24,2–10; F62,3.9

Περτίναξ imperator Romanus
    T1a,1; T1b,1; F65,392
Πετουβάτης F46,186
Πῆκος F24b,9
Πιερία F65,260
Πῖκος/Πῆκος (vide etiam Ζεύς)
    F24a,9; F24b,9
Πίσα F65,164
Πισαῖοι F60,1; F65,84.88.199
Πισιδία ad F23,18–20
Πιττακός F65,101
Πλάτων F15,6; ad F54a,10–13; ad
    F73,15–24; F81a,1
Πλημναῖος F51a,23
Πολέμων Πετραῖος F65,327
Πολίτης Κεραμίτης F65,349
Πολύβιος F34,17; F65,35
Πόλυβος (1) F51a,32.39
Πόλυβος (2) vide Θούωρις
Πολύδαμας Σκοτουσσαῖος
    F65,180
Πολυδεύκης ad F54a,20–24
Πολυκλῆς Κυρηναῖος F65,203
Πολυμήστωρ Μιλήσιος F65,118
Πολύμναστος Κυρηναῖος F65,166
Πολυνίκης Ἠλεῖος F65,103
Πολυφείδης F51a,36
Πολυχάρης Μεσήνιος F65,49
Πόντος T88
Πορφύριος T1b,2; F50,28
Ποσειδώνιος (1) T47,10
Ποσειδώνιος (2) F34,80
Πρίαμος ad F50,25–27
Πρόδικος F81a,12
Προῖτος F50,20
Προκλῆς Σπάρτης ad F58a,8–12
Πρόκνη ad F54a,10–13
Προμηθεύς F34,89.103; ad T36,1s;
    F54a,6; F56,3.10.12
Πρύμνης F59a,11
Πρωταγόρας F81b,5
Πρωτοφάνης Μάγνης F65,286

Πτολεμαῖοι T6,16; F84,3;
    F86,14.20; F89,55
Πτολεμαῖος I. ὁ Λάγου rex Aegypti
    F65,214; F86,2.5.7.21
Πτολεμαῖος II. ὁ Φιλάδελφος rex
    Aegypti F86,4.9
Πτολεμαῖος III. ὁ Εὐεργέτης rex
    Aegypti F86,10
Πτολεμαῖος IV. ὁ Φιλοπάτωρ rex
    Aegypti F86,11
Πτολεμαῖος V. ὁ Ἐπιφανής rex
    Aegypti F86,12
Πτολεμαῖος VI. ὁ Φιλομήτωρ rex
    Aegypti F86,13; T86a,2s
Πτολεμαῖος XII. Διόνυσος rex
    Aegypti F86,15
Πτολεμαῖος filius Ptolemaei Dionysii F86,16
Πτολεμαῖος I. rex Macedoniae
    F82,29
Πτολεμαῖος Κεραυνός rex Macedoniae F82,44
Πτολεμαῖος ὁ Μενδήσιος F34,86
Πυθαγόρας Λάκων F65,64
Πυθαγόρας Μάγνης F65,222.224
Πυθαγόρας ὁ Σάμιος F65,121; ad
    F73,9–14; F74,5
Πυθοκλῆς Σικυώνιος F65,242
Πυθόστρατος Ἐφέσιος F65,197
Πυρρίας Αἰτωλός F65,253
Πύρρος F82,42
Πῶλος Ἐπιδαύριος F65,65
Πῶρος Κυρηναῖος F65,200

Ῥαγαῦ T16c,8.9
Ῥαγουήλ F31,1
Ῥαθούρης F46,70
Ῥαθῶς F46,150
Ῥαμεσσῆς F46,154.161
Ῥατοίσης F46,58
Ῥαχήλ T28b,4; T28c,1; T33b,2
Ῥαψάκης F46,159

Ῥέα F24a,7.18; F24b,7
Ῥῆμος F53,2; F65,47
Ῥιψόλαος Λάκων F65,109
Ῥόδος ad F50,11-14; F66,2
Ῥόδων Κυμαῖος F65,351
Ῥωμαῖοι T6,2.17; T11,6; F14b,3;
    F29,3; T52,2; T54c,7.10;
    F65,42.304.306.323.335.337.
    341.350.353.355.360.367.
    373.382.387.392.397; T78a,3;
    F82,2; ad F87b,5; F89,3.56;
    T99,1
Ῥωμέλιος T68,1
Ῥώμη T52,1; F53,2; F65,53.291; ad
    F81b,4-7; F84,11; F89,5.23.40
Ῥῶμος vide Ῥῆμος
Ῥωμύλος F53,2.4; F65,47.53

Σαβάκων F46,194
Σαδυάτης F63a,13
Σαΐτης F46,119
Σακία F89,32
Σαλά T16c,3.4; T16i,2.3.4.7;
    T16k,1; T16l,3; T16m,1;
    T16n,2.6
Σαλμανασάρ T77a,4
Σαλμών T41a,22
Σαμανές ad T39,5s
Σαμάρεια T69,1; T77a,4; T85a,3;
    F89,59.63
Σαμαρεῖται T16e,7; T16h,5.7;
    T93d
Σάμιοι F74,1.5
Σαμουήλ T16k,5; F34,65; F35,1;
    T41b,2; F60,4
Σαμψών T39b,1; T41a,12
Σαούλ T41b,2; F58a,5; F59,1;
    F59a,20; F60,1.4; F76,2
Σαραπίων Ἀλεξανδρεύς F65,331
Σατορνίλος Κρὴς Γορτύνιος
    F65,396
Σεβεννύται F46,231

Σεβερχέρης F46,60
Σεβῆρος (L. Septimius Severus)
    T1a,1; F65,43.392
Σεβιχώς F46,196
Σεβωείμ F26,9
Σεδεκίας ad F76,4; T77a,5s; T77b
Σεθένης F46,25
Σεθροΐτης F46,120
Σέθως F46,158
Σειρῆνες ad F54a,20-24
Σέκτος T12,1
Σέλευκος I. rex Syriae F83
Σέλευκος IV. Φιλοπάτωρ rex
    Syriae F84,7.10s
Σέλευκος Μακεδών F65,231
Σέλευκος (M. Flavius Vitellius
    Seleucus) T54d,7
Σελήνη filia Cleopatrae F89,48
Σεμείγαρ ad T36,1s; ad T39b,1-4;
    T40,5
Σεμέλη ad F54a,10-13
Σεμέμψης F46,12
Σεμίραμις F24a,7; F24b,7; F34,51;
    T93c,12
Σερούχ T16c,9.10
Σεσόγχωσις F46,102
Σέσωγχις F46,179
Σέσωστρις F46,104
Σέσωχρις F46,29
Σευῆρος vide Σεβῆρος
Σεφρής F46,66
Σηγώρ F26,9
Σήθ T16a,2.4; F18; ad F19,1-4;
    F22,7; F23,3
Σήμ ad T16a,2-13; T16c,2;
    T16g,1; T16l,1; F24a,2; F24b,2
Σήμαχος ad F54a,10-13
Σήφουρις F46,46
Σθένελος F50,14
Σικελία F81,14
Σίκιμα F30a,2.4
Σικυών F51a,31

Σικυώνιοι F51a,1s.6s.40.52; F51b,1
Σιμίας F81a,1
Σίμμιας Σελευκεύς F65,283
Σιμύλος Νεαπολίτης F65,236
Σίμων F84,1.5.9; F85,1; T85a,1
Sinope T88
Σισίρης F46,68
Siunikʻ T88
Σκάμανδρος Ἀλεξανδρεύς F65,308
Σκάμανδρος Μιτυληναῖος F65,159
Σκεμίοφρις F46,113
Σκύλλα ad F54a,20-24
Σμενδής F46,170
Σμέρδις F73,10
Σογδιανός F46,220; F73,16
Σόδομα F26,8.9
Σολομών T41a,1.7.15; T41b,3; T42,1; T69,2; T85a,2
Σόλων F15,6; T54f,2
Σουσακείμ T47,18
Σουσάννα T3a,4
Σοῦφις (1) F46,52
Σοῦφις (2) F46,56
Σοφοκλῆς F81a,10; F81b,3
Σπαρτοί F34,90
Σταάν F46,124
Στέφανος Καππάδοξ F65,359
Στεφινάτης F46,200
Στόμας Ἀθηναῖος F65,97
Στρατόνικος Κορράγου Ἀλεξανδρεύς F65,295
Στράτων F89,60
Στράτων Ἀλεξανδρεύς F65,352
Σύλλα F65,291
Συμεών F30a,1; ad T39,3s; F90a,4
Σύμμαχος Μεσσήνιος F65,174
Σύμμαχος translator sacrae scripturae T1b,1

Συρία ad F24,2-10; F34,79; F56,10; T75a,4; F84,11; F89,25.32
Σύροι F26,10; T93d
Σύρος F56,9
Σφαῖρος Λάκων F65,98
Σφενδάτις ad F73,9-14
Σφίγξ T61,3
Σωκράτης F65,377; ad F73,15-24; F81a,1.9; F81b,7
Σώπατρος Ἀργεῖος F65,310
Σῶρις F46,51
Σῶς F43a,12; F43b,12
Σωσάννα T2b,4; T11,8; T12,4
Σώσαρμος F62,11
Σωσθένης F82,47
Σώσιος F89,26
Σώσιππος Δελφός F65,190
Σώϋφις F46,43
Σώφρων Ἀμβρακιώτης F65,172

Τακέλωθις F46,182
Τανῖται F46,169.185
Τανχέρης F46,72
Τάρκος F46,197
Ταρσός ad F89,18-22
Τατιανός ad F34,38; T48a,5; T48b,3
Τέθμωσις T46c,2; T47,23
Τελέστης F59a,18
Τέλλις Σικυώνιος F65,66
Τελχίν F51a,13
Τεριναῖος Ἠλεῖος F65,189
Τεώς F46,233
Τήλεκλος F58a,16
Τιβέριος F65,323.325; F78,5s.9s; T92,5; F93,14.52.58.80; T93b,1
Τίγρις F65,283
Τίμαιος Ἠλεῖος F65,187
Τιμόθεος Τραλλιανός F65,276
Τισικράτης Κροτωνιάτης F65,154
Τίτος F65,353

Τλάς F46,24
Τόμυρις T75a,1
Τορύμμας Θεσσαλός F65,163
Τοσέρτασις F46,44
Τόσορθρος F46,38
Τούθμωσις F46,145
Τραϊανός F65,360; F95,1
Τράχων F89,31
Τριόπας F50,12
Τροία vide Ἴλιον
Τρύφων Φιλαδελφεύς F65,346
Τρῶας F65,308
Τύρεις F46,41
Τυριμμᾶς F82,11
Τυφών F43a,17

Urha vide Ἔδεσσα
Yesov T13a
Ὑπέρβιος Συρακούσιος F65,176
Ὕπηνος Ἠλεῖος F65,61
Ὑρκανός I. summus sacerdos
 F85,2
Ὑρκανός II. summus sacerdos et
 rex F87a,15; F87b,1.17.20;
 F89,1.8.13; T89a,1s
Ὑστάσπης F46,215; ad F73,9-14

Φαέθων ad F54a,10-13
Φαίδιμος Ἀλεξανδρεύς F65,255
Φαῖδρος Φαρσάλιος F65,135
Φακεέ T68,1.5
Φακεσίας T67,1
Φαλέκ T16c,5.7s; T16e,1.8s;
 F25,2; F94,1
Φαλκίας (vide etiam Φακεσίας)
 ad T67,1; ad T68,4s
Φανᾶς Πελληνεύς F65,149
Faransun rex Persarum T91
Φασάιλος F89,8.12
Φαῦνος F24a,33; F24b,32
Φειδίας F81b,5

Φερεκλῆς princeps Atheniensium
 T49b,1; F54a,40; T54e,1
Φιλῖνος Κῶος F65,232
Φιλῖνος archon T54d,7
Φίλιππος I. rex Macedoniae
 F82,14
Φίλιππος II. rex Macedoniae
 ad F73,15-24; F82,31;
 ad F86,22s
Φίλιππος III. rex Macedoniae
 F82,36.38
Φίλιππος V. rex Macedoniae
 F82,51
Φιλόμβροτος Λάκων F65,80
Φιλομήλα ad F54a,10-13
Φιλόμηλος Φαρσάλιος F65,227
Φιλόχορος F34,32.73
Φιλύρα ad F24,10-14
Φιλώτας Συβαρίτης F65,112
Φιός F46,78
Φίωψ F46,80; ad F46,80
Φλάκκος Ἀσύλαιος T93b,1
Φλέγων F34,17; F93,14; T93a,1
Φοίνικες F15,9; F46,118; F84,6
Φόρβας F50,11; F54a,37
Φορωνεύς F34,28.54.55.78;
 T47,5.10.35.38; T48b,4; F50,5;
 T55,24.42
Φραάρτης ad F89,18-22
Φρυγία F23,20; ad F97,2-4
Φρύνων Ἀθηναῖος F65,100
Φυλιστιαῖοι ad F58b,1-5
Φωκίδης Ἀθηναῖος F65,198

Χαίρης F46,26
Χαλδαῖοι F15,1.9; ad T16c,2-6
Χάμ ad T16a,2-13; F44,1
Χαναάν T6,5.7; F26,7
Χανανίτις T16p,2; F26,2
Χαρίδημος F51a,49
Χάρμις Λάκων F65,83
Χάροψ F54a,51

Χάρυβδις   ad F54a,20–24
Χεβρής   F46,151
Χεβρώς   F46,136
Χελκίας   T71
Χενερής   F46,30
Χέοψ   F46,53
Χέρης   F46,69
Χίονις Λάκων   F65,86.89
Χοδολλαγομόρ   F26,11
Χρυσόγονος Νικαεύς   F65,279
Χρυσόμαξος Λάκων   F65,117

Ψαμμεχερίτης   F46,210
Ψαμμήτιχος   F46,203
Ψάμμουθις   F46,206.228
Ψαμμοῦς   F46,188

Ψιναχῆς   F46,175
Ψουσέννης   F46,171.176

Ὠβήδ   T41a,22
Ὤγυγος   F34,27.38.41.43.46.51.54. 57.71s.75.98; T47,36s; F54b,2.6; T54c,2; T55,10.16.20.24.31. 34.37.46
Ὠριγένης   T1a,6.8; T1b,4; T2b,4.7; T3a,2.4; T5,1.6; T8a,4; T11,8.11; T12,4; F97,3
Ὠριθυῖα   ad F54a,14–19
Ὧρος   F46,148
Ὧρος   F43a,15
Ὡσηέ   F66,1; T68,2
Ὦχος   F65,181; F73,19

3. Comparatio numerorum

nostrae editionis cum editionibus prioribus

3.1. Routh ²1846

Routh	GCS		
1	F14b,1s	31	T42
2	T17	32	F66
3	F19	33	T67
4	F20	34	T68
5	F22	35	F58b,5s
6	F16a	36 (p. 285,10–14)	T64d,8–14
7	F23	37	F64a.b
8	F16b	38 (p. 286,13–17)	T69
9 (p. 244,2–14)	F16c	39	F54d
9 (p. 244,15s)	T16p	40	F70
9 (p. 244,17–245,6)	F16d	41	T77a,5s
10	F15	42	T77a,2–4
11	F46	43	T75a,1–3
12	F24	44	F79
13	F26	45	F81a,2–5
14	(T27)	46	T86b,3
15	T28a	47	T85a
16	T28b	48	F87b
17	F29	49	F89
18	F30a,8–13	49*	F90
19	F31	50	F93
20	T32	51	T93c,7–10
21	F33	52	F97
22	F34	53	F96
23	T49a	54	F98
24	F56	55	F100
25	T36	56	T6
26 (p. 280,9–13)	T37		
26 (p. 280,14s)	T38		
27	T39a		
28	T40		
28*	–		
29	F51a		
30	T41b		

3. Comparatio numerorum

GCS	Routh
T6	56
F14b,1s	1
F15	10
F16a	6
F16b	8
F16c	9 (p. 244,2–14)
F16d	9 (p. 244,17–245,6)
T16p	9 (p. 244,15s)
T17	2
F19	3
F20	4
F22	5
F23	7
F24	12
F26	13
(T27)	14
T28a	15
T28b	16
F29	17
F30a,8–13	18
F31	19
T32	20
F33	21
F34	22
T36	25
T37	26 (p. 280,9–13)
T38	26 (p. 280,14s)
T39a	27
T40	28
T41b	30
T42	31
F46	11
T49a	23
F51a	29
F54d	39
F56	24
F58b,5s	35
F64a.b	37
T64d,8–14	36 (p. 285,10–14)
F66	32
T67	33
T68	34
T69	38 (p. 286,13–17)
F70	40
T75a,1–3	43
T77a,2–4	42
T77a,5s	41
F79	44
F81a,2–5	45
T85a	47
T86b,3	46
F87b	48
F89	49
F90	49*
F93	50
T93c,7–10	51
F96	53
F97	52
F98	54
F100	55
–	28*

3.2. Gallandi 1766 (= PG 10,63–94)

Gallandi	GCS	GCS	Gallandi
1	F15	F15	1
2	F23,1–11	F16a	3
3	F16a	F16b	5
4	F23,10–23	F16c,2–7	6
5	F16b	F16d	8
6	F16c,2–7	T16p	7
7	T16p	F23,1–11	2
8	F16d	F23,10–23	4
9	F26	F26	9
10a	F29	F29	10a
10b	F30a	F30a	10b
11	F33	F33	11
12	F34,38–60	F34,1–48.57–105	13
13	F34,1–48.57–105	F34,38–60	12
14	T64d,8–14	F64a.b	15
15	F64a.b	T64d,8–14	14
16	F93,22–66	F89	17
17	F89	F93,1–20.54–110	18
18	F93,1–20.54–110	F93,22–66	16
19	F100	F100	19

AFRICANUS' CHRONOLOGICAL SYSTEM

		Adam	Ol.	King/Emperor	BC/AD
	Creation of Adam	1			5502/01 BC
	Birth of Seth	230			
	Birth of Enosh	**435**			
	Birth of Kenan	625			
5	Birth of Mahalalel	795			
	Death of Adam	**930**			
	Birth of Jared	960			
	Birth of Enoch	1122			
	Birth of Methuselah	**1287**			
10	Birth of Lamech	1474			
	Disappearance of Enoch	1487			
	Birth of Noah	1662			
	Death of Methuselah	**2256**			
	Flood	2262			3241/40
15	Birth of Shelah	**2397**			
	Birth of Eber	**2527**			
	Birth of Peleg/Division of earth	**2661**			
	Birth of Reu	2791			
	Birth of Serug	2923			
20	**Death of Peleg**	**3000**			2503/02
	Birth of Nahor	3053			
	Birth of Terah	3132			
	Birth of Abraham	**3202**			
	Migration of Abraham	**3277**			
25	Birth of Isaac	3302			
	Birth of Jacob	3362			
	Beginning of Sicyonian kingdom	3391		1 Aegialeus	
	Migration of Jacob to Mesopotamia	3439			
	Birth of Levi	3449			
30	Birth of Joseph	3453			
	Entrance of Jacob into Egypt	3492			
	Death of Joseph	**3563**			
	Beginning of Argive kingdom	3602		1 Inachus	
	Birth of Moses	3627			
35	(Argive kingdom)	3652		1 Phoroneus	
	Exodus = 80 Moses	3707		55 Phoroneus	1796/95
	= Flood under Ogygus			= 43 Leucippus (Sicyonians)	
	Death of Ogygus	3724			
	Death of Moses	3747			

AFRICANUS' CHRONOLOGICAL SYSTEM

		Adam	Ol.	King/Emperor	BC/AD
40	Death of Joshua	3772			
	Prometheus	3801			
	Beginning of Athenian kingdom	3913		1 Cecrops	
	End of the Judges and Eli	4292			
	Fall of Troy	4320			1183/82
45	End of Samuel's rule	4382		1 Saul	1121/20
	End of Argive kingdom	4392			1111/10
	End of Sicyonian kingdom	4398			1105/04
	Beginning of Lacedaem. kingdom	4402		1 Eurystheus = 20 Saul	1101/00
	Building of the Temple	4457		8 Salomon	1046/45
50	**First Olympiad**	4727	1,1	1 Achaz	776/75
	= Beginning of Lydian kingdom			= 1 Ardysus	
	= End of Lacedaem. kingdom			= 2 Aeschylus	
	End of kingdom in Samaria	4750			753/52
	Archons/End of Athenian kingdom	4820	24,2	10 Eryginus	683/82
55	Beginning of Babylonian Captivity	4872		1 Sedekias	631/30
	Beginning of Persian kingdom	4942	{55,1}	1 Cyrus	561/60
	= End of Captivity				
	End of Lydian kingdom	4959	59,1		544/43
	Rebuilding of Jerusalem	5057	{83,4}	20 Artaxerxes min.	446/45
60	End of Persian kingdom	5172	112,2		331/30
	= Beginning of Ptolemaic dynasty				
	Beginning of Roman monarchy	5458		1 Augustus	45/44
	-----	5467		1 Herodes	36/35
	Death of Cleopatra/End of Ptolemies	5472	187,2	14 Augustus	31/30
65	**Incarnation**	5500	194,2	42 Augustus	3/2
	Death of Herod	5501			2/1 BC
	Beginning of public ministry of Jesus	5531		15 Tiberius	AD 29/30
	Resurrection	5532	202,2	16 Tiberius	30/31
	End of Chronographiae	5723	250,1	3 Elagabalus	221/22
70	= coss. C. Vettius Gratus Sabinianus/M. Flavius Vitellius Seleucus (AD 221)				

References:

2 F16a,2   **3** F16a,4f   **4** F16a,6; T16f   **5** F16a,7   **6** F16a,2f   **7** F16a,8   **8** F16a,9   **9** F16a,10; T22a   **10** F16a,12   **11** F16a,10f   **12** F16a,13   **13** T22a   **14** F16b; T16g; T16h; T16q; T22a; T45,9–11   **15** F16c,3   **16** F16c,4   **17** F16c,5   **18** F16c,7   **19** F16c,9   **20** F16c,8; F94,1   **21** F16c,10   **22** F16c,11   **23** F16c,12; T16o,4; T45,18   **24** T6,6; F16d,6; T16p; F25; F51,11: 114 years before 1 Aegialeus   **25** F51,10: 89 years before 1 Aegialeus   **26** F51,10   **27** F51,10f   **28** T28a,1: Jacob's age 77 years   **29** T28b,1; T28c,2f: Jacob's age 87 years   **30** Gen 50,26: 110 years before the death of Joseph, presumably 14 years after Jacob's arrival in Mesopotamia, see T28, note 1   **31** Gen 47,9: 130 years after the birth of Jacob; slight divergence from T32,4, see note 1   **32** T32,4f; F33; T33b   **33** F50,3.26–28   **34** 80 years before the Exodus (T47,1.38), see also F50,4   **35** F50,5   **36** F34,38–41.67–69; F46,132f; T47,1; F50,6f; F51,19f   **38** F34,71f; F54b   **39** F34,61   **40** F34,62; F35; F76,3   **41** F34,103: Prometheus lived 94 years after the Exodus   **42** F54a,47f   **43** T40,1f   **44** F50,26–28   **45** F35,2; F58a,5f; F76,3   **46** F50,35f   **47** F51,5   **48** F58a,5f   **49** T41,8; T42,4   **50** F34,41–43; F54a,46; F58,2f; F63,2–5; F64   **53** T69   **54** F54a,58–60: 907 years from Cecrops; F54d,6f: 903 archons to the year 5723   **55** T6,14; F76,3f   **56** F34,41f. 67–70; F73,2–6   **58** F63a,2–5.17f   **59** F73,14; F93,31–33.54–57   **60** T6,15f; F73,22–24; F93,51f   **62** T6,17; F89,54–57, see notes 5–6   **63** F89,33f   **64** F89,54–57   **65** F15,14f; T92,3f; F93c,8f   **66** T89a   **67** F93,109f; F94,1f   **68** F93,58f; F93d,8   **69** T6,20f; T11,7; F54d,9; F93,109f

For further explanation, see introduction, pp. XXIIIff.